Understanding Physics
JEE Main & Advanced

Optics and
Modern Physics

DC Pandey
[B.Tech, M.Tech, Pantnagar, ID 15722]

ARIHANT PRAKASHAN (Series), MEERUT

arihant

Arihant Prakashan (Series), Meerut

All Rights Reserved

ॐ **Administrative & Production Offices**

Regd. Office
'Ramchhaya' 4577/15, Agarwal Road, Darya Ganj, New Delhi -110002
Tele: 011- 47630600, 43518550

ॐ **Head Office**

Kalindi, TP Nagar, Meerut (UP) - 250002
Tel: 0121-7156203, 7156204

ॐ **Sales & Support Offices**
Agra, Ahmedabad, Bengaluru, Bareilly, Chennai, Delhi, Guwahati, Hyderabad, Jaipur, Jhansi, Kolkata, Lucknow, Nagpur & Pune.

ॐ **ISBN**   978-93-26191-59-3

PO No : TXT-XX-XXXXXXX-X-XX

Published by Arihant Publications (India) Ltd.

For further information about the books published by Arihant, log on to www.arihantbooks.com or e-mail at info@arihantbooks.com

Follow us on

PREFACE

The overwhelming response to the previous editions of this book gives me an immense feeling of satisfaction and I take this an opportunity to thank all the teachers and the whole student community who have found this book really beneficial.

In the present scenario of ever-changing syllabus and the test pattern of JEE Main & Advanced, the NEW EDITION of this book is an effort to cater all the difficulties being faced by the students during their preparation of JEE Main & Advanced. Almost all types and levels of questions are included in this book. My aim is to present the students a fully comprehensive textbook which will help and guide them for all types of examinations. An attempt has been made to remove all the printing errors that had crept in the previous editions.

I am very thankful to (Dr.) Mrs. Sarita Pandey and Mr. Anoop Dhyani for completing this book.

Comments and criticism from readers will be highly appreciated and incorporated in the subsequent editions.

I also request the readers to drop me a mail if you find any corrections in the book at mail id arihantcorrections@gmail.com

DC Pandey

CONTENTS

SYLLABUS

JEE Main

ELECTROMAGNETIC WAVES

Electromagnetic waves and their characteristics. Transverse nature of electromagnetic waves.

Electromagnetic spectrum (radio waves, microwaves, infrared, visible, ultraviolet, X-rays, γ- rays). Applications of e.m. waves.

OPTICS

Reflection and refraction of light at plane and spherical surfaces, Mirror formula, Total internal reflection and its applications, Deviation and Dispersion of light by a prism, Lens formula, Magnification, Power of a lens, Combination of thin lenses in contact, Microscope and astronomical telescope (reflecting and refracting) and their magnifying powers.

WAVE OPTICS

Wave front and Huygens' principle, Laws of reflection and refraction using Huygen's principle. Interference, Young's double slit experiment and expression for fringe width. Diffraction due to a single slit, width of central maximum. Resolving power of microscopes and astronomical telescopes, Polarisation, Plane polarized light; Brewster's law, uses of plane polarized light and polaroids.

DUAL NATURE OF MATTER AND RADIATION

Dual nature of radiation. Photoelectric effect, Hertz and Lenard's observations; Einstein's photoelectric equation; Particle nature of light. Matter waves-wave nature of particle, de-Broglie relation. Davisson-Germer experiment.

ATOMS AND NUCLEI

a-particle scattering experiment; Rutherford's model of atom; Bohr model, Energy levels, Hydrogen spectrum. Composition and size of nucleus, Atomic masses, Isotopes, Isobars; Isotones. Radioactivity - a, b and g particles/rays and their properties; radioactive decay law. Mass-energy relation, Mass defect; Binding energy per nucleon and its variation with mass number, Nuclear fission and fusion.

ELECTRONIC DEVICES

Semiconductors; semiconductor diode: I-V characteristics in forward and reverse bias; Diode as a rectifier; I-V characteristics of LED, photodiode, solar cell and Zener diode; Zener diode as a voltage regulator. Junction Transistor, transistor action, Characteristics of a transistor; transistor as an amplifier (common emitter configuration) and oscillator. Logic gates (OR, AND, NOT, NAND and NOR). Transistor as a switch.

COMMUNICATION SYSTEMS

Propagation of electromagnetic waves in the atmosphere; Sky and space wave propagation, Need for modulation, Amplitude and frequency modulation, Bandwidth of signals, Bandwidth of transmission medium, Basic elements of a communication system (block diagram only).

JEE Advanced

ELECTROMAGTIC WAVES

Electromagnetic waves and their characteristics. Electromagnetic spectrum (radio waves, microwaves, infrared, visible, ultraviolet, X-rays, γ-rays) including elementary facts about their uses.

OPTICS

Rectilinear propagation of light, Reflection and refraction at plane and spherical surfaces, Total internal reflection, Deviation and dispersion of light by a prism, Thin lenses, Combinations of mirrors and thin lenses, Magnification.

WAVE NATURE OF LIGHT

Huygens principle, Interference limited to Young's double-slit experiment. Diffraction due to a single slit. Polarization of light, plane polarized light; Brewster's law, Polaroids.

MODERN PHYSICS

Atomic nucleus, α, β and γ-radiations, Law of radioactive decay, Decay constant, Half-life and mean life, Binding energy and its calculation, Fission and fusion processes, Energy calculation in these processes.

Photoelectric effect, Bohr's theory of hydrogen-like atoms, Characteristic and continuous X-rays, Moseley's law, de-Broglie wavelength of matter waves.

This book is dedicated to my honourable grandfather

(Late) Sh. Pitamber Pandey

a Kumaoni poet and a resident of Village
Dhaura (Almora), Uttarakhand

DEAR STUDENTS...

Many a times I have seen that students have a phobia of Physics. Based on my experience in the field of teaching and writing for about more than 25 years, I am suggesting some of the strategies which can make your Physics subject very strong.

1. Physics is a subject of concepts. So, don't chase after too many problems. Make your concepts very strong. Each and every concept should be lucid clear. Let us take a small example of normal reaction, so what are the important points in it? Perpendicular to the surface; towards the surface, equal and opposite acting on two different bodies, just like pressure (or pressure force PA) between two bodies in contact; minimum value is zero where two bodies leave contact with each other, there is some maximum limit also where the weaker body breaks, electromagnetic and component of net contact force in normal direction; work done by normal reaction is not always zero etc.

2. Don't miss a single class wherever you are studying.

3. Your concentration level in class should be 100%.

4. Keep only one standard book with you. There are many drawbacks when you keep so many books in front of you. A lot of concepts and problems are usually repeated in different books. So basically you are just wasting your valuable time on similar types of concepts/problems if you are solving different books. You have to cover all chapters in all the subjects. If you have too many books then what generally would happen is; you complete a chapter from one book and then repeat the same chapter from the other book. By doing so your course lags and when your exams are near, you are disturbed because of incompletion of many chapters.

5. In this one book theory, selection of that book is very important. Number of problems in the book should neither be too less nor too much. If the level of IIT-JEE is x, then the problems should start from zero level and reach up to $1.25x$. There is no need of touching $1.5x$ level. In complete theory, examples and exercises almost all concepts and types of problems, which are normally asked in the examinations, should be covered. Level of examples and questions should increase very gradually.

6. I have tried my level best to incorporate all the measures mentioned above in point number 5 in my books.

7. There are total 1364 solved examples and 5169 problems in all my five text book. The total of these two is 6533.

8. If you start preparing for IIT-JEE from class 11th in the month of April then try to complete all five text books till the August next year. So you have total 480 days. Per day target of problems is 13.61 or 14.

9. After finishing one chapter in your classes, read each and every word of above mentioned books and complete your daily target of examples/problems by all means. Some problems/examples will be very simple, increasing your coverage that particular day and that saved time can be utilized in tough problems. If you are unable to solve a particular problem, just mark it and in your free time think over it like a philosopher. After two or three attempts if you are further unable to solve then, just see the solution of it which is given at the end of books. If you attend all classes, read complete theory, see all examples and solve all problems, then I am sure by the August month (next year) you will feel very comfortable in Physics. You can't do too many problems. So if you follow the above strategy then don't try any other book/material. Problems in the above mentioned books are given in a systematic increasing order of difficulty level. So if you move step by step then you will not feel any difficulty, I assure you that.

Note : *If you feel that theory of particular topic is very clear in your classes then you can skip theory of above books to save time and directly switch over to solved examples and exercises.*

10. From September to first Main Exam of January month, keep two more books in front of you. "New Pattern" written by myself and "IIT-JEE previous years' papers". Try to complete each and every problem of these two books. You can leave the subjective problems of IIT-JEE previous years' papers at this stage. If you qualify this stage then in the remaining months complete subjective problems of IIT-JEE previous years' papers, one another book written by me five hundred selected problems of Physics and all logical problems of Irodov. If you don't qualify JEE Main exam of January month then repeat those books once again (New Pattern and IIT-JEE previous years' papers, excluding its subjective problems) and just after the April Main exam, complete subjective problems of IIT-JEE previous years' papers, five hundred selected problems of Physics. That's it.

11. If you follow each and every word of above strategy, then I am sure you will give your best in the exams. And this is very important because due to wrong strategy and doing the things in mismanaged manner most of us are unable to deliver our best performance. Your personal talent in Physics subject and luck factor at the last moment also matters. That is beyond our control and I can't speak about it. Your school studies are also not covered in this message.

● ● ● *Good Luck Students* ● ● ●

DC Pandey

29

ELECTROMAGNETIC WAVES

29.1 **Introduction**

Earlier we have learned that a time varying magnetic field produces an electric field. Is the converse also true? Does a time varying electric field can produce a magnetic field? James Clerk Maxwell argued that not only an electric current but also a time varying electric field generates magnetic field.

Maxwell formulated a set of equations (known as Maxwell's equations) involving electric and magnetic fields. Maxwell's equations and Lorentz force formula make all the basic laws of electromagnetism.

The most important outcome of Maxwell's equations is the existence of electromagnetic waves.

The changing electric and magnetic fields form the basis of electromagnetic waves. A combination of time varying electric and magnetic fields (referred as electromagnetic wave) propagate in space very close to the speed of light ($= 3 \times 10^8$ m/s) obtained from optical measurements. We shall take a brief discussion of electromagnetic waves mainly developed by Maxwell around 1864.

29.2 **Displacement Current**

An electric current produces magnetic field. Value of magnetic field (due to an electric current) at some point can be obtained by Biot-Savart law or Ampere's circuital law.

We have stated Ampere's law as

$$\oint \mathbf{B} \cdot d\mathbf{l} = \mu_0 i \qquad \qquad ...(i)$$

where left hand side of this equation is the line integral of magnetic field over a closed path and i is the electric current crossing the surface bounded by that closed path.

Ampere's law in this form is not valid if the electric field at the surface varies with time. For an example if we place a magnetic needle in between the plates of a capacitor during its charging or discharging then it deflects. Although, there is no current between the plates, so magnetic field should be zero. Hence, the needle should not show any deflection. But deflection of needle shows that there is a magnetic field in the region between plates of capacitor during charging or discharging. So, there must be some other source (other than current) of magnetic field. This other source is nothing but the changing electric field. Because at the time of charging or discharging of capacitor electric field between the plates changes.

The relation between the changing electric field and the magnetic field resulting from it is given by

$$\oint \mathbf{B} \cdot d\mathbf{l} = \mu_0 \varepsilon_0 \frac{d\phi_E}{dt} \qquad \qquad ...(ii)$$

Here, ϕ_E is the flux of the electric field through the area bounded by the closed path along which line integral of **B** is calculated.

Combining Eqs. (i) and (ii), we can make a general expression of Ampere's circuital law and that is

$$\oint \mathbf{B} \cdot d\mathbf{l} = \mu_0 i + \mu_0 \varepsilon_0 \frac{d\phi_E}{dt} = \mu_0 \left(i + \varepsilon_0 \frac{d\phi_E}{dt} \right)$$

or

$$\oint \mathbf{B} \cdot d\mathbf{l} = \mu_0 \left(i + i_d \right) \qquad \qquad ...(iii)$$

Here,
$$i_d = \varepsilon_0 \frac{d\phi_E}{dt} \qquad \text{...(iv)}$$

is called the **displacement current** and which is produced by the change in electric field. The current due to the flow of charge is often called **conduction current** and is denoted by i_c. Thus, Eq. (iii) can also be written as

$$\oint \mathbf{B} \cdot d\mathbf{l} = \mu_0 \, (i_c + i_d) \qquad \text{...(v)}$$

Example

In the figure, a capacitor is charged by a battery through a resistance R. Charging of capacitor will be exponential. A time varying charging current i flows in the circuit (due to flow of charge) till charging continues. A time varying electric field is also produced between the plates. This causes a displacement current i_d between the plates. There is no current between the plates due to flow of charge, as a medium between the plates is insulator.

Consider two closed paths a and b as shown in figure. Ampere's circuital law in these two paths is

Along path a

$$\oint \mathbf{B} \cdot d\mathbf{l} = \mu_0 i \quad \text{or} \quad \oint \mathbf{B} \cdot d\mathbf{l} = \mu_0 i_c$$

Along path b

$$\oint \mathbf{B} \cdot d\mathbf{l} = \mu_0 \, i_d$$

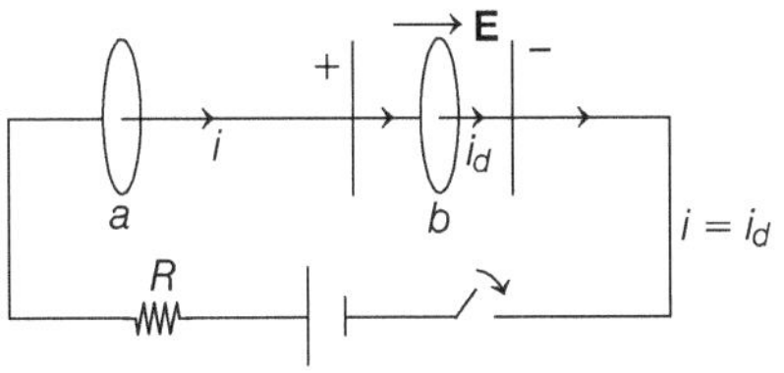

Fig. 29.1

Here, $i_d = \varepsilon_0 \dfrac{d\phi_E}{dt}$ is in the direction shown in figure. In sample example 29.1, we have shown that

$$i_c = i_d$$

⊘ *Extra Points to Remember*

Faraday's law of electromagnetic induction says that changing magnetic field gives rise to an electric field and its line integral (= *emf*) is given by the equation

$$\oint \mathbf{E} \cdot d\mathbf{l} = -\frac{d\phi_B}{dt}$$

A changing electric field gives rise to a magnetic field is the symmetrical counterpart of Faraday's law. This is a consequence of the displacement current and given by

$$\oint \mathbf{B} \cdot d\mathbf{l} = \mu_0 \varepsilon_0 \frac{d\phi_E}{dt} = \mu_0 i_d$$

Thus, time dependent electric and magnetic fields give rise to each other.

Maxwell's Equations

- $\oint \mathbf{E} \cdot d\mathbf{s} = q_{in}/\varepsilon_0$ (Gauss's law for electricity)

- $\oint \mathbf{B} \cdot d\mathbf{s} = 0$ (Gauss's law for magnetism)

- $\oint \mathbf{E} \cdot d\mathbf{l} = -\dfrac{d\phi_B}{dt}$ (Faraday's law)

- $\oint \mathbf{B} \cdot d\mathbf{l} = \mu_0(i_c + i_d) = \mu_0 i_c + \mu_0 \varepsilon_0 \dfrac{d\phi_E}{dt}$ (Ampere-Maxwell's law)

⊗ **Example 29.1** *During charging of a capacitor show that the displacement current between the plates is equal to the conduction current in the connecting wire.*

Solution Let A is the area of plates, q is the charge on capacitor at some instant and d the separation between the plates.

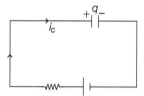

$$\text{Conduction current, } i_c = \frac{dq}{dt} \qquad \text{...(i)}$$

Electric field between the plates,

$$E = \frac{\sigma}{\varepsilon_0} = \frac{q/A}{\varepsilon_0} = \frac{q}{A\varepsilon_0}$$

Fig. 29.2

The flux of the electric field through the given area is

$$\phi_E = EA = \left(\frac{q}{A\,\varepsilon_0}\right) A = \frac{q}{\varepsilon_0}$$

∴

$$\frac{d\phi_E}{dt} = \frac{1}{\varepsilon_0}\left(\frac{dq}{dt}\right)$$

Displacement current,

$$i_d = \varepsilon_0 \frac{d\phi_E}{dt}$$

$$= \varepsilon_0 \left[\frac{1}{\varepsilon_0} \cdot \frac{dq}{dt}\right]$$

or

$$i_d = \frac{dq}{dt} \qquad \text{...(ii)}$$

From Eqs. (i) and (ii), we can see that

$$i_c = i_d$$

Hence Proved.

INTRODUCTORY EXERCISE 29.1

1. A parallel-plate capacitor with plate area A and separation between the plates d, is charged by a constant current i. Consider a plane surface of area $A/2$ parallel to the plates and drawn symmetrically between the plates. Find the displacement current through this area.

29.3 **Electromagnetic Waves**

Stationary charges produce only electric field. Charges in uniform motion (or steady currents) produce both electric and magnetic fields. **Accelerated charges radiate electromagnetic waves.** It is an important result of Maxwell's theory. Thus, an accelerated charge produces all three electric field, magnetic field and electromagnetic waves.

Consider an oscillating charged particle. Let f is the frequency of its oscillations. This oscillating charged particle produces an oscillating electric field (of same frequency f). Now, this oscillating electric field becomes a source of oscillating magnetic field (Ampere-Maxwell's law). This oscillating magnetic field again becomes a source of oscillating electric field (Faraday's law) and so on.

The oscillating electric and magnetic fields regenerate each other and electromagnetic wave propagates through the space. The frequency of the electromagnetic wave is equal to the frequency of oscillation of the charge.

Frequency of visible light is of the order of 10^{14} Hz, while the maximum frequency that we can get with modern electronic circuits is of the order of 10^{11} Hz. Therefore, it is difficult to experimentally demonstrate the production of visible light. **Hertz's** experiment (in 1887) demonstrated the production of electromagnetic waves of low frequency (in radio wave region). **Jagdish Chandra Bose** succeeded in producing the electromagnetic waves of much higher frequency in the laboratory.

✅ *Extra Points to Remember*

- When electromagnetic waves propagate in space then electric and magnetic fields oscillate in mutually perpendicular directions. Further, they are perpendicular to the direction of propagation of electromagnetic wave also.

- Consider a plane electromagnetic wave propagating along the z-direction. The electric field E_x is along the x-axis and varies sinusoidally. The magnetic field B_y is along the y-axis and again varies sinusoidally. We can write E_x and B_y as

$$E_x = E_0 \sin (\omega t - kz) \quad \text{and} \quad B_y = B_0 \sin (\omega t - kz)$$

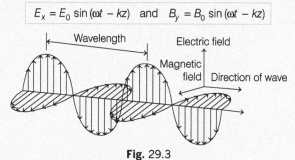

Fig. 29.3

Thus, electromagnetic wave travels in the direction of **E** × **B**.

- From Maxwell's equations and the knowledge of waves we can write the following expressions,

$$k = 2\pi/\lambda \quad \text{and} \quad \omega = 2\pi f \qquad \text{Speed of light (in vacuum)}$$
$$c = \frac{\omega}{k} = f\lambda = \frac{E_0}{B_0} = \frac{1}{\sqrt{\varepsilon_0 \mu_0}}$$

where, f is the frequency of electromagnetic wave and λ its wavelength.

- Unlike a mechanical wave (like sound wave) an electromagnetic wave does not require any material medium for the oscillations of electric and magnetic fields. They can travel in vacuum also. Oscillations of electric and magnetic fields are self sustaining in free space or vacuum.

- In a material medium (like glass, water etc.), electric and magnetic fields are different from the external fields. They are described in terms of permittivity ε and magnetic permeability μ. In Maxwell's equations, ε_0 and μ_0 are thus replaced by ε and μ and the velocity of light becomes,

$$v = \frac{1}{\sqrt{\varepsilon\mu}}$$

Thus, the velocity of light depends on electric and magnetic properties of the medium.

- Like other waves, electromagnetic waves also carry energy and momentum. In previous chapters, we have studied that, energy density in electric field $= \frac{1}{2}\varepsilon_0 E^2$ and energy density in magnetic field $= \frac{B^2}{2\mu_0}$.

An electromagnetic wave contains both electric and magnetic field. Therefore, energy density is associated with both the fields.

- Consider a plane perpendicular to the direction of propagation of the electromagnetic wave. If the total energy transferred to a surface in time t is E, then total momentum delivered to this surface for complete absorption is

$$\Delta p = \frac{E}{c} \qquad \text{(complete absorption)}$$

If the wave is totally reflected, the momentum delivered is

$$\Delta p = \frac{2E}{c} \qquad \text{(completely reflected)}$$

- The energy transferred per unit area per unit time perpendicular to the direction of propagation of electromagnetic wave is called the intensity of wave. It is given by

$$I = \frac{1}{2}\varepsilon_0 E^2 c$$

Here, E is the rms value of electric field or E_{rms}.

● **Example 29.2** *A plane electromagnetic wave of frequency 25 MHz travels in free space along the x-direction. At a particular point in space and time,* $E = (6.3\,\hat{\mathbf{j}})\,V/m$. *What is* $\mathbf{B}$ *at this point?*

Solution $$c = \frac{E_0}{B_0} \quad \text{or} \quad = \frac{E}{B}$$

$$\therefore \qquad\qquad B = \frac{E}{c}$$

Substituting the values in SI units,

$$B = \frac{6.3}{3 \times 10^8}$$

$$= 2.1 \times 10^{-8}\ \text{T}$$

From the relation $$\mathbf{c} = \mathbf{E} \times \mathbf{B}$$

We can see that $\mathbf{B}$ is along positive $\mathbf{z}$-direction. Because, $\mathbf{E}$ is along $\hat{\mathbf{j}}$ direction and $\mathbf{c}$ along $\hat{\mathbf{i}}$ direction.

$$\therefore \qquad\qquad \mathbf{B} = (2.1 \times 10^{-8}\ \text{T})\,\hat{\mathbf{k}} \qquad\qquad\qquad\qquad \textbf{Ans.}$$

⊘ **Example 29.3** *The magnetic field in a plane electromagnetic wave is given by*
$B_y = (2 \times 10^{-7} T) \sin (0.5 \times 10^3 x + 1.5 \times 10^{11} t) T$

(a) What is the wavelength and frequency of the wave?
(b) Write an expression for the electric field.

Solution (a) **Wavelength**

From the given equation, we can see that

$$k = 0.5 \times 10^3 \text{ m}^{-1}$$

But,

$$k = \frac{2\pi}{\lambda}$$

∴

$$\lambda = \frac{2\pi}{k} = \frac{2\pi}{0.5 \times 10^3}$$

$$= 1.25 \times 10^{-2} \text{ m}$$ **Ans.**

Frequency

Angular frequency,

$$\omega = 1.5 \times 10^{11} \text{ rad/s}$$

But,

$$\omega = 2\pi f$$

∴

$$f = \frac{\omega}{2\pi} = \frac{1.5 \times 10^{11}}{2\pi}$$ \

$$= 2.39 \times 10^{10} \text{ Hz}$$ **Ans.**

(b) $c = \dfrac{E_0}{B_0}$

∴

$$E_0 = cB_0$$

$$= (3.0 \times 10^8)(2 \times 10^{-7})$$

$$= 60 \text{ V/m}$$

From the relation,

$$\mathbf{c} = \mathbf{E} \times \mathbf{B}$$

We can see that **E** is along z-direction.

∴

$$E_z = (60 \text{ V/m}) \sin (0.5 \times 10^3 x + 1.5 \times 10^{11} t) \text{ V/m}$$ **Ans.**

⊘ **Example 29.4** *Light with an energy flux of* 18 *W/cm² falls on a non-reflecting surface at normal incidence. If the surface has an area of* 20 *cm², find the average force exerted on the surface during a* 30 *minute time span.*

Solution Total energy incident on the given surface in the given time interval is

$$E = (18 \times 10^4 \text{ W/m}^2)(20 \times 10^{-4} \text{ m}^2)(30 \times 60 \text{ s})$$

$$= 6.48 \times 10^5 \text{ J}$$

Therefore, the total momentum transferred to the given surface for complete absorption is

$$\Delta p = \frac{E}{c} = \frac{6.48 \times 10^5}{3.0 \times 10^8}$$

$$= 2.16 \times 10^{-3} \, \text{kg - m/s}$$

∴

$$F_{av} = \frac{\Delta p}{\Delta t} = \frac{2.16 \times 10^{-3}}{30 \times 60}$$

$$= 1.2 \times 10^{-6} \, \text{N}$$ **Ans.**

◉ **Example 29.5** *In the above example what is the average force if surface is perfectly reflecting?*

Solution (a) If the surface is perfectly reflecting, then

$$\Delta p = \frac{2E}{c}$$

Therefore, average force is doubled or

$$F_{av} = 2.4 \times 10^{-6} \, \text{N}$$ **Ans.**

◉ **Example 29.6** *Calculate the electric and magnetic fields produced by the radiation coming from a 100 W bulb at a distance of 3 m. Assume that the efficiency of the bulb is 2.5 % and it is a point source.*

Solution Intensity at a distance r from a point source of power P is given by

$$I = \frac{P}{4\pi r^2}$$

So, intensity at a distance of 3 m from the bulb with 2.5% efficiency will be

$$I = \frac{100}{4\pi \, (3)^2} \times \frac{2.5}{100}$$

$$= 0.022 \, \text{W/m}^2$$

Half of the intensity is provided by electric field and half by magnetic field.

∴

$$I_E = \frac{I}{2} = 0.011 \, \text{W/m}^2$$

But, I_E is given by $\frac{1}{2}\varepsilon_0 E^2 c$

∴

$$I_E = \frac{1}{2}\varepsilon_0 E^2 c \quad \text{or} \quad E = \sqrt{\frac{2 I_E}{\varepsilon_0 \, c}}$$

Substituting the values, we have

$$E = \sqrt{\frac{2 \times 0.011}{(8.85 \times 10^{-12})(3 \times 10^8)}}$$

$$= 2.9 \, \text{V/m}$$ **Ans.**

Note *that this is actually the rms value of electric field.*

From the equation, $c = E/B$

$$B = \frac{E}{c} = \frac{2.9}{3.0 \times 10^8}$$

$$= 9.6 \times 10^{-9} \text{ T} \qquad\qquad \textbf{Ans.}$$

This is again the rms value of magnetic field.

INTRODUCTORY EXERCISE 29.2

1. Show that the unit of $\dfrac{1}{\sqrt{\varepsilon_0 \mu_0}}$ is m/s.

2. A capacitor is connected to an alternating current source. Is there a magnetic field between the plates?

3. The sunlight reaching the earth has maximum electric field of 810 Vm^{-1}. What is the maximum magnetic field in this light?

4. The electric field in an electromagnetic wave is given by

$$E = (50 \text{ NC}^{-1}) \sin \omega (t - x/c) .$$

Find the energy contained in a cylinder of cross-section 10 cm^2 and length 50 cm along the x-axis.

29.4 Electromagnetic Spectrum

The basic source of electromagnetic wave is an accelerated charge. This produces the changing electric and magnetic fields which constitute an electromagnetic wave. An electromagnetic wave may have its wavelength varying from zero to infinity. Not all of them are known till date. Today, we are familiar with electromagnetic waves having wavelengths as small as 30 fm (1 fm $= 10^{-15}$ m) to as large as 30 km. The boundaries separating different regions of spectrum are not sharply defined, with visible light ranging from 4000 Å to 7000 Å. An approximate range of wavelengths associated with each colour are violet (4000 Å – 4500 Å), blue (4500 Å – 5200 Å), green (5200 Å – 5600 Å), yellow (5600 Å – 6000 Å), orange (6000 Å – 6250 Å) and red (6250 Å – 7000 Å).

The classification of electromagnetic waves according to frequency or wavelength is called electromagnetic spectrum. Table below gives range of wavelengths and frequencies for different waves.

Table 29.1

S.No.	Type	Wavelength range	Frequency range
1.	Radio waves	> 0.1 m	$< 3 \times 10^9$ Hz
2.	Micro waves	0.1 m to 1 mm	3×10^9 Hz to 3×10^{11} Hz
3.	Infrared	1 mm to 7000 Å	3×10^{11} Hz to 4.3×10^{14} Hz

S.No.	Type	Wavelength range	Frequency range
4.	Visible light	7000 Å to 4000 Å	4.3×10^{14} Hz to 7.5×10^{14} Hz
5.	Ultraviolet	4000 Å to 10 Å	7.5×10^{14} Hz to 3×10^{17} Hz
6.	X-rays	10 Å to 0.01 Å	3×10^{17} Hz to 3×10^{20} Hz
7.	Gamma rays	< 0.01 Å	$> 3 \times 10^{20}$ Hz

Note *In the above table, wavelength is decreasing from top to bottom. But, frequency is increasing. Now, let us discuss them in brief in the order of increasing wavelength.*

1. **Gamma Rays** These high frequency radiations are usually produced in nuclear reactions and also emitted by radioactive nuclei. They are used in medicines to destroy cancer cells.

2. **X-Rays** X-rays were discovered in 1895 by W.Roentgen. These are produced by the rapid deceleration of electrons that bombard a heavy metal target. These are also produced by electronic transitions between the energy levels in an atom. X-rays are used as a diagnostic tool in medicine and as a treatment for certain forms of cancer.

3. **Ultraviolet Rays** Ultraviolet radiation is produced by special lamps and very hot bodies. The sun is an important source of ultraviolet light. It plays an important role in the production of vitamin-D. But prolonged doses of UV radiation can induce skin cancers in human beings. Ozone layer in atmosphere at an altitude of about 40-50 km plays a protective role in this regarding. Depletion of this layer by chlorofluorocarbon (CFC) gas (such as Freon) is a matter of international concern now a days.

4. **Visible Light** It is most familiar form of electromagnetic waves.Our eye is sensitive to visible light. Visible light emitted or reflected from objects around us provides information about world. Process of photosynthesis in plants needs visible light. Visible light is produced by the transition of electrons in an atom from one energy level to other.

5. **Infrared Radiation** Infrared rays also sometimes referred as heat waves are produced by hot bodies. They are perceived by us as heat. In most of the materials, water molecules are present. These molecules readily absorb infrared rays. After absorption, their thermal motion increases, i.e. they heat up and heat their surroundings. Infrared rays are used for early detection of tumors. Infrared detectors are also used to observe growth of crops and for military purposes.

6. **Microwaves** Microwaves may be generated by the oscillations of electrons in a device called klystron. Microwave ovens are used in kitchens. In microwave ovens frequency of the microwaves is selected to match the resonant frequency of water molecules so that energy from the waves is transferred to the kinetic energy of the molecules. This raises the temperature of any food containing water.

7. **Radio Waves** Radio waves are generated when charges are accelerating through conducting wires. They are generated in L - C oscillators and are used in radio and television communication systems.

Extra Points to Remember

- Our eyes are sensitive to visible light (λ between 4000 Å to 7000 Å). Similarly, different animals are sensitive to different ranges of wavelengths. For example, snakes can detect infrared waves.

- The basic difference between different types of electromagnetic waves lies in their frequencies and wavelengths. All of them travel with same speed in vacuum. Further they differ in their mode of interaction with matter.

  For example infrared waves vibrate the electrons, atoms and molecules of a substance. These vibrations increase the internal energy and temperature of the substance. This is why infrared waves are also called heat waves.

- Electromagnetic waves interact with matter *via* their electric and magnetic fields, which set in oscillation with the charges present in all matter. This interaction depends on the wavelength of the electromagnetic wave and the nature of atoms or molecules in the medium.

- **Microwave Oven** In electromagnetic spectrum frequency and energy of microwaves is smaller than the visible light. Water content is required for cooking food in microwave oven. Almost all food items contain some water content. Microwaves interact with water molecules and atoms *via* their electric and magnetic fields. Temperature of water molecules increases by this. These water molecules share this energy with neighboring food molecules, heating up the food.

  Porcelain vessels are used for cooking food in microwave oven. Because its large molecules vibrate and rotate with much smaller frequencies and do not get heated up. We cannot use metal vessels. Metal vessels interact with microwaves. These vessels may melt due to heating.

Solved Examples

Example 1 *Long distance radio broadcasts use short wave bands. Explain why?*

Solution Short radio waves are reflected by ionosphere.

Example 2 *It is necessary to use satellites for long distance TV transmission. Explain why?*

Solution TV waves (part of radio waves) range from 54 MHz to 890 MHz. Unlike short wave bands (used in radio broadcasts) which are reflected by ionosphere, TV waves are not properly reflected by ionosphere. This is why, satellites are used for long distance TV transmission.

Example 3 *The ozone layer on the top of the stratosphere is crucial for human survival. Explain why?*

Solution Ozone layer protects ourselves from ultraviolet radiations. Over exposure to UV radiation can cause skin cancer in human beings. Ozone layer absorbs UV radiations. But unfortunately over use of Chlorofluoro Carbon Gases (CFCs) is depleting this ozone layer and it is a matter of international concern now a days.

Example 4 *Optical and radio telescopes are built on ground but X-ray astronomy is possible only from satellites orbiting the earth. Explain why?*

Solution Visible and radio waves can penetrate the atmosphere, while X-rays are absorbed by the atmosphere. This is why X-ray telescopes are installed in satellites orbiting the earth.

Example 5 *If the earth did not have an atmosphere, would its average surface temperature be higher or lower than what it is now?*

Solution Due to presence of atmosphere green house effect takes place. Heat radiated by earth is trapped due to green house effect. In the absence of atmosphere, temperature of the earth would be lower because the green house effect of the atmosphere would be absent.

Example 6 *Some scientists have predicted the global nuclear war on the earth would be followed by a severe nuclear winter with a devastating effect on life on earth. What might be the basis of this prediction?*

Solution After nuclear war, clouds would perhaps cover the atmosphere of earth preventing solar light from reaching many parts of earth. This would cause a winter.

Example 7 *Why is the orientation of the portable radio with respect to broadcasting station important?*

Solution Electromagnetic waves are plane polarised, so the receiving antenna should be parallel to electric and magnetic part of wave.

◉ **Example 8** *A plane electromagnetic wave propagating in the x-direction has a wavelength of 5.0 mm. The electric field is in the y-direction and its maximum magnitude is 30 Vm^{-1}. Write suitable equations for the electric and magnetic fields as a function of x and t.*

Solution Given,

$$\lambda = 5\,\text{mm} = 5 \times 10^{-3}\,\text{m}$$

$$k = \frac{2\pi}{\lambda} = \frac{2\pi}{5 \times 10^{-3}}\,\text{m}^{-1}$$

$$= 1257\,\text{m}^{-1}$$

From the equation,

$$c = \frac{\omega}{k}$$

$$\omega = c\,k = (3 \times 10^8)\,(1257)$$

$$= 3.77 \times 10^{11}\,\text{rad/s}$$

$$E_0 = 30\,\text{V/m}$$

$$c = \frac{E_0}{B_0}$$

∴

$$B_0 = \frac{E_0}{c} = \frac{30}{3 \times 10^8}$$

$$= 10^{-7}\,\text{T}$$

Now,

$$E_y = E_0 \sin(\omega t - kx)$$

$$= (30\,\text{V/m}) \sin[(3.77 \times 10^{11}\,\text{s}^{-1})\,t - (1257\,\text{m}^{-1})\,x]$$

and

$$B_z = (10^{-7}\,\text{T}) \sin[(3.77 \times 10^{11}\,\text{s}^{-1})\,t - (1257\,\text{m}^{-1})\,x] \qquad \textbf{Ans.}$$

◉ **Example 9** *A light beam travelling in the x-direction is described by the electric field $E_y = (300\,Vm^{-1}) \sin \omega(t - x/c)$. An electron is constrained to move along the y-direction with a speed of $2.0 \times 10^7\,ms^{-1}$. Find the maximum electric force and the maximum magnetic force on the electron.*

Solution **Maximum Electric Force**

Maximum electric field,

$$E_0 = 300\,\text{V/m}$$

∴ Maximum electric force

$$F = qE_0$$

$$= (1.6 \times 10^{-19})\,(300)$$

$$= 4.8 \times 10^{-17}\,\text{N} \qquad \textbf{Ans.}$$

Maximum Magnetic Force

From the equation,

$$c = \frac{E_0}{B_0}$$

Maximum magnetic field,

$$B_0 = \frac{E_0}{c}$$

or

$$B_0 = \frac{300}{3.0 \times 10^8} = 10^{-6}\,\text{T}$$

∴ Maximum magnetic force

$$= B_0 q v \sin 90° = B_0 q v$$

Substituting the values, we have

Maximum magnetic force

$$= (10^{-6})(1.6 \times 10^{-19})(2.0 \times 10^7)$$

$$= 3.2 \times 10^{-18}\,\text{N} \qquad \textbf{Ans.}$$

❯ *Example 10* *A parallel plate capacitor having plate area A and plate separation d is joined to a battery of emf V and internal resistance R at t = 0. Consider a plane surface of area A/2, parallel to the plates and situated symmetrically between them. Find the displacement current through this surface as a function of time. [The charge on the capacitor at time t is given by* $q = CV(1 - e^{-t/\tau})$, *where* $\tau = CR$]

Solution   Given,
$$q = CV(1 - e^{-t/\tau})$$

∴   Surface charge density,
$$\sigma = \frac{q}{A} = \frac{CV}{A}(1 - e^{-t/\tau})$$

Electric field between the plates of capacitor,
$$E = \frac{\sigma}{\varepsilon_0} = \frac{CV}{\varepsilon_0 A}(1 - e^{-t/\tau})$$

Electric flux from the given area,
$$\phi_E = \frac{EA}{2} = \frac{CV}{2\varepsilon_0}(1 - e^{-t/\tau})$$

Displacement current,
$$i_d = \varepsilon_0 \frac{d\phi_E}{dt}$$

or
$$i_d = \varepsilon_0 \frac{d}{dt}\left[\frac{CV}{2\varepsilon_0}(1 - e^{-t/\tau})\right] = \frac{CV}{2\tau}e^{-t/\tau}$$

Substituting,
$$\tau = CR$$

We have,
$$i_d = \frac{V}{2R}e^{-t/CR}$$

Again substituting,
$$C = \frac{\varepsilon_0 A}{d}$$

$$i_d = \frac{V}{2R}e^{-\frac{td}{\varepsilon_0 AR}}$$ **Ans.**

❯ *Example 11*   *About 5% of the power of a 100 W light bulb is converted to visible radiation. What is the average intensity of visible radiation*
(a) at a distance of 1 m from the bulb?
(b) at a distance of 10 m?
Assume that the radiation is emitted isotropically and neglect reflection.

Solution   Effective power (energy radiated per second)
$$= 5\% \text{ of } 100 \text{ W}$$
$$P = 5 \text{ W}$$

This energy will distribute on a sphere. At a distance r from the point source, area on which light is incident is

$$S = 4\,\pi r^2$$

∴ Intensity at distance r from the point source,

$$I = \frac{P}{S} = \frac{5}{4\pi r^2} = \text{Energy incident per unit area per unit time}$$

(a) At $r = 1\,\text{m}$,

$$I = \frac{5}{4\pi\,(1)^2}$$

$$= 0.4 \text{ W/m}^2 \qquad\qquad \textbf{Ans.}$$

(b) At $r = 10$ m,

$$I = \frac{5}{4\pi\,(10)^2}$$

$$= 0.004 \text{ W/m}^2 \qquad\qquad \textbf{Ans.}$$

⊘ **Example 12**   *Suppose that the electric field of an electromagnetic wave in vacuum is* $E = \{(3.0\ N/C)\cos[(1.8\ rad/m)\ y + (5.4 \times 10^6\ rad/s)\ t]\}\ \hat{i}.$

(a) What is the direction of propagation of wave?

(b) What is the wavelength λ?

(c) What is the frequency f?

(d) What is the amplitude of the magnetic field of the wave?

(e) Write an expression for the magnetic field of the wave.

Solution (a) From the knowledge of wave we can see that electromagnetic wave is travelling along negative y-direction, as ωt and ky both are positive.

(b) $k = 1.8$ rad/m

$$k = \frac{2\pi}{\lambda}$$

∴ $$\lambda = \frac{2\pi}{k} = \frac{2\pi}{1.8} = 3.5 \text{ m} \qquad\qquad \textbf{Ans.}$$

(c) $\omega = 5.4 \times 10^6$ rad/s

$$\omega = 2\pi f$$

∴ $$f = \frac{\omega}{2\pi} = \frac{5.4 \times 10^6}{2\pi}$$

$$= 8.6 \times 10^5 \text{ Hz} \qquad\qquad \textbf{Ans.}$$

(d) $\qquad\qquad E_0 = 3.0 \text{ N/C}$

From the relation, $\qquad\qquad c = \dfrac{E_0}{B_0}$

We have, $\qquad\qquad B_0 = \dfrac{E_0}{c} = \dfrac{3.0}{3.0 \times 10^8}$

$$= 10^{-8} \text{ T} \qquad\qquad \textbf{Ans.}$$

(e) **E** is along $\hat{i}$ direction, wave is travelling along negative y-direction. Therefore, oscillations of **B** are along z-direction or

$$\textbf{B} = (10^{-8} \text{ T}) \cos [(1.8 \text{ rad/m}) \ y + (5.4 \times 10^6 \text{ rad/s}) \ t] \ \hat{k} \qquad\qquad \textbf{Ans.}$$

◈ **Example 13** *A parallel plate capacitor made of circular plates each of radius R = 6.0 cm has a capacitance C = 100 pF. The capacitor is connected to a 230 V AC supply with a (angular) frequency of 300 rad/s.*

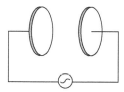

(a) *What is the rms value of the conduction current?*

(b) *Is the conduction current equal to the displacement current?*

(c) *Determine the amplitude of B at a point 3.0 cm from the axis between the plates.*

Solution (a) Capacitive reactance,

$$X_C = \frac{1}{\omega C}$$

$$= \frac{1}{300 \times 100 \times 10^{-12}}$$

$$= \frac{10^8}{3}\ \Omega$$

There is only capacitance in the circuit.

∴ $$i_{rms} = \frac{V_{rms}}{X_C}$$

$$= \frac{230}{(10^8/3)}$$

$$= 6.9 \times 10^{-6}\ \text{A} \qquad\qquad\qquad \textbf{Ans.}$$

(b) Yes, the derivation in example 29.1 is true even if current is alternating.

(c) Here, i_d is displacement current and i the conduction current. Magnetic field at a distance r from the axis,

$$B = \frac{\mu_0}{2\pi} \frac{i_d}{R^2} r$$

∴ $$B_{rms} = \frac{\mu_0}{2\pi} \frac{i_{rms}}{R^2} r \qquad\qquad\qquad (i_d = i = i_{rms})$$

Substituting the values, we have

$$B_{rms} = \frac{(2 \times 10^{-7})\,(6.9 \times 10^{-6})}{(6 \times 10^{-2})^2}\,(3 \times 10^{-2})$$

$$= 1.15 \times 10^{-11}\ \text{T}$$

∴ $$B_0 = \sqrt{2}\ B_{rms}$$

$$= (\sqrt{2})\,(1.15 \times 10^{-11})\ \text{T}$$

$$= 1.63 \times 10^{-11}\ \text{T} \qquad\qquad\qquad \textbf{Ans.}$$

Exercises

Single Correct Option

1. One requires 11eV of energy to dissociate a carbon monoxide molecule into carbon and oxygen atoms. The minimum frequency of the appropriate electromagnetic radiation to achieve the dissociation lies in
   (a) visible region
   (b) infrared region
   (c) ultraviolet region
   (d) microwave region

2. If **E** and **B** represent electric and magnetic field vectors of the electromagnetic wave, the direction of propagation of electromagnetic wave is along
   (a) **E**
   (b) **B**
   (c) **B** × **E**
   (d) **E** × **B**

3. The ratio of contributions made by the electric field and magnetic field components to the intensity of an EM wave is
   (a) $c:1$
   (b) $c^2:1$
   (c) $1:1$
   (d) $\sqrt{c}:1$

4. Light with an energy flux of 20 W/cm^2 falls on a non-reflecting surface at normal incidence. If the surface has an area of 30 cm^2. The total momentum delivered (for complete absorption) during 30 minutes is
   (a) 36×10^{-5} kg-m/s
   (b) 36×10^{-4} kg-m/s
   (c) 1.08×10^4 kg-m/s
   (d) 1.08×10^7 kg-m/s

More than One Correct Options

5. A plane electromagnetic wave propagating along x-direction can have the following pairs of **E** and **B**
   (a) E_x, B_y
   (b) E_y, B_z
   (c) B_x, E_y
   (d) E_z, B_y

6. The source of electromagnetic waves can be a charge
   (a) moving with a constant velocity
   (b) moving in a circular orbit
   (c) at rest
   (d) falling in an electric field

7. An electromagnetic wave of intensity I falls on a surface kept in vacuum and exerts radiation pressure p on it. Which of the following are true?
   (a) Radiation pressure is I/c if the wave is totally absorbed
   (b) Radiation pressure is I/c if the wave is totally reflected
   (c) Radiation pressure is $2I/c$ if the wave is totally reflected
   (d) Radiation pressure is in the range $I/c < p < 2I/c$ for real surfaces

8. A charged particle oscillates about its mean equilibrium position with a frequency of 10^9 Hz. The electromagnetic waves produced
   (a) will have frequency of 10^9 Hz
   (b) will have frequency of 2×10^9 Hz
   (c) will have a wavelength of 0.3 m
   (d) fall in the region of radio waves

Subjective Questions

9. Can an electromagnetic wave be deflected by an electric field? By a magnetic field?

10. What physical quantity is the same for X-rays of wavelength 10^{-10}m, red light of wavelength 6800 Å and radio waves of wavelength 500 m?

11. A plane electromagnetic wave travels in vacuum along z-direction. What can you say about the directions of its electric and magnetic field vectors? If the frequency of the wave is 30 MHz, what is its wavelength?

12. A radio can tune into any station in the 7.5 MHz to 12 MHz band. What is the corresponding wavelength of band?

13. The amplitude of the magnetic field part of a harmonic electromagnetic wave in vacuum is $B_0 = 510$ nT. What is the amplitude of the electric field part of the wave?

14. Figure shows a capacitor made of two circular plates each of radius 12 cm, and separated by 5.0 cm. The capacitor is being charged by an external source (not shown in the figure). The charging current is constant and equal to 0.15 A.

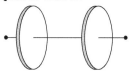

   (a) Calculate the capacitance and the rate of change of potential difference between the plates.
   (b) Obtain the displacement current across the plates.
   (c) Is Kirchhoff's first rule (junction rule) valid at each plate of the capacitor? Explain.

15. Suppose that the electric field amplitude of an electromagnetic wave is $E_0 = 120$N/C and that its frequency is 50.0 MHz. (a) Determine B_0, ω, k and λ, (b) Find expressions for **E** and **B**.

16. A variable frequency AC source is connected to a capacitor. How will the displacement current change with decrease in frequency?

17. A laser beam has intensity 2.5×10^{14} Wm^{-2}. Find the amplitudes of electric and magnetic fields in the beam.

18. In a plane electromagnetic wave, the electric field oscillates sinusoidally at a frequency of 2.0×10^{10} Hz and amplitude 48 Vm^{-1}.

   (a) What is the wavelength of the wave?
   (b) What is the amplitude of the oscillating magnetic field?
   (c) Show that the average energy density of the field **E** equals the average energy density of the field **B**. $[c = 3 \times 10^8$ ms$^{-1}]$.

19. The charge on a parallel plate capacitor varies as $q = q_0 \cos 2\pi ft$. The plates are very large and close together (area $= A$, separation $= d$). Neglecting the edge effects, find the displacement current through the capacitor.

Answers

Introductory Exercise 29.1

1. $i/2$

Introductory Exercise 29.2

2. Yes 3. $2.7\,\mu T$ 4. 5.55×10^{-12} J

Exercises

1. (c)   2 (d)   3. (c)   4. (b)
5. (b,d)   6. (b,d)   7. (a,c,d)   8. (a,c,d)
9. No, No
10. The speed in vacuum is the same for all
11. **E** and **B** lie in x-y plane and are mutually perpendicular, 10 m
12. Wavelength band from 40 m to 25 m
13. 153 N/C
14. (a) 8.0 pF, 1.87×10^{10} Vs^{-1} (b) 0.15 A

    (c) Yes, provided by current we mean the sum of conduction and displacement currents.
15. (a) 400 nT, 3.14×10^{8} rad/s, 1.05 rad/m, 6.00 m

    (b) $E = (120$ N/C$)$ sin $[(1.05$ rad/m$)]$ $x - (3.14 \times 10^{8}$ rad/s$)t]$

      $B = ($ 400 nT$)$ sin $[(1.05$ rad/m$)]$ $x - (3.14 \times 10^{8}$ rad/s$)$ $t]$
16. Displacement current will decrease
17. 4.3×10^{8} N/C , 1.44 T
18. (a) 1.5×10^{-2} m   (b) 1.6×10^{-7} T
19. $-2\pi q_{0} f$ sin $2\pi\,ft$

30

REFLECTION OF LIGHT

30.1 **Introduction**

The branch of physics called **optics** deals with the behaviour of light and other electromagnetic waves. Light is the principal means by which we gain knowledge of the world. Consequently, the nature of light has been the source of one of the longest debates in the history of science.

Electromagnetic radiation with wavelengths in the range of about 4000 Å to 7000 Å, to which eye is sensitive is called light.

In the present and next two chapters we investigate the behaviour of a beam of light when it encounters simple optical devices like mirrors, lenses and apertures. Under many circumstances, the wavelength of light is negligible compared with the dimensions of the device as in the case of ordinary mirrors and lenses. A light beam can then be treated as a ray whose propagation is governed by simple geometric rules. The part of optics that deals with such phenomena is known as **geometric optics.** However, if the wavelength is not negligible compared with the dimensions of the device (for example a very narrow slit), the ray approximation becomes invalid and we have to examine the behaviour of light in terms of its wave properties. This study is known as **physical optics.**

30.2 **General Concepts used in Geometrical Optics**

Some general concepts which are used in whole geometrical optics are given below.

1. Normal incidence means angle of incidence (with normal) is 0°. If angle of incidence is 90°, it is called grazing incidence.

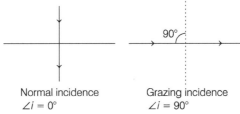

Normal incidence
$\angle i = 0°$

Grazing incidence
$\angle i = 90°$

Fig. 30.1

2. An image is formed either by reflection or refraction. Minimum two (reflected or refracted) rays are required for image formation. More the number of rays, more will be the intensity of image.

3. A light is reflected only from a silvered surface. Without any reflecting surface on the path of ray of light it keeps on moving ahead.

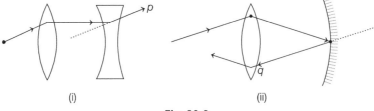

(i)

(ii)

Fig. 30.2

In figure (i) For image formation, if reflected ray-p is required to the left of concave lens, then we will take it as dotted line.

In figure (ii) For image formation, if reflected ray-q is required to the right of concave mirror, then we will take it as dotted line.

4. **Real object, virtual object, real image, virtual image** The point where the rays meet (or appear to meet) before refraction or reflection is called object and the point where the rays meet (or appear to meet) after refraction or reflection is called image. Further, object (or image) is real if dark lines meet and virtual if dotted lines meet.

In figure (a), object is real, while image is virtual. In figure (b), object is virtual while its image is real.

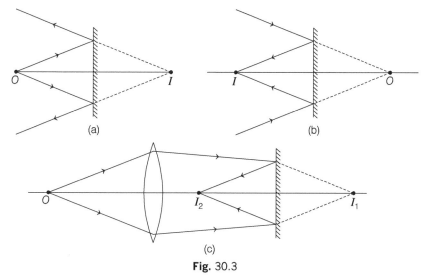

Fig. 30.3

In figure (c), the object O is real. Its image formed by the lens (i.e. I_1) is real. But, it acts as a virtual object for mirror which forms its real image I_2.

5. The virtual images cannot be taken on screen. But, they can be seen by our eye. Because our eye lens forms their real image on our retina. Thus, if we put a screen at I in the above figure (a) no image will be formed on it. At the same time if we put the screen at I in figure (b), image will be formed.

6. Normally, the object is kept on the left hand side of the optical instrument (mirror, lens etc.), i.e. the ray of light travels from left to right. Sometimes, it may happen that the light is travelling in opposite direction. See the figure.

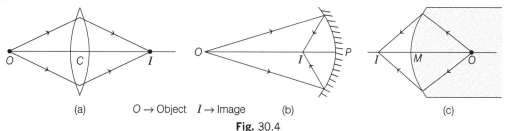

Fig. 30.4

In figures (a) and (b), light is travelling from left to right and in figure (c) it is travelling from right to left.

7. **Sign convention** The distances measured along the incident light are taken as positive while the distances measured against incident light are taken as negative. For example, in figures (a) and (b) the incident light travels from left to right. So, the distances measured in this direction are positive. While in figure (c) the incident light travels from right to left. So, in this case right to left direction will be positive. Distances are measured from pole of the mirror [point P in figure (b)], optical centre of the lens [point C in figure (a)] and the centre of the refracting surface [point M in figure (c)].

It may happen in some problem that sign convention does not remain same for the whole problem.

For example, in the Fig. 30.5 shown, the ray of light starting from O first undergoes refraction at A, then reflection at B and then finally refraction at C. For refraction and reflection at A and B the incident light is travelling from left to right, so distances measured along this direction are positive. For final refraction at C the incident light travels from right to left, so now the sign convention will change or right to left is positive.

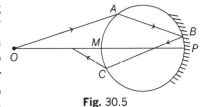

Fig. 30.5

8. Object distance (from P, C or M along the optic axis) in Fig. 30.4 is shown by u and image distance by v.

9. In front of mirror, object (or image) is always real, lines are always dark and u (or v) are always negative.

Behind the mirror object (or image) is always virtual, lines are always dotted and u (or v) are always positive.

This is because light always falls from front side of the mirror.

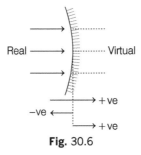

Fig. 30.6

10. In most of the cases, objects are real (whether refraction or reflection) and u for them is negative.

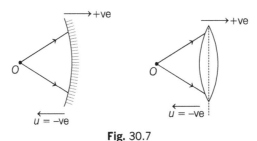

Fig. 30.7

11. In case of mirror light always falls from front of the mirror. But in a lens (or some other refracting surface like slab) light can fall from both sides.

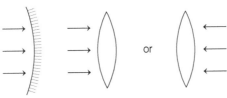

Fig. 30.8

12. **Total steps and reduced steps**
   In Fig. 30.9 total steps are five. Four of them are refraction. Only third is reflection. But we have made a lens formula for steps 1 and 2 or 4 and 5. So, the reduced steps are three,

   $$\text{lens} \rightarrow \text{mirror} \rightarrow \text{lens}.$$

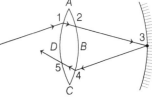

Fig. 30.9

13. **Image real or virtual** In Fig.30.9, if we wish to find the nature of I_2 (after 2nd refraction), then it is real if it is formed to the right of ABC because ray of light has moved to this side and it is virtual to the left of ABC. Similarly, I_5 is real to the left of ADC and virtual to the right of ADC.

14. **Final image coincides with the object** In most of these cases there will be one mirror, plane or spherical (convex or concave) and light will be falling normal ($\angle i = 0°$) to this mirror. In case of spherical mirror it is normal if ray of light passes through centre of curvature. In case of normal incidence, ray of light retraces its path and final image coincides with the object.

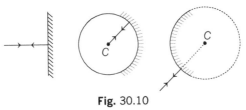

Fig. 30.10

In all above figures, $\angle i = 0°$ (normal incidence). Ray of light retraces its path.

15. Image at infinity means rays after refraction or reflection have become parallel to the optic axis. If a screen is placed directly in between these parallel rays no image will be formed on the screen. But if a lens (or a mirror) is placed on the path of these parallel rays, then image is formed at focus. Sometimes, our eye plays the role of this lens and the image is formed on our retina.

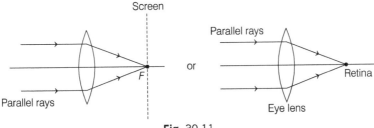

Fig. 30.11

16. **Visual angle θ** Angle subtended by an object on our eye is called the visual angle. The apparent size depends on the visual angle. As the object moves away from the eye, actual size remains the same but visual angle decreases. Therefore, apparent size decreases.

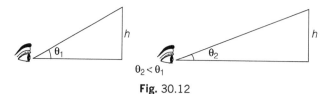

Fig. 30.12

30.3 **Reflection of Light**

When waves of any type strike the interface between two different materials, new waves are generated which move away from the interface. Experimentally, it is found that the rays corresponding to the incident and reflected waves make equal angles with the normal to the interface and that the reflected ray lies in the plane of incidence formed by the incident ray and the normal. Thus, the two laws of reflection can be summarised as under:

(i) $\angle i = \angle r$

(ii) Incident ray, reflected ray and normal lie on the same plane.

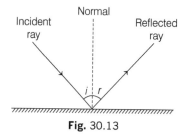

Fig. 30.13

Two Important Points in Reflection Laws

1. The first law $\angle i = \angle r$ can be applied for any type of surface. The main point is, normal at point of incidence. In spherical surface (convex mirror or concave mirror) normal at any point passes through centre of curvature.

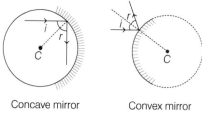

Concave mirror   Convex mirror

Fig. 30.14

2. Incident ray, reflected ray and normal are sometimes represented in the form of three vectors. Then, these three vectors should be coplanar.

Reflection from a Plane Surface (or Plane Mirror)

Almost everybody is familiar with the image formed by a plane mirror. If the object is real, the image formed by a plane mirror is virtual, erect, of same size and at the same distance from the mirror. The ray diagram of the image of a point object and of an extended object is as shown below.

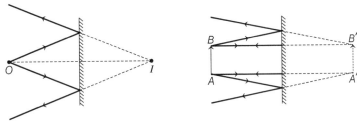

Fig. 30.15

Important Points in Reflection from Plane Mirror

1. Relation between object distance (u) and the image distance (v) in case of plane mirror is

    $$v = -u$$

    Here, v and u are measured from the plane surface. Two conclusions can be drawn from this equation.
    (i) Negative sign implies that object and image are on opposite sides of the mirror. So, if object is real then image is virtual and *vice-versa*.
    (ii) $|v| = |u|$
    And this implies that perpendicular distance of the object from the mirror is equal to the perpendicular distance of image from the mirror.

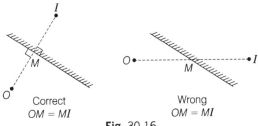

Correct
OM = MI

Wrong
OM = MI

Fig. 30.16

2. **Ray Diagram** Let us draw the ray diagram of a point object and an extended object.

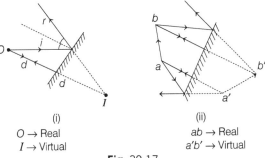

(i)
$O \rightarrow$ Real
$I \rightarrow$ Virtual

(ii)
$ab \rightarrow$ Real
$a'b' \rightarrow$ Virtual

Fig. 30.17

Just as we have drawn the ray diagram of point object O in figure (i), we can also draw the ray diagrams of points a and b in figure (ii).

3. **Field of view of an object for a given mirror**   Suppose a point object O is placed in front of a small mirror as shown in Fig. 30.18 (a), then a question arises in mind whether this mirror will make the image of this object or not. Or suppose an elephant is standing in front of a small mirror, will the mirror form the image of the elephant or not. The answer is yes, it will form. A mirror whatever may be the size of it forms the images of all objects lying in front of it. But every object has its own field of view for the given mirror. The field of view is the region between the extreme reflected rays and depends on the location of the object in front of the mirror. If our eye lies in the field of view then only we can see the image of the object otherwise not. The field of view of an object placed at different locations in front of a plane mirror are shown in Fig. 30.18 (b) and (c).

The region between extreme reflected rays (reflected from the end points of the mirror) is called the field of view. To see the image of object eye should lie in this region, as all reflected rays lie in this region.

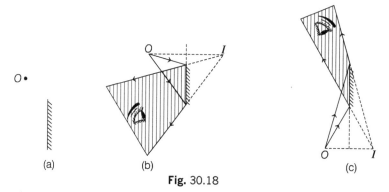

(a)   (b)   (c)

Fig. 30.18

4. Suppose a mirror is rotated by an angle θ (say anti-clockwise), keeping the incident ray fixed then the reflected ray rotates by 2θ along the same direction, i.e. anti-clockwise.

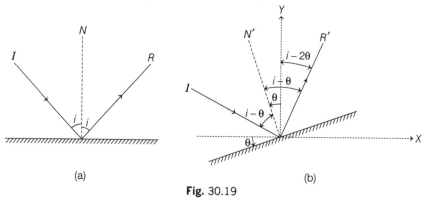

(a)   (b)

Fig. 30.19

In figure (a), I is the incident ray, N the normal and R the reflected ray.
In figure (b), I remains as it is N and R shift to N' and R'.
From the two figures, we can see that earlier the reflected ray makes an angle i with y-axis while after rotating the mirror it makes an angle $i - 2\theta$. Thus, we may conclude that the reflected ray has been rotated by an angle 2θ.

5. The minimum length of a plane mirror to see one's full height is $\dfrac{H}{2}$, where H is the height of person. But, the mirror should be placed in a fixed position which is shown in Fig. 30.20.

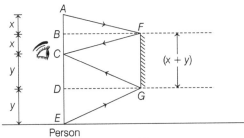

Fig. 30.20

A ray starting from head (A) after reflecting from upper end of the mirror (F) reaches the eye at C. Similarly, the ray starting from the foot (E) after reflecting from the lower end (G) also reaches the eye at C. In two similar triangles ABF and BFC, $AB = BC = x$ (say), Similarly in triangles CDG and DGE,

$$CD = DE = y \text{ (say)}$$

Now, we can see that height of the person is $2(x + y)$ and that of mirror is $(x + y)$, i.e. height of the mirror is half the height of the person.

Note *The mirror can be placed anywhere between the centre lines BF (of AC) and DG (of CE). As the mirror is moved away on this line, image also moves away from the person. So, apparent size keeps on decreasing.*

6. A person is standing exactly at midway between a wall and a mirror and he wants to see the full height of the wall (behind him) in a plane mirror (in front of him). The minimum length of mirror in this case should be $\dfrac{H}{3}$, where H is the height of wall. The ray diagram in this case is shown in Fig. 30.21

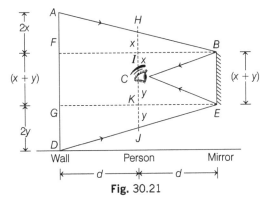

Fig. 30.21

In triangles HBI and IBC, $HI = IC = x$ (say). Now, in triangles HBI and ABF,

$$\frac{AF}{HI} = \frac{FB}{BI} \quad \text{or} \quad \frac{AF}{x} = \frac{2d}{d} \quad \text{or} \quad AF = 2x$$

Similarly, we can prove that $DG = 2y$ if, $CK = KJ = y$

Now, we can see that height of the wall is $3(x + y)$ while that of the mirror is $(x + y)$.

7. **Object and image velocity** There are four important points related to object and image velocity.

  (i) Image speed is equal to the object speed.

  (ii) Image velocity and object velocity make same angles from the plane mirror on two opposite sides of the mirror.

  (iii) Components of velocities which are along the mirror are equal.

  (iv) Components of velocities which are perpendicular to the mirror are equal and opposite.
    The following four figures demonstrate the above four points.

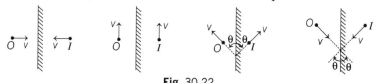

Fig. 30.22

Three Types of Problems in Reflection from Plane Mirror

Type 1. *Based on law of reflection* $\angle i = \angle r$

Concept

These problems are purely based on geometry. Proper normal at point of incidence is very important.

◉ **Example 30.1** *Two plane mirrors M_1 and M_2 are inclined at angle θ as shown. A ray of light 1, which is parallel to M_1 strikes M_2 and after two reflections, the ray 2 becomes parallel to M_2. Find the angle θ.*

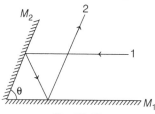

Fig. 30.23

Solution Different angles are as shown in Fig. 30.24. In triangle *ABC*,

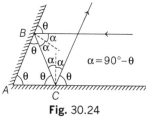

Fig. 30.24

$$\theta + \theta + \theta = 180°$$

∴ $$\theta = 60° \qquad\qquad\qquad \textbf{Ans.}$$

⊛ **Example 30.2** *Prove that for any value of angle i, rays 1 and 2 are parallel.*

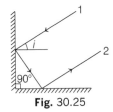

Fig. 30.25

Solution PQ and MN are mutually parallel. Rays 1 and 2 are making equal angles (= $\angle i$) from PQ and MN. So, they are mutually parallel.

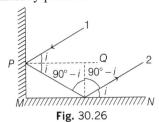

Fig. 30.26

Important Result Two plane mirrors kept at 90° deviate each ray of light by 180° from its original path.

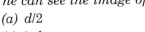

Concept

The region between extreme reflected rays is called field of view. To see the image of object our eye should lie in the field of view.

⊛ **Example 30.3** *A point source of light S, placed at a distance L in front of the centre of a mirror of width d, hangs vertically on a wall. A man walks in front of the mirror along a line parallel to the mirror at a distance 2L from it as shown. The greatest distance over which he can see the image of the light source in the mirror is*

(a) $d/2$ 　　　　　　　　(b) d

(c) $2d$ 　　　　　　　　(d) $3d$ 　　　　(JEE 2000)

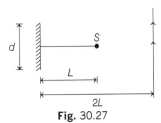

Fig. 30.27

Solution (d) The ray diagram will be as shown in Fig. 30.28.

$$HI = AB = d$$
$$DS = CD = \frac{d}{2}$$

Since, 　　　　　　　　$AH = 2AD$

∴ 　　　　　$GH = 2CD = 2\frac{d}{2} = d$

Similarly, 　　　　　　$IJ = d$

∴ 　　$GJ = GH + HI + IJ = d + d + d = 3d$

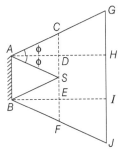

Fig. 30.28

⊚ **Example 30.4** *A pole of height 4 m is kept in front of a vertical plane mirror of length 2 m. The lower end of the mirror is at a height of 6 m from the ground. The horizontal distance between the mirror and the pole is 2 m. Upto what minimum and maximum heights a man can see the image of top of the pole at a horizontal distance of 4 m (from the mirror) standing on the same horizontal line which is passing through the pole and the horizontal point below the mirror?*

Solution PQ = Pole, MN = Image of pole

$$\frac{HG}{GN} = \frac{BD}{BN}$$

∴
$$BD = \frac{(HG)(BN)}{GN} = \frac{(2)(6)}{2}$$

$$= 6\,\text{m}$$

Minimum height required $= AD = BD + AB = 10\,\text{m}$

Further, $\dfrac{IG}{GN} = \dfrac{BE}{BN}$

∴
$$BE = \frac{(IG)(BN)}{GN} = \frac{(4)(6)}{2} = 12\,\text{m}$$

∴ Maximum height required $= AE$

$$= BE + AB = 16\,\text{m}$$

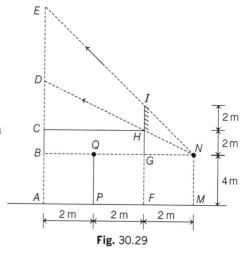

Fig. 30.29

Type 3.   *Based on object and image velocity*

Concept

We have already discussed four points on this topic.

⊚ **Example 30.5** *A plane mirror is lying in x-y plane. Object velocity is* $\mathbf{v}_0 = (2\hat{\mathbf{i}} - 3\hat{\mathbf{j}} + 4\hat{\mathbf{k}})\,m/s.$ *Find the image velocity.*

Solution   Components of object velocity parallel to plane mirror (or lying in x-y plane) remain unchanged. But, component perpendicular to plane mirror changes its direction but magnitude remains the same. Hence, the image velocity is

$$\mathbf{v}_I = (2\hat{\mathbf{i}} - 3\hat{\mathbf{j}} - 4\hat{\mathbf{k}})\,\text{m/s}$$ **Ans.**

⊚ **Example 30.6** *An object is falling vertically downwards with velocity 10 m/s. In terms of* $\hat{\mathbf{i}}$ *and* $\hat{\mathbf{j}},$ *find the image velocity.*

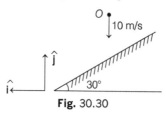

Fig. 30.30

Solution Image speed will also be 10 m/s. Further, image velocity will make same angle (= 60°) from the mirror on opposite side of it.

In terms of $\hat{\mathbf{i}}$ and $\hat{\mathbf{j}}$,

$$\mathbf{v}_I = 10\cos 30° \,\hat{\mathbf{i}} + 10\sin 30° \,\hat{\mathbf{j}}$$

or

$$\mathbf{v}_I = (5\sqrt{3}\,\hat{\mathbf{i}} + 5\,\hat{\mathbf{j}})\,\text{m/s} \qquad \textbf{Ans.}$$

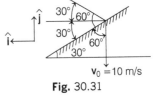

Fig. 30.31

> **Example 30.7** *A point object is moving with a speed v before an arrangement of two mirrors as shown in figure. Find the magnitude of velocity of image in mirror M_1 with respect to image in mirror M_2.*

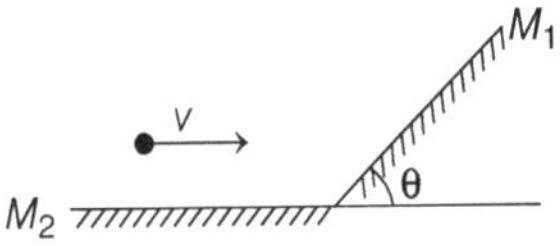

Solution Using the same concept used in above problem, we have to find magnitude of relative velocity between $\mathbf{v}_{I_1}$ and $\mathbf{v}_{I_2}$. The angle between these two vectors is 2θ.

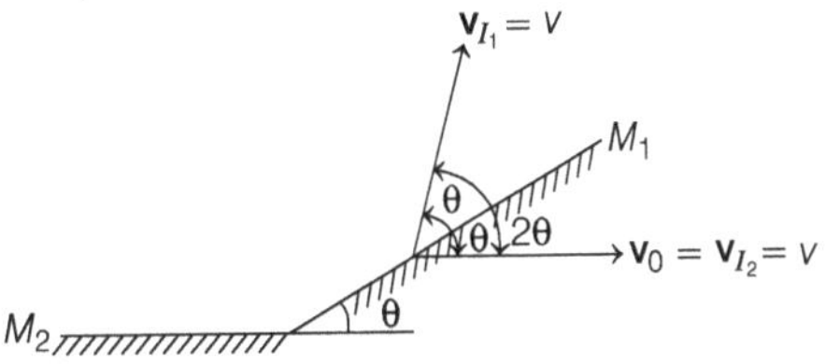

Fig. 30.32

Fig. 30.33

Hence, $$\mathbf{v}_r = \mathbf{v}_{I_1} - \mathbf{v}_{I_2}$$
$$\therefore \qquad |\mathbf{v}_r| = |\mathbf{v}_{I_1} - \mathbf{v}_{I_2}|$$

This is nothing but magnitude of subtraction of two velocity vectors of equal magnitudes v each and angle between them equal to 2θ.

Hence, $$|\mathbf{v}_r| = \sqrt{v^2 + v^2 - 2(v)(v)\cos 2\theta}$$

Solving these two equations, we get

$$|\mathbf{v}_2| = 2\,v\sin\theta \qquad\qquad \textbf{Ans.}$$

INTRODUCTORY EXERCISE 30.1

1. A man approaches a vertical plane mirror at speed of 2 m/s. At what rate does he approach his image?

2. An object M is placed at a distance of 3 m from a mirror with its lower end at 2 m from ground as shown in Fig. 30.34. There is a person at a distance of 4 m from object. Find minimum and maximum height of person to see the image of object.

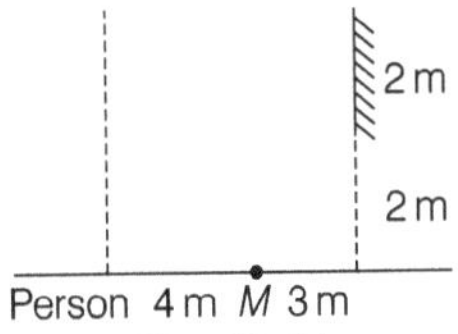

Fig. 30.34

3. In terms of θ find the value of i, so that ray of light retraces its path after third reflection.

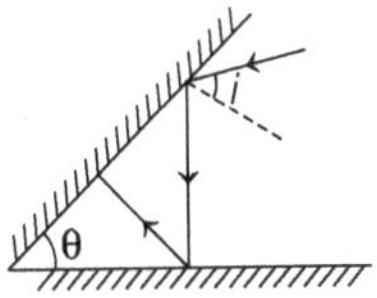

Fig. 30.35

30.4 **Reflection from a Spherical Surface**

We shall mainly consider the spherical mirrors, i.e. those which are part of a spherical surface.

Terms and Definitions

There are two types of spherical mirrors, concave and convex.

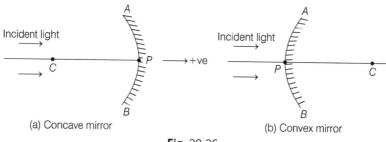

(a) Concave mirror   (b) Convex mirror

Fig. 30.36

Centre C of the sphere of which the mirror is a part is called the **centre of curvature** of the mirror and P the centre of the mirror surface, is called the **pole**. The line CP produced is the **principal axis** and AB is the **aperture** of the mirror. The distance CP is called the **radius of curvature (R).** All distances are measured from point P. We can see from the two figures that R is positive for convex mirror and negative for concave mirror.

Principal Focus

Observation shows that a narrow beam of rays, parallel and near to the principal axis, is reflected from a concave mirror so that all rays converge to a point F on the principal axis. F is called the **principal focus** of the mirror and it is a **real** focus, since, light actually passes through it. Concave mirrors are also known as converging mirrors because of their action on a parallel beam of light. They are used in car head-lights, search-lights and telescopes.

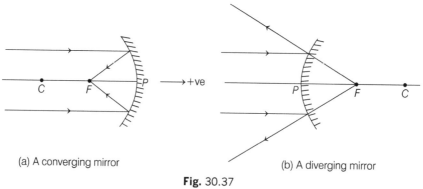

(a) A converging mirror   (b) A diverging mirror

Fig. 30.37

A narrow beam of rays, parallel and near to the principal axis, falling on a convex mirror is reflected to form a divergent beam which appears to come from a point F behind the mirror. A convex mirror thus has a virtual principal focus. It is also called a diverging mirror. The distance FP is called the **focal length (f)** of the mirror. Further, we can see that f is negative for a concave mirror and positive for convex mirror. Later, we will see that $f = R/2$.

Paraxial rays Rays which are close to the principal axis and make small angles with it, i.e. they are nearly parallel to the axis, are called paraxial rays. Our treatment of spherical mirrors will be restricted to such rays which means we shall consider only mirrors of small aperture. In diagrams, however, they will be made larger for clarity.

Images formed by Spherical Mirrors

In general position of image and its nature (i.e. whether it is real or virtual, erect or inverted, magnified or diminished) depend on the distance of object from the mirror.

Case 1 **Concave mirror**

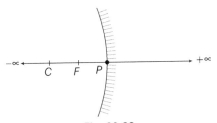

Fig. 30.38

Table 30.1

Object position	Image position	Image nature	Object speed and image speed
P	P	–	–
F	$\pm \infty$	–	–
C	C	Real, inverted and same size	$v_I = v_O$
Between P and F	Between P and $+\infty$	Virtual, erect and magnified	$v_I > v_O$
Between F and C	Between $-\infty$ and C	Real, inverted and magnified	$v_I > v_O$
Between C and $-\infty$	Between C and F	Real, inverted and diminished	$v_O > v_I$

Note (i) The above table is only for real objects lying in front of the mirror for which u is negative.

(ii) v_I and v_O are image and object speeds.

(iii) From the above table we can see that image and object always travel in opposite directions as long as they move along the principal axis.

Case 2 **Convex mirror** For real objects there is only one case

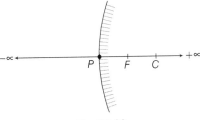

Fig. 30.39

Object lies between P and $-\infty$, then image lies between P and F. Image is virtual, erect and diminished. Object speed is greater than the image speed and they travel in opposite directions (along the principal axis).

Ray diagrams   We shall consider the small objects and mirrors of small aperture so that all rays are paraxial. To construct the image of a point object two of the following four rays are drawn passing through the object. To construct the image of an extended object, the image of two end points is only drawn. The image of a point object lying on principal axis is formed on the principal axis itself. The four rays are as under:

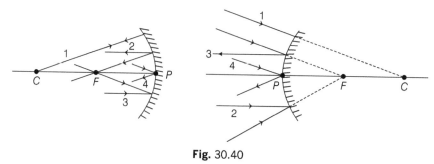

Fig. 30.40

Ray 1.   A ray through the centre of curvature which strikes the mirror normally and is reflected back along the same path.

Ray 2.   A ray parallel to principal axis after reflection either actually passes through the principal focus F or appears to diverge from it.

Ray 3.   A ray passing through the principal focus F or a ray which appears to converge at F is reflected parallel to the principal axis.

Ray 4.   A ray striking at pole P is reflected symmetrically back in the opposite side.

Convex Mirror

Image formed by convex mirror is always virtual, erect and diminished, no matter where the object is.

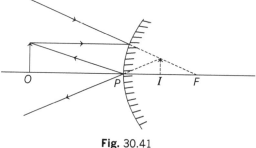

Fig. 30.41

Figure shows that convex mirror gives a wider **field of view** than a plane mirror, convex mirrors are therefore, used as rear view mirrors in cars or scooters. Although, they make the estimation of distances more difficult but still they are preferred because there is only a small movement of the image for a large movement of the object.

Concave Mirror

In case of a concave mirror the image is erect and virtual when the object is placed between F and P. In all other positions of object the image is real.

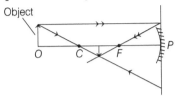

(a) Object beyond C
    Image between C and F, real, inverted, diminished

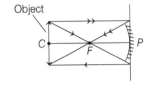

(b) Object at C
    Image at C, real, inverted, same size

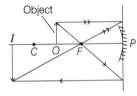

(c) Object between C and F
    Image beyond C, real inverted, magnified

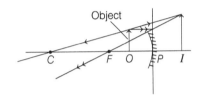

(d) Object between F and P
    Image behind mirror, virtual upright, magnified

Fig. 30.42

List of Formulae

(i) $f = \dfrac{R}{2}$

(ii) $\dfrac{1}{v} + \dfrac{1}{u} = \dfrac{1}{f} = \dfrac{2}{R}$

(iii) Lateral, transverse or linear magnification,

$$m = \frac{\text{Image height}}{\text{Object height}} = \frac{I}{O} = \frac{-v}{u}$$

(iv) Power of a mirror (in dioptre) $= \dfrac{1}{\text{Focal length (in metre)}}$

(v) Image velocity

Case 1 Along the principal axis, $\mathbf{v}_I = -m^2 \mathbf{v}_O$

Here, negative sign implies that object and image always travel in opposite directions.

Case 2 Perpendicular to principal axis,

$$\mathbf{v}_I = m\,\mathbf{v}_O$$

Here, m has to be substituted with sign. If m is positive, then $\mathbf{v}_I$ and $\mathbf{v}_O$ travel in same direction. If m is negative, then they travel in opposite directions.

Important Points in Formulae

(i) For plane mirror, $R = \infty$

$\therefore$ $\qquad f = \dfrac{R}{2}$ or $f = \infty$ and $\dfrac{1}{v} + \dfrac{1}{u} = \dfrac{2}{R} = \dfrac{2}{\infty} = 0$ or $v = -u$

(ii) From the value of m, we can know nature of image, type of mirror and an approximate location of object. But, always remind that real (and inverted) image is formed only by a concave mirror (for real objects) but virtual image is formed by all three mirrors. The only difference is, in their sizes. Magnified image is obtained from concave mirror, same size from plane mirror and diminished size from convex mirror. Let us make a table :

Table 30.2

Value of m	Nature of image	Type of mirror	Object position
-4	Inverted, real and magnified	Concave	Between F and C
-1	Inverted, real and same size	Concave	At C
$-\dfrac{1}{2}$	Inverted, real and diminished	Concave	Between C and $-\infty$
$+3$	Erect, virtual and magnified	Concave	Between P and F
$+1$	Erect, virtual and same size	Plane	For all positions
$+\dfrac{1}{2}$	Erect, virtual and diminished	Convex	Between P and $-\infty$

(iii) **Power** Optical power means power of bending of light. By convention, converging nature is taken as the positive power and diverging nature as negative power.

Power of a lens (in dioptre) $= + \dfrac{1}{f \text{ (in metre)}}$

Power of a mirror (in dioptre) $= - \dfrac{1}{f \text{ (in metre)}}$

Now, let us make a table :

Table 30.3

Lens/Mirror	f	P	Converging/Diverging	Diagram
Convex lens	+ ve	+ ve	Converging	
Concave lens	− ve	− ve	Diverging	

Lens/Mirror	f	P	Converging/Diverging	Diagram
Convex mirror	+ ve	– ve	Diverging	
Concave mirror	– ve	+ ve	Converging	

(iv) Image velocity

Case 1   **Along the principal axis**

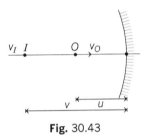

Fig. 30.43

By the motion of object and image v and u will change but focal length will remain unchanged. If we differentiate the mirror formula

$$\frac{1}{v} + \frac{1}{u} = \frac{1}{f}$$

with respect to time, we get

$$-v^{-2} \cdot \frac{dv}{dt} - u^{-2} \frac{du}{dt} = 0 \qquad\qquad \text{(as } f = \text{constant)}$$

or

$$\frac{dv}{dt} = -\left(\frac{v^2}{u^2}\right)\frac{du}{dt}$$

Here, $\dfrac{du}{dt}$ is the rate by which u is changing. Or it is the object speed if mirror is stationary.

Similarly, $\dfrac{dv}{dt}$ is the rate by which v (distance between image and mirror) is changing. Or it is image speed if mirror is stationary.

$$\frac{v^2}{u^2} = m^2$$

So, the above relation becomes :

$$\text{image speed} = m^2 \times \text{object speed}$$

As, object and image travel in opposite directions. So, in terms of velocity, the correct relation is

$$\boxed{\mathbf{v}_I = -m^2 \mathbf{v}_O}$$

Case 2 **Perpendicular to axis**

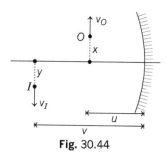

Fig. 30.44

This time v and u are constants. Therefore, $m = -\dfrac{v}{u}$ is also constant.

But, x and y are variables

$$m = \frac{I}{O} = \frac{y}{x}$$

$\Rightarrow$ $\qquad\qquad\qquad y = mx$

If we differentiate with respect to time,
we get,

$$\frac{dy}{dt} = m\frac{dx}{dt}$$

$\Rightarrow$ $\qquad\qquad\qquad \boxed{\mathbf{v}_I = m\mathbf{v}_O}$

Proofs of Different Formulae Discussed in Theory

(i) **Relation between f and R**   A ray AM parallel to the principal axis of a concave mirror of small aperture is reflected through the principal focus F. If C is the centre of curvature, CM is the normal to the mirror at M because the radius of a spherical surface is perpendicular to the surface. From first law of reflection,

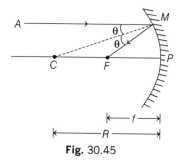

Fig. 30.45

$$\angle i = \angle r$$

or $\qquad\qquad\qquad \angle AMC = \angle CMF = \theta \qquad\qquad\qquad$ (say)

But, $\qquad\qquad\qquad \angle AMC = \angle MCF \qquad\qquad\qquad$ (alternate angles)

$\therefore \qquad\qquad\qquad \angle CMF = \angle MCF$

Therefore, ΔFCM is thus isosceles with $FC = FM$.

The rays are paraxial and so M is very close to P. Therefore,

$$FM \approx FP$$

$\therefore \qquad\qquad\qquad FC = FP$

or $\qquad\qquad\qquad FP = \dfrac{1}{2}CP$

or $\qquad\qquad\qquad \boxed{f = \dfrac{R}{2}}$

EXERCISE   Prove the above relation for convex mirror.

(ii) **The mirror formula**   In Fig. 30.46 (a) and (b), a ray OM from a point object O on the principal axis is reflected at M so that the angle θ, made by the incident and reflected rays with the normal CM are equal. A ray OP strikes the mirror normally and is reflected back along PO. The intersection I of the reflected rays MI and PO in figure (a) gives a **real** point image of O and in figure (b) gives a **virtual** point image of O. Let α, β and γ be the angles as shown. As the rays are paraxial, these angles are small, we can take

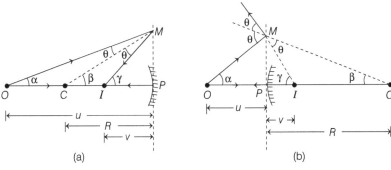

(a)   (b)

Fig. 30.46

$$\alpha \approx \tan \alpha = \frac{MP}{OP},$$

$$\beta = \frac{MP}{CP}$$

and $\qquad\qquad\qquad \gamma = \dfrac{MP}{IP}$

Now, let us take the two figures simultaneously.

Table 30.4

Concave	Convex
In triangle CMO, $\beta = \alpha + \theta$ (the exterior angle) or $\qquad \theta = \beta - \alpha$ ...(i)	In triangle CMO, $\qquad \theta = \alpha + \beta$ ...(iv) (the exterior angle)
In Δ CMI, $\qquad \gamma = \beta + \theta$ $\therefore \qquad \theta = \gamma - \beta$ ...(ii)	In ΔCMI $\quad \gamma = \theta + \beta$ or $\qquad \theta = \gamma - \beta$ ...(v)
From Eqs. (i) and (ii), we get $\qquad 2\beta = \gamma + \alpha$ ...(iii)	From Eqs. (iv) and (v), we get $\qquad 2\beta = \gamma - \alpha$ ...(vi)
Substituting the values of α, β and γ, we get $\dfrac{2}{CP} = \dfrac{1}{IP} + \dfrac{1}{OP}$ ...(A)	Substituting the values of α, β and γ, we get $\dfrac{2}{CP} = \dfrac{1}{IP} - \dfrac{1}{OP}$ ...(B)
If we now substitute the values with sign, i.e. $CP = -R$, $IP = -v$ and $OP = -u$ we get, $\qquad \dfrac{2}{R} = \dfrac{1}{v} + \dfrac{1}{u}$	If we now substitute the values with sign, i.e. $CP = +R$, $IP = +v$ and $OP = -u$, we get $\qquad \dfrac{2}{R} = \dfrac{1}{v} + \dfrac{1}{u}$
or $\qquad \dfrac{1}{v} + \dfrac{1}{u} = \dfrac{1}{f}$ $\quad \left(\text{as } f = \dfrac{R}{2}\right)$	or $\qquad \dfrac{1}{v} + \dfrac{1}{u} = \dfrac{1}{f}$ $\quad \left(\text{as } f = \dfrac{R}{2}\right)$

(iii) **Magnification** The lateral, transverse or linear magnification m is defined as

$$m = \frac{\text{Height of image}}{\text{Height of object}} = \frac{I'I}{O'O} = \frac{IP}{OP} \qquad \text{...(i)}$$

(From similar triangles)

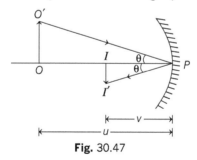

Fig. 30.47

Here, $IP = -v$ and $OP = -u$, further object is erect and image is inverted so we can take $I'I$ as negative and $O'O$ as positive and Eq. (i) will then become

$$\frac{I'I}{O'O} = -\frac{v}{u}$$

or

$$m = -\frac{v}{u}$$

Note *We have derived $\dfrac{1}{v} + \dfrac{1}{u} = \dfrac{1}{f}$ and $m = -\dfrac{v}{u}$ for special cases of the position of object but the same result can be derived for other cases also.*

Solved Examples

Types of Problems in Spherical Mirror

Type 1. *To find image distance and its magnification corresponding to given object distance and focal length of mirror*

How to Solve?

- In the mirror formula substitute signs of only u and f. Sign of v automatically comes after calculations. For real objects sign of u is always negative, sign of f is positive for convex mirror and negative for concave mirror.

Example 1 *An object is placed at a distance of 30 cm from a concave mirror of focal length 20 cm. Find image distance and its magnification. Also, draw the ray diagram.*

Solution Substituting $u = -30$ cm and $f = -20$ cm in the mirror formula $\dfrac{1}{v} + \dfrac{1}{u} = \dfrac{1}{f}$, we have

$$\frac{1}{v} + \frac{1}{-30} = \frac{1}{-20}$$

Solving, we get $\qquad\qquad v = -60 \text{ cm}$ **Ans.**

Magnification, $\quad m = \dfrac{-v}{u} = -\dfrac{(-60)}{(-30)}$

or $\qquad\qquad\qquad\qquad m = -2$ **Ans.**

Magnification is –2, which implies that image is inverted, real and two times magnified.
Ray diagram is as shown below.

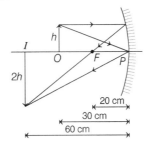

Example 2 *An object is placed at a distance of 40 cm from a convex mirror of focal length 40 cm. Find image position and its magnification. Also, draw its ray diagram.*

Solution Substituting, $u = -40$ cm and $f = +40$ cm in the mirror formula

$$\frac{1}{v} + \frac{1}{u} = \frac{1}{f}, \text{ we have}$$

$$\frac{1}{v} + \frac{1}{-40} = \frac{1}{+40}$$

We get,

$$v = +20 \text{ cm}$$

Ans.

Magnification, $m = -\dfrac{v}{u} = -\dfrac{(+20)}{(-40)} = +\dfrac{1}{2}$

Magnification is $+\dfrac{1}{2}$, which implies that image is erect, virtual and half in size.

Ray diagram is as shown.

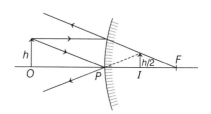

$$PO = PF = 40 \text{ cm}$$
$$PI = 20 \text{ cm}$$

Note *Here, PO = PF = 40 cm or object is placed at a distance of its focal length, but object is not actually kept at F. Otherwise, image would be formed at infinity.*

Type 2. *To find object/image distance corresponding to given magnification of image if focal length of mirror is also given*

How to Solve?

- In this type, substitute all three signs of u, v and f.
- Signs of u and f have been discussed in Type 1. Sign of v will be positive for virtual image and negative for real image.
- $m = -\dfrac{v}{u} \implies |v| = |mu|$

> **Example 3** *Find the distance of object from a concave mirror of focal length 10 cm so that image size is four times the size of the object.*

Solution Concave mirror can form real as well as virtual image. Here, nature of image is not given in the question. So, we will consider two possible cases.

Case 1 (When image is real) Real image is formed on the same side of the object, i.e. u, v and f all are negative. So let,

$$u = -x$$

then

$$v = -4x \quad \text{as} \quad \left|\frac{v}{u}\right| = |m| = 4$$

and

$$f = -10 \text{ cm}$$

Substituting in

$$\frac{1}{v} + \frac{1}{u} = \frac{1}{f}$$

We have

$$\frac{1}{-4x} - \frac{1}{x} = \frac{1}{-10}$$

or

$$\frac{5}{4x} = \frac{1}{10}$$

∴

$$x = 12.5 \text{ cm}$$

Ans.

Note *$|f| < |x| < |2f|$ and we know that in case of a concave mirror, image is real, inverted and magnified when object lies between F and C.*

Case 2 **(When image is virtual)**   In case of a mirror, image is virtual, when it is formed behind the mirror, i.e. u and f are negative, while v is positive. So let,

$$u = -y$$

then

$$v = +4y \quad \text{and} \quad f = -10 \text{ cm}$$

Substituting in

$$\frac{1}{v} + \frac{1}{u} = \frac{1}{f}$$

We have

$$\frac{1}{4y} - \frac{1}{y} = \frac{1}{-10}$$

or

$$\frac{3}{4y} = \frac{1}{10}$$

or

$$y = 7.5 \text{ cm}$$ **Ans.**

Note   *Here,* $|y| < |f|$, *as we know that image is virtual erect and magnified when the object lies between F and P.*

Type 3. *Based on making some condition*

How to Solve?

- Initially, substitute sign of f only.
- Make an equation of v.
- Now, for real image v should be negative and for virtual image v should be positive. With these concepts we can make the necessary condition.

➲ **Example 4**   *Find the condition under which a convex mirror can make a real image.*

Solution   Substituting the sign of f only in the mirror formula, we have

$$\frac{1}{v} + \frac{1}{u} = \frac{1}{+f} \quad \Rightarrow \quad \frac{1}{v} = \frac{1}{f} - \frac{1}{u}$$

For real image v should be negative and for this u should be positive and less than f. Object distance u is positive means object should be virtual and lying between P and F.

The ray diagram is as shown below.

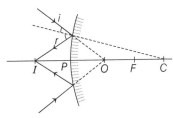

Here, $O =$ virtual between P and F

$I =$ real

Note   *Under normal conditions a concave mirror makes a real image. But, it makes a virtual image if a real object is kept between P and F. On the other hand a convex mirror makes a virtual image. But it makes a real image if a virtual object is kept between P and F.*

Type 4. *To find nature of image and type of mirror corresponding to given optic axis of mirror a point object and a point image. With the help of ray diagram we have to find focus and pole of the mirror also.*

◉ **Example 5** *An image I is formed of a point object O by a mirror whose principal axis is AB as shown in figure.*

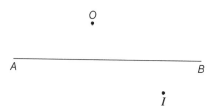

(a) *State whether it is a convex mirror or a concave mirror.*

(b) *Draw a ray diagram to locate the mirror and its focus. Write down the steps of construction of the ray diagram. Consider the possible two cases:*

(1) *When distance of I from AB is more than the distance of O from AB and*

(2) *When distance of O from AB is more than the distance of I from AB*

Solution

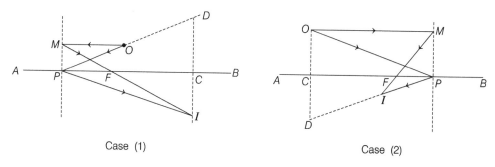

Case (1)   Case (2)

(a) As the image is on the opposite side of the principal axis, the mirror is concave. Because convex mirror always forms an erect image.

(b) Two different cases are shown in figure. Steps are as under :

(i) From *I* or *O* drop a perpendicular on principal axis, such that $CI = CD$ or $OC = CD$.

(ii) Draw a line joining *D* and *O* or *D* and *I* so that it meets the principal axis at *P*. The point *P* will be the pole of the mirror as a ray reflected from the pole is always symmetrical about principal axis.

(iii) From *O* draw a line parallel to principal axis towards the mirror so that it meets the mirror at *M*. Join *M* to *I*, so that it intersects the principal axis at *F*. *F* is the focus of the mirror as any ray parallel to principal axis after reflection from the mirror intersects the principal axis at the focus.

Note *In both figures, mirror should face towards the object.*

Exercise In the above problem, find centre of curvature of the mirror with the help of only ray diagram.

Type 5. *Based on velocity of image*

How to Solve?

- Using the steps discussed in Type 1, find v and then m
- Along the axis $\mathbf{v}_I = -m^2 \mathbf{v}_O$
- Perpendicular to axis $\mathbf{v}_I = m\mathbf{v}_O$
  Here, m has to be substituted with sign.

◉ **Example 6**   *Focal length of the mirror shown in figure is 20 cm. Find the image position and its velocity.*

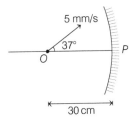

Solution   Substituting the values,

$$u = -30 \text{ cm and } f = -20 \text{ cm}$$

in the mirror formula, we have

$$\frac{1}{v} + \frac{1}{-30} = \frac{1}{-20}$$

Solving this equation, we get

$$v = -60 \text{ cm}$$

Further,

$$m = -\frac{v}{u} = -\frac{(-60)}{(-30)} = -2$$

and

$$m^2 = 4$$

Object velocity along the axis is $5 \cos 37° = 4$ mm/s (towards OP). Therefore, image velocity along the axis should be m^2 times or 16 mm/s in the opposite direction of object velocity. Object velocity perpendicular to axis is $5 \sin 37° = 3$ mm/s (upwards). Therefore, image velocity will be m times or −6 mm/s downwards. The position and velocity of image is shown below.

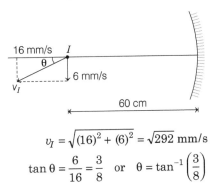

$$v_I = \sqrt{(16)^2 + (6)^2} = \sqrt{292} \text{ mm/s}$$

$$\tan \theta = \frac{6}{16} = \frac{3}{8} \quad \text{or} \quad \theta = \tan^{-1}\left(\frac{3}{8}\right)$$

Type 6. *To find a rough image of a square or rectangular type of object kept along the axis*

Concept

(i) If object is towards P or C, then its image is also towards P or C.

(ii) If object is towards F, then its image is towards infinity and it is more magnified.

◈ **Example 7** *A square mnqp is kept between F and C on the principal axis of a concave mirror as shown in figure. Find a rough image of this object.*

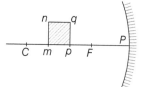

Solution Object is placed between F and C, therefore, image is real, inverted magnified and beyond C. Further pq is towards F. Therefore, its image $p'\,q'$ is towards infinity and it is more magnified. A rough image is as shown alongside.

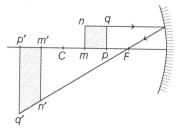

From the ray shown in figure, we can see that $n'\,q'$ will be a straight line.

Exercise In the given problem, focal length of mirror is 30 cm and side of square is 10 cm with $pP = 40$ cm. Find perimeter of the image

Ans $(90 + 15\sqrt{10})$ cm

Type 7. *Two mirror problems*

Concept

If an object is placed between two mirrors, then infinite reflections will take place. Therefore, infinite images are formed. But normally position of second image is asked. So, we have to apply mirror formula two times. Image from first mirror acts as an object for the second mirror. Sign convention for second reflection will change but sign of focal length will not change.

◈ **Example 8** *Focal length of convex mirror M_1 is 20 cm and that of concave mirror M_2 is 30 cm. Find position of second image I_2. Take first reflection from M_1.*

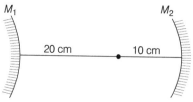

Solution

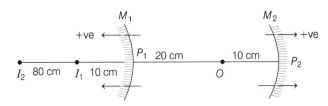

For M_1

$$u_1 = -20 \text{ cm}$$
$$f_1 = +20 \text{ cm}$$

Using the mirror formula,

$$\frac{1}{v} + \frac{1}{u} = \frac{1}{f}, \text{ we have}$$

$$\frac{1}{v_1} + \frac{1}{-20} = \frac{1}{+20}$$

Solving, we get

$$v_1 = +10 \text{ cm}$$

For M_2

$$u_2 = -40 \text{ cm} \qquad\qquad (PI_1 = 40 \text{ cm})$$
$$f_2 = -30 \text{ cm}$$

Using the mirror formula,

$$\frac{1}{v} + \frac{1}{u} = \frac{1}{f}$$

We have,

$$\frac{1}{v_2} + \frac{1}{-40} = \frac{1}{-30}$$

∴

$$v_2 = P_2 I_2 = -120 \text{ cm}$$

Note I_1 *is virtual from M_1 point of view (behind M_1). But it behaves like a real object for M_2 (in front of M_2).*

Type 8. *An extended object is kept perpendicular to principal axis and we have to make its image*

How to Solve?

With the help of type 1 first find v and then m. Now, suppose $m = -2$ and object is 2 mm above the principal axis, then its image will be formed 4 mm below its principal axis.

◉ *Example 9*

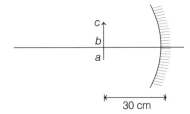

Focal length of the concave mirror shown in figure is 20 cm.

$$ab = 1 \text{ mm}$$

and

$$bc = 2 \text{ mm}$$

For the given situation, make its image

Solution

$$u = -30 \text{ cm} \quad \text{and} \quad f = -20 \text{ cm}$$

Using the mirror formula,

$$\frac{1}{v} + \frac{1}{u} = \frac{1}{f}, \text{ we have}$$

$$\frac{1}{v} + \frac{1}{-30} = \frac{1}{-20}$$

Solving this equation, we get

$$v = -60 \text{ cm}$$

Now,

$$m = -\frac{v}{u} = -\frac{(-60)}{(-30)} = -2$$

Now *c* point is 2 mm above the principal axis and magnification is –2. Hence, image *c'* will be formed 4 mm below the principal axis. Similarly *a* point is 1 mm below the principal axis and value of *m* is –2. Hence, image *a'* is formed 2 mm above the principal axis. Image with ray diagram of *c* is as shown below.

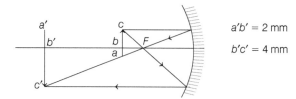

$a'b' = 2$ mm

$b'c' = 4$ mm

Type 9. *An extended object is kept along the principal axis. Now, in this type further two cases are possible.*

Case 1 When object size is very small.

In this case image length,

$$L_I = m^2(L_o)$$

Here, L_o is the object length. So, using type 1, we have to find v and then m.

Proof We have already proved that image speed.

$$v_I = m^2 v_O \qquad \qquad \text{(Along the axis)}$$

or

$$\frac{dv}{dt} = m^2 \left(\frac{du}{dt} \right)$$

For small change in the values of v and u, we can write

$$|\Delta v| = |m^2 \times \Delta u|$$

Δv is nothing but difference in two values of v or image length L_I. Similarly, Δu is object length L_o.

Case 2 When object size is large.

If an extended object is lying along the principal axis, then we will get two values of u corresponding to its two ends. Now, apply mirror formula two times and find two values of v. The image length now becomes,

$$L_I = |v_1 \sim v_2|$$

Note *If one end of the object is placed either at C or P, then its image will also be formed at C or P. So, we will have to apply the mirror formula only for the other end.*

◉ *Example 10*

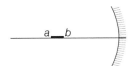

A small object ab of size 1 mm is kept at a distance of 40 cm from a concave mirror of focal length 30 cm. Make image of this object.

Solution   Here, object size is very small. So, this is case 1.

$$u = -40 \text{ cm}$$

and

$$f = -30 \text{ cm}$$

Applying the mirror formula

$$\frac{1}{v} + \frac{1}{u} = \frac{1}{f}, \text{ we have}$$

$$\frac{1}{v} + \frac{1}{-40} = \frac{1}{-30}$$

Solving this equation, we get

$$v = -120 \text{ cm}$$

Further,

$$m = -\frac{v}{u} = -\frac{(-120)}{(-40)} = -3$$

$$m^2 = 9$$

Now,

$$L_I = m^2 L_o = (9)(1 \text{ mm}) = 9 \text{ mm}$$

Image diagram is as shown below.

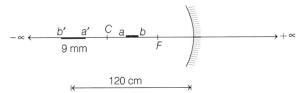

Note   *Point b is towards F, therefore its image b′ should be towards − ∞.*

◉ *Example 11*   *A thin rod of length $\frac{f}{3}$ is lying along the principal axis of a concave mirror of focal length f. Image is real, magnified and inverted and one of the end of rod coincides with its image itself. Find length of the image.*

Solution   Image is real, magnified and inverted. So, the given rod lies between F and C. Further, one end of the rod is coinciding with its image itself. Therefore, it is lying at C. So, the thin rod CR is kept as shown below.

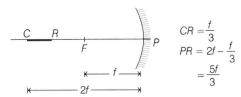

$$CR = \frac{f}{3}$$

$$PR = 2f - \frac{f}{3}$$

$$= \frac{5f}{3}$$

We have to apply mirror formula only for point R.

$$u = -\frac{5f}{3}, \text{ focal length} = -f$$

Using the mirror formula

$$\frac{1}{v} + \frac{1}{u} = \frac{1}{f},$$

We have,

$$\frac{1}{v} + \frac{1}{-\dfrac{5f}{3}} = \frac{1}{-f}$$

Solving this equation, we get

$$v = \frac{-5f}{2} \quad \text{or} \quad -2.5f$$

So, the image of rod CR is $C'R'$ as shown below.

So, image length $= C'R' = 0.5\,f$ or $\dfrac{f}{2}$.

Note *In this problem if magnification of rod is asked then we can write*

$$m = -\frac{L_I}{L_O} = -\frac{f/2}{f/3} = -\frac{3}{2}$$

Negative sign has been used for inverted image.

Type 10. *Based on u versus v graph or 1/u versus 1/v graph (only for real objects)*

⬖ **Example 12** *Draw u versus v graph or $\dfrac{1}{u}$ versus $\dfrac{1}{v}$ graph for a concave mirror of focal length f.*

Solution The mirror formula is

$$\frac{1}{v} + \frac{1}{u} = \frac{1}{f}$$

If we take $\dfrac{1}{v}$ along y-axis and $\dfrac{1}{u}$ along x-axis, then the above equation becomes

$$y + x = c \hspace{4cm} \left(\text{as } \frac{1}{f} = \text{constant}\right)$$

Therefore, $\dfrac{1}{v}$ *versus* $\dfrac{1}{u}$ graph will be a straight line. Let us take origin at pole.

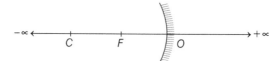

Table 30.5

S.No.	u	v	$\dfrac{1}{u}$	$\dfrac{1}{v}$
1.	0 to $-f$	-0 to $+\infty$	$-\infty$ to $-\dfrac{1}{f}$	$+\infty$ to 0
2.	$-f$ to $-2f$	$-\infty$ to $-2f$	$-\dfrac{1}{f}$ to $-\dfrac{1}{2f}$	0 to $-\dfrac{1}{2f}$
3.	$-2f$ to $-\infty$	$-2f$ to $-f$	$-\dfrac{1}{2f}$ to 0	$-\dfrac{1}{2f}$ to $-\dfrac{1}{f}$

u *versus* v and $\dfrac{1}{u}$ *versus* $\dfrac{1}{v}$ graphs are as shown below.

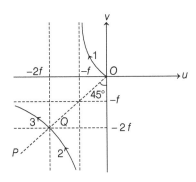

Note *OP line cuts the u - v graph at Q* $(-2f, -2f)$

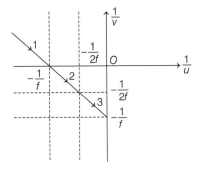

Exercise Draw above two graphs for convex mirror.

Miscellaneous Examples

Example 13 *An object is 30.0 cm from a spherical mirror, along the central axis. The absolute value of lateral magnification is $\frac{1}{2}$. The image produced is inverted. What is the focal length of the mirror?*

Solution Image is inverted, so it is real. u and v both are negative. Magnification is $\frac{1}{2}$, therefore, $v = \dfrac{u}{2}$.

Given, $u = -30$ cm, $v = -15$ cm

Using the mirror formula,

$$\frac{1}{v} + \frac{1}{u} = \frac{1}{f}$$

We have,

$$\frac{1}{f} = \frac{1}{-15} - \frac{1}{30} = -\frac{1}{10}$$

$\therefore$ $\qquad\qquad\qquad\qquad f = -10$ cm **Ans.**

Example 14 *A concave mirror has a radius of curvature of 24 cm. How far is an object from the mirror if an image is formed that is :*
(a) virtual and 3.0 times the size of the object,
(b) real and 3.0 times the size of the object and
(c) real and 1/3 the size of the object?

Solution Given, $R = -24$ cm (concave mirror)

Hence, $\qquad\qquad\qquad\qquad f = \dfrac{R}{2} = -12$ cm

(a) Image is virtual and 3 times larger. Hence, u is negative and v is positive.
   Simultaneously, $|v| = 3|u|$. So let,

$$u = -x$$

then $\qquad\qquad\qquad\qquad v = +3x$

Substituting in the mirror formula,

$$\frac{1}{v} + \frac{1}{u} = \frac{1}{f}$$

We have,

$$\frac{1}{3x} - \frac{1}{x} = \frac{1}{-12}$$

$\therefore$ $\qquad\qquad\qquad\qquad x = 8$ cm

   Therefore, object distance is 8 cm. **Ans.**

(b) Image is real and three times larger. Hence, u and v both are negative and $|v| = 3|u|$.
   So let,

$$u = -x$$

then $$v = -3x$$

Substituting in mirror formula, we have

$$\frac{1}{-3x} - \frac{1}{x} = -\frac{1}{12}$$

or $$x = 16 \text{ cm}$$

∴ Object distance should be 16 cm. **Ans.**

(c) Image is real and $\frac{1}{3}$rd the size of object. Hence, both u and v are negative and $|v| = \frac{|u|}{3}$.

So let, $$u = -x$$

then $$v = -\frac{x}{3}$$

Substituting in the mirror formula, we have

$$-\frac{3}{x} - \frac{1}{x} = -\frac{1}{12}$$

∴ $$x = 48 \text{ cm}$$

∴ Object distance should be 48 cm. **Ans.**

◉ **Example 15** *A ray of light is incident on a plane mirror along a vector* $\hat{\mathbf{i}} + \hat{\mathbf{j}} - \hat{\mathbf{k}}$. *The normal on incidence point is along* $\hat{\mathbf{i}} + \hat{\mathbf{j}}$. *Find a unit vector along the reflected ray.*

Solution Reflection of a ray of light is just like an elastic collision of a ball with a horizontal ground. Component of incident ray along the inside normal gets reversed while the component perpendicular to it remains unchanged. Thus, the component of incident ray vector $\mathbf{A} = \hat{\mathbf{i}} + \hat{\mathbf{j}} - \hat{\mathbf{k}}$ parallel to normal, i.e. $\hat{\mathbf{i}} + \hat{\mathbf{j}}$ gets reversed while perpendicular to it, i.e. $-\hat{\mathbf{k}}$ remains unchanged. Thus, the reflected ray can be written as

$$\mathbf{R} = -\hat{\mathbf{i}} - \hat{\mathbf{j}} - \hat{\mathbf{k}}$$

∴ A unit vector along the reflected ray will be

$$\hat{\mathbf{r}} = \frac{\mathbf{R}}{R} = \frac{-\hat{\mathbf{i}} - \hat{\mathbf{j}} - \hat{\mathbf{k}}}{\sqrt{3}}$$

or $$\hat{\mathbf{r}} = -\frac{1}{\sqrt{3}}(\hat{\mathbf{i}} + \hat{\mathbf{j}} + \hat{\mathbf{k}})$$ **Ans.**

Note *In this problem, given normal is inside the mirror surface. Think why?*

◉ **Example 16** *A gun of mass* m_1 *fires a bullet of mass* m_2 *with a horizontal speed* v_0. *The gun is fitted with a concave mirror of focal length* f *facing towards a receding bullet. Find the speed of separations of the bullet and the image just after the gun was fired.*

Solution Let v_1 be the speed of gun (or mirror) just after the firing of bullet. From conservation of linear momentum,

$$m_2 v_0 = m_1 v_1$$

or $$v_1 = \frac{m_2 v_0}{m_1}$$ ...(i)

Now, $\dfrac{du}{dt}$ is the rate at which distance between mirror and bullet is increasing $= v_1 + v_0$ ...(ii)

We have already read in extra points that :

$\therefore$
$$\frac{dv}{dt} = \left(\frac{v^2}{u^2}\right)\frac{du}{dt}$$

Here,
$$\frac{v^2}{u^2} = m^2 = 1 \quad \text{(as at the time of firing, bullet is at pole).}$$

$\therefore$
$$\frac{dv}{dt} = \frac{du}{dt} = v_1 + v_0 \qquad \text{...(iii)}$$

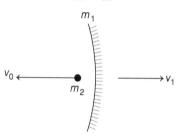

Here, $\dfrac{dv}{dt}$ is the rate at which distance between image (of bullet) and mirror is increasing. So, if v_2 is the absolute velocity of image (towards right), then

$$v_2 - v_1 = \frac{dv}{dt}$$
$$= v_1 + v_0$$

or
$$v_2 = 2v_1 + v_0 \qquad \text{...(iv)}$$

Therefore, speed of separation of bullet and image will be

$$v_r = v_2 + v_0$$
$$= 2v_1 + v_0 + v_0$$

or
$$v_r = 2\,(v_1 + v_0)$$

Substituting value of v_1 from Eq. (i), we have

$$v_r = 2\left(1 + \frac{m_2}{m_1}\right)v_0 \qquad\qquad \textbf{Ans.}$$

Exercises

LEVEL 1

Assertion and Reason

Directions : *Choose the correct option.*

(*a*) *If both **Assertion** and **Reason** are true and the **Reason** is correct explanation of the **Assertion**.*

(*b*) *If both **Assertion** and **Reason** are true but **Reason** is not the correct explanation of **Assertion**.*

(*c*) *If **Assertion** is true, but the **Reason** is false.*

(*d*) *If **Assertion** is false but the **Reason** is true.*

(*e*) *Both **Assertion** and **Reason** are false.*

1. **Assertion :** Focal length of a convex mirror is 20 cm. If a real object is placed at distance 20 cm from the mirror, its virtual erect and diminished image will be formed.

   Reason : If a virtual object is placed at 20 cm distance, its image is formed at infinity.

2. **Assertion :** Rear view mirror of vehicles is a convex mirror.

   Reason : It never makes real image of real objects.

3. **Assertion :** If magnification of a real object is – 2. Then, it is definitely a concave mirror.

   Reason : Only concave mirror can make real images of real objects.

4. **Assertion :** Any ray of light suffers a deviation of $(180° - 2i)$ after one reflection.

   Reason : For normal incidence of light deviation is zero.

5. **Assertion :** For real objects, image formed by a convex mirror always lies between pole and focus.

   Reason : When object moves from pole to infinity, its image will move from pole to focus.

6. **Assertion :** Light converges on a virtual object.

   Reason : Virtual object is always behind a mirror.

Objective Questions

1. A plane mirror reflects a beam of light to form a real image. The incident beam should be
   (a) parallel
   (b) convergent
   (c) divergent
   (d) not possible

2. When an object lies at the focus of a concave mirror, then the position of the image formed and its magnification are
   (a) pole and unity
   (b) infinity and unity
   (c) infinity and infinity
   (d) centre of curvature and unity

3. A concave mirror cannot form
   (a) virtual image of virtual object
   (b) virtual image of real object
   (c) real image of real object
   (d) real image of virtual object

4. All the following statements are correct except (for real objects)
   (a) the magnification produced by a convex mirror is always less than one
   (b) a virtual, erect and same sized image can be obtained using a plane mirror
   (c) a virtual, erect, magnified image can be formed using a concave mirror
   (d) a real, inverted same sized image can be formed using a convex mirror

5. The minimum distance between the object and its real image for concave mirror is
   (a) f　　　　　　(b) $2f$　　　　　　(c) $4f$　　　　　　(d) Zero

6. A watch shows the time as $3 : 25$. What will be the time that appears when seen through a plane mirror?
   (a) $8 : 35$　　　　(b) $9 : 35$　　　　(c) $7 : 35$　　　　(d) $8 : 25$

7. Two plane mirrors are inclined at $70°$. A ray incident on one mirror at incidence angle θ, after reflection falls on the second mirror and is reflected from there parallel to the first mirror. The value of θ is
   (a) $50°$　　　　　(b) $45°$　　　　　(c) $30°$　　　　　(d) $25°$

8. The radius of curvature of a convex mirror is 60 cm. When an object is placed at A, its image is formed at B. If the size of image is half that of the object, then the distance between A and B is
   (a) 30 cm　　　　(b) 60 cm　　　　(c) 45 cm　　　　(d) 90 cm

9. A boy of height 1.5 m with his eye level at 1.4 m stands before a plane mirror of length 0.75 m fixed on the wall. The height of the lower edge of the mirror above the floor is 0.8 m. Then,
   (a) the boy will see his full image 　　　(b) the boy cannot see his hair
   (c) the boy cannot see his feet 　　　　(d) the boy can see neither his hair nor his feet

10. A spherical mirror forms an erect image three times the size of the object. If the distance between the object and the image is 80 cm, the nature and the focal length of the mirror are
   (a) concave, 30 cm 　　　　　　(b) convex, 30 cm
   (c) concave, 15 cm 　　　　　　(d) convex, 15 cm

11. A convex mirror of focal length f produces an image $(1/n)^{\text{th}}$ of the size of the object. The distance of the object from the mirror is
   (a) nf　　　　　(b) f/n　　　　　(c) $(n + 1) f$　　　　(d) $(n - 1) f$

12. An object is moving towards a concave mirror of focal length 24 cm. When it is at a distance of 60 cm from the mirror, its speed is 9 cm/s. The speed of its image at that instant, is
   (a) 4 cm/s towards the mirror 　　　　(b) 6 cm/s towards the mirror
   (c) 4 cm/s away from the mirror 　　　(d) 6 cm/s away from the mirror

13. A particle moves perpendicularly towards a plane mirror with a constant speed of 4 cm/s. What is the speed of the image observed by an observer moving with 2 cm/s along the same direction? Mirror is also moving with a speed of 10 cm/s in the opposite direction.
   (All speeds are with respect to ground frame of reference)
   (a) 4 cm/s　　　　(b) 12 cm/s　　　　(c) 14 cm/s　　　　(d) 26 cm/s

14. A man is 180 cm tall and his eyes are 10 cm below the top of his head. In order to see his entire height from top to head, he uses a plane mirror kept at a distance of 1m from him. The minimum length of the plane mirror is
   (a) 180 cm　　　　(b) 90 cm　　　　(c) 85 cm　　　　(d) 170 cm

15. The focal length of a concave mirror is 50 cm. At what distance from the mirror an object be placed, so that its image is two times and inverted
   (a) 75 cm　　　　(b) 60 cm　　　　(c) 125 cm　　　　(d) 50 cm

16. Figure below shows two plane mirrors and an object O placed between them. What will be distance of the first three images from the mirror M_2?

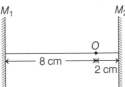

(a) 2 cm, 8 cm, 14 cm (b) 2 cm, 12 cm, 18 cm
(c) 2 cm, 18 cm, 22 cm (d) 2 cm, 24 cm, 38 cm

17. When a plane mirror is placed horizontally on level ground at a distance of 60 m from the foot of a tower, the top of the tower and its image in the mirror subtend an angle of 90° at the corner of the mirror nearer to the foot of tower. The height of the tower is
(a) 30 m (b) 60 m
(c) 90 m (d) 120 m

18. A point object is placed at a distance of 10 cm and its real image is formed at a distance of 20 cm from a concave mirror. If the object is moved by 0.1 cm towards the mirror, the image will shift by about
(a) 0.4 cm away from the mirror (b) 0.8 cm away from the mirror
(c) 0.4 cm towards the mirror (d) 0.8 cm towards the mirror

19. A convex and a concave mirror of radii 10 cm each are placed facing each other and 15 cm apart. An object is placed exactly between them. If the reflection first takes place in concave and then in convex mirror, the position of the final image will be
(a) 10 cm behind concave mirror (b) at the pole of the concave mirror
(c) at the pole of the convex mirror (d) 5 cm in front of concave mirror

20. A spherical mirror forms an erect image three times the size of the object. If the distance between the object and the image is 80 cm, the nature and the focal length of the mirror are
(a) concave, 15 cm (b) convex, 30 cm (c) concave, 30 cm (d) convex, 15 cm

21. In a concave mirror an object is placed at a distance x from the focus and the real image is formed at a distance y from the focus. The focal length of the mirror is
(a) $x \sim y$ (b) $\sqrt{xy}$
(c) $x + y$ (d) None of these

Subjective Questions

Note *You can take approximations in the answers.*

1. Figure shows two rays P and Q being reflected by a mirror and going as P' and Q'. State which type of mirror is this?

2. A candle 4.85 cm tall is 39.2 cm to the left of a plane mirror. Where does the mirror form the image, and what is the height of this image?

3. A plane mirror lies face up, making an angle of 15° with the horizontal. A ray of light shines down vertically on the mirror. What is the angle of incidence? What will be the angle between the reflected ray and the horizontal?

4. Two plane mirrors each 1.6 m long, are facing each other. The distance between the mirrors is 20 cm. A light incident on one end of one of the mirrors at an angle of incidence of 30°. How many times is the ray reflected before it reaches the other end?

5. Two plane mirrors are inclined to each other at an angle θ. A ray of light is reflected first at one mirror and then at the other. Find the total deviation of the ray.

6. Assume that a certain spherical mirror has a focal length of – 10.0 cm. Locate and describe the image for object distances of (a) 25.0 cm (b) 10.0 cm (c) 5.0 cm.

7. A ball is dropped from rest 3.0 m directly above the vertex of a concave mirror that has a radius of 1.0 m and lies in a horizontal plane.
   (a) Describe the motion of ball's image in the mirror.
   (b) At what time do the ball and its image coincide?

8. An object 6.0 mm is placed 16.5 cm to the left of the vertex of a concave spherical mirror having a radius of curvature of 22.0 cm.
   (a) Draw principal ray diagram showing formation of the image.
   (b) Determine the position, size, orientation, and nature (real or virtual) of the image.

9. An object 9.0 mm tall is placed 12.0 cm to the left of the vertex of a convex spherical mirror whose radius of curvature has a magnitude of 20.0 cm.
   (a) Draw a principal ray diagram showing formation of the image.
   (b) Determine the position, size, orientation, and nature (real or virtual) of the image.

10. An object is placed 42 cm, in front of a concave mirror of focal length 21 cm. Light from the concave mirror is reflected onto a small plane mirror 21 cm in front of the concave mirror. Where is the final image?

11. Prove that for spherical mirrors the product of the distance of the object and the image to the principal focus is always equal to the square of the principal focal length.

12. Convex and concave mirrors have the same radii of curvature R. The distance between the mirrors is $2R$. At what point on the common optical axis of the mirrors should a point source of light A be placed for the rays to coverage at the point A after being reflected first on the convex and then on the concave mirror?

13. A spherical mirror is to be used to form on a screen 5.0 m from the object an image five times the size of the object.
   (a) Describe the type of mirror required.
   (b) Where should the mirror be positioned relative to the object?

LEVEL 2

Single Correct Option

1. An insect of negligible mass is sitting on a block of mass M, tied with a spring of force constant k. The block performs simple harmonic motion with amplitude A in front of a plane mirror as shown. The maximum speed of insect relative to its image will be

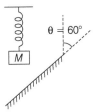

(a) $A\sqrt{\dfrac{k}{M}}$

(b) $\dfrac{A\sqrt{3}}{2}\sqrt{\dfrac{k}{M}}$

(c) $A\sqrt{3}\sqrt{\dfrac{k}{M}}$

(d) $2A\sqrt{\dfrac{M}{k}}$

2. A plane mirror is falling vertically as shown in the figure. If S is a point source of light, the rate of increase of the length AB is

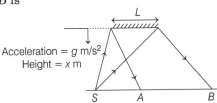

(a) directly proportional to x

(b) constant but not zero

(c) inversely proportional to x

(d) zero

3. Two plane mirrors L_1 and L_2 are parallel to each other and 3 m apart. A person standing x m from the right mirror L_2 looks into this mirror and sees a series of images. The distance between the first and second image is 4 m. Then, the value of x is

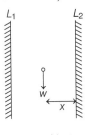

(a) 2 m   (b) 1.5 m   (c) 1 m   (d) 2.5 m

4. A piece of wire bent into an L shape with upright and horizontal portion of equal lengths 10 cm each is placed with the horizontal portion along the axis of the concave mirror towards pole of mirror whose radius of curvature is 10 cm. If the bend is 20 cm from the pole of the mirror, then the ratio of the lengths of the images of the upright and horizontal portion of the wire is

(a) $1:2$ (b) $1:3$ (c) $1:1$ (d) $2:1$

5. A point object at 15 cm from a concave mirror of radius of curvature 20 cm is made to oscillate along the principal axis with amplitude 2 mm. The amplitude of its image will be
   (a) 2 mm (b) 4 mm (c) 8 mm (d) None of these

6. A ray of light falls on a plane mirror. When the mirror is turned, by 20° the angle between the incident ray and new reflected ray is 45°. The angle between the incident ray and original reflected ray was therefore
   (a) 35° or 50° (b) 25° or 65° (c) 45° or 5° (d) None of these

7. A person AB of height 170 cm is standing in front of a plane mirror. His eyes are at height 164 cm. At what distance from P should a hole be made in mirror so that he cannot see his hair?
   (a) 167 cm (b) 161 cm
   (c) 163 cm (d) 165 cm

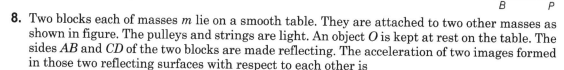

8. Two blocks each of masses m lie on a smooth table. They are attached to two other masses as shown in figure. The pulleys and strings are light. An object O is kept at rest on the table. The sides AB and CD of the two blocks are made reflecting. The acceleration of two images formed in those two reflecting surfaces with respect to each other is

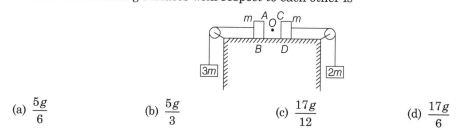

   (a) $\dfrac{5g}{6}$ (b) $\dfrac{5g}{3}$ (c) $\dfrac{17g}{12}$ (d) $\dfrac{17g}{6}$

9. An elevator at rest which is at 10th floor of a building is having a plane mirror fixed to its floor. A particle is projected with a speed $\sqrt{2}$ m/s and at 45° with the horizontal as shown in the figure. At the very instant of projection, the cable of the elevator breaks and the elevator starts falling freely. What will be the separation between the particle and is image 0.5 s after the instant of projection?

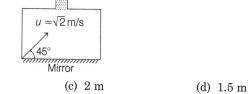

   (a) 0.5 m (b) 1 m (c) 2 m (d) 1.5 m

10. A plane mirror is moving with velocity $4\hat{i} + 4\hat{j} + 8\hat{k}$. A point object in front of the mirror moves with a velocity $3\hat{i} + 4\hat{j} + 5\hat{k}$. Here, $\hat{k}$ is along the normal to the plane mirror and facing towards the object. The velocity of the image is
    (a) $-3\hat{i} - 4\hat{j} + 5\hat{k}$ (b) $3\hat{i} + 4\hat{j} + 11\hat{k}$ (c) $-4\hat{i} + 5\hat{j} + 11\hat{k}$ (d) $7\hat{i} + 9\hat{j} + 3\hat{k}$

11. Point A (0, 1 cm) and B (12 cm, 5 cm) are the coordinates of object and image. x-axis is the principal axis of the mirror. Then, this object image pair is
    (a) due to a convex mirror of focal length 2.5 cm
    (b) due to a concave mirror having its pole at (2 cm, 0)
    (c) due to a concave mirror having its pole at (− 2 cm, 0)
    (d) Data is insufficient

12. Two plane mirrors AB and AC are inclined at an angle $\theta = 20°$. A ray of light starting from point P is incident at point Q on the mirror AB, then at R on mirror AC and again on S on AB. Finally, the ray ST goes parallel to mirror AC. The angle which the ray makes with the normal at point Q on mirror AB is

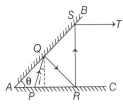

(a) 20°

(b) 30°

(c) 40°

(d) 60°

13. A convex mirror of radius of curvature 20 cm is shown in figure. An object O is placed in front of this mirror. Its ray diagram is shown. How many mistakes are there in the ray diagram (AB is principal axis)

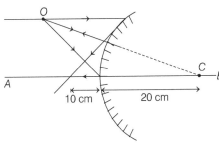

(a) 3

(b) 2

(c) 1

(d) 0

14. The graph shows part of variation of v with change in u for a concave mirror. Points plotted above the point P on the curve are for values of v :

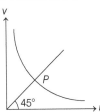

(a) smaller than f

(b) smaller than $2f$

(c) larger than $2f$

(d) larger than f but less than $2f$

15. A plane mirror is placed along the y-axis such that x-axis is normal to the plane of the mirror. The reflecting surface of the mirror is towards negative x-axis. The mirror moves in positive x-direction with uniform speed of 5 m/s and a point object P is moving with constant speed 3 m/s in negative x-direction. The speed of image with respect to mirror is

(a) 8 m/s

(b) 2 m/s

(c) 4 m/s

(d) 16 m/s

16. A mirror is inclined at an angle of θ with the horizontal. If a ray of light is incident at an angle of incidence θ, then the reflected ray makes the following angle with horizontal.

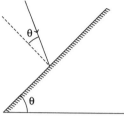

(a) θ
(b) 2θ
(c) $\dfrac{\theta}{2}$
(d) None of these

17. A ray of light makes an angle of 10° with the horizontal and strikes a plane mirror which is inclined at an angle θ to the horizontal. The angle θ for which the reflected ray becomes vertical, is
(a) 40°
(b) 50°
(c) 80°
(d) 100°

18. A ball is projected from top of the table with initial speed u at an angle of inclination θ, motion of image of ball w.r.t ball is

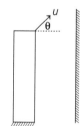

(a) a parabola
(b) a straight line and vertical
(c) a straight line and horizontal
(d) None of these

19. A ray of light travelling in the direction $\dfrac{1}{2}(\hat{\mathbf{i}} + \sqrt{3}\,\hat{\mathbf{j}})$ is incident on a plane mirror. After reflection, it travels along the direction $\dfrac{1}{2}(\hat{\mathbf{i}} - \sqrt{3}\,\hat{\mathbf{j}})$. The angle of incidence is
(a) 30°
(b) 45°
(c) 60°
(d) 75°

More than One Correct Options

1. The image formed by a concave mirror is twice the size of the object. The focal length of the mirror is 20 cm. The distance of the object from the mirror is/are
(a) 10 cm
(b) 30 cm
(c) 25 cm
(d) 15 cm

2. Magnitude of focal length of a spherical mirror is f and magnitude of linear magnification is $\dfrac{1}{2}$.

(a) If image is inverted, it is a concave mirror
(b) If image is erect, it is a convex mirror
(c) Object distance from the mirror may be $3f$
(d) Object distance from the mirror may be f

3. A point object is moving towards a plane mirror as shown in figure. Choose the correct options.

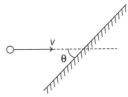

(a) Speed of image is also v
(b) Image velocity will also make an angle θ with mirror
(c) Relative velocity between object and image is $2v$
(d) Relative velocity between object and image is $2v \sin \theta$

4. AB is the principal axis of a spherical mirror. I is the point image corresponding to a point object O. Choose the correct options.

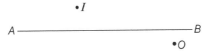

(a) Mirror is lying to the right hand side of O
(b) Focus of mirror is lying to the right hand side of O
(c) Centre of curvature of mirror is lying to the right hand side of O
(d) Centre of curvature of mirror is lying between I and O

5. A point object is placed on the principal axis of a concave mirror of focal length 20 cm. At this instant object is given a velocity v towards the axis (event-1) or perpendicular to axis (event-2). Then, speed of image

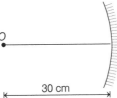

(a) in event-1 is $2v$
(b) in event-1 is $4v$
(c) in event-2 is $2v$
(d) in event-2 is $4v$

6. A point object is placed at equal distance $3f$ in front of a concave mirror, a convex mirror and a plane mirror separately (event-1). Now, the distance is decreased to $1.5\,f$ from all the three mirrors (event-2). Magnitude of focal length of convex mirror and concave mirror is f. Then, choose the correct options.

(a) Maximum distance of image in event-1 from the mirror is from plane mirror
(b) Minimum distance of image in event-1 from the mirror is from convex mirror
(c) Maximum distance of image in event-2 from the mirror is from concave mirror
(d) Minimum distance of image in event-2 from the mirror is from plane mirror

Comprehension Based Questions

Passage : (Q. No. 1 to 4)

A plane mirror (M_1) and a concave mirror (M_2) of focal length 10 cm are arranged as shown in figure. An object is kept at origin. Answer the following questions. (consider image formed by single reflection in all cases)

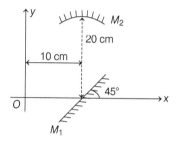

1. The coordinates of image formed by plane mirror are
   (a) $(-20\ \text{cm}, 0)$ (b) $(10\ \text{cm}, -60\ \text{cm})$ (c) $(10\ \text{cm}, -10\ \text{cm})$ (d) $(10\ \text{cm}, 10\ \text{cm})$

2. The coordinates of image formed by concave mirror are
   (a) $(10\ \text{cm}, -40\ \text{cm})$ (b) $(10\ \text{cm}, -60\ \text{cm})$ (c) $(10\ \text{cm}, 8\ \text{cm})$ (d) None of these

3. If concave mirror is replaced by convex mirror of same focal length, then coordinates of image formed by M_2 will be
   (a) $(10\ \text{cm}, 12\ \text{cm})$ (b) $(10\ \text{cm}, 22\ \text{cm})$ (c) $(10\ \text{cm}, 8\ \text{cm})$ (d) None of these

4. If concave mirror is replaced by another plane mirror parallel to x-axis, then coordinates of image formed by M_2 are
   (a) $(40\ \text{cm}, 20\ \text{cm})$ (b) $(20\ \text{cm}, 40\ \text{cm})$
   (c) $(-20\ \text{cm}, 20\ \text{cm})$ (d) None of these

Match the Columns

1. For real objects, match the following two columns corresponding to linear magnification m given in Column I.

	Column I	Column II
(a)	$m = -2$	(p) convex mirror
(b)	$m = -\dfrac{1}{2}$	(q) concave mirror
(c)	$m = +2$	(r) real image
(d)	$m = +\dfrac{1}{2}$	(s) virtual image

2. For virtual objects, match the following two columns.

Column I	Column II
(a) Plane mirror	(p) only real image
(b) Convex mirror	(q) only virtual image
(c) Concave mirror	(r) may be real or virtual image

3. Principal axis of a mirror (AB), a point object O and its image I are shown in Column I, match it with Column II.

	Column I	Column II
(a)	$O \bullet$ A————————B $\bullet I$	(p) plane mirror
(b)	$O \bullet$ A————————B $I \bullet$	(q) convex mirror
(c)	$O \bullet \qquad \bullet I$ A————————B	(r) concave mirror
(d)	$\bullet I$ $O \bullet$ ————————	(s) Not possible

4. Focal length of a concave mirror M_1 is -20 cm and focal length of a convex mirror M_2 is $+20$ cm. A point object is placed at a distance X in front of M_1 or M_2. Match the following two columns.

	Column I		Column II
(a)	$X = 20$, mirror is M_1	(p)	image is at infinity
(b)	$X = 20$, mirror is M_2	(q)	image is real
(c)	$X = 30$, mirror is M_1	(r)	image is virtual
(d)	$X = 30$, mirror is M_2	(s)	image is magnified

5. Focal length of a concave mirror is -20 cm. Match the object distance given in Column II corresponding to magnification (only magnitude) given is Column I.

	Column I		Column II
(a)	2	(p)	10 cm
(b)	1/2	(q)	30 cm
(c)	1	(r)	20 cm
(d)	1/4	(s)	None of these

Subjective Questions

1. A point source of light S is placed at a distance 10 cm in front of the centre of a mirror of width 20 cm suspended vertically on a wall. An insect walks with a speed 10 cm/s in front of the mirror along a line parallel to the mirror at a distance 20 cm from it as shown in figure. Find the maximum time during which the insect can see the image of the source S in the mirror.

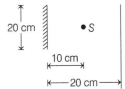

2. A concave mirror forms the real image of a point source lying on the optical axis at a distance of 50 cm from the mirror. The focal length of the mirror is 25 cm. The mirror is cut into and its halves are drawn a distance of 1 cm apart in a direction perpendicular to the optical axis. How will the image formed by the halves of the mirror be arranged?

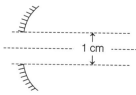

3. A point source of light S is placed on the major optical axis of the concave mirror at a distance of 60 cm. At what distance from the concave mirror should a flat mirror be placed for the rays to converge again at the point S having been reflected from the concave mirror and then from the flat one? Will the position of the point where the rays meet change if they are first reflected from the flat mirror? The radius of the concave mirror is 80 cm.

4. A balloon is moving upwards with a speed of 20 m/s. When it is at a height of 14 m from ground in front of a plane mirror in situation as shown in figure, a boy drops himself from the balloon. Find the time duration for which he will see the image of source S placed symmetrically before plane mirror during free fall.

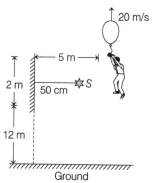

5. A plane mirror and a concave mirror are arranged as shown in figure and O is a point object. Find the position of image formed by two reflections, first one taking place at concave mirror.

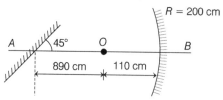

6. Figure shows a torch producing a straight light beam falling on a plane mirror at an angle 60°. The reflected beam makes a spot P on the screen along y-axis. If at $t = 0$, mirror starts rotating about the hinge A with an angular velocity $\omega = 1°$ per second clockwise. Find the speed of the spot on screen after time $t = 15$ s.

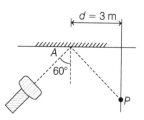

7. A thief is running away in a car with velocity of 20 m/s. A police jeep is following him, which is sighted by thief in his rear view mirror, which is a convex mirror of focal length 10 m. He observes that the image of jeep is moving towards him with a velocity of 1 cm/s. If the magnification of mirror for the jeep at that time is $\dfrac{1}{10}$. Find

(a) the actual speed of jeep,

(b) rate at which magnification is changing.

Assume the police's jeep is on the axis of the mirror.

8. A ball swings back and forth in front of a concave mirror. The motion of the ball is described approximately by the equation $x = f \cos \omega t$, where f is the focal length of the mirror and x is measured along the axis of mirror. The origin is taken at the centre of curvature of the mirror.

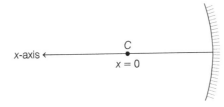

(a) Derive an expression for the distance from the mirror of the image of the swinging ball.

(b) At what point does the ball appear to coincide with its image?

(c) What will be the lateral magnification of the image of the ball at time $t = \dfrac{T}{2}$, where T is time period of oscillation?

9. Show that a parallel bundle of light rays parallel to the x-axis and incident on a parabolic reflecting surface given by $x = 2\,by^2$, will pass through a single point called focus of the reflecting surface. Also, find the focal length.

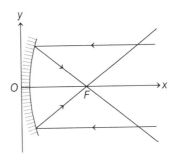

Answers

Introductory Exercise 30.1

1. 4 m/s
2. $\dfrac{20}{3}$ m, $\dfrac{40}{3}$ m
3. 2θ

Exercises

LEVEL 1

Assertion and Reason

1. (b)   2. (b)   3. (a or b)   4. (c)   5. (a, b)   6. (b)

Objective Questions

1. (b)   2. (c)   3. (a)   4. (d)   5. (d)   6. (a)   7. (a)   8. (c)   9. (c)   10. (a)
11. (d)   12. (c)   13. (d)   14. (b)   15. (a)   16. (c)   17. (b)   18. (a)   19. (c)   20. (c)
21. (b)

Subjective Questions

1. Plane mirror
2. 39.2 cm to the right of mirror, 4.85 cm
3. 15°, 60°
4. 14
5. $360° - 2\theta$
6. (a) -16.7 cm, real   (b) ∞ (c) $+10.0$ cm, virtual
7. (a) A real image moves from -0.6 m to $-\infty$, then a virtual image moves from $+\infty$ to 0.
   (b) 0.639 s and 0.782 s.
8. (b) 33.0 cm to the left of vertex 1.20 cm tall, inverted, real
9. (b) 5.46 cm to the right of vertex, 4.09 mm tall, erect, virtual
10. 21 cm in front of plane mirror
12. At a distance $\left(\dfrac{\sqrt{3}+1}{2}\right) R$ from convex mirror
13. (a) A concave mirror with radius of curvature 2.08 m   (b) 1.25 m from the object

LEVEL 2

Single Correct Option

1. (c)   2. (d)   3. (c)   4. (c)   5. (c)   6. (d)   7. (a)   8. (d)   9. (b)   10. (b)
11. (b)   12. (b)   13. (b)   14. (c)   15. (a)   16. (d)   17. (a)   18. (c)   19. (a)

More than One Correct Options

1. (a,b)   2. (a,b,c,d)   3. (a,b,d)   4. (a,b,d)   5. (b,c)   6. (a,b,c)

Comprehension Based Questions

  1. (c)   *2* (d)   *3.* (d)   *4.* (d)

Match the Columns

1.	(a) → q,r	(b) → q,r	(c) → q,s	(d) → p,s
2	(a) → p	(b) → r	(c) → p	
3.	(a) → r	(b) → r	(c) → p	(d) → r
4.	(a) → p,s	(b) → r	(c) → q,s	(d) → r
5.	(a) → p,q	(b) → s	(c) → s	(d) → s

Subjective Questions

  1. 6 s

  2 At a distance of 50 cm from mirror and 2 cm from each other

  3. 90 cm, Yes

  4. 1.7 s

  5. 100 cm vertically below A

  6. $\dfrac{2\pi}{15}$ m/s

  7. (a) 21 m/s   (b) 10^{-3}/s

  8. (a) Distance $= \left(\dfrac{2+\cos\omega t}{1+\cos\omega t}\right) f$ (b) At $x=0$ (c) $m = \infty$

  9. $f = \dfrac{1}{8b}$

31

REFRACTION OF LIGHT

31.1 **Refraction of Light and Refractive Index of a Medium**

When a ray of light travels from one medium to other medium with or without bending, the phenomenon is called refraction of light. Under following two conditions the ray of light does not bend in refraction.

(i) For normal incidence ($\angle i = 0$)

Fig. 31.1

(ii) If refractive index of both media is same, angle of incidence does not matter in this case.

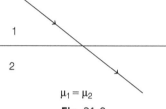

$\mu_1 = \mu_2$

Fig. 31.2

Here, μ = refractive index of medium

Refractive Index

(i) In general speed of light in any medium is less than its speed in vacuum. It is convenient to define refractive index μ of a medium as,

$$\mu = \frac{\text{Speed of light in vacuum}}{\text{Speed of light in medium}} = \frac{c}{v}$$

(ii) As a ray of light travels from medium 1 to medium 2, its wavelength changes but its frequency remains unchanged.

$$\mu_2 > \mu_1, v_1 > v_2, \lambda_1 > \lambda_2$$

1 | 2

λ_1 λ_2

Fig. 31.3

(iii) $_1\mu_2 = \dfrac{\mu_2}{\mu_1}$ = Refractive index of 2 w.r.t. 1

and $\qquad\qquad _2\mu_1 = \dfrac{\mu_1}{\mu_2}$ = Refractive index of 1 w.r.t. 2

∴ $\qquad\qquad _1\mu_2 = \dfrac{1}{_2\mu_1}$

(iv) $_1\mu_2 = \dfrac{\mu_2}{\mu_1}, \quad _2\mu_3 = \dfrac{\mu_3}{\mu_2} \quad$ and $\quad _3\mu_1 = \dfrac{\mu_1}{\mu_3}$

∴ $\qquad\qquad \boxed{_1\mu_2 \times _2\mu_3 \times _3\mu_1 = 1}$

(v) $v = \dfrac{c}{\mu} \quad$ and $\quad \lambda = \dfrac{\lambda_0}{\mu}$

Here, λ is the wavelength in a medium and λ_0 the wavelength in vacuum. Thus, in travelling from vacuum to a medium speed and wavelength decrease μ times but frequency remains unchanged.

(vi) $_1\mu_2 = \dfrac{\mu_2}{\mu_1} = \dfrac{c/v_2}{c/v_1} = \dfrac{v_1}{v_2} = \dfrac{f\lambda_1}{f\lambda_2} = \dfrac{\lambda_1}{\lambda_2}$

Here, f = frequency of light which remains same in both media.

Thus, $\qquad\qquad \boxed{_1\mu_2 = \dfrac{\mu_2}{\mu_1} = \dfrac{v_1}{v_2} = \dfrac{\lambda_1}{\lambda_2}}$

◉ **Example 31.1** *(a) Find the speed of light of wavelength $\lambda = 780\,nm$ (in air) in a medium of refractive index $\mu = 1.55$.*
(b) What is the wavelength of this light in the given medium?

Solution (a) $v = \dfrac{c}{\mu} = \dfrac{3.0 \times 10^8}{1.55} = 1.94 \times 10^8$ m/s   **Ans.**

(b) $\lambda_{\text{medium}} = \dfrac{\lambda_{\text{air}}}{\mu} = \dfrac{780}{1.55} = 503$ nm   **Ans.**

◉ **Example 31.2** *Refractive index of glass with respect to water is $(9/8)$. Refractive index of glass with respect to air is $(3/2)$. Find the refractive index of water with respect to air.*

Solution Given, $\quad _w\mu_g = 9/8 \quad$ and $\quad _a\mu_g = 3/2$

As, $\qquad\qquad _a\mu_g \times _g\mu_w \times _w\mu_a = 1$

∴ $\qquad\qquad \dfrac{1}{_w\mu_a} = _a\mu_w = _a\mu_g \times _g\mu_w = \dfrac{_a\mu_g}{_w\mu_g}$

∴ $\qquad\qquad _a\mu_w = \dfrac{3/2}{9/8} = \dfrac{4}{3}$ **Ans.**

⬢ **Example 31.3** *A ray of light passes through two slabs of same thickness. In the first slab n_1 waves are formed and in the second slab n_2. Find refractive index of second medium with respect to first.*

Solution   One wave means one wavelength. So, if t is the thickness of slab, λ the wavelength and n the number of waves, then

$$n\lambda = t \quad \Rightarrow \quad \lambda = \frac{t}{n}$$

or $\qquad\qquad \lambda \propto \frac{1}{n}$ (as t is same) $\quad$ or $\quad \dfrac{\lambda_1}{\lambda_2} = \dfrac{n_2}{n_1}$

Now, refractive index of second medium w.r.t. first medium is

$$_1\mu_2 = \frac{\lambda_1}{\lambda_2} = \frac{n_2}{n_1}$$ **Ans.**

INTRODUCTORY EXERCISE **31.1**

1. Given that $_1\mu_2 = 4/3$, $_2\mu_3 = 3/2$. Find $_1\mu_3$.

2. What happens to the frequency, wavelengths and speed of light that crosses from a medium with index of refraction μ_1 to one with index of refraction μ_2?

3. A monochromatic light beam of frequency 6.0×10^{14} Hz crosses from air into a transparent material where its wavelength is measured to be 300 nm. What is the index of refraction of the material?

31.2 **Law of Refraction (Snell's Law)**

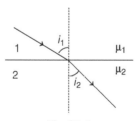

Fig. 31.4

If a ray of light passes through one medium to other medium, then according to Snell's law,

$$\boxed{\mu \sin i = \text{constant}}$$ ...(i)

For two media, $\qquad\qquad \mu_1 \sin i_1 = \mu_2 \sin i_2$

or $\qquad\qquad \boxed{\dfrac{\mu_2}{\mu_1} = \dfrac{\sin i_1}{\sin i_2} = {}_1\mu_2}$ ...(ii)

From Eq. (i) we can see that $i_1 > i_2$ if $\mu_2 > \mu_1$, i.e. if a ray of light passes from a rarer to a denser medium, it bends towards normal.

Eq. (ii) can be written as,

$$_1\mu_2 = \frac{\sin i_1}{\sin i_2} = \frac{v_1}{v_2} = \frac{\lambda_1}{\lambda_2} = \frac{\mu_2}{\mu_1} \qquad \qquad ...(iii)$$

Here, v_1 is the speed of light in medium 1 and v_2 in medium 2. Similarly, λ_1 and λ_2 are the corresponding wavelengths.

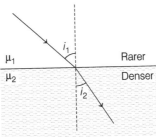

Fig. 31.5

If $\mu_2 > \mu_1$ then $v_1 > v_2$ and $\lambda_1 > \lambda_2$, i.e. in a rarer medium speed and hence, wavelength of light is more.

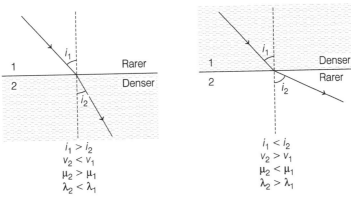

Fig. 31.6

Experiments show that if the boundaries of the media are **parallel**, the emergent ray CD although laterally displaced, is parallel to the incident ray AB if $\mu_1 = \mu_5$. We can also directly apply the Snell's law ($\mu \sin i = $ constant) in medium 1 and 5, i.e.

$$\mu_1 \sin i_1 = \mu_5 \sin i_5$$

So, $\qquad i_1 = i_5 \text{ if } \mu_1 = \mu_5$

If any of the boundary is not parallel we cannot use this law directly by jumping the intervening media.

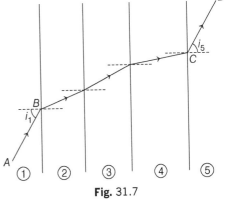

Fig. 31.7

✅ *Extra Points to Remember*

- $\mu = \dfrac{\sin i}{\sin r}$ is a special case of Snell's law when one medium is air.

  In Fig. 31.8, if we apply the Snell's law in original form then it is

  $$\mu_{air} \sin i_{air} = \mu_{medium} \sin i_{medium}$$

  or

  $$(1) \sin i = (\mu) \sin r$$

  ∴

  $$\mu = \frac{\sin i}{\sin r}$$

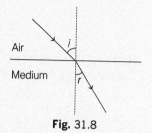

Fig. 31.8

- In $\mu = \dfrac{\sin i}{\sin r}$, angle i is not always the angle of incidence but it is the angle of

  ray of light in air (with normal).

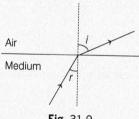

Fig. 31.9

  In the above figure, ray of light is travelling from medium to air. So, angle of incidence is actually r. But we have to take i angle in air and now we can apply $\mu = \dfrac{\sin i}{\sin r}$.

- In $\mu = \dfrac{\sin i}{\sin r}$, if i is changed, then r angle also changes. But $\dfrac{\sin i}{\sin r}$ remains constant and this constant is

  called refractive index of that medium.

- $\mu = \dfrac{\sin i}{\sin r}$ can be applied for any pair of angles i and r except the normal incidence for which $\angle i = \angle r = 0°$

  and $\mu = \dfrac{\sin i}{\sin r}$ is an indeterminant form.

◉ *Example 31.4* *A light beam passes from medium 1 to medium 2. Show that the emerging beam is parallel to the incident beam.*

Solution Applying Snell's law at A,

$$\mu_1 \sin i_1 = \mu_2 \sin i_2$$

or

$$\frac{\mu_1}{\mu_2} = \frac{\sin i_2}{\sin i_1} \qquad …(i)$$

Similarly at B,

$$\mu_2 \sin i_2 = \mu_1 \sin i_3$$

∴

$$\frac{\mu_1}{\mu_2} = \frac{\sin i_2}{\sin i_3} \qquad …(ii)$$

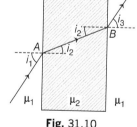

Fig. 31.10

From Eqs. (i) and (ii), we have

$$i_3 = i_1$$

i.e. the emergent ray is parallel to incident ray.

Proved.

Problems Based on $\mu = \dfrac{\sin i}{\sin r}$

◉ ***Example 31.5*** *A ray of light falls on a glass plate of refractive index* $\mu = 1.5$. *What is the angle of incidence of the ray if the angle between the reflected and refracted rays is* 90°?

Solution In the figure, $r = 90° - i$

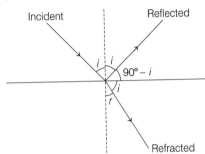

Fig. 31.11

From Snell's law,

$$1.5 = \frac{\sin i}{\sin r} = \frac{\sin i}{\sin (90° - i)} = \tan i$$

∴

$$i = \tan^{-1}(1.5) = 56.3°$$ **Ans.**

◉ ***Example 31.6*** *A pile* 4 *m high driven into the bottom of a lake is* 1 *m above the water. Determine the length of the shadow of the pile on the bottom of the lake if the sun rays make an angle of* 45° *with the water surface. The refractive index of water is* 4/3.

Solution From Snell's law, $\dfrac{4}{3} = \dfrac{\sin 45°}{\sin r}$

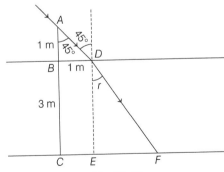

Fig. 31.12

Solving this equation, we get $\qquad r = 32°$

Further, $\qquad EF = (DE)\tan r = (3)\tan 32° = 1.88$ m

∴ Total length of shadow, $\qquad L = CF \quad$ or $\quad L = (1 + 1.88)$ m

$$= 2.88 \text{ m}$$ **Ans.**

⊙ **Example 31.7** *An observer can see through a pin-hole the top end of a thin rod of height h, placed as shown in the figure. The beaker height is 3h and its radius h. When the beaker is filled with a liquid up to a height 2h, he can see the lower end of the rod. Then, the refractive index of the liquid is* (JEE 2002)

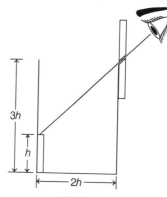

Fig. 31.13

(a) $\dfrac{5}{2}$ (b) $\sqrt{\dfrac{5}{2}}$ (c) $\sqrt{\dfrac{3}{2}}$ (d) $\dfrac{3}{2}$

Solution $PQ = QR = 2h$

∴

$$\angle i = 45°$$

∴

$$ST = RT = h = KM = MN$$

So,

$$KS = \sqrt{h^2 + (2h)^2} = h\sqrt{5}$$

∴

$$\sin r = \frac{h}{h\sqrt{5}} = \frac{1}{\sqrt{5}}$$

∴

$$\mu = \frac{\sin i}{\sin r} = \frac{\sin 45°}{1/\sqrt{5}} = \sqrt{\frac{5}{2}}$$

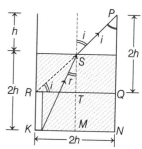

Fig. 31.14

∴   The correct answer is (b).

INTRODUCTORY EXERCISE **31.2**

1. In the figure shown, find $_1\mu_2$.

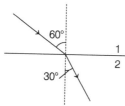

Fig. 31.15

2. If $_1\mu_2$ is 1.5, then find the value of $\dfrac{\lambda_1}{\lambda_2}$.

31.3 **Single Refraction from Plane Surface**

(i) If ray of light travels from first medium (refractive index μ_1) to second medium (refractive index μ_2), then image distance (or v) from the plane surface is given by

$$v = \frac{\mu_2}{\mu_1} u$$

(ii) From this equation, we can see that v and u are of same sign. This implies that object and image lie on same side of the plane surface. If one is real, then the other is virtual.

(iii) If ray of light travels from denser medium to rarer medium (or $\mu_1 > \mu_2$), then we can see that $v < u$) or the image distance is less than the object distance. If the light travels from rarer to denser medium ($\mu_1 < \mu_2$), then $v > u$ or the image distance is greater than the object distance.

Further, if rarer medium is air (or vacuum), then this decrease or increase in image distance will be μ times.

(iv) In all the four figures, single refraction is taking place through a plane surface. Refractive index of medium (may be glass, water etc.) is μ. In figures (a) and (d), the ray of light is travelling from denser to rarer medium and hence, it bends away from the normal. In figures (b) and (c), the ray of light is travelling from a rarer to a denser medium and hence, it bends towards the normal. Now, let us take the four figures individually.

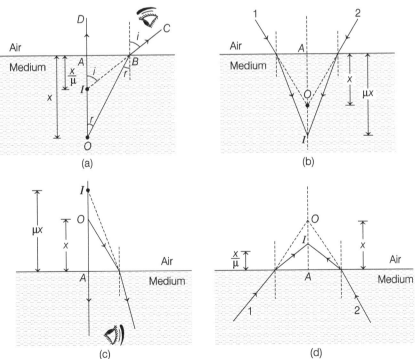

Fig. 31.16

Refer figure (a) Object O is placed at a distance x from A. Ray OA, which falls normally on the plane surface, passes undeviated as AD. Ray OB, which falls at angle r (with the normal) on the plane surface, bends away from the normal and passes as BC in air. Rays AD and BC meet at I after extending these two rays backwards. Let BC makes an angle i ($> r$) with normal.

In the figure, $\angle AOB$ will be r and $\angle AIB$ is i. For normal incidence (i.e. small angles of i and r)

$$\sin i \approx \tan i = \frac{AB}{AI} \qquad \qquad \ldots\text{(i)}$$

and

$$\sin r \approx \tan r = \frac{AB}{AO} \qquad \qquad \ldots\text{(ii)}$$

Dividing Eq. (i) by Eq. (ii), we have

$$\frac{\sin i}{\sin r} = \frac{AO}{AI} \quad \text{or} \quad \mu = \frac{AO}{AI} \qquad \qquad \left(\text{as} \; \frac{\sin i}{\sin r} = \mu \right)$$

$\therefore$

$$AI = \frac{AO}{\mu} = \frac{x}{\mu}.$$

If point O is at a depth of d from a water surface, then the above result is also sometimes written as,

$$\boxed{d_{\text{apparent}} = \frac{d_{\text{actual}}}{\mu}}$$

or the apparent depth is μ times less than the actual depth.

Refer figure (b)   In the absence of the plane refracting surface, the two rays 1 and 2 would have met at O. Proceeding in the similar manner we can prove that after refraction from the plane surface, they will now meet at a point I, where

$$AI = \mu x \qquad \qquad \text{(if } AO = x)$$

Refer figure (c)   In this case object is at O, a distance $AO = x$ from the plane surface. When seen from inside the medium, it will appear at I, where

$$AI = \mu x$$

If point O is at a height of h from the water surface, then the above relation is also written as

$$h_{\text{app}} = \mu h$$

Refer figure (d)   The two rays 1 and 2 meeting at O will now meet at I after refraction from the plane surface, where $AI = \dfrac{AO}{\mu} = \dfrac{x}{\mu}$.

Note   *In all the four cases, the change in the value of x is μ times whether it is increasing or decreasing. All the relations can be derived for small angles of incidence as done in part (a).*

EXERCISE   Three immiscible liquids of refractive indices μ_1, μ_2 and μ_3 (with $\mu_3 > \mu_2 > \mu_1$) are filled in a vessel. Their depths are d_1, d_2 and d_3 respectively. Prove that the apparent depth (for almost normal incidence) when seen from top of the first liquid will be

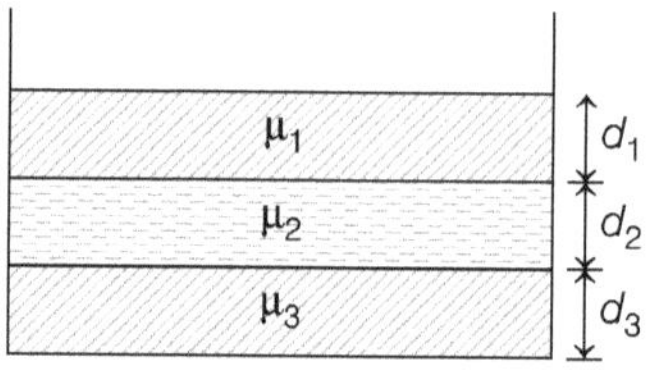

$$d_{\text{app}} = \frac{d_1}{\mu_1} + \frac{d_2}{\mu_2} + \frac{d_3}{\mu_3}$$

Fig. 31.17

◉ **Example 31.8** *In Fig. 31.18, find position of second image I_2 formed after two times refraction from two plane surfaces AB and CD.*

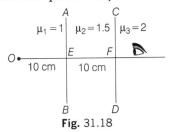

Fig. 31.18

Solution We will apply $v = \dfrac{\mu_2}{\mu_1} u$, two times with using the fact that object and image are on same side of the surface.

Refraction from *AB*

$$\mu_1 = 1$$
$$\mu_2 = 1.5$$
$$u = EO = 10\,\text{cm} \qquad\qquad \text{(towards left of } AB)$$

∴
$$v = \left(\frac{\mu_2}{\mu_1}\right) u = \frac{1.5}{1}(10)$$

or
$$v = EI_1 = 15\,\text{cm} \qquad\qquad \text{(towards left of } AB)$$

Refraction from *CD* I_1 will act as an object for refraction from CD

$$\mu_1 = 1.5 \quad \text{and} \quad \mu_2 = 2$$
$$u = FI_1 = FE + EI_1 = (10 + 15)\,\text{cm}$$
$$= 25\,\text{cm} \qquad\qquad \text{(towards left of } CD)$$

∴
$$v = \left(\frac{\mu_2}{\mu_1}\right)(u) = \left(\frac{2}{1.5}\right)(25)$$

$$= \frac{100}{3}\,\text{cm} \qquad\qquad \text{(towards left of } CD)$$

$$= FI_2$$

The correct figure is as shown below

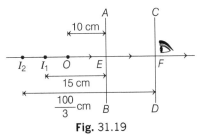

Fig. 31.19

Note I_1 and I_2 both are virtual as the light has moved towards right of AB and CD (because it is a refraction) but I_1 and I_2 are towards left of AB or CD.

● **Example 31.9** *Refractive index of the glass slab is 1.5. There is a point object O inside the slab as shown. To eye E_1 object appears at a distance of 6 cm (from the top surface) and to eye E_2 it appears at a distance of 8 cm (from the bottom surface). Find thickness of the glass slab.*

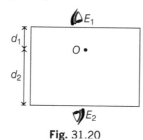

Fig. 31.20

Solution Applying $d_{app} = \dfrac{d}{\mu}$

$$d = (\mu)\, d_{app}$$

∴
$$d_1 = (1.5)(6) = 9 \, \text{cm}$$
$$d_2 = (1.5)(8) = 12 \, \text{cm}$$

Therefore, actual thickness of the glass slab is $d_1 + d_2 = 21$ cm. **Ans.**

INTRODUCTORY EXERCISE **31.3**

1. In the figure shown, at what distance

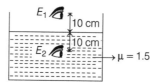

Fig. 31.21

(a) E_2 will appear to E_1
(b) E_1 will appear to E_2

31.4 **Shift due to a Glass Slab**

(i) It is a case of double refraction from two plane surfaces. So, we are talking about the second (or final) image and let us call it I.

(ii) If O is real then second image I is virtual and *vice-versa*.

(iii) I is shifted (w.r.t.) O by a distance $OI = \text{shift} = \left(1 - \dfrac{1}{\mu}\right) t$ in the direction of ray of light.

(iv) If E_1 observes E_2, then E_2 is object. So, light travels from E_2 towards E_1. So, shift is also in the same direction or E_1 will observe second image of E_2 at a distance
$$d_1 = d - \text{shift}$$

Same is the case when E_2 observes E_1.

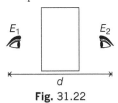

Fig. 31.22

(v) If two or more than two slabs are kept jointly or separately, then total shift is added.

∴
$$S_{\text{Total}} = S_1 + S_2 = \left(1 - \frac{1}{\mu_1}\right)t_1 + \left(1 - \frac{1}{\mu_2}\right)t_2$$

(vi)

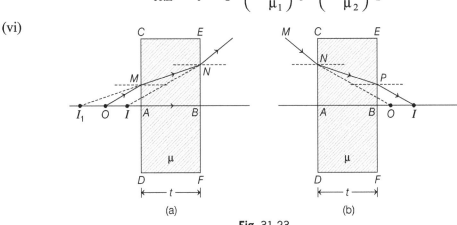

Fig. 31.23

Refer figure (a) An object is placed at O. Plane surface CD forms its image (virtual) at I_1. This image acts as an object for EF which finally forms the image (virtual) at I. Distance OI is called the normal shift and its value is

$$OI = \left(1 - \frac{1}{\mu}\right)t$$

This can be proved as under

Let $\qquad\qquad OA = x$

then $\qquad\qquad AI_1 = \mu x$ $\qquad\qquad$ (Refraction from CD)

$\qquad\qquad BI_1 = \mu x + t$

$\qquad\qquad BI = \dfrac{BI_1}{\mu} = x + \dfrac{t}{\mu}$ $\qquad\qquad$ (Refraction from EF)

∴ $\qquad\qquad OI = (AB + OA) - BI$

$\qquad\qquad\quad = (t + x) - \left(x + \dfrac{t}{\mu}\right) = \left(1 - \dfrac{1}{\mu}\right)t$ $\qquad$ **Hence Proved.**

Note *For two refractions (at CD and EF) we have used,*

$$v = \left(\frac{\mu_2}{\mu_1}\right)\mu$$

Refer figure (b) The ray of light which would have met line *AB* at *O* will now meet this line at *I* after two times refraction from the slab. Here,

$$OI = \left(1 - \frac{1}{\mu}\right)t$$

◉ **Example 31.10** *Refractive index of glass slab shown in figure is 1.5. Focal length of mirror is 20 cm. Find*

(a) *total number of refractions and reflections before final image is formed.*

(b) *reduced steps.*

(c) *value of x, so that final image coincides with the object.*

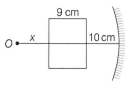

Fig. 31.24

Solution (a) There are total four refractions and one reflection.

(b) Reduced steps are three, first slab, then mirror and then again slab.

(c) Shift due to the slab,

$$s = \left(1 - \frac{1}{\mu}\right)t = \left(1 - \frac{2}{3}\right)(9) = 3 \text{ cm}$$

Actual distance from mirror to object is $(19 + x)$ cm. Slab will reduce this distance by 3 cm. So, apparent distance will be $(16 + x)$ cm.

Now, if $\qquad 16 + x = R = 2f = 40$ cm $\quad$ or $\quad x = 24$ cm

then ray of light will fall normal to the concave mirror. It will retrace its path and final image will coincide with the object

$\therefore \qquad\qquad\qquad\qquad x = 24$ cm $\qquad\qquad\qquad\qquad$ **Ans.**

Note *If ray of light falls normal to a mirror, then there is no need of applying the slab formula in return journey of ray of light. Path is retracing means, slab formula is automatically applied in return journey. But if it is not normal, then we will have to apply the slab formula in return journey too.*

◉ **Example 31.11** *A point object O is placed in front of a concave mirror of focal length 10 cm. A glass slab of refractive index $\mu = 3/2$ and thickness 6 cm is inserted between object and mirror. Find the position of final image when the distance x shown in figure is*

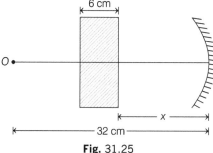

Fig. 31.25

(a) *5 cm* $\qquad\qquad\qquad\qquad\qquad\qquad$ (b) *20 cm*

Solution As we have read in the above article, the normal shift produced by a glass slab is

$$\Delta x = \left(1 - \frac{1}{\mu}\right)t = \left(1 - \frac{2}{3}\right)(6) = 2 \text{ cm}$$

i.e. for the mirror the object is placed at a distance $(32 - \Delta x) = 30$ cm from it. Applying mirror formula

$$\frac{1}{v} + \frac{1}{u} = \frac{1}{f} \quad \text{or} \quad \frac{1}{v} - \frac{1}{30} = -\frac{1}{10} \quad \text{or} \quad v = -15 \text{ cm}$$

(a) **When $x = 5$ cm** The light falls on the slab on its return journey as shown. But the slab will again shift it by a distance $\Delta x = 2$ cm. Hence, the final **real** image is formed at a distance $(15 + 2) = 17$ cm from the mirror.

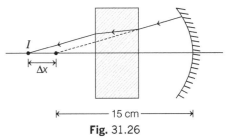

Fig. 31.26

(b) **When $x = 20$ cm** This time also the final image is at a distance 17 cm from the mirror but it is **virtual** as shown.

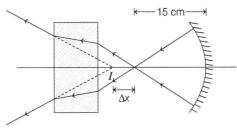

Fig. 31.27

INTRODUCTORY EXERCISE **31.4**

1. At what distance eye *E* will observe the fourth image (after four refractions from plane surfaces) of object *O* from itself.

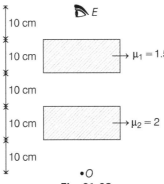

Fig. 31.28

31.5 Refraction from Spherical Surface

(i) There are two types of spherical surfaces, concave and convex.

(ii)

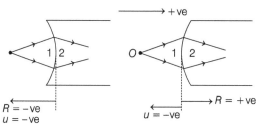

Fig. 31.29

If the ray of light is travelling from first medium to second medium, then for image distance v, we have the formula

$$\frac{\mu_2}{v} - \frac{\mu_1}{u} = \frac{\mu_2 - \mu_1}{R}$$

(iii) For plane surface $R = \infty$. Putting this value in the above formula, we get

$$v = \left(\frac{\mu_2}{\mu_1}\right)u$$

and this formula, we have already discussed in article 31.3.

(iv) Ray of light has moved in medium-2, so image formed in medium-2 will be real and v in this medium will be positive.

Proof

Consider two transparent media having indices of refraction μ_1 and μ_2, where the boundary between the two media is a spherical surface of radius R. We assume that $\mu_1 < \mu_2$. Let us consider a single ray leaving point O and focusing at point I. Snell's law applied to this refracted ray gives,

$$\mu_1 \sin\theta_1 = \mu_2 \sin\theta_2$$

Because θ_1 and θ_2 are assumed to be small, we can use the small angle approximation

$$\sin\theta \approx \theta \quad \text{(angles in radians)}$$

and say that

$$\mu_1\theta_1 = \mu_2\theta_2 \qquad \ldots\text{(i)}$$

From the geometry shown in the figure,

$$\theta_1 = \alpha + \beta \qquad \ldots\text{(ii)}$$

and

$$\beta = \theta_2 + \gamma \qquad \ldots\text{(iii)}$$

The above three equations can be rearranged as,

$$\beta = \frac{\mu_1}{\mu_2}(\alpha + \beta) + \gamma$$

So,

$$\mu_1\alpha + \mu_2\gamma = (\mu_2 - \mu_1)\beta \qquad \ldots\text{(iv)}$$

Since, the arc PM (of length s) subtends an angle β at the centre of curvature,

$$\beta = \frac{s}{R}$$

Also in the paraxial approximation, $\quad \alpha = \frac{s}{u}$ and $\quad \gamma = \frac{s}{v}$

Using these expressions in Eq. (iv) with proper signs, we are left with,

$$\frac{\mu_1}{-u} + \frac{\mu_2}{v} = \frac{\mu_2 - \mu_1}{R} \quad \text{or} \quad \boxed{\frac{\mu_2}{v} - \frac{\mu_1}{u} = \frac{\mu_2 - \mu_1}{R}} \quad \text{...(v)}$$

Although the formula (v) is derived for a particular situation, it is valid for all other situations of refraction at a single spherical surface.

> **Example 31.12** *A glass sphere of radius*
> *$R = 10$ cm is kept inside water. A point*
> *object O is placed at 20 cm from A as*
> *shown in figure. Find the position and*
> *nature of the image when seen from other*
> *side of the sphere. Also draw the ray*
> *diagram. Given, $\mu_g = 3/2$ and $\mu_w = 4/3$.*

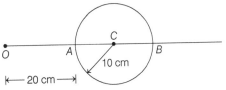

Fig. 31.31

Solution A ray of light starting from O gets refracted twice. The ray of light is travelling in a direction from left to right. Hence, the distances measured in this direction are taken positive.

Applying $\dfrac{\mu_2}{v} - \dfrac{\mu_1}{u} = \dfrac{\mu_2 - \mu_1}{R}$, twice with proper signs. We have,

$$\frac{3/2}{AI_1} - \frac{4/3}{-20} = \frac{3/2 - 4/3}{10} \quad \text{or} \quad AI_1 = -30\,\text{cm}$$

Now, the first image I_1 acts as an object for the second surface, where

$$BI_1 = u = -(30 + 20) = -50\,\text{cm}$$

$$\therefore \quad \frac{4/3}{BI_2} - \frac{3/2}{-50} = \frac{4/3 - 3/2}{-10}$$

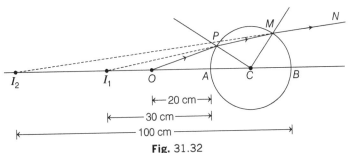

Fig. 31.32

$\therefore \quad BI_2 = -100$ cm,

i.e. the final image I_2 is **virtual** and is formed at a distance 100 cm (towards left) from B.

The ray diagram is as shown in Fig. 31.32

Following points should be noted while drawing the ray diagram.

(i) At P the ray travels from rarer to a denser medium. Hence, it will bend towards normal PC. At M, it travels from a denser to a rarer medium, hence, it moves away from the normal MC.

(ii) PM ray when extended backwards meets at I_1 and MN ray when extended meets at I_2.

INTRODUCTORY EXERCISE 31.5

1. If an object is placed at the centre of a glass sphere and it is seen from outside, then prove that its virtual image is also formed at centre.

2. A glass sphere ($\mu = 1.5$) with a radius of 15.0 cm has a tiny air bubble 5 cm above its centre. The sphere is viewed looking down along the extended radius containing the bubble. What is the apparent depth of the bubble below the surface of the sphere?

3. One end of a long glass rod ($\mu = 1.5$) is formed into a convex surface of radius 6.0 cm. An object is positioned in air along the axis of the rod. Find the image positions corresponding to object distances of (a) 20.0 cm, (b) 10.0 cm, (c) 3.0 cm from the end of the rod.

4. A dust particle is inside a sphere of refractive index $\dfrac{4}{3}$. If the dust particle is 10.0 cm from the wall of the 15.0 cm radius bowl, where does it appear to an observer outside the bowl.

5. A parallel beam of light enters a clear plastic bead 2.50 cm in diameter and index 1.44. At what point beyond the bead are these rays brought to a focus?

31.6 Lens Theory

(i) A lens is one of the most familiar optical devices for a human being. A lens is an optical system with two refracting surfaces. The simplest lens has two spherical surfaces close enough together that we can neglect the distance between them (the thickness of the lens). We call this a **thin lens.**

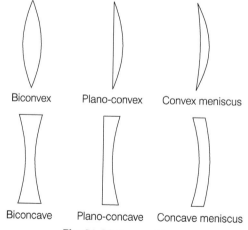

Fig. 31.33 Types of lens.

Lenses are of two basic types **convex** (converging) which are thicker in the middle than at the edges and **concave** (diverging) for which the reverse holds.

Figure shows examples of both types bounded by spherical or plane surfaces.

As there are two spherical surfaces, there are two centres of curvature C_1 and C_2 correspondingly two radii of curvature R_1 and R_2.

The line joining C_1 and C_2 is called the **principal axis** of the lens. The centre P of the thin lens which lies on the principal axis, is called the **optical centre.**

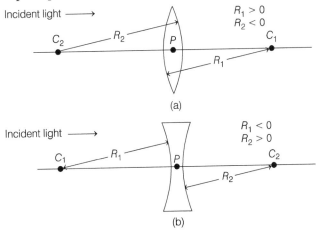

Fig. 31.34 (a) A converging thin lens and
(b) a diverging thin lens

(ii) All lens formulae (which we will use in this chapter) can be applied directly under following two conditions.

Condition 1 Lens should be thin or its thickness should be negligible.

Condition 2 On both sides of the lens, medium should be same (not necessarily air)

(iii) If either of the above two conditions are not satisfied, then apply refraction formulae $\left(\dfrac{\mu_2}{v} - \dfrac{\mu_1}{u} = \dfrac{\mu_2 - \mu_1}{R}\right.$ for spherical surface or $v = \dfrac{\mu_2}{\mu_1} u$ for plane surface$\left.\right)$ two times.

(iv) In a biconvex (or equiconvex) or biconcave (or equiconcave) lens,

$$|R_1| = |R_2|$$

(v) **Use of thin lens** If the lens is thin, then the first image distance v_1 is exactly equal to the second object distance u_2.

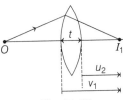

Fig. 31.35

In the figure, we can see that $\quad u_2 = v_1 - t$
But, $\quad\quad\quad\quad\quad\quad\quad\quad\quad u_2 = v_1 \quad$ if $\quad t = 0$

(vi) Unlike a mirror, a lens has two foci :

First focus (F_1) It is defined as a point at which if an object (real in case of a convex lens and virtual for concave) is placed, the image of this object is formed at infinity. Or we can say that rays passing through F_1 become parallel to the principal axis after refraction from the lens. The distance PF_1 is the first focal length f_1.

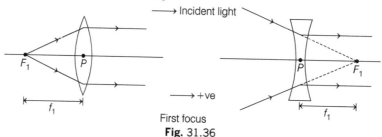

First focus
Fig. 31.36

Second focus or principal focus (F_2) A narrow beam of light travelling parallel to the principal axis either converge (in case of a convex lens) or diverge (in case of a concave lens) at a point F_2 after refraction from the lens. This point F_2 is called the second or principal focus. If the rays converge at F_2, the lens is said a converging lens and if they diverge, they are called diverging lens. Distance PF_2 is the second focal length f_2.

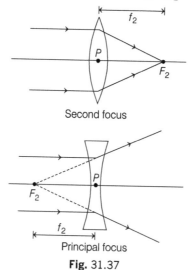

Second focus

Principal focus
Fig. 31.37

From the figure, we can see that f_1 is negative for a convex lens and positive for a concave lens. But, f_2 is positive for convex lens and negative for concave lens.

(vii) We are mainly concerned with the second focus f_2. Thus, wherever we write the focal length f, it means the second or principal focal length. Thus, $f = f_2$ and hence, f is positive for a convex lens and negative for a concave lens.

(viii) If the two conditions mentioned in point number (ii) are satisfied, then

$$|f_1| = |f_2|$$

although their signs are different.

(ix) If those two conditions are satisfied, then object can be placed on either side of the lens or light can fall from both sides of the lens. Following figures will help you to clear this concept.

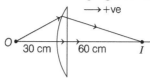

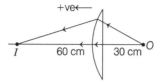

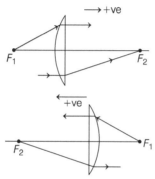

Fig. 31.38

Image Position, its Nature and Speed

Case 1 **Convex lens**

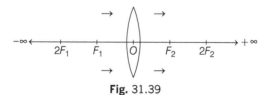

Fig. 31.39

Table 31.1

Object	Image	Nature of image	Speed
At F_1	$\pm \infty$	–	–
At $2F_1$	At $2F_2$	Real, Inverted and same size	$v_I = v_O$
At $-\infty$	At F_2	–	–
Between O and F_1	Between O and $-\infty$	Virtual, Erect and magnified	$v_O > v_I$
Between F_1 and $2F_1$	Between $+\infty$ and $2F_2$	Real, Inverted and magnified	$v_I > v_O$
Between $2F_1$ and $-\infty$	Between $2F_2$ and F_2	Real, Inverted and diminished	$v_O > v_I$

Note (i) *The above table has been made only for real objects (lying between O and −∞), object distance u for them is negative.*

(ii) *Since |f_1| = |f_2| (when two conditions discussed earlier are satisfied). Therefore, F_1 and F_2 are sometimes denoted by F and $2F_1$ (and $2F_2$) by 2F.*

(iii) *If object is travelling along the principal axis, then image also travels along the principal axis in the same direction.*

Case 2 **Concave lens** In case of concave lens there is only one case for real objects.

Object lies between O and $-\infty$, then image lies between O and F_2. Nature of image is virtual, erect and diminished. Object speed is always greater than image speed ($v_O > v_I$). Both travel in the same direction.

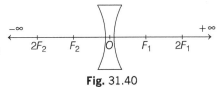

Fig. 31.40

Three Standard Rays for making Ray Diagrams

1. A ray parallel to the principal axis after refraction passes through the principal focus or appears to diverge from it.

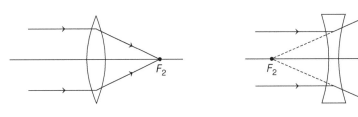

Fig. 31.41

2. A ray through the optical centre P passes undeviated because the middle of the lens acts like a thin parallel-sided slab.

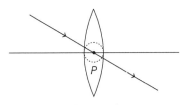

Fig. 31.42

3. A ray passing through the first focus F_1 becomes parallel to the principal axis after refraction.

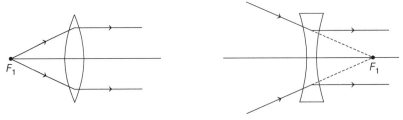

Fig. 31.43

Ray Diagrams

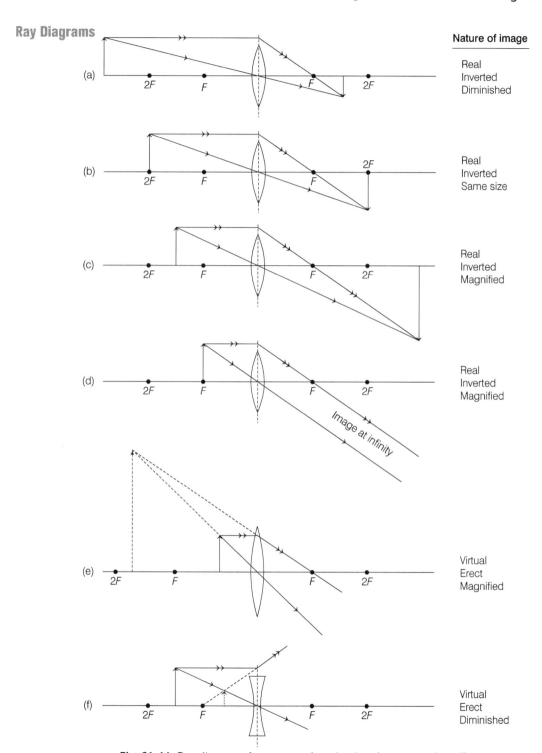

Nature of image

(a) Real
Inverted
Diminished

(b) Real
Inverted
Same size

(c) Real
Inverted
Magnified

(d) Real
Inverted
Magnified

(e) Virtual
Erect
Magnified

(f) Virtual
Erect
Diminished

Fig. 31.44 Ray diagrams for a convex lens (a–e) and a concave lens (f).

List of Formulae

(i) $\dfrac{1}{v} - \dfrac{1}{u} = \dfrac{1}{f}$

(ii) Linear magnification, $\quad m = \dfrac{\text{Image height}}{\text{Object height}} = \dfrac{I}{O} = \dfrac{v}{u}$

(iii) **Lens maker's formula**

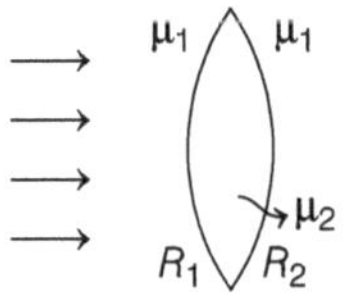

Fig. 31.45

$$\frac{1}{f} = \left(\frac{\mu_2}{\mu_1} - 1\right)\left(\frac{1}{R_1} - \frac{1}{R_2}\right)$$

In air, $\mu_1 = 1$ and $\mu_2 = \mu$. Therefore, $\dfrac{1}{f} = (\mu - 1)\left(\dfrac{1}{R_1} - \dfrac{1}{R_2}\right)$

(iv) Power of a lens (in dioptre) $= \dfrac{1}{\text{Focal length (in metre)}}$

(v) Two or more than two thin lenses in contact.

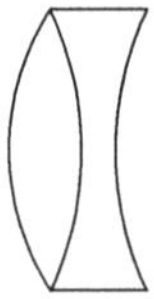

Fig. 31.46

$$\frac{1}{F} = \frac{1}{f_1} + \frac{1}{f_2} \quad \text{or} \quad P = P_1 + P_2$$

(vi) Two or more than two thin lenses at some distance

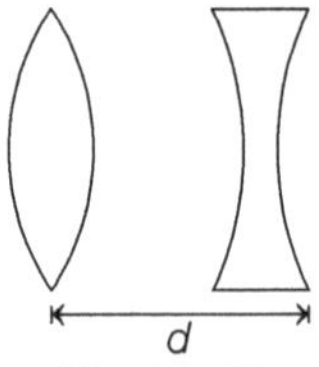

Fig. 31.47

$$\frac{1}{F} = \frac{1}{f_1} + \frac{1}{f_2} - \frac{d}{f_1 f_2}$$

or $\qquad P = P_1 + P_2 - dP_1P_2$

Note *In the above two equations if $d = 0$, then*

$$\frac{1}{F} = \frac{1}{f_1} + \frac{1}{f_2} \quad and \quad P = P_1 + P_2$$

(vii) Image velocity

(a) Along the principal axis,

$$\mathbf{v}_I = m^2 \mathbf{v}_0$$

$\mathbf{v}_I$ and $\mathbf{v}_0$ are in the same direction.

(b) Perpendicular to principal axis,

$$\mathbf{v}_I = m\mathbf{v}_0$$

If m is positive then $\mathbf{v}_I$ and $\mathbf{v}_0$ are in the same direction and if m is negative, then $\mathbf{v}_I$ and $\mathbf{v}_0$ are in opposite directions.

Note *The above two formulae have been derived in the previous chapter of reflection. So, same method can be applied here.*

Important points in formulae

(i) **On linear magnification m** From the value of m, we can determine nature of image, type of lens and an approximate position of object. Following table illustrates this point.

Table 31.2

Value of m	Nature of image	Type of lens	Object position
-3	Inverted, real and magnified	convex	Between F_1 and $2F_1$
-1	Inverted, real and same size	convex	at $2F_1$
$-\dfrac{1}{2}$	Inverted, real and diminished	convex	Between $2F_1$ and $-\infty$
$+2$	Erect, virtual and magnified	convex	Between O and F_1
$+\dfrac{1}{4}$	Erect, virtual and diminished	concave	Between O and $-\infty$

Note *For real objects, real image is formed only by convex lens. But virtual image is formed by both types of lenses. Their sizes are different. Magnified virtual image is formed by convex lens. Diminished virtual image is formed by concave lens.*

(ii) **On lens maker's formula**

$$\frac{1}{f} = \left(\frac{\mu_2}{\mu_1} - 1\right)\left(\frac{1}{R_1} - \frac{1}{R_2}\right) \qquad \ldots \text{(i)}$$

$$= (\mu - 1)\left(\frac{1}{R_1} - \frac{1}{R_2}\right) \text{ in air} \qquad \ldots \text{(ii)}$$

For a converging lens, R_1 is positive and R_2 is negative. Therefore, $\left(\dfrac{1}{R_1} - \dfrac{1}{R_2}\right)$ in Eq. (ii) comes out a positive quantity and if the lens is placed in air, $(\mu - 1)$ is also a positive quantity. Hence, the focal length f of a converging lens turns out to be positive. For a diverging lens however, R_1 is negative and R_2 is positive and the focal length f becomes negative.

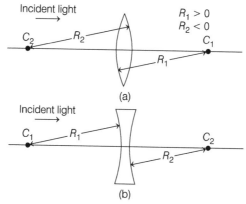

(a)

(b)

Fig. 31.48

Focal length of a mirror $\left(f_M = \dfrac{R}{2} \right)$ depends only upon the radius of curvature R while that of a lens [Eq. (i)] depends on μ_1, μ_2, R_1 and R_2. Thus, if a lens and a mirror are immersed in some liquid, the focal length of lens would change while that of the mirror will remain unchanged.

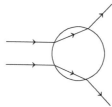

Fig. 31.49 Air bubble in water diverges the parallel beam of light incident on it.

Suppose $\mu_2 < \mu_1$ in Eq. (i), i.e. refractive index of the medium (in which lens is placed) is more than the refractive index of the material of the lens, then $\left(\dfrac{\mu_2}{\mu_1} - 1 \right)$ becomes a negative quantity, i.e. the lens changes its behaviour. A converging lens behaves as a diverging lens and *vice-versa*. An air bubble in water seems as a convex lens but behaves as a concave (diverging) lens.

(iii) **Power of lens** By optical power of an instrument (whether it is a lens, mirror or a refractive surface) we mean the ability of the instrument to deviate the path of rays passing through it. If the instrument converges the rays parallel to the principal axis its power is said to be positive and if it diverges the rays it is said a negative power.

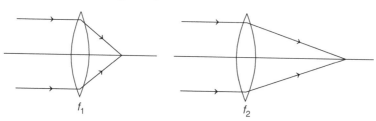

Fig. 31.50

The shorter the focal length of a lens (or a mirror) the more it converges or diverges the light. As shown in the figure,

$$f_1 < f_2$$

and hence the power $P_1 > P_2$, as bending of light in case 1 is more than that of case 2. For a lens,

$$P \text{ (in dioptre)} = \frac{1}{f \text{ (in metre)}}$$

and for a mirror,

$$P \text{ (in dioptre)} = \frac{-1}{f \text{ (in metre)}}$$

Following table gives the sign of P and f for different types of lens and mirror.

Table 31.3

Nature of lens/mirror	Focal length (f)	Power $P_L = \frac{1}{f}, P_M = -\frac{1}{f}$	Converging/ diverging	Ray diagram
Convex lens	+ ve	+ ve	converging	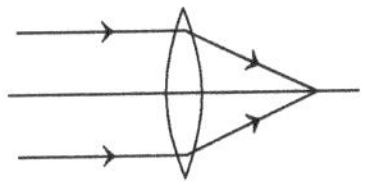
Concave mirror	– ve	+ ve	converging	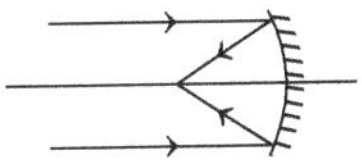
Concave lens	– ve	– ve	diverging	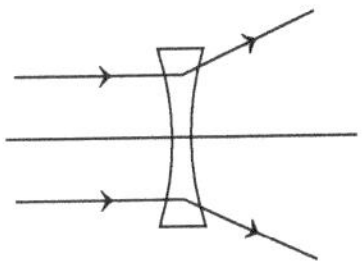
Convex mirror	+ ve	– ve	diverging	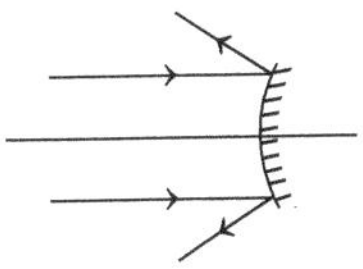

Thus, convex lens and concave mirror have positive power or they are converging in nature. Concave lens and convex mirror have negative power or they are diverging in nature.

(iv) **Based on two or more than two thin lenses in contact (or at some distance)**

If the lenses are kept in contact, then after finding the equivalent focal length F from the equation

$$\frac{1}{F} = \frac{1}{f_1} + \frac{1}{f_2}$$

We can directly apply the formula

$$\frac{1}{v} - \frac{1}{u} = \frac{1}{F}$$

for finding the image distance v, but we will have to apply lens formula, $\dfrac{1}{v} - \dfrac{1}{u} = \dfrac{1}{f}$ two times if the lenses are kept at some distance.

Proofs of Different Formulae

(i) Consider an object O placed at a distance u from a convex lens as shown in figure. Let its image I after two refractions from spherical surfaces of radii R_1 (positive) and R_2 (negative) be formed at a distance v from the lens. Let v_1 be the distance of image formed by refraction from the refracting surface of radius R_1. This image acts as an object for the second surface.

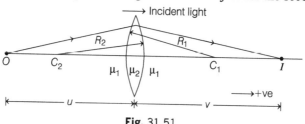

Fig. 31.51

Using,

$$\frac{\mu_2}{v} - \frac{\mu_1}{u} = \frac{\mu_2 - \mu_1}{R}$$

We have,

$$\frac{\mu_2}{v_1} - \frac{\mu_1}{u} = \frac{\mu_2 - \mu_1}{R_1} \qquad \text{...(i)}$$

and

$$\frac{\mu_1}{v} - \frac{\mu_2}{v_1} = \frac{\mu_1 - \mu_2}{-R_2} \qquad \text{...(ii)}$$

Adding Eqs. (i) and (ii) and then simplifying, we get

$$\frac{1}{v} - \frac{1}{u} = \left(\frac{\mu_2}{\mu_1} - 1\right)\left(\frac{1}{R_1} - \frac{1}{R_2}\right) \qquad \text{...(iii)}$$

This expression relates the image distance v of the image formed by a thin lens to the object distance u and to the thin lens properties (index of refraction and radii of curvature). It is valid only for paraxial rays and only when the lens thickness is much less than R_1 and R_2. The **focal length** f of a thin lens is the image distance that corresponds to an object at infinity. So, putting $u = \infty$ and $v = f$ in the above equation, we have

$$\frac{1}{f} = \left(\frac{\mu_2}{\mu_1} - 1\right)\left(\frac{1}{R_1} - \frac{1}{R_2}\right) \qquad \text{...(iv)}$$

If the refractive index of the material of the lens is μ and it is placed in air, $\mu_2 = \mu$ and $\mu_1 = 1$ so that Eq. (iv) becomes

$$\frac{1}{f} = (\mu - 1)\left(\frac{1}{R_1} - \frac{1}{R_2}\right) \qquad \text{...(v)}$$

This is called the **lens maker's formula** because it can be used to determine the values of R_1 and R_2 that are needed for a given refractive index and a desired focal length f.

Combining Eqs. (iii) and (v), we get

$$\frac{1}{v} - \frac{1}{u} = \frac{1}{f}$$

...(vi)

Which is known as the **lens formula.**

(ii) **Magnification** The lateral, transverse or linear magnification m produced by a lens is defined by

$$m = \frac{\text{Height of image}}{\text{Height of object}} = \frac{I}{O}$$

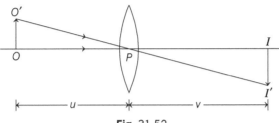

Fig. 31.52

A real image II' of an object OO' formed by a convex lens is shown in figure.

$$\frac{\text{Height of image}}{\text{Height of object}} = \frac{II'}{OO'} = \frac{v}{u}$$

Substituting v and u with proper sign,

$$\frac{II'}{OO'} = \frac{-I}{O} = \frac{v}{-u}$$

or

$$\frac{I}{O} = m = \frac{v}{u}$$

Thus,

$$m = \frac{v}{u}$$

(iii) **Focal length of two or more than two thin lenses in contact**

Combinations of lenses in contact are used in many optical instruments to improve their performance.

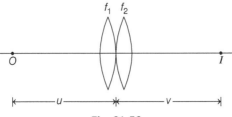

Fig. 31.53

Suppose two lenses of focal lengths f_1 and f_2 are kept in contact and a point object O is placed at a distance u from the combination. The first image (say I_1) after refraction from the first lens is formed at a distance v_1 (whatever may be the sign of v_1) from the combination. This image I_1 acts as an object for the second lens and let v be the distance of the final image from the combination. Applying the lens formula,

$$\frac{1}{v} - \frac{1}{u} = \frac{1}{f}$$

For the two lenses, we have
$$\frac{1}{v_1} - \frac{1}{u} = \frac{1}{f_1}$$ ...(i)

and
$$\frac{1}{v} - \frac{1}{v_1} = \frac{1}{f_2}$$ ...(ii)

Adding Eqs. (i) and (ii), we have
$$\frac{1}{v} - \frac{1}{u} = \frac{1}{f_1} + \frac{1}{f_2} = \frac{1}{F}$$ (say)

Here, F is the equivalent focal length of the combination. Thus,

$$\boxed{\frac{1}{F} = \frac{1}{f_1} + \frac{1}{f_2}}$$

Similarly for more than two lenses in contact, the equivalent focal length is given by the formula,

$$\boxed{\frac{1}{F} = \sum_{i=1}^{n} \frac{1}{f_i}}$$

Note *Here, f_1, f_2 etc., are to be substituted with sign.*

Types of Problems in Lens

Type 1. *Based on two or more than two thin lenses in contact*

How to Solve
$$\text{Apply, } \frac{1}{F} = \frac{1}{f_1} + \frac{1}{f_2}$$

and
$$P = P_1 + P_2$$

⊙ **Example 31.13** *A convex lens of power 2 D and a concave lens of focal length 40 cm are kept in contact, find*

    (a) Power of combination   *(b) Equivalent focal length*

Solution (a) Applying

$$P = P_1 + P_2 = P_{\text{convex}} + P_{\text{concave}}$$

$$= 2 + \frac{1}{(-0.4)} \qquad\qquad \left[P(\text{in } D) = \frac{1}{f(\text{in } m)} \right]$$

$$= 2 - 2.5 = -0.5 \, D \qquad\qquad\qquad\qquad\qquad\qquad\qquad \textbf{Ans.}$$

(b)
$$F = \frac{1}{P}$$

$$= \frac{1}{-0.5} = -2 \text{ m}$$

$$= -200 \text{ cm} \qquad \textbf{Ans.}$$

Note *F and P are negative so, the system behaves like a concave lens.*

⊚ **Example 31.14** *A converging lens of focal length 5.0 cm is placed in contact with a diverging lens of focal length 10.0 cm. Find the combined focal length of the system.*

Solution Here, $f_1 = +5.0$ cm and $f_2 = -10.0$ cm

Therefore, the combined focal length F is given by

$$\frac{1}{F} = \frac{1}{f_1} + \frac{1}{f_2} = \frac{1}{5.0} - \frac{1}{10.0} = +\frac{1}{10.0}$$

∴ $$F = +10.0 \text{ cm} \qquad \textbf{Ans.}$$

i.e. the combination behaves as a converging lens of focal length 10.0 cm.

Type 2. *Based on lens maker's formula*

How to Solve

Apply, $$\frac{1}{f} = \left(\frac{\mu_2}{\mu_1} - 1\right)\left(\frac{1}{R_1} - \frac{1}{R_2}\right) \quad \text{or} \quad \frac{1}{f} = (\mu - 1)\left(\frac{1}{R_1} - \frac{1}{R_2}\right)$$

Note *If initial two conditions are satisfied (thin lens and same medium on both sides,) then we can find focal length of the lens (f or f_2) from either side of the lens. Result comes out to be same.*

⊚ **Example 31.15**

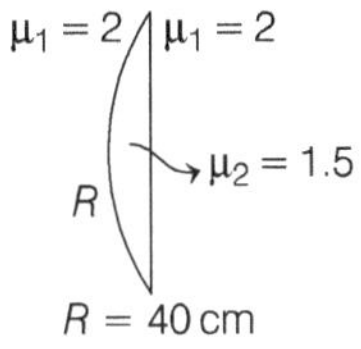

$\mu_1 = 2$ $\mu_1 = 2$

$\mu_2 = 1.5$

R

$R = 40$ cm

Fig. 31.54

Find focal length of the system shown in figure from left hand side.

Solution $\mu_1 = 2, \mu_2 = 1.5, R_1 = +40$ and $R_2 = \infty$

Using the equation

$$\frac{1}{f} = \left(\frac{\mu_2}{\mu_1} - 1\right)\left(\frac{1}{R_1} - \frac{1}{R_2}\right), \text{ we have}$$

R_1 R_2

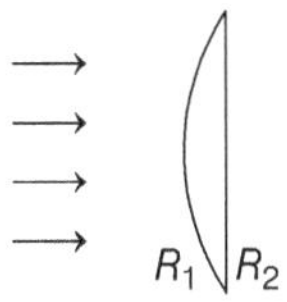

Fig. 31.55

$$\frac{1}{f} = \left(\frac{1.5}{2} - 1\right)\left(\frac{1}{+40} - \frac{1}{\infty}\right) \quad \Rightarrow \quad f = -160 \text{ cm}$$

Therefore, from left hand side it behaves like a concave lens of focal length 160 cm.

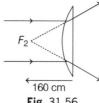

Fig. 31.56

Exercise Find focal length of the above system from right hand side and prove that it is also -160 cm.

◉ **Example 31.16** *Focal length of a convex lens in air is 10 cm. Find its focal length in water. Given that* $\mu_g = 3/2$ *and* $\mu_w = 4/3$.

Solution
$$\frac{1}{f_{air}} = (\mu_g - 1)\left(\frac{1}{R_1} - \frac{1}{R_2}\right) \qquad \qquad …(i)$$

and
$$\frac{1}{f_{water}} = \left(\frac{\mu_g}{\mu_w} - 1\right)\left(\frac{1}{R_1} - \frac{1}{R_2}\right) \qquad \qquad …(ii)$$

Dividing Eq. (i) by Eq. (ii), we get
$$\frac{f_{water}}{f_{air}} = \frac{(\mu_g - 1)}{(\mu_g/\mu_w - 1)}$$

Substituting the values, we have
$$f_{water} = \frac{(3/2 - 1)}{\left(\dfrac{3/2}{4/3} - 1\right)} f_{air}$$

$$= 4\, f_{air} = 4 \times 10 = 40\, cm \qquad \qquad \textbf{Ans.}$$

Note (i) *Students can remember the result* $f_{water} = 4\, f_{air}$, *if* $\mu_g = 3/2$ *and* $\mu_w = 4/3$.

(ii) *In water focal length has become four times and power (power of bending of light) remains* $\dfrac{1}{4}$ *th. This is because, difference in refractive index between glass and water has been decreased (compared to glass and air). So, there will be less bending of light.*

◉ **Example 31.17** *A biconvex lens* $(\mu = 1.5)$ *has radius of curvature* 20 *cm (both). Find its focal length.*

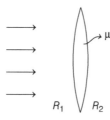

Fig. 31.57

Solution $R_1 = +20\,\text{cm}, R_2 = -20\,\text{cm}, \mu = 1.5$

Substituting the values in the equation

$$\frac{1}{f} = (\mu - 1)\left(\frac{1}{R_1} - \frac{1}{R_2}\right), \text{ we have}$$

$$\frac{1}{f} = (1.5 - 1)\left(\frac{1}{20} - \frac{1}{-20}\right)$$

or $\qquad\qquad\qquad f = +20\,\text{cm}$ **Ans.**

Note *If a biconvex or biconcave lens has refractive index* $\mu = 1.5$, *then*
$$|R_1| = |R_2| = |f|$$

Type 3. *To find image distance and its magnification corresponding to given object distance*

How to Solve?

• Substitute signs of *u* and *f*. Sign of *v* automatically comes after applying the lens formula. Sign of *u* is negative for real objects. Sign of *f* is positive for convex lens and negative for concave lens.

⊗ ***Example 31.18*** *Find distance of image from a convex lens of focal length 20 cm if object is placed at a distance of 30 cm from the lens. Also find its magnification.*

Solution $u = -30\,\text{cm}, f = +20\,\text{cm}$

Applying the lens formula

$$\frac{1}{v} - \frac{1}{u} = \frac{1}{f}$$

We have,

$$\frac{1}{v} - \frac{1}{-30} = \frac{1}{+20}$$

Solving, we get

$$v = +60\,\text{cm}$$ **Ans.**

$$m = \frac{v}{u} = \frac{+60}{-30} = -2$$ **Ans.**

m is − 2, it implies that image is real, inverted and two times magnified. The ray diagram is as shown below.

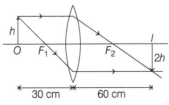

Fig. 31.58

Type 4. *To find object/image distance corresponding to given magnification of image and focal length of lens*

How to Solve?

● Substitute all three signs of *u*, *v* and *f*. Signs of *u* and *f* have been discussed in the above type. Sign of *v* is positive for real image (see the above example) and it is negative for virtual image.

● $m = \dfrac{v}{u} \implies |v| = |m \times u|$

⊗ **Example 31.19** *Find the distance of an object from a convex lens if image is two times magnified. Focal length of the lens is* 10 *cm.*

Solution Convex lens forms both types of images real as well as virtual. Since, nature of the image is not mentioned in the question, we will have to consider both the cases.

When image is real Means *v* is positive and *u* is negative with $|v| = 2|u|$. Thus, if

$$u = -x, \quad \text{then} \quad v = 2x \quad \text{and} \quad f = 10 \, \text{cm}$$

Substituting in

$$\frac{1}{v} - \frac{1}{u} = \frac{1}{f}$$

We have

$$\frac{1}{2x} + \frac{1}{x} = \frac{1}{10} \quad \text{or} \quad \frac{3}{2x} = \frac{1}{10}$$

∴ $\qquad\qquad\qquad\qquad\qquad\qquad x = 15 \, \text{cm}$ **Ans.**

$x = 15$ cm, means object lies between *F* and 2 *F*.

When image is virtual Means *v* and *u* both are negative. So let,

$$u = -y, \quad \text{then} \quad v = -2y \quad \text{and} \quad f = 10 \, \text{cm}$$

Substituting in,

$$\frac{1}{v} - \frac{1}{u} = \frac{1}{f}$$

We have,

$$\frac{1}{-2y} + \frac{1}{y} = \frac{1}{10} \quad \text{or} \quad \frac{1}{2y} = \frac{1}{10}$$

∴ $\qquad\qquad\qquad\qquad\qquad\qquad y = 5 \, \text{cm}$ **Ans.**

$y = 5$ cm, means object lies between *F* and *O*.

Type 5. *To make some conditions*

How to Solve?

● Initially, substitute sign of only *f*, then make equation of *v*. From this equation of *v*, find the asked condition.

⊗ **Example 31.20** *Under what condition, a concave lens can make a real image.*

Solution Substituting sign of *f* in the lens formula, we have

$$\frac{1}{v} - \frac{1}{u} = \frac{1}{-f} \quad \text{or} \quad \frac{1}{v} = \frac{1}{u} - \frac{1}{f} \qquad\qquad \dots(i)$$

For real image v should be positive. Therefore, from Eq. (i) we can see that u should be positive and less than f. Further, u is positive and less than f means a virtual object should lie between O and F_1.

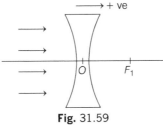

Fig. 31.59

Important Result

Under normal conditions, a convex lens makes a real image. But the image is virtual (and magnified) if a real object is placed between O and F_1. Opposite is the case with concave lens. Under normal conditions it makes a virtual image (for all real objects). But the image is real if a virtual object is placed between O and F_1.

Type 6. *To find image nature, type of lens, its optical centre and focus for given principal axis, point object and its point image.*

⊚ ***Example 31.21*** *An image I is formed of point object O by a lens whose optic axis is AB as shown in figure.*

Fig. 31.60

(a) State whether it is a convex lens or concave?

(b) Draw a ray diagram to locate the lens and its focus.

Solution (a) (i) Concave lens always forms an erect image. The given image I is on the other side of the optic axis. Hence, the lens is **convex.**

(ii) Join O with I. Line OI cuts the optic axis AB at optical centre (P) of the lens. The dotted line shows the position of lens.

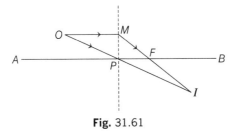

Fig. 31.61

From point O, draw a line parallel to AB. Let it cuts the dotted line at M. Join M with I. Line MI cuts the optic axis at focus (F) of the lens.

Type 7. *Two lens problems*

How to Solve?

- We have to apply lens formula two times. The first image behaves like an object for the second lens.

⊙ **Example 31.22** *Focal length of convex lens is 20 cm and of concave lens 40 cm. Find the position of final image.*

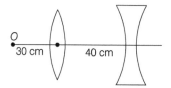

Fig. 31.62

Solution   Using the lens formula for convex lens,

$$u = -30 \text{ cm}, \ f = +20 \text{ cm}$$

∴

$$\frac{1}{v} - \frac{1}{-30} = \frac{1}{+20}$$

Solving this equation, we get $v = +60$ cm. Therefore, the first image is 60 cm to the right of convex lens or 20 cm to the right of concave lens. Again applying lens formula for concave lens,

$$u = +20 \text{ cm}, \ f = -40 \text{ cm, we have}$$

$$\frac{1}{v} - \frac{1}{+20} = \frac{1}{-40}$$

$$v = +40 \text{ cm}$$

So, the final image I_2 is formed at 40 cm to the right of concave lens as shown below.

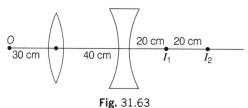

Fig. 31.63

Type 8. *Based on image velocity*

How to Solve?

- Using the methods discussed in Type 3, first find v and then m. Now,

(i) Along the axis, $\mathbf{v}_I = m^2 \mathbf{v}_0$

(ii) Perpendicular to axis, $\mathbf{v}_I = m \mathbf{v}_0$

⊜ **Example 31.23** *Focal length of the convex lens shown in figure is* 20 *cm. Find the image position and image velocity.*

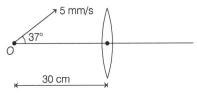

Fig. 31.64

Solution For the given condition,

$$u = -30\,\text{cm},\ f = +20\,\text{cm}$$

Using the lens formula, we have

$$\frac{1}{v} - \frac{1}{-30} = \frac{1}{+20}$$

Solving this equation, we get

$$v = +60\,\text{cm and}$$

$$m = \frac{v}{u} = \frac{+60}{-30} = -2$$

$$m^2 = 4$$

Component of velocity of object along the axis $= 5\cos 37° = 4$ mm/s (towards the lens) component of velocity of image along the axis $= m^2\,(4\ \text{mm/s}) = 4 \times 4 = 16$ mm/s. This component is away from the lens (in the same direction of object velocity component)

Component of velocity of object perpendicular to the axis $= 5\sin 37° = 3$ mm/s (upwards).

∴   Component of velocity of image perpendicular to axis $= m\,(3\ \text{mm/s})$ or $(-2)(3\ \text{mm/s})$ $= -6$ mm/s or this component is 6 mm/s downwards. These all points are shown in the figure given below.

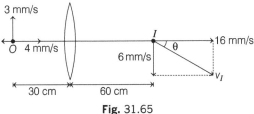

Fig. 31.65

$$v_I = \sqrt{(16)^2 + (6)^2}$$

$$= \sqrt{292}\ \text{mm/s}$$

$$\tan\theta = \frac{6}{16} = \frac{3}{8}$$

or

$$\theta = \tan^{-1}(3/8)$$

Type 9. *An extended object kept perpendicular to principal axis*

How to Solve?

- Using the methods discussed in Type 3, first find v and then m. Now, suppose m is -2 and object is 1 mm above the principal axis, then image will be 2 mm below the principal axis.

Example 31.24 *Focal length of concave lens shown in figure is 60 cm. Find image position and its magnification.*

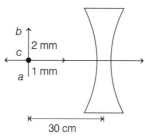

Fig. 31.66

Solution For the given situation,

$$u = -30 \, \text{cm}, \, f = -60 \, \text{cm}$$

Using the lens formula, we have

$$\frac{1}{v} - \frac{1}{-30} = \frac{1}{-60}$$

Solving this equation, we get

$$v = -20 \, \text{cm}$$

Further, $m = \dfrac{v}{u} = \dfrac{-20}{-30} = +\dfrac{2}{3}$. Point b is 2 mm above the principal axis. Therefore, its image b'

will be $(2)\left(\dfrac{2}{3}\right)$ or $\dfrac{4}{3}$ mm, above the principal axis.

Similarly, point a is 1 mm below the principal axis. Therefore, its image a' will be $(1)\left(\dfrac{2}{3}\right)$ or

$\dfrac{2}{3}$ mm below the principal axis. The final image is as shown in Fig. 31.67

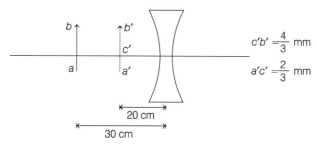

Fig. 31.67

Type 10. *To plot u versus v or $\dfrac{1}{u}$ versus $\dfrac{1}{v}$ graph*

Concept

In the previous chapter, we have seen that $\dfrac{1}{v}$ *versus* $\dfrac{1}{u}$ graph will be a straight line. Further for real

objects, u is always negative. So, u varies from 0 to $-\infty$. Therefore, $\dfrac{1}{u}$ will vary from $-\infty$ to 0.

● **Example 31.25** *Plot u versus v and* $\dfrac{1}{u}$ *versus* $\dfrac{1}{v}$ *graph for convex lens (only for*

real objects)

Solution

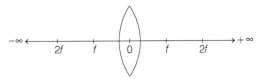

Fig. 31.68

Table 31.4

S.No.	u	v	$\dfrac{1}{u}$	$\dfrac{1}{v}$
1.	0 to $-f$	0 to $-\infty$	$-\infty$ to $-\dfrac{1}{f}$	$-\infty$ to 0
2.	$-f$ to $-2f$	$+\infty$ to $+2f$	$-\dfrac{1}{f}$ to $-\dfrac{1}{2f}$	0 to $+\dfrac{1}{2f}$
3.	$-2f$ to $-\infty$	$+2f$ to $+f$	$-\dfrac{1}{2f}$ to 0	$+\dfrac{1}{2f}$ to $+\dfrac{1}{f}$

u versus **graph**

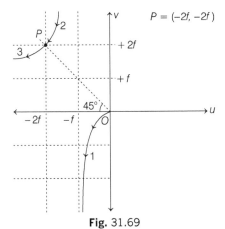

Fig. 31.69

$\dfrac{1}{u}$ *versus* $\dfrac{1}{v}$ **graph**

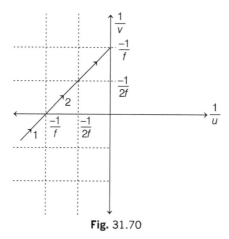

Fig. 31.70

Type 11. *Problems of inclined lenses*

● **Example 31.26**

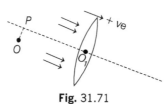

Fig. 31.71

O_1P *is the principal axis and* O *is the point object. Given,*
$O_1P = 30$ *cm,* $f = 20$ *cm and* $OP = 2$ *mm. Find the image distance and its position.*

Solution For the given situation,

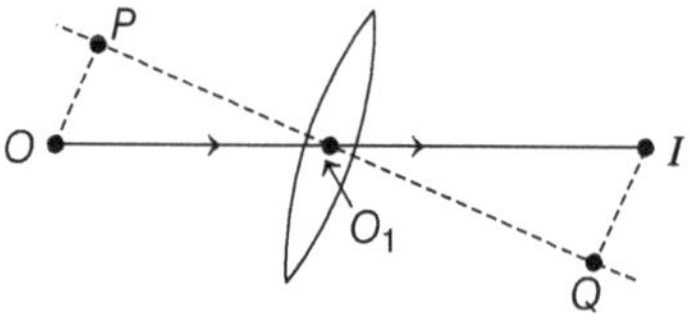

$O_1Q = 60$ cm
$QI = 4$ mm

Fig. 31.72

$$u = -30 \text{ cm}$$

and $$f = +20 \text{ cm}$$

Using the lens formula, we have

$$\frac{1}{v} - \frac{1}{-30} = \frac{1}{+20}$$

Solving this equation, we get

$$v = +60\,\text{cm}$$

Further,
$$m = \frac{v}{u} = \frac{+60}{-30} = -2$$

Therefore, image is at a distance of $+60$ cm from the lens at a distance of $(2 \text{ mm}) (-2)$ or 4 mm from the principal axis on other side of the object. The image is as shown above in Fig. 31.72.

Note *Image will always lie on the line joining O and O_1. This is because the ray OO_1 passes undeviated.*

Type 12. *To find focal length of an optical system for which either of the two conditions (thin lens and same medium on both sides) is not satisfied*

Concept

If focal length is asked then we have to find the second focal length f_2. The definition of F_2 is, if object is at infinity ($u_1 = \infty$) then final image after two refractions will be at F_2 ($v_2 = f_2$ or f). The use of thin lens is v_1 is exactly equal to u_2.

> **Example 31.27** *In the figure, light is incident on a thin lens as shown. The radius of curvature for both the surfaces is R. Determine the focal length of this system.* (JEE 2003)

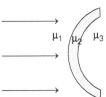

Fig. 31.73

Solution For refraction at first surface,
$$\frac{\mu_2}{v_1} - \frac{\mu_1}{-\infty} = \frac{\mu_2 - \mu_1}{+R} \qquad \text{...(i)}$$

For refraction at second surface,
$$\frac{\mu_3}{v_2} - \frac{\mu_2}{v_1} = \frac{\mu_3 - \mu_2}{+R} \qquad \text{... (ii)}$$

Adding Eqs. (i) and (ii), we get $\dfrac{\mu_3}{v_2} = \dfrac{\mu_3 - \mu_1}{R}$ or $v_2 = \dfrac{\mu_3 R}{\mu_3 - \mu_1}$

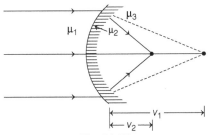

Fig. 31.74

Therefore, focal length of the given lens system is

$$f = \frac{\mu_3 R}{\mu_3 - \mu_1}$$

Note *If we find the focal length of the above system from right hand side, then it will be different because medium on both sides is not same.*

Important Points in Lens Theory

1.

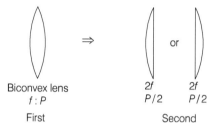

Fig. 31.75

In the first figure,

$$\frac{1}{f} = (\mu - 1)\left(\frac{1}{R} - \frac{1}{-R}\right) = (\mu - 1)\left(\frac{2}{R}\right)$$

∴

$$f = \frac{R}{2(\mu - 1)}$$

In the second figure,

$$\frac{1}{f'} = (\mu - 1)\left(\frac{1}{R} - \frac{1}{\infty}\right)$$

∴

$$f' = \frac{R}{\mu - 1}$$

or

$$f' = 2f$$

2.

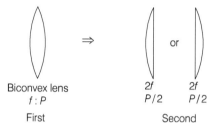

Fig. 31.76

3. The system shown in Fig. 31.77 has single value of u but two different parts will have two focal lengths. Therefore, we get two images I_1 and I_2, horizontally separated from each other. The two focal lengths are

$$\frac{1}{f_1} = (\mu_1 - 1)\left(\frac{1}{R_1} - \frac{1}{R_2}\right)$$

and
$$\frac{1}{f_2} = (\mu_2 - 1)\left(\frac{1}{R_1} - \frac{1}{R_2}\right)$$

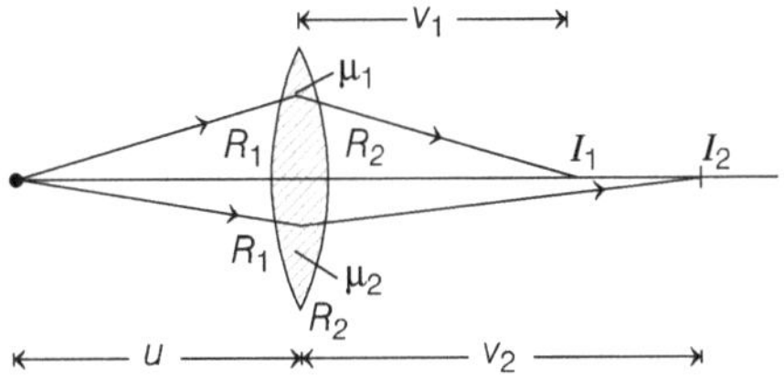

Fig. 31.77

4. This system shown in Fig. 31.78 has single values of u and f. Therefore, we will get single value of v. Still, we will get two images, vertically separated from each other. Let us take an example in support of this.

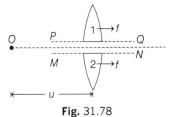

Fig. 31.78

If $u = 30\,\text{cm}$, f is 20 cm, principal axis PQ of upper part 1 is 1 mm above the object and principal axis MN of lower part 2 is 1 mm below the object O. Then, after applying lens formula, we get

$$v = +60\,\text{cm} \quad \text{and} \quad m = -2$$

Now, O is 1 mm below PQ and $m = -2$. Therefore, upper part will make I_1, 2 mm above PQ. Similarly, O is 1 mm above MN, therefore lower part will make I_2, 2 mm below MN. Ray diagram from the two parts is as shown in Fig. 31.79 below

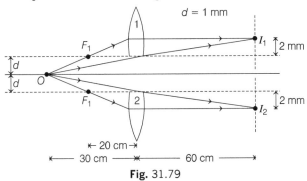

Fig. 31.79

5. If a liquid is filled between two thin convex glass lenses, then it is a group of three lenses as shown in figure.

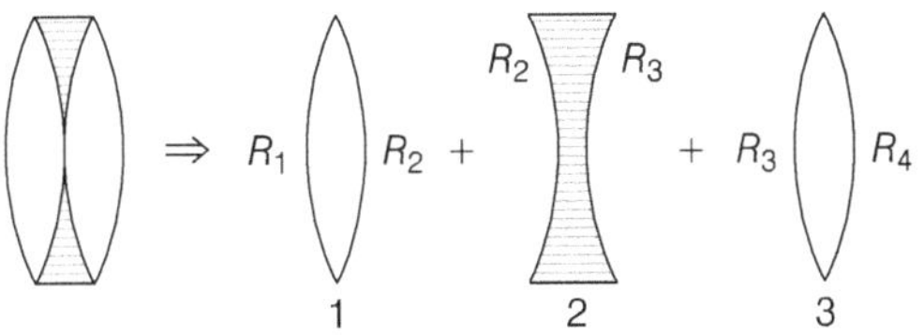

Fig. 31.80

∴
$$\frac{1}{F} = \frac{1}{f_1} + \frac{1}{f_2} + \frac{1}{f_3}$$

where,

$$\frac{1}{f_1} = (\mu_g - 1)\left(\frac{1}{R_1} - \frac{1}{R_2}\right)$$

$$\frac{1}{f_2} = (\mu_l - 1)\left(\frac{1}{R_2} - \frac{1}{R_3}\right) \quad \text{and}$$

$$\frac{1}{f_3} = (\mu_g - 1)\left(\frac{1}{R_3} - \frac{1}{R_4}\right)$$

6. The system shown in figure behaves like a lens of zero power (or $f = \infty$). This is because

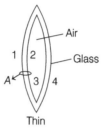

Fig. 31.81

$$R_1 \approx R_2 \quad \text{and} \quad R_3 \approx R_4$$

Now if we find focal length or power of part A, then

$$\frac{1}{f} \quad \text{or} \quad P = (\mu_g - 1)\left(\frac{1}{R_1} - \frac{1}{R_2}\right) = 0 \quad \text{as} \quad R_1 \approx R_2$$

Similarly, we can prove that power of other part is also zero.

7. Minimum distance between real object and its real image from a convex lens is $4f$.

   Exercise Prove the above result.

8. **Silvered lens** A point object O is placed in front of a silvered lens as shown in figure.

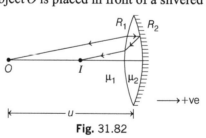

Fig. 31.82

Ray of light is first refracted, then reflected and then again refracted. In first two steps, light is travelling from left to right and in the last one direction of light is reversed. But we will take one sign convention, i.e. left to right as positive and in the last step will take v, u and R as negative.

$$\frac{\mu_2}{v_1} - \frac{\mu_1}{u} = \frac{\mu_2 - \mu_1}{R_1} \qquad \qquad \text{...(i)}$$

$$\frac{1}{v_2} + \frac{1}{v_1} = \frac{1}{f_{\text{mirror}}} = \frac{2}{R_2} \qquad \qquad \text{...(ii)}$$

$$\frac{\mu_1}{-v} - \frac{\mu_2}{-v_2} = \frac{\mu_1 - \mu_2}{-R_1} \qquad \ldots\text{(iii)}$$

Solving Eqs. (i), (ii) and (iii), we get

$$\frac{1}{v} + \frac{1}{u} = \frac{2(\mu_2/\mu_1)}{R_2} - \frac{2(\mu_2/\mu_1 - 1)}{R_1} \qquad \ldots\text{(iv)}$$

This is the desired formula for finding position of image for the given situation.

Note *The given system behaves as a mirror because the ray of light finally reflects in the same medium. Whose focal length can be found by comparing Eq. (iv) with mirror formula 1/v + 1/u = 1/f.*

$$\boxed{\frac{1}{f} = \frac{2(\mu_2/\mu_1)}{R_2} - \frac{2(\mu_2/\mu_1 - 1)}{R_1}} \qquad \ldots\text{(v)}$$

Let us take one example in support of this.

◉ **Example 31.28**

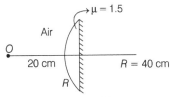

Fig. 31.83

(a) *Find focal length of the system as shown in figure.*
(b) *Find image position.*

Solution (a) $\mu_1 = 1, \mu_2 = 1.5, R_1 = R = +40\,\text{cm}$ and $R_2 = \infty$

Using the formula,

$$\frac{1}{f} = \frac{2(\mu_2/\mu_1)}{R_2} - \frac{2(\mu_2/\mu_1 - 1)}{R_1}$$

$$= \frac{2(1.5)}{\infty} - \frac{2(1.5 - 1)}{40}$$

or $\qquad\qquad f = -40\,\text{cm}$

Thus, the given system behaves like a concave mirror of focal length 40 cm.

(b) Using the mirror formula, we have

$$\frac{1}{v} + \frac{1}{u} = \frac{1}{f}$$

∴ $$\frac{1}{v} + \frac{1}{-20} = \frac{1}{-40}$$

∴ $\qquad\qquad v = +40\,\text{cm}$

Therefore, image will be formed at a distance of 40 cm to the right hand side of the given system.

9. **Displacement method of finding focal length of a convex lens** If the distance d between an object and screen is greater than 4 times the focal length of a convex lens, then there are two

positions of the lens between the object and the screen at which a sharp image of the object is formed on the screen. This method is called **displacement method** and is used in laboratory to determine the focal length of convex lens.

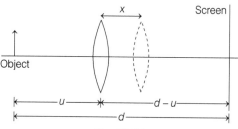

Fig. 31.84

To prove this, let us take an object placed at a distance u from a convex lens of focal length f. The distance of image from the lens $v = (d - u)$. From the lens formula,

$$\frac{1}{v} - \frac{1}{u} = \frac{1}{f}$$

We have,

$$\frac{1}{d - u} - \frac{1}{-u} = \frac{1}{f}$$

or

$$u^2 - du + df = 0$$

$\therefore$

$$u = \frac{d \pm \sqrt{d\,(d - 4f)}}{2}$$

Now, there are following possibilities:

(i) If $d < 4f$, then u is imaginary.

So, physically no position of the lens is possible.

(ii) If $d = 4f$, then $u = \dfrac{d}{2} = 2f$. So, only one position is possible. From here we can see that the

minimum distance between an object and its real image in case of a convex lens is 4 f.

(iii) If $d > 4f$, there are two positions of lens at distances

$$\frac{d + \sqrt{d\,(d - 4f)}}{2} \quad \text{and} \quad \frac{d - \sqrt{d\,(d - 4f)}}{2}$$

for which real image is formed on the screen.

(iv) Suppose I_1 is the image length in one position of the object and I_2 the image length in second position, then object length O is given by

$$\boxed{O = \sqrt{I_1 I_2}}$$

This can be proved as under

$$|u_1| = \frac{d + \sqrt{d\,(d - 4f)}}{2}$$

$\therefore$

$$|v_1| = d - |u_1| = \frac{d - \sqrt{d\,(d - 4f)}}{2}$$

$$|u_2| = \frac{d - \sqrt{d(d-4f)}}{2}$$

∴

$$|v_2| = d - |u_2| = \frac{d + \sqrt{d(d-4f)}}{2}$$

Now,

$$|m_1 m_2| = \frac{I_1}{O} \times \frac{I_2}{O} = \frac{|v_1|}{|u_1|} \times \frac{|v_2|}{|u_2|}$$

Substituting the values, we get

$$\frac{I_1 I_2}{O^2} = 1$$

or

$$O = \sqrt{I_1 I_2}$$

Hence Proved.

(v) Focal length of the lens is given by

$$f = \frac{d^2 - x^2}{4d}$$

Proof In the figure, we can see that difference of two values of u is x. Thus,

$$|u_1| - |u_2| = x$$

or

$$\left[\frac{d + \sqrt{d(d-4f)}}{2} \right] - \left[\frac{d - \sqrt{d(d-4f)}}{2} \right] = x$$

Solving this equation, we can find that

$$f = \frac{d^2 - x^2}{4d}$$

◉ *Example 31.29* *A thin plano-convex lens of focal length f is split into two halves. One of the halves is shifted along the optical axis as shown in figure. The separation between object and image planes is 1.8 m. The magnification of the image formed by one of the half lens is 2. Find the focal length of the lens and separation between the two halves. Draw the ray diagram for image formation.* (JEE 1996)

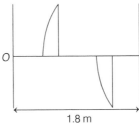

1.8 m

Fig. 31.85

Solution For both the halves, position of object and image is same. Only difference is of magnification. Magnification for one of the halves is given as 2 (> 1). This can be for the first one, because for this, $|v| > |u|$. Therefore, magnification, $|m| = |v/u| > 1$.

So, for the first half

$$|v/u| = 2$$

or

$$|v| = 2|u|$$

Let

$$u = -x,$$

then

$$v = +2x$$

and

$$|u| + |v| = 1.8\,\text{m}$$

i.e.

$$3x = 1.8\,\text{m}$$

or

$$x = 0.6\,\text{m}$$

Hence,

$$u = -0.6\,\text{m}$$

and

$$v = +1.2\,\text{m}$$

Using

$$\frac{1}{f} = \frac{1}{v} - \frac{1}{u} = \frac{1}{1.2} - \frac{1}{-0.6} = \frac{1}{0.4}$$

∴

$$f = 0.4\,\text{m}$$ **Ans.**

For the second half,

$$\frac{1}{f} = \frac{1}{1.2 - d} - \frac{1}{-(0.6 + d)}$$

or

$$\frac{1}{0.4} = \frac{1}{1.2 - d} + \frac{1}{(0.6 + d)}$$

Solving this, we get

$$d = 0.6\,\text{m}$$ **Ans.**

Magnification for the second half will be

$$m_2 = \frac{v}{u} = \frac{0.6}{-(1.2)} = -\frac{1}{2}$$

and magnification for the first half is

$$m_1 = \frac{v}{u} = \frac{1.2}{-(0.6)} = -2$$

The ray diagram is as follows:

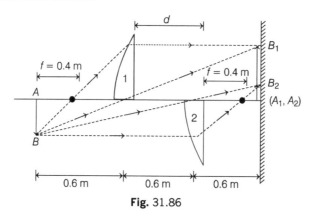

Fig. 31.86

INTRODUCTORY EXERCISE 31.6

1. When an object is placed 60 cm in front of a diverging lens, a virtual image is formed 20 cm from the lens. The lens is made of a material of refractive index $\mu = 1.65$ and its two spherical surfaces have the same radius of curvature. What is the value of this radius?

2. A converging lens has a focal length of 30 cm. Rays from a 2.0 cm high filament that pass through the lens form a virtual image at a distance of 50 cm from the lens. Where is the filament located? What is the height of the image?

3. Show that the focal length of a thin lens is not changed when the lens is rotated so that the left and the right surfaces are interchanged.

4. As an object is moved from the surface of a thin converging lens to a focal point, over what range does the image distance vary?

5. A diverging lens is made of material with refractive index 1.3 and has identical concave surfaces of radius 20 cm. The lens is immersed in a transparent medium with refractive index 1.8.
   (a) What is now the focal length of the lens?
   (b) What is the minimum distance that an immersed object must be from the lens so that a real image is formed?

6. An object is located 20 cm to the left of a converging lens with $f = 10$ cm. A second identical lens is placed to the right of the first lens and then moved until the image it produces is identical in size and orientation to the object. What is the separation between the lenses?

7. Suppose an object has thickness du so that it extends from object distance u to $u + du$. Prove that the thickness dv of its image is given by $\left(-\dfrac{v^2}{u^2}\right) du$, so the longitudinal magnification $\dfrac{dv}{du} = -m^2$, where m is the lateral magnification.

8. Two thin similar convex glass pieces are joined together front to front, with its rear portion silvered such that a sharp image is formed 0.2 m for an object at infinity. When the air between the glass pieces is replaced by water $\left(\mu = \dfrac{4}{3}\right)$, find the position of image.

9. When a pin is moved along the principal axis of a small concave mirror, the image position coincides with the object at a point 0.5 m from the mirror. If the mirror is placed at a depth of 0.2 m in a transparent liquid, the same phenomenon occurs when the pin is placed 0.4 m from the mirror. Find the refractive index of the liquid shown in Fig. 31.87.

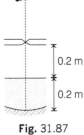
0.2 m
0.2 m
Fig. 31.87

10. When a lens is inserted between an object and a screen which are a fixed distance apart the size of the image is either 6 cm or $\dfrac{2}{3}$ cm. Find size of the object.

11. A lens of focal length 12 cm forms an upright image three times the size of a real object. Find the distance in cm between the object and image.

12. The distance between an object and its upright image is 20 cm. If the magnification is 0.5, what is the focal length of the lens that is being used to form the image?

13. A thin lens of focal length + 10.0 cm lies on a horizontal plane mirror. How far above the lens should an object be held if its image is to coincide with the object?

31.7 **Total Internal Reflection (TIR)**

(i) When a ray of light strikes the boundary separating two different media, then part of it is refracted and part is reflected.

(ii) If a ray of light is travelling from a denser to a rarer medium with angle of incidence greater than a critical angle $(i > \theta_C)$, then no refraction takes place but ray of light is 100% reflected in the same medium. This phenomenon is called TIR.

(iii) $\sin \theta_C = \dfrac{\mu_R}{\mu_D}$

Here, R stands for rarer medium and D for denser medium. If rarer medium is air, then

$$\sin \theta_C = \frac{1}{\mu}$$

∴
$$\boxed{\theta_C = \sin^{-1}\left(\frac{\mu_R}{\mu_D}\right) \quad \text{or} \quad \sin^{-1}\left(\frac{1}{\mu}\right)}$$

(iv) If value of μ increases, then critical angle θ_C decreases. Therefore, chances of TIR increase in travelling from denser to rarer medium.

(v)

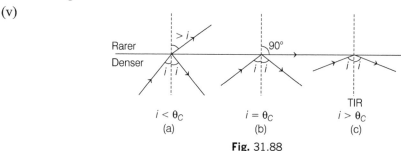

$$i < \theta_C \qquad\qquad i = \theta_C \qquad\qquad i > \theta_C$$
$$(a) \qquad\qquad\qquad (b) \qquad\qquad\qquad (c)$$

Fig. 31.88

Applying Snell's law of refraction in Fig. (b), we have

$$\mu_R \sin 90° = \mu_D \sin \theta_C$$

or
$$\sin \theta_C = \frac{\mu_R}{\mu_D}$$

or
$$\theta_C = \sin^{-1}\left(\frac{\mu_R}{\mu_D}\right)$$

(vi) In critical case (Fig. b), angle in denser medium is θ_C and angle in rarer medium is $90°$. TIR has following applications

(i) **Totally reflecting prisms** Refractive index of crown glass is 3/2. Hence,

$$\theta_C = \sin^{-1}\left(\frac{1}{\mu}\right) = \sin^{-1}\left(\frac{2}{3}\right) \approx 42°$$

A ray OA incident normally on face PQ of a crown glass prism suffers TIR at face PR since, the angle of incidence in the optically denser medium is $45°$. A bright ray AB emerges at right angles from face QR. The prism thus, reflects the ray through $90°$. Light can be reflected through $180°$

and an erect image can be obtained of an inverted one if the prism is arranged as shown in figure (b).

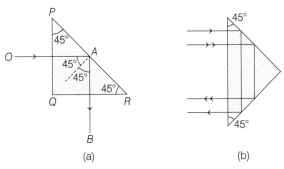

(a)   (b)

Fig. 31.89 Prism reflectors

(ii) **Optical fibres**   Light can be confined within a bent glass rod by TIR and so 'piped' along a twisted path as in figure. The beam is reflected from side to side practically without loss (except for that due to absorption in the glass) and emerges only at the end of the rod where it strikes the surface almost normally, i.e. at an angle less than the critical angle. A single, very thin, solid glass fibre behaves in the same way and if several thousands are taped together a flexible light pipe is obtained that can be used, for example in medicine and engineering to illuminate an inaccessible spot. Optical fibres are now a days used to carry telephone, television and computer signals from one place to the other.

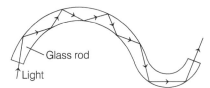

Fig. 31.90 Principle of an optical fibre

Note   *As we have seen*

$$\theta_C = \sin^{-1}\left(\frac{\mu_R}{\mu_D}\right)$$

Suppose we have two sets of media 1 and 2 and

$$\left(\frac{\mu_R}{\mu_D}\right)_1 < \left(\frac{\mu_R}{\mu_D}\right)_2$$

then $(\theta_C)_1 < (\theta_C)_2$

So, a ray of light has more chances to have TIR in case 1.

Examples of TIR

◉ **Example 31.30**   *An isotropic point source is placed at a depth h below the water surface. A floating opaque disc is placed on the surface of water so that the source is not visible from the surface. What is the minimum radius of the disc? Take refractive index of water = μ.*

Solution

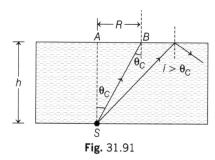

Fig. 31.91

As shown in figure light from the source will not emerge out of water if $i > \theta_C$.

Therefore, minimum radius R corresponds to $i = \theta_C$

In ΔSAB,

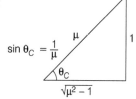

$$\sin \theta_C = \frac{1}{\mu}$$

Fig. 31.92

$$\frac{R}{h} = \tan \theta_C$$

$\therefore$ $$R = h \tan \theta_C$$

or $$R = \frac{h}{\sqrt{\mu^2 - 1}}$$ **Ans.**

Note *Only that portion of light refracts in air which falls on the circle (on the surface of water) with A as centre and AB as radius.*

⊘ **Example 31.31** *A point source of light is placed at a distance h below the surface of a large and deep lake. Show that the fraction f of light that escapes directly from water surface is independent of h and is given by*

$$f = \frac{[1 - \sqrt{1 - 1/\mu^2}]}{2}$$

Solution Due to TIR, light will be reflected back into the water if $i > \theta_C$. So, only that portion of incident light will escape which passes through the cone of angle $\theta = 2\theta_C$.

So, the fraction of light escaping

$$f = \frac{\text{area } ACB}{\text{Total area of sphere}} = \frac{2\pi R^2 (1 - \cos \theta_C)}{4\pi R^2} = \frac{1 - \cos \theta_C}{2}$$

Now, as f depends on θ_C and which depends only on μ, it is independent of h. **Proved.**

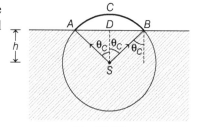

Fig. 31.93

Further $$\cos \theta_C = \frac{\sqrt{\mu^2 - 1}}{\mu} = \sqrt{1 - 1/\mu^2} \quad \Rightarrow \quad f = \frac{1 - \sqrt{1 - 1/\mu^2}}{2}$$ **Ans.**

Note *Area of $ACB = 2\pi R^2 (1 - \cos \theta_C)$ can be obtained by integration. In the above example, we have seen that light falling on the circle with centre at D and radius DB will only refract in air and in the absence of water surface only that light would fall on surface ACB of sphere.*

● **Example 31.32** *In the figure shown,* $\mu_1 > \mu_2$. *Find minimum value of i so that TIR never takes place at P.*

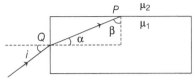

Fig. 31.94

Solution Let us take $\beta = \theta_C$. Then, $\alpha = 90° - \beta$ or $\alpha = 90° - \theta_C$

Here,
$$\sin \theta_C = \frac{\mu_R}{\mu_D} = \frac{\mu_2}{\mu_1}$$

∴
$$\theta_C = \sin^{-1}\left(\frac{\mu_2}{\mu_1}\right)$$

Applying Snell's law at point Q,
$$\mu_2 \sin i = \mu_1 \sin \alpha = \mu_1 \sin(90° - \theta_C)$$
$$= \mu_1 \cos \theta_C = \mu_1 \cos \sin^{-1}\left(\frac{\mu_2}{\mu_1}\right)$$

∴
$$i = \sin^{-1}\left[\frac{\mu_1}{\mu_2} \cos \sin^{-1}\left(\frac{\mu_2}{\mu_1}\right)\right] \qquad \textbf{Ans.}$$

Now, we can see that starting from this value of i, we get $\beta = \theta_C$.

If i is increased from this value, then α will also increase (becomes $> 90° - \theta_C$) and β decreases from θ_C (becomes $< \theta_C$) and no TIR takes place at P.

So far no TIR condition i has to be increased from the above value. Or this is the minimum value of i.

● **Example 31.33** *Monochromatic light is incident on a plane interface AB between two media of refractive indices μ_1 and μ_2 ($\mu_2 > \mu_1$) at an angle of incidence θ as shown in the figure.*

The angle θ is infinitesimally greater than the critical angle for the two media so that total internal reflection takes place. Now if a transparent slab DEFG of uniform thickness and of refractive index μ_3 is introduced on the interface (as shown in the figure), show that for any value of μ_3 all light will ultimately be reflected back again into medium II. Consider separately the cases.

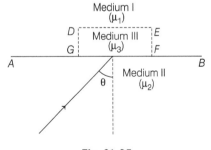

Fig. 31.95

(1986, 6M)

(a) $\mu_3 < \mu_1$ (b) $\mu_3 > \mu_1$

Solution Given, θ is slightly greater than $\sin^{-1}\left(\dfrac{\mu_1}{\mu_2}\right)$.

(a) **When** $\mu_3 < \mu_1$

i.e. $\mu_3 < \mu_1 < \mu_2$

or $\dfrac{\mu_3}{\mu_2} < \dfrac{\mu_1}{\mu_2}$ or $\sin^{-1}\left(\dfrac{\mu_3}{\mu_2}\right) < \sin^{-1}\left(\dfrac{\mu_1}{\mu_2}\right)$

Hence, critical angle for III and II will be less than the critical angle for II and I. So, if TIR is taking place between I and II, then TIR will definitely take place between II and III.

(b) **When** $\mu_3 > \mu_1$ Two cases may arise :

Case 1 $\mu_1 < \mu_3 < \mu_2$

In this case, there will be no TIR between II and III but TIR will take place between III and I. This is because

Ray of light first enters from II to III. i.e. from denser to rarer.

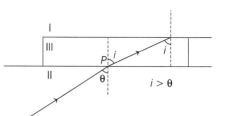

Fig. 31.96

$\therefore$ $i > \theta$

Applying Snell's law at P,

$$\mu_2 \sin\theta = \mu_3 \sin i \quad \text{or} \quad \sin i = \left(\dfrac{\mu_2}{\mu_3}\right)\sin\theta$$

Since, $\sin\theta$ is slightly greater than $\dfrac{\mu_1}{\mu_2}$.

$\therefore$ $\sin i$ is slightly greater than $\dfrac{\mu_2}{\mu_3} \times \dfrac{\mu_1}{\mu_2}$ or $\dfrac{\mu_1}{\mu_3}$

but $\dfrac{\mu_1}{\mu_3}$ is nothing but $\sin(\theta_C)_{\text{I, III}}$

$\therefore$ $\sin(i)$ is slightly greater than $\sin(\theta_C)_{\text{I, III}}$

or TIR will now take place on I and III and the ray of light will be reflected back.

Case 2 $\mu_1 < \mu_2 < \mu_3$

This time while moving from II to III, ray of light will bend towards normal. Again applying Snell's law at P,

$$\mu_2 \sin\theta = \mu_3 \sin i$$

$$\sin i = \dfrac{\mu_2}{\mu_3}\sin\theta$$

Since, $\sin\theta$ is slightly greater than $\dfrac{\mu_1}{\mu_2}$.

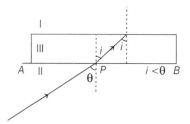

Fig. 31.97

Therefore, $\sin i$ will be slightly greater than $\dfrac{\mu_2}{\mu_3} \times \dfrac{\mu_1}{\mu_2}$ or $\dfrac{\mu_1}{\mu_3}$

But, $\dfrac{\mu_1}{\mu_3}$ is $\sin (\theta_C)_{I, III}$

i.e. $\sin i > \sin (\theta_C)_{I, III}$

or $i > (\theta_C)_{I, III}$

Therefore, TIR will again take place between I and III and the ray of light will be reflected back.

Note *Two cases of $\mu_3 > \mu_1$ can be explained by one single equation. But two cases are deliberately taken for better understanding of refraction, Snell's law and total internal reflection (TIR).*

◉ ***Example 31.34*** *A right angled prism is to be made by selecting a proper material and the angles A and B ($B \le A$), as shown in figure. It is desired that a ray of light incident on the face AB emerges parallel to the incident direction after two internal reflections.*

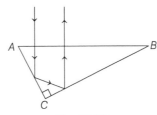

Fig. 31.98

(a) What should be the minimum refractive index n for this to be possible? (JEE 1987)

(b) For n = 5/3 is it possible to achieve this with the angle B equal to 30 degrees?

Solution (a) At P, angle of incidence $i_A = A$ and at Q, angle of incidence $i_B = B$

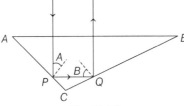

Fig. 31.99

If TIR satisfies for the smaller angle of incidence than for larger angle of incidence is automatically satisfied.

$$B \le A$$

∴ $$i_B \le i_A$$

Maximum value of B can be 45°. Therefore, if condition of TIR is satisfied for 45°, then condition of TIR will be satisfied for all value of i_A and i_B.

Thus, $45° \ge \theta_C$ or $\sin 45° \ge \sin \theta_C$

or $\dfrac{1}{\sqrt{2}} \ge \dfrac{1}{\mu}$ or $\mu \ge \sqrt{2}$

∴ Minimum value of μ is $\sqrt{2}$.

(b) For $\mu = \dfrac{5}{3}$, $\sin \theta_C = \dfrac{1}{\mu} = \sin^{-1}\left(\dfrac{3}{5}\right) \approx 37°$

If $B = 30°$, then $i_B = 30°$ and $A = 60°$ or $i_A = 60°$, $i_A > \theta_C$ but $i_B < \theta_C$
i.e. TIR will take place at A but not at B.

INTRODUCTORY EXERCISE 31.7

1. Light is incident normally on the short face of a $30° – 60° – 90°$ prism. A liquid is poured on the hypotenuse of the prism. If the refractive index of the prism is $\sqrt{3}$, find the maximum refractive index of the liquid so that light is totally reflected.

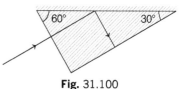

Fig. 31.100

2. If the speed of light in ice is 2.3×10^8 m/s, what is its index of refraction? What is the critical angle of incidence for light going from ice to air?

3. In figure, light refracts from material 1 into a thin layer of material 2, crosses that layer, and then is incident at the critical angle on the interface between materials 2 and 3.
   (a) What is the angle θ?
   (b) If θ is decreased, is there refraction of light into material 3?

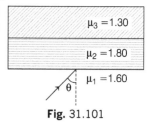

Fig. 31.101

31.8 Refraction Through Prism

A prism has two plane surfaces AB and AC inclined to each other as shown in figure. $\angle A$ is called the **angle of prism** or **refracting angle of prism**.

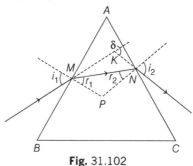

Fig. 31.102

General Formulae

(i) In quadrilateral $AMPN$, $\angle AMP + \angle ANP = 180°$

∴ $A + \angle MPN = 180°$ ...(i)

In triangle MNP, $r_1 + r_2 + \angle MPN = 180°$ ...(ii)

From Eqs. (ii) and (iii), we have $\boxed{r_1 + r_2 = A}$ ...(iii)

(ii) **Deviation** Deviation δ means angle between incident ray and emergent ray.

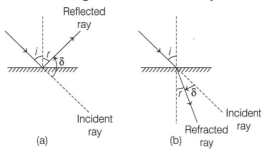

Fig. 31.103

In reflection,

$$\delta = 180° - 2i = 180° - 2r$$

In refraction,

$$\delta = |i - r|$$

In prism, a ray of light gets refracted twice one at M and other at N. At M its deviation is $i_1 - r_1$ and at N it is $i_2 - r_2$. These two deviations are added as both are clockwise. So, the net deviation is

$$\delta = (i_1 - r_1) + (i_2 - r_2) = (i_1 + i_2) - (r_1 + r_2) = (i_1 + i_2) - A$$

Thus, $\boxed{\delta = (i_1 + i_2) - A}$ ...(iv)

(iii) **If A and i_1 are small** The expression for the deviation in this case is basically used for developing the lens theory. Consider a ray falling almost normally in air on a prism of small angle A (less than about 6° or 0.1 radian) so that angle i_1 is small. Now, $\mu = \dfrac{\sin i_1}{\sin r_1}$ or $\sin i_1 = \mu \sin r_1$, therefore, r_1 will also be small. Since, sine of a small angle is nearly equal to the angle in radians, we have

$$i_1 \approx \mu r_1$$

Also, $A = r_1 + r_2$ and so if A and r_1 are small then r_2 and i_2 will also be small. From $\mu = \dfrac{\sin i_2}{\sin r_2}$, we can say $i_2 \approx \mu r_2$

Substituting these values in Eq. (iv), we have

$$\delta = (\mu r_1 + \mu r_2) - A$$
$$= \mu(r_1 + r_2) - A = \mu A - A$$

or $\boxed{\delta = (\mu - 1) A}$ ...(v)

This expression shows that all rays entering a small angle prism at small angles of incidence suffer the same deviation.

(iv) **Minimum deviation** It is found that the angle of deviation δ varies with the angle of incidence i_1 of the ray incident on the first refracting face of the prism. The variation is shown in figure and for one angle of incidence it has a minimum value δ_{min}. At this value, the ray passes symmetrically through the prism (a fact that can be proved theoretically as well as be shown experimentally), i.e. the angle of emergence of the ray from the second face equals the angle of incidence of the ray on the first face.

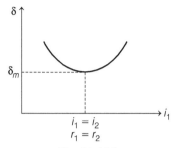

Fig. 31.104

$$i_2 = i_1 = i \qquad \qquad \text{...(vi)}$$

It therefore, follows that

$$r_1 = r_2 = r \qquad \qquad \text{...(vii)}$$

From Eqs. (iii) and (vii), we get $\quad r = \dfrac{A}{2}$

Further at $\qquad \qquad \delta = \delta_m = (i + i) - A$

or $\qquad \qquad i = \dfrac{A + \delta_m}{2} \qquad \qquad \text{...(viii)}$

$\therefore \qquad \qquad \mu = \dfrac{\sin i}{\sin r}$

or $\qquad \qquad \boxed{\mu = \dfrac{\sin\left(\dfrac{A + \delta_m}{2}\right)}{\sin \dfrac{A}{2}}} \qquad \qquad \text{...(ix)}$

(v) **Condition of no emergence** In this section, we want to find the condition such that a ray of light entering the face AB does not come out of the face AC for any value of angle i_1, i.e. TIR takes place on AC

$$r_1 + r_2 = A$$

$\therefore \qquad \qquad r_2 = A - r_1$

or $\qquad \qquad (r_2)_{\min} = A - (r_1)_{\max} \qquad \qquad \text{...(x)}$

Now, r_1 will be maximum when i_1 is maximum and maximum value of i_1 can be 90°.

Hence, $\qquad \qquad \mu = \dfrac{\sin(i_1)_{\max}}{\sin(r_1)_{\max}} = \dfrac{\sin 90°}{\sin (r_1)_{\max}}$

$\therefore \qquad \qquad \sin (r_1)_{\max} = \dfrac{1}{\mu} = \sin \theta_C$

$\therefore \qquad \qquad (r_1)_{\max} = \theta_C$

$\therefore$ From Eq. (x), $\qquad (r_2)_{\min} = A - \theta_C \qquad \qquad \text{...(xi)}$

Now, if minimum value of r_2 is greater than θ_C then obviously all values of r_2 will be greater than θ_C and TIR will take place under all conditions. Thus, the condition of no emergence is

$$(r_2)_{\min} > \theta_C \quad \text{or} \quad A - \theta_C > \theta_C$$

or
$$\boxed{A > 2\theta_C} \qquad \qquad \text{...(xii)}$$

(vi) **Dispersion and deviation of light by a prism**   White light is a superposition of waves with wavelengths extending throughout the visible spectrum. The speed of light in vacuum is the same for all wavelengths, but the speed in a material substance is different for different wavelengths. Therefore, the index of refraction of a material depends on wavelength. In most materials, the value of refractive index μ decreases with increasing wavelength.

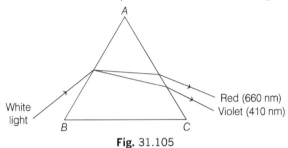

Fig. 31.105

If a beam of white light, which contains all colours, is sent through the prism, it is separated into a spectrum of colours. The spreading of light into its colour components is called **dispersion.**

Dispersive Power

When a beam of white light is passed through a prism of transparent material, light of different wavelengths are deviated by different amounts. If δ_r, δ_y and δ_v are the deviations for red, yellow and violet components then average deviation is measured by δ_y as yellow light falls in between red and violet. $\delta_v - \delta_r$ is called **angular dispersion.** The **dispersive power** of a material is defined as the ratio of angular dispersion to the average deviation when a white beam of light is passed through it. It is denoted by ω. As we know

$$\delta = (\mu - 1)\,A$$

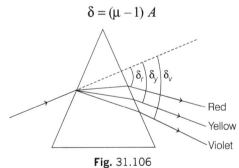

Fig. 31.106

This equation is valid when A and i are small. Suppose, a beam of white light is passed through such a prism, the deviation of red, yellow and violet light are

$$\delta_r = (\mu_r - 1)A, \ \delta_y = (\mu_y - 1)A$$

and
$$\delta_v = (\mu_v - 1)\,A$$

The angular dispersion is $\delta_v - \delta_r = (\mu_v - \mu_r) A$ and the average deviation is $\delta_y = (\mu_y - 1) A$. Thus, the dispersive power of the medium is

$$\omega = \frac{\mu_v - \mu_r}{\mu_y - 1} \qquad \text{...(i)}$$

Dispersion without Average Deviation and Average Deviation without Dispersion

Figure shows two prisms of refracting angles A and A' and dispersive powers ω and ω' respectively. They are placed in contact in such a way that the two refracting angles are reversed with respect to each other. A ray of light passes through the combination as shown. The deviations produced by the two prisms are

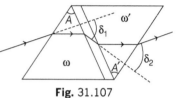

Fig. 31.107

$$\delta_1 = (\mu - 1) A \quad \text{and} \quad \delta_2 = (\mu' - 1) A'$$

As the two deviations are opposite to each other, the net deviation is

$$\delta = \delta_1 - \delta_2 = (\mu - 1)A - (\mu' - 1) A' \qquad \text{...(ii)}$$

Using this equation, the average deviation produced by the combination if white light is passed is

$$\delta_y = (\mu_y - 1)A - (\mu'_y - 1) A' \qquad \text{...(iii)}$$

and the net angular dispersion is

$$\delta_v - \delta_r = (\mu_v - \mu_r)A - (\mu'_v - \mu'_r)A'$$

But, as $\mu_v - \mu_r = \omega(\mu_y - 1)$ from Eq. (i), we have

$$\delta_v - \delta_r = (\mu_y - 1)\omega A - (\mu'_y - 1) \omega' A' \qquad \text{...(iv)}$$

Dispersion without average deviation   From Eq. (iii),

$$\delta_y = 0 \quad \text{if}$$

$$\frac{A}{A'} = \frac{\mu'_y - 1}{\mu_y - 1} \qquad \text{...(v)}$$

This is the required condition of dispersion without average deviation. Using this in Eq. (iv), the net angular dispersion produced is

$$\delta_v - \delta_r = (\mu_y - 1)A (\omega - \omega')$$

Average deviation without dispersion

From Eq. (iv),

$$\delta_v - \delta_r = 0 \quad \text{if}$$

$$\frac{A}{A'} = \frac{(\mu'_y - 1)\omega'}{(\mu_y - 1) \omega} = \frac{\mu'_v - \mu'_r}{\mu_v - \mu_r} \qquad \text{...(vi)}$$

This is the required condition of average deviation without dispersion. Using the above condition in Eq. (iii), the net average deviation is

$$\delta_y = (\mu_y - 1)A \left(1 - \frac{\omega}{\omega'}\right)$$

Important Points in Prism

1. Equation $r_1 + r_2 = A$ can be applied at any of the three vertices. For example in the figure shown, $r_1 + r_2 = B$.

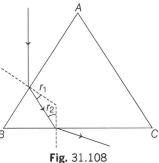

Fig. 31.108

2. Sometimes a part of a prism is given as shown in Fig. 31.109 (a). To solve such problems, first complete the prism then solve as the problems of prism are solved.

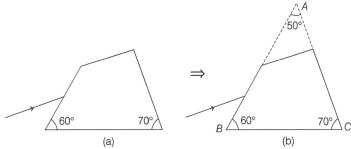

Fig. 31.109

3. For isosceles or equilateral triangle ($\angle B = \angle C$), ray of light is parallel to base of the prism at minimum deviation condition.

   Under minimum deviation condition, we know that $r_1 = r_2 \Rightarrow \alpha = \beta$. Because, $\alpha = 90° + r_1$ and $\beta = 90° + r_2$.

   Further, it is given that $\angle B = \angle C$. Therefore, MN is parallel to BC.

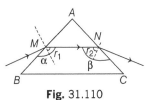

Fig. 31.110

4. In some cases, when deviation at M is clockwise and deviation at N is anti-clockwise, then

$$r_1 - r_2 = A$$

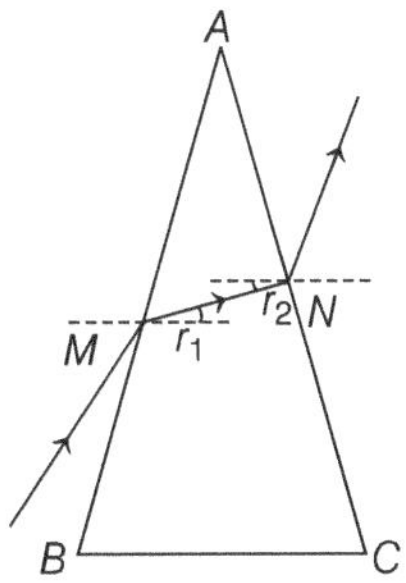

Fig. 31.111

This condition is normally obtained with thin angle prisms as shown above:
At M, deviation is clockwise and at N deviation is anti-clockwise. In triangle AMN,

$$A + (90° - r_1) + (90° + r_2) = 180°$$

$\therefore$ $$r_1 - r_2 = A$$

5. In the ray diagram shown in Fig. 31.112, we can treat it like a prism ABC of $\angle A = 90°$

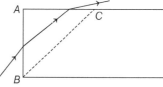

Fig. 31.112

6. Different identical equilateral triangles are arranged as shown in Fig. 31.113. Deviation by prism(s) in each case will be same, if angle of incidence is same.

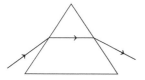  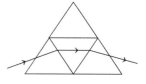

Fig. 31.113

Examples of Prism

● ***Example 31.35*** *One face of a prism with a refractive angle of* $30°$ *is coated with silver. A ray of light incident on another face at an angle of* $45°$ *is refracted and reflected from the silver coated face and retraces its path. What is the refractive index of the prism?*

Solution

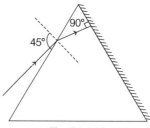

Fig. 31.114

Given, $A = 30°$, $i_1 = 45°$ and $r_2 = 0$

Since, $$r_1 + r_2 = A$$

$\therefore$ $$r_1 = A = 30°$$

Now, refractive index of the prism,

$$\mu = \frac{\sin i_1}{\sin r_1} = \frac{\sin 45°}{\sin 30°} = \frac{\dfrac{1}{\sqrt{2}}}{\dfrac{1}{2}} = \sqrt{2}$$ **Ans.**

⊙ **Example 31.36** *In the shown figure, mirror is rotated by an angle θ. Find θ if*

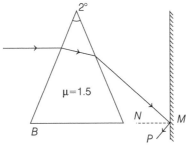

Fig. 31.115

(a) ray of light retraces its path after reflection from M
(b) ray of light MP turns in the direction of MN.

Solution In this case, A and i_1 are small. Therefore, deviation by prism can be obtained by

$$\delta = (\mu - 1)\,A = (1.5 - 1)(2°) = 1°$$

Hence, the prism will deviate the ray of light by 1° from its original path as shown in Fig. 31.116.

(a) In the absence of prism, ray of light was falling normal to the mirror. So, ray of light was already retracing its path. Prism has rotated the ray by 1° in clockwise direction. So if we rotate the mirror also by 1° in clockwise direction, then ray of light will further fall normal to the mirror and it again retraces its path. Therefore, the correct answer is

$$\theta = 1° ,\text{clockwise} \qquad\qquad \textbf{Ans.}$$

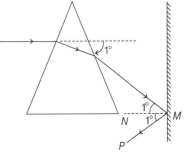

Fig. 31.116

(b) If we rotate a plane mirror by θ in clockwise direction, then reflected ray also rotates in clockwise direction by an angle 2θ.

Here, we have to rotate reflected ray MP by 1° in clockwise direction to make it in the direction of MN. Therefore, we will have to rotate the mirror by 0.5° in clockwise direction. Therefore, the correct answer is

$$\theta = 0.5° , \text{ clockwise} \qquad\qquad \textbf{Ans.}$$

⊙ **Example 31.37** **General method of finding deviation by prism.**

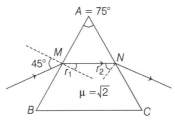

Fig. 31.117

In the ray diagram shown in figure, find total deviation by prism.

Solution Deviation by a prism is given by

$$\delta = (i_1 + i_2) - A \qquad \qquad ..(i)$$

Here, $i_1 = 45°$ and $A = 75°$

Therefore, the main objective is to find i_2 and this angle i_2 can be obtained under following three steps.

(i) Applying Snell's law at point M, we have

$$\mu = \frac{\sin i_1}{\sin r_1} \quad \text{or} \quad \sqrt{2} = \frac{\sin 45°}{\sin r_1}$$

Solving this equation, we get $\qquad r_1 = 30°$

(ii) $\qquad\qquad\qquad\qquad r_1 + r_2 = A$

$\therefore \qquad\qquad\qquad\qquad 30° + r_2 = 75°$

$\therefore \qquad\qquad\qquad\qquad r_2 = 45°$

(iii) Further applying Snell's law at N,

$$\mu = \frac{\sin i_2}{\sin r_2} \quad \Rightarrow \quad \sqrt{2} = \frac{\sin i_2}{\sin 45°}$$

Solving this equation, we get $\qquad i_2 = 90°$

Now, substituting the values in Eq. (i), we have

$$\delta = 45° + 90° - 75°$$
$$= 60° \qquad\qquad\qquad \textbf{Ans.}$$

⊙ *Example 31.38* ***Based on the condition of no emergence from face AC***

In the shown figure,

$$A = 110°, B = 20°, C = 50°, i_1 = 45° \text{ and } \mu = \sqrt{2}$$

Find the total deviation by prism.

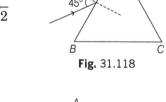

Fig. 31.118

Solution $\theta_C = \sin^{-1}\left(\frac{1}{\mu}\right) = \sin^{-1}\left(\frac{1}{\sqrt{2}}\right) = 45°$

Here, $A > 2\theta_C$

Therefore, TIR will take place at AC and the ray of light emerges from the prism as shown in figure.

Applying, $\mu = \frac{\sin i}{\sin r}$ at M and Q, we can find the respective angles as shown in figure.

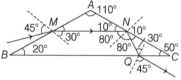

Fig. 31.119

Now, deviation at M is clockwise, deviation at N is clockwise but deviation at Q is anti-clockwise.

$\therefore \qquad\qquad \delta_{\text{Total}} = \delta_M + \delta_N - \delta_Q$

$$= (45° - 30°) + (180° - 2 \times 80°) - (45° - 30°)$$
$$= 20° \qquad\qquad\qquad \textbf{Ans.}$$

INTRODUCTORY EXERCISE **31.8**

1. The prism shown in figure has a refractive index of 1.60 and the angles A are 30°. Two light rays P and Q are parallel as they enter the prism. What is the angle between them after they emerge? $[\sin^{-1}(0.8) = 53°]$

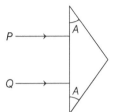

Fig. 31.120

2. A glass vessel in the shape of a triangular prism is filled with water, and light is incident normally on the face xy. If the refractive indices for water and glass are 4/3 and 3/2 respectively, total internal reflection will occur at the glass-air surface xz only for $\sin \theta$ greater than

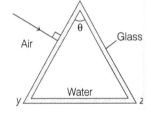

A 1/2   **B** 2/3

C 3/4   **D** 8/9

E 16/27.

Fig. 31.121

3. A light ray going through a prism with the angle of prism 60°, is found to deviate at least by 30°. What is the range of the refractive index of the prism?

4. A ray of light falls normally on a refracting face of a prism. Find the angle of prism if the ray just fails to emerge from the prism ($\mu = 3/2$).

5. A ray of light is incident at an angle of 60° on one face of a prism which has an angle of 30°. The ray emerging out of the prism makes an angle of 30° with the incident ray. Show that the emergent ray is perpendicular to the face through which it emerges and calculate the refractive index of the material of prism.

6. A ray of light passing through a prism having refractive index $\sqrt{2}$ suffers minimum deviation. It is found that the angle of incidence is double the angle of refraction within the prism. What is the angle of prism?

7. A ray of light undergoes deviation of 30° when incident on an equilateral prism of refractive index $\sqrt{2}$. What is the angle subtended by the ray inside the prism with the base of the prism?

8. Light is incident at an angle i on one planar end of a transparent cylindrical rod of refractive index μ. Find the least value of μ so that the light entering the rod does not emerge from the curved surface of the rod irrespective of the value of i.

Fig. 31.122

9. The refractive index of the material of a prism of refracting angle 45° is 1.6 for a certain monochromatic ray. What will be the minimum angle of incidence of this ray on the prism so that no TIR takes place as the ray comes out of the prism.

31.9 **Deviation**

1. **In reflection** In reflection, the deviation is given by

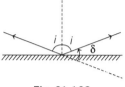

Fig. 31.123

$$\delta = 180° - 2i$$

Therefore, δ *versus* i graph is a straight line. The range of i is from $0°$ to $90°$.
At $i = 0°$, $\delta = 180°$
At $i = 90°$, $\delta = 0°$
δ *versus* i graph is as shown below:

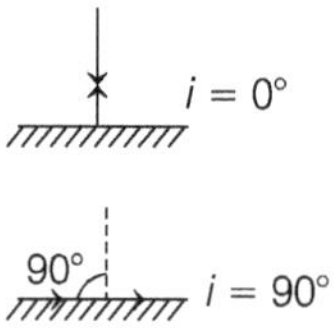

Fig. 31.124

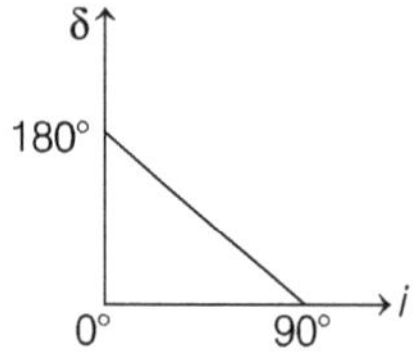

Fig. 31.125

2. Two plane mirrors at $90°$, deviate all rays by $180°$ from their original path.

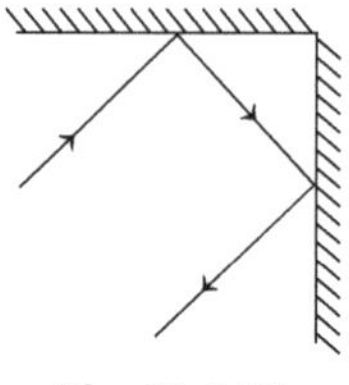

Fig. 31.126

3. **In refraction** Deviation in refraction is given by

$$\delta = i - r$$ (where, $i > r$)

Fig. 31.127

Note *(i) To plot δ versus i graph, first we will have to convert r into i with the help of Snell's law, otherwise there are three variables in the equation,*
$$\delta = i - r$$
(ii) In general, deviation in reflection is more than the deviation in refraction.

4. Deviation by a sphere after two refractions is

$$\delta = 2(i - r)$$

This can be proved as under :

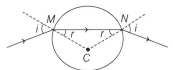

Fig. 31.128

$$MC = NC$$

Therefore, both angles inside the sphere are same $(= r)$. Hence, angles outside the sphere will also be same $(= i)$. Deviation at M as well as N is clockwise.

∴ $$\delta = \delta_M + \delta_N = (i - r) + (i - r) \quad \text{or} \quad \delta = 2(i - r)$$

5. **Deviation by a prism**

$$\delta = (i_1 + i_2) - A$$

If A and i_1 are small, then

$$\delta \approx (\mu - 1) A$$

◉ *Example 31.39 Theory*

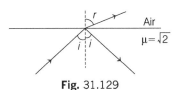

Fig. 31.129

In the figure, i is increased from $0°$ to $90°$. But ray of light is travelling from denser to rarer medium. Therefore, TIR will take place when $i > \theta_C$, where

$$\theta_C = \sin^{-1}\left(\frac{1}{\mu}\right) = \sin^{-1}\left(\frac{1}{\sqrt{2}}\right) = 45°$$

From $0° - 45°$, refraction and reflection both will take place. After $45°$, only reflection will take place.

***Question** Plot δ versus i graph between incident ray and refracted ray, for $i \le 45°$ and with reflected ray for $i \ge 45°$.*

Solution **For $i \le 45°$**

$$\delta = \delta_{\text{Refraction}} = r - i \qquad \text{(as } r > i)$$

Applying Snell's law, we have

$$\mu = \frac{\sin r}{\sin i} \quad \text{or} \quad \sqrt{2} = \frac{\sin r}{\sin i}$$

∴ $$r = \sin^{-1}(\sqrt{2} \sin i)$$

Substituting this value of r in the equation, we have

$$\delta = \sin^{-1}(\sqrt{2} \sin i) - i \qquad \qquad \text{...(i)}$$

Now, variables are only two δ and *i* but this is not a known equation. So, we can find some of the coordinates from where graph must pass.

At $i = 0°$, $\delta = 0°$

At $i = 45° = \theta_C$, $\delta = 45°$

For $i \geq 45°$

$$\delta = \delta_{\text{Reflection}}$$

∴ $$\delta = 180° - 2i$$

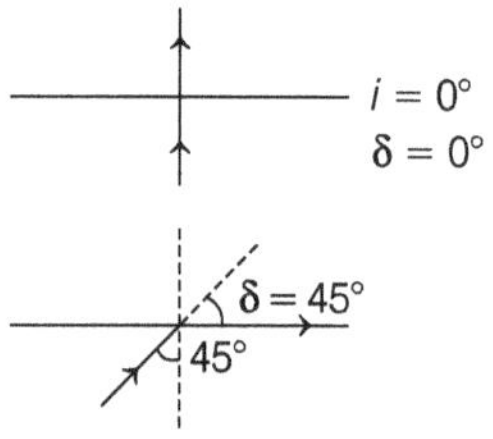

Fig. 31.130

Now, δ *versus i* graph is a straight line.

At $i = 45°$, $\delta = 90°$

At $i = 90°$, $\delta = 0°$

Now, δ *versus i* graph is as shown in Fig. 31.131:

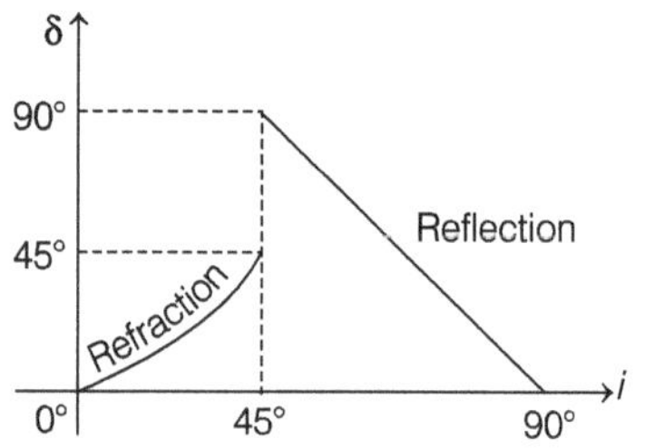

Note At $\quad i = 45° = \theta_C$

$\delta_{\text{Refraction}} = 45°$

but $\delta_{\text{Reflection}} = 90°$

This is because deviation in reflection is more than deviation in refraction.

31.10 **Optical Instruments**

Optical instruments are used to assist the eye in viewing an object. Our eye lens has a power to adjust its focal length to see the nearer objects. This process of adjusting focal length is called accommodation. However, if the object is brought too close to the eye, the focal length cannot be adjusted to form the image on the retina. Thus, there is a minimum distance for the clear vision of an object. This distance is called **least distance of distinct vision (+D).** For normal eye this distance is generally taken to be 25 cm.

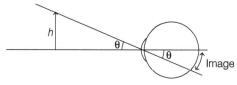

Fig. 31.132

Visual angle The size of an object as sensed by us is related to the size of the image formed on the retina.

The size of the image on the retina is roughly proportional to the angle subtended by the object on the eye. This angle is known as the visual angle. Optical instruments are used to increase this angle artificially in order to improve the clarity.

Magnifying power (M) Magnifying power is the factor by which the image on the retina can be enlarged by using the microscope or telescope. For a microscope and for a telescope the definition of M is slightly different.

For a microscope, $\quad M = \dfrac{\text{Visual angle formed by final image}}{\text{Visual angle formed by the object when kept at distance } D}$

For a telescope, $$M = \frac{\text{Visual angle formed by final image}}{\text{Visual angle subtended by the object directly when seen from naked eye}}$$

Note that M is different from linear magnification $m \left(= \pm \dfrac{v}{u} \right)$ which is the ratio of height of image to that of object while M is the ratio of apparent increase in size of image seen by the eye. Unit of M is X, thus we write an angular magnification of 10 as $10X$.

Simple microscope   To view an object with naked eyes, the object must be placed between D and infinity. The maximum angle is subtended when it is placed at D.

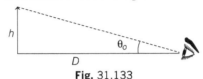

Fig. 31.133

Say this angle is θ_o. Then, $\theta_o = \dfrac{h}{D}$

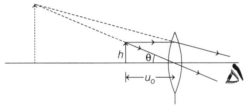

Fig. 31.134

This angle can be further increased if a converging lens of short focal length is placed just in front of the eye. The lens used for this purpose is called simple microscope or a magnifier.

The object is placed at a distance u_o from the lens (between pole and focus of lens). The virtual magnified image is formed as shown. This image subtends a visual angle say θ on the eye. Then,

$$\theta = \frac{h}{u_o}$$

From the definition of magnifying power for a microscope,

$$M = \frac{\theta}{\theta_o} = \frac{h/u_o}{h/D}$$

$\therefore$

$$M = \frac{D}{u_o}$$

For relaxed eye   The final image should be at infinity. Thus, $u_o = f$

$\therefore$

$$M_\infty = \frac{D}{f}$$

This is also called magnifying power for normal adjustment.

We can see that $M_\infty > 1$ if $f < D$.

Magnifying power when final image is at D   In the above case, we saw that M is equal $\dfrac{D}{f}$. The magnification can be made large by choosing the focal length f small.

The magnifying power can be increased in an another way by moving the object still closer to the lens. Suppose, the final virtual image is formed at a distance D. Then, from the equation $\dfrac{1}{v} - \dfrac{1}{u} = \dfrac{1}{f}$, we have

$$\frac{1}{-D} + \frac{1}{u_o} = \frac{1}{f}$$

or

$$\frac{1}{u_o} = \frac{1}{D} + \frac{1}{f}$$

Substituting this value in the equation, $M = \dfrac{D}{u_o}$, we have

$$M_D = 1 + \frac{D}{f}$$

Note   (i) *That $M_D > M_\infty$, i.e. when final image is formed at 25 cm, angular magnification is increased but eye is most strained. On the other hand when final image is at infinity, angular magnification is slightly less but eye is relaxed. So, the choice is yours whether you want to see bigger size with strained eye or smaller size with relaxed eye.*

(ii) *That M can be increased by decreasing f, but due to several other aberrations the image becomes too defective at large magnification with a simple microscope. Roughly speaking a magnification upto 4 is trouble free.*

Compound Microscope   Figure shows a simplified version of a compound microscope. It consists of two converging lenses arranged coaxially. The one facing the object is called objective and the one close to eye is called eyepiece. The objective has a smaller aperture and smaller focal length than those of the eyepiece.

The separation between the objective and the eyepiece (called the length of the microscope L) can be varied by appropriate screws fixed on the panel of microscope.

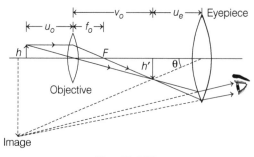

Fig. 31.135

The object is placed beyond first focus of objective, so that an inverted and real image (intermediate image) is formed by the objective. This intermediate image acts as an object for the eyepiece and lies between first focus and pole of eye piece. The final magnified virtual image is formed by the eyepiece. Let θ be the angle subtended by the final image on the eye, then,

$$\theta = \frac{h'}{u_e}$$

Here, h' is the height of the first image and u_e is its distance from the eyepiece.

Further

$$\theta_o = \frac{h}{D}$$

$\therefore$ Magnifying power of the compound microscope will be

$$M = \frac{\theta}{\theta_o} = \frac{h'}{u_e} \times \frac{D}{h} = \left(\frac{h'}{h}\right)\left(\frac{D}{u_e}\right)$$

Here, $\dfrac{h'}{h}$ is the linear magnification by the objective. Thus,

$$\frac{h'}{h} = |m_0| = \frac{v_0}{u_0}$$

$\therefore$

$$\boxed{M = \frac{v_0}{u_0}\left(\frac{D}{u_e}\right)}$$

Length of the microscope will be

$$\boxed{L = v_0 + u_e}$$

For relaxed eye   For relaxed eye final image should be at infinity. Or,

$$\boxed{u_e = f_e \quad \therefore \quad M_\infty = \frac{v_0}{u_0}\frac{D}{f_e}}$$

and

$$L_\infty = v_0 + f_e$$

Final image at D   When the final image (by eyepiece) is formed at D. Then, by the formula $\dfrac{1}{v} - \dfrac{1}{u} = \dfrac{1}{f}$ we have

$$\frac{1}{-D} + \frac{1}{u_e} = \frac{1}{f_e}$$

$\therefore$

$$\frac{1}{u_e} = \frac{1}{D} + \frac{1}{f_e}$$

or

$$u_e = \frac{Df_e}{D + f_e}$$

Thus,

$$\boxed{M_D = \frac{v_0}{u_0}\left(1 + \frac{D}{f_e}\right)}$$

and

$$\boxed{L_D = v_0 + \frac{Df_e}{D + f_e}}$$

Telescopes A microscope is used to view the objects placed closed to it. To look at distant objects such as a star, a planet or a distant tree etc., we use telescopes. There are three types of telescopes in use.

(i) Astronomical telescope,

(ii) Terrestrial telescope and

(iii) Galilean telescope.

(i) **Astronomical telescope** Figure shows the construction and working of an astronomical telescope.

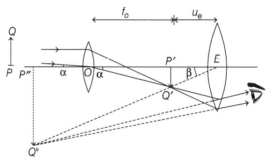

Fig. 31.136

It consists of two converging lenses placed coaxially. The one facing the distant object is called the objective and has a large aperture and large focal length. The other is called the eyepiece, as the eye is placed closed to it. The eyepiece tube can slide within the objective tube, so that the separation between the objective and the eyepiece may be varied.

Magnifying power Although a telescope can also be used to view the objects of few kilometers away but the magnifying power calculated below is for the case when object is at infinity. Rays coming from the object in that case will be almost parallel.

The image formed by objective will be at its second focus. This image called the intermediate image will act as the object for eyepiece. This usually lies between pole and first focus of eyepiece. So that eyepiece forms a virtual and magnified image of it.

$|\alpha|$ = angle subtended by object on objective (or you can say at eye)

$$= \frac{P'Q'}{f_o}$$

$|\beta|$ = angle subtended by final image at eyepiece (or at eye)

$$= \frac{P'Q'}{u_e}$$

From the definition of magnifying power (for telescope),

$$M = \frac{|\beta|}{|\alpha|} = \frac{f_o}{u_e} \qquad \text{or} \qquad \boxed{M = \frac{f_o}{u_e}}$$

and length of telescope,

$$L = f_o + u_e$$

For relaxed eye For relaxed eye, intermediate image should lie at first focus of eyepiece or

$$u_e = f_e$$

$\therefore$

$$\boxed{M_\infty = \frac{f_o}{f_e} \quad \text{and} \quad L_\infty = f_o + f_e}$$

Final image at D When the final image is at D, then using the formula $\dfrac{1}{v} - \dfrac{1}{u} = \dfrac{1}{f}$ for eyepiece we have,

$$\frac{1}{-D} + \frac{1}{u_e} = \frac{1}{f_e}$$

$\therefore$

$$\frac{1}{u_e} = \frac{1}{D} + \frac{1}{f_e}$$

or

$$\boxed{u_e = \frac{Df_e}{D + f_e}}$$

Therefore,

$$M_D = \frac{f_o}{f_e}\left(1 + \frac{f_e}{D}\right)$$

and

$$L_D = f_o + \frac{Df_e}{D + f_e}$$

(ii) Terrestrial telescope In an astronomical telescope, the final image is inverted with respect to the object. To remove this difficulty, a convex lens of focal length f is included between the objective and the eyepiece in such a way that the focal plane of the objective is a distance $2f$ away from this lens.

The role of the intermediate lens L is only to invert the image. The magnification produced by it is -1. The formula of M does not change at all. They remain as it is, as were derived for astronomical telescope. The length of telescope will however increase by $4f$. Here, you should note that we are talking only about magnitude of M. Thus,

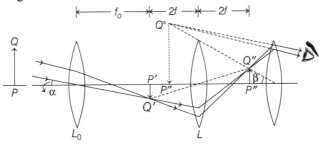

Fig. 31.137

$$M_\infty = \frac{f_o}{f_e} \quad \text{and} \quad M_D = \frac{f_o}{f_e}\left(1 + \frac{f_e}{D}\right)$$

$$L_\infty = f_o + 4f + f_e \quad \text{and} \quad L_D = f_o + 4f + \frac{Df_e}{D + f_e}$$

(iii) Galilean telescope Figure shows a simple model of Galilean telescope. A convergent lens is used as the objective and a divergent lens as the eyepiece. The objective lens forms a real and inverted image $P'Q'$ but the divergent lens comes in between. This intermediate image acts as virtual object for eyepiece. Final image $P''Q''$ is erect and magnified as shown in figure. The intermediate image is formed at second focus of objective.

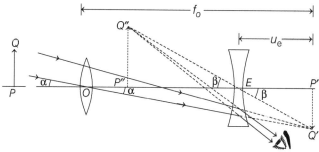

Fig. 31.138

Magnifying power From the figure, we can see that

$$|\alpha| = \frac{P'Q'}{f_O} \quad \text{and} \quad |\beta| = \frac{P'Q'}{u_e}$$

From the definition of magnifying power for telescope,

$$M = \frac{|\beta|}{|\alpha|} = \frac{f_O}{u_e}$$

and length of the telescope, $\qquad L = f_O - u_e$

For relaxed eye For relaxed eye intermediate image should lie at first focus of eyepiece. Or,

$$u_e = f_e$$

Hence, $\qquad\qquad M_\infty = \frac{f_o}{f_e} \quad \text{and} \quad L_\infty = f_o - f_e$

Final image at D For the final image to be at a distance D from the eyepiece, we have from the formula $\dfrac{1}{v} - \dfrac{1}{u} = \dfrac{1}{f}$

$$\frac{1}{-D} - \frac{1}{u_e} = \frac{1}{-f_e} \quad \Rightarrow \quad \frac{1}{u_e} = \frac{1}{f_e} - \frac{1}{D}$$

or $\qquad\qquad\qquad u_e = \dfrac{Df_e}{D - f_e}$

Thus, $\qquad\qquad M_D = \dfrac{f_o}{f_e}\left(1 - \dfrac{f_e}{D}\right)$

and $\qquad\qquad L_D = f_o - \dfrac{f_e D}{D - f_e}$

Note   (i) *In all above formulae of M, we are considering only the magnitude of M.*
(ii) *For telescopes, formulae have been derived when the object is at infinity. For the object at some finite distance different formulae will have to be derived.*
(iii) *Given below are formulae derived above of M and L in tabular form.*

Table 31.5

Name of optical instruments	M	L	M_∞	M_D	L_∞	L_D
Simple microscope	$\dfrac{D}{u_o}$	—	$\dfrac{D}{f}$	$1+\dfrac{D}{f}$	—	—
Compound microscope	$\dfrac{v_o}{u_o}\dfrac{D}{u_e}$	v_o+u_e	$\dfrac{v_o}{u_o}\dfrac{D}{f_e}$	$\dfrac{v_o}{u_o}\left(1+\dfrac{D}{f_e}\right)$	v_o+f_e	$v_o+\dfrac{Df_e}{D+f_e}$
Astronomical telescope	$\dfrac{f_o}{u_e}$	f_o+u_e	$\dfrac{f_o}{f_e}$	$\dfrac{f_o}{f_e}\left(1+\dfrac{f_e}{D}\right)$	f_o+f_e	$f_o+\dfrac{Df_e}{D+f_e}$
Terrestrial telescope	— do —	f_o+4f+u_e	— do —	— do —	f_o+4f+f_e	$f_o+4f+\dfrac{Df_e}{D+f_e}$
Galilean telescope	$\dfrac{f_o}{u_e}$	f_o-u_e	$\dfrac{f_o}{f_e}$	$\dfrac{f_o}{f_e}\left(1-\dfrac{f_e}{D}\right)$	f_o-f_e	$f_o-\dfrac{f_eD}{D-f_e}$

Resolving Power of a Microscope and a Telescope

Microscope   The resolving power of a microscope is defined as the reciprocal of the distance between two objects which can be just resolved when seen through the microscope. It depends on the wavelength λ of the light, the refractive index μ of the medium between the object and the objective and the angle θ subtended by a radius of the objective on one of the objects.

$$R=\frac{1}{\Delta d}=\frac{2\mu\sin\theta}{\lambda}$$

To increase R, objective and object are immersed in oil.

Telescope   The resolving power of a telescope is defined as the reciprocal of the angular separation between two distant objects which are just resolved by a telescope.

It is given by

$$R=\frac{1}{\Delta\theta}=\frac{a}{1.22\lambda}$$

Here, a is the diameter of the objective. That is why, telescopes with larger objective aperture are used.

⊚ ***Example 31.40***   *An astronomical telescope has an angular magnification of magnitude 5 for distant objects. The separation between the objective and eyepiece is 36 cm and the final image is formed at infinity. Determine the focal length of objective and eyepiece.*

Solution For final image at infinity,

$$M_\infty = \frac{f_o}{f_e} \quad \text{and} \quad L_\infty = f_o + f_e$$

$\therefore$
$$5 = \frac{f_o}{f_e} \qquad \qquad ...(i)$$

and
$$36 = f_o + f_e \qquad \qquad ...(ii)$$

Solving these two equations, we have

$$f_o = 30 \, \text{cm} \quad \text{and} \quad f_e = 6 \, \text{cm} \qquad \textbf{Ans.}$$

⊘ **Example 31.41** *A telescope has an objective of focal length 50 cm and an eyepiece of focal length 5 cm. The least distance of distinct vision is 25 cm. The telescope is focused for distinct vision on a scale 2 m away from the objective. Calculate (a) magnification produced and (b) separation between objective and eyepiece.*

Solution Given, $f_o = 50 \, \text{cm}$ and $f_e = 5 \, \text{cm}$

Note *Here, object is placed at finite distance from the objective. Hence, formulae derived for angular magnification M cannot be applied directly as they have been derived for the object to be at infinity. Here, it will be difficult to find angular magnification. So, only linear magnification can be obtained.*

For objective
$$\frac{1}{v_o} - \frac{1}{-200} = \frac{1}{50}$$

$\therefore$
$$v_o = \frac{200}{3} \, \text{cm}$$

$$m_o = \frac{v_o}{u_o} = \frac{(200/3)}{-200} = -\frac{1}{3}$$

For eyepiece
$$\frac{1}{-25} - \frac{1}{u_e} = \frac{1}{5}$$

$\therefore$
$$u_e = -\frac{25}{6} \, \text{cm}$$

and
$$m_e = \frac{v_e}{u_e} = \frac{-25}{-(25/6)} = 6$$

(a) Magnification,
$$m = m_o \times m_e = -2 \qquad \textbf{Ans.}$$

(b) Separation between objective and eyepiece,

$$L = v_o + |u_e| = \frac{200}{3} + \frac{25}{6} = \frac{425}{6}$$

$$= 70.83 \, \text{cm} \qquad \textbf{Ans.}$$

Core Concepts

Fermat's principle :

1. A ray of light follows that path in reaching from one point to another point along which it takes the shortest time. Let us take an example.

In figure, P is a point in air and Q a point in a medium of refractive index μ.

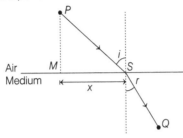

In air, speed of light is c and in the medium speed of light is $v = c/\mu$. Suppose that, the ray of light follows a path PSQ where S is at a distance x from M. Then, time taken by the ray of light in reaching from P to Q is

$$t = \frac{PS}{c} + \frac{SQ}{v} = \frac{PS}{c} + \frac{SQ}{(c/\mu)} \quad \text{or} \quad t = \frac{PS}{c} + \frac{\mu SQ}{c}$$

To make the time minimum one has to differentiate it with respect to x and find the point S when t is a minimum. From differentiation (we are skipping here) we find that t is minimum when,

$$\frac{\sin i}{\sin r} = \mu$$

This is nothing but the Snell's law.

2. **Lateral shift** We have already discussed that ray MA is parallel to ray BN. But the emergent ray is displaced laterally by a distance d, which depends on μ, t and i and its value is given by the relation,

$$d = t \left(1 - \frac{\cos i}{\sqrt{\mu^2 - \sin^2 i}} \right) \sin i$$

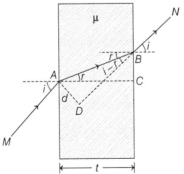

Proof

$$AB = \frac{AC}{\cos r} = \frac{t}{\cos r} \qquad (\text{as } AC = t)$$

Now,

$$d = AB \sin (i - r)$$

$$= \frac{t}{\cos r} [\sin i \cos r - \cos i \sin r]$$

or $\qquad$ $d = t\,[\sin i - \cos i\,\tan r]$ $\qquad$ ...(i)

Further, $\qquad$ $\mu = \dfrac{\sin i}{\sin r}$ or $\sin r = \dfrac{\sin i}{\mu}$

∴ $\qquad$ $\tan r = \dfrac{\sin i}{\sqrt{\mu^2 - \sin^2 i}}$

Substituting in Eq. (i), we get $\quad d = \left[1 - \dfrac{\cos i}{\sqrt{\mu^2 - \sin^2 i}}\right] t \sin i$ $\qquad$ **Hence Proved.**

EXERCISE Show that for small angles of incidence, $d = t i \left(\dfrac{\mu - 1}{\mu}\right)$.

3. In case of spherical mirrors if object distance x_1 and image distance x_2 are measured from focus instead of pole, $u = (f + x_1)$ and $v = (f + x_2)$ the mirror formula,

$$\frac{1}{v} + \frac{1}{u} = \frac{1}{f} \text{ reduces to, } \frac{1}{f + x_2} + \frac{1}{f + x_1} = \frac{1}{f}$$

which on simplification gives,

$$x_1 x_2 = f^2$$

This formula is called **Newton's formula.**

This formula applies to a lens also, but in that case x_1 is the object distance from first focus and x_2 the image distance from second focus.

4. Eye is most sensitive to yellow-green light ($\lambda = 5550$ Å).

5. Frequency of visible light is of the order of 10^{15} Hz.

6. Colour of light is determined by its frequency and not the wavelength. During refraction of light frequency and colour of light do not change.

7. **Twinkling of stars** Due to fluctuations in refractive index of atmosphere the refraction of light (reaching to our eye from the star) becomes irregular and the light sometimes reaches the eye and sometimes it does not. This gives rise to twinkling of stars.

8. **Oval shape of sun in the morning and evening** In the morning or evening, the sun is at the horizon. The refractive index decreases with height. Light reaching earth's atmosphere from different parts of vertical diameter of the sun enters at different heights in earth's atmosphere and so travels in media of different refractive indices at the same instant and hence, bends unequally. Due to this unequal bending of light from vertical diameter, the image of the sun gets distorted and it appears oval and larger. However, at noon when the sun is overhead, then due to normal incidence there will be no bending and the sun will appear circular.

9. The sparkling of diamond is due to total internal reflection inside it.

10. **Mirage** Mirage in deserts is caused by total internal reflection.

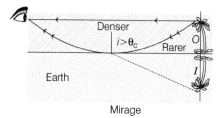

Mirage

Due to heating of the earth, the refractive index of air near the surface of earth becomes lesser than above it. Light from distant objects reaches the surface of earth with $i > \theta_C$. So that total internal reflection will take place and we see the image of an object along with the object as seen in figure, creating an illusion of water near the object.

11. **Advance sunrise and delayed sunset** Apparent shift in the position of sun at sunrise and sunset. The sun is visible before actual sunrise and after actual sunset, because of atmospheric refraction. With altitude, the density and hence refractive index of air-layer decreases. As shown in Fig. the light rays starting from the sun travel from rarer to denser layers. They bend more and more towards the normal. To an observer on the earth, light rays appears to come from position S'. The sun which is actually in position S below the horizon, appears in position S' above the horizon. Thus the sun appears to rise early by about two minutes and for the same reason, it appears to set late by about two minutes. This increases the length of the day by about four minutes.

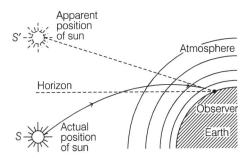

12. **Looming** It is also due to **total internal reflection**. This phenomenon is observed in cold deserts and is opposite to that of mirage.

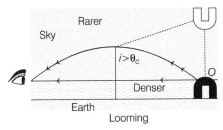

Looming

13. **Scattering of light** If the molecules of a medium after absorbing incoming radiations (light) emit them in all possible directions, the process is called scattering. In scattering if the wavelength of radiation remains unchanged the scattering is called elastic otherwise inelastic.

Rayleigh has shown, theoretically that in case of elastic scattering of light by molecules, the intensity of scattered light depends on both nature of molecules and wavelength of light. According to him,

Intensity of scattered light $\propto \dfrac{1}{\lambda^4}$

Raman effect was based on inelastic scattering. For this **C.V. Raman** was awarded the Nobel Prize in 1930.

Scattering helps us in understanding the following:

Why sky is Blue When white light from the sun enters the earth's atmosphere, scattering takes place. As scattering is proportional to $\dfrac{1}{\lambda^4}$, blue is scattered most. When we look at the sky we receive scattered light which is rich in blue and hence, the sky appears blue.

Why sun appears red during sunset and sunrise In the morning and evening when sun is at the horizon, due to oblique incidence, light reaches earth after traversing maximum path in the atmosphere and so suffers maximum scattering. Now, as scattering $\propto \dfrac{1}{\lambda^4}$, shorter wavelengths are scattered most leaving the longer one. As red light has longest wavelength in the visible region, it is scattered least. This is why sun appears red in the morning and evening. The same reason is why red light is used for danger signals.

14. **Defects of images** Actual image formed by an optical system is usually imperfect. The defects of images are called **aberrations**. The defect may be due to light or optical system. If the defect is due to light, it is called **chromatic aberration,** and if due to optical system, **monochromatic aberration.**

   (a) **Chromatic aberration** The image of an object formed by a lens is usually coloured and blurred. This defect of image is called chromatic aberration. This defect arises due to the fact that focal length of a lens is different for different colours. For a lens,

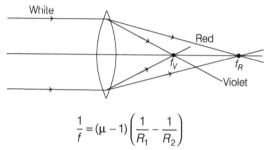

$$\frac{1}{f} = (\mu - 1)\left(\frac{1}{R_1} - \frac{1}{R_2}\right)$$

As μ is maximum for violet while minimum for red, violet is focused nearest to the lens while red farthest from it.

The difference between f_R and f_V is a measure of longitudinal chromatic aberration. Thus,

$$LCA = f_R - f_V$$

Condition of achromatism To get achromatism, we use a pair of two lenses in contact. For two thin lenses in contact we have,

∴

$$\boxed{\frac{\omega_1}{f_1} + \frac{\omega_2}{f_2} = 0}$$

This is the **condition of achromatism.** From the condition of achromatism, following conclusions can be drawn:

   (i) As ω_1 and ω_2 are positive quantities, f_1 and f_2 should have opposite signs, i.e. if one lens is convex, the other must be concave.

   (ii) If $\omega_1 = \omega_2$, means both the lenses are of same material. Then,

$$\frac{1}{f_1} + \frac{1}{f_2} = 0 \quad \text{or} \quad \frac{1}{F} = 0 \quad \text{or} \quad F = \infty$$

   Thus, the combination behaves as a plane glass plate. So, we can conclude that both the lenses should be of different materials or $\omega_1 \neq \omega_2$

   (iii) Dispersive power of crown glass (ω_C) is less than that of flint glass (ω_F).

   (iv) If we want the combination to behave as a convergent lens, then convex lens should have lesser focal length or its dispersive power should be more. Thus, convex lens should be made of flint glass and concave lens of crown. Thus, combination is converging if convex is made of flint glass and concave of crown. Similarly, for the combination to behave as diverging lens, convex is made of crown glass and concave of flint glass.

(b) **Monochromatic aberration** This is the defect in image due to optical system. Monochromatic aberration is of many types such as, spherical, coma, distortion, curvature and astigmatism. Here, we shall limit ourselves to spherical aberration only.

Spherical aberration Spherical aberration arises due to spherical nature of lens (or mirror).

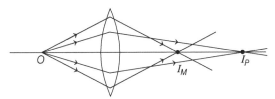

The paraxial rays (close to optic axis) get focused at I_P and marginal rays (away from the optic axis) are focused at I_M. Thus, image of a point object O is not a point.

The inability of the lens to form a point image of an axial point object is called spherical aberration. Spherical aberration can never be eliminated but can be minimised by the following methods:

(i) **By using stops** By using stops either paraxial or marginal rays are cut-off.

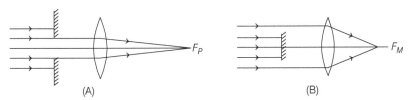

(A) (B)

(ii) **Using two thin lenses separated by a distance** Two thin lenses separated by a distance $d = f_2 - f_1$ has the minimum spherical aberration.

(iii) **Using parabolic mirrors** If spherical mirror is replaced by parabolic mirror, spherical aberration is minimised.

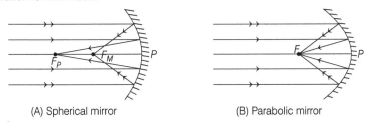

(A) Spherical mirror (B) Parabolic mirror

(iv) **Using lens of large focal length** It has been found that spherical aberration varies inversely as the cube of the focal length. So, if f is large, spherical aberration will be reduced.

(v) **Using plano-convex lens** In case of plano-convex lens, spherical aberration is minimised, if its curved surface faces the incident or emergent ray whichever is more parallel.

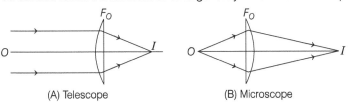

(A) Telescope (B) Microscope

This is why in telescope, the curved surface faces the object while in microscope curved surface is towards the image.

(vi) Using crossed lens For a single lens with object at infinity, spherical aberration is found to be minimum when R_1 and R_2 have the following ratio,

$$\frac{R_1}{R_2} = \frac{2\mu^2 - \mu - 4}{\mu \, (2\mu + 1)}$$

A lens which satisfies this condition is called a crossed lens.

Defects of vision Regarding eye, the following points are worthnoting:

(a) The human eye is most sensitive to yellow-green light ($\lambda = 5550$ Å).

(b) The persistance of vision is $\frac{1}{10}$ sec, i.e. if time interval between two consecutive light pulses is less than 0.1 sec, eye cannot distinguish them separately.

(c) By the eyelens, real, inverted and diminished image is formed on retina.

(d) While testing your eye through reading chart if doctor finds it to 6/12, it implies that you can read a letter from 6 m which the normal eye can read from 12 m. Thus, 6/6 means normal eye sight.

The common defects of vision are as follows:

(i) Myopia or short-sightedness Distant objects are not clearly visible in this defect. The image of distant object is formed before the retina.

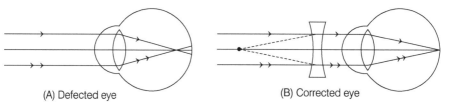

(A) Defected eye   (B) Corrected eye

The defect can be remedied by using a concave lens.

(ii) Hyperopia or far-sightedness The near objects are not clearly visible. Image of near object is formed behind the retina.

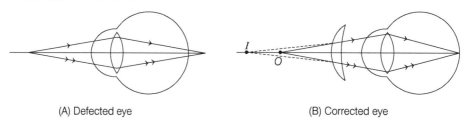

(A) Defected eye   (B) Corrected eye

This defect is remedied by using a convex lens.

(iii) Presbyopia In it both near and far objects are not clearly visible. This is remedied either by using two separate lenses or by using single spectacle having bifocal lenses.

(iv) Astigmatism In this defect, eye cannot see objects in two orthogonal (perpendicular) directions clearly simultaneously. This defect is remedied by using cylindrical lens.

Solved Examples

Example 1 *A spherical convex surface separates object and image space of refractive index 1.0 and $\dfrac{4}{3}$. If radius of curvature of the surface is 10 cm, find its power.*

Solution Let us see where does the parallel rays converge (or diverge) on the principal axis. Let us call it the focus and the corresponding length the focal length f. Using $\dfrac{\mu_2}{v} - \dfrac{\mu_1}{u} = \dfrac{\mu_2 - \mu_1}{R}$ with proper values and signs, we have

$$\frac{4/3}{f} - \frac{1.0}{\infty} = \frac{4/3 - 1.0}{+10} \quad \text{or} \quad f = 40 \text{ cm} = 0.4 \text{ m}$$

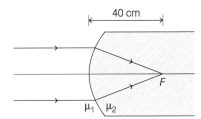

Since, the rays are converging, its power should be positive. Hence,

$$P \text{ (in dioptre)} = \frac{+1}{f \text{ (metre)}} = \frac{1}{0.4}$$

or $$P = 2.5 \text{ dioptre}$$ **Ans.**

Example 2 *A ray of light is incident at an angle of $60°$ on the face of a prism having refracting angle $30°$. The ray emerging out of the prism makes an angle $30°$ with the incident ray. Show that the emergent ray is perpendicular to the face through which it emerges.*

Solution Given, $i_1 = 60°$, $A = 30°$ and $\delta = 30°$.

From the relation, $$\delta = (i_1 + i_2) - A$$
we have, $$i_2 = 0$$

This means that the emergent ray is perpendicular to the face through which it emerges. **Ans.**

Example 3 *The angle of minimum deviation for a glass prism with $\mu = \sqrt{3}$ equals the refracting angle of the prism. What is the angle of the prism?*

Solution Given, $A = \delta_m$

Using, $$\mu = \frac{\sin\left(\dfrac{A + \delta_m}{2}\right)}{\sin\left(\dfrac{A}{2}\right)}$$

We have,
$$\sqrt{3} = \frac{\sin\left(\dfrac{A+A}{2}\right)}{\sin\left(\dfrac{A}{2}\right)}$$

or
$$\sqrt{3} = \frac{\sin A}{\sin\left(\dfrac{A}{2}\right)} = \frac{2\sin\dfrac{A}{2}\cdot\cos\dfrac{A}{2}}{\sin\left(\dfrac{A}{2}\right)}$$

$\therefore$
$$\cos\frac{A}{2} = \frac{\sqrt{3}}{2}$$

$\therefore$
$$\frac{A}{2} = 30°$$

or
$$A = 60°$$ **Ans.**

Example 4 *The distance between two point sources of light is* 24 *cm. Find out where would you place a converging lens of focal length* 9 *cm, so that the images of both the sources are formed at the same point.*

Solution **For S_1:** $\dfrac{1}{v_1} - \dfrac{1}{-x} = \dfrac{1}{9}$

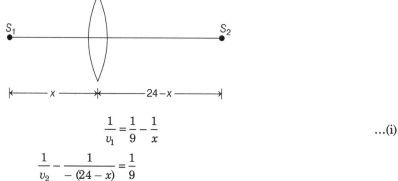

$\therefore$
$$\frac{1}{v_1} = \frac{1}{9} - \frac{1}{x}$$ ...(i)

For S_2:
$$\frac{1}{v_2} - \frac{1}{-(24-x)} = \frac{1}{9}$$

$\therefore$
$$\frac{1}{v_2} = \frac{1}{9} - \frac{1}{24-x}$$ ...(ii)

Since, sign convention for S_1 and S_2 are just opposite. Hence,
$$v_1 = -v_2$$

or
$$\frac{1}{v_1} = -\frac{1}{v_2}$$

$\therefore$
$$\frac{1}{9} - \frac{1}{x} = \frac{1}{24-x} - \frac{1}{9}$$

Solving this equation we get, $x = 6$ cm. Therefore, the lens should be kept at a distance of 6 cm from either of the object. **Ans.**

● **Example 5**   *A source of light is located at double focal length from a convergent lens. The focal length of the lens is f = 30 cm. At what distance from the lens should a flat mirror be placed, so that the rays reflected from the mirror are parallel after passing through the lens for the second time?*

Solution   Object is at a distance of $2f = 60$ cm from the lens. Image I_1 formed by lens, should be at a distance 60 cm from the lens. Now I_2, the image formed by plane mirror should lie at focus or at a distance of 30 cm from the lens. Hence, the mirror should be placed at distance 45 cm from the lens as shown in figure.

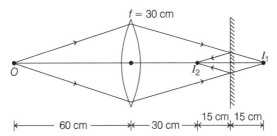

● **Example 6**   *Two equi-convex lenses of focal lengths 30 cm and 70 cm, made of material of refractive index = 1.5, are held in contact coaxially by a rubber band round their edges. A liquid of refractive index 1.3 is introduced in the space between the lenses filling it completely. Find the position of the image of a luminous point object placed on the axis of the combination lens at a distance of 90 cm from it.*

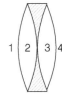

Solution $|R_1| = |R_2| = f_1 = 30$ cm   (As $\mu = 1.5$)

Similarly, $|R_3| = |R_4| = f_2 = 70$ cm

The focal length of the liquid lens (in air).

$$\frac{1}{f_3} = (\mu - 1)\left(\frac{1}{R_2} - \frac{1}{R_3}\right)$$

$$= (1.3 - 1)\left(\frac{1}{-30} - \frac{1}{+70}\right)$$

$$= -\frac{1}{70}$$

Further, equivalent focal length of the combination,

$$\frac{1}{F} = \frac{1}{f_1} + \frac{1}{f_2} + \frac{1}{f_3}$$

$$= \frac{1}{30} + \frac{1}{70} - \frac{1}{70} = \frac{1}{30}$$

Using the lens formula $\dfrac{1}{v} - \dfrac{1}{u} = \dfrac{1}{F}$, we have

$$\frac{1}{v} - \frac{1}{-90} = \frac{1}{30}$$

∴ $v = +45$ cm

Thus, image will be formed at a distance of 45 cm from the combination.

⊙ **Example 7** *Two thin converging lenses are placed on a common axis, so that the centre of one of them coincides with the focus of the other. An object is placed at a distance twice the focal length from the left hand lens. Where will its image be? What is the lateral magnification? The focal of each lens is f.*

Solution

The image formed by first lens will be at a distance $2f$ with lateral magnification $m_1 = -1$. For the second lens this image will behave as a virtual object. Using the lens formula, $\dfrac{1}{v} - \dfrac{1}{u} = \dfrac{1}{f}$ we have,

$$\frac{1}{v} - \frac{1}{f} = \frac{1}{f} \quad \Rightarrow \quad v = \frac{f}{2}$$

$$m_2 = \frac{v_2}{u_2} = \frac{(f/2)}{f} = \frac{1}{2}$$

Therefore, final image is formed at a distance $\dfrac{f}{2}$ from the second lens with total lateral magnification,

$$m = m_1 \times m_2 = (-1) \times \left(\frac{1}{2}\right) = -\frac{1}{2}$$ **Ans.**

⊙ **Example 8** *The refracting angle of a glass prism is 30°. A ray is incident onto one of the faces perpendicular to it. Find the angle δ between the incident ray and the ray that leaves the prism. The refractive index of glass is μ = 1.5.*

Solution Given, $A = 30°, \mu = 1.5$ and $i_1 = 0°$

Since, $i_1 = 0°$, therefore, r_1 is also equal to $0°$.

Further, since, $r_1 + r_2 = A$

∴ $$r_2 = A = 30°$$

Using, $$\mu = \frac{\sin i_2}{\sin r_2}$$

We have, $$1.5 = \frac{\sin i_2}{\sin 30°}$$

or $$\sin i_2 = 1.5 \sin 30°$$

$$= 1.5 \times \frac{1}{2} = 0.75$$

∴ $$i_2 = \sin^{-1}(0.75) = 48.6°$$

Now, the deviation, $\delta = (i_1 + i_2) - A$

$$= (0 + 48.6) - 30$$

or $$\delta = 18.6°$$ **Ans.**

Example 9 *A biconvex thin lens is prepared from glass of refractive index 3/2. The two bounding surfaces have equal radii of 25 cm each. One of the surfaces is silvered from outside to make it reflecting. Where should an object be placed before this lens so that the image coincides with the object.*

Solution Equivalent focal length of this system which behaves like a mirror is given by

$$\frac{1}{f} = \frac{2\,(\mu_2/\mu_1)}{R_2} - \frac{2\,(\mu_2/\mu_1 - 1)}{R_1}$$

Here, $R_1 = +25$ cm, $R_2 = -25$ cm, $\mu_1 = 1$

and $\mu_2 = 3/2$

Image coincides with object, hence, $u = v = -x$ (say)

Substituting in mirror formula, we have

$$\frac{1}{-x} - \frac{1}{x} = \frac{2(3/2)}{-25} - \frac{2(3/2 - 1)}{25}$$

or $$\frac{2}{x} = \frac{3}{25} + \frac{1}{25} = \frac{4}{25}$$

∴ $x = 12.5$ cm **Ans.**

Hence, the object should be placed at a distance 12.5 cm in front of the silvered lens.

Example 10 *An object is 5.0 m to the left of a flat screen. A converging lens for which the focal length is $f = 0.8$ m is placed between object and screen.*

(a) *Show that two lens positions exist that form images on the screen and determine how far these positions are from the object?*

(b) *How do the two images differ from each other?*

Solution (a) Using the lens formula,

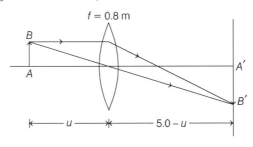

$$\frac{1}{v} - \frac{1}{u} = \frac{1}{f}$$

We have, $$\frac{1}{5.0 - u} - \frac{1}{-u} = \frac{1}{0.8} \quad \text{or} \quad \frac{1}{5 - u} + \frac{1}{u} = 1.25$$

∴ $u + 5 - u = 1.25\,u\,(5 - u) \quad \text{or} \quad 1.25\,u^2 - 6.25\,u + 5 = 0$

∴ $$u = \frac{6.25 \pm \sqrt{39.0625 - 25}}{2.5}$$

or $u = 4$ m and 1 m **Ans.**

Both the values are real, which means there exist two positions of lens that form images of object on the screen.

(b) $m = \dfrac{v}{u}$

∴ $\quad m_1 = \dfrac{(5.0 - 4.0)}{(-4.0)} = -0.25$

and $\quad m_2 = \dfrac{(5.0 - 1.0)}{(-1.0)} = -4.00$

Hence, both the images are real and inverted, the first has magnification -0.25 and the second -4.00. **Ans.**

Example 11 *An object is midway between the lens and the mirror as shown. The mirror's radius of curvature is* 20.0 *cm and the lens has a focal length of* -16.7 *cm. Considering only the rays that leaves the object and travels first toward the mirror, locate the final image formed by this system. Is this image real or virtual? Is it upright or inverted? What is the overall magnification?*

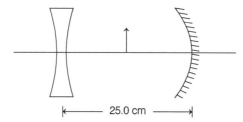

$\overset{\longmapsto}{\underset{25.0\ \text{cm}}{\longmapsto}}$

Solution **Image formed by mirror** Using mirror formula

$$\frac{1}{v} + \frac{1}{u} = \frac{1}{f} = \frac{2}{R} \qquad \left(\text{as } f = \frac{R}{2} \right)$$

We have, $\qquad \dfrac{1}{v_1} + \dfrac{1}{-12.5} = \dfrac{2}{-20}$

∴ $\qquad v_1 = -50 \text{ cm}$

$$m_1 = -\frac{v}{u} = -\frac{(-50)}{(-12.5)} = -4$$

i.e. image formed by the mirror is at a distance of 50 cm from the mirror to the left of it. It is inverted and four times larger.

Image formed by lens Image formed by mirror acts as an object for lens. It is at a distance of 25.0 cm to the left of lens. Using the lens formula,

$$\frac{1}{v} - \frac{1}{u} = \frac{1}{f}$$

We have, $\qquad \dfrac{1}{v_2} - \dfrac{1}{25} = \dfrac{1}{-16.7}$

∴ $\qquad v_2 = -50.3 \text{ cm}$

and $\qquad m_2 = \dfrac{v}{u} = \dfrac{-50.3}{25} = -2.012$

overall magnification is

$$m = m_1 \times m_2 = 8.048$$

Thus, the final image is at a distance 25.3 cm to the right of the mirror, virtual, upright enlarged and 8.048 times. Positions of the two images are shown in figure.

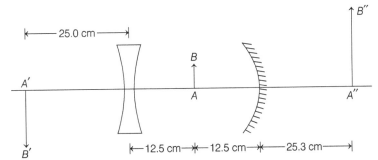

● **Example 12** *An object is placed 12 cm to the left of a diverging lens of focal length − 6.0 cm. A converging lens with a focal length of 12.0 cm is placed at a distance d to the right of the diverging lens. Find the distance d that corresponds to a final image at infinity.*

Solution

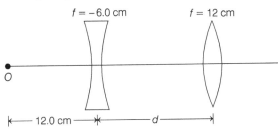

Applying lens formula $\dfrac{1}{v} - \dfrac{1}{u} = \dfrac{1}{f}$ twice we have,

$$\frac{1}{v_1} - \frac{1}{-12} = \frac{1}{-6} \qquad\qquad \text{...(i)}$$

$$\frac{1}{\infty} - \frac{1}{v_1 - d} = \frac{1}{12} \qquad\qquad \text{...(ii)}$$

Solving Eqs. (i) and (ii), we have

$$v_1 = -4 \text{ cm} \quad \text{and} \quad d = 8 \text{ cm} \qquad\qquad \textbf{Ans.}$$

● **Example 13** *A solid glass sphere with radius R and an index of refraction 1.5 is silvered over one hemisphere. A small object is located on the axis of the sphere at a distance 2R to the left of the vertex of the unsilvered hemisphere. Find the position of final image after all refractions and reflections have taken place.*

Solution The ray of light first gets refracted then reflected and then again refracted. For first refraction and then reflection the ray of light travels from left to right while for the last refraction it travels from right to left. Hence, the sign convention will change accordingly.

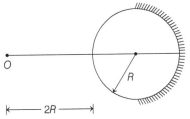

First refraction Using $\dfrac{\mu_2}{v} - \dfrac{\mu_1}{u} = \dfrac{\mu_2 - \mu_1}{R}$ with proper sign conventions, we have

$$\frac{1.5}{v_1} - \frac{1.0}{-2R} = \frac{1.5 - 1.0}{+R}$$

∴
$$v_1 = \infty$$

Second reflection Using $\frac{1}{v} + \frac{1}{u} = \frac{1}{f} = \frac{2}{R}$ with proper sign conventions, we have

$$\frac{1}{v_2} + \frac{1}{\infty} = -\frac{2}{R}$$

∴
$$v_2 = -\frac{R}{2}$$

Third refraction Again using $\frac{\mu_2}{v} - \frac{\mu_1}{u} = \frac{\mu_2 - \mu_1}{R}$ with reversed sign convention, we have

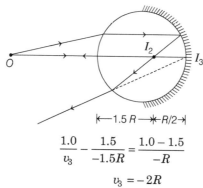

$$\frac{1.0}{v_3} - \frac{1.5}{-1.5R} = \frac{1.0 - 1.5}{-R}$$

or
$$v_3 = -2R$$

i.e. final image is formed on the vertex of the silvered face.

◉ **Example 14** *A converging lens forms a five fold magnified image of an object. The screen is moved towards the object by a distance d = 0.5 m, and the lens is shifted so that the image has the same size as the object. Find the power of lens and the initial distance between the object and the screen.*

Solution In the first case image is five times magnified. Hence, $|v| = 5|u|$. In the second case, image and object are of equal size. Hence, $|v| = |u|$. From the two figures,

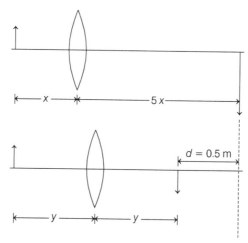

$$6x = 2y + d \quad \text{or} \quad 6x - 2y = 0.5 \qquad \qquad \text{...(i)}$$

Using the lens formula for both the cases,

$$\frac{1}{5x} - \frac{1}{-x} = \frac{1}{f} \quad \text{or} \quad \frac{6}{5x} = \frac{1}{f} \qquad \qquad \text{...(ii)}$$

$$\frac{1}{y} - \frac{1}{-y} = \frac{1}{f} \quad \text{or} \quad \frac{2}{y} = \frac{1}{f} \qquad \qquad \text{...(iii)}$$

Solving these three equations, we get

$$x = 0.1875 \text{ m} \quad \text{and} \quad f = 0.15625 \text{ m}$$

Therefore, initial distance between the object and the screen $= 6x = 1.125$ m **Ans.**

Power of the lens,
$$P = \frac{1}{f}$$

$$= \frac{1}{0.15625} = 6.4 \text{ D} \qquad \qquad \textbf{Ans.}$$

◉ **Example 15** *Surfaces of a thin equi-convex glass lens have radius of curvature R. Paraxial rays are incident on it. If the final image is formed after n internal reflections, calculate distance of this image from pole of the lens. Refractive index of glass is* μ.

Solution The rays will first get refracted, then *n*-times reflected and finally again refracted. So, using $\frac{\mu_2}{v} - \frac{\mu_1}{u} = \frac{\mu_2 - \mu_1}{R}$ for first refraction, we have

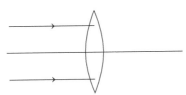

$$\frac{\mu}{v_i} - \frac{1}{\infty} = \frac{\mu - 1}{R} \quad \Rightarrow \quad v_i = \left(\frac{\mu}{\mu - 1} \right) R$$

For first reflection, let us use $\frac{1}{v} + \frac{1}{u} = \frac{1}{f} = \frac{2}{R}$

∴
$$\frac{1}{v_1} + \left(\frac{\mu - 1}{\mu R} \right) = \frac{-2}{R} \quad \text{or} \quad \frac{1}{v_1} = -\left(\frac{3\mu - 1}{\mu R} \right)$$

For second reflection,
$$\frac{1}{v_2} + \frac{3\mu - 1}{\mu R} = \frac{-2}{R} \quad \text{or} \quad \frac{1}{v_2} = -\left(\frac{5\mu - 1}{\mu R} \right)$$

Similarly, after n^{th} reflection,
$$\frac{1}{v_n} = -\left[\frac{(2n + 1)\mu - 1}{\mu R} \right]$$

Finally, using $\frac{\mu_2}{v} - \frac{\mu_1}{u} = \frac{\mu_2 - \mu_1}{R}$, we have

$$\frac{1}{v_f} - \left\{ \frac{(2n + 1)\mu - 1}{R} \right\} = \frac{1 - \mu}{-R}$$

or
$$v_f = \frac{R}{2 (\mu n + \mu - 1)} \qquad \qquad \textbf{Ans.}$$

Exercises

LEVEL 1

Note *In different books refractive index has been represented by the symbol n and μ. So, in our book we have used both symbols at different places.*

Assertion and Reason

Directions : *Choose the correct option.*

(*a*) *If both **Assertion** and **Reason** are true and the **Reason** is correct explanation of the **Assertion**.*
(*b*) *If both **Assertion** and **Reason** are true but **Reason** is not the correct explanation of **Assertion**.*
(*c*) *If **Assertion** is true, but the **Reason** is false.*
(*d*) *If **Assertion** is false but the **Reason** is true.*
(*e*) *Both **Assertion** and **Reason** are false.*

1. **Assertion :** There is a glass slab between Ram and Anoop. Then, Ram appears nearer to Anoop as compared to the actual distance between them.

   Reason : Ray of light starting from Ram will undergo two times refraction before reaching Anoop.

2. **Assertion :** Minimum distance between object and its real image by a convex lens is 4*f*.

   Reason : If object distance from a convex lens is 2*f*, then its image distance is also 2*f*.

3. **Assertion :** If object is placed at infinity, then a virtual image will be formed at first focus of a concave lens.

   Reason : First focal length of a concave lens is positive.

4. **Assertion :** A convex lens and a concave lens are kept in contact. They will behave as a diverging lens if focal length of convex lens is more.

   Reason : Power of a concave lens is always less than the power of a convex lens, as power of concave lens is negative whereas power of convex lens is positive.

5. **Assertion :** In the figure shown $|R_1|>|R_2|$. Two point objects O_1 and O_2 are kept at same distance from the lens. Image distance of O_1 from the lens will be more compared to the image distance of O_2.

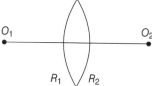

   Reason : If medium on two sides of the lens is different, we cannot apply lens formulae directly.

6. **Assertion :** White light is incident on face *AB* of an isosceles right angled prism as shown. Colours, for which refractive index of material of prism is more than 1.414, will be able to emerge from the face *AC*.

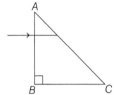

Reason : Total internal reflection cannot take place for the light travelling from a rarer medium to a denser medium.

7. **Assertion :** Although the surfaces of goggle lens are curved, it does not have any power.

   Reason : In case of goggles, both the curved surfaces have equal radii of curvature and have centre of curvature on the same side.

8. **Assertion :** A diverging lens (in air) cannot be made more diverging whatever be the medium we choose to completely cover the lens.

   Reason : The minimum refractive index of any medium is 1.

9. **Assertion :** Focal length of a lens depends on the wavelength of light used.

   Reason : The more the wavelength lesser is the focal length.

10. **Assertion :** In front of a concave mirror a point object is placed between focus and centre of curvature. If a glass slab is placed between object and mirror then image from mirror may become virtual.

    Reason : Glass slab always makes a virtual image of a virtual object.

Objective Questions

1. An endoscope is employed by a physician to view the internal parts of body organ. It is based on the principle of
   (a) refraction
   (b) reflection
   (c) total internal reflection
   (d) dispersion

2. An object is placed at a distance of 12 cm from a convex lens on its principal axis and a virtual image of certain size is formed. If the object is moved 8 cm away from the lens, a real image of the same size as that of the virtual image is formed. The focal length of the lens in cm is
   (a) 15
   (b) 16
   (c) 18
   (d) 20

3. A plane glass slab is placed over various coloured letters. The letter which appears to be raised the least is
   (a) violet
   (b) yellow
   (c) red
   (d) green

4. Critical angle of light passing from glass to air is least for
   (a) red
   (b) green
   (c) yellow
   (d) violet

5. The power in dioptre of an equi-convex lens with radii of curvature of 10 cm and refractive index 1.6 is
   (a) +12
   (b) +18
   (c) +1.2
   (d) +1.8

6. The refractive index of water is 4/3. The speed of light in water is
   (a) 1.50×10^8 m/s
   (b) 1.78×10^8 m/s
   (c) 2.25×10^8 m/s
   (d) 2.67×10^8 m/s

7. White light is incident from under water on the water-air interface. If the angle of incidence is slowly increased from zero, the emergent beam coming out into the air will turn from

(a) white to violet
(b) white to red
(c) white to black
(d) None of these

8. When light enters from air to water, then its

(a) frequency increases and speed decreases
(b) frequency is same, but the wavelength is smaller in water than in air
(c) frequency is same but the wavelength in water is greater than in air
(d) frequency decreases and wavelength is smaller in water than in air

9. In the figure shown $\dfrac{\sin i}{\sin r}$ is equal to

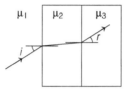

(a) $\dfrac{\mu_2^2}{\mu_3\,\mu_1}$
(b) $\dfrac{\mu_3}{\mu_1}$
(c) $\dfrac{\mu_3\,\mu_1}{\mu_2^2}$
(d) $\dfrac{\mu_1}{\mu_3}$

10. In figure, the reflected ray B makes an angle $90°$ with the ray C. If i, r_1 and r_2 are the angles of incidence, reflection and refraction, respectively. Then, the critical angle of the medium is

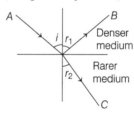

(a) $\sin^{-1}(\tan i)$
(b) $\sin^{-1}(\cot i)$
(c) r_1
(d) r_2

11. A prism of apex angle $A = 60°$ has the refractive index $\mu = \sqrt{2}$. The angle of incidence for minimum deviation is

(a) $30°$
(b) $45°$
(c) $60°$
(d) None of these

12. A thin equi-convex lens is made of glass of refractive index 1.5 and its focal length is 0.2 m. If it acts as a concave lens of 0.5 m focal length when dipped in a liquid, the refractive index of the liquid is

(a) $\dfrac{17}{8}$
(b) $\dfrac{15}{8}$
(c) $\dfrac{13}{8}$
(d) $\dfrac{9}{8}$

13. A ray of light, travelling in a medium of refractive index μ, is incident at an angle i on a composite transparent plate consisting of three plates of refractive indices μ_1, μ_2 and μ_3. The ray emerges from the composite plate into a medium of refractive index μ_4, at angle x. Then,

(a) $\sin x = \sin i$
(b) $\sin x = \dfrac{\mu}{\mu_4}\sin i$

(c) $\sin x = \dfrac{\mu_4}{\mu}\sin i$
(d) $\sin x = \dfrac{\mu_1\mu_3\,\mu}{\mu_2\,\mu_2\mu_4}\sin i$

14. The given equi-convex lens is broken into four parts and rearranged as shown. If the initial focal length is f, then after rearrangement the equivalent focal length is

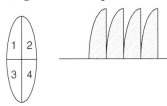

(a) f (b) $f/2$ (c) $f/4$ (d) $4f$

15. A glass slab of thickness 4 cm contains the same number of waves as 5 cm of water, when both are traversed by the same monochromatic light. If the refractive index of water is 4/3, then refractive index of glass is

(a) 5/3   (b) 5/4   (c) 16/15   (d) 1.5

16. Two convex lenses of focal length 10 cm and 20 cm respectively placed coaxially and are separated by some distance d. The whole system behaves like a concave lens . One of the possible value of d is

(a) 15 cm   (b) 20 cm   (c) 25 cm   (d) 40 cm

17. For no TIR to take place, a prism can have a maximum refracting angle of (θ_C = critical angle for the material of prism)

(a) 60°   (b) θ_C (c) $2\theta_C$ (d) slightly less than 180°

18. A ray of light is incident at small angle I on the surface of prism of small angle A and emerges normally from the opposite surface. If the refractive index of the material of the prism is μ, the angle of incidence is nearly equal to

(a) $\dfrac{A}{\mu}$ (b) $\dfrac{A}{2\mu}$ (c) μA (d) $\mu A/2$

19. The refractive angle of a prism is A, and the refractive index of the material of the prism is $\cot (A/2)$. The angle of minimum deviation is

(a) $180° - 3A$ (b) $180° + 2A$ (c) $90° - A$ (d) $180° - 2A$

20. The focal length of a convex lens is f and the distance of an object from the first focus is x. The ratio of the size of the real image to the size of the object is

(a) $\dfrac{f}{x}$ (b) $\dfrac{x}{f}$ (c) $\dfrac{f+x}{f}$ (d) $\dfrac{f}{f+x}$

21. The focal length of a combination of two lenses is doubled if the separation between them is doubled. If the separation is increased to 4 times, the magnitude of focal length is (as compared to original)

(a) doubled   (b) quadrupled   (c) halved   (d) same

22. A convexo-concave convergent lens is made of glass of refractive index 1.5 and focal length 24 cm. Radius of curvature for one surface is double than that of the other. Then, radii of curvature for the two surfaces are (in cm)

(a) 6, 12   (b) 12, 24   (c) 3, 6   (d) 18, 36

23. An optical system consists of a thin convex lens of focal length 30 cm and a plane mirror placed 15 cm behind the lens. An object is placed 15 cm in front of the lens. The distance of the final image from the object is

(a) 60 cm   (b) 30 cm   (c) 75 cm   (d) 45 cm

24. In the figure shown, the angle made by the light ray with the normal in the medium of refractive index $\sqrt{2}$ is

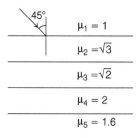

(a) 30° (b) 60° (c) 90° (d) None of these

25. For refraction through a small angled prism, the angle of minimum deviation
(a) increases with increase in refractive index of a prism
(b) will be 2δ for a ray of refractive index 2.4 if it is δ for a ray of refractive index 1.2
(c) is directly proportional to the angle of the prism
(d) will decrease with increase in refractive index of the prism

26. A ray of light passes from vacuum into a medium of refractive index n. If the angle of incidence is twice the angle of refraction, then the angle of incidence is
(a) $\cos^{-1}(n/2)$ (b) $\sin^{-1}(n/2)$ (c) $2\cos^{-1}(n/2)$ (d) $2\sin^{-1}(n/2)$

27. A thin convex lens of focal length 30 cm is placed in front of a plane mirror. An object is placed at a distance x from the lens (not in between lens and mirror) so that its final image coincides with itself . Then, the value of x is
(a) 15 cm (b) 30 cm (c) 60 cm (d) Insufficient data

28. One side of a glass slab is silvered as shown in the figure. A ray of light is incident on the other side at angle of incidence 45°. Refractive index of glass is given as $\sqrt{2}$. The deflection suffered by the ray when it comes out of the slab is

(a) 90° (b) 180° (c) 120° (d) 45°

29. A prism has refractive index $\sqrt{\dfrac{3}{2}}$ and refractive angle 90°. Find the minimum deviation produced by prism
(a) 60° (b) 45°
(c) 30° (d) 15°

30. An achromatic convergent doublet of two lenses in contact has a power of + 2 D. The convex lens has a power + 5 D. What is the ratio of the dispersive powers of the convergent and divergent lenses?
(a) 2 : 5 (b) 3 : 5
(c) 5 : 2 (d) 5 : 3

31. A point object is placed at a distance of 12 cm from a convex lens of focal length 10 cm. On the other side of the lens, a convex mirror is placed at a distance of 10 cm from the lens such that the image formed by the combination coincides with the object itself. The focal length of the convex mirror is

(a) 20 cm   (b) 25 cm

(c) 15 cm   (d) 30 cm

32. An object, a convex lens of focal length 20 cm and a plane mirror are arranged as shown in the figure. How far behind the mirror is the second image formed?

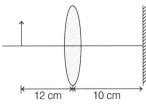

12 cm   10 cm

(a) 30 cm   (b) 20 cm

(c) 40 cm   (d) 50 cm

33. In Fig. (i), a lens of focal length 10 cm is shown. It is cut into two parts and placed as shown in Fig. (ii). An object AB of height 1 cm is placed at a distance of 7.5 cm. The height of the image will be

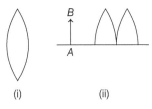

(i)   (ii)

(a) 2 cm   (b) 1 cm   (c) 1.5 cm   (d) 3 cm

34. The image for the converging beam after refraction through the curved surface is formed at

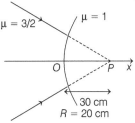

$\mu = 3/2$ $\mu = 1$

O P X

30 cm

$R = 20$ cm

(a) $x = 40$ cm   (b) $x = 40/3$ cm   (c) $x = -40/3$ cm   (d) $x = 20$ cm

35. From the figure shown, establish a relation between μ_1, μ_2 and μ_3

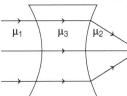

μ_1 μ_3 μ_2

(a) $\mu_1 < \mu_2 < \mu_3$ (b) $\mu_3 < \mu_2 ; \mu_3 = \mu_1$ (c) $\mu_3 > \mu_2 ; \mu_3 = \mu_1$ (d) None of these

36. When light of wavelength λ is incident on an equilateral prism, kept on its minimum deviation position, it is found that the angle of deviation equals the angle of the prism itself. The refractive index of the material of the prism for the wavelength λ is

(a) $\sqrt{3}$ (b) $\sqrt{3}/2$

(c) 2   (d) $\sqrt{2}$

37. White light is incident on the interface of glass and air as shown in the figure. If green light is just totally internally reflected, then the emerging ray in air contains

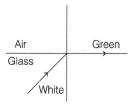

(a) yellow, orange, red   (b) violet, indigo, blue

(c) all colours   (d) all colours except green

38. An under water swimmer is at a depth of 12 m below the surface of water. A bird is at a height of 18 m from the surface of water, directly above his eyes. For the swimmer, the bird appears to be at a distance from the surface of water equal to (Refractive index of water is 4/3)

(a) 24 m   (b) 12 m

(c) 18 m   (d) 9 m

39. In the figure, an air lens of radii of curvature $10\, \text{cm}\,(R_1 = R_2 = 10\, \text{cm})$ is cut in a cylinder of glass $\left(\mu = \dfrac{3}{2}\right)$. The focal length and the nature of the lens is

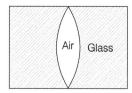

(a) 15 cm, concave

(b) 15 cm, convex

(c) ∞, neither concave nor convex

(d) 10 cm, concave

40. A ray of light is incident at the glass-water interface at an angle i, it emerges finally parallel to the surface of water then the value of μ_g would be

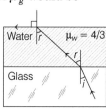

(a) (4/3) sin i (b) 1/sin i

(c) 4/3   (d) 1

41. P is a point on the axis of a concave mirror. The image of P, formed by the mirror, coincides with P. A rectangular glass slab of thickness t and refractive index μ is now introduced between P and the mirror. For the image of P to coincide with P again, the mirror must be moved.

(a) towards P by $(\mu - 1)t$
(b) away from P by $(\mu - 1)t$
(c) away from P by $t\left(1 - \dfrac{1}{\mu}\right)$
(d) towards P by $t\left(1 - \dfrac{1}{\mu}\right)$

42. In a plano-convex lens the radius of curvature of the convex lens is 10 cm. If the plane side is polished, then the focal length of this combination will be (Refractive index $= 1.5$)

(a) 20.5 cm
(b) 10 cm
(c) 15.5 cm
(d) 5 cm

43. A convex lens forms an image of an object on a screen 30 cm from the lens. When the lens is moved 90 cm towards the object, the image is again formed on the screen. Then, the focal length of the lens is

(a) 13 cm
(b) 24 cm
(c) 33 cm
(d) 40 cm

44. A point object O is placed on the principal axis of a convex lens of focal length $f = 20$ cm at a distance of 40 cm to the left of it. The diameter of the lens is 10 cm. An eye is placed 60 cm to right of the lens and a distance h below the principal axis. The maximum value of h to see the image is

(a) 7.5 cm
(b) 2.5 cm
(c) 5 cm
(d) 10 cm

45. Given a slab with index $n = 1.33$ and incident light striking the top horizontal face at angle i as shown in figure. The maximum value of i for which total internal reflection occurs at P is

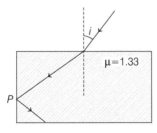

(a) $\sin^{-1}(\sqrt{0.77})$
(b) $\cos^{-1}(\sqrt{0.77})$
(c) $\sin^{-1}(0.77)$
(d) $\sin^{-1}(0.38)$

46. A plane mirror is placed horizontally inside water ($\mu = 4/3$). A ray falls normally on it. Then, mirror is rotated through an angle θ. The minimum value of θ for which ray does not come out of the water surface, is

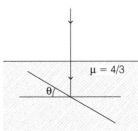

(a) $\pi/4$
(b) $\sin^{-1}\left(\dfrac{3}{4}\right)$
(c) $\dfrac{1}{2}\sin^{-1}\left(\dfrac{3}{4}\right)$
(d) $2\sin^{-1}\left(\dfrac{3}{4}\right)$

47. A, B and C are three optical media of respective critical angles C_1, C_2 and C_3 w.r.t. air. Total internal reflection of light can occur from A to B and also from B to C but not from C to A. Then, the correct relation between critical angles is
(a) $C_1 > C_2 > C_3$ (b) $C_1 = C_2 = C_3$ (c) $C_3 > C_1 > C_2$ (d) $C_1 < C_2 < C_3$

48. A point object O is placed in front of a glass rod having spherical end of radius of curvature 30 cm. The image would be formed at $(\mu_g = 3/2)$

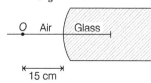

(a) 30 cm to the left   (b) infinity
(c) 10 cm to the right   (d) 18 cm to the left

49. A glass prism of refractive index 1.5 is immersed in water of refractive index 4/3. A light ray incident normally on face AB is totally reflected at face AC if

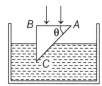

(a) $\sin \theta > 8/9$ (b) $\sin \theta < 2/3$
(c) $\sin \theta = \sqrt{3}/2$ (d) $2/3 < \sin \theta \leq 8/9$

50. A thin lens, made of glass of refractive index 3/2, produces a real and magnified image of an object in air. If the whole system, maintaining the same distance between the object and the lens, is immersed in water (RI = 4/3), then the image formed will be
(a) real, magnified   (b) real, diminished
(c) virtual, magnified   (d) virtual, diminished

51. The maximum value of refractive index of a prism which permits the transmission of light through it when the refracting angle of the prism is 90°, is given by
(a) 1.500   (b) 1.414   (c) 2.000   (d) 1.732

Subjective Questions

1. The laws of reflection or refraction are the same for sound as for light. The index of refraction of a medium (for sound) is defined as the ratio of the speed of sound in air 343 m/s to the speed of sound in the medium.
(a) What is the index of refraction (for sound) of water ($v = 1498$ m/s)?
(b) What is the critical angle θ, for total reflection of sound from water?

2. Light from a sodium lamp ($\lambda_0 = 589$ nm) passes through a tank of glycerin (refractive index = 1.47) 20 m long in a time t_1. If it takes a time t_2 to transverse the same tank when filled with carbon disulfide (index = 1.63), determine the difference $t_2 - t_1$.

3. A light beam of wavelength 600 nm in air passes through film 1 ($n_1 = 1.2$) of thickness 1.0 μm, then through film 2 (air) of thickness 1.5 μm, and finally through film 3 ($n_3 = 1.8$) of thickness 1.0 μm
(a) Which film does the light cross in the least time, and what is that least time?
(b) What are the total number of wavelengths (at any instant) across all three films together?

4. A plate with plane parallel faces having refractive index 1.8 rests on a plane mirror. A light ray is incident on the upper face of the plate at 60°. How far from the entry point will the ray emerge after reflection by the mirror. The plate is 6 cm thick.

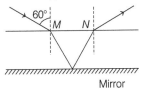

Mirror

5. In a certain spectrum produced by a glass prism of dispersive power 0.0305, it is found that the refractive index for the red ray is 1.645 and that for the violet ray is 1.665. What is the refractive index for the yellow ray?

6. The index of refraction of heavy flint glass is 1.68 at 434 nm and 1.65 at 671 nm. Calculate the difference in the angle of deviation of blue (434 nm) and red (671 nm) light incident at 65° on one side of a heavy flint glass prism with apex angle 60°.

7. Find the position of final image of an object O as shown in figure.

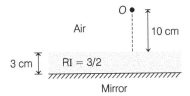

Mirror

8. One face of a rectangular glass plate 6 cm thick is silvered. An object held 8 cm in front of the unsilvered face forms an image 10 cm behind the silvered face. Find the refractive index of glass. Consider all the three steps.

9. A shallow glass dish is 4.00 cm wide at the bottom as shown in figure. When an observer's eye is positioned as shown, the observer sees the edge of the bottom of the empty dish. When this dish is filled with water, the observer sees the centre of the bottom of the dish. Find the height of the dish $\mu_w = 4/3$.

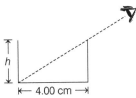

10. A glass prism in the shape of a quarter cylinder lies on a horizontal table. A uniform, horizontal light beam falls on its vertical plane surface as shown in the figure. If the radius of the cylinder is $R = 5$ cm and the refractive index of the glass is $n = 1.5$, where on the table beyond the cylinder, will a path of light be found?

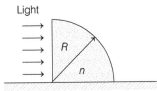

11. A glass sphere with 10 cm radius has a 5 cm radius spherical hole at its centre. A narrow beam of parallel light is directed into the sphere. Where, if anywhere, will the sphere produce an image? The index of refraction of the glass is 1.50.

12. A glass sphere has a radius of 5.0 cm and a refractive index of 1.6. A paperweight is constructed by slicing through the sphere on a plate that is 2.0 cm from the centre of the sphere and perpendicular to a radius of the sphere that passes through the centre of the circle formed by the intersection of the plane and the sphere. The paperweight is placed on a table and viewed from directly above an observer who is 8.0 cm from the table top, as shown in figure. When viewed through the paperweight, how far away does the table top appear to the observer?

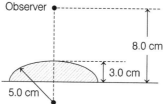

13. A fish is rising up vertically inside a pond with velocity 4 cm/s, and notices a bird, which is diving downward and its velocity appears to be 16 cm/s (to the fish). What is the real velocity of the diving bird, if refractive index of water is 4/3?

14. A lens with a focal length of 16 cm produces a sharp image of an object in two positions, which are 60 cm apart. Find the distance from the object to the screen.

15. Two glasses with refractive indices of 1.5 and 1.7 are used to make two identical double convex lenses.
    (a) Find the ratio between their focal lengths.
    (b) How will each of these lenses act on a ray parallel to its optical axis if the lenses are submerged into a transparent liquid with a refractive index of 1.6?

16. A converging beam of rays is incident on a diverging lens. Having passed through the lens the rays intersect at a point 15 cm from the lens. If the lens is removed, the point where the rays meet, move 5 cm closer to the mounting that holds the lens. Find the focal length of the lens.

17. A parallel beam of rays is incident on a convergent lens with a focal length of 40 cm. Where a divergent lens with a focal length of 15 cm be placed for the beam of rays to remain parallel after passing through the two lenses.

18. An achromatic convergent lens of focal length 150 cm is made by combining flint and crown glass lenses. Calculate the focal lengths of both the lenses and point out which one is divergent if the ratio of the dispersive power of flint and crown glasses is 3 : 2.

19. Determine the position of the image produced by an optical system consisting of a concave mirror with a focal length of 10 cm and a convergent lens with a focal length of 20 cm. The distance from the mirror to the lens is 30 cm and from the lens to the object is 40 cm. Consider only two steps. Plot the image.

20. A parallel beam of light is incident on a system consisting of three thin lenses with a common optical axis. The focal lengths of the lenses are equal to $f_1 = +10$ cm and $f_2 = -20$ cm, and $f_3 = +9$ cm respectively. The distance between the first and the second lens is 15 cm and between the second and the third is 5 cm. Find the position of the point at which the beam converges when it leaves the system of lenses.

21. A point source of light S is placed at the bottom of a vessel containing a liquid of refractive index 5/3. A person is viewing the source from above the surface. There is an opaque disc of radius 1 cm floating on the surface. The centre of the disc lies vertically above the source S. The liquid from the vessel is gradually drained out through a tap. What is the maximum height of the liquid for which the source cannot at all be seen from above?

22. A ray of light travelling in glass (μ_g = 3/2) is incident on a horizontal glass-air surface at the critical angle θ_C. If a thin layer of water (μ_w = 4/3) is now poured on the glass-air surface. At what angle will the ray of light emerges into water at glass-water surface?

23. An achromatic lens-doublet is formed by placing in contact a convex lens of focal length 20 cm and a concave lens of focal length 30 cm. The dispersive power of the material of the convex lens is 0.18.
(a) Determine the dispersive power of the material of the concave lens.
(b) Calculate the focal length of the lens-doublet.

24. Light is incident from glass $\left(\mu_g = \dfrac{3}{2}\right)$ to water $\left(\mu_w = \dfrac{4}{3}\right)$. Find the range of the angle of deviation for refracted light.

25. In an equilateral prism of $\mu = 1.5$, the condition for minimum deviation is fulfilled. If face AC is polished

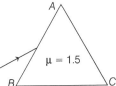

(a) Find the net deviation.
(b) If the system is placed in water what will be the net deviation for same angle of incidence?
Refractive index of water $= \dfrac{4}{3}$.

LEVEL 2

Single Correct Option

1. A bird is flying over a swimming pool at a height of 2 m from the water surface. If the bottom is perfectly plane reflecting surface and depth of swimming pool is 1 m, then the distance of final image of bird from the bird itself is μ_w = 4/3

(a) $\dfrac{11}{3}$ m   (b) $\dfrac{23}{3}$ m   (c) $\dfrac{11}{4}$ m   (d) $\dfrac{11}{2}$ m

2. A parallel narrow beam of light is incident on the surface of a transparent hemisphere of radius R and refractive index $\mu = 1.5$ as shown. The position of the image formed by refraction at the spherical surface only is

(a) $\dfrac{R}{2}$ (b) $3R$

(c) $\dfrac{R}{3}$ (d) $2R$

3. Consider the situation as shown in figure. The point O is the centre . The light ray forms an angle of 60° with the normal. The normal makes an angle 60° with the horizontal and each mirror makes an angle 60° with the normal. The value of refractive index of that spherical portion so that light ray retraces its path is

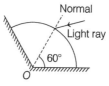

(a) $\sqrt{2}$

(b) $\dfrac{2}{\sqrt{3}}$

(c) $\dfrac{3}{2}$

(d) $\sqrt{3}$

4. The figure shows an equi-convex lens. What should be the condition of the refractive indices so that the lens becomes diverging?

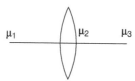

(a) $2\mu_3 > \mu_1 - \mu_2$
(c) $2\mu_2 > 2\mu_1 - \mu_3$

(b) $2\mu_2 < \mu_1 + \mu_3$
(d) None of these

5. An object is kept at a distance of 16 cm from a thin lens and the image formed is real. If the object is kept at a distance of 6 cm from the same lens, the image formed is virtual. If the sizes of the image formed are equal, the focal length of the lens will be

(a) 19 cm
(c) 21 cm

(b) 17 cm
(d) 11 cm

6. The apparent depth of water in cylindrical water tank of diameter $2R$ cm is reducing at the rate of x cm/min when water is being drained out at a constant rate. The amount of water drained in cc/min is (n_1 = refractive index of air, n_2 = refractive index of water)

(a) $\dfrac{x\pi R^2 n_1}{n_2}$

(b) $\dfrac{x\pi R^2 n_2}{n_1}$

(c) $\dfrac{2\pi R n_1}{n_2}$

(d) $\pi R^2 x$

7. A ray of light makes normal incidence on the diagonal face of a right angled prism as shown in figure. If $\theta = 37°$, then the angle of deviation after second step (from AB) is ($\sin 37° = 3/5$)

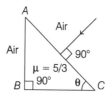

(a) 53°
(c) 106°

(b) 74°
(d) 90°

8. A bird in air looks at a fish directly below it inside in a transparent liquid in a tank. If the distance of the fish as estimated by the bird is h_1 and that of the bird as estimated by the fish is h_2, then the refractive index of the liquid is

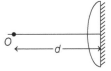

(a) $\dfrac{h_2}{h_1}$

(b) $\dfrac{h_1}{h_2}$

(c) $\dfrac{h_1 + h_2}{h_1 - h_2}$

(d) $\dfrac{h_1 - h_2}{h_1 + h_2}$

9. Diameter of the flat surface of a circular plano-convex lens is 6 cm and thickness at the centre is 3 mm. The radius of curvature of the curved part is

(a) 15 cm (b) 20 cm (c) 30 cm (d) 10 cm

10. When the object is at distances u_1 and u_2 from the optical centre of a convex lens, a real and a virtual image of the same magnification are obtained. The focal length of the lens is

(a) $\dfrac{u_1 - u_2}{2}$

(b) $u_1 + u_2$

(c) $\sqrt{u_1 u_2}$

(d) $\dfrac{u_1 + u_2}{2}$

11. Two convex lenses placed in contact form the image of a distant object at P. If the lens B is moved to the right, the image will

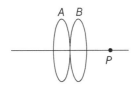

(a) move to the left
(b) move to the right
(c) remain at P
(d) move either to the left or right, depending upon focal lengths of the lenses

12. Two light rays 1 and 2 are incident on two faces AB and AC on an isosceles prism as shown in the figure. The rays emerge from the side BC. Then,

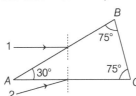

(a) minimum deviation of ray 1 > minimum deviation of ray 2
(b) minimum deviation of ray 1 < minimum deviation of ray 2
(c) minimum deviation of ray 1 = minimum deviation of ray 2
(d) Cannot be determined

13. Refractive index of a prism is $\sqrt{\dfrac{7}{3}}$ and the angle of prism is 60°. The limiting angle of incidence of a ray that will be transmitted through the prism is approximately

(a) 30° (b) 45° (c) 15° (d) None of these

14. A plano-convex thin lens of focal length 10 cm is silvered at its plane surface. The distance d at which an object must be kept in order to get its image on itself is

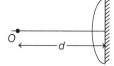

(a) 5 cm   (b) 20 cm

(c) 10 cm   (d) 2.5 cm

15. There is a small black dot at the centre C of a solid glass sphere of refractive index μ. When seen from outside, the dot will appear to be located

(a) away from the C for all values of μ

(b) at C for all values of μ.

(c) at C for $\mu = 1.5$, but away from C for μ not equal to 1.5

(d) at C for $2 < \mu < 1.5$

16. In the figure ABC is the cross-section of a right angled prism and $BCDE$ is the cross-section of a glass slab. The value of θ so that light incident normally on the face AB does not cross the face BC is (Given $\sin^{-1} 3/5 = 37°$)

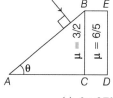

(a) $\theta < 37°$ (b) $\theta < 53°$ (c) $\theta \geq 37°$ (d) $\theta \geq 53°$

17. An object O is kept in air in front of a thin plano-convex lens of radius of curvature 10 cm. Its refractive index is 3/2 and the medium towards right of the plane surface is water of refractive index 4/3. What should be distance x of the object so that the rays become parallel finally?

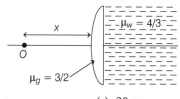

(a) 5 cm   (b) 10 cm   (c) 20 cm   (d) 15 cm

18. If a symmetrical bi-concave thin lens is cut into two identical halves, and they are placed in different ways as shown, then

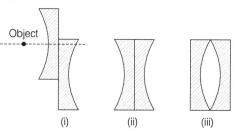

(a) three images will be formed in case (i)

(b) two images will be formed in case (ii)

(c) the ratio of focal lengths in (ii) and (iii) is 1

(d) the ratio of focal lengths in (ii) and (iii) is 2

19. If an object is placed at $A\,(OA > f)$; where f is the focal length of the lens, the image is formed at B. A perpendicular is erected at O and C is chosen on it such that the angle $\angle BCA$ is a right angle. Then, the value of f will be

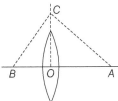

(a) $\dfrac{AB}{OC^2}$ (b) $\dfrac{(AC)\,(BC)}{OC}$ (c) $\dfrac{OC^2}{AB}$ (d) $\dfrac{(OC)\,(AB)}{AC + BC}$

20. An object is seen through a glass slab of thickness 36 cm and refractive index 3/2. The observer, and the slab are dipped in water ($\mu = 4/3$). The shift produced in the position of the object is
(a) 12 cm   (b) 4 cm   (c) 6 cm   (d) 8 cm

21. How much water should be filled in a container of height 21 cm, so that it appears half filled to the observer when viewed from the top of the container ($\mu = 4/3$).
(a) 8 cm   (b) 10.5 cm   (c) 12 cm   (d) 14 cm

22. Optic axis of a thin equi-convex lens is the x-axis. The co-ordinates of a point object and its image are $(-40\text{ cm}, 1\text{ cm})$ and $(50\text{ cm}, -2\text{ cm})$, respectively. Lens is located at
(a) $x = 20$ cm   (b) $x = -30$ cm   (c) $x = -10$ cm   (d) origin

23. A thin plano-convex lens acts like a concave mirror of radius of curvature 20 cm when its plane surface is silvered. The radius of curvature of the curved surface if index of refraction of its material is 1.5 will be
(a) 40 cm   (b) 30 cm   (c) 10 cm   (d) 20 cm

24. If the optic axis of convex and concave lenses are separated by a distance 5 mm as shown in the figure. Find the coordinate of the final image formed by the combination if parallel beam of light is incident on lens. Origin is at the optical centre of convex lens

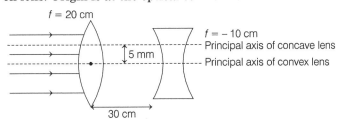

(a) (25 cm, 0.5 cm)   (b) (25 cm, 0.25 cm)   (c) (25 cm, -0.5 cm)   (d) (25 cm, -2.5 cm)

25. A light source S is placed at the centre of a glass sphere of radius R and refractive index μ. The maximum angle θ with the x-axis (as shown in the figure) an incident light ray can make without suffering total internal reflection is

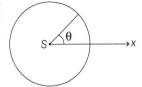

(a) $\cos^{-1}\left(\dfrac{1}{\mu}\right)$ (b) $\sin^{-1}\left(\dfrac{1}{\mu}\right)$

(c) $\tan^{-1}\left(\dfrac{1}{\mu}\right)$ (d) there will never be total internal reflection

26. A sphere $\left(\mu = \dfrac{4}{3}\right)$ of radius 1 m has a small cavity of diameter 1 cm at its centre. An observer who is looking at it from right, sees the magnification of diameter of the cavity as

(a) $\dfrac{4}{3}$ (b) $\dfrac{3}{4}$

(c) 1 (d) 0.5

27. An equi-convex lens of $\mu = 1.5$ and $R = 20$ cm is cut into two equal parts along its axis. Two parts are then separated by a distance of 120 cm (as shown in figure). An object of height 3 mm is placed at a distance of 30 cm to the left of first half lens. The final image will form at

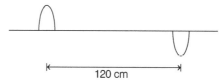

(a) 120 cm to the right of first half lens, 3 mm in size and inverted
(b) 150 cm to the right of first half lens, 3 mm in size and erect
(c) 120 cm to the right of first half lens, 4 mm in size and inverted
(d) 150 cm to the right of first half lens, 4 mm in size and erect

28. As shown in the figure, region *BCDEF* and *ABFG* are of refractive index 2.0 and 1.5 respectively. A particle *O* is kept at the mid of *DH*. Image of the object as seen by the eye is at a distance

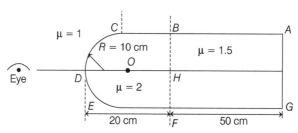

(a) 10 cm from point *D* (b) 22.5 cm from point *D*
(c) 30 cm from point *D* (d) 20 cm from point *D*

29. A point object *O* is placed at a distance of 20 cm from a convex lens of focal length 10 cm as shown in the figure. At what distance *x* from the lens should a convex mirror of focal length 60 cm, be placed so that final image coincide with the object?

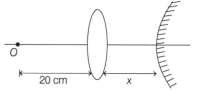

(a) 10 cm
(b) 40 cm
(c) 20 cm
(d) Final image can never coincide with the object in the given conditions

30. A flat glass slab of thickness 6 cm and index 1.5 is placed in front of a plane mirror. An observer is standing behind the glass slab and looking at the mirror. The actual distance of the observer from the mirror is 50 cm. The distance of his image from himself, as seen by the observer is

(a) 94 cm (b) 96 cm
(c) 98 cm (d) 100 cm

31. Distance of an object from the first focus of an equi-convex lens is 10 cm and the distance of its real image from second focus is 40 cm. The focal length of the lens is
(a) 25 cm (b) 10 cm (c) 20 cm (d) 40 cm

32. A cubical block of glass of refractive index n_1 is in contact with the surface of water of refractive index n_2. A beam of light is incident on vertical face of the block. After refraction a total internal reflection at the base and refraction at the opposite face take place. The ray emerges at angle θ as shown. The value of θ is given by

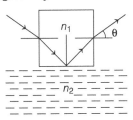

(a) $\sin \theta < \sqrt{n_1^2 - n_2^2}$

(b) $\cos \theta < \sqrt{n_1^2 - n_2^2}$

(c) $\sin \theta < \dfrac{1}{\sqrt{n_1^2 - n_2^2}}$

(d) $\cos \theta < \dfrac{1}{\sqrt{n_1^2 - n_2^2}}$

33. A concave mirror of focal length 2 cm is placed on a glass slab as shown in the figure. The image of point object O formed due to reflection at mirror and then refraction by the slab
(a) is virtual and at 2 cm from pole of the concave mirror
(b) is virtual and on the pole of mirror
(c) is real and on the object itself
(d) None of the above

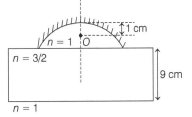

34. Two refracting media are separated by a spherical interface as shown in the figure. AB is the principal axis, μ_1 and μ_2 are the refractive indices of medium of incidence and medium of refraction respectively. Then,

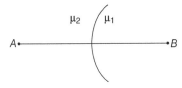

(a) if $\mu_2 > \mu_1$, then there cannot be a real image of real object
(b) if $\mu_2 > \mu_1$, then there cannot be a real image of virtual object
(c) if $\mu_1 > \mu_2$, then there cannot be a real image of virtual object
(d) if $\mu_1 > \mu_2$, then there cannot be a virtual image of virtual object

35. A convex spherical refracting surface separates two media glass and air ($\mu_g = 1.5$). If the image is to be real, at what minimum distance u should the object be placed in air if R is the radius of curvature
(a) $u > 3R$ (b) $u > 2R$ (c) $u < 4R$ (d) $u < R$

36. An object is moving towards a converging lens on its axis. The image is also found to be moving towards the lens. Then, the object distance u must satisfy
(a) $2f < u < 4f$ (b) $f < u < 2f$ (c) $u > 4f$ (d) $u < f$

37. Two diverging lenses are kept as shown in figure. The final image formed will be

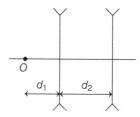

(a) virtual for any value of d_1 and d_2
(b) real for any value of d_1 and d_2
(c) virtual or real depends on d_1 and d_2 only
(d) virtual or real depends on d_1 and d_2 and also on the focal lengths of the lens

38. In the figure shown, a point object O is placed in air on the principal axis. The radius of curvature of the spherical surface is 60 cm. I is the final image formed after all reflections and refractions.

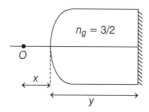

(a) If $x = 120$ cm, then I is formed on O for any value of y
(b) If $x = 240$ cm, then I is formed on O only if $y = 360$ cm
(c) If $x = 240$ cm, then I is formed on O for any value of y
(d) None of the above

39. In the figure, a point object O is placed in air. A spherical boundary separates two media of radius of curvature 1.0 m. AB is principal axis. The separation between the images formed due to refraction from two halves of the spherical surface is

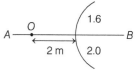

(a) 12 m   (b) 20 m
(c) 14 m   (d) 10 m

40. A ray incident at a point at an angle of incidence of 60° enters a glass sphere of refractive index $n = \sqrt{3}$ and is reflected and refracted at the other surface of the sphere. The angle between the reflected and refracted rays at this surface is
(a) 50°   (b) 60°   (c) 90°   (d) 40°

41. If the distances of an object and its virtual image from the focus of a convex lens of focal length f are 1 cm each, then f is
(a) 4 cm   (b) $(\sqrt{2} + 1)$ cm
(c) $2\sqrt{2}$ cm   (d) $(2 + \sqrt{2})$ cm

42 A circular beam of light (diameter $= d$) falls on a plane surface of a liquid. The angle of incidence is 45° and refractive index of the liquid is μ. The diameter of the refracted beam is
(a) d (b) $(\mu - 1)d$ (c) $\dfrac{\sqrt{2\mu^2 - 1}}{\mu} d$ (d) $\dfrac{\sqrt{\mu^2 - 1}}{\mu} d$

43. A convex lens of focal length 30 cm forms a real image three times larger than the object on a screen. Object and screen are moved until the image becomes twice the size of the object. If the shift of the object is 5 cm, then the shift of screen is
(a) 30 cm (b) 14 cm (c) 18 cm (d) 16 cm

44. A concave mirror is placed at the bottom of an empty tank with face upwards and axis vertical. When sunlight falls normally on the mirror, it is focussed at distance of 32 cm from the mirror. If the tank is filled with water $\left(\mu = \dfrac{4}{3}\right)$ upto a height of 20 cm, then the sunlight will now get focussed at
(a) 16 cm above water level (b) 9 cm above water level
(c) 24 cm below water level (d) 9 cm below water level

45. The graph shows how the inverse of magnification $\dfrac{1}{m}$ produced by a convex thin lens varies with object distance u. What was the focal length of the lens used?

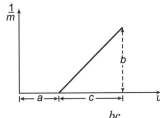

(a) $\dfrac{b}{c}$ (b) $\dfrac{b}{ca}$ (c) $\dfrac{bc}{a}$ (d) $\dfrac{c}{b}$

46. A ball is dropped from a height of 20 m above the surface of water in a lake. The refractive index of water is 4/3. A fish inside the lake, in the line of fall of the ball, is looking at the ball. At an instant, when the ball is 12.8 m above the water surface, the fish sees the speed of ball as $(g = 10 \, \text{m/s}^2)$
(a) 9 m/s (b) 12 m/s
(c) 16 m/s (d) 21.33 m/s

47. The diagram shown in figure represents a wavefront AB which passes from air to another transparent medium and produces a new wavefront CD after refraction.

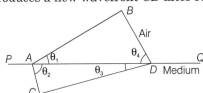

The refractive index of the medium is (PQ is the boundary between air and the medium)
(a) $\dfrac{\cos \theta_1}{\cos \theta_3}$ (b) $\dfrac{\cos \theta_4}{\cos \theta_1}$ (c) $\dfrac{\sin \theta_1}{\sin \theta_3}$ (d) $\dfrac{\sin \theta_2}{\sin \theta_3}$

48. The xz-plane separates two media A and B with refractive indices μ_1 and μ_2, respectively. A ray of light travels from A and B. Its directions in the two media are given by the unit vectors $\hat{r}_A = a\hat{i} + b\hat{j}$ and $\hat{r}_B = \alpha\hat{i} + \beta\hat{j}$ respectively, where $\hat{i}$ and $\hat{j}$ are unit vectors in the x and y-directions. Then,
(a) $\mu_1 a = \mu_2 \alpha$ (b) $\mu_1 \alpha = \mu_2 a$
(c) $\mu_1 b = \mu_2 \beta$ (d) None of these

49. In a lake, a fish rising vertically to the surface of water uniformly at the rate of 3 m/s, observes a bird diving vertically towards the water at the rate of 9 m/s. The actual velocity of the dive of the bird is (Given, refractive index of water = 4/3)

    (a) 3.6 m/s   (b) 4.5 m/s   (c) 6.0 m/s   (d) 12.0 m/s

50. A ray of light travels from an optically denser medium towards rarer medium. The critical angle for the two media is C. The maximum possible angle of deviation of the ray is

    (a) $\dfrac{\pi}{2} - C$ (b) $\dfrac{\pi}{2} - 2C$ (c) $2C$ (d) $\dfrac{\pi}{2} + C$

51. To remove myopia (short sightedness) a lens of power 0.66 D is required. The distant point of the eye is approximately

    (a) 100 cm   (b) 151.5 cm   (c) 50 cm   (d) 25 cm

52. A spherical surface of radius of curvature R, separates air (refractive index 1.0) from glass (refractive index 1.5). The centre of curvature is in the glass. A point object P placed in air is found to have a real image Q in the glass. The line PQ cuts the surface at a point O and $PO = OQ$. The distance PO is equal to

    (a) 5 R (b) 3 R (c) 2 R (d) 1.5 R

More than One Correct Option

1. n number of identical equilateral prisms are kept in contact as shown in figure. If deviation through a single prism is δ. Then, (n, m are integers)

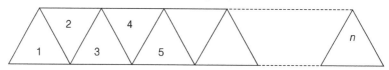

    (a) if $n = 2m$, deviation through n prisms is zero
    (b) if $n = 2m + 1$, deviation through system of n prisms is δ
    (c) if $n = 2m$, deviation through system of n prisms is δ
    (d) if $n = 2m + 1$, deviation through system of n prisms is zero

2. A ray of monochromatic light is incident on the plane surface of separation between two media x and y with angle of incidence i in the medium x and angle of refraction r in the medium y. The graph shows the relation between $\sin i$ and $\sin r$.

    (a) The speed of light in the medium y is $\sqrt{3}$ times than in medium x
    (b) The speed of light in the medium y is $\dfrac{1}{\sqrt{3}}$ times than in medium x

    (c) The total internal reflection can take place when the incidence is in x
    (d) The total internal reflection can take place when the incidence is in y

3. Which of the following statement(s) is/are true?
    (a) In vacuum the speed of red colour is more than that of violet colour
    (b) An object in front of a mirror is moved towards the pole of a spherical mirror from infinity, it is found that image also moves towards the pole. The mirror must be convex
    (c) There exist two angles of incidence in a prism for which angles of deviation are same except minimum deviation
    (d) A ray travels from a rarer medium to denser medium. There exist three angles of incidence for which the deviation is same

4. A lens of focal length f is placed in between an object and screen at a distance D. The lens forms two real images of object on the screen for two of its different positions, a distance x apart. The two real images have magnifications m_1 and m_2 respectively ($m_1 > m_2$). Choose the correct statement(s).

(a) $m_1 m_2 = -1$

(b) $m_1 m_2 = 1$

(c) $f = \dfrac{D^2 - x^2}{4D}$

(d) $D > 4f$

5. Which of the following quantities increase when wavelength of light is increased? Consider only the magnitudes.

(a) The power of a converging lens

(b) The focal length of a converging lens

(c) The power of a diverging lens

(d) The focal length of a diverging lens

Comprehension Based Questions

Passage : (Q. No. 1 to 3)

A plano-convex lens P and a concavo-convex lens Q are in contact as shown in figure. The refractive index of the material of the lens P and Q is 1.8 and 1.2 respectively. The radius of curvature of the concave surface of the lens Q is double the radius of curvature of the convex surface. The convex surface of Q is silvered.

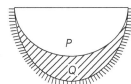

1. An object is placed on the principal axis at a distance 10 cm from the plane surface. The image is formed at a distance 40 cm from the plane surface on the same side. The focal length of the system is

(a) -8 cm

(b) 8 cm

(c) $-\dfrac{40}{3}$ cm

(d) $\dfrac{40}{3}$ cm

2. The radius of curvature of common surface is

(a) 48 cm

(b) 24 cm

(c) 12 cm

(d) 8 cm

3. If the plane surface of P is silvered as shown in figure, the system acts as

(a) convex mirror of focal length 24 cm

(b) concave mirror of focal length 8 cm

(c) concave mirror of focal length 24 cm

(d) convex mirror of focal length 8 cm

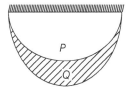

Match the Columns

1. Match the following two columns for a convex lens corresponding to object position shown in Column I.

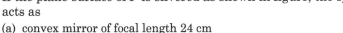

	Column I		Column II
(a)	Between O and F_1	(p)	Real
(b)	Between F_1 and $2F_1$	(q)	Virtual
(c)	Between O and F_2	(r)	Erect
(d)	Between F_2 and $2F_2$	(s)	Inverted

Note $O \to$ optical centre, $F_1 \to$ first focus and $F_2 \to$ second focus.

2. Match the following two columns for a concave lens corresponding to object position shown in Column II.

Column I	Column II
(a) Between O and F_1	(p) Real
(b) Between F_1 and $2F_1$	(q) Virtual
(c) Between O and F_2	(r) Erect
(d) Between F_2 and $2F_2$	(s) Inverted

3. Match the following two columns corresponding to single refraction from plane surface. In all cases shown in Column I, $\mu_1 > \mu_2$.

Column I	Column II
(a)	(p) Image distance greater than x from plane surface
(b)	(q) Image distance less than x from plane surface
(c)	(r) Real image
(d)	(s) Virtual image

4. Match the following two columns.

Column I	Column II
(a)	(p) Real image
(b)	(q) Virtual image

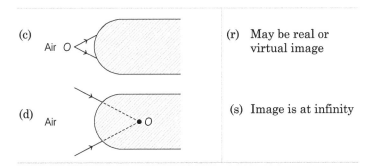

(c)	(r)	May be real or virtual image
(d)	(s)	Image is at infinity

5. A convex lens L_1 and a concave lens L_2 have refractive index 1.5. Match the following two columns.

Column I	Column II
(a) L_1 is immersed in a liquid of refractive index 1.4	(p) Lens will behave as convex lens
(b) L_1 is immersed in a liquid of refractive index 1.6	(q) Lens will behave as concave lens
(c) L_2 is immersed in a liquid of refractive index 1.4	(r) Magnitude of power of lens will increase
(d) L_2 is immersed in a liquid of refractive index 1.6	(s) Magnitude of power of lens will decrease

6. Consider a linear extended object that could be real or virtual with its length at right angles to the optic axis of a lens. With regard to image formation by lenses.

Column I	Column II
(a) Image of the same size as the object	(p) Concave lens in case of real object
(b) Virtual image of a size greater than the object	(q) Convex lens in case of real object
(c) Real image of a size smaller than the object	(r) Concave lens in case of virtual object
(d) Real and magnified image	(s) Convex lens in case of virtual object

7. Match Column I (Phenomenon) with Column II (Principle) and select the correct answer using the codes given below the lists.

Column I (Phenomenon)	Column II (Principle)
(a) Blue colour of a sky	(p) Total internal reflection
(b) Glittering of diamond	(q) Dispersion of light
(c) Formation of rainbow	(r) Scattering of light
(d) In the evening when the sun goes down below the horizon, it continues to remain visible for sometime	(s) Refraction of light

Subjective Questions

1. Figure shows the optical axis of a lens, the point source of light A and its virtual image A'. Trace the rays to find the position of the lens and of its principal focus. What type of lens is it?

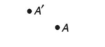

2. Solve the problem similar to the previous one if A and A' are interchanged.

3. In figure, a fish watcher watches a fish through a 3.0 cm thick glass wall of a fish tank. The watcher is in level with the fish; the index of refraction of the glass is 8/5 and that of the water is 4/3.

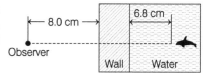

    (a) To the fish, how far away does the watcher appear to be?

    (b) To the watcher, how far away does the fish appear to be?

4. A concave spherical mirror with a radius of curvature of 0.2 m is filled with water. What is the focal length of this system? Refractive index of water is 4/3.

5. A convexo-convex lens has a focal length of $f_1 = 10$ cm. One of the lens surfaces having a radius of curvature of $R = 10$ cm is coated with silver. Construct the image of the object produced by the given optical system and determine the position of the image if the object is at a distance of $a = 15$ cm from the lens. Refractive index of lens $= 1.5$.

6. A lens with a focal length of $f = 30$ cm produces on a screen a sharp image of an object that is at a distance of $a = 40$ cm from the lens. A plane parallel plate with thickness of $d = 9$ cm is placed between the lens and the object perpendicular to the optical axis of the lens. Through what distance should the screen be shifted for the image of the object to remain distinct? The refractive index of the glass of the plate is $\mu = 1.8$.

7. One side of radius of curvature $R_2 = 120$ cm of a convexo-convex lens of material of refractive index $\mu = 1.5$ and focal length $f_1 = 40$ cm is slivered. It is placed on a horizontal surface with silvered surface in contact with it. Another convex lens of focal length $f_2 = 20$ cm is fixed coaxially $d = 10$ cm above the first lens. A luminous point object O on the axis gives rise to an image coincident with it. Find its height above the upper lens.

8. A small object is placed on the principal axis of concave spherical mirror of radius 20 cm at a distance of 30 cm. By how much will the position of the image alter only after mirror, when a parallel-sided slab of glass of thickness 6 cm and refractive index 1.5 is introduced between the centre of curvature and the object? The parallel sides are perpendicular to the principal axis.

9. A thin glass lens of refractive index $\mu_2 = 1.5$ behaves as an interface between two media of refractive indices $\mu_1 = 1.4$ and $\mu_3 = 1.6$ respectively. Determine the focal length of the lens for the shown arrangement of radius of curvature of both the surfaces 20 cm.

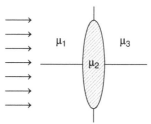

10. A glass hemisphere of radius 10 cm and $\mu = 1.5$ is silvered over its curved surface. There is an air bubble in the glass 5 cms from the plane surface along the axis. Find the position of the images of this bubble seen by observer looking along the axis into the flat surface of the atmosphere.

11. An equilateral prism of flint glass ($\mu_g = 3/2$) is placed inside water ($\mu_w = 4/3$).

(a) At what angle should a ray of light fall on the face of the prism so that inside the prism the ray is perpendicular to the bisector of the angle of the prism.

(b) Through what angle will the ray turn after passing through both faces of the prism?

12. Rays of light fall on the plane surface of a half cylinder at an angle 45° in the plane perpendicular to the axis (see figure). Refractive index of glass is $\sqrt{2}$. Discuss the condition that the rays do not suffer total internal reflection.

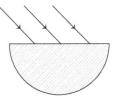

13. The figure shows an arrangement of an equi-convex lens and a concave mirror. A point object O is placed on the principal axis at a distance 40 cm from the lens such that the final image is also formed at the position of the object. If the radius of curvature of the concave mirror is 80 cm, find the distance d. Also draw the ray diagram. The focal length of the lens in air is 20 cm.

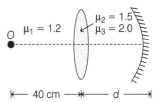

14. A convex lens is held 45 cm above the bottom of an empty tank. The image of a point at the bottom of a tank is formed 36 cm above the lens. Now, a liquid is poured into the tank to a depth of 40 cm. It is found that the distance of the image of the same point on the bottom of the tank is 48 cm above the lens. Find the refractive index of the liquid.

15. A parallel beam of light falls normally on the first face of a prism of a small angle. At the second face it is partly transmitted and partly reflected. The reflected beam striking at the first face again emerges from it in a direction making an angle of 6° 30′ with the reversed direction of the incident beam. The refracted beam is found to have undergone a deviation of 1°15 from the original direction. Calculate the refractive index of the glass and the angle of the prism.

16. Two converging lenses of the same focal length f are separated by a distance $2f$. The axis of the second lens is inclined at angle $\theta = 60°$ with respect to the axis of the first lens. A parallel paraxial beam of light is incident from left side of the lens. Find the coordinates of the final image with respect to the origin of the first lens.

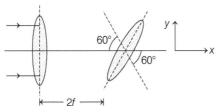

17. A thin converging lens of focal length $f = 1.5$ m is placed along y-axis such that its optical centre coincides with the origin. A small light source S is placed at $(-2.0$ m, 0.1 m$)$. Where should a plane mirror inclined at an angle θ, $\tan \theta = 0.3$ be placed such that y-coordinate of final image is 0.3 m, i.e. find d. Also find x-coordinate of final image.

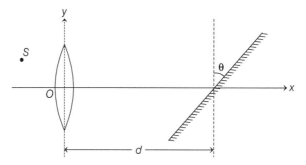

18. A spherical ball of transparent material has index of refraction μ. A narrow beam of light AB is aimed as shown. What must the index of refraction be in order that the light is focused at the point C on the opposite end of the diameter from where the light entered? Given that $x \ll R$.

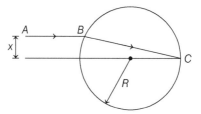

19. A ray incident on a droplet of water at an angle of incidence i undergoes two reflections (not total) and emerges. If the deviation suffered by the ray is minimum and the refractive index of the droplet be μ, then show that $\cos i = \sqrt{\dfrac{\mu^2 - 1}{8}}$.

20. A convex lens of focal length 15 cm is split into two halves and the two halves are placed at a separation of 120 cm. Between the two halves of convex lens a plane mirror is placed horizontally and at a distance of 4 mm below the principal axis of the lens halves. An object of length 2 mm is placed at a distance of 20 cm from one half lens as shown in figure.

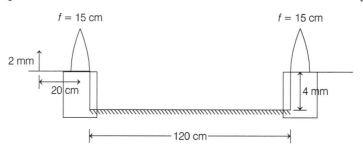

(a) Find the position and size of the final image.
(b) Trace the path of rays forming the image.

21. A cylindrical glass rod of radius 0.1 m and refractive index $\sqrt{3}$ lies on a horizontal plane mirror. A horizontal ray of light moving perpendicular to the axis of the rod is incident on it. At what height from the mirror should the ray be incident so that it leaves the rod at a height of 0.1 m above the plane mirror? At what centre to centre distance a second similar rod, parallel to the first, be placed on the mirror, such that the emergent ray from the second rod is in line with the incident ray on the first rod?

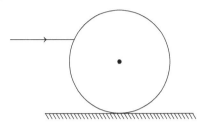

22. A transparent solid sphere of radius 2 cm and density ρ floats in a transparent liquid of density 2ρ kept in a beaker. The bottom of the beaker is spherical in shape with radius of curvature 8 cm and is silvered to make it concave mirror as shown in the figure. When an object is placed at a distance of 10 cm directly above the centre of the sphere C, its final image coincides with it. Find h (as shown in the figure), the height of the liquid surface in the beaker from the apex of the bottom. Consider the paraxial rays only. The refractive index of the sphere is 3/2 and that of the liquid is 4/3.

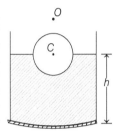

23. A hollow sphere of glass of refractive index μ has a small mark on its interior surface which is observed from a point outside the sphere on the side opposite the centre. The inner cavity is concentric with external surface and the thickness of the glass is everywhere equal to the radius of the inner surface. Prove that the mark will appear nearer than it really is, by a distance $\dfrac{(\mu - 1)\, R}{(3\mu - 1)}$, where R is the radius of the inner surface.

24. A ray of light is refracted through a sphere whose material has a refractive index μ in such a way that it passes through the extremities of two radii which make an angle β with each other. Prove that if α is the deviation of the ray caused by its passage through the sphere, then

$$\cos\left(\frac{\beta - \alpha}{2}\right) = \mu\ \cos\left(\frac{\beta}{2}\right)$$

25. A man of height 2.0 m is standing on a level road where because of temperature variation the refractive index of air is varying as $\mu = \sqrt{1 + ay}$, where y is height from road. If $a = 2.0 \times 10^{-6}\,\mathrm{m^{-1}}$. Then, find distant point that he can see on the road.

26. A glass rod has ends as shown in figure. The refractive index of glass is μ. The object O is at a distance $2R$ from the surface of larger radius of curvature. The distance between apexes of ends is $3R$. Find the distance of image formed of the point object from right hand vertex. What is the condition to be satisfied if the image is to be real?

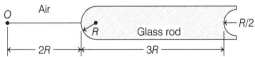

Answers

Introductory Exercise 31.1

1. 2

2. The frequency does not change, while the wavelength and speed change by the factor μ_1 / μ_2.

3. 1.67

Introductory Exercise 31.2

1. $\sqrt{3}$

2. $\dfrac{3}{2}$

Introductory Exercise 31.3

1. (a) $\dfrac{50}{3}$ cm   (b) 25 cm

Introductory Exercise 31.4

1. $\dfrac{125}{3}$ cm

Introductory Exercise 31.5

2. 8.57 cm

3. (a) 45.0 cm (b) −90.0 cm (c) −6.0 cm

4. Inside the bowl at −9.0 cm

5. 4.0 cm

Introductory Exercise 31.6

1. 39 cm

2. 18.75 cm from the lens, 5.3 cm

4. From the surface to infinity on object side

5. (a) 36 cm (b) 36 cm

6. 40 cm

8. 12 cm

9. 1.5

10. 2 cm

11. 16 cm

12. −40.0 cm

13. 10.0 cm.

Introductory Exercise 31.7

1. 1.5

2. $\mu = 1.3, \theta_C = \sin^{-1}(0.77)$

3. (a) $\theta = \sin^{-1}\left(\dfrac{13}{16}\right)$ (b) Yes

Introductory Exercise 31.8

1. 46°

2. C

3. $\mu \leq \sqrt{2}$

4. $\sin^{-1}(2/3) = 42°$

5. $\mu = \sqrt{3}$

6. 90°

7. 0°

8. $\sqrt{2}$

9. 9°

Exercises

LEVEL 1

Assertion and Reason

1. (b)   *2.* (a,b)   *3.* (d)   *4.* (c)   *5.* (d)   *6.* (d)   *7.* (a)   *8.* (a or b)   *9.* (c)   *10.* (c)

Objective Questions

1. (c)	2. (b)	3. (c)	4. (d)	5. (a)	6. (c)	7. (c)	8. (b)	9. (b)	10. (a)
11. (b)	12. (b)	13. (b)	14. (b)	15. (a)	16. (d)	17. (c)	18. (c)	19. (d)	20. (a)
21. (a)	22. (a)	23. (d)	24. (a)	25. (a)	26. (c)	27. (b)	28. (a)	29. (c)	30. (b)
31. (b)	32. (c)	33. (a)	34. (a)	35. (b)	36. (a)	37. (a)	38. (a)	39. (a)	40. (b)
41. (c)	42. (b)	43. (b)	44. (b)	45. (a)	46. (c)	47. (d)	48. (a)	49. (a)	50. (c)
51. (b)									

Subjective Questions

1. (a) 0.229 (b) 13.2°   2. 1.07×10^{-8} s
3. (a) First film, $t_{min} = 4 \times 10^{-15}$ s (b) 7.5
4. 6.6 cm
5. $\mu_y = 1.656$
6. 2.8°   7. 11 cm behind mirror   8. 1.5
9. 2.4 cm   10. 1.71 cm   11. 4.67 cm to the left of extreme right edge
12. 7.42 cm   13. 9 cm/s   14. 100 cm
15. (a) 1.4 (b) The first lens will be a diverging and the second a converging one
16. $f = -30$ cm   17. 25 cm   18. 50 cm, −75 cm, divergent lens is of flint glass
19. 5 cm from mirror towards the lens
20. Ray will become parallel to the optic axis.   21. $\frac{4}{3}$ cm   22. $\sin^{-1}(3/4)$
23. (a) 0.27 (b) 60 cm   24. 0 to $\cos^{-1}(8/9)$ 25. (a) 157.2° (b) 157.2°

LEVEL 2

Single Correct Option

1. (d)	2. (b)	3. (d)	4. (b)	5. (d)	6. (b)	7. (b)	8. (a)	9. (a)	10. (d)
11. (b)	12. (c)	13. (a)	14. (c)	15. (b)	16. (a)	17. (c)	18. (c)	19. (c)	20. (b)
21. (d)	22. (c)	23. (c)	24. (b)	25. (d)	26. (a)	27. (b)	28. (a)	29. (c)	30. (b)
31. (c)	32. (a)	33. (d)	34. (d)	35. (b)	36. (d)	37. (a)	38. (a)	39. (a)	40. (c)
41. (b)	42. (c)	43. (a)	44. (b)	45. (d)	46. (c)	47. (c)	48. (a)	49. (b)	50. (a)
51. (b)	52. (a)								

More than One Correct Options

1. (a,b)   2. (b,d)   3. (b,c)   4. (b,c,d)   5. (b,d)

Comprehension Based Questions

1. (a)   2. (a)   3. (c)

Match the Columns

1. (a) → q,r   (b) → p,s   (c) → p,r   (d) → p,r
2. (a) → p,r   (b) → q,s   (c) → q,r   (d) → q,r
3. (a) → q,s   (b) → q,r   (c) → p,s   (d) → p,r
4. (a) → q   (b) → r   (c) → r   (d) → p
5. (a) → p,s   (b) → q,s   (c) → q,s   (d) → p,s
6. (a) → q,r   (b) → q,r   (c) → q,r   (d) → q,r
7. (a) → r   (b) → p   (c) → q   (d) → s

Subjective Questions

1. Lens is convex
2. Lens is concave
3. (a) 20.0 cm   (b) 14.975 cm
4. $F = -7.5$ cm (concave mirror)
5. At a distance of 3.0 cm from the system
6. 60 cm away from the lens
7. 10 cm
8. $\Delta v = 0.55$ cm
9. $f = \infty$
10. First image at a distance of 3.33 cm from flat surface and the second at infinity
11. (a) 34.2°   (b) 8.4°
12. Maximum distance of the incident rays from the centre should be $\sqrt{\dfrac{2}{3}} R$, where R is the radius of hemisphere
13. 30 cm
14. 1.37
15. $A = 2°, \mu = 1.62$
16. (0, 0)
17. $d = 5.0$ m, x co-ordinate of final image = 4.0 m
18. $\mu = 2$
20. (a) Final image is at a distance of 20 cm behind the second half lens and at a distance of 2/3 mm above the principal axis. The size of image is 2 mm and is inverted as compared to the given object
21. 0.186 m, 0.315 m
22. $h \approx 15$ cm
25. $x_{max} = 2000$ m = 2 km
26. Distance $= \dfrac{R(9 - 4\mu)}{(10\mu - 9)(\mu - 2)}$, for final image to be real μ should lie between 2 and 2.25

32

INTERFERENCE AND DIFFRACTION OF LIGHT

32.1 **Principle of Superposition**

Suppose there are two sources of waves S_1 and S_2.

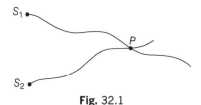

Fig. 32.1

Now, the two waves from S_1 and S_2 meet at some point (say P). Then, according to principle of superposition net displacement at P (from its mean position) at any time is given by

$$y = y_1 + y_2$$

Here, y_1 and y_2 are the displacements of P due to two waves individually.

For example, suppose at 9 AM, displacement of P above its mean position should be 6 mm accordingly to wave-1 and at the same time its displacement should be 2 mm below its mean position accordingly to wave-2, then at 9 AM net displacement of P will be 4 mm above its mean position.

Now, based upon the principle of superposition we have two phenomena in physics, interference and beats. Stationary waves (or standing waves) and Young's double slit experiment (or YDSE) are two examples of interference.

Based on principle of superposition means two or more than two waves meet at one point or several points and at every point net displacement is $y = y_1 + y_2$ or $y = y_1 + y_2 + y_3$ etc.

32.2 **Resultant Amplitude and Intensity due to Coherent Sources**

In article 32.1, we have seen that the two waves from two sources S_1 and S_2 were meeting at point P. Suppose they meet at P in a phase difference $\Delta\phi$ (or ϕ). If this phase difference remains constant with time, then sources are called coherent, otherwise incoherent.

For sources to be coherent, the frequencies (f, ω or T) of the two sources must be same. This can be understood by the following example.

Suppose the phase difference is $0°$. It means they are in same phase. Both reaches their extremes ($+A$ or $-A$) simultaneously. They cross their mean positions (in the same direction) simultaneously. Now, if we want their phase difference to remain constant or we want that the above situation is maintained all the time, then obviously their time periods (or frequencies) must be same.

Resultant Amplitude

1. Consider the superposition of two sinusoidal waves of same frequency (means sources are coherent) at some point. Let us assume that the two waves are travelling in the same direction with same velocity. The equation of the two waves reaching at a point can be written as

$$y_1 = A_1 \sin (kx - \omega t)$$

and
$$y_2 = A_2 \sin (kx - \omega t + \phi)$$

The resultant displacement of the point where the waves meet, is

$$y = y_1 + y_2$$
$$= A_1 \sin(kx - \omega t) + A_2 \sin(kx - \omega t + \phi)$$
$$= A_1 \sin(kx - \omega t) + A_2 \sin(kx - \omega t)\cos\phi + A_2 \cos(kx - \omega t)\sin\phi$$
$$= (A_1 + A_2 \cos\phi)\sin(kx - \omega t) + A_2 \sin\phi \cos(kx - \omega t)$$
$$= A\cos\theta \sin(kx - \omega t) + A\sin\theta \cos(kx - \omega t)$$

or $$y = A\sin(kx - \omega t + \theta)$$

Here, $$A_1 + A_2 \cos\phi = A\cos\theta$$
and $$A_2 \sin\phi = A\sin\theta$$
or $$A^2 = (A_1 + A_2 \cos\phi)^2 + (A_2 \sin\phi)^2$$

or $$\boxed{A = \sqrt{A_1^2 + A_2^2 + 2A_1 A_2 \cos\phi}}$$ ...(i)

and $$\tan\theta = \frac{A\sin\theta}{A\cos\theta} = \frac{A_2 \sin\phi}{A_1 + A_2 \cos\phi}$$

2. The above result can be obtained by graphical method also. Assume a vector $\mathbf{A}_1$ of length A_1 to represent the amplitude of first wave.

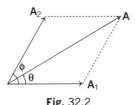

Fig. 32.2

Another vector $\mathbf{A}_2$ of length A_2, making an angle ϕ with $\mathbf{A}_1$ represent the amplitude of second wave. The resultant of $\mathbf{A}_1$ and $\mathbf{A}_2$ represents the amplitude of resulting function y. The angle θ represents the phase difference between the resulting function and the first wave.

Resultant Intensity

In the previous chapter, we have read that intensity of a wave is given by

$$I = \frac{1}{2}\rho\omega^2 A^2 v \quad \text{or} \quad I \propto A^2$$

So, if ρ, ω and v are same for the both interfering waves then Eq. (i) can also be written as

$$\boxed{I = I_1 + I_2 + 2\sqrt{I_1 I_2}\cos\phi}$$ ...(ii)

Here, proportionality constant ($I \propto A^2$) cancels out on right hand side and left hand side.

Note *(i) Eqs. (i) and (ii) are two equations for finding resultant amplitude and resultant intensity at some point due to two coherent sources.*

(ii) In the above equations ϕ is the constant phase difference at that point as the sources are coherent. Value of this constant phase difference will be different at different points.

(iii) The special case of above two equations is, when the individual amplitudes (or intensities) are equal.

(iii) The special case of above two equations is, when the individual amplitudes (or intensities) are equal.

or $\qquad\qquad A_1 = A_2 = A_0$ *(say)*

∴ $\qquad\qquad I_1 = I_2 = I_0$ *(say)*

In this case, Eqs. (i) and (ii) become

$$A = 2A_0 \cos \frac{\phi}{2} \qquad\qquad\qquad ...(iii)$$

and $\qquad\qquad$ $$I = 4I_0 \cos^2 \frac{\phi}{2} \qquad\qquad\qquad ...(iv)$$

(iv) From Eqs. (i) to (iv), we can see that, for given values of A_1, A_2, I_1 and I_2 the resultant amplitude and the resultant intensity are the functions of only ϕ.

(v) If three or more than three waves (due to coherent sources) meet at some point then there is no direct formula for finding resultant amplitude or resultant intensity. In this case, first of all we will find resultant amplitude by vector method (either by using polygon law of vector addition or component method) and then by the relation $I \propto A^2$, we can also determine the resultant intensity.

For example, if resultant amplitude comes out to be $\sqrt{2}$ times then resultant intensity will become two times.

32.3 **Interference**

For interference phenomena to take place, sources must be coherent. So, phase difference at some point should remain constant. Value of this constant phase difference will be different at different points. And since the sources are coherent, therefore following four equations can be applied for finding resultant amplitude and intensity (in case of two sources)

$$A = \sqrt{A_1^2 + A_2^2 + 2A_1 A_2 \cos \phi} \qquad\qquad ...(i)$$

$$I = I_1 + I_2 + 2\sqrt{I_1 I_2} \cos \phi \qquad\qquad ...(ii)$$

$$A = 2A_0 \cos \frac{\phi}{2} \qquad (\text{if } A_1 = A_2 = A_0) \qquad\qquad ...(iii)$$

$$I = 4I_0 \cos^2 \frac{\phi}{2} \qquad (\text{if } I_1 = I_2 = I_0) \qquad\qquad ...(iv)$$

For given values of A_1, A_2, I_1 and I_2 the resultant amplitude and resultant intensity are the functions of only ϕ.

Now, suppose S_1 and S_2 are two coherent sources, then we can see that the two waves are meeting at several points (P_1, P_2, P_3 ... etc). At different points path difference Δx will be different and therefore phase difference $\Delta \phi$ or ϕ will also be different. Because the phase difference depends on the path difference ($\Delta \phi$ or $\phi = \dfrac{2\pi}{\lambda} \cdot \Delta x$).

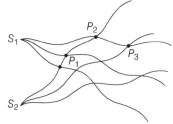

Fig. 32.3

And since phase difference at different points is different, therefore from the above four equations we can see that resultants amplitude and intensity will also be different. But whatever is the intensity at some point, it will remain constant at that point because the sources are coherent and the phase difference is constant at that point.

Constructive Interference

These are the points where resultant amplitude or intensity is maximum or

$$A_{max} = A_1 + A_2 \qquad \text{[from Eq. (i)]}$$

or $\quad A_{max} = \pm 2A_0 \qquad$ [from Eq. (iii)]

and $\quad I_{max} = (\sqrt{I_1} + \sqrt{I_2})^2 \qquad$ [from Eq. (ii)]

or $\quad I_{max} = 4I_0 \qquad$ [from Eq. (iv)]

at those points where, $\quad \cos\phi = +1 \qquad$ [from Eqs. (i) or (ii)]

or $\quad \phi = 0, 2\pi, 4\pi, \ldots, 2n\pi \qquad$ (where $n = 0, 1, 2$)

$\therefore \quad \Delta x = 0, \lambda, 2\lambda, \ldots, n\lambda \qquad \left[\text{as } \Delta x = \phi \left(\dfrac{\lambda}{2\pi} \right) \right]$

Destructive Interference

These are the points where resultant amplitude or intensity is minimum or

$$A_{min} = A_1 \sim A_2 \qquad \text{[from Eq. (i)]}$$

or $\quad A_{min} = 0 \qquad$ [from Eq. (iii)]

and $\quad I_{min} = (\sqrt{I_1} - \sqrt{I_2})^2 \qquad$ [from Eq. (ii)]

or $\quad I_{min} = 0 \qquad$ [from Eq. (iv)]

at those points where, $\quad \cos\phi = -1 \qquad$ [from Eqs. (i) or (ii)]

or $\quad \phi = \pi, 3\pi \ldots (2n-1)\pi \qquad$ (where $n = 1, 2 \ldots$)

$\therefore \quad \Delta x = \dfrac{\lambda}{2}, \dfrac{3\lambda}{2} \ldots (2n-1)\dfrac{\lambda}{2} \qquad \left[\text{as } \Delta x = \phi \left(\dfrac{\lambda}{2\pi} \right) \right]$

✅ *Extra Points to Remember*

- In amplitude, it hardly matters whether it is $+2A_0$ or $-2A_0$. This is the reason we have taken, $A_{max} = \pm 2A_0$

- In interference, two or more than two waves from coherent sources meet at several points. At different points Δx, $\Delta\phi$ or ϕ, resultant amplitude and therefore resultant intensity will be different (varying from I_{max} to I_{min}). But, whatever is the resultant intensity at some point, it remains constant at that point.

- In interference,

$$\frac{I_{max}}{I_{min}} = \left(\frac{\sqrt{I_1} + \sqrt{I_2}}{\sqrt{I_1} - \sqrt{I_2}} \right)^2 = \left(\frac{\sqrt{I_1/I_2} + 1}{\sqrt{I_1/I_2} - 1} \right)^2 = \left(\frac{A_1/A_2 + 1}{A_1/A_2 - 1} \right)^2 = \left(\frac{A_1 + A_2}{A_1 - A_2} \right)^2$$

- **Coherent sources** In order to produce a stable interference pattern the individual waves must maintain a **constant phase** relationship with one another, i.e. the two interfering sources must emit waves having a constant phase difference between them.

  If the phase difference between two sources does not remain constant, then the places of maxima and minima shift. In case of mechanical waves it is possible to keep a constant phase relationship between two different sources. But in case of light two different light sources can't be coherent This is because of the way light is emitted. In ordinary light sources, atoms gain excess energy by thermal agitation or by impact with accelerated electrons. An atom that is 'excited' in such a way begins to radiate energy and continues until it has lost all the energy it can, typically in a time of the order of 10^{-8} s.

The many atoms in a source ordinarily radiate in an unsynchronized and random phase relationship, and the light that is emitted from two such sources has no definite phase relationship. Hence, to obtain a stable interference in light a single source is split into two coherent sources.

Following are shown some of the methods by which we can split a single light source into two.

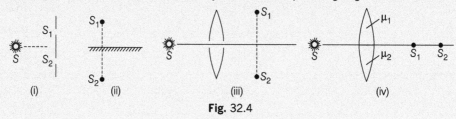

Fig. 32.4

● **Example 32.1** *In interference, two individual amplitudes are A_0 each and the intensity is I_0 each. Find resultant amplitude and intensity at a point, where:*

(a) phase difference between two waves is $60°$

(b) path difference between two waves is $\dfrac{\lambda}{3}$.

Solution (a) Substituting $\phi = 60°$ in the equations,

$$A = 2A_0 \cos \frac{\phi}{2} \quad \text{and} \quad I = 4I_0 \cos^2 \frac{\phi}{2}$$

We get, $\qquad\qquad\qquad\qquad A = \sqrt{3}A_0 \ \text{and} \ I = 3I_0$ **Ans.**

(b) Given, $\qquad\qquad\qquad\qquad \Delta x = \dfrac{\lambda}{3}$

∴ $\qquad\qquad\qquad \phi \ \text{or} \ \Delta\phi = \left(\dfrac{2\pi}{\lambda}\right) \cdot \Delta x$

$$= \left(\frac{2\pi}{\lambda}\right)\left(\frac{\lambda}{3}\right) = \frac{2\pi}{3} \ \text{or} \ 120°$$

Now, substituting $\phi = 120°$ in the above two equations, we get

$$A = A_0 \ \text{and} \ I = I_0$$ **Ans.**

● **Example 32.2** *Three waves from three coherent sources meet at some point. Resultant amplitude of each is A_0. Intensity corresponding to A_0 is I_0. Phase difference between first wave and the second wave is $60°$. Path difference between first wave and the third wave is $\dfrac{\lambda}{3}$. The first wave lags behind in phase angle from second and the third wave. Find resultant intensity at this point.*

Solution Here, the sources are three. So, we don't have any direct formula for finding the resultant intensity. First we will find the resultant amplitude by vector method and then, by the relation $I \propto A^2$, we can also find the resulting intensity.

Further, a path difference of $\dfrac{\lambda}{3}$ is equivalent to a phase difference of $120°$ $\left(\Delta\phi \ \text{or} \ \phi = \dfrac{2\pi}{\lambda} \cdot \Delta x\right)$.

Hence, the phase difference first and second is 60° and between first and third is 120°. So, vector diagram for amplitude is as shown below.

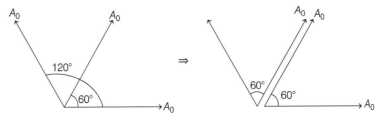

Fig. 32.5

Now, resultant of first and third acting at 120° is also A_0 (as $A = 2A_0 \cos \dfrac{\phi}{2}$ and $\phi = 120°$) and

since the first and third are equal, so this resultant A_0 passes through the bisector line of these two or in the direction of second amplitude vector. Therefore, the resultant amplitude is

$$A = A_0 + A_0 = 2A_0$$

and the resultant intensity is

$$I = 4I_0 \qquad \text{(as } I \propto A^2\text{)} \qquad \textbf{Ans.}$$

◉ ***Example 32.3*** *Two waves of equal frequencies have their amplitudes in the ratio of* 3 : 5. *They are superimposed on each other. Calculate the ratio of maximum and minimum intensities of the resultant wave.*

Solution Given, $\dfrac{A_1}{A_2} = \dfrac{3}{5}$

∴ $$\sqrt{\dfrac{I_1}{I_2}} = \dfrac{3}{5} \qquad \text{(as } I \propto A^2\text{)}$$

Maximum intensity is obtained, where

$$\cos \phi = 1$$

and $$I_{\max} = (\sqrt{I_1} + \sqrt{I_2})^2$$

Minimum intensity is found, where

$$\cos \phi = -1$$

and $$I_{\min} = (\sqrt{I_1} - \sqrt{I_2})^2$$

Hence, $$\dfrac{I_{\max}}{I_{\min}} = \left(\dfrac{\sqrt{I_1} + \sqrt{I_2}}{\sqrt{I_1} - \sqrt{I_2}}\right)^2 = \left(\dfrac{\sqrt{\dfrac{I_1}{I_2}} + 1}{\sqrt{\dfrac{I_1}{I_2}} - 1}\right)^2$$

$$= \left(\dfrac{3/5 + 1}{3/5 - 1}\right)^2 = \dfrac{64}{4} = \dfrac{16}{1} \qquad \textbf{Ans.}$$

● **Example 32.4** *In interference,* $\dfrac{I_{max}}{I_{min}} = \alpha,$ *find*

(a) $\dfrac{A_{max}}{A_{min}}$ (b) $\dfrac{A_1}{A_2}$ (c) $\dfrac{I_1}{I_2}$

Solution (a) $\dfrac{A_{max}}{A_{min}} = \sqrt{\dfrac{I_{max}}{I_{min}}} = \sqrt{\alpha}$ **Ans.**

(b) $\dfrac{A_{max}}{A_{min}} = \sqrt{\alpha} = \dfrac{A_1 + A_2}{A_1 - A_2} = \dfrac{A_1 / A_2 + 1}{A_1 / A_2 - 1}$

Solving this equation, we get $\dfrac{A_1}{A_2} = \dfrac{\sqrt{\alpha} + 1}{\sqrt{\alpha} - 1}$ **Ans.**

(c) $\dfrac{I_1}{I_2} = \left(\dfrac{A_1}{A_2}\right)^2 = \left(\dfrac{\sqrt{\alpha} + 1}{\sqrt{\alpha} - 1}\right)^2$ **Ans.**

INTRODUCTORY EXERCISE 32.1

1. The ratio of intensities of two waves is 9:16. If these two waves interfere, then determine the ratio of the maximum and minimum possible intensities.

2. In interference, two individual amplitudes are 5 units and 3 units. Find

   (a) $\dfrac{A_{max}}{A_{min}}$ (b) $\dfrac{I_{max}}{I_{min}}$

3. Three waves due to three coherent sources meet at one point. Their amplitudes are $\sqrt{2}A_0, 3A_0$ and $\sqrt{2}A_0$. Intensity corresponding to A_0 is I_0. Phase difference between first and second is $45°$. Path difference between first and third is $\dfrac{\lambda}{4}$. In phase angle, first wave lags behind from the other two waves. Find resultant intensity at this point.

32.4 Young's Double Slit Experiment (YDSE)

(i) YDSE is an experiment (or an example) of interference in light.

(ii) For interference, two coherent sources are required and in light two different light sources are never coherent. Therefore, a single source S is split into two sources as shown below.

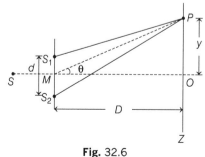

Fig. 32.6

(iii) Z is a two-dimensional screen and OP the centre line of this screen. On different points of this screen, two rays of light (from two coherent sources S_1 and S_2) will interfere. At different points of the screen path difference (and therefore) phase difference will be different. Therefore, resultant intensity will be different. But whatever is the resultant intensity at any point, it remains constant at that point.

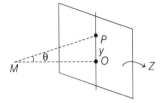

Fig. 32.7

(iv) Mathematically, we will find the resultant intensity at any point on the centre line OP of the screen, as it will have only one variable y (or θ).

(v) The order of λ, d and D is normally

$$\lambda << d << D$$

(vi) Since $d << D$, we can assume that intensities at P due to independent sources S_1 and S_2 are almost equal, or

$$I_1 \approx I_2 = I_0 \quad \text{(say)}$$

Therefore, for resultant intensity we can apply

$$I = 4I_0 \cos^2 \frac{\phi}{2} \qquad \ldots \text{(i)}$$

(vii) In YDSE, our main objective is to find resultant intensity at a general point P on the centre line of the screen. Point P can be generalised in the following four ways.

(a) Directly phase difference ϕ (between two rays interfering at P) can be given. This is the simplest one. As, we can directly apply

$$I = 4I_0 \cos^2 \frac{\phi}{2}$$

for the resultant intensity.

(b) Path difference Δx (between two interfering rays) can be given at P. In this case, first we will convert Δx into phase difference ϕ by the relation,

$$\phi = \frac{2\pi}{\lambda} \Delta x$$

and then, we will apply

$$I = 4I_0 \cos^2 \frac{\phi}{2}$$

(c) Distance OP or y-coordinate of point P can be given.

(d) Angular position θ of point P will be given.

Note *In last two cases, first we will find the path difference Δx in terms of y and θ and then we will find the resultant intensity.*

Path Difference in Terms of *y* and θ

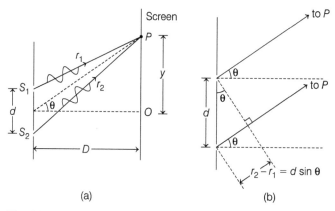

(a)   (b)

Fig. 32.8 (a) To reach P, the light waves from S_1 and S_2 must travel different distances. (b) The path difference between the two rays is $d \sin \theta$.

Figure shows the light waves from S_1 and S_2 meeting at an arbitrary point P on the screen. Since, $D \gg d$, the two light rays are approximately parallel, with a path difference,

$$\Delta x = S_2 P - S_1 P$$

$$\boxed{\Delta x \approx d \sin \theta} \qquad \qquad \ldots\text{(ii)}$$

This is basically the expression of Δx in terms of θ.

If θ is small, then
$$\sin \theta \approx \tan \theta = \frac{y}{D}$$

Substituting in Eq. (ii), we get

$$\boxed{\Delta x = \frac{yd}{D}} \qquad \qquad \ldots\text{(iii)}$$

This is the expression of path difference Δx in terms of y.

Maximum and Minimum Intensity

Maximum Intensity

In Eq. (i), we know that maximum intensity is $4I_0$ at points where

$$\Delta x = n\lambda \qquad \qquad (n = 0, \pm 1, \pm 2 \ldots)$$

or
$$d \sin \theta = n\lambda$$

or
$$\frac{yd}{D} = n\lambda$$

or
$$\boxed{y = \frac{n\lambda D}{d} = Y_n} \qquad \qquad \ldots\text{(iv)}$$

Here, Y_n may be called as y-coordinate (with respect to point O) of nth order maxima, where

$$n = 0, \pm 1, \pm 2 \ldots$$

For example,

$$Y_0 = 0 \rightarrow y\text{-coordinate of zero order maxima (for } n = 0)$$

$$Y_1 \text{ or } Y_1' = \pm \frac{\lambda D}{d} \rightarrow y\text{-coordinate of first order maxima (for } n = \pm 1)$$

$$Y_2 \text{ or } Y_2' = \pm \frac{2\lambda D}{D} \rightarrow y\text{-coordinate of second order maxima (for } n = \pm 2)$$

and so on.

Minimum Intensity

In Eq. (i), we know that minimum intensity is zero at points where

$$\Delta x = (2n - 1)\frac{\lambda}{2} \qquad\qquad (n = \pm 1, \pm 2 \ldots)$$

or

$$d \sin \theta = (2n - 1)\frac{\lambda}{2}$$

or

$$\frac{yd}{D} = (2n - 1)\frac{\lambda}{2}$$

or

$$\boxed{y = \frac{(2n - 1)\,\lambda D}{2d} = y_n} \qquad\qquad \ldots\text{(v)}$$

Here, y_n may be called as y-coordinate (with respect to point O) of nth order minima, where $n = \pm 1, \pm 2 \ldots$

For example,

$$y_1 \text{ or } y_1' = \pm \frac{\lambda D}{2d} \rightarrow y\text{-coordinate of first order minima (for } n = \pm 1)$$

$$y_2 \text{ or } y_2' = \pm \frac{3\lambda D}{2d} \rightarrow y\text{-coordinate of second order minima (for } n = \pm 2)$$

Fringe Width (ω)

Distance between two adjacent maxima or minima (or bright/dark fringes) is called the fringe width. Thus,

$$\omega = Y_n - Y_{n-1} = \text{ distance between two adjacent maxima}$$

$$= \frac{n\lambda D}{d} - \frac{(n-1)\lambda D}{d}$$

$$= \frac{\lambda D}{d}$$

or

$$\boxed{\omega = \frac{\lambda D}{d}} \qquad\qquad \ldots \text{(vi)}$$

We can see that distance between two successive minima is also $\dfrac{\lambda D}{d}$.

Intensity Distribution

In the shown figure, let us discuss one maxima (say Y_2) on upper side of centre line MO and one minima (say y_2') on lower side.

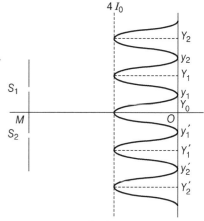

Fig. 32.9

Y_2 This may be called second order maxima on upper side of line MO. Here, the intensity is $4I_0$. Path difference is

$$\Delta x = S_2 P - S_1 P = 2\lambda$$

and the phase difference is 4π. Further, y-coordinate of this point is

$$y = \frac{2\lambda D}{d} = 2\omega$$

y_2' This may be called the second order minima on lower side of line MO. Here, the intensity is zero. Path difference is

$$\Delta x = S_1 P - S_2 P = \frac{3\lambda}{2}$$

and the phase difference is 3π. Further, y-coordinate of this point is

$$y = -\frac{3\lambda D}{2d} = -\frac{3}{2}\omega$$

Intensity Variation within One Fringe

Let us first make the following table corresponding to this point.

Table 32.1

Intensity	Amplitude $A \propto \sqrt{I}$	Phase difference (ϕ) where $A = 2A_0 \cos\frac{\phi}{2}$	Path difference $\Delta x = \frac{\lambda}{2\pi}\phi$	y-coordinate $\Delta x = \frac{yd}{D}$ $\Rightarrow \quad y = \Delta x \left(\frac{D}{d}\right)$
$4I_0$	$2A_0$	2π or $360°$	λ	$\lambda D/d = \omega$
$3I_0$	$\sqrt{3}A_0$	$\frac{\pi}{3}$ or $60°$	$\lambda/6$	$\lambda D/6d = \omega/6$
$2I_0$	$\sqrt{2}A_0$	$\frac{\pi}{2}$ or $90°$	$\lambda/4$	$\lambda D/4d = \omega/4$
I_0	A_0	$\frac{2\pi}{3}$ or $120°$	$\lambda/3$	$\lambda D/3d = \omega/3$
0	0	π or $180°$	$\lambda/2$	$\lambda D/2d = \omega/2$

Now, according to above table we can make the following figure.

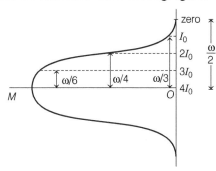

Fig. 32.10

● **Example 32.5** *In YDSE, the two slits are separated by 0.1 mm and they are 0.5 m from the screen. The wavelength of light used is 5000 Å. Find the distance between 7th maxima and 11th minima on the upper side of screen.*

Solution Given, $d = 0.1\,mm = 10^{-4}$ m, $D = 0.5$ m and $\lambda = 5000$ Å $= 5.0 \times 10^{-7}$ m

$$\Delta y = y_{11} - Y_7 = \frac{(2 \times 11 - 1)\lambda D}{2d} - \frac{7\lambda D}{d}$$

or $$\Delta y = \frac{7\lambda D}{2d} = \frac{7 \times 5.0 \times 10^{-7} \times 0.5}{2 \times 10^{-4}}$$

$$= 8.75 \times 10^{-3} \text{ m}$$

$$= 8.75 \text{ mm} \qquad \textbf{Ans.}$$

● **Example 32.6** *Maximum intensity in YDSE is I_0. Find the intensity at a point on the screen where*

(a) the phase difference between the two interfering beams is $\dfrac{\pi}{3}$.

(b) the path difference between them is $\dfrac{\lambda}{4}$.

Solution (a) We know that

$$I = I_{max} \cos^2 \left(\frac{\phi}{2} \right)$$

Here, I_{max} is I_0 (i.e. intensity due to independent sources is $I_0/4$). Therefore, at

$$\phi = \frac{\pi}{3}$$

or $$\frac{\phi}{2} = \frac{\pi}{6}$$

$$I = I_0 \cos^2 \left(\frac{\pi}{6} \right) = \frac{3}{4} I_0 \qquad \textbf{Ans.}$$

(b) Phase difference corresponding to the given path difference $\Delta x = \dfrac{\lambda}{4}$ is

$$\phi = \left(\dfrac{2\pi}{\lambda}\right)\left(\dfrac{\lambda}{4}\right) = \dfrac{\pi}{2} \quad \text{or} \quad \dfrac{\phi}{2} = \dfrac{\pi}{4}$$

$$\therefore \qquad I = I_0 \cos^2\left(\dfrac{\pi}{4}\right) = \dfrac{I_0}{2} \qquad\qquad \textbf{Ans.}$$

Dependence of Fringe Width on λ

Fringe width (ω) is given by

$$\omega = \dfrac{\lambda D}{d} \quad \text{or} \quad \boxed{\omega \propto \lambda}$$

Two conclusions can be drawn from this relation.

(i) If YDSE apparatus is immersed in a liquid of refractive index μ, then wavelength of light and hence, fringe width decreases μ times.

(ii) If white light is used in place of a monochromatic light then coloured fringes are obtained on the screen with red fringes of larger size than that of violet, because $\lambda_{red} > \lambda_{violet}$.

But note that centre is still white because path difference there is zero for all colours. Hence, all the wavelengths interfere constructively. At other points light will interfere destructively for those wavelengths for whom path difference is $\lambda/2, 3\lambda/2, \ldots$ etc. and they will interfere constructively for the wavelengths for whom path difference is $\lambda, 2\lambda, \ldots$ etc.

This point can be explained as under,

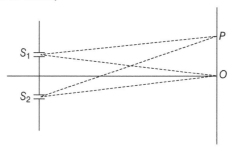

Fig. 32.11

In YDSE let us take a bichromatic light (having two wavelengths). Suppose one wavelength is $\lambda_1 = \lambda$ and the other wavelength is $\lambda_2 = 2\lambda$. At point O,

$S_1 O = S_2 O \Rightarrow \Delta x = O$ for both wavelengths. Therefore, both wavelengths interfere constructively.

At any other point (say at P) $S_1 P \neq S_2 P \Rightarrow \Delta x \neq O$ and suppose $\Delta x = \lambda$. Then, this Δx is

$$\Delta x = \lambda_1 \quad \text{and} \quad \Delta x = \dfrac{\lambda_2}{2}$$

Therefore at P, wavelength λ_1 interferes constructively and λ_2 destructively. Same is the case with white light. At point O, all wavelengths interfere constructively. Therefore, white is produced. At any other point some of the wavelengths interfere constructively, (produce $4 I_0$) some destructively (produce zero intensity) and rest intermediately (between zero to $4 I_0$ intensity).

⊙ ***Example 32.7***   *White light is used to illuminate the two slits in a Young's double slit experiment. The separation between the slits is b and the screen is at a distance d ($>> b$) from the slits. At a point on the screen directly in front of one of the slits, certain wavelengths are missing. Some of these missing wavelengths are*   (JEE 1984)
(a) $\lambda = b^2 /d$ (b) $\lambda = 2b^2 /d$ (c) $\lambda = b^2 /3d$ (d) $\lambda = 2b^2 /3d$

Solution   At P (directly in front of S_1) $y = b/2$

∴ Path difference, $\Delta x = S_2 P - S_1 P = \dfrac{y \cdot (b)}{d} = \dfrac{\left(\dfrac{b}{2}\right)(b)}{d} = \dfrac{b^2}{2d}$

Those wavelengths will be missing for which

$$\Delta x = \frac{\lambda_1}{2}, \frac{3\lambda_2}{2}, \frac{5\lambda_3}{2} \ldots$$

∴

$$\lambda_1 = 2\Delta x = \frac{b^2}{d}$$

$$\lambda_2 = \frac{2\Delta x}{3} = \frac{b^2}{3d}$$

$$\lambda_3 = \frac{2\Delta x}{5} = \frac{b^2}{5d}$$

Therefore, the correct options are (a) and (c).

⊙ ***Example 32.8***   *Bichromatic light is used in YDSE having wavelengths $\lambda_1 = 400\ nm$ and $\lambda_2 = 700\ nm$. Find minimum order of bright fringe of λ_1 which overlaps with bright fringe of λ_2.*

Solution   Let n_1 bright fringe of λ_1 overlaps with n_2 bright fringe of λ_2. Then,

$$\frac{n_1 \lambda_1 D}{d} = \frac{n_2 \lambda_2 D}{d} \quad \text{or} \quad \frac{n_1}{n_2} = \frac{\lambda_2}{\lambda_1} = \frac{700}{400} = \frac{7}{4}$$

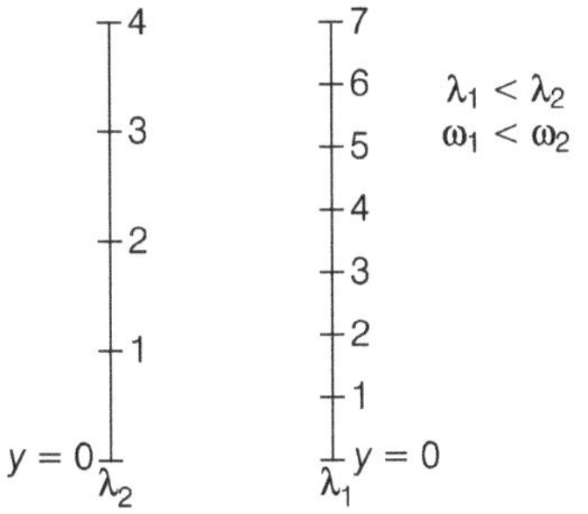

$\lambda_1 < \lambda_2$
$\omega_1 < \omega_2$

Fig. 32.12

The ratio $\dfrac{n_1}{n_2} = \dfrac{7}{4}$ implies that 7th bright fringe of λ_1 will overlap with 4th bright fringe of λ_2.

Similarly, 14th of λ_1 will overlap with 8th of λ_2 and so on.

So, the minimum order of λ_1 which overlaps with λ_2 is 7.

Note *In the above example,*

$$\frac{n_1}{n_2} = \frac{7}{4}, \frac{14}{8}, \frac{21}{12} \ \text{etc.}$$

So, to overlap maximas, we can take either of the ratios $\frac{7}{4}$ or $\frac{14}{8}$ or $\frac{21}{12}$ etc.

But in the next example, we will see that if we wish to overlap minimas we cannot take each successive ratio. The reason behind this is that order of fringe n (whether it is order of maxima or minima) should always be an integer.

⟫ **Example 32.9** *In YDSE, bichromatic light of wavelengths* 400 *nm and* 560 *nm are used. The distance between the slits is* 0.1 *mm and the distance between the plane of the slits and the screen is* 1 *m. The minimum distance between two successive regions of complete darkness is*   (JEE 2004)
(a) 4 *mm*   *(b)* 5.6 *mm*   *(c)* 14 *mm*   *(d)* 28 *mm*

Solution   Let nth minima of 400 nm coincides with mth minima of 560 nm, then

$$\frac{(2n-1)\lambda_1 D}{2d} = \frac{(2m-1)\lambda_2 D}{2d}$$

or

$$(2n-1)\left(\frac{400}{2}\right) = (2m-1)\left(\frac{560}{2}\right)$$

$$\frac{2n-1}{2m-1} = \frac{7}{5} = \frac{14}{10} = \frac{21}{15}$$

If we take the first ratio, then $n = 4$ and $m = 3$.

If we take the second ratio, then $n = 7.5$ and $m = 5.5$.

This is not acceptable. If we take the third ratio, then $n = 11$ and $m = 8$

i.e. 4th minima of 400 nm coincides with 3rd minima of 560 nm.

Location of this minima is

$$y_1 = \frac{(2 \times 4 - 1)(1000)(400 \times 10^{-6})}{2 \times 0.1} = 14 \ \text{mm}$$

Next 11th minima of 400 nm will coincide with 8th minima of 560 nm.

Location of this minima is

$$y_2 = \frac{(2 \times 11 - 1)(1000)(400 \times 10^{-6})}{2 \times 0.1} = 42 \ \text{mm}$$

∴   Required distance $= y_2 - y_1 = 28 \, \text{mm}$ **Ans.**

∴   The correct option is (d).

Path Difference Produced by a Slab

Consider two light rays 1 and 2 moving in air parallel to each other. If a slab of refractive index μ and thickness t is inserted between the path of one of the rays, then a path difference

$$\boxed{\Delta x = (\mu - 1)\, t}$$ ...(i)

is produced between them. This can be shown as under,

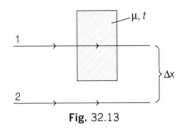

Fig. 32.13

$$\text{Speed of light in air} = c$$

$$\text{Speed of light in medium} = \frac{c}{\mu}$$

Time taken by ray 1 to cross the slab, $\quad t_1 = \dfrac{t}{c/\mu} = \dfrac{\mu t}{c}$

and time taken by ray 2 to cross the same thickness t in air will be,

$$t_2 = \frac{t}{c} \quad \text{as} \quad t_1 > t_2$$

Difference in time $\qquad \Delta t = t_1 - t_2 = (\mu - 1)\dfrac{t}{c}$

During this time ray 2 will travel an extra distance, $\Delta x = (\Delta t)\, c = (\mu - 1)\, t$, which is same as Eq. (i).

EXERCISE 1 A slab of thickness t and refractive index μ_2 is kept in a medium of refractive index $\mu_1 \,(<\mu_2)$. Prove that, if two rays parallel to each other passes through such a system, with one ray passing through the slab, then the path difference produced between them due to the slab will be:

$$\Delta x = \left(\frac{\mu_2}{\mu_1} - 1 \right) t$$

EXERCISE 2

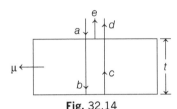

Fig. 32.14

In the figure shown, a is the incident ray, e is reflected from top surface of the slab but d comes after reflecting from bottom surface. Then, prove that path difference between e and d is

$$\Delta x = 2\mu t$$

Shifting of Fringes

Suppose a glass slab of thickness t and refractive index μ is inserted onto the path of the ray emanating from source S_1, then the whole fringe pattern shifts upwards by a distance $\dfrac{(\mu - 1)\, tD}{d}$. This can be shown as under,

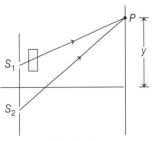

Fig. 32.15

Geometric path difference between $S_2 P$ and $S_1 P$ is

$$\Delta x_1 = S_2 P - S_1 P = \frac{yd}{D}$$

Path difference produced by the glass slab,

$$\Delta x_2 = (\mu - 1)\, t$$

Note *Due to the glass slab path of ray 1 gets increased by* Δx_2.

Therefore, net path difference between the two rays is,

$$\Delta x = \Delta x_1 - \Delta x_2 \quad \text{or} \quad \Delta x = \frac{yd}{D} - (\mu - 1)\, t$$

For n^{th} order maxima on upper side, $\qquad\qquad \Delta x = n\lambda$

or $\qquad\qquad \dfrac{yd}{D} - (\mu - 1)\, t = n\,\lambda$

$\therefore \qquad\qquad y = \dfrac{n\lambda D}{d} + \dfrac{(\mu - 1)\, tD}{d} = Y_n$

Earlier without slab it was $\dfrac{n\lambda D}{d}$

$\therefore \qquad\qquad \boxed{\text{Shift} = \dfrac{(\mu - 1)t\, D}{d}} \qquad\qquad\qquad \dots\text{(ii)}$

Following three points are important with regard to Eq. (ii).

(a) Shift is independent of n, (the order of the fringe), i.e.

shift of zero order maximum = shift of 7th order maximum

or   shift of 5th order maximum = shift of 9th order minimum and so on

(b) Shift is independent of λ, i.e. if white light is used then,

shift of red colour fringe = shift of violet colour fringe

(c) Number of fringes shifted $= \dfrac{\text{shift}}{\text{fringe width}}$

$$= \frac{(\mu - 1)\, t\, D/d}{\lambda D/d} = \frac{(\mu - 1)t}{\lambda}$$

These numbers are inversely proportional to λ. This is because shift is same for all colours but fringe width of the colour having smaller value of λ is small, so more number of fringes will shift for this colour.

◉ **Example 32.10** *In YDSE, find the thickness of a glass slab* ($\mu = 1.5$) *which should be placed in front of the upper slit* S_1 *so that the central maximum now lies at a point where 5th bright fringe was lying earlier (before inserting the slab). Wavelength of light used is 5000 Å.*

Solution According to the question,

$$\text{Shift} = 5\,(\text{fringe width})$$

$\therefore \qquad\qquad \dfrac{(\mu - 1)\, tD}{d} = \dfrac{5\lambda D}{d}$

$\therefore \qquad\qquad t = \dfrac{5\lambda}{\mu - 1} = \dfrac{25000}{1.5 - 1}$

$$= 50000 \ \text{Å} \qquad\qquad\qquad\qquad \textbf{Ans.}$$

◉ **Example 32.11** *Interference fringes are produced by a double slit arrangement and a piece of plane parallel glass of refractive index 1.5 is interposed in one of the interfering beam. If the fringes are displaced through 30 fringe widths for light of wavelength* 6×10^{-5} *cm, find the thickness of the plate.*

Solution Path difference due to the glass slab,

$$\Delta x = (\mu - 1)t$$

Thirty fringes are displaced due to the slab. Hence,

$$\Delta x = 30\lambda \quad \Rightarrow \quad (\mu - 1)t = 30\lambda$$

∴

$$t = \frac{30\lambda}{\mu - 1} = \frac{30 \times 6 \times 10^{-5}}{1.5 - 1}$$

$$= 3.6 \times 10^{-3} \text{ cm} \qquad \text{**Ans.**}$$

INTRODUCTORY EXERCISE **32.2**

1. Explain why two flashlights held close together do not produce an interference pattern on a distant screen?

2. Why it is so much easier to perform interference experiments with a laser than with an ordinary light source?

3. In YDSE, $D = 1.2$ m and $d = 0.25$ cm, the slits are illuminated with coherent 600 nm light. Calculate the distance y above the central maximum for which the average intensity on the screen is 75% of the maximum.

4. Slit 1 of a double slit is wider than slit 2, so that the light from slit 1 has an amplitude three times that of the light from slit 2. Show that equation $I = I_{max} \cos^2 \frac{\phi}{2}$ is replaced by the equation,

$$I = \left(\frac{I_{max}}{4}\right)\left(1 + 3\cos^2 \frac{\phi}{2}\right)$$

5. In a two-slit interference pattern, the maximum intensity is I_0.
   (a) At a point in the pattern where the phase difference between the waves from the two slits is 60°, what is the intensity?
   (b) What is the path difference for 480 nm light from the two slits at a point where the phase angle is 60°?

6. Two waves of the same frequency and same amplitude 'a' are reaching a point simultaneously. What should be the phase difference between the waves so that the amplitude of the resultant wave be :
   (i) $2a$ (ii) $\sqrt{2}\,a$ (iii) a (iv) zero

32.5 Introduction to Diffraction

When light waves pass through two slits in YDSE, an interference pattern is observed rather than a sharp spot of light. This behaviour indicates that light, once it has passed through the aperture, spreads beyond the narrow path defined by the aperture into regions that would be in shadow if light travelled in straight lines. Other waves, such as sound waves and water waves, also have this property of spreading when passing through apertures or by sharp edges. This phenomenon, known as diffraction, can be described only with a wave model for light.

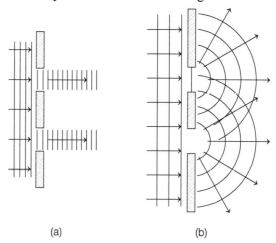

(a)   (b)

Fig. 32.16 (a) If light waves did not spread out after passing through the slits, no interference would occur (b) The light waves from the two slits overlap as they spread out, filling what we expect to be shadowed regions with light and producing interference fringes.

In general, diffraction occurs when waves pass through small openings, around obstacles, or past sharp edges. As shown in figure, when an opaque object is placed between a point source of light and a screen, no sharp boundary exists on the screen between a shadowed region and an illuminated region. The illuminated region above the shadow of the object contains alternating light and dark fringes. Such a display is called a **diffraction pattern.**

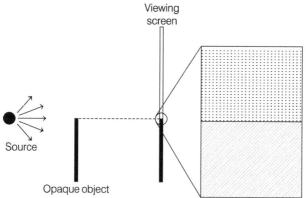

Viewing
screen

Source

Opaque object

Fig. 32.17 Light from a small source passes by the edge of an opaque object. We might expect no light to appear on the screen below the position of the edge of the object. In reality, light bends around the top edge of the object and enter this region. Because of these effects, a diffraction pattern consisting of bright and dark fringes appears in the region above the edge of the object.

In this chapter, we restrict our attention to **Fraunhofer diffraction**, which occurs, for example, when all the rays passing through a narrow slit are approximately parallel to one another. This can be achieved experimentally either by placing the screen far from the opening used to create the diffraction or by using a converging lens to focus the rays once they pass through the opening, as shown in Fig. 32.18.

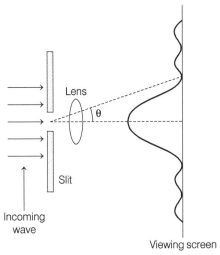

Fig. 32.18 Fraunhofer diffraction pattern of a single slit.

32.6 **Diffraction from a Narrow Slit**

Until now, we have assumed that slits are point sources of light. In this section, we abandon that assumption and see how the finite width of slits is the basis for understanding Fraunhofer diffraction.

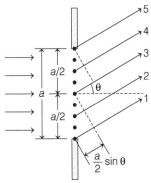

Fig. 32.19 Diffraction of light by a narrow slit of width a. Each portion of the slit acts as a point source of light waves. The path difference between rays 1 and 3 or between rays 2 and 4 is $(a/2) \sin \theta$ (drawing not to scale).

We can deduce some important features of this phenomenon by examining waves coming from various portions of the slit, as shown in Fig. 32.19 According to Huygens's principle, **each portion of the slit acts as a source of light waves.** Hence, light from one portion of the slit can interfere with light from another portion, and the resultant light intensity on a viewing screen depends on the direction θ.

To analyze the diffraction pattern, it is convenient to divide the slit into two halves, as shown in Fig. 32.19. Keeping in mind that all the waves are in phase as they leave the slit, consider rays 1 and 3. As these two rays travel toward a viewing screen far to the right of the Fig. 32.19, ray 1 travels farther than ray 3 by an amount equal to the path difference $(a/2) \sin \theta$, where a is the width of the slit. Similarly, the path difference between rays 2 and 4 is also $(a/2) \sin \theta$. If this path difference is exactly half a wavelength (corresponding to a phase difference of 180°), then the two waves cancel each other and destructive interference results. This is true for any two rays that originate at points separated by half the slit width because the phase difference between two such points is 180°. Therefore, waves from the upper half of the slit interfere destructively with waves from the lower half when

$$\frac{a}{2} \sin \theta = \frac{\lambda}{2} \quad \text{or when} \quad \sin \theta = \frac{\lambda}{a}$$

If we divide the slit into four equal parts and use similar reasoning, we find that the viewing screen is also dark when

$$\sin \theta = \frac{2\lambda}{a}$$

Likewise, we can divide the slit into six equal parts and show that darkness occurs on the screen when

$$\sin \theta = \frac{3\lambda}{a}$$

Therefore, the general condition for destructive interference is

$$\boxed{\sin \theta = m \frac{\lambda}{a}} \quad m = \pm 1, \ \pm 2, \pm 3, \dots \qquad \dots \text{(i)}$$

This equation gives the values of θ for which the diffraction pattern has zero light intensity—that is, when a dark fringe is formed. However, it tells us nothing about the variation in light intensity along the screen. The general features of the intensity distribution are shown in Fig. 32.20. A broad central bright fringe is observed; this fringe is flanked by much weaker bright fringes alternating with dark fringes. The various dark fringes occur at the values of θ that satisfy Eq. (i). Each bright fringe peak lies approximately halfway between its bordering dark fringe minima. Note that the central bright maximum is twice as wide as the secondary maxima.

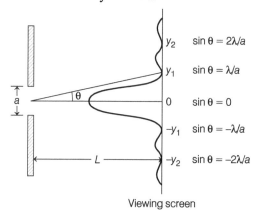

Fig. 32.20 Intensity distribution for a Fraunhofer diffraction pattern from a single slit of width a

Intensity of Single Slit Diffraction Patterns

We can use phasor to determine the light intensity distribution for a single slit diffraction pattern. The proof is beyond our syllabus, we are just writing here the intensity at angle θ.

$$I = I_0 \left[\frac{\sin \beta/2}{\beta/2} \right]^2$$

Here,

$$\frac{\beta}{2} = \frac{\pi \, a \sin \theta}{\lambda}$$

or

$$I = I_0 \left[\frac{\sin (\pi \, a \sin \theta/\lambda)}{(\pi \, a \sin \theta)/\lambda} \right]^2 \qquad \text{(at angle θ)}$$

Here, I_0 is the intensity at $\theta = 0°$ (the central maximum).

From this result, we see that minima occurs when

$$\frac{\pi \, a \sin \theta}{\lambda} = m\pi$$

or

$$\sin \theta = m \frac{\lambda}{a} \qquad\qquad m = \pm 1, \pm 2, \ldots$$

This is in agreement with Eq. (i).

Note *That $\sin \theta = 0$, corresponds to central maxima while $\dfrac{\pi \, a \sin \theta}{\lambda} = \pi$, corresponds to first minima.*

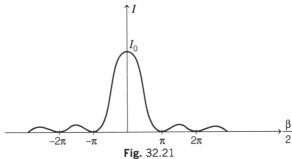

Fig. 32.21

⊗ **Example 32.12** *A beam of light of wavelength 600 nm from a distant source falls on a single slit 1.0 mm wide and the resulting diffraction pattern is observed on a screen 2 m away. What is the distance between the first dark fringe on either side of the central bright fringe?*

Solution For the diffraction at a single slit, the position of minima is given by

$$d \sin \theta = n\lambda$$

For small value of θ,

$$\sin \theta \approx \theta = \frac{y}{D}$$

∴

$$d \frac{y}{D} = \lambda \quad \text{or} \quad y = \frac{D}{d} \lambda$$

Substituting the values, we have

$$y = \frac{2 \times 6 \times 10^{-7}}{1 \times 10^{-3}}$$

$$= 1.2 \times 10^{-3} \text{ m}$$

$$= 1.2 \text{ mm}$$

∴ Distance between first minima on either side of central maxima $= 2y = 2.4$ mm **Ans.**

◉ **Example 32.13** *A parallel beam of monochromatic light of wavelength* 450 *nm passes through a slit of width* 0.2 *mm. Find the angular divergence in which most of the light is diffracted.*

Solution Most of the light is diffracted between the two first order minima. These minimas occur at angle given by

$$d \sin \theta = \pm \, n\lambda$$

∴ $$\sin \theta = \pm \frac{\lambda}{d}$$

$$= \pm \frac{450 \times 10^{-9}}{0.2 \times 10^{-3}}$$

$$= \pm \, 2.25 \times 10^{-3} \text{ rad}$$

∴ The angular divergence $= 4.5 \times 10^{-3}$ rad. **Ans.**

Core Concepts

1. In YDSE, if one slit is closed then we will not get interference on screen and intensity at every point is almost uniform ($= I_0$) and this is due to only one slit.

2. In YDSE, if both sources are incoherent, then again we will not get interference and intensity at every point is again uniform ($= I_1 + I_2$ or $2I_0$).

3. In YDSE, if width of one slit is slightly increased then I_{max} and I_{min} both will increase. This is because intensity due to the slit of increased width will increase or

$$I_1 = I_0 \text{ but } I_2 = nI_0 \qquad \text{(where } n > 1\text{)}$$

$$\therefore \quad I_{min} = (\sqrt{I_1} - \sqrt{I_2})^2 > 0$$

and

$$I_{max} = (\sqrt{I_1} + \sqrt{I_2})^2 > 4I_0$$

4. **Shape of fringes on complete screen** Until now, we have discussed the fringe pattern on the centre line of the screen. On this centre line maximas (like Y_0, Y_1, Y_2 etc.) or minimas (like y_1, y_2 etc.) are just points. But on the whole screen fringes make a curve and this curve is a locus of points where path difference from two slits is a constant. Or

$$\Delta x = S_1 P - S_2 P = C \qquad \text{...(i)}$$

$C = 0$, gives Y_0 fringe. Similarly, $C = \pm \lambda$ gives Y_1 or Y_1' fringe etc.

Now on the centre line, Δx was a function of only one variable coordinate $y \left(\Delta x = \dfrac{yd}{D} \right)$. But on the whole screen it will become a function of two variable coordinates (say y and z). Therefore, Eq. (i) becomes

$$\Delta x = f(y, z) = C \qquad \text{...(ii)}$$

After proper calculations, we can show that this comes out to be a family of curves of hyperbolas. Thus, on the complete screen, fringes are of the shape of hyperbolas.

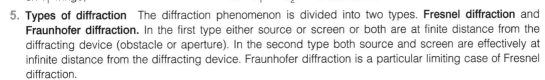

For $C = 0$, this hyperbola converts into a straight line. Hence, only Y_0 fringe is a straight line. The fringe pattern is as shown in figure.

MN is the centre line of screen,

on Y_0 fringe, $\qquad\qquad \Delta x = S_1 P - S_2 P = 0$

on Y_1 fringe, $\qquad\qquad \Delta x = S_2 P - S_1 P = \lambda$

on Y_1' fringe, $\qquad\qquad \Delta x = S_1 P - S_2 P = \lambda$ and so on

5. **Types of diffraction** The diffraction phenomenon is divided into two types. **Fresnel diffraction** and **Fraunhofer diffraction.** In the first type either source or screen or both are at finite distance from the diffracting device (obstacle or aperture). In the second type both source and screen are effectively at infinite distance from the diffracting device. Fraunhofer diffraction is a particular limiting case of Fresnel diffraction.

6. **Difference between interference and diffraction** Both interference and diffraction are the results of superposition of waves, so they are often present simultaneously as in Young's double slit experiment. However, interference is the result of superposition of waves from two different wavefronts while diffraction results due to superposition of wavelets from different points of the same wavefronts.

Solved Examples

PATTERNED PROBLEMS

Based on YDSE

Note *Unless mentioned in the question consider two sources S_1 and S_2 as coherent.*

Type 1. *Based on interference by thin films*

Concept

Interference effects are commonly observed in thin films, such as thin layers of oil on water or the thin surface of a soap bubble.

The varied colours observed when white light is incident on such films result from the interference of waves reflected from the two surfaces of the film.

Consider a film of uniform thickness t and index of refraction μ, as shown in figure. Let us assume that the light rays travelling in air are nearly normal to the two surfaces of the film. To determine whether the reflected rays interfere constructively or destructively, we first note the following facts.

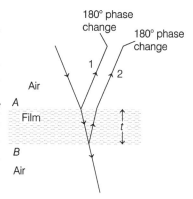

(i) The wavelength of light in a medium whose refractive index is μ, is

$$\lambda_\mu = \frac{\lambda}{\mu}$$

where, λ is the wavelength of light in vacuum (or air).

(ii) If a wave is reflected from a denser medium, it undergoes a phase change of 180°. Let us apply these rules to the film shown in figure. The path difference between the two rays 1 and 2 is $2t$ while the phase difference between them is 180°. Hence, condition of **constructive** interference will be

$$2t = (2n - 1)\frac{\lambda_\mu}{2} \qquad\qquad (n = 1, 2, 3,...)$$

or
$$2\mu t = \left(n - \frac{1}{2}\right)\lambda \qquad\qquad \left(\text{as } \lambda_\mu = \frac{\lambda}{\mu}\right)$$

Similarly, condition of **destructive** interference will be
$$2\mu t = n\lambda \qquad\qquad (n = 0, 1, 2,...)$$

Note *Where there is a phase difference of π between two interfering rays, conditions of maximas and minimas are interchanged.*

⦿ **Example 1** *Calculate the minimum thickness of a soap bubble film ($\mu = 1.33$) that results in constructive interference in the reflected light if the film is illuminated with light whose wavelength in free space is $\lambda = 600$ nm.*

Solution For constructive interference in case of soap film,

$$2\mu t = \left(n - \frac{1}{2}\right)\lambda \qquad\qquad (n = 1, 2, 3, \ldots)$$

For minimum thickness t, $n = 1$

or

$$2\mu t = \frac{\lambda}{2} \quad \text{or} \quad t = \frac{\lambda}{4\mu} = \frac{600}{4 \times 1.33}$$

$$= 112.78 \text{ nm} \qquad\qquad\qquad\qquad \textbf{Ans.}$$

⦿ **Example 2** *In solar cells, a silicon solar cell ($\mu = 3.5$) is coated with a thin film of silicon monoxide SiO ($\mu = 1.45$) to minimize reflective losses from the surface. Determine the minimum thickness of SiO that produces the least reflection at a wavelength of 550 nm, near the centre of the visible spectrum. Assume approximately normal incidence.*

Solution The reflected light is a minimum when rays 1 and 2 (shown in figure) meet the condition of destructive interference.

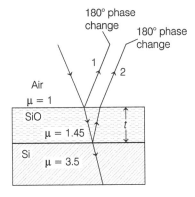

Note Both rays undergo a 180° phase change upon reflection. The net change in phase due to reflection is therefore zero, and the condition for a reflection minimum requires a path difference of $\lambda_\mu / 2$. Hence,

$$2t = \frac{\lambda}{2\mu} \quad \text{or} \quad t = \frac{\lambda}{4\mu} = \frac{550}{4\,(1.45)}$$

$$= 94.8 \text{ nm} \qquad\qquad\qquad\qquad \textbf{Ans.}$$

Type 2. *Based on conditions of maxima or minima*

Concept

(i) In the problems of YDSE, our first task is to find the path difference. Let us take a typical case. In the figure shown, path of ray 1 is more than path of ray 2 by a distance,

$$\Delta x_1 = d \sin\alpha$$

and

$$\Delta x_2 = (\mu_1 - 1)\, t_1$$

and path of ray 2 is greater than path of ray 1 by a distance,

$$\Delta x_3 = \frac{yd}{D} \quad \text{and} \quad \Delta x_4 = (\mu_2 - 1) t_2$$

Therefore, net path difference is

$$\Delta x = (\Delta x_1 + \Delta x_2) \sim (\Delta x_3 + \Delta x_4)$$

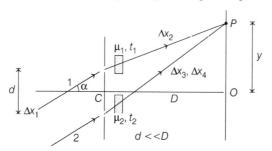

(ii) Once the path difference is known, put

$$\Delta x = n\lambda \qquad \text{(for maximum intensity)}$$

and

$$\Delta x = (2n - 1) \frac{\lambda}{2} \qquad \text{(for minimum intensity)}$$

Note *If medium is not air or medium is different on two sides of the slits, then for conditions of maxima/minima phase difference between two interfering beams is more important rather than the path difference. For phase difference, we will use*

$$\Delta\phi \quad or \quad \phi = \frac{2\pi}{\lambda}(\Delta x)$$

Here, λ is the wavelength in that particular medium.

⊚ **Example 3** *Distance between two slits is d. Wavelength of light is λ. There is a source of light S behind S_2 at a distance D_1. A glass slab of thickness t and refractive index μ is kept in front of S_1. Find*

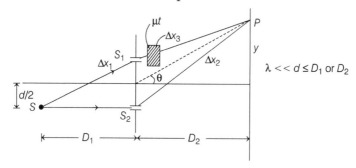

(a) *Net path difference at point P at an angular position θ.*
(b) *Write the equation for finding two angular positions corresponding to second order minima (y_2 and $y_2{}'$).*
(c) *If θ in part (b) does not come out to be small, then find two y-coordinates corresponding to them.*

Solution (a) $\Delta x_1 = SS_1 - SS_2 = \dfrac{(d/2)(d)}{D_1}$ $\qquad\qquad\left(\text{Using } \Delta x = \dfrac{yd}{D}\right)$

$$= \dfrac{d^2}{2D_1}$$

$$\Delta x_2 = d \sin \theta$$

$$\Delta x_3 = (\mu - 1)\, t$$

$\therefore\qquad\qquad \Delta x_{\text{net}} = (\Delta x_1 + \Delta x_3) \sim \Delta x_2$

$$= \left\{\dfrac{d^2}{2D_1} + (\mu - 1)\, t\right\} \sim d \sin \theta$$

(b) Corresponding to second order minima, net path difference should be $\dfrac{3\lambda}{2}$. So, let θ_1 and θ_2 be the two angular positions, then

$$\left\{\dfrac{d^2}{2D_1} + (\mu - 1)\, t\right\} - d \sin \theta_1 = \dfrac{3\lambda}{2}$$

and $\qquad\qquad d \sin \theta_2 - \left\{\dfrac{d^2}{2D_1} + (\mu - 1)\, t\right\} = \dfrac{3\lambda}{2}$

From these two equations, we can find θ_1 and θ_2.

(c) Even if θ is not small, we can write

$$\tan \theta = \dfrac{y}{D_2}$$

$\therefore\qquad\qquad y = D_2 \tan \theta$

Therefore, two y-coordinates are

$$y_1 = D_2 \tan \theta_1$$

and $\qquad\qquad y_2 = D_2 \tan \theta_2$

◉ **Example 4** *In the figure shown, a parallel beam of light (of wavelength λ_1 in medium μ_1) is incident at an angle θ. Distance $S_1 O = S_2 O$. Distance between the slits is d.*

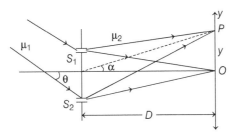

Using $d = 1\, mm, D = 1\, m, \theta = 30°, \lambda_1 = 0.3\, mm, \mu_1 = 4/3$ and $\mu_2 = 10/9$, find

(a) *the y-coordinate of the point where the total phase difference between the interfering waves is zero.*

(b) *If the intensity due to each light wave at point O is I_0, then find the resultant intensity at O.*

(c) *Find y-coordinate of the nearest maxima above O.*

Solution (a) Wavelength of light in air,

$$\lambda_0 = \mu_1 \lambda_1 = 0.4 \text{ mm}$$

Wavelength of light in medium-2,

$$\lambda_2 = \frac{\lambda_0}{\mu_2} = \frac{0.4}{(10/9)} = 0.36 \text{ mm}$$

Let net path difference at some angle α is zero, then

$$\Delta\phi_1 + \Delta\phi_2 = 0$$

or $$\frac{2\pi}{\lambda_1}(\Delta x_1) + \frac{2\pi}{\lambda_2}(\Delta x_2) = 0$$

or $$\frac{\Delta x_1}{\lambda_1} + \frac{\Delta x_2}{\lambda_2} = 0$$

or $$\frac{d \sin\theta}{\lambda_1} + \frac{d \sin\alpha}{\lambda_2} = 0$$

∴ $$\sin\alpha = -\frac{\lambda_2}{\lambda_1}\sin\theta$$

$$= -\frac{0.36}{0.4} \times \frac{1}{2} = -0.45$$

∴ $$\alpha \approx -26.74°$$

$$y = D \tan\alpha$$

$$= (1 \text{ m}) \tan(-26.74°)$$

$$\approx -\frac{1}{2} m \qquad \qquad \textbf{Ans.}$$

(b) At O, net phase difference,

$$\Delta\phi \ \text{ or } \ \phi = \left(\frac{2\pi}{\lambda_1}\right)\Delta x_1$$

$$= \frac{2\pi}{\lambda_1}(d \sin\theta)$$

$$= \frac{2\pi}{0.3}(1)\sin 30°$$

$$= \frac{10\pi}{3} = 600°$$

Using the equation $\quad I = 4 I_0 \cos^2\dfrac{\phi}{2}$, we have

$$I = 4 I_0 \cos^2(300°)$$

$$= I_0 \qquad \qquad \textbf{Ans.}$$

(c) At O, phase difference $\Delta\phi_1$ is $\dfrac{10\pi}{3}$ which is greater than 2π but less than 4π. So, to make it 4π, we must have

$$\Delta\phi_1 + \Delta\phi_2 = 4\pi$$

$$\Delta\phi_2 = 4\pi - \frac{10\pi}{3} = \frac{2\pi}{3}$$

$$\Delta\phi_2 = \frac{2\pi}{3} = \frac{2\pi}{\lambda_2}(\Delta x_2) = \frac{2\pi}{\lambda_2}(d \sin\alpha)$$

or $$\sin \alpha = \frac{\lambda_2}{3d} = \frac{0.36}{3 \times 1} = 0.12$$

∴ $$\alpha \approx 6.89°$$

Now, $$y = D \tan \alpha$$
$$= (1 \text{ m}) \tan (6.89°)$$
$$= 0.12 \text{ m} \qquad\qquad \textbf{Ans.}$$

Type 3. *Based on the concept of $\Delta x = d \cos\theta$ and number of maxima or minima on the screen*

Concept

(i) If the slits are vertical [as in figure (a)], path difference is
$$\Delta x = d \sin\theta$$

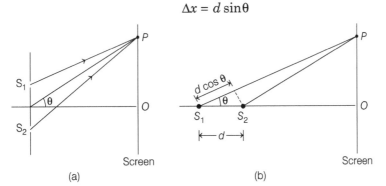

(a)   (b)

This path difference increases as θ increases. Hence, order of fringe ($d \sin\theta = n\lambda$ or $n = \frac{d \sin\theta}{\lambda}$) increases as we move away from point O on the screen.

Opposite is the case when the slits are horizontal [as in figure (b)]. Here, path difference is
$$\Delta x = d \cos\theta$$

This path difference decreases as θ increases. Hence, order of fringe $\left(n = \frac{d \cos\theta}{\lambda} \right)$

decreases as we move away from point O.
See the figure below,

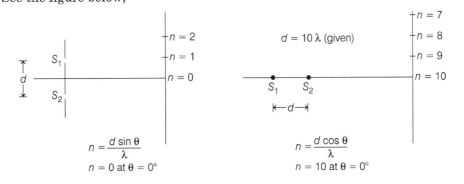

(ii) Sometimes maximum number of maximas or minimas are asked in the question which can be obtained on the screen. For this, we use the fact that value of $\sin\theta$ (or $\cos\theta$) can't be greater than 1. For example, in the first case when the slits are vertical,

$$d\sin\theta = n\lambda \quad \text{or} \quad \sin\theta = \frac{n\lambda}{d} \qquad \text{(for maximum intensity)}$$

$$\sin\theta \ngtr 1$$

$\therefore$

$$\frac{n\lambda}{d} \ngtr 1 \quad \text{or} \quad n \ngtr \frac{d}{\lambda}$$

Suppose in some question $\dfrac{d}{\lambda}$ is 4.6, then total number of maximas on the screen will be 9. Corresponding to $n = 0, \pm 1, \pm 2, \pm 3$ and ± 4.

(iii) Number of maximas or minimas are normally asked when λ is of the order of d. In this case, fringe size will be large and limited number of maximas and minimas will be obtained on the screen. If $\lambda << d$, then fringe size $\left(\omega = \dfrac{\lambda D}{d}\right)$ is very small (of the order of μm). So, millions of fringes can be obtained on the screen. So, number of maximas or minimas are normally not asked.

(iv) If $d << D$, then we can apply

$$\Delta x = d\sin\theta \quad \text{or} \quad d\cos\theta$$

If θ is large, then we cannot use the approximation

$$\sin\theta \approx \tan\theta = \frac{y}{D} \quad \text{or} \quad \Delta x = \frac{yd}{D}$$

But we can use

$$\tan\theta = \frac{y}{D} \quad \text{or} \quad y = D\tan\theta$$

▶ **Example 5** *In the YDSE apparatus shown in figure, $d << D$ and $d = 6\lambda$. Find*

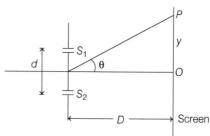

(a) total number of maximas and minimas on the screen
(b) two y-coordinates corresponding to third order maxima

Solution (a) In the given set up, $d << D$

Therefore, we can apply

$$\Delta x = d\sin\theta$$

$$(\Delta x)_{\min} = 0 \text{ at } \theta = 0° \text{ and}$$

$$(\Delta x)_{\max} = 6\lambda \text{ at } \theta = 90°$$

Therefore, total number of maximas are **eleven** corresponding to,

$$\Delta x = 0, \pm\lambda, \pm 2\lambda, \pm 3\lambda, \pm 4\lambda \text{ and } \pm 5\lambda$$

Note $\Delta x = 6\lambda$ *will also produce maxima but it is corresponding to* $\theta = 90°$ *and in the figure, we can see that* $\theta = 90°$ *point lies outside the screen. So, we will have to ignore this maxima. Similarly, total number of minimas are* **twelve** *corresponding to :*

$$\Delta x = \pm\,0.5\,\lambda,\pm\,1.5\,\lambda,\pm\,2.5\,\lambda,\pm\,3.5\,\lambda,\pm\,4.5\,\lambda \;\; and \;\; \pm\,5.5\,\lambda$$

(b) Third order minima lies at

$$\Delta x = \pm\,3\,\lambda$$

$\therefore$ $$d\sin\theta = \pm\,3\,\lambda \quad or \quad 6\lambda\sin\theta = \pm\,3\,\lambda$$

or $$\sin\theta = \pm\frac{1}{2} \quad or \quad \theta = \pm\,30°$$

Now, $$\frac{y}{D} = \tan\theta \;\; and \;\; y = D\tan\theta$$

$\therefore$ $$y = \pm\,D\tan 30° \quad or \quad y = \pm\frac{D}{\sqrt 3}$$ **Ans.**

◉ **Example 6** *In the set up shown in figure $d \ll D$ and $d = 4\lambda$, find*

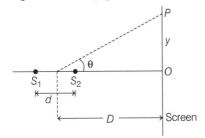

(a) total number of maximas and minimas on the screen

(b) y-coordinates corresponding to minima nearest to O.

Solution (a) In the given set up, $d \ll D$, therefore we can use

$$\Delta x = d\cos\theta$$
$$(\Delta x)_{min} = 0 \;\; at \;\; \theta = 90°$$
$$(\Delta x)_{max} = d = 4\lambda \;\; at \;\; \theta = 0°$$

Therefore, total number of maximas are **seven** corresponding to

$$\Delta x = 4\lambda, \pm\,3\,\lambda, \pm\,2\,\lambda \;\; and \;\; \pm\,\lambda$$

Note $\Delta x = 0$ *also produce maxima. But this is corresponding to* $\theta = 90°$*, which does not lie on screen.*

Similarly, total number of minimas are **eight** corresponding to

$$\Delta x = \pm\,3.5\,\lambda, \pm\,2.5\,\lambda, \pm\,1.5\,\lambda \;\; and \;\; \pm\,0.5\,\lambda$$

(b) Minima nearest to O are corresponding to

$$\Delta x = \pm\,3.5\,\lambda$$

$\therefore$ $$d\cos\theta = \pm\,3.5\,\lambda \quad or \quad 4\lambda\cos\theta = \pm\,3.5\,\lambda$$

or $$\theta = \pm\cos^{-1}\left(\frac{3.5\,\lambda}{4\,\lambda}\right) \quad or \quad \theta = \pm\cos^{-1}\left(\frac{7}{8}\right)$$

Now, $$\frac{y}{D} = \tan\theta \quad \Rightarrow \quad y = D\tan\theta$$

$\therefore$ $$y = \pm\,D\tan\left\{\cos^{-1}\left(\frac{7}{8}\right)\right\}$$ **Ans.**

● **Example 7** *There is a large circle (not a screen this time) around two coherent sources S_1 and S_2 kept at a distance $d = 3.4\lambda$.*

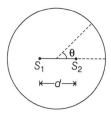

(a) Find total number of maximas on this circle.

(b) Four angular positions corresponding to third order maxima on this circle.

Solution (a) Since, radius of circle >> d, therefore we can apply

$$\Delta x = d \cos\theta$$

Corresponding to given figure

$$(\Delta x)_{min} = 0 \text{ at } \theta = 90°$$

and

$$(\Delta x)_{max} = d = 3.4\lambda \text{ at } \theta = 0°$$

Note *This time, $\theta = 90°$ lies on the circle. Therefore, $\Delta x = 0$ corresponding to zero order maxima lie on circle (two in numbers). Hence, the total number of maximas are fourteen as shown below.*

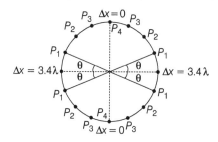

At P_1, $\Delta x = 3\lambda$

At P_2, $\Delta x = 2\lambda$

At P_3, $\Delta x = \lambda$

At P_4, $\Delta x = 0$

(b) Corresponding to third order maxima, (At P_1)

$$\Delta x = 3\lambda$$

or

$$d \cos\theta = 3\lambda$$

or

$$3.4 \cos\theta = 3\lambda$$

∴

$$\theta = \cos^{-1}\left(\frac{3}{3.4}\right)$$

Ans.

Four angular positions are as shown in figure.

Note *At $\theta = 0°$, $\Delta x = d = 3.4\lambda$. So, this is neither a maxima nor a minima.*

Exercise Find number of minimas on the circle in the above problem.

Type 4. *When one of the interfering rays is reflected from a denser medium*

Concept

In the shown figure, a virtual image S_2 is formed of the real source S_1. Further, $\lambda \ll d \ll D$. At any point P on the screen two rays interfere. One is direct from S_1 and other is reflected (or we can assume that it comes from S_2) from a denser medium. So, they will have a phase difference of π or 180° between them.

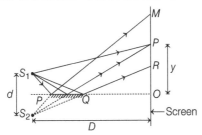

Whenever there exists a phase difference of π between the two interfering beams of light, conditions of maxima and minima are interchanged, i.e.

$$\Delta x = n\lambda \qquad \text{(for minimum intensity)}$$

and
$$\Delta x = (2n - 1)\,\lambda/2 \qquad \text{(for maximum intensity)}$$

Further, *PQRM* is the field of view corresponding to S_2 and the plane mirror. Or all reflected rays fall on this region. So, interference will be obtained only between *M* and *R* on the screen. Fringe width is still,

$$\omega = \frac{\lambda D}{d}$$

Total number of fringes obtained on the screen will be

$$N = \frac{MR}{\omega}$$

Suppose *OP* is
$$y = \frac{n\lambda D}{d} \qquad \text{(where, } n \text{ is an integer)}$$

$$= n\omega$$

and *P* lies between *M* and *R*, then it will become a dark fringe because conditions of maxima and minima have been interchanged.

◉ **Example 8** *A source of light of wavelength 5000 Å is placed as shown in figure. Considering interference of direct and reflected rays, determine the position of the region where the fringes will be visible and calculate the number of fringes.*

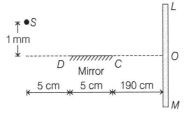

Solution Interference will be obtained between direct rays from S and reflected rays from S' (image of S on mirror).

Since, the reflected rays will lie between region P and Q on the screen. So, interference is obtained in this region only. From geometry will can show that,

$$OP = 1.9 \text{ cm} \quad \text{and} \quad OQ = 3.9 \text{ cm}$$

∴ $$PQ = 2 \text{ cm} \qquad \textbf{Ans.}$$

Fringe width , $\omega = \dfrac{\lambda D}{d} = \dfrac{(5000 \times 10^{-8})(200)}{(2 \times 10^{-1})} \text{ cm} = 0.05 \text{ cm}$

Total number of fringes in the region PQ,

$$N = \frac{PQ}{\omega} = \frac{2}{0.05} = 40 \qquad \textbf{Ans.}$$

Type 5. *Based on conditions of double interference*

Concept

On screen-1 interference takes place first time and intensity varies between 0 and $4I_0$. There are further two slits on screen-1 at S_3 and S_4. Therefore, second time interference takes place on screen-2 due to two rays of light from S_3 and S_4.

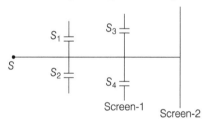

⦿ **Example 9** *Consider the situation shown in figure. The two slits S_1 and S_2 placed symmetrically around the centre line are illuminated by a monochromatic light of wavelength λ. The separation between the slits is d. The light transmitted by the slits falls on a screen M_1 placed at a distance D from the slits. The slit S_3 is at the centre line and the slit S_4 is at a distance y from S_3. Another screen M_2 is placed at a further distance D away from M_1. Find the ratio of the maximum to minimum intensity observed on M_2 if y is equal to ($d \ll D$)*

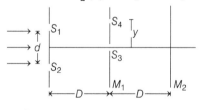

(a) $\dfrac{\lambda D}{2d}$ (b) $\dfrac{\lambda D}{d}$ (c) $\dfrac{\lambda D}{4d}$

Solution $S_1S_3 = S_2S_3$

∴ Δx at S_3 is zero. Therefore, intensity at S_3 will be $4I_0$. Let us call it I_1. Thus,

$$I_{S_3} = I_1 = 4I_0$$

Now, I_{S_4} (or I_2) depends on the value of y.

(a) When $y = \dfrac{\lambda D}{2d}$

$$\Delta x = \frac{yd}{D} = \frac{\lambda}{2}$$

∴ $$I_{S_4} = I_2 = 0$$

or $$\frac{I_{max}}{I_{min}} = \left(\frac{\sqrt{I_1} + \sqrt{I_2}}{\sqrt{I_1} - \sqrt{I_2}}\right)^2 = 1$$ **Ans.**

(b) When $y = \dfrac{\lambda D}{d}$

$$\Delta x = \frac{yd}{D} = \lambda$$

∴ $$I_{S_4} = I_2 = 4I_0$$

or $$\frac{I_{max}}{I_{min}} = \left(\frac{\sqrt{I_1} + \sqrt{I_2}}{\sqrt{I_1} - \sqrt{I_2}}\right)^2 = \infty$$

(c) When $y = \dfrac{\lambda D}{4d}$

$$\Delta x = \frac{yd}{D} = \frac{\lambda}{4}$$

⇒ $$\Delta\phi = \phi = 90°$$

∴ $$I_{S_4} = I_2 = 4I_0 \cos^2\frac{\phi}{2} = 2I_0$$

or $$\frac{I_{max}}{I_{min}} = \left(\frac{\sqrt{I_1} + \sqrt{I_2}}{\sqrt{I_1} - \sqrt{I_2}}\right)^2 = 34$$ **Ans.**

⊙ **Example 10** *Consider the arrangement shown in figure. By some mechanism, the separation between the slits S_3 and S_4 can be changed. The intensity is measured at the point P which is at the common perpendicular bisector of S_1S_2 and S_3S_4. When $z = \dfrac{D\lambda}{2d}$, the intensity measured at P is I. Find the intensity when z is equal to*

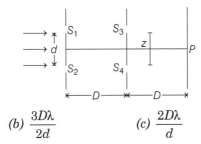

(a) $\dfrac{D\lambda}{d}$ (b) $\dfrac{3D\lambda}{2d}$ (c) $\dfrac{2D\lambda}{d}$

Solution $|y_{S_3}| = |y_{S_4}| = \dfrac{z}{2} = y$ (say)

When $\hspace{4cm} z = \dfrac{D\lambda}{2d}, \ \dfrac{z}{2} = y = \dfrac{D\lambda}{4d}$

∴ $\hspace{4.5cm} \Delta x = \dfrac{yd}{D} = \dfrac{\lambda}{4}$

and we have seen in the above example that, at $\Delta x = \dfrac{\lambda}{4}$, intensity is $2I_0$.

∴ $\hspace{4.5cm} I_{S_3} = I_{S_4} = 2I_0$

Now, P is at the perpendicular bisector of $S_3 S_4$. Therefore, intensity at P will be four times of $2I_0$ or $8I_0$.

∴ $\hspace{4.5cm} 8I_0 = I$ $\hspace{5cm}$ (Given)

Hence, $\hspace{4.5cm} I_0 = \dfrac{I}{8}$

(a) When $z = \dfrac{D\lambda}{d}$

$\hspace{4.5cm} y = \dfrac{z}{2} = \dfrac{D\lambda}{2d}$

∴ $\hspace{4.5cm} \Delta x = \dfrac{yd}{D} = \dfrac{\lambda}{2}$

or $\hspace{4.5cm} I_{S_3} = I_{S_4} = 0$

Hence, $\hspace{4.5cm} I_P = 0$ $\hspace{5cm}$ **Ans.**

(b) When $\hspace{4.5cm} z = \dfrac{3D\lambda}{2d}$

$\hspace{4.5cm} y = \dfrac{z}{2} = \dfrac{3D\lambda}{4d}$

$\hspace{4.5cm} \Delta x = \dfrac{yd}{D} = \dfrac{3\lambda}{4}$

∴ $\hspace{3.5cm} \Delta\phi \ \text{ or } \ \phi = \dfrac{2\pi}{\lambda}(\Delta x) = \dfrac{3\pi}{2}$

Using $\hspace{4.5cm} I = 4I_0 \cos^2 \dfrac{\phi}{2}$

We have, $\hspace{4.5cm} I_{S_3} = I_{S_4} = 2I_0$

∴ $\hspace{4.5cm} I_P = 4(2I_0) = 8I_0 = I$ $\hspace{4cm}$ **Ans.**

(c) When $z = \dfrac{2D\lambda}{d}$

$\hspace{4.5cm} y = \dfrac{z}{2} = \dfrac{D\lambda}{d}$

∴ $\hspace{4.5cm} \Delta x = \dfrac{yd}{D} = \lambda$

∴ $\hspace{4.5cm} I_{S_3} = I_{S_4} = 4I_0$

$\hspace{4.5cm} I_P = 4(4I_0) = 16 I_0 = 2I$ $\hspace{4cm}$ **Ans.**

> **Type 6.** *When no approximation can be taken in finding the path difference*

Concept

If D is not very very greater than d, then we cannot apply $\Delta x = d \sin\theta$ or $d\cos\theta$ or $\dfrac{yd}{D}$. In this case, we will have to find the path difference by using geometry.

⊚ **Example 11** *Two coherent point sources S_1 and S_2 emit light of wavelength λ. The separation between sources is 2λ. Consider a line passing through S_2 and perpendicular to the line $S_1 S_2$. What is the smallest distance on this line from S_2 where a minimum of intensity occurs?*

Solution At S_2, $\qquad\qquad\qquad\qquad \Delta x = 2\lambda$

Therefore, the minima closest to S_2 will be corresponding to the path difference $\Delta x = \dfrac{3\lambda}{2}$. Suppose this point is P at a distance y from S_2. Then,

$$S_1 P - S_2 P = \frac{3\lambda}{2}$$

$$\sqrt{y^2 + (S_1 S_2)^2} - y = \frac{3\lambda}{2}$$

or $\qquad\qquad \sqrt{y^2 + (2\lambda)^2} = \left(y + \frac{3\lambda}{2}\right)$

Squaring and then solving this equation, we get

$$y = \frac{7\lambda}{12} \qquad\qquad\qquad \textbf{Ans.}$$

> **Type 7.** *Based on single slit diffraction*

⊚ **Example 12** *A screen is placed 50 cm from a single slit, which is illuminated with 6000 Å light. If distance between the first and third minima in the diffraction pattern is 3.0 mm, what is the width of the slit?*

Solution Position of first minima on a single slit diffraction pattern is given by

$$d \sin\theta = n\lambda$$

For small value of θ, $\sin\theta \approx \theta = \dfrac{y}{D}$

∴ $\qquad\qquad\qquad \dfrac{yd}{D} = n\lambda \quad$ or $\quad y = \dfrac{n\lambda D}{d}$

∴ Distance between third order minima and first order minima will be

$$\Delta y = y_3 - y_1 = \frac{(3-1)\,(\lambda D)}{d} = \frac{2\lambda D}{d}$$

Substituting the values, we have

$$\Delta y = \frac{(2)\,(6 \times 10^{-7})\,(0.5)}{3 \times 10^{-3}}$$

$$= 2 \times 10^{-4} \text{ m}$$

$$= 0.2 \text{ mm} \qquad\qquad\qquad \textbf{Ans.}$$

⊚ **Example 13** *In a single slit diffraction experiment first minima for* $\lambda_1 = 660$ *nm coincides with first maxima for wavelength* λ_2. *Calculate the value of* λ_2.

Solution Position of minima in diffraction pattern is given by

$$d \sin \theta = n\lambda$$

For first minima of λ_1, we have

$$d \sin \theta_1 = (1) \lambda_1$$

or

$$\sin \theta_1 = \frac{\lambda_1}{d} \qquad \ldots(\text{i})$$

The first maxima approximately lies between first and second minima. For wavelength λ_2, its position will be

$$d \sin \theta_2 = \frac{3}{2} \lambda_2$$

∴

$$\sin \theta_2 = \frac{3\lambda_2}{2d} \qquad \ldots(\text{ii})$$

The two will coincide if

$$\theta_1 = \theta_2$$

or

$$\sin \theta_1 = \sin \theta_2$$

∴

$$\frac{\lambda_1}{d} = \frac{3\lambda_2}{2d}$$

or

$$\lambda_2 = \frac{2}{3} \lambda_1$$

$$= \frac{2}{3} \times 660 \text{ nm}$$

$$= 440 \text{ nm} \qquad \qquad \textbf{Ans.}$$

Miscellaneous Examples

⊚ **Example 14** *Figure shows three equidistant slits illuminated by a monochromatic parallel beam of light. Let* $BP_0 - AP_0 = \lambda/3$ *and* $D \gg \lambda$

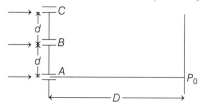

(a) *Show that* $d = \sqrt{2\lambda D/3}$

(b) *Show that the intensity at* P_0 *is three times the intensity due to any of the three slits individually.*

Solution (a) Given, $\qquad\qquad BP_0 - AP_0 = \lambda/3$

∴ $\qquad\qquad \sqrt{D^2 + d^2} - D = \frac{\lambda}{3}$

or
$$\sqrt{D^2 + d^2} = \left(D + \frac{\lambda}{3}\right)$$

Squaring both sides, we get
$$D^2 + d^2 = D^2 + \frac{\lambda^2}{9} + \frac{2D\lambda}{3}$$

Since $\lambda \ll D$, we can ignore the term $\dfrac{\lambda^2}{9}$. By ignoring this term, we get the desired result.
$$d = \sqrt{\frac{2\lambda D}{3}}$$

(b) Given,
$$BP_0 - AP_0 = \Delta x_{12} = \frac{\lambda}{3}$$

$\therefore$
$$\Delta\phi_{12} \quad \text{or} \quad \phi_{12} = 120°$$

Now,
$$CP_0 - AP_0 = \Delta x_{13} = \sqrt{(2d)^2 + D^2} - D$$

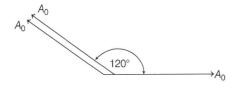

$$= D\left[1 + \left(\frac{2d}{D}\right)^2\right]^{\frac{1}{2}} - D$$

$$\approx D\left[1 + \frac{1}{2} \times \frac{4d^2}{D^2}\right] - D$$

$$= \frac{2d^2}{D}$$

Substituting, $d = \sqrt{\dfrac{2\lambda D}{3}} \quad$ or $\quad d^2 = \dfrac{2\lambda D}{3}$

We get,
$$\Delta x_{13} = \frac{4}{3}\lambda$$

$\therefore$
$$\Delta\phi_{13} \quad \text{or} \quad \phi_{13} = \frac{4}{3}(360°) = 480°$$
$$= 480° - 360° = 120°$$

Now, we know that in case of coherent sources amplitudes are first added by vector method. So, let individual amplitude is A_0.

The resultant amplitude will be given by
$$A = \sqrt{A_0^2 + (2A_0)^2 + 2(A_0)(2A_0)\cos 120°}$$
$$= \sqrt{3}\, A_0$$
$$I \propto A^2$$

and amplitude has become $\sqrt{3}$ times, therefore resultant intensity will become 3 times.

⊘ **Example 15** *Young's double slit experiment is carried out using microwaves of wavelength* $\lambda = 3\,cm$. *Distance between the slits is* $d = 5\,cm$ *and the distance between the plane of slits and the screen is* $D = 100\,cm$.

(a) *Find total number of maximas and*

(b) *their positions on the screen.*

Solution (a) The maximum path difference that can be produced = distance between the sources or 5 cm.

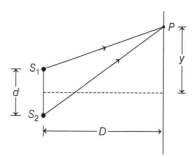

Thus, in this case we can have only three maximas, one central maxima and two on its either side for a path difference of λ or 3 cm.

(b) For maximum intensity at P,

$$S_2P - S_1P = \lambda$$

or $$\sqrt{(y + d/2)^2 + D^2} - \sqrt{(y - d/2)^2 + D^2} = \lambda$$

Substituting $d = 5$ cm, $D = 100$ cm and $\lambda = 3$ cm we get,

$$y = \pm\,75\,\text{cm}$$

Thus, the three maximas will be at

$$y = 0$$

and $$y = \pm\,75\,\text{cm}$$ **Ans.**

⊘ **Example 16** *Two coherent sources are 0.3 mm apart. They are 0.9 m away from the screen. The second dark fringe is at a distance of 0.3 cm from the centre. Find the distance of fourth bright fringe from the centre. Also, find the wavelength of light used.*

Solution Given, $d = 0.3 \times 10^{-3}$ m, $D = 0.9$ m

$$\frac{3\lambda D}{2d} = 0.3 \times 10^{-2}\,\text{cm} \qquad \text{(the distance of second dark fringe)}$$

∴. $$\frac{\lambda D}{d} = (0.3 \times 10^{-2})\left(\frac{2}{3}\right)$$

$$= 0.2 \times 10^{-2}\,\text{m} = 0.2\,\text{cm}$$

(i) Distance of fourth bright fringe from centre $= \dfrac{4\lambda D}{d} = 0.8$ cm **Ans.**

(ii) $\lambda = \left(\dfrac{d}{D}\right)(0.2 \times 10^{-2})\,\text{m} = \left(\dfrac{0.3 \times 10^{-3}}{0.9}\right)(0.2 \times 10^{-2})$

$$= 6.67 \times 10^{-7}\,\text{m}$$ **Ans.**

● **Example 17** *In a Young's double slit set up, the wavelength of light used is*
546 nm. The distance of screen from slits is 1 m. The slit separation is 0.3 mm.

(a) *Compare the intensity at a point P distant 10 mm from the central fringe where the*
intensity is I_0.

(b) *Find the number of bright fringes between P and the central fringe.*

Solution Given, $\lambda = 546$ nm $= 5.46 \times 10^{-7}$ m, $D = 1.0$ m and $d = 0.3$ mm $= 0.3 \times 10^{-3}$ m

(a) At a distance $y = 10$ mm $= 10 \times 10^{-3}$ m, from central fringe, the path difference will be

$$\Delta x = \frac{yd}{D} = \frac{(10 \times 10^{-3})(0.3 \times 10^{-3})}{1.0} = 3.0 \times 10^{-6} \text{ m}$$

The corresponding phase difference between the two interfering beams will be

$$\phi = \frac{2\pi}{\lambda} \cdot \Delta x$$

$$= \left(\frac{2\pi}{5.46 \times 10^{-7}} \right) (3.0 \times 10^{-6}) \text{ radian}$$

$$= 1978°$$

∴ $$\frac{\phi}{2} = 989°$$

∴ $$I = I_0 \cos^2 \frac{\phi}{2}$$

$$= I_0 \cos^2 (989)$$

$$= 3.0 \times 10^{-4} I_0 \qquad \qquad \textbf{Ans.}$$

(b) Fringe width, $\omega = \dfrac{\lambda D}{d} = \dfrac{(5.46 \times 10^{-7})(1.0)}{0.3 \times 10^{-3}}$ m

$$= 1.82 \text{ mm}$$

Since, $$\frac{y}{\omega} = \frac{10}{1.82} = 5.49$$

Therefore, number of bright fringes between P and central fringe will be 5 (excluding the
central fringe). **Ans.**

● **Example 18** *In a double slit pattern* ($\lambda = 6000$ Å)*, the first order and tenth order*
maxima fall at 12.50 mm and 14.75 mm from a particular reference point. If λ is
changed to 5500 Å, find the position of zero order and tenth order fringes, other
arrangements remaining the same.

Solution Distance between 10 fringes is

$$9\omega = (14.75 - 12.50) \text{ mm} = 2.25 \text{ mm}$$

∴ Fringe width, $$\omega = 0.25 \text{ mm}$$

When the wavelength is changed from 6000 Å to 5500 Å, the new fringe width will become,

$$\omega' = \left(\frac{5500}{6000} \right) \omega = \left(\frac{5500}{6000} \right) (0.25)$$

as fringe width $\propto \lambda$

∴ $$\omega' = 0.23 \text{ mm}$$

The position of central (or zero order) maxima will remain unchanged. Earlier it was at a
position,

$$Y_0 = Y_1 - \omega = (12.50 - 0.25) = 12.25 \text{ mm} \qquad \textbf{Ans.}$$

The new position of tenth order maxima will be

$$Y_{10} = Y_0 + 10\,\omega' = (12.25) + (10)\,(0.23) = 14.55 \text{ mm} \qquad \textbf{Ans.}$$

◈ **Example 19** *Two coherent narrow slits emitting light of wavelength λ in the same phase are placed parallel to each other at a small separation of 2 λ. The light is collected on a screen S which is placed at a distance D(>> λ) from the slit S_1 as shown in figure. Find the finite distance x such that the intensity at P is equal to intensity at O.*

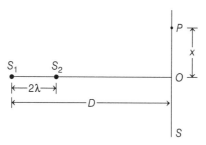

Solution Path difference at O,

$$S_1O - S_2O = 2\lambda$$

i.e. maximum intensity is obtained at O. Next maxima will be obtained at point P where,

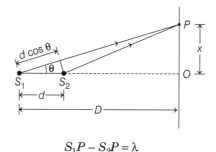

$$S_1P - S_2P = \lambda$$

or $$d \cos\theta = \lambda$$

or $$2\lambda \cos\theta = \lambda$$

or $$\cos\theta = \frac{1}{2}$$

∴ $$\theta = 60°$$

Now in ΔS_1PO, $$\frac{PO}{S_1O} = \tan\theta \quad \text{or} \quad \frac{x}{D} = \tan 60° = \sqrt{3}$$

∴ $$x = \sqrt{3}D \qquad \textbf{Ans.}$$

Note *At point O, path difference is 2λ, i.e. we get second order maxima. At point P, where path difference is λ (i.e x = √3D) we get first order maxima. The next, i.e. zero order maxima will be obtained where path difference, i.e. d cos θ = 0 or θ = 90°. At θ = 90°, x = ∞. So, our answer, i.e. finite distance of x should be x = √3D, corresponding to first order maxima.*

◉ **Example 20** *An interference is observed due to two coherent sources S_1 placed at origin and S_2 placed at $(0, 3\lambda, 0)$. Here, λ is the wavelength of the sources. A detector D is moved along the positive x-axis. Find x-coordinates on the x-axis (excluding $x = 0$ and $x = \infty$) where maximum intensity is observed.*

Solution At $x = 0$, path difference is 3λ. Hence, third order maxima will be obtained. At $x = \infty$, path difference is zero. Hence, zero order maxima is obtained. In between, first and second order maxima will be obtained.

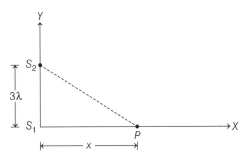

First order maxima
$$S_2P - S_1P = \lambda \quad \text{or} \quad \sqrt{x^2 + 9\lambda^2} - x = \lambda \quad \text{or} \quad \sqrt{x^2 + 9\lambda^2} = x + \lambda$$

Squaring on both sides, we get
$$x^2 + 9\lambda^2 = x^2 + \lambda^2 + 2x\lambda$$

Solving this, we get
$$x = 4\lambda$$

Second order maxima
$$S_2P - S_1P = 2\lambda \quad \text{or} \quad \sqrt{x^2 + 9\lambda^2} - x = 2\lambda \quad \text{or} \quad \sqrt{x^2 + 9\lambda^2} = (x + 2\lambda)$$

Squaring on both sides, we get
$$x^2 + 9\lambda^2 = x^2 + 4\lambda^2 + 4x\lambda$$

Solving, we get
$$x = \frac{5}{4}\lambda = 1.25\,\lambda$$

Hence, the desired x-coordinates are
$$x = 1.25\,\lambda \quad \text{and} \quad x = 4\,\lambda \qquad\qquad \textbf{Ans.}$$

Note (i) As we move along positive x-axis (from origin) order of maxima decreases from $n = 3$ to $n = 0$.
(ii) Here, we cannot take the path difference $d \cos\theta$ or $d \sin\theta$. Think why?

◉ **Example 21** *In a Young's double slit experiment, the light sources is at distance $l_1 = 20\,\mu m$ and $l_2 = 40\,\mu m$ from the main slit. The light of wavelength $\lambda = 500\,nm$ is incident on slits separated at a distance $10\,\mu m$. A screen is placed at a distance $D = 2\,m$ away from the slits as shown in figure. Find*

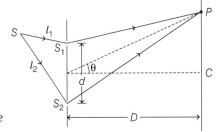

(a) *the values of θ relative to the central line where maxima appear on the screen?*

(b) *how many maxima will appear on the screen?*

(c) *what should be the minimum thickness of a slab of refractive index 1.5 placed on the path of one of the ray so that minima occurs at C?*

Solution (a) The optical path difference between the beams arriving at P,

$$\Delta x = (l_2 - l_1) + d \sin \theta$$

The condition for maximum intensity is

$$\Delta x = n\lambda \qquad\qquad [n = 0, \pm 1, \ \pm 2, \ldots]$$

Thus,

$$\sin \theta = \frac{1}{d} [\Delta x - (l_2 - l_1)] = \frac{1}{d} [n\lambda - (l_2 - l_1)]$$

$$= \frac{1}{10 \times 10^{-6}} [n \times 500 \times 10^{-9} - 20 \times 10^{-6}]$$

$$= 2 \left[\frac{n}{40} - 1 \right]$$

Hence,

$$\theta = \sin^{-1} \left[2 \left(\frac{n}{40} - 1 \right) \right] \qquad\qquad \textbf{Ans.}$$

(b) $|\sin \theta| \leq 1$

$\therefore$

$$-1 \leq 2 \left[\frac{n}{40} - 1 \right] \leq 1$$

or

$$-20 \leq (n - 40) \leq 20$$

or

$$20 \leq n \leq 60$$

Hence, number of maximas will be 41 between $n = 20$ and $n = 60$, if we take all maximas corresponding to $\theta = \pm 90°$ also.

(c) At C, phase difference

$$\phi = \left(\frac{2\pi}{\lambda} \right) (l_2 - l_1) = \left(\frac{2\pi}{500 \times 10^{-9}} \right) (20 \times 10^{-6})$$

$$= 80 \pi$$

Hence, maximum intensity will appear at C. For minimum intensity at C,

$$(\mu - 1) t = \frac{\lambda}{2}$$

or

$$t = \frac{\lambda}{2 (\mu - 1)} = \frac{500 \times 10^{-9}}{2 \times 0.5} = 500 \text{ nm} \qquad\qquad \textbf{Ans.}$$

Exercises

LEVEL 1

Assertion and Reason

Directions : *Choose the correct option.*

(*a*) *If both **Assertion** and **Reason** are true and the **Reason** is correct explanation of the **Assertion.***

(*b*) *If both **Assertion** and **Reason** are true but **Reason** is not the correct explanation of **Assertion.***

(*c*) *If **Assertion** is true, but the **Reason** is false.*

(*d*) *If **Assertion** is false but the **Reason** is true.*

(*e*) *Both **Assertion** and **Reason** are false.*

1. Assertion : In the figure shown, zero order maxima will lie above the point O.

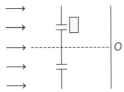

    Reason : Zero order maxima normally means a point where path difference is zero.

2. Assertion : If width of one slit in Young's double slit experiment is slightly increased, then maximum and minimum both intensities will increase.

    Reason : Intensity reaching from that slit on screen will slightly increase.

3. Assertion : A glass hemisphere is placed on a flat plate as shown. The observed interference fringes from this combination shall be circular.

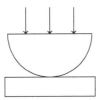

    Reason : In all cases fringes are circular .

4. Assertion : Two coherent sources S_1 and S_2 are placed in front of a screen as shown in figure. At point P, 10th order maxima is obtained . Then, 11th order maxima will be obtained above P.

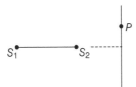

    Reason : For 11th order maxima path difference should be more.

5. Assertion : In the YDSE apparatus shown in figure $d \ll D$ and $\dfrac{d}{\lambda} = 4$, then second order maxima will be obtained at $\theta = 30°$.

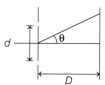

Reason : Total seven maximas will be obtained on screen.

Objective Questions

1. The colours are characterised by which of following character of light.
(a) Frequency (b) Amplitude (c) Wavelength (d) Velocity

2. The main difference in the phenomenon of interference and diffraction is that
(a) diffraction is due to interaction of light from the same wavefront, whereas interference is the interaction of waves from two isolated sources
(b) diffraction is due to interaction of light from same wavefront, whereas the interference is the interaction of two waves derived from two incoherent sources
(c) diffraction is due to interaction of waves derived from the same source, whereas the interference is the bending of light from the same wavefront
(d) diffraction is caused by the reflected waves from a source, whereas interference is caused due to refraction of waves from a source

3. Interference was observed in interference chamber when air is present. Now, the chamber is evacuated and if the same light is used, then for the same arrangement
(a) no interference pattern will be obtained
(b) exactly same interference pattern will be obtained with better contrast
(c) the fringe width is slightly decreased
(d) the fringe width is slightly increased

4. Three coherent waves having amplitudes 12 mm, 6 mm and 4 mm arrive at a given point with successive phase difference of $\pi / 2$. Then, the amplitude of the resultant wave is
(a) 7 mm (b) 10 mm
(c) 5 mm (d) 4.8 mm

5. The ratio of maximum to minimum intensity due to superposition of two waves is $\dfrac{49}{9}$. Then, the ratio of the intensity of component waves is
(a) $\dfrac{25}{4}$ (b) $\dfrac{5}{4}$
(c) $\dfrac{25}{6}$ (d) $\dfrac{7}{5}$

6. Two coherent sources of intensity ratio β^2 interfere. Then, the value of $(I_{max} - I_{min})/(I_{max} + I_{min})$ is
(a) $\dfrac{1 + \beta}{\sqrt{\beta}}$ (b) $\sqrt{\dfrac{1 + \beta}{\beta}}$
(c) $\dfrac{1 + \beta}{\beta}$ (d) None of these

7. In Young's double slit experiment, distance between two sources is 0.1 mm. The distance of screen from the sources is 20 cm. Wavelength of light used is 5460 Å. Then, angular position of first dark fringe is approximately

(a) 0.08°

(b) 0.16°

(c) 0.20°

(d) 0.32°

8. Young's double slit experiment is made in a liquid. The tenth bright fringe in liquid lies in screen where 6th dark fringe lies in vacuum. The refractive index of the liquid is approximately

(a) 1.8

(b) 1.54

(c) 1.67

(d) 1.2

9. A plane monochromatic light wave falls normally on a diaphragm with two narrow slits separated by 2.5 mm. The fringe pattern is formed on a screen 100 cm behind the diaphragm. By what distance will these fringes be displaced, when one of the slits is covered by a glass plate ($\mu = 1.5$) of thickness $10\,\mu m$?

(a) 2 mm

(b) 1 mm

(c) 3 mm

(d) 4 mm

10. In Young's double slit experiment, 60 fringes are observed in the central view zone with light of wavelength 4000 Å. The number of fringes that will be observed in the same view zone with the light of wavelength 6000 Å, is

(a) 40

(b) 90

(c) 60

(d) None of these

11. In a two slit experiment with monochromatic light, fringes are obtained on a screen placed at some distance from the slits. If the screen is moved by 5×10^{-2} m, towards the slits, the change in fringe width is 3×10^{-5} m. If separation between the slits is 10^{-3} m, the wavelength of light used is

(a) 6000 Å

(b) 5000 Å

(c) 3000 Å

(d) 4500 Å

12. A beam of light parallel to central line AB is incident on the plane of slits. The number of minima obtained on the large screen is n_1. Now, if the beam is tilted by some angle ($\neq 90°$) as shown in figure, then the number of minima obtained is n_2. Then,

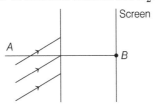

(a) $n_1 = n_2$

(b) $n_1 > n_2$

(c) $n_2 > n_1$

(d) n_2 will be zero

13. Young's double slit experiment is performed with blue and green light of wavelengths 4360 Å and 5460 Å, respectively. If x is the distance of 4th maxima from the central one, then

(a) $x\,(\text{blue}) = x\,(\text{green})$

(b) $x\,(\text{blue}) > x\,(\text{green})$

(c) $x\,(\text{blue}) < x\,(\text{green})$

(d) $\dfrac{x\,(\text{blue})}{x\,(\text{green})} = \dfrac{5460}{4360}$

14. In the diffraction pattern of single slit under bichromatic illumination, the first minimum with the wavelength λ_1 is found to be coincident with the third minimum at λ_2. So,

(a) $\lambda_1 = 3\lambda_2$

(b) $3\lambda_1 = \lambda_2$

(c) $\lambda_1 = 3.5\lambda_2$

(d) None of these

15. Light of wavelength λ in air enters a medium of refractive index μ. Two points in this medium, lying along the path of this light, are at a distance of x apart. The phase difference between these points is

    (a) $\mu\left(\dfrac{2\pi}{\lambda}\right)x$

    (b) $\dfrac{1}{\mu}\left(\dfrac{2\pi}{\lambda}\right)x$

    (c) $(\mu-1)\left(\dfrac{2\pi}{\lambda}\right)x$

    (d) $\dfrac{1}{\mu-1}\left(\dfrac{2\pi}{\lambda}\right)x$

16. In a Young's double-slit experiment D equals the distance of screen and d is the separation between the slits. The distance of the nearest point to the centre maximum where the intensity is same as that due to a single slit, is equal to

    (a) $\dfrac{D\lambda}{4d}$

    (b) $\dfrac{D\lambda}{2d}$

    (c) $\dfrac{D\lambda}{3d}$

    (d) $\dfrac{2D\lambda}{3d}$

17. Two beams of light having intensities I and $4I$ interfere to produce a fringe pattern on a screen. The phase difference between the beams is $\pi/2$ at point A and π at point B. Then, the difference between the resultant intensities at A and B is

    (a) $2I$ (b) $4I$ (c) $5I$ (d) $9I$

18. In Young's double slit experiment, the angular width of a fringe formed on a distant screen is $1°$, the wavelength of light used is $6000\,\text{Å}$. The spacing between the slits is

    (a) $6 \times 10^{-7}\,\text{m}$

    (b) $6.8 \times 10^{-5}\,\text{m}$

    (c) $3.4 \times 10^{-5}\,\text{m}$

    (d) $3.4 \times 10^{-4}\,\text{m}$

19. In the Young's double-slit experiment, the intensity of light at a point on the screen where the path difference is λ is K, (λ being the wave length of light used). The intensity at a point where the path difference is $\lambda/4$, will be

    (a) K (b) $K/4$ (c) $K/2$ (d) Zero

20. In the Young's double slit experiment, the intensities at two points P_1 and P_2 on the screen are respectively I_1 and I_2. If P_1 is located at the centre of a bright fringe and P_2 is located at a distance equal to a quarter of fringe width from P_1, then $\dfrac{I_1}{I_2}$ is

    (a) 2

    (b) 3

    (c) 4

    (d) None of these

Subjective Questions

Note   *You can take approximations in the answers.*

1. Consider an interference experiment using eight equally spaced slits. Determine the smallest phase difference in the waves from adjacent slits such that the resultant wave has zero amplitude.

2. Two coherent sources A and B of radio waves are 5.00 m apart. Each source emits waves with wavelength 6.00 m. Consider points along the line between the two sources. At what distances, if any, from A is the interference (a) constructive (b) destructive?

3. A radio transmitting station operating at a frequency of 120 MHz has two identical antennas that radiate in phase. Antenna B is 9.00 m to the right of antenna A. Consider point P between the antennas and along the line connecting them, a horizontal distance x to the right of antenna A. For what values of x will constructive interference occur at point P?

4. Coherent light from a sodium-vapour lamp is passed through a filter that blocks everything except for light of a single wavelength. It then falls on two slits separated by 0.460 mm. In the resulting interference pattern on a screen 2.20 m away, adjacent bright fringes are separated by 2.82 mm. What is the wavelength?

5. Find the angular separation between the consecutive bright fringes in a Young's double slit experiment with blue-green light of wavelength 500 nm. The separation between the slits is 2.0×10^{-3} m.

6. A Young's double slit apparatus has slits separated by 0.25 mm and a screen 48 cm away from the slits. The whole apparatus is immersed in water and the slits are illuminated by the red light ($\lambda = 700$ nm in vacuum). Find the fringe width of the pattern formed on the screen. ($\mu_w = 4/3$)

7. In a double slit experiment, the distance between the slits is 5.0 mm and the slits are 1.0 m from the screen. Two interference patterns can be seen on the screen one due to light with wavelength 480 nm, and the other due to light with wavelength 600 nm. What is the separation on the screen between the third order bright fringes of the two interference patterns?

8. Two slits 4.0×10^{-6} m apart are illuminated by light of wavelength 600 nm. What is the highest order fringe in the interference pattern?

9. Coherent light with wavelength 600 nm passes through two very narrow slits and the interference pattern is observed on a screen 3.00 m from the slits. The first order bright fringe is at 4.94 mm from the centre of the central bright fringe. For what wavelength of light will the first order dark fringe be observed at this same point on the screen?

10. Two very narrow slits are spaced 1.80 μm apart and are placed 35.0 cm from a screen. What is the distance between the first and second dark lines of the interference pattern when the slits are illuminated with coherent light of $\lambda = 550$ nm? (Hint : The angle θ is not small).

11. A narrow beam of 100 eV electrons is fired at two parallel slits very close to each other. The distance between the slits is 10 Å. The electron waves after passing through the slits interfere on a screen 3 m away from slits and form interference fringes. Find the width of the fringe.

12. In a Young's double slit set up, the wavelength of light used is 546 nm. The distance of screen from slits is 1 m. The slit separation is 0.3 mm.
    (a) Compare the intensity at a point P distant 10 mm from the central fringe where the intensity is I_0.
    (b) Find the number of bright fringes between P and the central fringe.

13. Interference pattern with Young's double slits 1.5 mm apart are formed on a screen at a distance 1.5 m from the plane of slits. In the path of the beam of one of the slits, a transparent film of 10 micron thickness and of refractive index 1.6 is interposed while in the path of the beam from the other slit a transparent film of 15 micron thickness and of refractive index 1.2 is interposed. Find the displacement of the fringe pattern.

14. In a Young's double slit experiment using monochromatic light, the fringe pattern shifts by a certain distance on the screen when a mica sheet of refractive index 1.6 and thickness 1.964 microns is introduced in the path of one of the interfering waves. The mica sheet is then removed and the distance between the slits and screen is doubled. It is found that the distance between successive maxima (or minima) now is the same as observed fringe shift upon the introduction of the mica sheet. Calculate the wavelength of the monochromatic light used in the experiment.

15. Interference effects are produced at point P on a screen as a result of direct rays from a 500 nm source and reflected rays from a mirror, as shown in figure. If the source is 100 m to the left of the screen and 1.00 cm above the mirror, find the distance y (in milimetres) to the first dark band above the mirror.

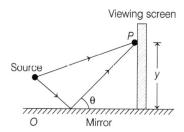

16. What is the thinnest film of coating with $n = 1.42$ on glass ($n = 1.52$) for which destructive interference of the red component (650 nm) of an incident white light beam in air can take place by reflection?

17. A glass plate ($n = 1.53$) that is $0.485 \, \mu m$ thick and surrounded by air is illuminated by a beam of white light normal to the plate.

(a) What wavelengths (in air) within the limits of the visible spectrum ($\lambda = 400$ to 700 nm) are intensified in the reflected beam?

(b) What wavelengths within the visible spectrum are intensified in the transmitted light?

18. A thick glass slab ($\mu = 1.5$) is to be viewed in reflected white light. It is proposed to coat the slab with a thin layer of a material having refractive index 1.3 so that the wavelength 6000 Å is suppressed. Find the minimum thickness of the coating required.

19. An oil film covers the surface of a small pond. The refractive index of the oil is greater than that of water. At one point on the film, the film has the smallest non-zero thickness for which there will be destructive interference in the reflected light when infrared radiation with wavelength 800 nm is incident normal to the film. When this film is viewed at normal incidence at this same point, for what visible wavelengths, if any, will there be constructive interference? (Visible light has wavelengths between 400 nm and 700 nm)

20. A possible means for making an airplane invisible to radar is to coat the plane with an anti reflective polymer. If radar waves have a wavelength of 3.00 cm and the index of refraction of the polymer is $\mu = 1.5$. How thick is the oil film? Refractive index of the material of airplane wings is greater than the refractive index of polymer.

21. Determine what happens to the double slit interference pattern if one of the slits is covered with a thin, transparent film whose thickness is $\dfrac{\lambda}{2(\mu - 1)}$, where λ is the wavelength of the incident light and μ is the index of refraction of the film.

LEVEL 2

Single Correct Option

1. The intensity of each of the two slits in Young's double slit experiment is I_0. Calculate the minimum separation between the two points on the screen where intensities are $2I_0$ and I_0. Given, the fringe width equal to β.

   (a) $\dfrac{\beta}{4}$ (b) $\dfrac{\beta}{3}$

   (c) $\dfrac{\beta}{12}$ (d) None of these

2. In Young's double slit experiment, the intensity of light at a point on the screen where path difference is λ is I. If intensity at another point is $I/4$, then possible path differences at this point are

   (a) $\lambda/2$, $\lambda/3$ (b) $\lambda/3$, $2\lambda/3$

   (c) $\lambda/3$, $\lambda/4$ (d) $2\lambda/3$, $\lambda/4$

3. White light is incident normally on a glass plate (in air) of thickness 500 nm and refractive index of 1.5. The wavelength (in nm) in the visible region (400 nm-700 nm) that is strongly reflected by the plate is

   (a) 450   (b) 600

   (c) 400   (d) 500

4. In a YDSE experiment, $d = 1$mm, $\lambda = 6000$ Å and $D = 1$ m. The minimum distance between two points on screen having 75% intensity of the maximum intensity will be

   (a) 0.50 mm   (b) 0.40 mm

   (c) 0.30 mm   (d) 0.20 mm

5. Let S_1 and S_2 be the two slits in Young's double slit experiment . If central maxima is observed at P and angle $S_1 P S_2 = \theta$, (θ is small) find the y-coordinates of the 3rd minima assuming the origin at the central maxima . (λ = wavelength of monochromatic light used).

   (a) $\pm \dfrac{2\lambda}{\theta}$ (b) $\pm \dfrac{5\lambda}{2\theta}$

   (c) $\pm \dfrac{5}{2}\lambda\theta$ (d) $\pm 2\lambda\theta$

6. The ratio of the intensity at the centre of a bright fringe to the intensity at a point one quarter of the fringe width from the centre is

   (a) 3   (b) 2

   (c) 4   (d) 1

7. In YDSE if a slab whose refractive index can be varied is placed in front of one of the slits . Then, the variation of resultant intensity at mid-point of screen with μ will be best represented by (μ is greater than or equal to 1)

   (a) 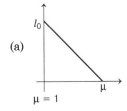   (b) 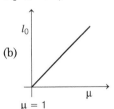   (c) 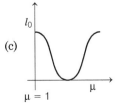   (d)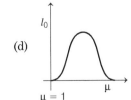

8. In YDSE, both slits produce equal intensities on the screen. A 100% transparent thin film is placed in front of one of the slits. Now, the intensity on the centre becomes 75% of the previous intensity. The wavelength of light is 6000 Å and refractive index of glass is 1.5. The minimum thickness of the glass slab is
   (a) $0.2\,\mu m$ (b) $0.3\,\mu m$ (c) $0.4\,\mu m$ (d) $0.5\,\mu m$

9. YDSE is carried with two thin sheets of thickness $10.4\,\mu m$ each and refractive index $\mu_1 = 1.52$ and $\mu_2 = 1.40$ covering the slits S_1 and S_2, respectively. If white light of range 400 nm to 780 nm is used, then which wavelength will form maxima exactly at point O, the centre of the screen

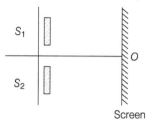

Screen

  (a) 416 nm only   (b) 624 nm only
  (c) 416 nm and 624 nm only   (d) None of these

10. Two light rays having the same wavelength λ in vacuum are in phase initially. Then, the first ray travels a path L_1 through a medium of refractive index n_1 while the second ray travels a path of length L_2 through a medium of refractive index n_2. The two waves are then combined to produce interference. The phase difference between the two waves is
   (a) $\dfrac{2\pi}{\lambda}(L_2 - L_1)$ (b) $\dfrac{2\pi}{\lambda}(n_1 L_1 - n_2 L_2)$ (c) $\dfrac{2\pi}{\lambda}(n_2 L_1 - n_1 L_2)$ (d) $\dfrac{2\pi}{\lambda}\left(\dfrac{L_1}{n_1} - \dfrac{L_2}{n_2}\right)$

11. An interference is observed due to two coherent sources separated by a distance 5λ along positive y-axis, where λ is the wavelength of light. A detector D is moved along the positive x-axis. The number of points on the x-axis excluding the points $x = 0$ and $x = \infty$ at which resultant intensity will be maximum, are
   (a) 4   (b) 5   (c) ∞ (d) zero

12. In Young's double-slit experiment, the y-coordinates of central maxima and 10th maxima are 2 cm and 5 cm respectively. When the YDSE apparatus is immersed in a liquid of refractive index 1.5, then corresponding y-coordinates will be
   (a) 2 cm, 7.5 cm   (b) 3 cm, 6 cm   (c) 2 cm, 4 cm   (d) 4/3 cm, 10/3 cm

13. In Young's double-slit experiment how many maximas can be obtained on a screen (including the central maximum) on both sides of the central fringes if $\lambda = 2000\,\text{Å}$ and $d = 7000\,\text{Å}$
   (a) 12   (b) 7   (c) 18   (d) 4

14. Two ideal slits S_1 and S_2 are at a distance d apart and illuminated by light of wavelength λ passing through an ideal source slit S placed on the line through S_2 as shown. The distance between the planes of slits and the source slit is D.

   A screen is held at a distance D from the plane of the slits. The minimum value of d for which there is darkness at O is

   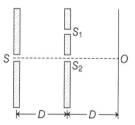

   (a) $\sqrt{\dfrac{3\lambda D}{2}}$ (b) $\sqrt{\lambda D}$

   (c) $\sqrt{\dfrac{\lambda D}{2}}$ (d) $\sqrt{3\lambda D}$

15. In the figure Young's double-slit experiment is shown. Q is the position of the first bright fringe on the one side of O. P is the 11th bright fringe on the other side, as measured from Q. If the wavelength of the light used is 600 nm, then S_1B will be equal to

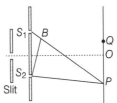

(a) 6×10^{-6} m
(c) 3.138×10^{-7} m

(b) 6.6×10^{-6} m
(d) 3.144×10^{-7} m

16. Two coherent light sources A and B are at a distance 3λ from each other (λ = wavelength). The distance from A on the x-axis at which the interference is constructive is

(a) 3λ
(c) $3.5\,\lambda$

(b) 4λ
(d) $1.5\,\lambda$

17. In the Young's double-slit experiment using a monochromatic light of wavelength λ, the path difference (in terms of an integer n) corresponding to any point   having half the peak intensity is

(a) $(2n + 1)\dfrac{\lambda}{2}$

(b) $(2n + 1)\dfrac{\lambda}{4}$

(c) $(2n + 1)\dfrac{\lambda}{8}$

(d) $(2n + 1)\dfrac{\lambda}{16}$

18. If two sources (each having intensity I_0) have a randomly varying phase difference $\phi(t)$, the resultant intensity will be given by

(a) $4I_0$
(c) $2I_0$

(b) $I_0/2$
(d) $I_0\sqrt{2}$

19. Two coherent point sources S_1 and S_2 are separated by a small distance d as shown. The fringes obtained on the screen will be

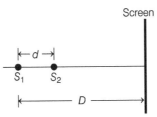

(a) points
(c) semi-circle

(b) straight lines
(d) concentric circles

20. In the below diagram, CP represents a wavefront and AO and BP, the corresponding two rays. Find the condition of θ for constructive interference at P between the ray BP and reflected ray OP.

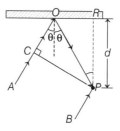

(a) $\cos\theta = \dfrac{3\lambda}{2d}$

(b) $\cos\theta = \dfrac{\lambda}{4d}$

(c) $\sec\theta - \cos\theta = \dfrac{\lambda}{d}$

(d) $\sec\theta - \cos\theta = \dfrac{4\lambda}{d}$

More than One Correct Options

1. If one of the slit of a standard Young's double slit experiment is covered by a thin parallel sided glass slab so that it transmits only one-half the light intensity of the other, then
   (a) the fringe pattern will get shifted towards the covered slit
   (b) the fringe pattern will get shifted away from the covered slit
   (c) the bright fringes will be less bright and the dark ones will be more bright
   (d) the fringe width will remain unchanged

2. A parallel beam of light ($\lambda = 5000$ Å) is incident at an angle $\theta = 30°$ with the normal to the slit plane in a Young's double slit experiment. The intensity due to each slit is I_0. Point O is equidistant from S_1 and S_2. The distance between slits is 1 mm.

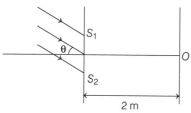

   (a) The intensity at O is $4I_0$
   (b) The intensity at O is zero
   (c) The intensity at a point on the screen 4 mm above O is $4I_0$
   (d) The intensity at a point on the screen 4 mm above O is zero

3. In YDSE set up shown in figure,

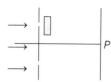

   (a) zero order maxima will lie above point P
   (b) first order maxima may lie above point P
   (c) first order maxima may lie below point P
   (d) zero order maxima may lie at point P

4. Bichromatic light of wavelengths $\lambda_1 = 5000$ Å and $\lambda_2 = 7000$ Å are used in YDSE. Then,
  (a) 14th order maxima of λ_1 will coincide with 10th order maxima of λ_2
  (b) 21st order maxima of λ_2 will coincide with 15th order maxima of λ_1
  (c) 11th order minima of λ_1 will coincide with 8th order minima of λ_2
  (d) 3rd order minima of λ_1 will coincide with 4th order minima of λ_2

Match the Columns

1. Two waves from coherent sources meet at a point in a phase difference of ϕ. Both the waves have same intensities. Match the following two columns.

Column I		Column II
(a) If $\phi = 60°$	(p)	Resultant intensity will become four times
(b) If $\phi = 90°$	(q)	Resultant intensity will become two times
(c) If $\phi = 0°$	(r)	Resultant intensity will remain unchanged
(d) If $\phi = 120°$	(s)	Resultant intensity will become three times

2. Two waves from coherent sources meet at a point in a path difference of Δx. Both the waves have same intensities. Match the following two columns.

Column I		Column II
(a) If $\Delta x = \lambda/3$	(p)	Resultant intensity will become three times
(b) If $\Delta x = \lambda/6$	(q)	Resultant intensity will remain same
(c) If $\Delta x = \lambda/4$	(r)	Resultant intensity will become two times
(d) If $\Delta x = \lambda/2$	(s)	Resultant intensity will become zero.

3. In terms of fringe width ω, match the following two columns.

Column I	Column II
(a) Distance between central maxima and third order maxima	(p) $2.5\,\omega$
(b) Distance between central maxima and third order minima	(q) $3.0\,\omega$
(c) Distance between first minima and fourth order maxima	(r) $3.5\,\omega$
(d) Distance between second order maxima and fifth order minima	(s) None of these

4. Match the following two columns.

Column I		Column II
(a)		(p) The zero order maxima will lie above point O
(b)		(q) The zero order maxima will lie below point O
(c)		(r) The zero order maxima may lie above or below point O
(d)		(s) The zero order maxima may lie at point O

5. In the figure shown, Z_1 and Z_2 are two screens. Line PO is the bisector line of S_1S_2 and S_3S_4. When Z_1 is removed, resultant intensity at O due to slits S_1 and S_2 is I. Now, Z_1 is placed. For different values of y given in Column I, match the resultant intensity at O given in Column II.

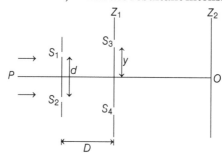

Column I		Column II	
(a)	$y = \dfrac{\lambda D}{2d}$	(p)	$3I$
(b)	$y = \dfrac{\lambda D}{6d}$	(q)	zero
(c)	$y = \dfrac{\lambda D}{4d}$	(r)	I
(d)	$y = \dfrac{\lambda D}{3d}$	(s)	None of these

Subjective Questions

1. A ray of light is incident on the left vertical face of the glass slab. If the incident light has an intensity I and on each reflection the intensity decreases by 90% and on each refraction the intensity decreases by 10%, find the ratio of the intensities of maximum to minimum in reflected pattern.

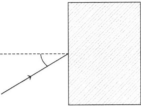

2. A parallel beam of white light falls on a thin film whose refractive index is equal to 4/3. The angle of incidence $i = 53°$. What must be the minimum film thickness if the reflected light is to be coloured yellow (λ of yellow $= 0.6\,\mu m$) most intensively? ($\tan 53° = 4/3$)

3. A convergent lens with a focal length of $f = 10\,cm$ is cut into two halves that are then moved apart to a distance of $d = 0.5\,mm$ (a double lens). Find the fringe width on screen at a distance of 60 cm behind the lens if a point source of monochromatic light ($\lambda = 5000\,Å$) is placed in front of the lens at a distance of $a = 15\,cm$ from it.

4. In the figure shown, a screen is placed normal to the line joining the two point coherent sources S_1 and S_2. The interference pattern consists of concentric circles.

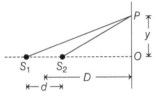

   (a) Find the radius of the nth bright ring.
   (b) If $d = 0.5\,mm$, $\lambda = 5000\,Å$ and $D = 100\,cm$, find the radius of the closest second bright ring.
   (c) Also, find the value of n for this ring.

5. In the Young's double slit experiment, a point source of $\lambda = 5000\,Å$ is placed slightly above the central axis as shown in the figure.

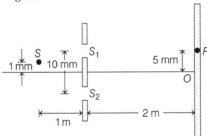

   (a) Find the nature and order of the interference at the point P.
   (b) Find the nature and order of the interference at O.
   (c) Where should we place a film of refractive index $\mu = 1.5$ and what should be its thickness so that maxima of zero order is obtained at O?

6. Light of wavelength $\lambda = 500$ nm falls on two narrow slits placed a distance $d = 50 \times 10^{-4}$ cm apart, at an angle $\phi = 30°$ relative to the slits as shown in figure. On the lower slit a transparent slab of thickness 0.1 mm and refractive index $\dfrac{3}{2}$ is placed. The interference pattern is observed at a distance $D = 2$ m from the slits. Then, calculate

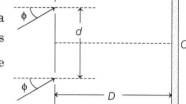

(a) position of the central maxima.
(b) the order of maxima at point C of screen.
(c) how many fringes will pass C, if we remove the transparent slab from the lower slit?

7. In the YDSE, the monochromatic source of wavelength λ is placed at a distance $\dfrac{d}{2}$ from the central axis (as shown in the figure), where d is the separation between the two slits S_1 and S_2.

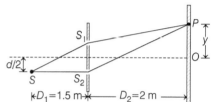

(a) Find the position of the central maxima.
(b) Find the order of interference formed at O.
(c) Now, S is placed on centre dotted line. Find the minimum thickness of the film of refractive index $\mu = 1.5$ to be placed in front of S_2 so that intensity at O becomes $\dfrac{3}{4}$ th of the maximum intensity.

(Take, $\lambda = 6000$ Å ; $d = 6$ mm)

8. YDSE is carried out in a liquid of refractive index $\mu = 1.3$ and a thin film of air is formed in front of the lower slit as shown in the figure. If a maxima of third order is formed at the origin O, find the thickness of the air film. Find the positions of the fourth maxima. The wavelength of light in air is $\lambda_0 = 0.78 \mu$m and $D/d = 1000$.

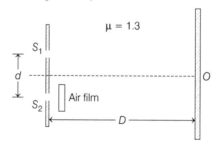

Answers

Introductory Exercise 32.1

1. $49 : 1$ *2.* (a) $4 : 1$ (b) $16 : 1$ *3.* $25 I_0$

Introductory Exercise 32.2

1. Because they are incoherent   *2.* Because they are highly coherent

3. $48.0\,\mu m$ *5.* (a) $0.75 I_0$ (b) $80\,nm$ *6.* (i) $0°$ (ii) $90°$ (iii) $120°$ (iv) $180°$

Exercises

LEVEL 1

Assertion and Reason

1. (b)   *2.* (a)   *3.* (c)   *4.* (d)   *5.* (b)

Objective Questions

1. (a)   *2.* (a)   *3.* (d)   *4.* (b)   *5.* (a)   *6.* (d)   *7.* (b)   *8.* (a)   *9.* (a)   *10.* (a)

11. (a)   *12.* (a)   *13.* (c)   *14.* (a)   *15.* (a)   *16.* (c)   *17.* (b)   *18.* (c)   *19.* (c)   *20.* (a)

Subjective Questions

1. $45°$ *2.* (a) $2.50\,m$ (b) $1.0\,m, 4.0\,m$ *3.* $0.75\,m, 2.0\,m, 3.25\,m, 4.50\,m, 5.75\,m, 7.0\,m, 8.25\,m$

4. $590\,nm$ *5.* $0.014°$ *6.* $1.0\,mm$ *7.* $0.072\,mm$

8. 6   *9.* $1200\,nm$ *10.* $12.6\,cm$ *11.* $36.6\,cm$

12. (a) $I_p = 3.0 \times 10^{-4} I_0$ (b) Five   *13.* $3\,mm$ *14.* $589\,nm$

15. $2.5\,mm$ *16.* $114\,nm$ *17.* (a) $424\,nm, 594\,nm$ (b) $495\,nm$

18. $1154\,Å$ *19.* $533\,nm$ *20.* $0.5\,cm$ *21.* Bright and dark fringes interchange positions

LEVEL 2

Single Correct Option

1. (c)   *2.* (b)   *3.* (b)   *4.* (d)   *5.* (b)   *6.* (b)   *7.* (c)   *8.* (a)   *9.* (c)   *10.* (b)

11. (a)   *12.* (c)   *13.* (b)   *14.* (c)   *15.* (a)   *16.* (b)   *17.* (b)   *18.* (c)   *19.* (d)   *20.* (b)

More than One Correct Options

1. (a,c,d)   *2.* (a,c)   *3.* (a,b,c)   *4.* (a,c)

Match the Columns

1. (a) → s   (b) → q   (c) → p   (d) → r   *2.* (a) → q   (b) → p   (c) → r   (d) → s

3. (a) → q   (b) → p   (c) → r   (d) → p   *4.* (a) → p   (b) → r,s   (c) → p   (d) → p

5. (a) → q   (b) → p   (c) → s   (d) → r

Subjective Questions

1. 361   *2.* $0.14\,\mu m$ *3.* $0.1\,mm$ *4.* (a) $D\sqrt{2\left(1 - \dfrac{n\lambda}{d}\right)}$ (b) $6.32\,cm$ (c) 998

5. (a) 70th order maxima (b) 20th order maxima (c) $t = 20\,\mu m$, in front of S_1

6. (a) At $\theta = 30°$ below C (b) 50 (c) 100   *7.* (a) $4\,mm$ above O (b) 20 (c) $2000\,Å$

8. (a) $7.8\,\mu m$ (b) $4.2\,mm, -0.6\,mm$

33

MODERN PHYSICS - I

33.1 Dual Nature of Electromagnetic Waves

Classical physics treats particles and waves as separate components. The mechanics of particles and the optics of waves are traditionally independent disciplines, each with its own chain of principles based on their results. We regard electrons as particles because they possess charge and mass and behave according to the laws of particle mechanics in such familiar devices as television picture tubes. We shall see, however, that it is just as correct to interpret a moving electron as a wave manifestation as it is to interpret it as a particle manifestation. We regard electromagnetic waves as waves because under suitable circumstances they exhibit diffraction, interference and polarization. Similarly, we shall see that under other circumstances they behave as a stream of particles. Rather we can say that they have the **dual nature.**

The wave nature of light (a part of electromagnetic waves) was first demonstrated by Thomas Young, who observed the interference pattern of two coherent sources. The particle nature of light was first proposed by Albert Einstein in 1905 in his explanation of the photoelectric effect. A particle of light called a **photon** has energy E that is related to the frequency f and wavelength λ of light wave by the Einstein equation,

$$E = hf = \frac{hc}{\lambda} \qquad \qquad \text{...(i)}$$

where, c is the speed of light (in vacuum) and h is Planck's constant.

$$h = 6.626 \times 10^{-34} \text{ J-s}$$
$$= 4.136 \times 10^{-15} \text{ eV-s}$$

Since, energies are often given in electron volt $(1 \text{ eV} = 1.6 \times 10^{-19} \text{ J})$ and wavelengths are in Å, it is convenient to the combination hc in eV-Å. We have,

$$hc = 12375 \text{ eV-Å}$$

Hence, Eq. (i) in simpler form can be written as

$$E \text{ (in eV)} = \frac{12375}{\lambda \text{ (in Å)}} \qquad \qquad \text{...(ii)}$$

The propagation of light is governed by its wave properties, whereas the exchange of energy between light with matter is governed by its particle properties. The wave particle duality is a general property of nature. For example, electrons (and other so called particles) also propagate as waves and exchange energy as particles.

33.2 Electromagnetic Spectrum

The basic source of electromagnetic wave is an accelerated charge. This produces the changing electric and magnetic fields which constitute an electromagnetic wave. An electromagnetic wave may have its wavelength varying from zero to infinity. Not all of them are known till date. Today we are familiar with electromagnetic waves having wavelengths as small as 30 fm $(1 \text{ fm} = 10^{-15} \text{ m})$ to as large as 30 km. The boundaries separating different regions of spectrum are not sharply defined, with the exception of the visible part of the spectrum. The visible part of the electromagnetic spectrum covers from 4000 Å to 7000 Å. An approximate range of wavelengths is associated with each colour :

violet (4000 Å– 4500 Å), blue (4500 Å–5200 Å), green (5200 Å–5600 Å), yellow (5600 Å–6000 Å), orange (6000 Å– 6250 Å) and red (6250 Å–7000 Å).

Figure shows the spectrum of electromagnetic waves. The classification is based roughly on how the waves are produced and or detected.

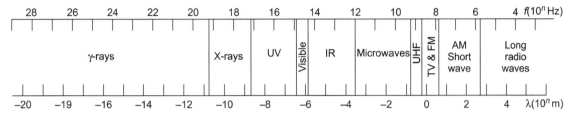

Fig. 33.1. The electromagnetic spectrum

γ-Rays   These were identified by P. Villiard in 1900. These are usually produced within the nucleus of an atom and extremely energetic by atomic standards. They cover the range from 0.1 Å down or equivalently from 10^{20} Hz up.

X-Rays   X-rays, discovered in 1895 by W. Roentgen extend from 100 Å to 0.1 Å. These are produced by the rapid deceleration of electrons that bombard a heavy metal target. These are also produced by electronic transitions between the energy levels in an atom. X-rays are used to study the atomic structure of crystals or molecules such as DNA. Besides their diagnostic and therapeutic use in medicine they have become an important tool in studying the universe.

Ultraviolet radiation   Ultraviolet (UV) rays were first discovered by J.W. Ritter in 1801. The ultraviolet region extends from 4000 Å to 100 Å. It plays a role in the production of vitamin D in our skins. But prolonged doses of UV radiation can induce cancers in humans. Glass absorbs UV radiation and hence, can provide some protection against the sun's rays. If the ozone in our atmosphere did not absorb the UV below 3000 Å, there would be a large number of cell mutations, especially cancerous ones, in humans. For this reason, the depletion of the ozone in our atmosphere by chlorofluorocarbons (CFCs) is now a matter of international concern.

Visible light   A lot of discussion has already been done on visible light in previous chapters. As electrons undergo transitions between energy levels in an atom, light is produced at well defined wavelengths. Light covering a continuous range of wavelengths is produced by the random acceleration of electrons in hot bodies. Our sense of vision and the process of photosynthesis in plants have evolved within the range of those wavelengths of sunlight that our atmosphere does not absorb.

Infrared radiation   The infrared region (IR) starts at 7000 Å and extends to about 1 mm. It was discovered in 1800 by M. Herchel. It is associated with the vibration and rotation of molecules and is perceived by us as heat. IR is used in the early detection of tumours.

Microwaves   Microwaves cover wavelengths from 1 mm to about 15 cm. Microwaves upto about 30 GHz (1 cm) may be generated by the oscillations of electrons in a device called klystron. Microwave ovens are used in kitchens. Modern intercity communications such as phone conversations and TV programs are often carried *via* a cross country network of microwave antennas.

Radio and TV signals   Radio waves are generated when charges are accelerating through conducting wires. Their wavelengths lie in the range 10^{14} m to 10 cm. They are generated by *LC* oscillators and are used in radio and television communication systems.

33.3 **Momentum and Radiation Pressure**

An electromagnetic wave transports linear momentum. We state, without proof that the linear momentum carried by an electromagnetic wave is related to the energy it transports according to

$$p = \frac{E}{c} \qquad \text{...(i)}$$

If the wave is incident in the direction perpendicular to a surface and is completely absorbed, then Eq. (i) tells us the linear momentum imparted to the surface. If surface is perfectly reflecting, the momentum change of the wave is doubled. Consequently, the momentum imparted to the surface is also doubled.

According to Newton's second law, the force exerted by an electromagnetic wave on a surface may be related by the equation

$$F = \frac{\Delta p}{\Delta t}$$

From Eq. (i),
$$\frac{\Delta p}{\Delta t} = \frac{1}{c}\left(\frac{\Delta E}{\Delta t}\right)$$

$$\therefore \qquad F = \frac{1}{c}\left(\frac{\Delta E}{\Delta t}\right) \qquad \text{...(ii)}$$

Intensity (I) of a wave is the energy transported per unit area per unit time.

or
$$I = \left(\frac{1}{S}\right)\frac{\Delta E}{\Delta t}$$

$$\therefore \qquad \frac{\Delta E}{\Delta t} = IS$$

Substituting in Eq. (ii),
$$F = \frac{IS}{c}$$

or
$$\frac{F}{S} = \text{pressure} = \frac{I}{c}$$

or
$$P_{\text{rad}} = \frac{I}{c}$$

$\dfrac{I}{c}$ is also equal to the energy density (energy per unit volume) u.

Hence,
$$P_{\text{rad}} = u \qquad \text{...(iii)}$$

The radiation pressure is thus equal to the energy density ($\text{N/m}^2 = \text{J/m}^3$). At a perfectly reflecting surface, the pressure on the surface is doubled. Thus, we can write

$$P_{\text{rad}} = \frac{I}{c} = u \qquad \text{(wave totally absorbed)}$$

and
$$P_{\text{rad}} = \frac{2I}{c} = 2u \qquad \text{(wave totally reflected)}$$

⊛ **Example 33.1** *The intensity of direct sunlight before it passes through the earth's atmosphere is* 1.4 *kW/m²*. *If it is completely absorbed, find the corresponding radiation pressure.*

Solution For completely absorbing surface,

$$p_{rad} = \frac{I}{c} = \frac{1.4 \times 10^3}{3.0 \times 10^8}$$

$$= 4.7 \times 10^{-6} \, Nm^{-2} \qquad \textbf{Ans.}$$

33.4 de-Broglie Wavelength of Matter Wave

The wave particle nature of electromagnetic waves discussed in article 33.1, led de-Broglie (pronounced de Broy) to suggest that matter might also exhibit this duality and have wave properties. His ideas can be expressed quantitatively by first considering electromagnetic radiation. A photon of frequency f and wavelength λ has energy.

$$E = hf = \frac{hc}{\lambda}$$

By Einstein's energy mass relation, $E = mc^2$ the equivalent mass m of the photon is given by

$$m = \frac{E}{c^2} = \frac{hf}{c^2} = \frac{h}{\lambda c} \qquad \dots(i)$$

or

$$\lambda = \frac{h}{mc} \quad \text{or} \quad \frac{h}{p} \qquad \dots(ii)$$

Here, p is the momentum of photon. By analogy de-Broglie suggested that a particle of mass m moving with speed v behaves in some ways like waves of wavelength λ given by

$$\lambda = \frac{h}{mv} = \frac{h}{p} \qquad \dots(iii)$$

where, p is the momentum of the particle. Momentum is related to the kinetic energy by the equation,

$$p = \sqrt{2Km}$$

and a charge q when accelerated by a potential difference V gains a kinetic energy $K = qV$. Combining all these relations Eq. (iii) can be written as

$$\lambda = \frac{h}{mv} = \frac{h}{p} = \frac{h}{\sqrt{2Km}} = \frac{h}{\sqrt{2qVm}} \quad \text{(de-Broglie wavelength)} \qquad \dots(iv)$$

de-Broglie Wavelength for an Electron

If an electron (charge $= e$) is accelerated by a potential difference of V volts, it acquires a kinetic energy,

$$K = eV$$

Substituting the values of *h*, *m* and *q* in Eq. (iv), we get a simple formula for calculating de-Broglie wavelength of an electron. This is

$$\lambda \text{ (in Å)} = \sqrt{\frac{150}{V \text{ (in volts)}}} \qquad \qquad ...(v)$$

Note *If an electron is accelerated by 1 volt, then its kinetic energy becomes 1 eV. Therefore, the above formula can also be written as*

$$\lambda \text{ (in Å)} = \sqrt{\frac{150}{KE(\text{in } eV)}}$$

○ **Example 33.2** *An electron is accelerated by a potential difference of 25 volt. Find the de-Broglie wavelength associated with it.*

Solution For an electron, de-Broglie wavelength is given by

$$\lambda = \sqrt{\frac{150}{V}} = \sqrt{\frac{150}{25}}$$
$$= \sqrt{6} \approx 2.5 \text{ Å} \qquad \qquad \textbf{Ans.}$$

○ **Example 33.3** *A particle of mass M at rest decays into two particles of masses* m_1 *and* m_2 *having non-zero velocities. The ratio of the de-Broglie wavelengths of the particles* λ_1/λ_2 *is* (JEE 1999)

(a) m_1/m_2 (b) m_2/m_1 (c) 1   (d) $\sqrt{m_2}/\sqrt{m_1}$

Solution From the law of conservation of momentum,

$$p_1 = p_2 \qquad \qquad (\text{ in opposite directions})$$

Now, de-Broglie wavelength is given by

$$\lambda = \frac{h}{p}, \text{ where } h = \text{Planck constant}$$

Since magnitude of momentum (*p*) of both the particles is equal, therefore $\lambda_1 = \lambda_2$

or $\qquad \qquad \qquad \lambda_1/\lambda_2 = 1$

Therefore, the correct option is (c).

○ **Example 33.4** *The energy of a photon is equal to the kinetic energy of a proton. The energy of the photon is E. Let* λ_1 *be the de-Broglie wavelength of the proton and* λ_2 *be the wavelength of the photon. The ratio* $\dfrac{\lambda_1}{\lambda_2}$ *is proportional to*

(a) E^0 (b) $E^{1/2}$ (c) E^{-1} (d) E^{-2} (JEE 2004)

Solution $\dfrac{\lambda_1}{\lambda_2} = \dfrac{\dfrac{h}{\sqrt{2mE}}}{\dfrac{hc}{E}}$ or $\dfrac{\lambda_1}{\lambda_2} \propto E^{1/2}$

Therefore, the correct option is (b).

⊘ **Example 33.5** *An α-particle and a proton are accelerated from rest by a potential difference of* 100 *V. After this, their de-Broglie wavelengths are* λ_α *and* λ_p *respectively. The ratio* $\dfrac{\lambda_p}{\lambda_\alpha}$, *to the nearest integer, is* (JEE 2010)

Solution $\because$ $\lambda = \dfrac{h}{p} = \dfrac{h}{\sqrt{2qVm}}$

or $$\lambda \propto \dfrac{1}{\sqrt{qm}}$$

$$\dfrac{\lambda_p}{\lambda_\alpha} = \sqrt{\dfrac{q_\alpha}{q_p} \cdot \dfrac{m_\alpha}{m_p}}$$

$$= \sqrt{\dfrac{(2)(4)}{(1)(1)}} = 2.828$$

The nearest integer is 3.

$\therefore$ Answer is 3.

⊘ **Example 33.6** *The potential energy of a particle varies as*

$$U(x) = E_0 \quad for \ \ 0 \le x \le 1$$
$$= 0 \quad for \ \ x > 1$$

For $0 \le x \le 1$, *de-Broglie wavelength is* λ_1 *and for* $x > 1$ *the de-Broglie wavelength is* λ_2. *Total energy of the particle is* $2E_0$. *Find* $\dfrac{\lambda_1}{\lambda_2}$. (JEE 2005)

Solution   For $0 \le x \le 1$, PE $= E_0$

$\therefore$ Kinetic energy K_1 = Total energy $-$ PE

$$= 2E_0 - E_0 = E_0$$

$\therefore$ $$\lambda_1 = \dfrac{h}{\sqrt{2mE_0}}$$ ...(i)

For $x > 1$, PE $= 0$

$\therefore$ Kinetic energy K_2 = Total energy $= 2E_0$

$\therefore$ $$\lambda_2 = \dfrac{h}{\sqrt{4mE_0}}$$ ...(ii)

From Eqs. (i) and (ii), we have

$$\dfrac{\lambda_1}{\lambda_2} = \sqrt{2}$$

INTRODUCTORY EXERCISE 33.1

1. Find the energy and momentum of a photon of ultraviolet radiation of 280 nm wavelength.

2. A small plate of a metal is placed at a distance of 2 m from a monochromatic light source of wavelength 4.8×10^{-7} m and power 1.0 Watt. The light falls normally on the plate. Find the number of photons striking the metal plate per square metre per second.

3. A proton and a deuteron are accelerated by same potential difference. Find the ratio of their de-Broglie wavelengths.

4. A deuteron and an α-particle have same kinetic energy. Find the ratio of their de-Broglie wavelengths.

5. Two protons are having same kinetic energy. One proton enters a uniform magnetic field at right angles to it. Second proton enters a uniform electric field in the direction of field. After some time their de-Broglie wavelengths are λ_1 and λ_2, then
   (a) $\lambda_1 = \lambda_2$ (b) $\lambda_1 < \lambda_2$ (c) $\lambda_1 > \lambda_2$
   (d) some more information is required

6. Find the de-Broglie wavelengths of
   (a) a 46 g golf ball with a velocity of 30 m/s   (b) an electron with a velocity of 10^7 m/s.

33.5 Early Atomic Structures

Every atom consists of a small nucleus of protons and neutrons with a number of electrons some distance away.

In the present article and in the next, our chief concern will be the structure of the atom, since it is this structure that is responsible for nearly all the properties of matter. In nineteenth century many models were present by different scientists, but ultimately the first theory of the atom to meet with any success was put forward in 1913 by Neils Bohr. But before studying Bohr's model of atom let us have a look on other two models of the period one presented by J.J. Thomson in 1898 and the other by Ernest Rutherford in 1911.

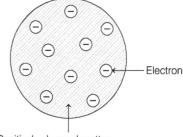

Positively charged matter

Fig. 33.2 The Thomson model of the atom. The Rutherford scattering experiment showed it to be incorrect.

J.J. Thomson suggested that atoms are just positively charged lumps of matter with electrons embedded in them like raisins in a fruit cake. Thomson's model called the 'plum pudding' model is illustrated in Fig. 33.2.

Thomson had played an important role in discovering the electron, his idea was taken seriously. But, the real atom turned out to be quite different.

Rutherford's Nuclear Atom

The nuclear atom is the basis of the modern theory of atomic structure and was proposed by Rutherford in 1911. He, with his two assistants Geiger and Marsden did an experiment in which they directed a narrow beam of α-particles onto gold foil about 1 μm thick and found that while most of the particles passed straight through, some were scattered appreciably and a very few about 1 in 8000 suffered deflection of more than 90°.

To account for this very surprising result Rutherford suggested that : "All the positive charge and nearly all the mass were concentrated in a very small volume or nucleus at the centre of the atom. The electrons were supposed to move in circular orbits round the nucleus (like planets round the sun). The electrostatic attraction between the two opposite charges being the required centripetal force for such motion.

The large angle scattering of α-particles would then be explained by the strong electrostatic repulsion from the nucleus.

Rutherford's model of the atom, although strongly supported by evidence for the nucleus, is inconsistent with classical physics. An electron moving in a circular orbit round a nucleus is accelerating and according to electromagnetic theory it should therefore, emit radiation continuously and thereby lose energy. If this happened the radius of the orbit would decrease and the electron would spiral into the nucleus in a fraction of second. But atoms do not collapse. In 1913, an effort was made by Neils Bohr to overcome this paradox.

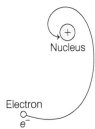

Fig. 33.3 An atomic electron should, classically, spiral rapidly into the nucleus as it radiates energy due to its acceleration

33.6 **The Bohr Hydrogen Atom**

After Neils Bohr obtained his doctorate in 1911, he worked under Rutherford for a while. In 1913, he presented a model of the hydrogen atom, which has one electron and one proton. He postulated that an electron moves only in certain circular orbits, called stationary orbits. In stationary orbits, electron does not emit radiation, contrary to the predictions of classical electromagnetic theory. According to Bohr, there is a definite energy associated with each stable orbit and an atom radiates energy only when it makes a transition from one of these orbits to another. The energy is radiated in the form of a photon with energy and frequency given by

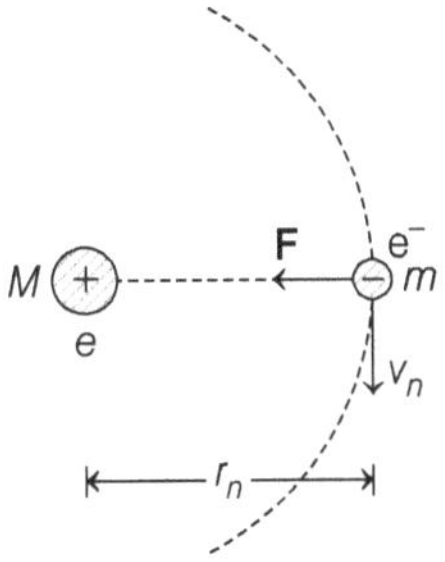

Fig. 33.4

$$\boxed{\Delta E = hf = E_i - E_f} \qquad \ldots(\text{i})$$

Bohr found that the magnitude of the electron's angular momentum is quantised, and this magnitude for the electron must be integral multiple of $\dfrac{h}{2\pi}$. The magnitude of the angular momentum is $L = mvr$ for a particle with mass m moving with speed v in a circle of radius r. So, according to Bohr's postulate,

$$mvr = \frac{nh}{2\pi} \qquad (n = 1, 2, 3 \ldots)$$

Each value of n corresponds to a permitted value of the orbit radius, which we will denote by r_n and the corresponding speed v_n. The value of n for each orbit is called **principal quantum number** for the orbit. Thus,

$$\boxed{mv_n r_n = \frac{nh}{2\pi}} \qquad \ldots(\text{ii})$$

According to Newton's second law, a radially inward centripetal force of magnitude $F = \dfrac{mv^2}{r_n}$ is needed to the electron which is being provided by the electrical attraction between the positive proton and the negative electron.

Thus,

$$\frac{mv_n^2}{r_n} = \frac{1}{4\pi\varepsilon_0}\frac{e^2}{r_n^2}$$

...(iii)

Solving Eqs. (ii) and (iii), we get

$$r_n = \frac{\varepsilon_0 n^2 h^2}{\pi m e^2} \quad \left(\begin{array}{c} n\text{th orbit radius} \\ \text{in Bohr model} \end{array}\right)$$

...(iv)

and

$$v_n = \frac{e^2}{2\varepsilon_0 nh} \quad \left(\begin{array}{c} n\text{th orbit speed} \\ \text{in Bohr model} \end{array}\right)$$

...(v)

The smallest orbit radius corresponds to $n = 1$. We'll denote this minimum radius, called the **Bohr radius** as a_0. Thus,

$$a_0 = \frac{\varepsilon_0 h^2}{\pi m e^2}$$

Substituting values of ε_0, h, π, m and e, we get

$$a_0 = 0.529 \times 10^{-10} \text{ m} = 0.529 \text{ Å}$$

...(vi)

Eq. (iv), in terms of a_0 can be written as

$$r_n = n^2 a_0 \quad \text{or} \quad r_n \propto n^2$$

...(vii)

Similarly, substituting values of e, ε_0 and h with $n = 1$ in Eq. (v), we get

$$v_1 = 2.19 \times 10^6 \text{ m/s} \approx \frac{c}{137}$$

...(viii)

This is the greatest possible speed of the electron in the hydrogen atom. Which is approximately equal to $c/137$, where c is the speed of light in vacuum.

Eq. (v), in terms of v_1 can be written as

$$v_n = \frac{v_1}{n} \quad \text{or} \quad v_n \propto \frac{1}{n}$$

...(ix)

Energy levels Kinetic and potential energies K_n and U_n in nth orbit are

$$K_n = \frac{1}{2} mv_n^2 = \frac{me^4}{8\varepsilon_0^2 n^2 h^2}$$

and

$$U_n = -\frac{1}{4\pi\varepsilon_0}\frac{(e)(e)}{r_n} = -\frac{me^4}{4\varepsilon_0^2 n^2 h^2}$$

The total energy E_n is the sum of the kinetic and potential energies.

$$E_n = K_n + U_n = -\frac{me^4}{8\varepsilon_0^2 n^2 h^2}$$

Substituting values of m, e, ε_0 and h with $n = 1$, we get the least energy of the atom in first orbit, which is -13.6 eV. Hence,

$$E_1 = -13.6 \, \text{eV} \qquad \qquad \qquad \text{...(x)}$$

and

$$E_n = \frac{E_1}{n^2} = -\frac{13.6}{n^2} \, \text{eV} \qquad \qquad \text{...(xi)}$$

Substituting $n = 2, 3, 4 \ldots$, etc., we get energies of atom in different orbits.

$$E_2 = -3.40 \, \text{eV}, \; E_3 = -1.51 \, \text{eV}, \ldots E_\infty = 0$$

Ionization energy of the hydrogen atom is the energy required to remove the electron completely. In ground state ($n = 1$), energy of atom is -13.6 eV and energy corresponding to $n = \infty$ is zero. Hence, energy required to remove the electron from ground state is 13.6 eV.

Emission spectrum of hydrogen atom

Under normal conditions the single electron in hydrogen atom stays in ground state ($n = 1$). It is excited to some higher energy state when it acquires some energy from external source. But, it hardly stays there for more than 10^{-8} second.

A photon corresponding to a particular spectrum line is emitted when an atom makes a transition from a state in an excited level to a state in a lower excited level or the ground level.

Let n_i be the initial and n_f the final energy state, then depending on the final energy state following series are observed in the emission spectrum of hydrogen atom.

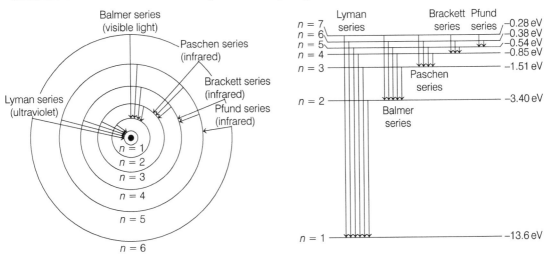

Fig. 33.5

For the Lyman series $n_f = 1$, for Balmer series $n_f = 2$ and so on. The relation of the various spectral series to the energy levels and to electron orbits is shown in figure.

Wavelength of Photon Emitted in De-excitation

According to Bohr when an atom makes a transition from higher energy level to a lower energy level it emits a photon with energy equal to the energy difference between the initial and final levels. If E_i is the initial energy of the atom before such a transition, E_f is its final energy after the transition, and the photon's energy is $hf = \dfrac{hc}{\lambda}$, then conservation of energy gives

$$hf = \frac{hc}{\lambda} = E_i - E_f \qquad \text{(energy of emitted photon)} \quad \dots\text{(xii)}$$

By 1913, the spectrum of hydrogen had been studied intensively. The visible line with longest wavelength, or lowest frequency is in the red and is called H_α, the next line, in the blue-green is called H_β and so on. In 1885, Johann Balmer, a swiss teacher found a formula that gives the wave lengths of these lines. This is now called the Balmer series. The Balmer's formula is

$$\frac{1}{\lambda} = R\left(\frac{1}{2^2} - \frac{1}{n^2}\right) \qquad \dots\text{(xiii)}$$

Here, $n = 3, 4, 5 \dots$, etc.

$R = $ Rydberg constant $= 1.097 \times 10^7 \text{ m}^{-1}$

and λ is the wavelength of light/photon emitted during transition.

For $n = 3$, we obtain the wavelength of H_α line. Similarly, for $n = 4$, we obtain the wavelength of H_β line. For $n = \infty$, the smallest wavelength ($= 3646$ Å) of this series is obtained. Using the relation $E = \dfrac{hc}{\lambda}$, we can find the photon energies corresponding to the wavelength of the Balmer series.

Multiplying Eq. (xiii) by hc, we find

$$E = \frac{hc}{\lambda} = hcR\left(\frac{1}{2^2} - \frac{1}{n^2}\right) = \frac{Rhc}{2^2} - \frac{Rhc}{n^2} = E_n - E_2$$

This formula suggests that

$$E_n = -\frac{Rhc}{n^2}, n = 1, 2, 3 \dots \qquad \dots\text{(xiv)}$$

Comparing this with Eq. (xi) of the same article, we have

$$Rhc = 13.60 \text{ eV} \qquad \dots\text{(xv)}$$

The wavelengths corresponding to other spectral series (Lyman, Paschen , etc.) can be represented by formula similar to Balmer formula.

Lyman series
$$\frac{1}{\lambda} = R\left(\frac{1}{1^2} - \frac{1}{n^2}\right), n = 2, 3, 4 \dots$$

Paschen series
$$\frac{1}{\lambda} = R\left(\frac{1}{3^2} - \frac{1}{n^2}\right), n = 4, 5, 6 \dots$$

Brackett series
$$\frac{1}{\lambda} = R\left(\frac{1}{4^2} - \frac{1}{n^2}\right), n = 5, 6, 7 \dots$$

Pfund series

$$\frac{1}{\lambda} = R\left(\frac{1}{5^2} - \frac{1}{n^2}\right), n = 6, 7, 8\dots$$

The Lyman series is in the ultraviolet, and the Paschen, Brackett and Pfund series are in the infrared region.

33.7 Hydrogen Like Atoms

The Bohr model of hydrogen can be extended to hydrogen like atoms, i.e. one electron atoms such as singly ionized helium (He^+), doubly ionized lithium (Li^{+2}) and so on. In such atoms, the nuclear charge is $+Ze$, where Z is the atomic number, equal to the number of protons in the nucleus.

The effect in the previous analysis is to replace e^2 everywhere by Ze^2. Thus, the equations for, r_n, v_n and E_n are altered as under

$$r_n = \frac{\varepsilon_0 n^2 h^2}{\pi m Z e^2} = \frac{n^2}{Z} a_0 \quad \text{or} \quad r_n \propto \frac{n^2}{Z} \qquad \dots(i)$$

where, $a_0 = 0.529 \text{ Å}$ (radius of first orbit of H)

$$v_n = \frac{Ze^2}{2\varepsilon_0 nh} = \frac{Z}{n} v_1 \quad \text{or} \quad v_n \propto \frac{Z}{n} \qquad \dots(ii)$$

where, $v_1 = 2.19 \times 10^6 \text{ m/s}$ (speed of electron in first orbit of H)

$$E_n = -\frac{mZ^2 e^4}{8\varepsilon_0^2 n^2 h^2} = \frac{Z^2}{n^2} E_1 \quad \text{or} \quad E_n \propto \frac{Z^2}{n^2} \qquad \dots(iii)$$

where, $E_1 = -13.60 \text{ eV}$ (energy of atom in first orbit of H)

Fig. 33.6 compares the energy levels of H and He^+ which has $Z = 2$. H and He^+ have many spectrum lines that have almost the same wavelengths

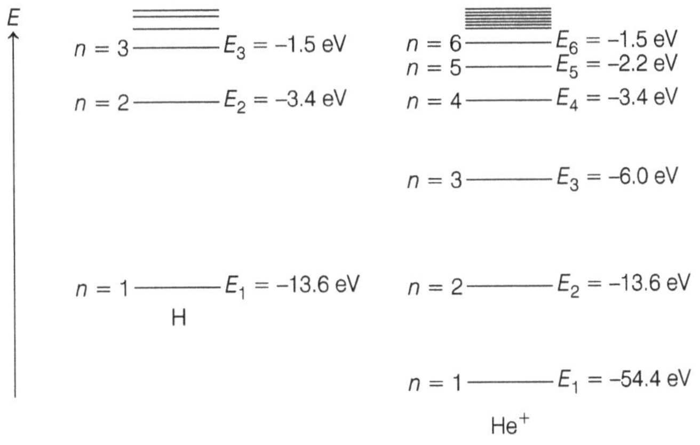

Fig. 33.6 Energy levels of H and He^+. Because of the additional factor Z^2 in the energy expression, the energy of the He^+ ion with a given n is almost exactly four times that of the H-atom with the same n. There are small differences (of the order of 0.05%) because of the different masses.

✅ *Extra Points to Remember*

- Bohr's theory is applicable for hydrogen and hydrogen like atoms/ions. For such types of atoms/ions number of electron is one. Although, atomic numbers may be different.

  e.g, For $_1H^1$, atomic number $Z = 1$, For He^+, atomic number $Z = 2$ and

  For Li^{+2}, atomic number $Z = 3$

  But for all three number of electron is one.

- In nth orbit

$$\frac{mv^2}{r} = \frac{1}{4\pi \varepsilon_0} \cdot \frac{(e)(Ze)}{r^2} \quad \text{and} \quad L_n = mvr = \frac{nh}{2\pi}$$

  After solving these two equations, we will get following results.

  (a) $r \propto \dfrac{n^2}{Z}$ and $r \propto \dfrac{1}{m}$

  (b) $v \propto \dfrac{Z}{n}$ and $v \propto m^0$

  (c) $E \propto \dfrac{Z^2}{n^2}$ and $E \propto m$

  (d) $r_1^H = 0.529$ Å

  (e) $v_1^H = 2.19 \times 10^6$ m/s $= \dfrac{c}{137}$

  (f) $E_1^H = -13.6$ eV

  (g) $K = |E|$ and $U = 2E$

Note *With the help of above results, we can find any value in any orbit of hydrogen like atoms. In the above expressions, m is the mass of electron*

- Total number of emission lines from some higher energy state n_1 to lower energy state n_2 $(< n_1)$ is given by $\dfrac{(n_1 - n_2)(n_1 - n_2 + 1)}{2}$.

  For example, total number of lines from $n_1 = n$ to $n_2 = 1$ are $\dfrac{n(n-1)}{2}$.

- As the principal quantum number n is increased in hydrogen and hydrogen like atoms, some quantities are decreased and some are increased. The table given below shows which quantities are increased and which are decreased.

Table 33.1

Increased	Decreased
Radius	Speed
Potential energy	Kinetic energy
Total energy	Angular speed
Time period	Frequency
Angular momentum	

- Whenever the force obeys inverse square law $\left(F \propto \dfrac{1}{r^2}\right)$ and potential energy is inversely proportional to $r \left(U \propto \dfrac{1}{r}\right)$, kinetic energy (K), potential energy (U) and total energy (E) have the following relationships.

$$K = \frac{|U|}{2} \quad \text{and} \quad E = -K = \frac{U}{2}$$

  If force is not proportional to $\dfrac{1}{r^2}$ or potential energy is not proportional to $\dfrac{1}{r}$, the above relations do not hold good.

- Total energy of a closed system is always negative and the modulus of this is the binding energy of the system. For instance, suppose a system has a total energy of –100 J. It means that this system will separate if 100 J of energy is supplied to this. Hence, binding energy of this system is 100 J. Thus, total energy of an open system is either zero or greater than zero.

- Kinetic energy of a particle can't be negative, while the potential energy can be zero, positive or negative. It basically depends on the reference point where we have taken it zero. It is customary to take zero potential energy when the electron is at infinite distance from the nucleus. In some problem, suppose we take zero potential energy in first orbit ($U_1 = 0$), then the modulus of actual potential energy in first orbit (when reference point was at infinity) is added in U and E in all energy states, while K remains unchanged. See sample example number 33.11.

- In the transition from n_2 to $n_1 (< n_1)$. The wavelength of emitted photon can be given by the following shortcut formula,

$$\lambda \text{ (in Å)} = \frac{12375}{E_{n_2} - E_{n_1}}$$

where, E_{n_1} and E_{n_2} are in eV. In general, E_n in eV is given by

$$E_n = -(13.6)\frac{Z^2}{n^2}$$

- In hydrogen emission spectrum, Balmer series was first discovered as it lies in visible light.

⊚ **Example 33.7**   *Using the known values for hydrogen atom, calculate*
   (a) *radius of third orbit for* Li^{+2}
   (b) *speed of electron in fourth orbit for* He^+
   (c) *angular momentum of electron in* 3*rd orbit of* He^+

Solution   (a) $Z = 3$ for Li^{+2}. Further we know that $r_n = \dfrac{n^2}{Z} a_0$

Substituting, $n = 3$, $Z = 3$ and $a_0 = 0.529$ Å

We have r_3 for $Li^{+2} = \dfrac{(3)^2}{(3)} (0.529)$ Å $= 1.587$ Å   **Ans.**

(b) $Z = 2$ for He^+. Also we know that

$$v_n = \frac{Z}{n} v_1$$

Substituting, $n = 4$, $Z = 2$ and $v_1 = 2.19 \times 10^6$ m/s

We get, v_4 for $He^+ = \left(\dfrac{2}{4}\right)(2.19 \times 10^6)$ m/s

$$= 1.095 \times 10^6 \text{ m/s}$$ **Ans.**

(c) $L_n = n\left(\dfrac{h}{2\pi}\right)$

For $n = 3$, $L_3 = 3\left(\dfrac{h}{2\pi}\right)$ **Ans.**

Note   *This result is independent of value of Z.*

● **Example 33.8** *A doubly ionized lithium atom is hydrogen like with atomic number 3. Find the wavelength of the radiation required to excite the electron in* Li^{++} *from the first to the third Bohr orbit. The ionization energy of the hydrogen atom is 13.6 eV.*

Solution $\because$ $E_n = -\dfrac{Z^2}{n^2}(13.6\,\text{eV})$

By putting $Z = 3$, we have $\qquad$ $E_n = -\dfrac{122.4}{n^2}\,\text{eV}$

$$E_1 = -\dfrac{122.4}{(1)^2} = -122.4\,\text{eV}$$

and $\qquad\qquad\qquad\qquad$ $E_3 = -\dfrac{122.4}{(3)^2} = -13.6\,\text{eV}$

$\therefore$ $\qquad\qquad\qquad\qquad\qquad$ $\Delta E = E_3 - E_1 = 108.8\,\text{eV}$

The corresponding wavelength is

$$\lambda = \dfrac{12375}{\Delta E\ (\text{in eV})}\,\text{Å} = \dfrac{12375}{108.8}\,\text{Å}$$

$$= 113.74\,\text{Å} \qquad\qquad\qquad\qquad\textbf{Ans.}$$

● **Example 33.9** *Find variation of angular speed and time period of single electron of hydrogen like atoms with n and Z.*

Solution Angular speed, $\qquad$ $\omega = \dfrac{v}{r}$

Now, $\qquad\qquad\qquad\qquad$ $v \propto \dfrac{Z}{n}$ and $r \propto \dfrac{n^2}{Z}$

$\therefore$ $\qquad\qquad\qquad$ $\omega \propto \dfrac{(Z/n)}{(n^2/Z)}$ or $\omega \propto \dfrac{Z^2}{n^3}$ $\qquad\qquad$ **Ans.**

Time period, $\qquad\qquad\qquad$ $T = \dfrac{2\pi}{\omega}$ or $T \propto \dfrac{1}{\omega}$

$\therefore$ $\qquad\qquad\qquad\qquad\qquad$ $T \propto \dfrac{n^3}{Z^2}$ $\qquad\qquad\qquad\qquad$ **Ans.**

● **Example 33.10** *Find kinetic energy, electrostatic potential energy and total energy of single electron in 2nd excited state of* Li^{+2} *atom.*

Solution $\because$ $E_I^H = -13.6\,\text{eV}$

Further, $E \propto \dfrac{Z^2}{n^2}$, For Li^{+2}, $Z = 3$

and for 2nd excited state $n = 3$

$\therefore$ $$E = -13.6 \left(\frac{3}{3}\right)^2 = -13.6 \text{ eV}$$ **Ans.**

$$K = |E| = 13.6 \text{ eV}$$ **Ans.**

$$U = 2E = -27.2 \text{ eV}$$ **Ans.**

Note *In the above expressions E is the total energy, K is the kinetic energy and U is the potential energy.*

● **Example 33.11** *Find the kinetic energy, potential energy and total energy in first and second orbit of hydrogen atom if potential energy in first orbit is taken to be zero.*

Solution $E_1 = -13.60 \text{ eV}, \quad K_1 = -E_1 = 13.60 \text{ eV}, \quad U_1 = 2E_1 = -27.20 \text{ eV}$

$E_2 = \dfrac{E_1}{(2)^2} = -3.40 \text{ eV}, \quad K_2 = 3.40 \text{ eV} \quad \text{and} \quad U_2 = -6.80 \text{ eV}$

Now, $U_1 = 0$, i.e. potential energy has been increased by 27.20 eV. So, we will increase U and E in all energy states by 27.20 eV, while kinetic energy will remain unchanged. Changed values in tabular form are as under.

Table 33.2

Orbit	K (eV)	U (eV)	E (eV)
First	13.60	0	13.60
Second	3.40	20.40	23.80

● **Example 33.12** *A small particle of mass m moves in such a way that the potential energy $U = ar^2$, where a is constant and r is the distance of the particle from the origin. Assuming Bohr model of quantization of angular momentum and circular orbits, find the radius of nth allowed orbit.*

Solution The force at a distance r is

$$F = -\frac{dU}{dr} = -2ar$$

Suppose r be the radius of nth orbit. Then, the necessary centripetal force is provided by the above force. Thus,

$$\frac{mv^2}{r} = 2ar \qquad \qquad \ldots\text{(i)}$$

Further, the quantization of angular momentum gives

$$mvr = \frac{nh}{2\pi} \qquad \qquad \ldots\text{(ii)}$$

Solving Eqs. (i) and (ii) for r, we get

$$r = \left(\frac{n^2 h^2}{8 \, am \, \pi^2}\right)^{\frac{1}{2}} \qquad \qquad \textbf{Ans.}$$

◈ **Example 33.13** *Calculate (a) the wavelength and (b) the frequency of the H_β line of the Balmer series for hydrogen.*

Solution (a) H_β line of Balmer series corresponds to the transition from $n = 4$ to $n = 2$ level.

Using Eq. (xiii), the corresponding wavelength for H_β line is

$$\frac{1}{\lambda} = (1.097 \times 10^7)\left(\frac{1}{2^2} - \frac{1}{4^2}\right) = 0.2056 \times 10^7$$

∴ $\qquad\qquad \lambda = 4.9 \times 10^{-7}$ m $\qquad\qquad\qquad$ **Ans.**

(b) $\qquad\qquad f = \dfrac{c}{\lambda} = \dfrac{3.0 \times 10^8}{4.9 \times 10^{-7}} = 6.12 \times 10^{14}$ Hz $\qquad$ **Ans.**

◈ **Example 33.14** *Find the largest and shortest wavelengths in the Lyman series for hydrogen. In what region of the electromagnetic spectrum does each series lie?*

Solution The transition equation for Lyman series is given by

$$\frac{1}{\lambda} = R\left(\frac{1}{1^2} - \frac{1}{n^2}\right), \ n = 2, 3, \dots$$

The largest wavelength is corresponding to $n = 2$

∴ $\qquad\qquad \dfrac{1}{\lambda_{\text{max}}} = 1.097 \times 10^7 \left(\dfrac{1}{1} - \dfrac{1}{4}\right) = 0.823 \times 10^7$

∴ $\qquad\qquad \lambda_{\text{max}} = 1.2154 \times 10^{-7}$ m $= 1215$ Å $\qquad\qquad$ **Ans.**

The shortest wavelength corresponds to $n = \infty$

∴ $\qquad\qquad \dfrac{1}{\lambda_{\text{min}}} = 1.097 \times 10^7 \left(\dfrac{1}{1} - \dfrac{1}{\infty}\right)$

or $\qquad\qquad \lambda_{\text{min}} = 0.911 \times 10^{-7}$ m $= 911$ Å $\qquad\qquad$ **Ans.**

Both of these wavelengths lie in ultraviolet (UV) region of electromagnetic spectrum.

◈ **Example 33.15** *In a hypothetical atom, mass of electron is doubled, value of atomic number is $Z = 4$. Find wavelength of photon when this electron jumps from 3rd excited state to 2nd orbit.*

Solution $E \propto \dfrac{Z^2}{n^2} \propto m$

Mass is doubled, $Z = 4$ and 3rd excited state means $n = 4$, second orbit means $n = 2$. For these values, we have

$$E_4 = -13.6 \times 2\left(\frac{4}{4}\right)^2 = -27.2 \text{ eV} \quad \text{and} \quad E_2 = -13.6 \times 2\left(\frac{4}{2}\right)^2 = -108.8 \text{ eV}$$

$$\lambda \text{ (in Å)} = \frac{12375}{\Delta E(\text{in eV})} = \frac{12375}{E_4 - E_2} = \frac{12375}{-27.2 + 108.8}$$

∴ $\qquad\qquad \lambda = 151.65$ Å $\qquad\qquad\qquad$ **Ans.**

INTRODUCTORY EXERCISE 33.2

1. Find the ionisation energy of a doubly ionized lithium atom.

2. A hydrogen atom is in a state with energy -1.51 eV. In the Bohr model, what is the angular momentum of the electron in the atom with respect to an axis at the nucleus?

3. As an electron makes a transition from an excited state to the ground state of a hydrogen like atom/ion   (JEE 2015)
   (a) kinetic energy, potential energy and total energy decrease
   (b) kinetic energy decreases, potential energy increases but total energy remains same
   (c) kinetic energy and total energy decrease but potential energy increases
   (d) its kinetic energy increases but potential energy and total energy decrease

4. The wavelength of the first spectral line in the Balmer series of hydrogen atom is 6561 Å. The wavelength of the second spectral line in the Balmer series of singly ionized helium atom is
   (a) 1215 Å   (b) 1640 Å   (c) 2430 Å   (d) 4687 Å (JEE 2011)

5. The largest wavelength in the ultraviolet region of the hydrogen spectrum is 122 nm. The smallest wavelength in the infrared region of the hydrogen spectrum (to the nearest integer) is
   (a) 802 nm   (b) 823 nm
   (c) 1882 nm   (d) 1648 nm   (JEE 2007)

6. A photon collides with a stationary hydrogen atom in ground state inelastically. Energy of the colliding photon is 10.2 eV. After a time interval of the order of micro second another photon collides with same hydrogen atom inelastically with an energy of 15 eV. What will be observed by the detector?   (JEE 2005)
   (a) 2 photons of energy 10.2 eV
   (b) 2 photons of energy 1.4 eV
   (c) One photon of energy 10.2 eV and an electron of energy 1.4 eV
   (d) One photon of energy 10.2 eV and another photon of energy 1.4 eV

7. A hydrogen atom and a Li^{2+} ion are both in the second excited state. If l_H and l_{Li} are their respective electronic angular momenta, and E_H and E_{Li} their respective energies, then
   (a) $l_H > l_{Li}$ and $|E_H| > |E_{Li}|$ (b) $l_H = l_{Li}$ and $|E_H| < |E_{Li}|$ (JEE 2002)
   (c) $l_H = l_{Li}$ and $|E_H| > |E_{Li}|$ (d) $l_H < l_{Li}$ and $|E_H| < |E_{Li}|$

8. The transition from the state $n = 4$ to $n = 3$ in a hydrogen like atom results in ultraviolet radiation. Infrared radiation will be obtained in the transition   (JEE 2001)
   (a) $2 \to 1$ (b) $3 \to 2$ (c) $4 \to 2$ (d) $5 \to 4$

9. As per Bohr model, the minimum energy (in eV) required to remove an electron from the ground state of doubly ionized Li atom ($Z = 3$) is   (JEE 1997)
   (a) 1.51   (b) 13.6
   (c) 40.8   (d) 122.4

10. Consider the spectral line resulting from the transition $n = 2 \to n = 1$ in the atoms and ions given below. The shortest wavelength is produced by   (JEE 1983)
    (a) hydrogen atom   (b) deuterium atom
    (c) singly ionized helium   (d) doubly ionized lithium

11. The energy levels of a certain atom are shown in figure. If a photon of frequency f is emitted when there is an electron transition from $5E$ to E, what frequencies of photons could be produced by other energy level transitions?

    ———————— 5E
    ———————— 4E

    ———————— E

12. Find the longest wavelength present in the Balmer series of hydrogen.

33.8 **X-Rays**

Electromagnetic radiation with wavelengths from 0.1 Å to 100 Å falls into the category of X-rays. The boundaries of this category are not sharp. The shorter wavelength end overlaps gamma rays and the longer wavelength end overlaps ultraviolet rays. Photoelectric effect (will be discussed later) provides convincing evidence that photons of light can transfer energy to electrons. Is the inverse process also possible? That is, can part or all of the kinetic energy of a moving electron be converted into a photon? Yes, it is possible. In 1895 **Wilhelm Roentgen** found that a highly penetrating radiation of unknown nature is produced when fast moving electrons strike a target of high atomic number and high melting point. These radiations were given a name X-rays as their nature was unknown (in mathematics an unknown quantity is normally designated by X). Later, it was discovered that these are high energy photons (or electromagnetic waves).

Production of X-Rays Figure shows a diagram of a X-ray tube, called the coolidge tube. A cathode (a plate connected to negative terminal of a battery), heated by a filament through which an electric current is passed, supplies electrons by thermionic emission. The high potential difference V maintained between the cathode and a metallic target accelerate the electrons toward the later. The face of the target is at an angle relative to the electron beam, and the X-rays that leave the target pass through the side of the tube. The tube is evacuated to permit the electrons to get to the target unimpedded.

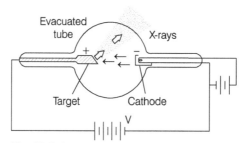

Fig. 33.7 An X-ray tube. The higher the accelerating voltage V, the faster the

Continuous and characteristic X-rays X-rays so produced by the coolidge tube are of two types, continuous and characteristic. While the former depends only on the accelerating voltage V, the later depends on the target used.

Continuous X-rays Electromagnetic theory predicts that an accelerated electric charge will radiate electromagnetic waves, and a rapidly moving electrons when suddenly brought to rest is certainly accelerated (of course negative). X-rays produced under these circumstances is given the German name **bremsstrahlung** (braking radiation). Energy loss due to bremsstrahlung is more important for electrons than for heavier particles because electrons are more violently accelerated when passing near nuclei in their paths. The continuous X-rays (or bremsstrahlung X-rays) produced at a given accelerating potential V vary in wavelength, but none has a wavelength shorter than a certain value λ_{min}. This minimum wavelength corresponds to the maximum energy of the X-rays which in turn is equal to the maximum kinetic energy qV or eV of the striking electrons. Thus,

$$\frac{hc}{\lambda_{min}} = eV \quad \text{or} \quad \lambda_{min} = \frac{hc}{eV}$$

After substituting values of h, c and e we obtain the following simple formula for λ_{min}.

$$\lambda_{min} \text{ (in Å)} = \frac{12375}{V \text{ (in volts)}} \qquad \text{...(i)}$$

Increasing V decreases λ_{min}. This wavelength is also known as the cut off wavelength or the threshold wavelength.

Characteristic X-rays The X-ray spectrum typically consists of a broad continuous band containing a series of sharp lines as shown in Fig. 33.8.

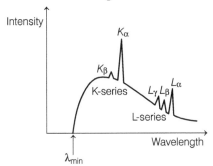

Fig. 33.8 X-ray spectrum

As discussed above the continuous spectrum is the result of collisions between incoming electrons and atoms in the target. The kinetic energy lost by the electrons during the collisions emerges as the energy of the X-ray photons radiated from the target.

The sharp lines superimposed on the continuous spectrum are known as **characteristic X-rays** because they are characteristic of the target material. They were discovered in 1908, but their origin remained unexplained until the details of atomic structure, particularly the shell structure of the atom, were discovered.

Characteristic X-ray emission occurs when a bombarding electron that collides with a target atom has sufficient energy to remove an inner shell electron from the atom. The vacancy created in the shell is filled when an electron from a higher level drops down into it. This transition is accompanied by the emission of a photon whose energy equals the difference in energy between the two levels.

Let us assume that the incoming electron has dislodged an atomic electron from the innermost shell-the K shell. If the vacancy is filled by an electron dropping from the next higher shell the L shell, the photon emitted has an energy corresponding to the K_α characteristic X-ray line. If the vacancy is filled by an electron dropping from the M shell, the K_β line is produced. An L_α line is produced as an electron drops from the M shell to the L-shell, and an L_β line is produced by a transition from the N-shell to the L-shell.

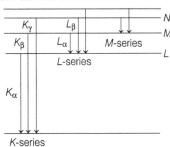

Fig. 33.9

Moseley's Law for Characteristic Spectrum

Although multi-electron atoms cannot be analyzed with the Bohr model, Henery G.J. Moseley in 1914 made an effort towards this. Moseley measured the frequencies of characteristic X-rays from a large number of elements and plotted the square root of the frequency $\sqrt{f}$ against the atomic number

Z of the element. He discovered that the plot is very close to a straight line. He plotted the square root of the frequency of the K_α line *versus* the atomic number Z.

As figure shows, Moseley's plot did not pass through the origin. Let us see why. It can be understood from Gauss's law. Consider an atom of atomic number Z in which one of the two electrons in the K-shell has been ejected. Imagine that we draw a Gaussian sphere just inside the most probable radius of the L-electrons. The effective charge inside the Gaussian surface is the positive nuclear charge and one negative charge due to the single K-electron. If we ignore the interactions between L-electrons, a single L electron behaves as if it experiences an electric field due to a charge $(Z-1)$ enclosed by the Gaussian surface.

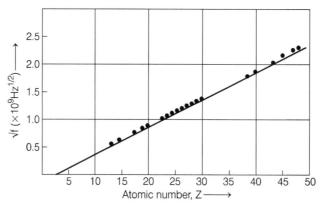

Fig. 33.10   A plot of the square root of the frequency of the K_α lines *versus* atomic number using Moseley's data

Thus, Moseley's law of the frequency of K_α line is

$$\sqrt{f_{K_\alpha}} = a\,(Z-1) \qquad\qquad \text{...(ii)}$$

where, a is a constant that can be related to Bohr theory. The above law in general can be stated as under

$$\sqrt{f} = a\,(Z-b) \quad \text{or} \quad \boxed{\sqrt{f} \propto (Z-b)} \qquad\qquad \text{...(iii)}$$

For K_α line, $\qquad\qquad \Delta E = hf = Rhc\,(Z-1)^2 \left(\dfrac{1}{1^2} - \dfrac{1}{2^2}\right)$

or $\qquad\qquad\qquad \sqrt{f} = \sqrt{\dfrac{3Rc}{4}}\,(Z-1)$

or $\qquad\qquad\qquad a = \sqrt{\dfrac{3Rc}{4}} \quad \text{and} \quad b=1$

After substituting values of R and c, we get $\qquad a = 4.98 \times 10^7 \ (\text{Hz})^{1/2}$

Eq. (iii) can also be written as $\qquad\qquad f = a^2\,(Z-b)^2 \qquad\qquad \text{...(iv)}$

For K_α line, $\qquad\qquad a^2 = \dfrac{3Rc}{4} = (2.48 \times 10^{15} \ \text{Hz}) \quad \text{and} \quad b=1$

Hence, $\qquad\qquad\qquad f_{K_\alpha} = (2.48 \times 10^{15} \ \text{Hz})\,(Z-1)^2$

💮 *Extra Points to Remember*

- In continuous X-ray spectrum, all wavelengths greater than λ_{min} are obtained. Characteristic X-ray spectrum is discrete. Certain fixed wavelengths like λ_{K_α}, λ_{K_β} etc. are obtained and these wavelengths are different for different target elements. The mixed spectrum of continuous and characteristic X-rays is as shown in figure 33.8.

- In general, if we compare between different series, then
$$E_K > E_L > E_M \quad \text{or} \quad f_K > f_L > f_M \quad \text{or} \quad \lambda_K < \lambda_L < \lambda_M$$
And if we compare between α, β and γ, then
$$E_\alpha < E_\beta < E_\gamma \quad \text{or} \quad f_\alpha < f_\beta < f_\gamma \quad \text{or} \quad \lambda_\alpha > \lambda_\beta > \lambda_\gamma$$

- In Moseley's law,
$$\sqrt{f} \propto (Z - b)$$
$$b = 1 \quad \text{for} \quad K_\alpha \text{ line}$$
and
$$b = 7.4 \quad \text{for} \quad L_\alpha \text{ line}$$
Thus, $\sqrt{f} = 0$ at $Z = b = 1$ for K_α line
and $\sqrt{f} = 0$ at $Z = b = 7.4$ for K_β line

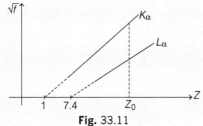

Fig. 33.11

For lower atomic numbers lines are shown dotted. This is because X-rays are obtained only at high atomic numbers. Further, we can see that for a given atomic number (say Z_0).
$$\sqrt{f_K} > \sqrt{f_L}$$

- **Screening effect** The energy levels, in general, depend on the principal quantum number (n) and orbital quantum number (l). Let us take sodium ($Z = 11$) as an example. According to Gauss's law, for any spherically symmetric charge distribution the electric field magnitude at a distance r from the centre is $\dfrac{1}{4\pi\varepsilon_0}\dfrac{q_{encl}}{r^2}$, where q_{encl} is the total charge enclosed within a sphere with radius r. Mentally, remove the outer (valence) electron from a sodium atom. What you have left is a spherically symmetric collection of 10 electrons (filling the K and L shells) and 11 protons. So,
$$q_{encl} = -10e + 11e = +e$$
If the eleventh is completely outside this collection of charges, it is attracted by an effective charge of $+e$, not $+11e$.

This effect is called **screening**, the 10 electrons screen 10 of the 11 protons leaving an effective net charge of $+e$. In general, an electron that spends all its time completely outside a positive charge $Z_{eff}e$ has energy levels given by the hydrogen expression with e^2 replaced by $Z_{eff}\,e^2$. i.e.
$$E_n = -\frac{Z_{eff}^2}{n^2}\,(13.6 \text{ eV}) \quad \text{(energy levels with screening)}$$

If the eleventh electron in the sodium atom is completely outside the remaining charge distribution, then $Z_{eff} = 1$.

We can estimate the frequency of K_α X-ray photons using the concept of screening. A K_α X-ray photon is emitted when an electron in the L-shell ($n = 2$) drops down to fill a hole in the K-shell ($n = 1$). As the electron drops down, it is attracted by the Z protons in the nucleus screened by one remaining electron in the K-shell. Thus,

$$Z_{eff} = (Z - 1), \quad n_i = 2 \quad \text{and} \quad n_f = 1$$

The energy before transition is

$$E_i = -\frac{(Z-1)^2}{2^2}(13.6 \text{ eV}) = -(Z-1)^2 (3.4 \text{ eV})$$

and energy after transition is

$$E_f = -\frac{(Z-1)^2}{1^2}(13..6 \text{ eV}) = -(Z-1)^2 (13.6 \text{ eV})$$

The energy of the K_α X-ray photon is

$$E_{K_\alpha} = E_i - E_f = (Z-1)^2 (10.2 \text{ eV})$$

The frequency of K_α X-ray photon is therefore,

$$f_{K_\alpha} = \frac{E_{K_\alpha}}{h} = \frac{(Z-1)^2 (10.2 \text{ eV})}{(4.136 \times 10^{-15} \text{ eV-s})}$$

$$= (2.47 \times 10^{15} \text{ Hz})(Z-1)^2$$

This relation agrees almost exactly with Moseley's experimental law.

- The target (or anode) used in the Coolidge tube should be of high melting point. This is because less than 0.5% of the kinetic energy of the electrons is converted into X-rays. The rest of the kinetic energy converts into internal energy of the target which simultaneously has to be kept cool by circulating oil or water.

- Atomic number of the target material should be high. This is because X-rays are high energy photons and as we have seen above energy of the X-rays increases as Z increases.

- X-rays are basically electromagnetic waves. So, they possess all the properties of electromagnetic waves.

⊙ **Example 33.16** *Find the cut off wavelength for the continuous X-rays coming from an X-ray tube operating at 40 kV.*

Solution Cut off wavelength λ_{min} is given by

$$\lambda_{min} \text{ (in Å)} = \frac{12375}{V(\text{in volts})} = \frac{12375}{40 \times 10^3}$$

$$= 0.31 \text{ Å} \qquad\qquad \textbf{Ans.}$$

⊙ **Example 33.17** *Use Moseley's law with $b = 1$ to find the frequency of the K_α X-rays of La $(Z = 57)$ if the frequency of the K_α X-rays of Cu $(Z = 29)$ is known to be 1.88×10^{18} Hz.*

Solution Using the equation, $\sqrt{f} = a(Z - b) \qquad (b = 1)$

$$\frac{f_{La}}{f_{Cu}} = \left(\frac{Z_{La} - 1}{Z_{Cu} - 1}\right)^2 \quad \text{or} \quad f_{La} = f_{Cu}\left(\frac{Z_{La} - 1}{Z_{Cu} - 1}\right)^2$$

$$= 1.88 \times 10^{18}\left(\frac{57-1}{29-1}\right)^2$$

$$= 7.52 \times 10^{18} \text{ Hz} \qquad\qquad \textbf{Ans.}$$

⊛ **Example 33.18** *Electrons with de-Broglie wavelength λ fall on the target in an X-ray tube. The cut off wavelength of the emitted X-rays is* (JEE 2007)

(a) $\lambda_0 = \dfrac{2mc\lambda^2}{h}$

(b) $\lambda_0 = \dfrac{2h}{mc}$

(c) $\lambda_0 = \dfrac{2m^2c^2\lambda^3}{h^2}$

(d) $\lambda_0 = \lambda$

Solution Momentum of bombarding electrons,

$$p = \frac{h}{\lambda}$$

∴ Kinetic energy of bombarding electrons,

$$K = \frac{p^2}{2m} = \frac{h^2}{2m\lambda^2}$$

This is also maximum energy of X-ray photons.

Therefore,

$$\frac{hc}{\lambda_0} = \frac{h^2}{2m\lambda^2}$$

or

$$\lambda_0 = \frac{2m\lambda^2 c}{h}$$

∴ Correct option is (a).

⊛ **Example 33.19** *Electrons with energy 80 keV are incident on the tungsten target of an X-ray tube. K-shell electrons of tungsten have 72.5 keV energy. X-rays emitted by the tube contain only* (JEE 2000)

(a) *a continuous X-ray spectrum (Bremsstrahlung) with a minimum wavelength of* $\approx 0.155\,\text{Å}$

(b) *a continuous X-ray spectrum (Bremsstrahlung) with all wavelengths*

(c) *the characteristic X-ray spectrum of tungsten*

(d) *a continuous X-ray spectrum (Bremsstrahlung) with a minimum wavelength of* $\approx 0.155\,\text{Å}$ *and the characteristic X-ray spectrum of tungsten*

Solution Minimum wavelength of continuous X-ray spectrum is given by λ_{min} (in Å)

$$= \frac{12375}{E\,(\text{in eV})}$$

Here, E = energy of incident electrons (in eV)

= energy corresponding to minimum wavelength λ_{min} of X-ray

$$E = 80\,\text{keV} = 80 \times 10^3 \text{ eV}$$

∴

$$\lambda_{min}\,(\text{in Å}) = \frac{12375}{80 \times 10^3} \approx 0.155$$

Also the energy of the incident electrons (80 keV) is more than the ionization energy of the K-shell electrons (i.e. 72.5 keV). Therefore, characteristic X-ray spectrum will also be obtained because energy of incident electron is high enough to knock out the electron from K or L-shells.

∴ The correct option is (d).

INTRODUCTORY EXERCISE 33.3

1. If λ_{Cu} is the wavelength of K_α, X-ray line of copper (atomic number 29) and λ_{Mo} is the wavelength of the K_α X-ray line of molybdenum (atomic number 42), then the ratio $\lambda_{Cu}/\lambda_{Mo}$ is close to   (JEE 2014)
   (a) 1.99   (b) 2.14
   (c) 0.50   (d) 0.48

2. Which one of the following statements is wrong in the context of X-rays generated from an X-ray tube?   (JEE 2008)
   (a) Wavelength of characteristic X-rays decreases when the atomic number of the target increases
   (b) Cut off wavelength of the continuous X-rays depends on the atomic number of the target
   (c) Intensity of the characteristic X-rays depends on the electrical power given to the X-ray tube
   (d) Cut off wavelength of the continuous X-rays depends on the energy of the electrons in the X-ray tube

3. K_α wavelength emitted by an atom of atomic number $Z = 11$ is λ. Find the atomic number for an atom that emits K_α radiation with wavelength 4λ (JEE 2005)
   (a) $Z = 6$ (b) $Z = 4$
   (c) $Z = 11$ (d) $Z = 44$

4. The intensity of X-rays from a coolidge tube is plotted against wavelength λ as shown in the figure. The minimum wavelength found is λ_c and the wavelength of the K_α line is λ_k. As the accelerating voltage is increased   (JEE 2001)

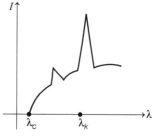

Fig. 33.12

   (a) $\lambda_k - \lambda_c$ increases   (b) $\lambda_k - \lambda_c$ decreases
   (c) λ_k increases   (d) λ_k decreases

5. X-rays are produced in an X-ray tube operating at a given accelerating voltage. The wavelength of the continuous X-rays has values from   (JEE 1998)
   (a) 0 to ∞
   (b) λ_{min} to ∞, where $\lambda_{min} > 0$
   (c) 0 to λ_{max}, where $\lambda_{max} < \infty$
   (d) λ_{min} to λ_{max}, where $0 < \lambda_{min} < \lambda_{max} < \infty$

6. Characteristic X-rays of frequency 4.2×10^{18} Hz are produced when transitions from L-shell to K-shell take place in a certain target material. Use Mosley's law to determine the atomic number of the target material. Given Rydberg constant $R = 1.1 \times 10^7 \, m^{-1}$.   (JEE 2003)

33.9 **Emission of Electrons**

At room temperature the free electrons move randomly within the conductor, but they don't leave the surface of the conductor due to attraction of positive charges. Some external energy is required to emit electrons from a metal surface. Minimum energy is required to emit the electrons which are just on the surface of the conductor. This minimum energy is called the **work-function** (denoted by W) of the conductor. Work-function is the property of the metallic surface.

The energy required to liberate an electron from metal surface may arise from various sources such as heat, light, electric field etc. Depending on the nature of source of energy, the following methods are possible :

(i) **Thermionic emission**   The energy to the free electrons can be given by heating the metal. The electrons so emitted are known as **thermions**.

(ii) **Field emission**   When a conductor is put under strong electric field, the free electrons on it experience an electric force in the opposite direction of field. Beyond a certain limit, electrons start coming out of the metal surface. Emission of electrons from a metal surface by this method is called the field emission.

(iii) **Secondary emission**   Emission of electrons from a metal surface by the bombardment of high speed electrons or other particles is known as secondary emission.

(iv) **Photoelectric emission**   Emission of free electrons from a metal surface by falling light (or any other electromagnetic wave which has an energy greater than the work-function of the metal) is called photoelectric emission. The electrons so emitted are called **photoelectrons**.

33.10 **Photoelectric Effect**

When light of an appropriate frequency (or correspondingly of an appropriate wavelength) is incident on a metallic surface, electrons are liberated from the surface. This observation is known as **photoelectric effect**. Photoelectric effect was first observed in 1887 by Hertz. For photoemission to take place, energy of incident light photons should be greater than or equal to the work-function of the metal.

or
$$E \geq W \qquad \qquad \ldots(\text{i})$$

$\therefore$
$$hf \geq W$$

or
$$f \geq \frac{W}{h}$$

Here, $\dfrac{W}{h}$ is the minimum frequency required for the emission of electrons. This is known as threshold frequency f_0.

Thus,
$$f_0 = \frac{W}{h} \quad \text{(threshold frequency)} \qquad \qquad \ldots(\text{ii})$$

Further, Eq. (i) can be written as

$$\frac{hc}{\lambda} \geq W \quad \text{or} \quad \lambda \leq \frac{hc}{W}$$

Here, $\dfrac{hc}{W}$ is the largest wavelength beyond which photoemission does not take place. This is called the threshold wavelength λ_0.

Thus,
$$\lambda_0 = \frac{hc}{W} \quad \text{(threshold wavelength)}$$
...(iii)

Hence, for the photoemission to take place either of the following conditions must be satisfied.

$$E \geq W \quad \text{or} \quad f \geq f_0 \quad \text{or} \quad \lambda \leq \lambda_0$$
...(iv)

Stopping Potential and Maximum Kinetic Energy of Photoelectrons

When the frequency f of the incident light is greater than the threshold frequency, some electrons are emitted from the metal with substantial initial speeds. Suppose E is the energy of light incident on a metal surface and $W (< E)$ the work-function of metal. As minimum energy is required to extract electrons from the surface, they will have the maximum kinetic energy which is $E - W$.

Thus,
$$K_{max} = E - W$$
...(v)

This value K_{max} can experimentally be found by keeping the metal plate P (from which electrons are emitting) at higher potential relative to an another plate Q placed in front of P. Some electrons after emitting from plate P, reach the plate Q despite the fact that Q is at lower potential and it is repelling the electrons from reaching in itself. This is because the electrons emitted from plate P possess some kinetic energy and due to this energy they reach the plate Q and current i flows in the circuit in the direction shown in figure.

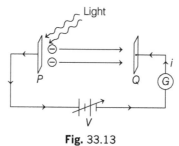

Fig. 33.13

As the potential V is increased, the force of repulsion to the electrons gets increased and less number of electrons reach the plate Q and current in the circuit gets decreased. At a certain value V_0 electrons having maximum kinetic energy (K_{max}) also get stopped and current in the circuit becomes zero. This is called the **stopping potential**.

As an electron moves from P to Q, the potential decreases by V_0 and negative work $-eV_0$ is done on the (negatively charged) electron, the most energetic electron leaves plate P with kinetic energy $K_{max} = \dfrac{1}{2} mv_{max}^2$ and has zero kinetic energy at Q. Using the work energy theorem, we have

$$W_{ext} = -eV_0 = \Delta K = 0 - K_{max}$$

or
$$K_{max} = \frac{1}{2} mv_{max}^2 = eV_0$$
...(vi)

Photoelectric Current

Figure shows an apparatus used to study the variation of photocurrent i with the intensity and frequency of light falling on metal plate P. Photoelectrons are emitted from plate P which are being attracted by the positive plate Q and a photoelectric current i flows in the circuit, which can be measured by the galvanometer G.

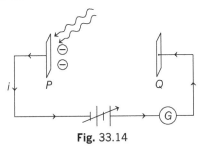

Fig. 33.14

Figure 33.15 (a) shows graphs of photocurrent as a function of potential difference V_{QP} for light of constant frequency and two different intensities. When V_{QP} is sufficiently large and positive the current becomes constant, showing that all the emitted electrons are being collected by the anode plate Q. The stopping potential difference $-V_0$ needed to reduce the current to zero is shown. If the intensity of light is increased, (or we can say the number of photons incident per unit area per unit time is increased) while its frequency is kept the same, the current becomes constant at a higher value, showing that more electrons are being emitted per unit time. But the stopping potential is found to be the same.

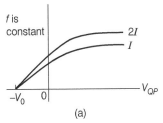

(a)

Photocurrent i as a function of the potential V_{QP} of the anode with respect to the cathode for a constant light frequency f, the stopping potential V_0 is independent of the light intensity I.

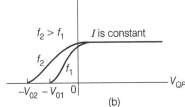

(b)

Photocurrent i as a function of the potential V_{QP} of the anode with respect to a cathode for two different light frequencies f_1 and f_2 with the same intensity. The stopping potential V_0 (and therefore the maximum kinetic energy of the photoelectrons) increases linearly with frequency.

Fig. 33.15

Figure 33.15 (b) shows current as a function of potential difference for two different frequencies with the same intensity in each case. We see that when the frequency of the incident monochromatic light is increased, the stopping potential V_0 gets increased. Of course, V_0 turn out to be a linear function of the frequency f.

Graph between K_{max} and f

Let us plot a graph between maximum kinetic energy K_{max} of photoelectrons and frequency f of incident light. The equation between K_{max} and f is

$$K_{max} = hf - W$$

Comparing it with $y = mx + c$, the graph between K_{max} and f is a straight line with positive slope and negative intercept.

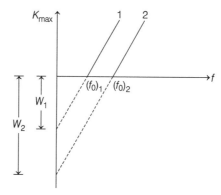

Fig. 33.16

From the graph, we can note the following points

(i) $K_{max} = 0$ at $f = f_0$

(ii) Slope of the straight line is h, a universal constant, i.e. if graph is plotted for two different metals 1 and 2, slope of both the lines is same.

(iii) The negative intercept of the line is W, the work-function which is characteristic of a metal, i.e. intercepts for two different metals will be different. Further,

$$W_2 > W_1$$

$\therefore \qquad\qquad (f_0)_2 > (f_0)_1 \qquad\qquad$ [as $W = hf_0$]

Here, $\qquad\qquad f_0 =$ threshold frequency

Graph between V_0 and f

Let us now plot a graph between the stopping potential V_0 and the incident frequency f. The equation between them is

$$eV_0 = hf - W$$

or $\qquad\qquad V_0 = \left(\dfrac{h}{e}\right)f - \left(\dfrac{W}{e}\right)$

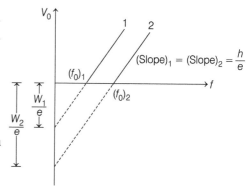

Fig. 33.17

Again comparing with $y = mx + c$, the graph between V_0 and f is a straight line with positive slope $\dfrac{h}{e}$ (a universal constant) and negative intercept $\dfrac{W}{e}$ (which depends on the metal). The corresponding graph is shown in figure.

✅ *Extra Points to Remember*

- The major features of the photoelectric effect could not be explained by the wave theory of light which were later explained by Einstein's photon theory.
  - (i) Wave theory suggests that the kinetic energy of the photoelectrons should increase with the increase in intensity of light. However equation, $K_{max} = eV_0$ suggests that it is independent of the intensity of light.
  - (ii) According to wave theory, the photoelectric effect should occur for any frequency of the light, provided that the light is intense enough. However, the above equation suggests that photoemission is possible only when frequency of incident light is either greater than or equal to the threshold frequency f_0.
  - (iii) If the energy to the photoelectrons is obtained by soaking up from the incident wave, it is not likely that the effective target area for an electron in the metal is much more than a few atomic diameters. (see example 33.20) between the impinging of the light on the surface and the ejection of the photoelectrons. During this interval the electron should be "soaking up" energy from the beam until it had accumulated enough energy to escape. However, no detectable time lag has ever been measured.
- **Einstein's photon theory** Einstein succeeded in explaining the photoelectric effect by making a remarkable assumption, that the energy in a light beam travels through space in concentrated bundles, called photons. The energy E of a single photon is given by

$$E = hf$$

Applying the photon concept to the photoelectric effect, Einstein wrote

$$hf = W + K_{max} \qquad \text{(already discussed)}$$

Consider how Einstein's photon hypothesis meets the three objections raised against the wave theory interpretation of the photoelectric effect.

As for objection 1 (the lack of dependence of K_{max} on the intensity of illumination), doubling the light intensity merely doubles the number of photons and thus doubles the photoelectric current, it does not change the energy of the individual photons

Objection 2 (the existence of a cutoff frequency) follows from equation $hf = W + K_{max}$. If K_{max} equals zero, We have $hf_0 = W$ which asserts that the photon has just enough energy to eject the photoelectrons and none extra to appear as kinetic energy. The quantity W is called the work-function of the substance. If f is reduced below f_0, the individual photons, no matter how many of them there are (that is, no matter how intense the illumination), will not have enough energy to eject photo electrons.

Objection 3 (the absence of a time lag) follows from the photon theory because the required energy is supplied in a concentrated bundle. It is not spread uniformly over a large area, as in the wave theory. Although, the photon hypothesis certainly fits the facts of photoelectricity, it seems to be in direct conflict with the wave theory of light. Out modern view of the nature of light is that it has a dual character, behaving like a wave under some circumstances and like a particle or photon under others.

◉ *Example 33.20* *A metal plate is placed* 5 *m from a monochromatic light source whose power output is* 10^{-3} *W. Consider that a given ejected photoelectron may collect its energy from a circular area of the plate as large as ten atomic diameters* $(10^{-9}\, m)$ *in radius. The energy required to remove an electron through the metal surface is about* 5.0 *eV. Assuming light to be a wave, how long would it take for such a 'target' to soak up this much energy from such a light source.*

Solution The target area is $S_1 = \pi (10^{-9})^2 = \pi \times 10^{-18}$ m^2. The area of a 5 m sphere centered on the light source is, $S_2 = 4\pi (5)^2 = 100\, \pi$ m^2. Thus, if the light source radiates uniformly in all directions the rate P at which energy falls on the target is given by

$$P = (10^{-3} \text{ watt}) \left(\frac{S_1}{S_2} \right) = (10^{-3}) \left(\frac{\pi \times 10^{-18}}{100 \times \pi} \right) = 10^{-23} \text{ J/s}$$

Assuming that all power is absorbed, the required time is

$$t = \left(\frac{5 \text{ eV}}{10^{-23} \text{ J/s}} \right) \left(\frac{1.6 \times 10^{-19} \text{ J}}{1 \text{ eV}} \right) \approx 22 \text{ h} \qquad \text{Ans.}$$

⊗ **Example 33.21** *The photoelectric work-function of potassium is 2.3 eV. If light having a wavelength of 2800 Å falls on potassium, find*

(a) the kinetic energy in electron volts of the most energetic electrons ejected.
(b) the stopping potential in volts

Solution Given, $W = 2.3 \text{ eV}, \quad \lambda = 2800 \text{ Å}$

$$\therefore \qquad E \text{ (in eV)} = \frac{12375}{\lambda \text{ (in Å)}} = \frac{12375}{2800} = 4.4 \text{ eV}$$

(a) $K_{max} = E - W$

$$= (4.4 - 2.3) \text{eV} = 2.1 \text{ eV} \qquad \text{Ans.}$$

(b) $K_{max} = eV_0$

$$\therefore \qquad 2.1 \text{eV} = eV_0 \quad \text{or} \quad V_0 = 2.1 \text{ volt} \qquad \text{Ans.}$$

⊗ **Example 33.22** *When a beam of 10.6 eV photons of intensity 2.0 W/m² falls on a platinum surface of area 1.0×10^{-4} m² and work-function 5.6 eV, 0.53% of the incident photons eject photoelectrons. Find the number of photoelectrons emitted per second and their minimum and maximum energies (in eV). Take $1 eV = 1.6 \times 10^{-19}$ J.*

Solution Number of photoelectrons emitted per second

$$= \frac{(\text{Intensity})(\text{Area})}{(\text{Energy of each photon})} \times \frac{0.53}{100}$$

$$= \frac{(2.0)(1.0 \times 10^{-4})}{(10.6 \times 1.6 \times 10^{-19})} \times \frac{0.53}{100}$$

$$= 6.25 \times 10^{11} \qquad \text{Ans.}$$

Minimum kinetic energy of photoelectrons,

$$K_{min} = 0$$

and maximum kinetic energy is, $\qquad K_{max} = E - W = (10.6 - 5.6) \text{eV}$

$$= 5.0 \text{ eV} \qquad \text{Ans.}$$

⊗ **Example 33.23** *Maximum kinetic energy of photoelectrons from a metal surface is K_0 when wavelength of incident light is λ. If wavelength is decreased to $\lambda/2$, the maximum kinetic energy of photoelectrons becomes*

(a) $= 2K_0$ (b) $> 2K_0$ (c) $< 2K_0$

Solution Using the equation,

$$K_{max} = E - W, \text{ we have}$$

$$K_0 = \frac{hc}{\lambda} - W \qquad \qquad ...(i)$$

with wavelength $\dfrac{\lambda}{2}$, suppose the maximum kinetic energy is K_0' , then

$$K_0' = \frac{hc}{\lambda/2} - W = 2\frac{hc}{\lambda} - W$$

$$= 2\left(\frac{hc}{\lambda} - W\right) + W$$

but $\dfrac{hc}{\lambda} - W$ is K_0. Therefore,

$$K_0' = 2K_0 + W$$
or
$$K_0' > 2K_0$$

∴ The correct option is (b). **Ans.**

◉ **Example 33.24** *Intensity and frequency of incident light both are doubled. Then, what is the effect on stopping potential and saturation current.*

Solution By increasing the frequency of incident light energy of incident light will increase. So, maximum kinetic energy of photoelectrons will also increase. Hence, stopping potential will increase.

Further, by doubling the frequency of incident light energy of each photon will be doubled. So, intensity itself becomes two times without increasing number of photons incident per unit area per unit time. Therefore, saturation current will remain unchanged.

◉ **Example 33.25** *When a monochromatic point source of light is at a distance of 0.2 m from a photoelectric cell, the cut off voltage and the saturation current are respectively 0.6 V and 18.0 mA. If the same source is placed 0.6 m away from the photoelectric cell, then* (JEE 1992)

(a) the stopping potential will be 0.2 V

(b) the stopping potential will be 0.6 V

(c) the saturation current will be 6.0 mA

(d) the saturation current will be 2.0 mA

Solution (b) Stopping potential depends on two factors – one the energy of incident light and the other the work-function of the metal. By increasing the distance of source from the cell, neither of the two change. Therefore, stopping potential remains the same.

(d) Saturation current is directly proportional to the intensity of light incident on cell and for a point source, intensity $I \propto 1/r^2$

When distance is increased from 0.2 m to 0.6 m (three times), the intensity and hence the saturation current will decrease 9 times, i.e. the saturation current will be reduced to 2.0 mA.

∴ The correct options are (b) and (d).

⊗ **Example 33.26** *The threshold wavelength for photoelectric emission from a material is* 5200 Å. *Photoelectrons will be emitted when this material is illuminated with monochromatic radiation from a* (1982, 3M)

(a) 50 *W infrared lamp*   (b) 1 *W infrared lamp*

(c) 50 *W ultraviolet lamp*   (d) 1 *W ultraviolet lamp*

Solution   For photoemission to take place, wavelength of incident light should be less than the threshold wavelength. Wavelength of ultraviolet light < 5200 Å while that of infrared radiation > 5200 Å.

∴ The correct options are (c) and (d).

INTRODUCTORY EXERCISE 33.4

1. Light of wavelength 2000 Å is incident on a metal surface of work-function 3.0 eV. Find the minimum and maximum kinetic energy of the photoelectrons.

2. Is it correct to say that K_{max} is proportional to f? If not, what would a correct statement of the relationship between K_{max} and f?

3. When a metal is illuminated with light of frequency f, the maximum kinetic energy of the photoelectrons is 1.2 eV. When the frequency is increased by 50%, the maximum kinetic energy increases to 4.2 eV. What is the threshold frequency for this metal?

4. A metal surface is illuminated by light of two different wavelengths 248 nm and 310 nm. The maximum speeds of the photoelectrons corresponding to these wavelengths are u_1 and u_2, respectively. If the ratio $u_1 : u_2 = 2 : 1$ and $hc = 1240$ eV nm, the work-function of the metal is nearly (JEE 2014)

   (a) 3.7 eV   (b) 3.2 eV   (c) 2.8 eV   (d) 2.5 eV

5. The figure shows the variation of photocurrent with anode potential for a photosensitive surface for three different radiations. Let I_a, I_b and I_c be the intensities and f_a, f_b and f_c be the frequencies for the curves a, b and c, respectively (JEE 2004)

   (a) $f_a = f_b$ and $I_a \neq I_b$ (b) $f_a = f_c$ and $I_a = I_c$

   (c) $f_a = f_b$ and $I_a = I_b$ (d) $f_b = f_c$ and $I_b = I_c$

6. The work-function of a substance is 4.0 eV. The longest wavelength of light that can cause photoelectron emission from this substance is approximately (JEE 1998)

   (a) 540 nm   (b) 400 nm   (c) 310 nm   (d) 220 nm

7. The maximum kinetic energy of photoelectrons emitted from a surface when photons of energy 6 eV fall on it is 4 eV. The stopping potential in volt is (JEE 1997)

   (a) 2   (b) 4   (c) 6   (d) 10

8. Photoelectric effect supports quantum nature of light because (JEE 1987)

   (a) there is a minimum frequency of light below which no photoelectrons are emitted

   (b) the maximum kinetic energy of photoelectrons depends only on the frequency of light and not on its intensity

   (c) even when the metal surface is faintly illuminated, the photoelectrons leave the surface immediately

   (d) electric charge of the photoelectrons is quantised

Core Concepts

1. In hydrogen and hydrogen like atoms :

   Circumference of nth orbit $= n$ (wavelength of single electron in that orbit)

   Proof

   According to Bohr's assumption,

   $$L_n = n\left(\frac{h}{2\pi}\right)$$

   or

   $$mvr = n\left(\frac{h}{2\pi}\right)$$

   $\therefore$

   $$(2\pi r) = n\left(\frac{h}{mv}\right)$$

   or circumference $= n$(de-Broglie wavelength of electron)

2. $Rhc = 13.6\,eV$

   Therefore, Rhc has the dimensions of energy or

   $$[Rhc] = [ML^2T^{-2}]$$

3. 1 Rhc is also called 1 Rydberg. It is not Rydberg constant R.

Solved Examples

PATTERNED PROBLEMS

Type 1. *Based on de-Broglie wavelength*

Example 1 *A proton is fired from very far away towards a nucleus with charge $Q = 120\ e$, where e is the electronic charge. It makes a closest approach of 10 fm to the nucleus. The de-Broglie wavelength (in units of fm) of the proton at its start is [Take the proton mass, $m_p = (5/3) \times 10^{-27}$ kg, $h/e = 4.2 \times 10^{-15}$ J-s/C,*

$\dfrac{1}{4\pi\varepsilon_0} = 9 \times 10^9$ m/F, 1 fm $= 10^{-15}$ m]

(JEE 2013)

Solution $r =$ closest distance $= 10$ fm

From energy conservation, we have

$$K_i + U_i = K_f + U_f$$

or $$K + 0 = 0 + \frac{1}{4\pi\varepsilon_0} \cdot \frac{q_1 q_2}{r}$$

or $$K = \frac{1}{4\pi\varepsilon_0} \cdot \frac{(120\ e)\ (e)}{r} \quad \text{...(i)}$$

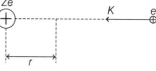

de-Broglie wavelength,

$$\lambda = \frac{h}{\sqrt{2Km}} \quad \text{...(ii)}$$

Substituting the given values in above two equations, we get

$$\lambda = 7 \times 10^{-15}\ \text{m} = 7\ \text{fm}$$

Example 2 *Find de-Broglie wavelength of single electron in 2 nd orbit of hydrogen atom by two methods.*

Solution **Method 1** Kinetic energy of single electron in 2nd orbit is 3.4 eV using the equation,

$$\lambda = \sqrt{\frac{150}{KE\,(\text{in eV})}} = \sqrt{\frac{150}{3.4}} = 6.64\ \text{Å} \qquad \textbf{Ans.}$$

Method 2 Circumference of nth orbit $= n\lambda$

∴ $$2\,\pi r = 2\,\lambda$$

or $$\lambda = \pi\,r$$

Now, $$r \propto n^2$$

$$r_1 = 0.529\,\text{Å}$$

∴ $$\lambda = \pi\,(0.529)(2)^2 \text{Å}$$

$$= 6.64\ \text{Å} \qquad \textbf{Ans.}$$

Type 2. *Based on Bohr's atomic models*

❯ **Example 3** *The electric potential between a proton and an electron is given by*
$V = V_0 \ln \dfrac{r}{r_0}$, *where r_0 is a constant. Assuming Bohr model to be applicable,*
write variation of r_n with n, being the principal quantum number. (JEE 2003)

(a) $r_n \propto n$ (b) $r_n \propto \dfrac{1}{n}$ (c) $r_n \propto n^2$ (d) $r_n \propto \dfrac{1}{n^2}$

Solution ∵ $U = eV = eV_0 \ln\left(\dfrac{r}{r_0}\right)$

$$|F| = \left|-\frac{dU}{dr}\right| = \frac{eV_0}{r}$$

This force will provide the necessary centripetal force. Hence, $\dfrac{mv^2}{r} = \dfrac{eV_0}{r}$

or $$v = \sqrt{\frac{eV_0}{m}} \qquad \text{...(i)}$$

Moreover, $$mvr = \frac{nh}{2\pi} \qquad \text{...(ii)}$$

Dividing Eq. (ii) by Eq. (i), we have

$$mr = \left(\frac{nh}{2\pi}\right)\sqrt{\frac{m}{eV_0}} \quad \text{or} \quad r_n \propto n$$

❯ **Example 4** *Imagine an atom made up of proton and a hypothetical particle of double the mass of the electron but having the same charge as the electron. Apply the Bohr atom model and consider all possible transitions of this hypothetical particle to the first excited level. The longest wavelength photon that will be emitted has wavelength λ (given in terms of the Rydberg constant R for the hydrogen atom) equal to* (JEE 2000)

(a) $9/5R$ (b) $36/5R$ (c) $18/5R$ (d) $4/R$

Solution In hydrogen atom, $E_n = -\dfrac{Rhc}{n^2}$

Also, $$E_n \propto m$$

where, m is the mass of the electron.
Here, the electron has been replaced by a particle whose mass is double of an electron.
Therefore, for this hypothetical atom energy in nth orbit will be given by

$$E_n = -\frac{2Rhc}{n^2}$$

The longest wavelength $\lambda_{\max}$ (or minimum energy) photon will correspond to the transition of particle from $n = 3$ to $n = 2$.

∴ $$\frac{hc}{\lambda_{\max}} = E_3 - E_2 = 2Rhc\left(\frac{1}{2^2} - \frac{1}{3^2}\right)$$

This gives, $\lambda_{\max} = 18/5R$

∴ The correct option is (c).

⊘ **Example 5** *The recoil speed of a hydrogen atom after it emits a photon is going from $n = 5$ state to $n = 1$ state is .... m/s.* (JEE 1997)

Solution From conservation of linear momentum,

| Momentum of recoil hydrogen atom | = | Momentum of emitted photon |

or $$mv = \frac{\Delta E}{c}$$

Here, $$\Delta E = E_5 - E_1 = -13.6 \left[\frac{1}{5^2} - \frac{1}{1^2} \right] \text{eV}$$

$$= (13.6)(24/25) \text{ eV} = 13.056 \text{ eV}$$

$$= 13.056 \times 1.6 \times 10^{-19} \text{ J} = 2.09 \times 10^{-18} \text{ J}$$

and $$m = \text{mass of hydrogen atom} = 1.67 \times 10^{-27} \text{ kg}$$

∴ $$v = \frac{\Delta E}{mc} = \frac{2.09 \times 10^{-18}}{(1.67 \times 10^{-27})(3 \times 10^8)}$$

$$v \approx 4.17 \text{ m/s}$$

⊘ **Example 6** *A hydrogen like atom (described by the Bohr model) is observed to emit six wavelengths, originating from all possible transitions between a group of levels. These levels have energies between − 0.85 eV and −0.544 eV (including both these values).* (JEE 2002)

(a) *Find the atomic number of the atom.*

(b) *Calculate the smallest wavelength emitted in these transitions.*

(Take, hc = 1240 eV-nm, ground state energy of hydrogen atom = −13.6 eV)

Solution (a) Total 6 lines are emitted. Therefore,

$$\frac{n(n-1)}{2} = 6 \quad \text{or} \quad n = 4$$

So, transition is taking place between mth energy state and $(m + 3)$th energy state.

$$E_m = -0.85 \text{ eV} \quad \text{or} \quad -13.6 \left(\frac{Z^2}{m^2} \right) = -0.85$$

or $$\frac{Z}{m} = 0.25 \qquad \qquad \text{...(i)}$$

Similarly, $E_{m+3} = -0.544$ eV

or $$-13.6 \frac{Z^2}{(m+3)^2} = -0.544$$

or $$\frac{Z}{(m+3)} = 0.2 \qquad \qquad \text{...(ii)}$$

Solving Eqs. (i) and (ii) for Z and m, we get

$$m = 12 \text{ and } Z = 3 \qquad \qquad \textbf{Ans.}$$

(b) Smallest wavelength corresponds to maximum difference of energies which is obviously $E_{m+3} - E_m$

∴ $$\Delta E_{\text{max}} = -0.544 - (-0.85) = 0.306 \text{ eV}$$

∴ $$\lambda_{\text{min}} = \frac{hc}{\Delta E_{\text{max}}} = \frac{1240}{0.306} = 4052.3 \text{ nm} \qquad \textbf{Ans.}$$

⦿ **Example 7** *A hydrogen like atom of atomic number Z is in an excited state of quantum number 2n. It can emit a maximum energy photon of 204 eV. If it makes a transition to quantum state n, a photon of energy 40.8 eV is emitted. Find n, Z and the ground state energy (in eV) of this atom. Also calculate the minimum energy (in eV) that can be emitted by this atom during de-excitation. Ground state energy of hydrogen atom is –13.6 eV.* (JEE 2000)

Solution Let ground state energy (in eV) be E_1.

Then, from the given condition

$$E_{2n} - E_1 = 204 \text{ eV}$$

or

$$\frac{E_1}{4n^2} - E_1 = 204 \text{ eV}$$

or

$$E_1 \left(\frac{1}{4n^2} - 1 \right) = 204 \text{ eV} \qquad \text{...(i)}$$

and

$$E_{2n} - E_n = 40.8 \text{ eV}$$

or

$$\frac{E_1}{4n^2} - \frac{E_1}{n^2} = 40.8 \text{ eV}$$

or

$$E_1 \left(\frac{-3}{4n^2} \right) = 40.8 \text{ eV} \qquad \text{...(ii)}$$

From Eqs. (i) and (ii), we get

$$\frac{1 - \dfrac{1}{4n^2}}{\dfrac{3}{4n^2}} = 5 \quad \text{or} \quad 1 = \frac{1}{4n^2} + \frac{15}{4n^2}$$

or

$$\frac{4}{n^2} = 1 \quad \text{or} \quad n = 2$$

From Eq. (ii),

$$E_1 = -\frac{4}{3} n^2 (40.8) \text{ eV}$$

$$= -\frac{4}{3} (2)^2 (40.8) \text{ eV}$$

or

$$E_1 = -217.6 \text{ eV}$$

$$E_1 = -(13.6) Z^2$$

∴

$$Z^2 = \frac{E_1}{-13.6} = \frac{-217.6}{-13.6} = 16$$

∴

$$Z = 4$$

$$E_{\min} = E_{2n} - E_{2n-1} = \frac{E_1}{4n^2} - \frac{E_1}{(2n-1)^2}$$

$$= \frac{E_1}{16} - \frac{E_1}{9} = -\frac{7}{144} E_1$$

$$= -\left(\frac{7}{144} \right) (-217.6) \text{ eV}$$

∴

$$E_{\min} = 10.58 \text{ eV}$$

Example 8 *A hydrogen like atom (atomic number Z) is in a higher excited state of quantum number n. The excited atom can make a transition to the first excited state by successively emitting two photons of energy 10.2 eV and 17.0 eV, respectively. Alternatively, the atom from the same excited state can make a transition to the second excited state by successively emitting two photons of energies 4.25 eV and 5.95 eV, respectively.* (JEE 1994)

Determine the values of n and Z.

(Ionization energy of H-atom – 13.6 eV)

Solution From the given conditions,

$$E_n - E_2 = (10.2 + 17)\text{ eV} = 27.2\text{ eV} \qquad \text{...(i)}$$

and

$$E_n - E_3 = (4.25 + 5.95)\text{ eV} = 10.2\text{ eV} \qquad \text{...(ii)}$$

Eq. (i) – Eq. (ii) gives

$$E_3 - E_2 = 17.0\text{ eV} \quad \text{or} \quad Z^2\,(13.6)\left(\frac{1}{4} - \frac{1}{9}\right) = 17.0$$

$$\Rightarrow \qquad Z^2\,(13.6)\,(5/36) = 17.0$$

$$\Rightarrow \qquad Z^2 = 9 \quad \text{or} \quad Z = 3$$

From Eq. (i),

$$Z^2\,(13.6)\left(\frac{1}{4} - \frac{1}{n^2}\right) = 27.2 \quad \text{or} \quad (3)^2\,(13.6)\left(\frac{1}{4} - \frac{1}{n^2}\right) = 27.2$$

or

$$\frac{1}{4} - \frac{1}{n^2} = 0.222 \quad \text{or} \quad 1/n^2 = 0.0278$$

or

$$n^2 = 36 \quad \Rightarrow \quad n = 6$$

Type 3. *Based on X-rays*

Example 9 *The potential difference applied to an X-ray tube is 5 kV and the current through it is 3.2 mA. Then, the number of electrons striking the target per second is* (JEE 2002)

(a) 2×10^{16} (b) 5×10^6

(c) 1×10^{17} (d) 4×10^{15}

Solution ∵ $i = \dfrac{q}{t} = \dfrac{ne}{t}$

∴

$$n = \frac{i\,t}{e}$$

Substituting

$$i = 3.2 \times 10^{-3}\text{ A,}$$
$$e = 1.6 \times 10^{-19}\text{ C}$$

and

$$t = 1\text{ s}$$

We get,

$$n = 2 \times 10^{16}$$

∴ The correct answer is (a).

⊗ **Example 10** *X-rays are incident on a target metal atom having 30 neutrons.*
The ratio of atomic radius of the target atom and $_2^4$ He is $(14)^{1/3}$. (JEE 2005)

(a) *Find the mass number of target atom.*

(b) *Find the frequency of K_α line emitted by this metal.*

Hint : *Radius of a nucleus (r) has the following relation with mass number (A).*

$$r \propto A^{1/3}$$

$(R = 1.1 \times 10^7 \, m^{-1}, c = 3 \times 10^8 \, m/s)$

Solution (a) From the relation $r \propto A^{1/3}$,

We have,
$$\frac{r_2}{r_1} = \left(\frac{A_2}{A_1}\right)^{1/3}$$

or
$$\left(\frac{A_2}{4}\right)^{1/3} = (14)^{1/3}$$

∴
$$A_2 = 56$$

(b) $Z_2 = A_2 - $ number of neutrons

$$= 56 - 30 = 26$$

∴
$$f = Rc \, (Z - 1)^2 \left(\frac{1}{1^2} - \frac{1}{2^2}\right)$$

$$= \frac{3Rc}{4} \, (Z - 1)^2$$

Substituting the given values of R, c and Z, we get

$$f = 1.55 \times 10^{18} \text{ Hz}$$

⊗ **Example 11** *Stopping potential of* 24, 100, 110 *and* 115 *kV are measured for*
photoelectrons emitted from a certain element when it is radiated with
monochromatic X-ray. If this element is used as a target in an X-ray tube, what
will be the wavelength of K_α -line?

Solution Stopping potentials are 24, 100, 110 and 115 kV, i.e. if the electrons are emitted
from conduction band, maximum kinetic energy of photoelectrons would be 115×10^3 eV. If they
are emitted from next inner shell, maximum kinetic energy of photoelectrons would be
110×10^3 eV and so on.

For photoelectrons of L- shell it would be 100×10^3 eV and for K-shell it is 24×10^3 eV.
Therefore, difference between energy of L-shell and K-shell is

$$\Delta E = E_L - E_K$$

$$= (100 - 24) \times 10^3 \text{ eV}$$

$$= 76 \times 10^3 \text{ eV}$$

∴ Wavelength of K_α-line (transition of electron from L-shell to K-shell) is,

$$\lambda_{K_\alpha} \text{ (in Å)} = \frac{12375}{\Delta E \text{ (in eV)}}$$

$$= \frac{12375}{76 \times 10^3}$$

$$= 0.163 \text{ Å} \qquad\qquad \textbf{Ans.}$$

⊘ **Example 12** *In Moseley's equation* $\sqrt{f} = a(Z - b)$, *a and b are constants. Find their values with the help of the following data.*

Element	Z	Wavelength of K_α X-rays
Mo	42	0.71 Å
Co	27	1.785 Å

Solution $\sqrt{f} = a(Z - b)$

or
$$\sqrt{\frac{c}{\lambda_1}} = a(Z_1 - b) \qquad \qquad \dots\text{(i)}$$

and
$$\sqrt{\frac{c}{\lambda_2}} = a(Z_2 - b) \qquad \qquad \dots\text{(ii)}$$

From Eqs. (i) and (ii), we have

$$\sqrt{c}\left[\frac{1}{\sqrt{\lambda_1}} - \frac{1}{\sqrt{\lambda_2}}\right] = a(Z_1 - Z_2) \qquad \qquad \dots\text{(iii)}$$

Solving above three equations with $c = 3.0 \times 10^8$ m/s, $\lambda_1 = 0.71 \times 10^{-10}$ m
$\lambda_2 = 1.785 \times 10^{-10}$ m, $Z_1 = 42$ and $Z_2 = 27$, we get
$$a = 5 \times 10^7 \text{ (Hz)}^{1/2} \qquad \text{and} \qquad b = 1.37 \qquad \qquad \textbf{Ans.}$$

Type 4. *Based on photoelectric effect*

⊘ **Example 13** *A monochromatic light source of frequency f illuminates a metallic surface and ejects photoelectrons. The photoelectrons having maximum energy are just able to ionize the hydrogen atoms in ground state. When the whole experiment is repeated with an incident radiation of frequency $\frac{5}{6}f$, the photoelectrons so emitted are able to excite the hydrogen atom beam which then emits a radiation of wavelength 1215 Å.*

(a) What is the frequency of radiation?

(b) Find the work-function of the metal.

Solution (a) Using Einstein's equation of photoelectric effect,
$$K_{max} = hf - W$$
Here,
$$K_{max} = 13.6 \text{ eV}$$
∴
$$hf - W = 13.6 \text{ eV} \qquad \qquad \dots\text{(i)}$$
Further,
$$h\left(\frac{5}{6}f\right) - W = \frac{12375}{1215} = 10.2 \text{ eV} \qquad \qquad \dots\text{(ii)}$$

Solving Eqs. (i) and (ii), we have
$$\frac{hf}{6} = 3.4 \text{ eV} \quad \text{or} \quad f = \frac{(6)(3.4)(1.6 \times 10^{-19})}{(6.63 \times 10^{-34})}$$
$$= 4.92 \times 10^{15} \text{ Hz} \qquad \qquad \textbf{Ans.}$$
(b)
$$W = hf - 13.6 \qquad \qquad \text{[from Eq. (i)]}$$
$$= 6(3.4) - 13.6 = 6.8 \text{ eV} \qquad \qquad \textbf{Ans.}$$

⊚ **Example 14** *The graph between* $1/\lambda$ *and stopping potential* (V) *of three metals having work-functions* ϕ_1, ϕ_2 *and* ϕ_3 *in an experiment of photoelectric effect is plotted as shown in the figure. Which of the following statement(s) is/are correct? (Here,* λ *is the wavelength of the incident ray).* (JEE 2006)

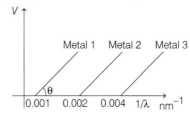

(a) Ratio of work-functions $\phi_1 : \phi_2 : \phi_3 = 1 : 2 : 4$

(b) Ratio of work-functions $\phi_1 : \phi_2 : \phi_3 = 4 : 2 : 1$

(c) $\tan \theta$ *is directly proportional to* hc/e, *where h is Planck constant and c is the speed of light*

(d) The violet colour light can eject photoelectrons from metals 2 and 3

Solution From the relation,

$$eV = \frac{hc}{\lambda} - \phi \quad \text{or} \quad V = \left(\frac{hc}{e}\right)\left(\frac{1}{\lambda}\right) - \frac{\phi}{e}$$

This is equation of straight line. Slope is $\tan \theta = \dfrac{hc}{e}$.

Further $V = 0$ at $\phi = \dfrac{hc}{\lambda}$

∴ $$\phi_1 : \phi_2 : \phi_3 = \frac{hc}{\lambda_{01}} : \frac{hc}{\lambda_{02}} : \frac{hc}{\lambda_{03}} = \frac{1}{\lambda_{01}} : \frac{1}{\lambda_{02}} : \frac{1}{\lambda_{03}} = 1 : 2 : 4$$

$$\frac{1}{\lambda_{01}} = 0.001 \text{ nm}^{-1}$$

or $$\lambda_{01} = 10000 \text{ Å}$$

$$\frac{1}{\lambda_{02}} = 0.002 \text{ nm}^{-1}$$

or $$\lambda_{02} = 5000 \text{ Å}$$

$$\frac{1}{\lambda_{03}} = 0.004 \text{ nm}^{-1}$$

or $$\lambda_{03} = 2500 \text{ Å}$$

Violet colour has wavelength 4000 Å.

So, violet colour can eject photoelectrons from metal 1 and metal 2.

∴ The correct options are (a) and (c).

⊚ **Example 15** *A beam of light has three wavelengths 4144 Å, 4972 Å and 6216 Å with a total intensity of* 3.6×10^{-3} *Wm*$^{-2}$ *equally distributed amongst the three wavelengths. The beam falls normally on an area 1.0 cm*^{2} *of a clean metallic surface of work-function 2.3 eV. Assume that there is no loss of light by reflection and that each energetically capable photon ejects one electron. Calculate the number of photoelectrons liberated in two seconds.* (JEE 1989)

Solution　Energy of photon having wavelength 4144 Å,

$$E_1 = \frac{12375}{4144} \text{ eV}$$

$$= 2.99 \text{ eV}$$

Similarly,

$$E_2 = \frac{12375}{4972} \text{ eV}$$

$$= 2.49 \text{ eV and}$$

$$E_3 = \frac{12375}{6216} \text{ eV}$$

$$= 1.99 \text{ eV}$$

Since, only E_1 and E_2 are greater than the work-function $W = 2.3$ eV , only first two wavelengths are capable for ejecting photoelectrons. Given intensity is equally distributed in all wavelengths. Therefore, intensity corresponding to each wavelength is

$$\frac{3.6 \times 10^{-3}}{3} = 1.2 \times 10^{-3} \text{ W/m}^2$$

Or energy incident per second in the given area $(A = 1.0 \text{ cm}^2 = 10^{-4} \text{ m}^2)$ is

$$P = 1.2 \times 10^{-3} \times 10^{-4}$$

$$= 1.2 \times 10^{-7} \text{ J/s}$$

Let n_1 be the number of photons incident per unit time in the given area corresponding to first wavelength. Then,

$$n_1 = \frac{P}{E_1}$$

$$= \frac{1.2 \times 10^{-7}}{2.99 \times 1.6 \times 10^{-19}}$$

$$= 2.5 \times 10^{11}$$

Similarly,

$$n_2 = \frac{P}{E_2}$$

$$= \frac{1.2 \times 10^{-7}}{2.49 \times 1.6 \times 10^{-19}}$$

$$= 3.0 \times 10^{11}$$

Since, each energetically capable photon ejects one electron, total number of photoelectrons liberated in 2 s.

$$= 2(n_1 + n_2)$$

$$= 2 \ (2.5 + 3.0) \times 10^{11}$$

$$= 1.1 \times 10^{12} \qquad\qquad\qquad \textbf{Ans.}$$

Miscellaneous Examples

⊙ **Example 16** *Two metallic plates A and B each of area 5×10^{-4} m^2, are placed parallel to each other at a separation of 1 cm. Plate B carries a positive charge of 33.7×10^{-12} C. A monochromatic beam of light, with photons of energy 5 eV each, starts falling on plate A at $t = 0$ so that 10^{16} photons fall on it per square metre per second. Assume that one photoelectron is emitted for every 10^6 incident photons. Also assume that all the emitted photoelectrons are collected by plate B and the work-function of plate A remains constant at the value 2 eV.*

Determine (JEE 2002)

(a) the number of photoelectrons emitted upto $t = 10$ s,

(b) the magnitude of the electric field between the plates A and B at $t = 10$ s and

(c) the kinetic energy of the most energetic photoelectrons emitted at $t = 10$ s when it reaches plate B.

Neglect the time taken by the photoelectron to reach plate B.

(Take, $\varepsilon_0 = 8.85 \times 10^{-12} C^2/N\text{-}m^2$).

Solution   Area of plates, $= 5 \times 10^{-4}$ m^2

Distance between the plates, $d = 1$ cm $= 10^{-2}$ m

(a) Number of photoelectrons emitted upto $t = 10$ s are

$$n = \frac{\text{(number of photons falling on unit area in unit time)} \times \text{(area} \times \text{time)}}{10^6}$$

$$= \frac{1}{10^6} [(10)^{16} \times (5 \times 10^{-4}) \times (10)]$$

$$= 5.0 \times 10^7 \qquad\qquad \textbf{Ans.}$$

(b) At time $t = 10$ s,

Charge on plate A, $\qquad q_A = + ne = (5.0 \times 10^7)(1.6 \times 10^{-19})$

$$= 8.0 \times 10^{-12} \text{ C}$$

and charge on plate B,

$$q_B = (33.7 \times 10^{-12} - 8.0 \times 10^{-12})$$

$$= 25.7 \times 10^{-12} \text{ C}$$

∴ Electric field between the plates, $E = \dfrac{(q_B - q_A)}{2A\varepsilon_0}$

or $\qquad\qquad\qquad E = \dfrac{(25.7 - 8.0) \times 10^{-12}}{2 \times (5 \times 10^{-4})(8.85 \times 10^{-12})}$

$$= 2 \times 10^3 \text{ N/C}$$

(c) Energy of most energetic photoelectrons at plate A,

$$= E - W = (5 - 2) \text{ eV} = 3 \text{ eV}$$

Increase in energy of photoelectrons

$$= (eEd) \text{ joule} = (Ed) \text{ eV}$$
$$= (2 \times 10^3)\,(10^{-2}) \text{ eV} = 20 \text{ eV}$$

Energy of photoelectrons at plate B

$$= (20 + 3) \text{ eV} = 23 \text{ eV}$$ **Ans.**

> **Example 17** *Photoelectrons are emitted when 400 nm radiation is incident on a surface of work-function 1.9 eV. These photoelectrons pass through a region containing α-particles. A maximum energy electron combines with an α-particle to form a He$^+$ ion, emitting a single photon in this process. He$^+$ ions thus formed are in their fourth excited state. Find the energies in eV of the photons lying in the 2 to 4 eV range, that are likely to be emitted during and after the combination.* [*Take, $h = 4.14 \times 10^{-15}$ eV-s*]
>
> (JEE 1999)

Solution Given work-function $W = 1.9$ eV

Wavelength of incident light, $\lambda = 400$ nm

∴ Energy of incident light, $E = \dfrac{hc}{\lambda} = 3.1$ eV

(Substituting the values of h, c and λ)

Therefore, maximum kinetic energy of photoelectrons

$$K_{\max} = E - W = (3.1 - 1.9) = 1.2 \text{ eV}$$

Now, the situation is as shown in figure.

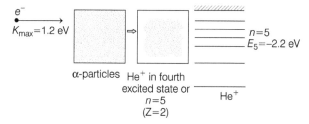

Energy of electron in 4th excited state of He$^+$ ($n = 5$) will be

$$E_5 = -13.6\,\dfrac{Z^2}{n^2} \text{ eV}$$

$\Rightarrow$
$$E_5 = -(13.6)\,\dfrac{(2)^2}{(5)^2} = -2.2 \text{ eV}$$

Therefore, energy released during the combination

$$= 1.2 - (-2.2) = 3.4 \text{ eV}$$

Similarly, energies in other energy states of He$^+$ will be

$$E_4 = -13.6\,\dfrac{(2)^2}{(4)^2} = -3.4 \text{ eV}$$

$$E_3 = -13.6\,\dfrac{(2)^2}{(3)^2} = -6.04 \text{ eV}$$

$$E_2 = -13.6\,\dfrac{(2)^2}{(2)^2} = -13.6 \text{ eV}$$

The possible transitions are

$$\Delta E_{5 \rightarrow 4} = E_5 - E_4 = 1.2 \text{ eV} < 2 \text{ eV}$$
$$\Delta E_{5 \rightarrow 3} = E_5 - E_3 = 3.84 \text{ eV}$$
$$\Delta E_{5 \rightarrow 2} = E_5 - E_2 = 11.4 \text{ eV} > 4 \text{ eV}$$
$$\Delta E_{4 \rightarrow 3} = E_4 - E_3 = 2.64 \text{ eV}$$
$$\Delta E_{4 \rightarrow 2} = E_4 - E_2 = 10.2 \text{ eV} > 4 \text{ eV}$$

Hence, the energy of emitted photons in the range of 2 eV and 4 eV are 3.4 eV during combination and 3.84 eV and 2.64 after combination.

● **Example 18** *Light from a discharge tube containing hydrogen atoms falls on the surface of a piece of sodium. The kinetic energy of the fastest photoelectrons emitted from sodium is 0.73 eV. The work-function for sodium is 1.82 eV.* (JEE 1992)
Find

(a) the energy of the photons causing the photoelectrons emission.

(b) the quantum numbers of the two levels involved in the emission of these photons.

(c) the change in the angular momentum of the electron in the hydrogen atom, in the above transition, and

(d) the recoil speed of the emitting atom assuming it to be at rest before the transition. (Ionization potential of hydrogen is 13.6 eV.)

Solution (a) From Einstein's equation of photoelectric effect,

Energy of photons causing the photoelectric emission

$$= \text{Maximum kinetic energy of emitted photons} + \text{work-function}$$

or $$E = K_{\max} + W = (0.73 + 1.82) \text{ eV}$$

or $$E = 2.55 \text{ eV}$$ **Ans.**

(b) In case of a hydrogen atom,

$$E_1 = -13.6 \text{ eV}, E_2 = -3.4 \text{ eV}, E_3 = -1.5 \text{ eV}$$
$$E_4 = -0.85 \text{ eV}$$

Since, $$E_4 - E_2 = 2.55 \text{ eV}$$

Therefore, quantum numbers of the two levels involved in the emission of these photons are 4 and 2 $(4 \rightarrow 2)$.

(c) Change in angular momentum in transition from 4 to 2 will be

$$\Delta L = L_2 - L_4 = 2 \left(\frac{h}{2\pi} \right) - 4 \left(\frac{h}{2\pi} \right) \quad \text{or} \quad \Delta L = -\frac{h}{\pi}$$

(d) From conservation of linear momentum

$$|\text{Momentum of hydrogen atom}| = |\text{Momentum of emitted photon}|$$

or $$mv = \frac{E}{c} \qquad (m = \text{mass of hydrogen atom})$$

or $$v = \frac{E}{mc} = \frac{(2.55 \times 1.6 \times 10^{-19} \text{ J})}{(1.67 \times 10^{-27} \text{kg}) (3.0 \times 10^8 \text{ m/s})}$$

$$v = 0.814 \text{ m/s}$$ **Ans.**

⊙ **Example 19** *If an X-ray tube operates at the voltage of 10 kV, find the ratio of the de-Broglie wavelength of the incident electrons to the shortest wavelength of X-rays produced. The specific charge of electron is* $1.8 \times 10^{11} C/kg$.

Solution de-Broglie wavelength when a charge q is accelerated by a potential difference of V volts is

$$\lambda_b = \frac{h}{\sqrt{2qVm}} \qquad \ldots(i)$$

For cut off wavelength of X-rays, we have $qV = \frac{hc}{\lambda_m}$

or

$$\lambda_m = \frac{hc}{qV} \qquad \ldots(ii)$$

From Eqs. (i) and (ii), we get $\dfrac{\lambda_b}{\lambda_m} = \dfrac{\sqrt{\dfrac{qV}{2m}}}{c}$

For electron $\dfrac{q}{m} = 1.8 \times 10^{11}$ C/kg (given). Substituting the values the desired ratio is

$$\frac{\lambda_b}{\lambda_m} = \frac{\sqrt{\dfrac{1.8 \times 10^{11} \times 10 \times 10^3}{2}}}{3 \times 10^8} = 0.1 \qquad \textbf{Ans.}$$

⊙ **Example 20** *The wavelength of the first line of Lyman series for hydrogen is identical to that of the second line of Balmer series for some hydrogen like ion x. Calculate energies of the first four levels of x.*

Solution Wavelength of the first line of Lyman series for hydrogen atom will be given by the equation

$$\frac{1}{\lambda_1} = R\left(\frac{1}{1^2} - \frac{1}{2^2}\right) = \frac{3R}{4} \qquad \ldots(i)$$

The wavelength of second Balmer line for hydrogen like ion x is

$$\frac{1}{\lambda_2} = RZ^2\left(\frac{1}{2^2} - \frac{1}{4^2}\right) = \frac{3RZ^2}{16} \qquad \ldots(ii)$$

Given that $\lambda_1 = \lambda_2$ or $\dfrac{1}{\lambda_1} = \dfrac{1}{\lambda_2}$

i.e. $\dfrac{3R}{4} = \dfrac{3RZ^2}{16}$

∴ $Z = 2$

i.e. x ion is He^+. The energies of first four levels of x are

$$E_1 = -(13.6)\,Z^2 = -54.4 \text{ eV}$$

$$E_2 = \frac{E_1}{(2)^2} = -13.6 \text{ eV}$$

$$E_3 = \frac{E_1}{(3)^2} = -6.04 \text{ eV}$$

and

$$E_4 = \frac{E_1}{(4)^2} = -3.4 \text{ eV} \qquad \textbf{Ans.}$$

⊛ **Example 21** *A moving hydrogen atom makes a head on collision with a stationary hydrogen atom. Before collision both atoms are in ground state and after collision they move together. What is the minimum value of the kinetic energy of the moving hydrogen atom, such that one of the atoms reaches one of the excited state?*

Solution Let K be the kinetic energy of the moving hydrogen atom and K', the kinetic energy of combined mass after collision.

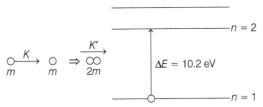

From conservation of linear momentum,

$$p = p' \quad \text{or} \quad \sqrt{2Km} = \sqrt{2K'\,(2m)}$$

or $\qquad\qquad\qquad\qquad\qquad K = 2K'$ ...(i)

From conservation of energy, $\qquad\qquad K = K' + \Delta E$ ...(ii)

Solving Eqs. (i) and (ii), we get $\qquad\qquad \Delta E = \dfrac{K}{2}$

Now, minimum value of ΔE for hydrogen atom is 10.2 eV.

or $\qquad\qquad\qquad\qquad\qquad \Delta E \geq 10.2 \text{ eV}$

∴ $\qquad\qquad\qquad\qquad\qquad \dfrac{K}{2} \geq 10.2$

∴ $\qquad\qquad\qquad\qquad\qquad K \geq 20.4 \text{ eV}$

Therefore, the minimum kinetic energy of moving hydrogen is 20.4 eV.   **Ans.**

⊛ **Example 22** *An imaginary particle has a charge equal to that of an electron and mass 100 times the mass of the electron. It moves in a circular orbit around a nucleus of charge $+4e$. Take the mass of the nucleus to be infinite. Assuming that the Bohr model is applicable to this system.*

(a) *Derive an expression for the radius of nth Bohr orbit.*

(b) *Find the wavelength of the radiation emitted when the particle jumps from fourth orbit to the second orbit.*

Solution (a) We have $\qquad\qquad \dfrac{m_p v^2}{r_n} = \dfrac{1}{4\pi\varepsilon_0}\dfrac{Ze^2}{r_n^2}$ ...(i)

The quantization of angular momentum gives

$$m_p v r_n = \dfrac{nh}{2\pi}$$ ...(ii)

Solving Eqs. (i) and (ii), we get

$$r = \dfrac{n^2 h^2 \varepsilon_0}{Z\pi m_p e^2}$$

Substituting $\qquad\qquad\qquad m_p = 100\, m$

where, m = mass of electron and $Z = 4$

We get, $$r_n = \frac{n^2 h^2 \varepsilon_0}{400 \, \pi \, me^2}$$ **Ans.**

(b) As we know, $$E_1^H = -13.60 \text{ eV}$$

and $$E_n \propto \left(\frac{Z^2}{n^2}\right) m$$

For the given particle, $$E_4 = \frac{(-13.60) \, (4)^2}{(4)^2} \times 100$$

$$= -1360 \text{ eV}$$

and $$E_2 = \frac{(-13.60) \, (4)^2}{(2)^2} \times 100$$

$$= -5440 \text{ eV}$$

$$\Delta E = E_4 - E_2$$

$$= 4080 \text{ eV}$$

∴ $$\lambda \text{ (in Å)} = \frac{12375}{\Delta E \text{ (in eV)}}$$

$$= \frac{12375}{4080}$$

$$= 3.0 \text{ Å}$$ **Ans.**

Example 23 *The energy levels of a hypothetical one electron atom are given by*

$$E_n = -\frac{18.0}{n^2} \, eV$$

where $n = 1, 2, 3,...$

(a) Compute the four lowest energy levels and construct the energy level diagram.

(b) What is the first excitation potential

(c) What wavelengths (Å) can be emitted when these atoms in the ground state are bombarded by electrons that have been accelerated through a potential difference of 16.2 V?

(d) If these atoms are in the ground state, can they absorb radiation having a wavelength of 2000 Å?

(e) What is the photoelectric threshold wavelength of this atom?

Solution (a) $E_1 = \dfrac{-18.0}{(1)^2} = -18.0$ eV

$$E_2 = \frac{-18.0}{(2)^2} = -4.5 \text{ eV}$$

$$E_3 = \frac{-18.0}{(3)^2} = -2.0 \text{ eV}$$

and $$E_4 = \frac{-18.0}{(4)^2} = -1.125 \text{ eV}$$

The energy level diagram is shown in figure.

$$\begin{array}{l} \underline{} E_4 = -1.125 \text{ eV} \\ \underline{} E_3 = -2.0 \text{ eV} \\[8pt] \underline{} E_2 = -4.5 \text{ eV} \\[40pt] \underline{} E_1 = -18.0 \text{ eV} \end{array}$$

(b) $E_2 - E_1 = 13.5$ eV

$\therefore$ First excitation potential is 13.5 V.

(c) Energy of the electron accelerated by a potential difference of 16.2 V is 16.2 eV. With this energy the electron can excite the atom from $n = 1$ to $n = 3$ as

$$E_4 - E_1 = -1.125 - (-18.0) = 16.875 \text{ eV} > 16.2 \text{ eV}$$

and $$E_3 - E_1 = -2.0 - (-18.0) = 16.0 \text{ eV} < 16.2 \text{ eV}$$

Now, $$\lambda_{32} = \frac{12375}{E_3 - E_2} = \frac{12375}{-2.0 - (-4.5)}$$

$$= 4950 \text{ Å} \qquad\qquad \textbf{Ans.}$$

$$\lambda_{31} = \frac{12375}{E_3 - E_1} = \frac{12375}{16} = 773 \text{ Å} \qquad\qquad \textbf{Ans.}$$

and $$\lambda_{21} = \frac{12375}{E_2 - E_1} = \frac{12375}{-4.5 - (-18.0)}$$

$$= 917 \text{ Å} \qquad\qquad \textbf{Ans.}$$

(d) No, the energy corresponding to $\lambda = 2000$ Å is

$$E = \frac{12375}{2000} = 6.1875 \text{ eV} \qquad\qquad \textbf{Ans.}$$

The minimum excitation energy is 13.5 eV $(n = 1 \text{ to } n = 2)$.

(e) Threshold wavelength for photoemission to take place from such an atom is

$$\lambda_{\min} = \frac{12375}{18}$$

$$= 687.5 \text{ Å} \qquad\qquad \textbf{Ans.}$$

● **Example 24** *In a photocell the plates P and Q have a separation of 5 cm, which are connected through a galvanometer without any cell. Bichromatic light of wavelengths 4000 Å and 6000 Å are incident on plate Q whose work-function is 2.39 eV. If a uniform magnetic field B exists parallel to the plates, find the minimum value of B for which the galvanometer shows zero deflection.*

Solution Energy of photons corresponding to light of wavelength $\lambda_1 = 4000$ Å is

$$E_1 = \frac{12375}{4000} = 3.1 \text{ eV}$$

and that corresponding to $\lambda_2 = 6000$ Å is

$$E_2 = \frac{12375}{6000} = 2.06 \text{ eV}$$

As, $$E_2 < W \quad \text{and} \quad E_1 > W \qquad\qquad (W = \text{work-function})$$

Photoelectric emission is possible with λ_1 only.

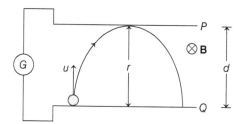

Photoelectrons experience magnetic force and move along a circular path. The galvanometer will indicate zero deflection if the photoelectrons just complete semicircular path before reaching the plate P.

Thus,

$$d = r = 5 \text{ cm}$$

$\therefore$

$$r = 5 \text{ cm} = 0.05 \text{ m}$$

Further,

$$r = \frac{mv}{Bq} = \frac{\sqrt{2Km}}{Bq}$$

$\therefore$

$$B_{\text{min}} = \frac{\sqrt{2Km}}{rq}$$

Here,

$$K = E_1 - W = (3.1 - 2.39)$$
$$= 0.71 \text{ eV}$$

Substituting the values, we have

$$B_{\text{min}} = \frac{\sqrt{2 \times 0.71 \times 1.6 \times 10^{-19} \times 9.109 \times 10^{-31}}}{(0.05)(1.6 \times 10^{-19})}$$

$$= 5.68 \times 10^{-5} \text{ T}$$ **Ans.**

Exercises

LEVEL 1

Assertion and Reason

Directions : *Choose the correct option.*
(a) *If both **Assertion** and **Reason** are true and the **Reason** is correct explanation of the **Assertion**.*
(b) *If both **Assertion** and **Reason** are true but **Reason** is not the correct explanation of **Assertion**.*
(c) *If **Assertion** is true, but the **Reason** is false.*
(d) *If **Assertion** is false but the **Reason** is true.*
(e) *Both **Assertion** and **Reason** are false.*

1. **Assertion :** X-rays cannot be deflected by electric or magnetic fields.

   Reason : These are electromagnetic waves.

2. **Assertion :** If wavelength of light is doubled, energy and momentum of photons are reduced to half.

   Reason : By increasing the wavelength, speed of photons will decrease.

3. **Assertion :** Photoelectric effect proves the particle nature of light.

   Reason : Photoemission starts as soon as light is incident on the metal surface, provided frequency of incident light is greater than or equal to the threshold frequency.

4. **Assertion :** X-rays cannot be obtained in the emission spectrum of hydrogen atom.

   Reason : Maximum energy of photons emitted from hydrogen spectrum is 13.6 eV.

5. **Assertion :** If light continuously falls on a metal surface then emission of electrons will stop after some time.

   Reason : We cannot extract electrons from a metal.

6. **Assertion :** It is essential that all the lines available in the emission spectrum will also be available in the absorption spectrum.

   Reason : The spectrum of hydrogen atom is only absorption spectrum.

7. **Assertion :** Work function of a metal is 8 eV. Two photons each having energy 5 eV cannot eject the electron from the metal.

   Reason : This proves the particle nature of light.

8. **Assertion :** We can increase the saturation current in photoelectric experiment without increasing the intensity of light.

   Reason : Intensity can be increased by increasing the frequency of incident photons.

Objective Questions

1. The radius of an atom is approximately equal to
   (a) 10^{-8}cm
   (b) 10^{-4}cm
   (c) 10^{-10}cm
   (d) 10^{-6}cm

2. In Thomson's method of determining e/m of electrons
   (a) electric and magnetic fields are parallel to electron beam
   (b) electric and magnetic fields are perpendicular to each other and perpendicular to electron beam
   (c) magnetic field is parallel to the electron beam
   (d) electric field is parallel to the electron beam

3. According to Einstein's photoelectric equation, the plot of the maximum kinetic energy of the emitted photoelectrons from a metal *versus* frequency of the incident radiation gives a straight line whose slope
   (a) depends on the nature of metal used
   (b) depends on the intensity of radiation
   (c) depends on both intensity of radiation and the nature of metal used
   (d) is the same for all metals and independent of the intensity of radiation

4. Which of the folllowing products in a hydrogen atom are independent of the principal quantum number n?
   (a) vr (b) Er (c) Ev (d) None of these

5. An X-ray tube is operated at 18 kV. The maximum velocity of electron striking the target is
   (a) 8×10^7 m/s   (b) 6×10^7 m/s
   (c) 5×10^7 m/s   (d) None of these

6. What is the ratio of de-Broglie wavelength of electron in the second and third Bohr orbits in the hydrogen atoms?
   (a) 2/3   (b) 3/2
   (c) 4/3   (d) 3/4

7. The velocity of the electron in the first Bohr orbit as compared to that of light is about
   (a) 1/300   (b) 1/500
   (c) 1/137   (d) 1/187

8. The energy of an atom or ion in the first excited state is -13.6 eV. It may be
   (a) He^+ (b) Li^{++}
   (c) hydrogen   (d) deuterium

9. In order that the short wavelength limit of the continuous X-ray spectrum be 1 Å, the potential difference through which an electron must be accelerated is
   (a) 124 kV   (b) 1.24 kV
   (c) 12.4 kV   (d) 1240 kV

10. The momentum of an X-ray photon with $\lambda = 0.5$ Å is
    (a) 13.26×10^{-26} kg-m/s   (b) 1.326×10^{-26} kg-m/s
    (c) 13.26×10^{-24} kg-m/s   (d) 13.26×10^{-22} kg-m/s

11. The work-function of a substance is 1.6 eV. The longest wavelength of light that can produce photoemission from the substance is
    (a) 7734 Å   (b) 3875 Å
    (c) 5812 Å   (d) 2964 Å

12. If the potential energy of a hydrogen atom in the ground state is assumed to be zero, then total energy of $n = \infty$ is equal to
    (a) 13.6 eV   (b) 27.2 eV
    (c) zero   (d) None of these

13. The energy of a hydrogen atom in its ground state is − 13.6 eV. The energy of the level corresponding to the quantum number $n = 5$ is
(a) − 0.54 eV   (b) − 5.40 eV
(c) − 0.85 eV   (d) − 2.72 eV

14. Photoelectric effect supports quantum nature of light because
(a) the energy of released electron is discrete
(b) the maximum kinetic energy of photoelectrons depends only on the frequency of light and not on its intensity
(c) even when the metal surface is faintly illuminated, the photoelectrons leave the surface immediately
(d) electric charge of the photoelectrons is quantized

15. In which of the following systems will the radius of the first orbit ($n = 1$) be minimum?
(a) Hydrogen atom   (b) Deuterium atom
(c) Singly ionized helium   (d) Doubly ionized lithium

16. The excitation energy of a hydrogen like ion to its first excited state is 40.8 eV. The energy needed to remove the electron from the ion in the ground state is
(a) 54.4 eV   (b) 62.6 eV
(c) 72.6 eV   (d) 58.6 eV

17. If the de-Broglie wavelength of a proton is 10^{-13} m, the electric potential through which it must have been accelerated is
(a) 4.07×10^4 V   (b) 8.15×10^4 V
(c) 8.15×10^3 V   (d) 4.07×10^5 V

18. The operating potential in an X-ray tube is increased by 2%. The percentage change in the cut off wavelength is
(a) 1% increase   (b) 2% increase
(c) 2% decrease   (d) 1% decrease

19. The frequency of the first line in Lyman series in the hydrogen spectrum is v. What is the frequency of the corresponding line in the spectrum of doubly ionized Lithium?
(a) v   (b) 3 v   (c) 9 v   (d) 2 v

20. Which energy state of doubly ionized lithium (Li^{++}) has the same energy as that of the ground state of hydrogen?
(a) $n = 1$ (b) $n = 2$
(c) $n = 3$ (d) $n = 4$

21. The longest wavelength of the Lyman series for hydrogen atom is the same as the wavelength of a certain line in the spectrum of He^+ when the electron makes a transition from $n \rightarrow 2$. The value of n is
(a) 3   (b) 4
(c) 5   (d) 6

22. Electromagnetic radiation of wavelength 3000 Å is incident on an isolated platinum surface of work-function 6.30 eV. Due to the radiation, the
(a) sphere becomes positively charged
(b) sphere becomes negatively charged
(c) sphere remains neutral
(d) maximum kinetic energy of the ejected photoelectrons would be 2.03 eV

23. Ultraviolet radiation of 6.2 eV falls on an aluminium surface (work-function = 4.2 eV). The kinetic energy in joule of the fastest electrons emitted is
(a) 3.2×10^{-21}
(b) 3.2×10^{-19}
(c) 3.2×10^{-17}
(d) 3.2×10^{-15}

24. What should be the velocity of an electron so that its momentum becomes equal to that of a photon of wavelength 5200 Å?
(a) 700 m/s
(b) 1000 m/s
(c) 1400 m/s
(d) 2800 m/s

25. An electron with kinetic energy 5 eV is incident on a H-atom in its ground state. The collision
(a) must be elastic
(b) may be partially elastic
(c) must be completely inelastic
(d) may be completely inelastic

26. A proton accelerated through a potential difference of 100 V has de-Broglie wavelength λ_0. The de-Broglie wavelength of an α-particle, accelerated through 800 V is
(a) $\dfrac{\lambda_0}{\sqrt{2}}$
(b) $\dfrac{\lambda_0}{2}$
(c) $\dfrac{\lambda_0}{4}$
(d) $\dfrac{\lambda_0}{8}$

27. The minimum wavelength of X-rays produced by electrons accelerated by a potential difference of V volt is equal to
(a) $\dfrac{eV}{hc}$
(b) $\dfrac{eh}{cV}$
(c) $\dfrac{hc}{eV}$
(d) $\dfrac{cV}{eh}$

28. The wavelength of K_α, X-rays for lead isotopes Pb^{208}, Pb^{206}, Pb^{204} are λ_1, λ_2 and λ_3 respectively. Then,
(a) $\lambda_1 = \lambda_2 > \lambda_3$
(b) $\lambda_1 > \lambda_2 > \lambda_3$
(c) $\lambda_1 < \lambda_2 < \lambda_3$
(d) $\lambda_2 = \sqrt{\lambda_1 \lambda_3}$

29. Moseley's law for characteristic X-rays is $\sqrt{v} = a(Z - b)$. In this,
(a) both a and b are independent of the material
(b) a is independent but b depends on the material
(c) b is independent but a depends on the material
(d) both a and b depends on the material

30. Find the binding energy of an electron in the ground state of a hydrogen like atom in whose spectrum the third Balmer line is equal to 108.5 nm.
(a) 54.4 eV
(b) 13.6 eV
(c) 112.4 eV
(d) None of these

31. Light of wavelength 330 nm falling on a piece of metal ejects electrons with sufficient energy with required voltage V_0 to prevent them from reaching a collector. In the same set up, light of wavelength 220 nm ejects electrons which require twice the voltage V_0 to stop them in reaching a collector. The numerical value of voltage V_0 is
(a) $\dfrac{16}{15} V$
(b) $\dfrac{15}{16} V$
(c) $\dfrac{15}{8} V$
(d) $\dfrac{8}{15} V$

32. Maximum kinetic energy of a photoelectron is E when the wavelength of incident light is λ. If energy becomes four times when wavelength is reduced to one-third, then work-function of the metal is

(a) $\dfrac{3\,hc}{\lambda}$

(b) $\dfrac{hc}{3\lambda}$

(c) $\dfrac{hc}{\lambda}$

(d) $\dfrac{hc}{2\lambda}$

33. If the frequency of K_α X-ray emitted from the element with atomic number 31 is f, then the frequency of K_α X-ray emitted from the element with atomic number 51 would be

(a) $\dfrac{5f}{3}$

(b) $\dfrac{51f}{31}$

(c) $\dfrac{9f}{25}$

(d) $\dfrac{25f}{9}$

34. According to Moseley's law, the ratio of the slope of graph between $\sqrt{f}$ and Z for K_β and K_α is

(a) $\sqrt{\dfrac{32}{27}}$

(b) $\sqrt{\dfrac{27}{32}}$

(c) $\sqrt{\dfrac{5}{36}}$

(d) $\sqrt{\dfrac{36}{5}}$

35. A potential of 10000 V is applied across an X-ray tube. Find the ratio of de-Broglie wavelength associated with incident electrons to the minimum wavelength associated with X-rays. (Given, $e/m = 1.8 \times 10^{11}$ C/kg for electrons)

(a) 10

(b) 20

(c) 1/10

(d) 1/20

36. When a metallic surface is illuminated with monochromatic light of wavelength λ, the stopping potential is $5\,V_0$. When the same surface is illuminated with the light of wavelength 3λ, the stopping potential is V_0. Then, the work-function of the metallic surface is

(a) $hc/6\lambda$

(b) $hc/5\lambda$

(c) $hc/4\lambda$

(d) $2hc/4\lambda$

37. The threshold frequency for a certain photosensitive metal is v_0. When it is illuminated by light of frequency $v = 2v_0$, the stopping potential for photoelectric current is V_0. What will be the stopping potential when the same metal is illuminated by light of frequency $v = 3v_0$?

(a) $1.5\,V_0$

(b) $2\,V_0$

(c) $2.5\,V_0$

(d) $3\,V_0$

38. Two identical photo-cathodes receive light of frequencies v_1 and v_2. If the velocities of the photoelectrons (of mass m) coming out are v_1 and v_2 respectively, then

(a) $v_1 - v_2 = \left[\dfrac{2h}{m}(v_1 - v_2)\right]^{1/2}$

(b) $v_1^2 - v_2^2 = \dfrac{2h}{m}(v_1 - v_2)$

(c) $v_1 + v_2 = \left[\dfrac{2h}{m}(v_1 - v_2)\right]^{1/2}$

(d) $v_1^2 + v_2^2 = \dfrac{2h}{m}(v_1 - v_2)$

39. The frequencies of K_α, K_β and L_α X-rays of a material are γ_1, γ_2 and γ_3 respectively. Which of the following relation holds good?

(a) $\gamma_2 = \sqrt{\gamma_1\,\gamma_3}$

(b) $\gamma_2 = \gamma_1 + \gamma_3$

(c) $\gamma_2 = \dfrac{\gamma_1 + \gamma_3}{2}$

(d) $\gamma_3 = \sqrt{\gamma_1\,\gamma_2}$

40. If E_1, E_2 and E_3 represent respectively the kinetic energies of an electron , an α-particle and a proton each having same de-Broglie wavelength, then
   (a) $E_1 > E_3 > E_2$
   (b) $E_2 > E_3 > E_1$
   (c) $E_1 > E_2 > E_3$
   (d) $E_1 = E_2 = E_3$

41. For the Bohr's first orbit of circumference $2\pi r$, the de-Broglie wavelength of revolving electron will be
   (a) $2\pi r$
   (b) πr
   (c) $\dfrac{1}{2\pi r}$
   (d) $\dfrac{1}{4\pi r}$

42. In a hypothetical Bohr hydrogen, the mass of the electron is doubled. The energy E_0 and radius r_0 of the first orbit will be (a_0 is the Bohr radius)
   (a) $E_0 = -27.2$ eV, $r_0 = a_0/2$
   (b) $E_0 = -27.2$ eV, $r_0 = a_0$
   (c) $E_0 = -13.6$ eV, $r_0 = a_0/2$
   (d) $E_0 = -13.6$ eV, $r_0 = a_0$

43. An electron makes a transition from orbit $n = 4$ to the orbit $n = 2$ of a hydrogen atom. The wave number of the emitted radiations (R = Rydberg's constant) will be
   (a) $\dfrac{16}{3R}$
   (b) $\dfrac{2R}{16}$
   (c) $\dfrac{3R}{16}$
   (d) $\dfrac{4R}{16}$

44. The wavelength of radiation emitted is λ_0 when an electron jumps from the third to the second orbit of hydrogen atom. For the electron jump from the fourth to the second orbit of the hydrogen atom, the wavelength of radiation emitted will be
   (a) $\dfrac{16}{25}\lambda_0$
   (b) $\dfrac{20}{27}\lambda_0$
   (c) $\dfrac{27}{20}\lambda_0$
   (d) $\dfrac{25}{16}\lambda_0$

45. The electron in a hydrogen atom makes transition from M shell to L-shell. The ratio of magnitude of initial to final acceleration of the electron is
   (a) $9 : 4$
   (b) $81 : 16$
   (c) $4 : 9$
   (d) $16 : 81$

46. The work functions of metals A and B are in the ratio $1 : 2$. If light of frequencies f and $2f$ are incident on metal surfaces of A and B respectively, the ratio of the maximum kinetic energies of photoelectron emitted is (f is greater than threshold frequency of A, $2f$ is greater than threshold frequency of B)
   (a) $1 : 1$
   (b) $1 : 2$
   (c) $1 : 3$
   (d) $1 : 4$

47. An electron of mass m when accelerated through a potential difference V has de-Broglie wavelength λ. The de-Broglie wavelength associated with a proton of mass M accelerated through the same potential difference will be
   (a) $\lambda\dfrac{m}{M}$
   (b) $\lambda\sqrt{\dfrac{m}{M}}$
   (c) $\lambda\dfrac{M}{m}$
   (d) $\lambda\sqrt{\dfrac{M}{m}}$

48. A beam of white light is incident normally on a plane surface absorbing 70% of the light and reflecting the rest. If the incident beam carries 20 W of power, the force exerted by it on the surface is
(a) 5.6×10^{-7} N   (b) 2.6×10^{-7} N
(c) 1×10^{-7} N   (d) None of these

49. An α-particle of 5 MeV energy strikes with a stationary nucleus of uranium at an scattering angle of $180°$. The nearest distance upto which α-particle reaches the nucleus will be of the order of
(a) 1 Å   (b) 10^{-10} cm
(c) 10^{-12} cm   (d) 10^{-15} cm

50. Hydrogen (H), deuterium (D), singly ionized helium (He^+) and doubly ionized lithium (Li^{++}) all have one electron around the nucleus. Consider $n = 2$ to $n = 1$ transition. The wavelengths of emitted radiations are $\lambda_1, \lambda_2, \lambda_3$ and λ_4 respectively. Then, approximately
(a) $\lambda_1 = \lambda_2 = 4\lambda_3 = 9\lambda_4$ (b) $4\lambda_1 = 2\lambda_2 = 2\lambda_3 = \lambda_4$
(c) $\lambda_1 = 2\lambda_2 = 2\sqrt{2}\lambda_3 = 3\sqrt{2}\lambda_4$ (d) $\lambda_1 = \lambda_2 = 2\lambda_3 = 3\sqrt{2}\lambda_4$

Subjective Questions

Note   *You can take approximations in the answers.*
  $h = 6.62 \times 10^{-34}$ J-s, $c = 3.0 \times 10^8$ m/s, $m_e = 9.1 \times 10^{-31}$ kg and 1 eV $= 1.6 \times 10^{-19}$ J

1. For a given element the wavelength of the K_α-line is 0.71 nm and of the K_β-line it is 0.63 nm. Use this information to find wavelength of the L_α-line.

2. The energy of the $n = 2$ state in a given element is $E_2 = -2870$ eV. Given that the wavelengths of the K_α and K_β-lines are 0.71 nm and 0.63 nm respectively, determine the energies E_1 and E_3.

3. 1.5 mW of 400 nm light is directed at a photoelectric cell. If 0.1% of the incident photons produce photoelectrons, find the current in the cell.

4. A photon has momentum of magnitude 8.24×10^{-28} kg-m/s.
(a) What is the energy of this photon? Give your answer in joules and in electron volts.
(b) What is the wavelength of this photon? In what region of the electromagnetic spectrum does it lie?

5. A 75 W light source emits light of wavelength 600 nm.
(a) Calculate the frequency of the emitted light.
(b) How many photons per second does the source emit?

6. An excited nucleus emits a gamma-ray photon with energy of 2.45 MeV.
(a) What is the photon frequency? (b) What is the photon wavelength?

7. (a) A proton is moving at a speed much less than the speed of light. It has kinetic energy K_1 and momentum p_1. If the momentum of the proton is doubled, so $p_2 = 2p_1$, how is its new kinetic energy K_2 related to K_1?
(b) A photon with energy E_1 has momentum p_1. If another photon has momentum p_2 that is twice p_1, how is the energy E_2 of the second photon related to E_1?

8. A parallel beam of monochromatic light of wavelength 500 nm is incident normally on a perfectly absorbing surface. The power through any cross-section of the beam is 10 W. Find
(a) the number of photons absorbed per second by the surface and
(b) the force exerted by the light beam on the surface.

9. A parallel beam of monochromatic light of wavelength 663 nm is incident on a totally reflecting plane mirror. The angle of incidence is 60° and the number of photons striking the mirror per second is 1.0×10^{19}. Calculate the force exerted by the light beam on the mirror.

10. An electron has a de-Broglie wavelength of 2.80×10^{-10} m. Determine
    (a) the magnitude of its momentum,
    (b) its kinetic energy (in joule and in electron volt).

11. Find de-Broglie wavelength corresponding to the root-mean square velocity of hydrogen molecules at room temperature (20°C).

12. In the Bohr model of the hydrogen atom, what is the de-Broglie wavelength for the electron when it is in
    (a) the $n = 1$ level?
    (b) the $n = 4$ level? In each case, compare the de-Broglie wavelength to the circumference $2\pi r_n$ of the orbit.

13. Hydrogen atom in its ground state is excited by means of monochromatic radiation of wavelength 1023 Å. How many different lines are possible in the resulting spectrum? Calculate the longest wavelength among them. You may assume the ionization energy of hydrogen atom as 13.6 eV.

14. A doubly ionized lithium atom is hydrogen like with atomic number 3. Find the wavelength of the radiation required to excite the electron in Li^{++} from the first to the third Bohr orbit (ionization energy of the hydrogen atom equals 13.6 eV).

15. Find the quantum number n corresponding to nth excited state of He^+ ion if on transition to the ground state the ion emits two photons in succession with wavelengths 108.5 nm and 30.4 nm. The ionization energy of the hydrogen atom is 13.6 eV.

16. A hydrogen like atom (described by the Bohr model) is observed to emit ten wavelengths, originating from all possible transitions between a group of levels. These levels have energies between –0.85 eV and –0.544 eV (including both these values).
    (a) Find the atomic number of the atom.
    (b) Calculate the smallest wavelength emitted in these transitions.
    (Take ground state energy of hydrogen atom = -13.6 eV)

17. The energy levels of a hypothetical one electron atom are shown in the figure.
    (a) Find the ionization potential of this atom.
    (b) Find the short wavelength limit of the series terminating at $n = 2$.
    (c) Find the excitation potential for the state $n = 3$.
    (d) Find wave number of the photon emitted for the transition $n = 3$ to $n = 1$.

∞	0 eV
$n = 5$	–0.80 eV
$n = 4$	–1.45 eV
$n = 3$	–3.08 eV
$n = 2$	–5.30 eV
$n = 1$	–15.6 eV

18. (a) An atom initially in an energy level with $E = -6.52$ eV absorbs a photon that has wavelength 860 nm. What is the internal energy of the atom after it absorbs the photon?
    (b) An atom initially in an energy level with $E = -2.68$ eV emits a photon that has wavelength 420 nm. What is the internal energy of the atom after it emits the photon?

19. A silver ball is suspended by a string in a vacuum chamber and ultraviolet light of wavelength 2000 Å is directed at it. What electrical potential will the ball acquire as a result? Work function of silver is 4.3 eV.

20. A small particle of mass m moves in such a way that the potential energy $U = \dfrac{1}{2}m^2\omega^2 r^2$, where ω is a constant and r is the distance of the particle from the origin. Assuming Bohr model of quantization of angular momentum and circular orbits, show that radius of the nth allowed orbit is proportional to $\sqrt{n}$.

21. X-rays are produced in an X-ray tube by electrons accelerated through an electric potential difference of 50.0 kV. An electron makes three collisions in the target coming to rest and loses half its remaining kinetic energy in each of the first two collisions. Determine the wavelength of the resulting photons. (Neglecting the recoil of the heavy target atoms).

22. A voltage applied to an X-ray tube being increased $\eta = 1.5$ times, the short wave limit of an X-ray continuous spectrum shifts by $\Delta\lambda = 26$ pm. Find the initial voltage applied to the tube.

23. The K_α X-rays of aluminium ($Z = 13$) and zinc ($Z = 30$) have wavelengths 887 pm and 146 pm, respectively. Use Moseley's equation $\sqrt{v} = a(Z - b)$ to find the wavelength of the K_a X-ray of iron ($Z = 26$).

24. Characteristic X-rays of frequency 4.2×10^{18} Hz are produced when transitions from L shell take place in a certain target material. Use Moseley's law and determine the atomic number of the target material. Given, Rydberg constant is $R = 1.1 \times 10^7$ m^{-1}.

25. The electric current in an X-ray tube operating at 40 kV is 10 mA. Assume that on an average 1% of the total kinetic energy of the electrons hitting the target are converted into X-rays.
(a) What is the total power emitted as X-rays and
(b) How much heat is produced in the target every second?

26. The stopping potential for the photoelectrons emitted from a metal surface of work-function 1.7 eV is 10.4 V. Find the wavelength of the radiation used. Also, identify the energy levels in hydrogen atom, which will emit this wavelength.

27. What will be the maximum kinetic energy of the photoelectrons ejected from magnesium (for which the work-function $W = 3.7$ eV) when irradiated by ultraviolet light of frequency 1.5×10^{15} s^{-1}.

28. A metallic surface is irradiated with monochromatic light of variable wavelength. Above a wavelength of 5000 Å, no photoelectrons are emitted from the surface. With an unknown wavelength, stopping potential of 3 V is necessary to eliminate the photocurrent. Find the unknown wavelength.

29. A graph regarding photoelectric effect is shown between the maximum kinetic energy of electrons and the frequency of the incident light . On the basis of data as shown in the graph, calculate

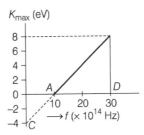

(a) threshold frequency,
(b) work-function,
(c) planck constant

30. A metallic surface is illuminated alternatively with light of wavelengths 3000 Å and 6000 Å. It is observed that the maximum speeds of the photoelectrons under these illuminations are in the ratio 3 : 1. Calculate the work-function of the metal and the maximum speed of the photoelectrons in two cases.

31. Light of wavelength 180 nm ejects photoelectrons from a plate of metal whose work-function is 2 eV. If a uniform magnetic field of 5×10^{-5} T be applied parallel to the plate, what would be the radius of the path followed by electrons ejected normally from the plate with maximum energy.

32. Light described at a place by the equation $E = (100 \text{ V/m}) [\sin(5 \times 10^{15} \text{ s}^{-1})t + \sin(8 \times 10^{15} \text{ s}^{-1})t]$ falls on a metal surface having work-function 2.0 eV. Calculate the maximum kinetic energy of the photoelectrons.

33. The electric field associated with a light wave is given by $E = E_0 \sin [(1.57 \times 10^7 \text{ m}^{-1})(x - ct)]$. Find the stopping potential when this light is used in an experiment on photoelectric effect with a metal having work-function 1.9 eV.

LEVEL 2

Single Correct Option

1. If we assume only gravitational attraction between proton and electron in hydrogen atom and the Bohr quantization rule to be followed, then the expression for the ground state energy of the atom will be (the mass of proton is M and that of electron is m.)

(a) $\dfrac{G^2 M^2 m^2}{h^2}$

(b) $-\dfrac{2\pi^2 G^2 M^2 m^3}{h^2}$

(c) $-\dfrac{2\pi^2 G M^2 m^3}{h^2}$

(d) None of these

2. An electron in a hydrogen atom makes a transition from first excited state to ground state. The magnetic moment due to circulating electron

(a) increases two times

(b) decreases two times

(c) increases four times

(d) remains same

3. An electron in a hydrogen atom makes a transition from first excited state to ground state. The equivalent current due to circulating electron

(a) increases 4 times

(b) decreases 4 times

(c) increases 8 times

(d) decreases 8 times

4. In a sample of hydrogen like atoms all of which are in ground state, a photon beam containing photons of various energies is passed. In absorption spectrum, five dark lines are observed. The number of bright lines in the emission spectrum will be
(assume that all transitions take place)

(a) 21

(b) 10

(c) 15

(d) None of these

5. Let A_n be the area enclosed by the nth orbit in a hydrogen atom. The graph of $\ln (A_n / A_1)$ against $\ln (n)$

(a) will not pass through origin

(b) will be a straight line with slope 4

(c) will be a rectangular hyperbola

(d) will be a parabola

6. In the hydrogen atom, an electron makes a transition from $n = 2$ to $n = 1$. The magnetic field produced by the circulating electron at the nucleus
   (a) decreases 16 times
   (b) increases 4 times
   (c) decreases 4 times
   (d) increases 32 times

7. A stationary hydrogen atom emits photon corresponding to the first line of Lyman series. If R is the Rydberg constant and M is the mass of the atom, then the velocity acquired by the atom is
   (a) $\dfrac{3Rh}{4M}$
   (b) $\dfrac{4M}{3Rh}$
   (c) $\dfrac{Rh}{4M}$
   (d) $\dfrac{4M}{Rh}$

8. The time period of the electron in the ground state of hydrogen atom is two times the time period of the electron in the first excited state of a certain hydrogen like atom (Atomic number Z). The value of Z is
   (a) 2
   (b) 3
   (c) 4
   (d) None of these

9. In case of hydrogen atom, whenever a photon is emitted in the Balmer series,
   (a) there is a probability of emitting another photon in the Lyman series
   (b) there is a probability of emitting another photon of wavelength 1213 Å
   (c) the wavelength of radiation emitted in Lyman series is always shorter than the wavelength emitted in the Balmer series
   (d) All of the above

10. An electron of kinetic energy K collides elastically with a stationary hydrogen atom in the ground state. Then,
    (a) $K > 13.6$ eV
    (b) $K > 10.2$ eV
    (c) $K < 10.2$ eV
    (d) data insufficient

11. In a stationary hydrogen atom, an electron jumps from $n = 3$ to $n = 1$. The recoil speed of the hydrogen atom is about
    (a) 4 m/s
    (b) 4 cm/s
    (c) 4 mm/s
    (d) 4×10^{-4} m/s

12. An X-ray tube is operating at 150 kV and 10 mA. If only 1% of the electric power supplied is converted into X-rays, the rate at which the target is heated in calorie per second is
    (a) 3.55
    (b) 35.5
    (c) 355
    (d) 3550

13. An electron revolves round a nucleus of atomic number Z. If 32.4 eV of energy is required to excite an electron from the $n = 3$ state to $n = 4$ state, then the value of Z is
    (a) 5
    (b) 6
    (c) 4
    (d) 7

14. If E_n and L_n denote the total energy and the angular momentum of an electron in the nth orbit of Bohr atom, then
    (a) $E_n \propto L_n$
    (b) $E_n \propto \dfrac{1}{L_n}$
    (c) $E_n \propto L_n^2$
    (d) $E_n \propto \dfrac{1}{L_n^2}$

15. A moving hydrogen atom makes a head-on collision with a stationary hydrogen atom. Before collision, both atoms are in ground state and after collision they move together. The minimum value of the kinetic energy of the moving hydrogen atom, such that one of the atoms reaches one of the excitation state is
    (a) 20.4 eV
    (b) 10.2 eV
    (c) 54.4 eV
    (d) 13.6 eV

16. In an excited state of hydrogen like atom an electron has total energy of -3.4 eV. If the kinetic energy of the electron is E and its de-Broglie wavelength is λ, then
(a) $\lambda = 6.6$ Å
(b) $E = 3.4$ eV
(c) Both are correct
(d) Both are wrong

17. A ray of light of wavelength 5030 Å is incident on a totally reflecting surface. The momentum delivered by the ray is equal to
(a) 6.63×10^{-27} kg-m/s
(b) 2.63×10^{-27} kg-m/s
(c) 1.25×10^{-24} kg-m/s
(d) None of these

18. If the radius of first Bohr's orbit is x, then de-Broglie wavelength of electron in 3rd orbit is nearly
(a) $2\pi x$
(b) $6\pi x$
(c) $9x$
(d) $\dfrac{x}{3}$

19. A H-atom moving with speed v makes a head on collision with a H-atom at rest. Both atoms are in ground state. The minimum value of velocity v for which one of the atom may excite is
(a) 6.25×10^4 m/s
(b) 8×10^4 m/s
(c) 7.25×10^4 m/s
(d) 13.6×10^4 m/s

Note : $m_H = 1.67 \times 10^{-27}$ kg

20. An excited hydrogen atom emits a photon of wavelength λ in jumping to the ground state. The quantum number n of the excited state is given by (R = Rydberg constant)
(a) $\sqrt{\lambda R(\lambda R - 1)}$
(b) $\sqrt{\dfrac{\lambda R}{(\lambda R - 1)}}$
(c) $\sqrt{\dfrac{(\lambda R - 1)}{\lambda R}}$
(d) $\sqrt{\dfrac{1}{\lambda R(\lambda R - 1)}}$

21. Magnetic moment of an electron in nth orbit of hydrogen atom is
(a) $\dfrac{neh}{\pi m}$
(b) $\dfrac{neh}{4\pi m}$
(c) $\dfrac{meh}{2\pi n}$
(d) $\dfrac{meh}{4\pi n}$

[where, m = mass of electron, h = Planck's constant]

22. When the voltage applied to an X-ray tube is increased from $V_1 = 10$ kV to $V_2 = 20$ kV, the wavelength difference between the K_α line and the short wavelength limit of the continuous X-ray spectrum increases by a factor 3. The atomic number of the target element is :
(a) 62
(b) 56
(c) 45
(d) 29

23. A photon has the same wavelength as the de-Broglie wavelength of electron. Given that c = speed of light and v = speed of electron. Which of the following relation is correct?
[Here, E_e = Kinetic energy of electron, E_{ph} = energy of photon, p_e = momentum of electron and p_{ph} = momentum of photon]
(a) $\dfrac{E_e}{E_{ph}} = \dfrac{2c}{v}$
(b) $\dfrac{E_e}{E_{ph}} = \dfrac{v}{2c}$
(c) $\dfrac{p_e}{p_{ph}} = \dfrac{2c}{v}$
(d) $\dfrac{p_e}{p_{ph}} = \dfrac{c}{2v}$

24. The ratio of speed of the electron in the first Bohr orbit of hydrogen and the speed of light is equal to (where e, h and c have their usual meanings)
(a) $\dfrac{2\pi hc}{e^2}$
(b) $\dfrac{e^2 c}{2\pi h}$
(c) $\dfrac{e^2 h}{2\pi c}$
(d) $\dfrac{e^2}{2\varepsilon_0 hc}$

25. In a hydrogen atom, the binding energy of the electron in the ground state is E_1. Then, the frequency of revolution of the electron in the nth orbit is

(a) $\dfrac{2E_1}{n^3 h}$ (b) $\dfrac{2E_1 n^3}{h}$ (c) $\sqrt{\dfrac{2mE_1}{n^3 h}}$ (d) $\dfrac{E_1 n^2}{h}$

26. A photon of energy E ejects a photoelectron from a metal surface whose work function is W_0. If electron having maximum kinetic energy enters into a uniform magnetic field of induction B in a direction perpendicular to the field and describes a circular path of radius r, then the radius r is given by (in the usual notation)

(a) $\dfrac{\sqrt{2m(E - W_0)}}{eB}$ (b) $\sqrt{2m(E - W_0)}\, eB$

(c) $\dfrac{\sqrt{2e(E - W_0)}}{mB}$ (d) None of these

27. The acceleration of electron in the first orbit of hydrogen atom is

(a) $\dfrac{4\pi^2 m}{h^3}$ (b) $\dfrac{h^2}{4\pi^2 mr}$ (c) $\dfrac{h^2}{4\pi^2 m^2 r^3}$ (d) $\dfrac{m^2 h^2}{4\pi^2 r^3}$

28. An α-particle accelerated through V volts is fired towards a nucleus. Its distance of closest approach is r. If a proton accelerated through the same potential is fired towards the same nucleus, the distance of closest approach of proton will be

(a) r (b) $2r$ (c) $\dfrac{r}{2}$ (d) $\dfrac{r}{4}$

29. In an experiment on photoelectric effect, light of wavelength 400 nm is incident on a cesium plate at the rate of 5.0 W. The potential of the collector plate is made sufficiently positive with respect to the emitter so that the current reaches its saturation value. Assuming that on the average one out of every 10^6 photons is able to eject a photoelectron, the photocurrent in the circuit is

(a) $0.4\,\mu$A (b) $0.8\,\mu$A (c) $1.2\,\mu$A (d) $1.6\,\mu$A

30. The de-Broglie wavelength of a neutron at 27°C is λ. What will be its wavelength at 927°C ?

(a) $\dfrac{\lambda}{2}$ (b) λ (c) 2λ (d) 4λ

31. In the Bohr's model of a hydrogen atom, the centripetal force is furnished by the coulomb attraction between the proton and the electron. If a_0 is the radius of the ground state orbit, m is the mass, e is the charge on electron and ε_0 is the permittivity of free space, the speed of the electron is

(a) $\dfrac{e}{\sqrt{\varepsilon_0 a_0 m}}$ (b) zero (c) $\dfrac{e}{\sqrt{4\pi\varepsilon_0 a_0 m}}$ (d) $\dfrac{\sqrt{4\,\varepsilon_0 a_0 m}}{e}$

32. The intensity of light pulse travelling in an optical fibre decreases according to the relation $I = I_0 e^{-\alpha x}$. The intensity of light is reduced to 20% of its initial value after a distance x equal to

(a) $\ln (1/\alpha)$ (b) $\ln \alpha$
(c) $(\ln 5)/\alpha$ (d) $\ln (5/\alpha)$

33. If momentum of an electron is changed by Δp, then the de-Broglie wavelength associated with it changes by 0.50%. The initial momentum of the electron will be

(a) $\dfrac{\Delta p}{200}$ (b) $\dfrac{\Delta p}{199}$

(c) $199\,\Delta p$ (d) $400\,\Delta p$

More than One Correct Options

1. In Bohr model of the hydrogen atom, let R, v and E represent the radius of the orbit, speed of the electron and the total energy of the electron respectively. Which of the following quantities are directly proportional to the quantum number n?

   (a) vR (b) RE (c) $\dfrac{v}{E}$ (d) $\dfrac{R}{E}$

2. The magnitude of angular momentum, orbital radius and time period of revolution of an electron in a hydrogen atom corresponding to the quantum number n are L, r and T respectively. Which of the following statement(s) is/are correct?

   (a) $\dfrac{rL}{T}$ is independent of n (b) $\dfrac{L}{T} \propto \dfrac{1}{n^2}$

   (c) $\dfrac{T}{r} \propto n$ (d) $Lr \propto \dfrac{1}{n^3}$

3. In which of the following cases the heavier of the two particles has a smaller de-Broglie wavelength? The two particles
   (a) move with the same speed
   (b) move with the same linear momentum
   (c) move with the same kinetic energy
   (d) have the same change of potential energy in a conservative field

4. Hydrogen atom absorbs radiations of wavelength λ_0 and consequently emit radiations of 6 different wavelengths, of which two wavelengths are longer than λ_0. Choose the correct alternative(s).
   (a) The final excited state of the atoms is $n = 4$
   (b) The initial state of the atoms is $n = 2$
   (c) The initial state of the atoms is $n = 3$
   (d) There are three transitions belonging to Lyman series

5. In coolidge tube, if f and λ represent the frequency and wavelength of K_α-line for a metal of atomic number Z, then identify the statement which represents a straight line

   (a) $\sqrt{f}$ versus Z (b) $\dfrac{1}{\sqrt{\lambda}}$ versus Z

   (c) f versus Z (d) λ versus Z

Comprehension Based Questions

Passage I (Q. No. 1 to 3)

When a surface is irradiated with light of wavelength 4950 Å, a photocurrent appears which vanishes if a retarding potential greater than 0.6 volt is applied across the phototube. When a second source of light is used, it is found that the critical retarding potential is changed to 1.1 volt.

1. The work-function of the emitting surface is
   (a) 2.2 eV   (b) 1.5 eV
   (c) 1.9 eV   (d) 1.1 eV

2. The wavelength of the second source is
   (a) 6150 Å   (b) 5150 Å
   (c) 4125 Å   (d) 4500 Å

3. If the photoelectrons (after emission from the source) are subjected to a magnetic field of 10 tesla, the two retarding potentials would
(a) uniformly increase
(b) uniformly decrease
(c) remain the same
(d) None of these

Passage II (Q. No. 4 to 6)

In an experimental set up to study the photoelectric effect a point source of light of power 3.2×10^{-3} W was taken. The source can emit monoenergetic photons of energy 5 eV and is located at a distance of 0.8 m from the centre of a stationary metallic sphere of work-function 3.0 eV . The radius of the sphere is $r = 8 \times 10^{-3}$ m. The efficiency of photoelectric emission is one for every 10^6 incident photons.
Based on the information given above answer the questions given below.
(Assume that the sphere is isolated and photoelectrons are instantly swept away after the emission).

4. de-Broglie wavelength of the fastest moving photoelectron is
(a) 6.63 Å
(b) 8.69 Å
(c) 2 Å
(d) 5.26 Å

5. It was observed that after some time emission of photoelectrons from the sphere stopped. Charge on the sphere when the photon emission stops is
(a) $16\pi\varepsilon_0 r$ coulomb
(b) $8\pi\varepsilon_0 r$ coulomb
(c) $15\pi\varepsilon_0 r$ coulomb
(d) $20\pi\varepsilon_0 r$ coulomb

6. Time after which photoelectric emission stops is
(a) 100 s
(b) 121 s
(c) 111 s
(d) 141 s

Match the Columns

1. Match the following two columns for hydrogen spectrum.

Column I	Column II
(a) Lyman series	(p) infrared region
(b) Balmer series	(q) visible region
(c) Paschen series	(r) ultraviolet region
(d) Brackett series	(s) X-rays

2. Ionization energy from first excited state of hydrogen atom is E. Match the following two columns for He^+ atom.

Column I	Column II
(a) Ionization energy from ground state	(p) $4E$
(b) Electrostatic potential energy in first excited state.	(q) $-16E$
(c) Kinetic energy of electron in ground state.	(r) $-8E$
(d) Ionization energy from first excited state.	(s) $16E$

3.

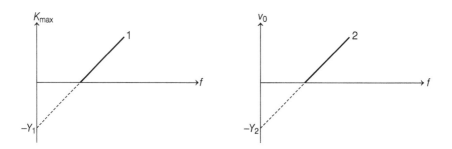

Maximum kinetic energy *versus* frequency of incident light and stopping potential *versus* frequency of incident light graphs are shown in figure. Match the following two columns.

Column I	Column II
(a) Slope of line-1	(p) h/e
(b) Slope of line-2	(q) h
(c) Y_1	(r) W
(d) Y_2	(s) W/e

Here, h = Planck constant, $e = 1.6 \times 10^{-19}$ C and W = work-function.

4. For hydrogen and hydrogen type atoms, match the following two columns.

Column I	Column II
(a) Time period	(p) Proportional to n/Z
(b) Angular momentum	(q) Proportional to n^2/Z
(c) Speed	(r) Proportional to n^3/Z^2
(d) Radius	(s) None of these

5. In hydrogen atom wavelength of second line of Balmer series is λ. Match the following two columns corresponding to the wavelength.

Column I	Column II
(a) First line of Balmer series	(p) $(27/20)\,\lambda$
(b) Third line of Balmer series	(q) $(\lambda/4)$
(c) First line of Lyman series	(r) $(25/12)\,\lambda$
(d) Second line of Lyman series	(s) None of these

6. Match the following (Give most appropriate one matching)

Column I	Column II
(a) Characteristic X-ray	(p) Inverse process of photoelectric effect
(b) X-ray production	(q) Potential difference
(c) Cut off wavelength	(r) Moseley's law
(d) Continuous X-ray	(s) None of these

7. In a photoelectric effect experiment. If f is the frequency of radiations incident on the metal surface and I is the intensity of the incident radiations, then match the following columns.

Column I	Column II
(a) If f is increased keeping I and work-function constant	(p) Stopping potential increases
(b) If distance between cathode and anode is increased	(q) Saturation current increases
(c) If I is increased keeping f and work-function constant	(r) Maximum kinetic energy of photoelectron increases
(d) Work-function is decreased keeping f and I constant	(s) Stopping potential remains same

Subjective Questions

1. The wavelength for $n = 3$ to $n = 2$ transition of the hydrogen atom is 656.3 nm. What are the wavelengths for this same transition in (a) positronium, which consists of an electron and a positron (b) singly ionized helium (**Note:** A positron is a positively charged electron).

2. (a) Find the frequencies of revolution of electrons in $n = 1$ and $n = 2$ Bohr orbits.

(b) What is the frequency of the photon emitted when an electron in an $n = 2$ orbit drops to an $n = 1$ hydrogen orbit?

(c) An electron typically spends about 10^{-8}s in an excited state before it drops to a lower state by emitting a photon. How many revolutions does an electron in an $n = 2$ Bohr hydrogen orbit make in 1.00×10^{-8} s?

3. A **muon** is an unstable elementary particle whose mass is $207\, m_e$ and whose charge is either e^+ or e^-. A negative muon (μ^-) can be captured by a nucleus to form a muonic atom.

(a) A proton captures a μ^-. Find the radius of the first Bohr orbit of this atom.

(b) Find the ionization energy of the atom.

4. (a) A gas of hydrogen atoms in their ground state is bombarded by electrons with kinetic energy 12.5 eV. What emitted wavelengths would you expect to see?

(b) What if the electrons were replaced by photons of same energy?

5. A source emits monochromatic light of frequency 5.5×10^{14} Hz at a rate of 0.1 W. Of the photons given out, 0.15% fall on the cathode of a photocell which gives a current of $6\,\mu A$ in an external circuit.

(a) Find the energy of a photon.

(b) Find the number of photons leaving the source per second.

(c) Find the percentage of the photons falling on the cathode which produce photoelectrons.

6. The hydrogen atom in its ground state is excited by means of monochromatic radiation. Its resulting spectrum has six different lines. These radiations are incident on a metal plate. It is observed that only two of them are responsible for photoelectric effect. If the ratio of maximum kinetic energy of photoelectrons in the two cases is 5 then find the work-function of the metal.

7. Electrons in hydrogen like atoms $(Z = 3)$ make transitions from the fifth to the fourth orbit and from the fourth to the third orbit. The resulting radiations are incident normally on a metal plate and eject photoelectrons. The stopping potential for the photoelectrons ejected by the shorter wavelength is 3.95 volts. Calculate the work-function of the metal and the stopping potential for the photoelectrons ejected by the longer wavelength.

8. Find an expression for the magnetic dipole moment and magnetic field induction at the centre of Bohr's hypothetical hydrogen atom in the nth orbit of the electron in terms of universal constant.

9. An electron and a proton are separated by a large distance and the electron approaches the proton with a kinetic energy of 2 eV. If the electron is captured by the proton to form a hydrogen atom in the ground state, what wavelength photon would be given off?

10. Hydrogen gas in the atomic state is excited to an energy level such that the electrostatic potential energy of H-atom becomes -1.7 eV. Now, a photoelectric plate having work-function $W = 2.3$ eV is exposed to the emission spectra of this gas. Assuming all the transitions to be possible, find the minimum de-Broglie wavelength of the ejected photoelectrons.

11. A gas of hydrogen like atoms can absorb radiation of 68 eV. Consequently, the atom emits radiations of only three different wavelengths. All the wavelengths are equal or smaller than that of the absorbed photon.

(a) Determine the initial state of the gas atoms.

(b) Identify the gas atoms.

(c) Find the minimum wavelength of the emitted radiations.

(d) Find the ionization energy and the respective wavelength for the gas atoms.

12. A photon with energy of 4.9 eV ejects photoelectrons from tungsten. When the ejected electron enters a constant magnetic field of strength $B = 2.5$ mT at an angle of 60° with the field direction, the maximum pitch of the helix described by the electron is found to be 2.7 mm. Find the work-function of the metal in electron-volt. Given that specific charge of electron is 1.76×10^{11} C/kg.

13. For a certain hypothetical one-electron atom, the wavelength (in Å) for the spectral lines for transitions originating at $n = p$ and terminating at $n = 1$ are given by

$$\lambda = \frac{1500\,p^2}{p^2 - 1}, \quad \text{where} \quad p = 2, 3, 4$$

(a) Find the wavelength of the least energetic and the most energetic photons in this series.

(b) Construct an energy level diagram for this element showing the energies of the lowest three levels.

(c) What is the ionization potential of this element?

14. A photocell is operating in saturation mode with a photocurrent 4.8 mA when a monochromatic radiation of wavelength 3000 Å and power of 0.388 W is incident. When another monochromatic radiation of wavelength 1650 Å and power 5 mW is incident, it is observed that maximum velocity of photoelectron increases to two times. Assuming efficiency of photoelectron generation per incident photon to be same for both the cases, calculate

(a) the threshold wavelength for the cell

(b) the efficiency of photoelectron generation per incident photon

(c) the saturation current in second case

15. Wavelengths belonging to Balmer series for hydrogen atom lying in the range of 450 nm to 750 nm were used to eject photoelectrons from a metal surface whose work-function is 2.0 eV. Find (in eV) the maximum kinetic energy of the emitted photoelectrons.

16. Assume that the de-Broglie wave associated with an electron can form a standing wave between the atoms arranged in a one-dimensional array with nodes at each of the atomic sites. It is found that one such standing wave is formed if the distance d between the atoms of the array is 2 Å. A similar standing wave is again formed if d is increased to 2.5 Å but not for any intermediate value of d. Find the energy of the electron in eV and the least value of d for which the standing wave of the type described above can form.

17. The negative muon has a charge equal to that of an electron but a mass that is 207 times as great. Consider hydrogen like atom consisting of a proton and a muon.

(a) What is the reduced mass of the atom?

(b) What is the ground-level energy (in eV)?

(c) What is the wavelength of the radiation emitted in the transition from the $n = 2$ level to the $n = 1$ level?

18. Assume a hypothetical hydrogen atom in which the potential energy between electron and proton at separation r is given by $U = [k \ln r - (k/2)]$, where k is a constant. For such a hypothetical hydrogen atom, calculate the radius of nth Bohr orbit and energy levels.

19. An electron is orbiting in a circular orbit of radius r under the influence of a constant magnetic field of strength B. Assuming that Bohr postulate regarding the quantisation of angular momentum holds good for this electron, find

(a) the allowed values of the radius r of the orbit.

(b) the kinetic energy of the electron in orbit

(c) the potential energy of interaction between the magnetic moment of the orbital current due to the electron moving in its orbit and the magnetic field B.

(d) the total energy of the allowed energy levels.

(e) the total magnetic flux due to the magnetic field B passing through the nth orbit.

(Assume that the charge on the electron is $-e$ and the mass of the electron is m).

20. A mixture of hydrogen atoms (in their ground state) and hydrogen like ions (in their first excited state) are being excited by electrons which have been accelerated by same potential difference V volts. After excitation when they come directly into ground state, the wavelengths of emitted light are found in the ratio 5 : 1. Then, find

(a) the minimum value of V for which both the atoms get excited after collision with electrons.

(b) atomic number of other ion.

(c) the energy of emitted light.

21. When a surface is irradiated with light of $\lambda = 4950$ Å a photocurrent appears which vanishes if a retarding potential 0.6 V is applied. When a different source of light is used, it is found that critical retarding potential is changed to 1.1 volt. Find the work-function of emitting surface and wavelength of second source. If photoelectrons after emission from surface are subjected to a magnetic field of 10 tesla, what changes will be observed in the above two retarding potentials?

22. In an experiment on photoelectric effect light of wavelength 400 nm is incident on a metal plate at the rate of 5 W. The potential of the collector plate is made sufficiently positive with respect to emitter so that the current reaches the saturation value. Assuming that on the average one out of every 10^6 photons is able to eject a photoelectron, find the photocurrent in the circuit.

23. A light beam of wavelength 400 nm is incident on a metal of work-function 2.2 eV. A particular electron absorbs a photon and makes 2 collisions before coming out of the metal

(a) Assuming that 10% of existing energy is lost to the metal in each collision find the final kinetic energy of this electron as it comes out of the metal.

(b) Under the same assumptions find the maximum number of collisions, the electron should suffer before it becomes unable to come out of the metal.

Answers

Introductory Exercise 33.1

1. 4.6eV, $2.45 \times 10^{-27} \dfrac{\text{kg-m}}{\text{s}}$ **2.** 4.82×10^{16} per m^2-s **3.** $\sqrt{2}$

4. $\sqrt{2}$ **5.** (c) **6.** (a) 4.81×10^{-34} m (b) 7.12×10^{-11} m

Introductory Exercise 33.2

1. 122.4 eV **2.** 3.16×10^{-34} kg-m^2/s **3.** (d) **4.** (a) **5.** (b)

6. (c) **7.** (b) **8.** (d) **9.** (d) **10.** (d) **11.** $\dfrac{3f}{4}, \dfrac{f}{4}$

12. 651 nm

Introductory Exercise 33.3

1. (b) **2.** (b) **3.** (a) **4.** (a) **5.** (b) **6.** 42

Introductory Exercise 33.4

1. Zero, 3.19 eV **2.** $K_{\max} \propto (f - f_0)$ **3.** 1.16×10^{15} Hz **4.** (a)

5. (a) **6.** (c) **7.** (b) **8.** (a)

Exercises

LEVEL 1

Assertion and Reason

1. (a) **2.** (c) **3.** (a) **4.** (a) **5.** (c) **6.** (d) **7.** (b) **8.** (a or b)

Objective Questions

1. (a) **2.** (b) **3.** (d) **4.** (b) **5.** (a) **6.** (a) **7.** (c) **8.** (a) **9.** (c) **10.** (c)
11. (a) **12.** (b) **13.** (a) **14.** (b) **15.** (d) **16.** (a) **17.** (b) **18.** (c) **19.** (c) **20.** (c)
21. (b) **22.** (c) **23.** (b) **24.** (c) **25.** (a) **26.** (d) **27.** (c) **28.** (d) **29.** (a) **30.** (a)
31. (c) **32.** (b) **33.** (d) **34.** (a) **35.** (c) **36.** (a) **37.** (b) **38.** (b) **39.** (b) **40.** (a)
41. (a) **42.** (a) **43.** (c) **44.** (b) **45.** (d) **46.** (b) **47.** (b) **48.** (d) **49.** (c) **50.** (a)

Subjective Questions

1. 5.59 nm **2.** $E_1 = -4613$ eV, $E_3 = -2650$ eV **3.** $0.48\,\mu$A

4. (a) 2.47×10^{-19} J $= 1.54$ eV (b) 804 nm, infrared

5. (a) 5.0×10^{14} Hz (b) 2.3×10^{20} photons/s **6.** (a) 5.92×10^{20} Hz (b) 5.06×10^{-13} m

7. (a) $K_2 = 4K_1$ (b) $E_2 = 2E_1$ **8.** (a) 2.52×10^{19} (b) 3.33×10^{-8} N

9. 10^{-8} N

10. (a) $2.37 \times 10^{-24} \dfrac{\text{kg-m}}{\text{s}}$ (b) 3.07×10^{-18} J $= 19.2$ eV **11.** 1.04 Å

12. (a) 3.32×10^{-10} m (b) 1.33×10^{-9} m **13.** 3, 6513 Å **14.** 113.74 Å

15. $n = 5$ **16.** (a) $Z = 4$ (b) $\lambda_{\min} = 40441$ Å

17. (a) 15.6 volt (b) 2335 Å (c) 12.52 V (d) 1.01×10^7 m^{-1} **18.** (a) -5.08 eV (b) -5.63 eV

19. 1.9 V **21.** 49.5 pm, 99.0 pm **22.** 15865 V

23. 198 pm   **24.** $Z = 42$ **25.** (a) 4 W (b) 396 J/s   **26.** 1022 Å, $n = 3$ to $n = 1$

27. 2.51 eV   **28.** 2260 Å   **29.** (a) 10^{15} Hz (b) 4eV (c) 6.4×10^{-34} J-s

30. 1.81 eV, 9.0×10^5 ms, 3.0×10^5 m/s   **31.** 0.148 m   **32** 3.27 eV   **33.** 1.2 V

LEVEL 2

Single Correct Option

1. (b)	**2** (b)	**3.** (c)	**4.** (c)	**5.** (b)	**6.** (d)	**7.** (a)	**8.** (c)	**9.** (d)	**10.** (c)
11. (a)	**12.** (c)	**13.** (d)	**14.** (d)	**15.** (a)	**16.** (c)	**17.** (b)	**18.** (b)	**19.** (a)	**20.** (b)
21. (b)	**22.** (d)	**23.** (b)	**24.** (d)	**25.** (a)	**26.** (a)	**27.** (c)	**28.** (a)	**29.** (d)	**30.** (a)
31. (c)	**32.** (c)	**33.** (c)							

More than One Correct Options

1. (a,c)   **2** (a,b,c)   **3.** (a,c)   **4.** (a,b,d)   **5.** (a,b)

Comprehension Based Questions

1. (c)   **2.** (c)   **3.** (c)   **4.** (b)   **5.** (b)   **6.** (c)

Match the Columns

1. (a) → r   (b) → q   (c) → p   (d) → p   **2** (a) → s   (b) → r   (c) → s   (d) → p

3. (a) → q   (b) → p   (c) → r   (d) → s   **4.** (a) → r   (b) → s   (c) → s   (d) → q

5. (a) → p   (b) → s   (c) → q   (d) → s   **6.** (a) → r   (b) → p   (c) → q   (d) → q

7. (a) → p,r   (b) → s   (c) → q,s (d) → p,r

Subjective Questions

1. (a) 1.31 μm (b) 164 nm

2 (a) 6.58×10^{15} Hz, 0.823×10^{15} Hz (b) 2.46×10^{15} Hz (c) 8.23×10^6 revolutions

3. (a) 2.55×10^{-13} m (b) 2.81 keV   **4.** (a) 102 nm, 122 nm, 651 nm (b) No lines

5. (a) 2.27 eV (b) 2.75×10^{17} (c) 9%   **6.** $W = 11.925$ eV   **7.** 2 eV, 0.754 V

8. $\dfrac{neh}{4\pi m}, \dfrac{\mu_0 \pi m^2 e^7}{8\varepsilon_0 h^5 n^5}$ **9.** 793.3 Å   **10.** 3.8 Å

11. (a) $n_i = 2$ (b) $Z = 6$ (c) 28.43 Å (d) 489.6 eV, 25.3 Å   **12** 4.5 eV

13. (a) 2000 Å, 1500 Å (b) $E_1 = -8.25$ eV, $E_2 = -2.05$ eV and $E_3 = -0.95$ eV (c) 8.25 V

14. (a) 4125 Å (b) 34 μA (c) 5.1%   **15.** 0.55 eV   **16.** 150 eV, 0.5 Å

17. (a) 1.69×10^{-28} kg (b) − 2.53 keV (c) 0.653 nm   **18.** $r_n = \dfrac{nh}{2\pi\sqrt{mk}}$, $E_n = k \ln \left\{ \dfrac{nh}{2\pi\sqrt{mk}} \right\}$

19. (a) $r_n = \sqrt{\dfrac{nh}{2\pi Be}}$ (b) $K = \dfrac{nhBe}{4\pi m}$ (c) $U = \dfrac{nheB}{4\pi m}$ (d) $E = \dfrac{nheB}{2\pi m}$ (e) $\dfrac{nh}{2e}$

20. (a) 10.2 volt (b) $Z = 2$ (c) 10.2 eV and 51 eV   **21.** 1.9 eV, 4125 Å, No change is observed

22 1.6 μA   **23.** (a) 0.31 eV (b) 4

34

MODERN PHYSICS - II

34.1 **Nuclear Stability and Radioactivity**

Among about 1500 known nuclides, less than 260 are stable. The others are unstable that decay to form other nuclides by emitting α and β-particles and γ-electromagnetic waves. This process is called radioactivity. It was discovered in 1896 by Henry Becquerel.

Whilst the chemical properties of an atom are governed entirely by the number of protons in the nucleus (i.e. the proton number Z), the stability of an atom appears to depend on both the number of protons and the number of neutrons. For light nuclei, the greatest stability is achieved when the numbers of protons and neutrons are approximately equal $(N \approx Z)$.

For heavier nuclei, instability caused by electrostatic repulsion between the protons is minimized when there are more neutrons than protons.

Figure shows a plot of N versus Z for the stable nuclei. For mass numbers upto about $A = 40$, we see that $N \approx Z$. $_{40}$Ca is the heaviest stable nucleus for which $N = Z$. For larger values of Z, the (short range) nuclear force is unable to hold the nucleus together against the (long range) electrical repulsion of the protons unless the number of neutrons exceeds the number of protons. At Bi $(Z = 83, A = 209)$, the neutron excess is $N - Z = 43$. There are no stable nuclides with $Z > 83$.

The nuclide $_{83}^{209}$Bi is the heaviest stable nucleus.

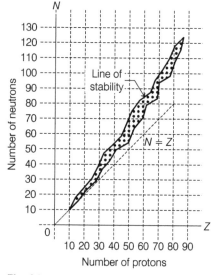

Fig. 34.1 The stable nuclides plotted on a graph of neutron number, N, *versus* proton number, Z. Note that for heavier nuclides, N is larger relative to Z. The stable nuclides group along a curve called the line of stability.

Atoms are radioactive if their nuclei are unstable and spontaneously (and randomly) emit various particles, the α, β and or γ radiations. When naturally occurring nuclei are unstable, we call the phenomena **natural radioactivity.** Other nuclei can be transformed into radioactive nuclei by various means, typically involving irradiation by neutrons, this is called **artificial radioactivity.**

A radioactive nucleus is called a **parent nucleus,** the nucleus resulting from its decay by particle emission is called **daughter nucleus.** Daughter nuclei also might be granddaughter nuclei, and so on. There are no son or grandson nuclei. For unstable nuclides and radioactivity, the following points can be made.

 (i) Disintegrations tend to produce new nuclides near the stability line and continue until a stable nuclide is formed.

 (ii) Radioactivity is a nuclear property, i.e. α, β and γ emission take place from the nucleus.

(iii) Nuclear processes involve huge amount of energy so the particle emission rate is independent of temperature and pressure. The rate depends solely on the concentration of the number of atoms of the radioactive substance.

 (iv) A radioactive substance is either an α-emitter or a β-emitter, γ-rays emit with both.

Alpha Decay

An alpha particle is a helium nucleus. Thus, a nucleus emitting an alpha particle loses two protons and two neutrons. Therefore, the atomic number Z decreases by 2, the mass number A decreases by 4 and the neutron number N decreases by 2. The decay can be written as

$$\underset{Z}{\overset{A}{}} X = \underset{Z-2}{\overset{A-4}{}} Y + \underset{2}{\overset{4}{}} \text{He}$$

where, X is the parent nucleus and Y the daughter nucleus. As examples U^{238} and Ra^{226} are both alpha emitters and decay according to

$$\underset{92}{\overset{238}{}} \text{U} \longrightarrow \underset{90}{\overset{234}{}} \text{Th} + \underset{2}{\overset{4}{}} \text{He}$$

$$\underset{88}{\overset{226}{}} \text{Ra} \longrightarrow \underset{86}{\overset{222}{}} \text{Rn} + \underset{2}{\overset{4}{}} \text{He}$$

As a general rule, in any decay sum of mass numbers A and atomic numbers Z must be the same on both sides.

Note that a nuclide below the stability line in Fig. 34.2 disintegrates in such a way that its proton number decreases and its neutron to proton ratio increases. In heavy nuclides, this can occur by alpha emission.

If the original nucleus has a mass number A that is 4 times an integer, the daughter nucleus and all those in the chain will also have mass numbers equal to 4 times an integer. (Because in α-decay A decreases by 4 and in β-decay it remains the same). Similarly, if the mass number of the original nucleus is $4n + 1$, where n is an integer, all the nuclei in the decay chain will have mass numbers given by $4n + 1$ with n decreasing by 1 in each α-decay. We can see therefore, that there are four possible α-decay chains, depending on whether A equals $4n, 4n + 1, 4n + 2$ or $4n + 3$, where n is an integer.

Series $4n + 1$ is now not found. Because its longest lived member (other than the stable end product Bi^{209}) is Np^{237} which has a half-life of only 2×10^6 years. Because this is much less than the age of the earth, this

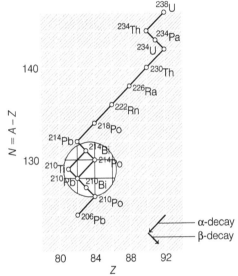

Fig. 34.2 The uranium decay series $(A = 4n + 2)$. The decay of $\underset{83}{\overset{214}{}}\text{Bi}$ may proceed either by alpha emission and then beta emission or in the reverse order.

series has disappeared. Figure shows the uranium $(4n + 2)$ series. The series branches at Bi^{214}, which decays either by α-decay to Ti^{210} or β-decay to Po^{214}. The branches meet at the lead isotope Pb^{210}. Table 34.1 lists the four radioactive series.

Table 34.1 Four Radioactive Series

Mass numbers	Series	Parent	Half-life, Years	Stable product
$4n$	Thorium	$\underset{90}{\overset{232}{}}\text{Th}$	1.39×10^{10}	$\underset{82}{\overset{208}{}}\text{Pb}$
$4n + 1$	Neptunium	$\underset{93}{\overset{237}{}}\text{Np}$	2.25×10^6	$\underset{83}{\overset{209}{}}\text{Bi}$
$4n + 2$	Uranium	$\underset{92}{\overset{238}{}}\text{U}$	4.47×10^9	$\underset{82}{\overset{206}{}}\text{Pb}$
$4n + 3$	Actinium	$\underset{92}{\overset{235}{}}\text{U}$	7.07×10^8	$\underset{82}{\overset{207}{}}\text{Pb}$

Beta Decay

Beta decay can involve the emission of either electrons or positrons. A positron is a form of antimatter which has a charge equal to $+e$ and mass equal to that of an electron. The electrons or positrons emitted in β-decay do not exist inside the nucleus. They are only created at the time of emission, just as photons are created when an atom makes a transition from a higher to a lower energy state.

In β⁻ decay a neutron in the nucleus is transformed into a proton, an electron and an antineutrino.

$$n \longrightarrow p + e^- + \overline{v}$$

To conserve energy and momentum in the process, the emission of an antineutrino $(\overline{v})$ (alongwith proton and electron) was first suggested by W. Pauli in 1930, but it was first observed experimentally in 1957.

Thus, a parent nucleus with atomic number Z and mass number A decays by β⁻ emission into a daughter with atomic number $Z + 1$ and the same mass number A.

$$_Z^A X \xrightarrow{\beta^-} {}_{Z+1}^A Y$$

β⁻ decay occurs in nuclei that have too many neutrons. An example of β⁻ decay is the decay of carbon-14 into nitrogen,

$$_6^{14}C \longrightarrow {}_7^{14}N + e^- + \overline{v}$$

In β⁺ decay, a proton changes into a neutron with the emission of a positron (and a neutrino)

$$p \longrightarrow n + e^+ + v$$

Positron (e^+) emission from a nucleus decreases the atomic number Z by 1 while keeping the same mass number A.

$$_Z^A X \xrightarrow{\beta^+} {}_{Z-1}^A Y$$

B^+ decay occurs in nuclei that have too few neutrons. A typical β⁺ decay is

$$_7^{13}N \longrightarrow {}_6^{13}C + e^+ + v$$

Electron capture Electron capture is competitive with positron emission since both processes lead to the same nuclear transformation. This occurs when a parent nucleus captures one of its own orbital electrons and emits a neutrino.

$$_Z^A X + e^{-1} \longrightarrow {}_{Z-1}^A Y + v$$

In most cases, it is a K-shell electron that is captured, and for this reason the process is referred to as **K-capture.** One example is the capture of an electron by $_4\text{Be}^7$

$$_4^7\text{Be} + e^- \longrightarrow {}_3^7\text{Li} + v$$

Gamma Decay

Very often a nucleus that undergoes radioactive decay (α or β-decay) is left in an excited energy state (analogous to the excited states of the orbiting electrons, except that the energy levels associated with the nucleus have much larger energy differences than those involved with the atomic electrons). The typical half-life of an excited nuclear state is 10^{-10} s. The excited nucleus (X^*) then undergoes to a lower energy state by emitting a high energy photon, called the γ-ray photon. The following sequence of events represents a typical situation in which γ-decay occurs.

$$^{12}_{5}B \longrightarrow {}^{12}_{6}C^* + e^- + \bar{v}$$

$$^{12}_{6}C^* \longrightarrow {}^{12}_{6}C + \gamma$$

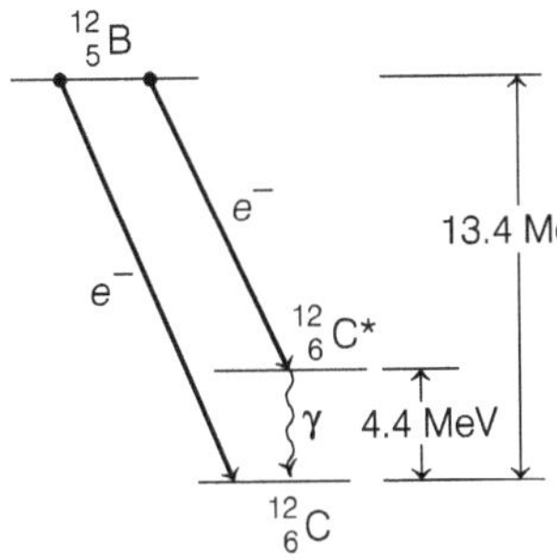

Gamma decay
Fig. 34.3

Figure shows decay of B^{12} nucleus, which undergoes β-decay to either of two levels of C^{12}. It can either decay directly to the ground state of C^{12} by emitting a 13.4 MeV electron or undergo β-decay to an excited state of $^{12}_{6}C^*$ followed by γ-decay to the ground state. The later process results in the emission of a 9.0 MeV electron and a 4.4 MeV photon. The various pathways by which a radioactive nucleus can undergo decay are summarized in Table 34.2.

Note *In both α and β-decay, the Z value of a nucleus changes and the nucleus of one element becomes the nucleus of a different element. In γ-decay, the element does not change, the nucleus merely goes from an excited state to a less excited state.*

Table 34.2 **Various Decay Pathways**

Alpha decay	$^{A}_{Z}X \longrightarrow {}^{A-4}_{Z-2}Y + {}^{4}_{2}He$
Beta decay (β^-)	$^{A}_{Z}X \longrightarrow {}^{A}_{Z+1}Y + e^- + \bar{v}$
Beta decay (β^+)	$^{A}_{Z}X \longrightarrow {}^{A}_{Z-1}Y + e^+ + v$
Electron capture	$^{A}_{Z}X + e^- \longrightarrow {}^{A}_{Z-1}Y + v$
Gamma decay	$^{A}_{Z}X^* \longrightarrow {}^{A}_{Z}X + \gamma$

🔘 *Extra Points to Remember*

- After emission of one alpha particle and two beta particles isotopes are produced. This is because after the emission of one alpha particle, atomic number decreases by 2. Further, after the emission of two beta particles atomic number increases by 2. So, finally atomic number remains unchanged.
- From beta emission mass number does not change. Therefore, isobars will be produced.

⊛ **Example 34.1** *Mass number of a nucleus X is A and atomic number is Z. Find mass number and atomic number of the new nucleus (say Y) after the emission of m-alpha particles and n-beta particles.*

Solution By the emission of one alpha particle, atomic number decreases by 2 and by the emission of one beta particle atomic number increases by 1. Therefore, the atomic number of nucleus Y is $Z = Z - 2m + n$

Further, by the emission of one alpha particle mass number decreases by 4 and by the emission of beta particle, mass number does not change. Therefore, the mass number of Y is

$$A' = A - 4m$$

34.2 **Radioactive Decay Law**

Radioactive decay is a random process. Each decay is an independent event and one cannot tell when a particular nucleus will decay. When a particular nucleus decays, it is transformed into another nuclide, which may or may not be radioactive. When there is a very large number of nuclei in a sample, the rate of decay is proportional to the number of nuclei, N, that are present

$$\left(-\frac{dN}{dt} \right) \propto N$$

or

$$\left(-\frac{dN}{dt} \right) = \lambda N$$

where, λ is called the **decay constant.** This equation may be expressed in the form $\dfrac{dN}{N} = -\lambda dt$ and integrated,

$$\int_{N_0}^{N} \frac{dN}{N} = -\lambda \int_{0}^{t} dt$$

or

$$\ln \left(\frac{N}{N_0} \right) = -\lambda t$$

where, N_0 is the initial number of parent nuclei at $t = 0$. The number that survives at time t is therefore,

$$\boxed{N = N_0 e^{-\lambda t}} \qquad \qquad \ldots(i)$$

This function is plotted in Fig. 34.4.

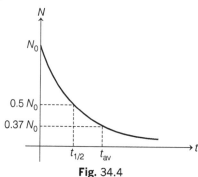

Fig. 34.4

Half-life The time required for the number of parent nuclei to fall to 50% is called half-life $t_{1/2}$ and may be related to λ as follows.

$$0.5N_0 = N_0 e^{-\lambda t_{1/2}}$$

We have $$\lambda t_{1/2} = \ln(2) = 0.693$$

$\therefore$ $$\boxed{t_{1/2} = \frac{\ln(2)}{\lambda} = \frac{0.693}{\lambda}}$$ ...(ii)

Mean life The average or mean life t_{av} is the reciprocal of the decay constant.

$$\boxed{t_{av} = \frac{1}{\lambda}}$$ ...(iii)

The mean life is analogous to the time constant in the exponential decrease in the charge on a capacitor in an RC circuit. After a time equal to the mean life time, the number of radioactive nuclei decreases to $\frac{1}{e}$ times or approximately 37% of their original values.

Activity of a Radioactive Substance

The decay rate R of a radioactive substance is the number of decays per second. And as we have seen above

$$-\frac{dN}{dt} \propto N \quad \text{or} \quad -\frac{dN}{dt} = \lambda N$$

Thus, $$R = -\frac{dN}{dt} \quad \text{or} \quad R \propto N$$

or $$R = \lambda N \quad \text{or} \quad R = \lambda N_0 e^{-\lambda t}$$

or $$\boxed{R = R_0 e^{-\lambda t}}$$ ...(iv)

where, $R_0 = \lambda N_0$ is the activity of the radioactive substance at time $t = 0$. The activity *versus* time graph is shown in Fig. 34.5.

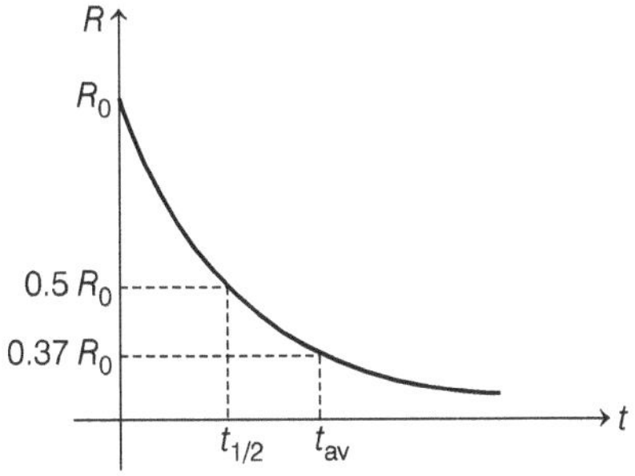

Fig. 34.5

Thus, the number of nuclei and hence the activity of the radioactive substance also decreases exponentially with time.

Units of activity The SI unit for the decay rate is the Becquerel (Bq), but the curie (Ci) and rutherford (rd) are often used in practice.

$$\boxed{1\,\text{Bq} = 1\,\text{decays/s}, \quad 1\,\text{Ci} = 3.7 \times 10^{10}\,\text{Bq} \quad \text{and} \quad 1\,\text{rd} = 10^6\,\text{Bq}}$$

✔ *Extra Points to Remember*

- After n half-lives,

  (a) number of nuclei left $= N_0 \left(\dfrac{1}{2}\right)^n$

  (b) fraction of nuclei left $= \left(\dfrac{1}{2}\right)^n$ and

  (c) percentage of nuclei left $= 100 \left(\dfrac{1}{2}\right)^n$

- Number of nuclei decayed after time t,

$$= N_0 - N$$
$$= N_0 - N_0 e^{-\lambda t} = N_0 (1 - e^{-\lambda t})$$

  The corresponding graph is as shown in Fig. 34.6.

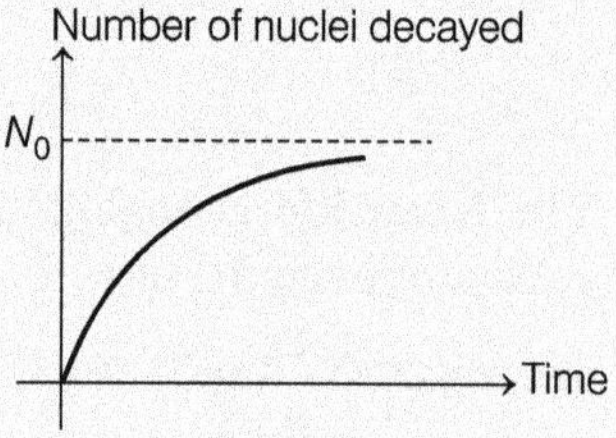

- Probability of a nucleus for survival upto time t,

$$P\,(\text{survival}) = \frac{N}{N_0} = \frac{N_0 e^{-\lambda t}}{N_0} = e^{-\lambda t}$$

  The corresponding graph is shown in Fig. 34.7.

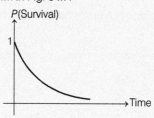

Number of nuclei decayed

Fig. 34.6

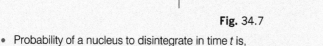

P(Survival)

Fig. 34.7

- Probability of a nucleus to disintegrate in time t is,

$$P\,(\text{disintegration}) = 1 - P\,(\text{survival}) = 1 - e^{-\lambda t}$$

  The corresponding graph is as shown in Fig. 34.8.

- Half-life and mean life are related to each other by the relation,

$$\boxed{t_{1/2} = 0.693\,t_{av} \quad \text{or} \quad t_{av} = 1.44\,t_{1/2}}$$

- As we discussed above number of nuclei decayed in time t are $N_0 (1 - e^{-\lambda t})$. This expression involves power of e.

  So, to avoid it we can use

$$\boxed{\Delta N = \lambda N \Delta t}$$

  where, ΔN are the number of nuclei decayed in time Δt at the instant when total number of nuclei are N. But, this can be applied only when $\Delta t \ll t_{1/2}$.

  Proof
$$-\frac{dN}{dt} = \lambda N \quad \Rightarrow \quad -dN = \lambda N dt$$

  or
$$\Delta N = \lambda N \Delta t$$

- In same interval of time, equal percentage (or fraction) of nuclei are decayed (or left undecayed).

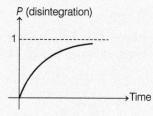

P (disintegration)

Fig. 34.8

⊘ **Example 34.2**   *At time $t = 0$, number of nuclei of a radioactive substance are 100. At $t = 1$ s these numbers become 90. Find the number of nuclei at $t = 2$ s.*

Solution   In 1 second, 90% of the nuclei have remained undecayed, so in another 1 second 90% of 90, i.e. 81 nuclei will remain undecayed.

⊘ **Example 34.3**   *At time $t = 0$, activity of a radioactive substance is 1600 Bq, at $t = 8$ s activity remains 100 Bq. Find the activity at $t = 2$ s.*

Solution $R = R_0 \left(\dfrac{1}{2} \right)^n$

Here, n is the number of half-lives.

Given, $R = \dfrac{R_0}{16}$

∴ $\dfrac{R_0}{16} = R_0 \left(\dfrac{1}{2} \right)^n$ or $n = 4$

Four half-lives are equivalent to 8 s. Hence, 2 s is equal to one half-life. So, in one half-life activity will remain half of 1600 Bq, i.e. 800 Bq.

⊘ **Example 34.4**   *From a radioactive substance n_1 nuclei decay per second at an instant when total number of nuclei are n_2. Find half-life of the radioactive substance.*

Solution   Using the equation,

$$- \frac{dN}{dt} - = \lambda N$$

We have, $n_1 = \lambda n_2$

∴ $\lambda = \dfrac{n_1}{n_2}$

Now, half-life is given by

$$t_{1/2} = \frac{\ln 2}{\lambda} = \frac{\ln 2}{(n_1 / n_2)}$$

$$= \left(\frac{n_2}{n_1} \right) \ln 2 \qquad \textbf{Ans.}$$

⊘ **Example 34.5**   *Half-life of a radioactive substance is T. At time t_1 activity of a radioactive substance is R_1 and at time t_2 it is R_2. Find the number of nuclei decayed in this interval of time.*

Solution   Half-life is given by

$$t_{1/2} = \frac{\ln 2}{\lambda}$$

∴ $\lambda = \dfrac{\ln 2}{t_{1/2}} = \dfrac{\ln 2}{T}$

Activity $R = \lambda N$

$\therefore$ $$N = \frac{R}{\lambda} = \frac{RT}{\ln 2}$$

When activity is R_1, numbers of nuclei are

$$N_1 = \frac{R_1 T}{\ln 2}$$

Similarly, $$N_2 = \frac{R_2 T}{\ln 2}$$

$\therefore$ Numbers decayed $= N_1 - N_2 = \dfrac{(R_1 - R_2)T}{\ln 2}$ **Ans.**

⊛ **Example 34.6** *Two radioactive materials X_1 and X_2 have decay constants 10λ and λ, respectively. If initially they have the same number of nuclei, then the ratio of the number of nuclei of X_1 to that of X_2 will be $1/e$ after a time* (JEE 2000)
(a) $1/10\lambda$ (b) $1/11\lambda$ (c) $11/10\lambda$ (d) $1/9\lambda$

Solution $\dfrac{N_{x_1}(t)}{N_{x_2}(t)} = \dfrac{1}{e}$

or $\dfrac{N_0 \, e^{-10\lambda t}}{N_0 \, e^{-\lambda t}} = \dfrac{1}{e}$ (Initially, both have same number of nuclei say N_0)

or $e^{-9\lambda t} = e^{-1}$ or $e = e^{9\lambda t}$

or $9\lambda t = 1$ or $t = \dfrac{1}{9\lambda}$

$\therefore$ The correct option is (d).

⊛ **Example 34.7** *The half-life period of a radioactive element x is same as the mean life time of another radioactive element y. Initially, both of them have the same number of atoms. Then,* (JEE 1999)
(a) *x and y have the same decay rate initially*
(b) *x and y decay at the same rate always*
(c) *y will decay at a faster rate than x*
(d) *x will decay at a faster rate than y*

Solution $(t_{1/2})_x = (t_{\text{mean}})_y$

or $$\frac{0.693}{\lambda_x} = \frac{1}{\lambda_y}$$

$\therefore$ $$\lambda_x = 0.693 \, \lambda_y$$
$$\lambda_x < \lambda_y$$

or Rate of decay $= \lambda N$

Initially, number of atoms (N) of both are equal but since $\lambda_y > \lambda_x$, therefore, y will decay at a faster rate than x.

$\therefore$ The correct option is (c).

◈ ***Example 34.8*** *A radioactive sample consists of two distinct species having equal number of atoms initially. The mean life of one species is τ and that of the other is 5τ. The decay products in both cases are stable. A plot is made of the total number of radioactive nuclei as a function of time. Which of the following figure best represents the form of this plot?* (JEE 2001)

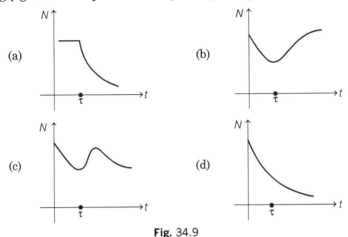

Fig. 34.9

Solution   The total number of atoms can neither remain constant (as in option a) nor can ever increase (as in options b and c). They will continuously decrease with time. Therefore, (d) is the appropriate option.

INTRODUCTORY EXERCISE 34.1

1. The decay constant of a radioactive sample is λ. The half-life and mean life of the sample are respectively given by (JEE 1989)
   (a) $1/\lambda$ and $(\ln 2)/\lambda$
   (b) $(\ln 2)/\lambda$ and $1/\lambda$
   (c) $\lambda (\ln 2)$ and $1/\lambda$
   (d) $\lambda/(\ln 2)$ and $1/\lambda$

2. Consider α-particles, β-particles and γ-rays each having an energy of 0.5 MeV. In increasing order of penetrating powers, the radiations are (JEE 1994)
   (a) α, β, γ
   (b) α, γ, β
   (c) β, γ, α
   (d) γ, β, α

3. Which of the following is a correct statement? (JEE 1999)
   (a) Beta rays are same as cathode rays
   (b) Gamma rays are high energy neutrons
   (c) Alpha particles are singly ionized helium atoms
   (d) Protons and neutrons have exactly the same mass

4. The electron emitted in beta radiation originates from (JEE 2001)
   (a) inner orbits of atom
   (b) free electrons existing in nuclei
   (c) decay of a neutron in a nucleus
   (d) photon escaping from the nucleus

5. During a negative beta decay, (JEE 1987)
   (a) an atomic electron is ejected
   (b) an electron which is already present within the nucleus is ejected
   (c) a neutron in the nucleus decays emitting an electron
   (d) a part of the binding energy of the nucleus is converted into an electron

6. A freshly prepared radioactive source of half-life 2 h emits radiation of intensity which is 64 times the permissible safe level. The minimum time after which it would be possible to work safely with this source is (JEE 1988)
   (a) 6 h   (b) 12 h   (c) 24 h   (d) 128 h

7. A radioactive sample S_1 having an activity of 5 μCi has twice the number of nuclei as another sample S_2 which has an activity of 10 μCi. The half-lives of S_1 and S_2 can be (JEE 2008)
   (a) 20 yr and 5 yr, respectively   (b) 20 yr and 10 yr, respectively
   (c) 10 yr each   (d) 5 yr each

8. Half-life of a radioactive substance A is 4 days. The probability that a nucleus will decay in two half-lives is (JEE 2006)
   (a) $\dfrac{1}{4}$ (b) $\dfrac{3}{4}$ (c) $\dfrac{1}{2}$ (d) 1

9. After 280 days, the activity of a radioactive sample is 6000 dps. The activity reduces to 3000 dps after another 140 days. The initial activity of the sample in dps is (JEE 2004)
   (a) 6000   (b) 9000   (c) 3000   (d) 24000

10. The half-life of ^{215}At is 100 μs. The time taken for the activity of a sample of ^{215}At to decay to $\dfrac{1}{16}$ th of its initial value is (JEE 2002)
    (a) 400 μs   (b) 63 μs
    (c) 40 μs   (d) 300 μs

11. The half-life of the radioactive radon is 3.8 days. The time, at the end of which 1/20 th of the radon sample will remain undecayed, is (given $\log_{10} e = 0.4343$) (JEE 1981)
    (a) 3.8 days   (b) 16.5 days
    (c) 33 days   (d) 76 days

12. Activity of a radioactive substance decreases from 8000 Bq to 1000 Bq in 9 days. What is the half-life and average life of the radioactive substance?

13. A radioactive substance has a half-life of 64.8 h. A sample containing this isotope has an initial activity ($t = 0$) of 40 μCi. Calculate the number of nuclei that decay in the time interval between $t_1 = 10.0$ h and $t_2 = 12.0$ h.

14. A freshly prepared sample of a certain radioactive isotope has an activity of 10 mCi. After 4.0 h its activity is 8.00 mCi.
    (a) Find the decay constant and half-life
    (b) How many atoms of the isotope were contained in the freshly prepared sample?
    (c) What is the sample's activity 30.0 h after it is prepared?

15. A radioactive substance contains 10^{15} atoms and has an activity of 6.0×10^{11} Bq. What is its half-life?

16. Two radioactive elements X and Y have half-life periods of 50 minutes and 100 minutes, respectively. Initially, both of them contain equal number of atoms. Find the ratio of atoms left N_X / N_Y after 200 minutes.

34.3 **Successive Disintegration**

Suppose a parent radioactive nucleus A (decay constant $= \lambda_a$) has number of atoms N_0 at time $t = 0$. After disintegration it converts into a nucleus B (decay constant $= \lambda_b$) which is further radioactive. Initially ($t = 0$), number of atoms of B are zero. We are interested in finding N_b, the number of atoms of B at time t.

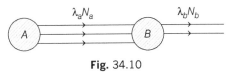

Fig. 34.10

	A	**B**
At $t = 0$	N_0	0
At $t = t$	$N_a = N_0 e^{-\lambda_a t}$	$N_b = ?$

At time t, net rate of formation of B = rate of disintegration of A − rate of disintegration of B

$\therefore \qquad \dfrac{dN_b}{dt} = \lambda_a N_a - \lambda_b N_b$

or $\qquad \dfrac{dN_b}{dt} = \lambda_a N_0 e^{-\lambda_a t} - \lambda_b N_b \qquad\qquad\qquad$ (as $N_a = N_0 e^{-\lambda_a t}$)

or $\qquad dN_b + \lambda_b N_b \, dt = \lambda_a N_0 e^{-\lambda_a t}$

Multiplying this equation by $e^{\lambda_b t}$, we have

$$e^{\lambda_b t} dN_b + e^{\lambda_b t} \lambda_b N_b \, dt = \lambda_a N_0 e^{(\lambda_b - \lambda_a)t}$$

$\therefore \qquad\qquad\qquad d\{N_b e^{\lambda_b t}\} = \lambda_a N_0 e^{(\lambda_b - \lambda_a)t} \, dt$

Integrating both sides, we get

$$N_b e^{\lambda_b t} = \left(\frac{\lambda_a}{\lambda_b - \lambda_a} \right) N_0 e^{(\lambda_b - \lambda_a)t} + C \qquad\qquad \ldots(\text{i})$$

where, C is the constant of integration, which can be found as under.

At time, $\quad t = 0, \quad N_b = 0$

$\therefore \qquad\qquad\qquad C = -\left(\frac{\lambda_a}{\lambda_b - \lambda_a} \right) N_0$

Substituting this value in Eq. (i), we have

$$N_b = \frac{N_0 \lambda_a}{\lambda_b - \lambda_a} (e^{-\lambda_a t} - e^{-\lambda_b t}) \qquad\qquad \ldots(\text{ii})$$

Now, the following conclusions may be drawn from the above discussion.

1. From Eq. (ii) we can see that $N_b = 0$ at time $t = 0$ (it was given) and at $t = \infty$ (because B is also radioactive)

2. N_a will continuously decrease with time while N_b will first increase (until $\lambda_a N_a > \lambda_b N_b$), reaches to a maximum value (when $\lambda_a N_a = \lambda_b N_b$) and then decreases (when $\lambda_b N_b > \lambda_a N_a$). The two graphs for N_a and N_b with time are shown below.

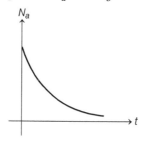 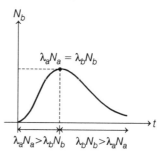

Fig. 34.11

⊚ **Example 34.9** *A radio nuclide X is produced at constant rate* α. *At time* $t = 0$, *number of nuclei of X are zero. Find*
(a) the maximum number of nuclei of X.
(b) the number of nuclei at time t.
Decay constant of X is λ.

Solution (a) Let N be the number of nuclei of X at time t.

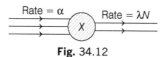

Fig. 34.12

Rate of formation of $X = \alpha$ (given)

Rate of disintegration $= \lambda N$

Number of nuclei of X will increase until both the rates will become equal. Therefore,

$$\alpha = \lambda N_{max}$$

$\therefore$
$$N_{max} = \frac{\alpha}{\lambda}$$ **Ans.**

(b) Net rate of formation of X at time t is

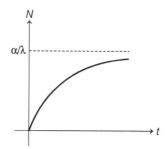

Fig. 34.13

$$\frac{dN}{dt} = \alpha - \lambda N$$

∴ $$\frac{dN}{\alpha - \lambda N} = dt$$

Integrating with proper limits, we have

$$\int_0^N \frac{dN}{\alpha - \lambda N} = \int_0^t dt$$

or $$N = \frac{\alpha}{\lambda}(1 - e^{-\lambda t})$$ **Ans.**

This expression shows that number of nuclei of X are increasing exponentially from 0 to $\frac{\alpha}{\lambda}$.

● **Example 34.10** *In the above problem if each decay produces E_0 energy, then find*
(a) power produced at time t
(b) total energy produced upto time t

Solution (a) ∵ $N = \frac{\alpha}{\lambda}(1 - e^{-\lambda t})$

At time t, number of decays per second $= \lambda N = \alpha(1 - e^{-\lambda t})$.

Each decay produces E_0 energy. Therefore, energy produced per second or power.

= (number of decays per second) (energy produced in each decay)

$$= (\lambda N)E_0$$
$$= \alpha E_0 (1 - e^{-\lambda t})$$

or $$P = \alpha E_0 (1 - e^{-\lambda t})$$ **Ans.**

(b) Power is a function of time. Therefore, total energy produced upto time t can be obtained by integrating this power or

$$E_{\text{Total}} = \int_0^t P \, dt$$

Alternate Method

Energy is produced only in decay. Upto time t total αt nuclei are produced and N nuclei are left. So, total number of nuclei decayed.

$$N_d = \alpha t - N = \alpha t - \frac{\alpha}{\lambda}(1 - e^{-\lambda t})$$
$$= \alpha \left[t - \frac{1}{\lambda}(1 - e^{-\lambda t}) \right]$$

Each decay produces E_0 energy. Therefore, total energy produced upto time t,

$$E_{\text{Total}} = N_d E_0$$
$$= \alpha E_0 \left[t - \frac{1}{\lambda}(1 - e^{-\lambda t}) \right]$$ **Ans.**

34.4 Equivalence of Mass and Energy

In 1905, while developing his special theory of relativity, Einstein made the suggestion that energy and mass are equivalent. He predicted that if the energy of a body changes by an amount E, its mass changes by an amount m given by the equation,

$$E = mc^2$$

where, c is the speed of light. Everyday examples of energy gain are much too small to produce detectable changes of mass. But in nuclear physics this plays an important role. Mass appears as energy and the two can be regarded as equivalent. In nuclear physics, mass is measured in **unified atomic mass units (u)**, $1 u$ being one-twelfth of the mass of carbon-12 atom and equals 1.66×10^{-27} kg. It can readily be shown using $E = mc^2$ that, 1 u mass has energy 931.5 MeV.

Thus,

$$1 u = 931.5 \text{ MeV/c}^2 \quad \text{or} \quad c^2 = 931.5 \text{ MeV/u}$$

A unit of energy may therefore be considered to be a unit of mass. For example, the electron has a rest mass of about 0.5 MeV.

If the principle of conservation of energy is to hold for nuclear reactions it is clear that mass and energy must be regarded as equivalent. The implication of $E = mc^2$ is that any reaction producing an appreciable mass decrease is a possible source of energy.

> ⊘ **Example 34.11** *Find the increase in mass of water when* 1.0 *kg of water absorbs* 4.2×10^3 *J of energy to produce a temperature rise of* 1 *K.*
>
> *Solution*
> $$m = \frac{E}{c^2} = \frac{4.2 \times 10^3}{(3.0 \times 10^8)^2} \text{ kg}$$
> $$= 4.7 \times 10^{-14} \text{ kg} \qquad\qquad\qquad \textbf{Ans.}$$

34.5 Binding Energy and Nuclear Stability

The existence of a stable nucleus means that the nucleons (protons and neutrons) are in a bound state. Since, the protons in a nucleus experience strong electrical repulsion, there must exist a stronger attractive force that holds the nucleus together. The **nuclear force** is a short range interaction that extends only to about 2 fm. (In contrast, the electromagnetic interaction is a long-range interaction). An important feature of the nuclear force is that it is essentially the same for all nucleons, independent of charge.

The **binding energy** (E_b) of a nucleus is the energy required to completely separate the nucleons. The origin of the binding energy may be understood with the help of mass-energy relation, $\Delta E = \Delta m c^2$, where Δm is the difference between the total mass of the separated nucleons and the mass of the stable nucleus. The mass of the stable nucleus is less than the sum of the mass of its nucleons. The binding energy of a nuclide $_Z X^A$ is thus,

$$E_b = [Z m_P + (A - Z) m_N - m_X] c^2 \qquad\qquad \text{...(i)}$$

where, m_P = mass of proton, m_N = mass of neutron and m_X = mass of nucleus

Note (i) $\Delta m = [Zm_P + (A - Z)\, m_N - m_X]$ is called the mass defect. This much mass is lost during the formation of a nucleus. Energy $\Delta E = (\Delta m)\, c^2$ is liberated during the making of the nucleus. This is the energy due to which nucleons are bound together. So, to break the nucleus in its constituent nucleons this much energy has to be given to the nucleus.

(ii) **Stability** : Although nuclides with Z values upto $Z = 92$ (uranium) occur naturally, not all of these are stable. The nuclide $^{209}_{83}$Bi is the heaviest stable nucleus. Even though uranium is not stable, however, its long lived isotope ^{238}U, has a half-life of some 4 billion year.

Binding energy per nucleon If the binding energy of a nucleus is divided by its mass number, the binding energy per nucleon is obtained. A plot of binding energy per nucleon E_b / A as a function of mass number A for various stable nuclei is shown in figure.

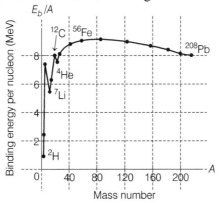

Fig. 34.14 The binding energy per nucleon, E_b / A, as a function of the mass number A

Note That it is the binding energy per nucleon which is more important for stability of a nucleus rather than the total binding energy.

Following conclusions can be drawn from the above graph.

1. The greater the binding energy per nucleon the more stable is the nucleus. The curve reaches a maximum of about 8.75 MeV in the vicinity of $^{56}_{26}$Fe and then gradually falls to 7.6 MeV for $^{238}_{92}$U.

2. In a nuclear reaction energy is released if total binding energy is increasing. Let us take an example.

Suppose a nucleus X, which has total binding energy of 100 MeV converts into some another nucleus Y which has total binding energy 120 MeV. Then, in this process 20 MeV energy will be released. This is because 100 MeV energy has already been released during the formation of X while in case of Y it is 120 MeV. So, the remaining 20 MeV will be released now.

> Energy is released if ΣE_b is increasing.

3. ΣE_b in a nuclear process is increased if binding energy per nucleon of the daughter products gets increased. Let us take an example. Consider a nucleus $X\ (A_X = 100)$ breaks into lighter nuclei $Y\ (A_Y = 60)$ and $Z(A_Z = 40)$.

$$X \rightarrow Y + Z$$

Binding energy per nucleon of these three are say, 7 MeV, 7.5 MeV and 8.0 MeV. Then, total binding energy of X is $100 \times 7 = 700$ MeV and that of $Y + Z$ is $(60 \times 7.5) + (40 \times 8.0) = 770$ MeV. So, in this process 70 MeV energy will be released.

4. Binding energy per nucleon is increased if two or more lighter nuclei combine to form a heavier nucleus. This process is called **nuclear fusion.**

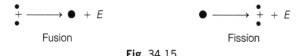

Fig. 34.15

In **nuclear fission** a heavy nucleus splits into two or more lighter nuclei of almost equal mass.

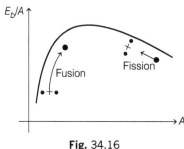

Fig. 34.16

In both the processes E_b / A is increasing. Thus, energy will be released.

34.6 Nuclear Fission (Divide and Conquer)

As we saw in the above article nuclear fission occurs when a heavy nucleus such as ^{235}U, splits into two lighter nuclei. In nuclear fission, the combined mass of the daughter nuclei is less than the mass of the parent nucleus. The difference is called the mass defect. Fission is initiated when a heavy nucleus captures a thermal neutron (slow neutrons). Multiplying the mass defect by c^2 gives the numerical value of the released energy. Energy is released because the binding energy per nucleon of the daughter nuclei is about 1 MeV greater than that of the parent nucleus.

The fission of ^{235}U by thermal neutrons can be represented by the equation,

$$_0^1 n + {}_{92}^{235}U \longrightarrow {}_{92}^{236}U^* \longrightarrow X + Y + \text{neutrons}$$

where, $^{236}U^*$ is an intermediate excited state that lasts only for 10^{-12} s before breaking into nuclei X and Y, which are called fission fragments. In any fission equation there are many combinations of X and Y that satisfy the requirements of conservation of energy and charge with uranium, for example, there are about 90 daughter nuclei that can be formed. Fission also results in the production of several neutrons, typically two or three. On the average, about 2.5 neutrons are released per event.

A typical fission reaction for uranium is

$$_0^1 n + {}_{92}^{235}U \longrightarrow {}_{56}^{141}Ba + {}_{36}^{92}Kr + 3{}_0^1 n$$

About 200 MeV is released in the fission of a heavy nucleus. The fission energy appears mostly as kinetic energy of the fission fragments (e.g. barium and krypton nuclei) which fly apart at great speed. The kinetic energy of the fission neutrons also makes a slight contribution. In addition one or both of the large fragments are highly radioactive and small amount of energy takes the form of beta and gamma radiation.

Chain Reaction Shortly after nuclear fission was discovered, it was realized that, the fission neutrons can cause further fission of ^{235}U and a chain reaction can be maintained.

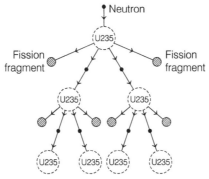

Fig. 34.17 A chain reaction

In practice only a proportion of the fission neutrons is available for new fissions since, some are lost by escaping from the surface of the uranium before colliding with another nucleus. The ratio of neutrons escaping to those causing fission decreases as the size of the piece of uranium-235 increases and there is a **critical size** (about the size of a cricket ball) which must be attained before a chain reaction can start.

In the **'atomic bomb'** an increasing uncontrolled chain reaction occurs in a very short time when two pieces of uranium-235 are rapidly brought together to form a mass greater than the critical size.

Nuclear Reactors In a nuclear reactor the chain reaction is steady and controlled so that on average only one neutron from each fission produces another fission. The reaction rate is adjusted by inserting neutron absorbing rods of boron steel into the uranium 235.

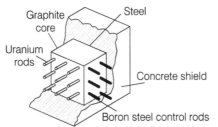

Fig. 34.18 Nuclear reactor

Graphite core is used as a **moderator** to slow down the neutrons. Natural uranium contains over 99% of ^{238}U and less than 1% of ^{235}U. The former captures the medium speed fission neutrons without fissioning. It fissions with very fast neutrons. On the other hand ^{235}U (and plutonium-239) fissions with slow neutrons and the job of moderator is to slow down the fission neutrons very quickly so that most escape capture by ^{238}U and then cause the fission of ^{235}U.

A bombarding particle gives up most energy when it has an elastic collision with a particle of similar mass. For neutrons, hydrogen atoms would be most effective but they absorb the neutrons. But deuterium (in heavy water) and carbon (as graphite) are both suitable as moderator.

To control the power level **control rods** are used. These rods are made of materials such as cadmium, that are very efficient in absorbing neutrons. The first nuclear reactor was built by Enrico Fermi and his team at the University of Chicago in 1942.

34.7 Nuclear Fusion

Binding energy for light nuclei ($A < 20$) is much smaller than the binding energy for heavier nuclei. This suggests a process that is the reverse of fission. When two light nuclei combine to form a heavier nucleus, the process is called nuclear fusion. The union of light nuclei into heavier nuclei also lead to a transfer of mass and a consequent liberation of energy. Such a reaction has been achieved in **'hydrogen bomb'** and it is believed to be the principal source of the sun's energy.

A reaction with heavy hydrogen or deuterium which yields 3.3 MeV per fusion is

$$_1^2 H + _1^2 H \rightarrow {}_2^3 He + {}_0^1 n$$

By comparison with the 200 MeV per fission of ^{235}U this seems small, but per unit mass of material it is not. Fusion of two deuterium nuclei, i.e. deuterons, will only occur if they overcome their mutual electrostatic repulsion. This may happen, if they collide at very high speed when, for example, they are raised to a very high temperature ($10^8 - 10^9$ K). So much high temperature is obtained by using an atomic (fission) bomb to trigger off fusion. If a controlled fusion reaction can be achieved, an almost unlimited supply of energy will become available from deuterium in the water of the oceans.

Extra Points to Remember

- **Q-value of a nuclear reaction (optional)** Consider a nuclear reaction in which a target nucleus X is bombarded by a particle 'a' resulting in a daughter nucleus Y and a particle b.

$$a + X \rightarrow Y + b$$

Sometimes this reaction is written as $X(a, b)Y$

The reaction energy Q associated with a nuclear reaction is defined as the total energy released as a result of the reaction. Thus,

$$Q = (M_a + M_X - M_Y - M_b)c^2$$

A reaction for which Q is positive is called **exothermic.** A reaction for which Q is negative is called **endothermic.**

In an exothermic reaction, the total mass of incoming particles is greater than that of the outgoing particles and the Q-value is positive. If the total mass of the incoming particles is less than that of the outgoing particles, energy is required for reaction to take place and the reaction is said to be endothermic. Thus, an endothermic reaction does not occur unless the bombarding particle has a kinetic energy greater than $|Q|$. The minimum energy necessary for such a reaction to occur is called **threshold energy K_{th}**. The threshold energy is somewhat greater than $|Q|$ because the outgoing particles must have some kinetic energy to conserve momentum.

Thus, $K_{th} > |Q|$ (in endothermic reaction)

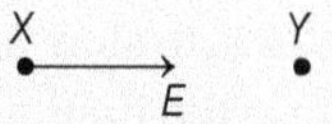

Fig. 34.19

Consider a bombarding particle X of mass m_1 and a target Y of mass m_2 (at rest). The threshold energy of X for endothermic reaction (negative value of Q) to take place is

$$K_{th} = |Q|\left(\frac{m_1}{m_2} + 1\right)$$

● **Example 34.12** *In the fusion reaction* $_1^2 H + _1^2 H \longrightarrow _2^3 He + _0^1 n$, *the masses of deuteron, helium and neutron expressed in amu are* 2.015, 3.017 *and* 1.009 *respectively. If* 1 *kg of deuterium undergoes complete fusion, find the amount of total energy released.* 1 *amu* $\equiv 931.5$ *MeV* $/c^2$.

Solution $\Delta m = 2 (2.015) - (3.017 + 1.009) = 0.004$ amu

∴   Energy released $= (0.004 \times 931.5)$ MeV $= 3.726$ MeV

   Energy released per deuteron $= \dfrac{3.726}{2} = 1.863$ MeV

   Number of deuterons in 1 kg $= \dfrac{6.02 \times 10^{26}}{2} = 3.01 \times 10^{26}$

∴   Energy released per kg of deuterium fusion $= (3.01 \times 10^{26} \times 1.863) = 5.6 \times 10^{26}$ MeV

$$\approx 9.0 \times 10^{13} \text{ J} \qquad\qquad \textbf{Ans.}$$

● **Example 34.13** *A nucleus with mass number* 220 *initially at rest emits an* α-*particle. If the Q-value of the reaction is* 5.5 *MeV, calculate the kinetic energy of the* α-*particle.*   (JEE 2003)

(a) 4.4 MeV   (b) 5.4 MeV   (c) 5.6 MeV   (d) 6.5 MeV

Solution   Given that $K_1 + K_2 = 5.5$ MeV   ...(i)

From conservation of linear momentum,

$$p_1 = p_2 \quad \text{or} \quad \sqrt{2 K_1 (216 m)} = \sqrt{2 K_2 (4 m)} \quad \text{as} \quad p = \sqrt{2 K m}$$

∴ $K_2 = 54 K_1$ ...(ii)

Solving Eqs. (i) and (ii), we get $K_2 = $ KE of α-particle $= 5.4$ MeV

∴   The correct option is (b).

● **Example 34.14** *Binding energy per nucleon versus mass number curve for nuclei is shown in figure. W, X, Y and Z are four nuclei indicated on the curve. The process that would release energy is*   (JEE 1999)

(a) $Y \rightarrow 2Z$

(b) $W \rightarrow X + Z$

(c) $W \rightarrow 2Y$

(d) $X \rightarrow Y + Z$

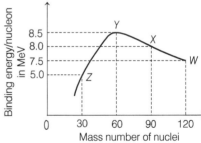

Fig. 34.20

Solution   Energy is released in a process when total binding energy of the nucleus (= binding energy per nucleon × number of nucleons) is increased or we can say, when total binding energy of products is more than the reactants. By calculation we can see that only in option (c), this happens. Given, $W \rightarrow 2Y$

Binding energy of reactants $= 120 \times 7.5 = 900$ MeV

and binding energy of products $= 2 (60 \times 8.5) = 1020$ MeV > 900 MeV

∴   The correct option is (c).

⊙ **Example 34.15** *A star initially has 10^{40} deuterons. It produces energy via the processes $_1H^2 + _1H^2 \rightarrow _1H^3 + p$ and $_1H^2 + _1H^3 \rightarrow _2He^4 + n$. If the average power radiated by the star is 10^{16} W, the deuteron supply of the star is exhausted in a time of the order of* (JEE 1993)

(a) 10^6 s   (b) 10^8 s   (c) 10^{12} s   (d) 10^{16} s

The masses of the nuclei are as follows
$$M(H^2) = 2.014 \text{ amu}; \ M(n) = 1.008 \text{ amu},$$
$$M(p) = 1.007 \text{ amu}; \ M(He^4) = 4.001 \text{ amu}$$

Solution The given reactions are
$$_1H^2 + _1H^2 \longrightarrow _1H^3 + p$$
$$_1H^2 + _1H^3 \longrightarrow _2He^4 + n$$
$$\Rightarrow \qquad\qquad 3\,_1H^2 \longrightarrow _2He^4 + n + p$$

Mass defect, $\qquad\qquad \Delta m = (3 \times 2.014 - 4.001 - 1.007 - 1.008)$ amu
$$= 0.026 \text{ amu}$$

$$\text{Energy released} = 0.026 \times 931 \text{ MeV}$$
$$= 0.026 \times 931 \times 1.6 \times 10^{-13} \text{ J}$$
$$= 3.87 \times 10^{-12} \text{ J}$$

This is the energy produced by the consumption of three deuteron atoms.

∴ Total energy released by 10^{40} deuterons
$$= \frac{10^{40}}{3} \times 3.87 \times 10^{-12} \text{ J} = 1.29 \times 10^{28} \text{ J}$$

The average power radiated is $P = 10^{16}$ W or 10^{16} J/s.

Therefore, total time to exhaust all deuterons of the star will be
$$t = \frac{1.29 \times 10^{28}}{10^{16}} = 1.29 \times 10^{12} \text{s} \approx 10^{12} \text{s}$$

∴   The correct option is (c).

⊙ **Example 34.16** *Assume that the nuclear binding energy per nucleon (B/A) versus mass number (A) is as shown in the figure. Use this plot to choose the correct choice(s) given below.* (JEE 2008)

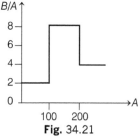

Fig. 34.21

(a) *Fusion of two nuclei with mass numbers lying in the range of $1 < A < 50$ will release energy.*

(b) *Fusion of two nuclei with mass numbers lying in the range of $51 < A < 100$ will release energy.*

(c) *Fission of a nucleus lying in the mass range of $100 < A < 200$ will release energy when broken into two equal fragments.*

(d) *Fission of a nucleus lying in the mass range of $200 < A < 260$ will release energy when broken into two equal fragments.*

Solution In fusion, two or more lighter nuclei combine to make a comparatively heavier nucleus. In fission, a heavy nucleus breaks into two or more comparatively lighter nuclei. Further, energy will be released in a nuclear process if total binding energy increases.

∴ The correct options are (b) and (d).

INTRODUCTORY EXERCISE 34.2

1. If a star can convert all the He nuclei completely into oxygen nuclei. The energy released per oxygen nuclei is (Mass of the helium nucleus is 4.0026 amu and mass of oxygen nucleus is 15.9994 amu) *(JEE 2005)*
   (a) 7.6 MeV
   (b) 56.12 MeV
   (c) 10.24 MeV
   (d) 23.4 MeV

2. Fast neutrons can easily be slowed down by *(JEE 1994)*
   (a) the use of lead shielding
   (b) passing them through heavy water
   (c) elastic collisions with heavy nuclei
   (d) applying a strong electric field

3. During a nuclear fusion reaction, *(JEE 1987)*
   (a) a heavy nucleus breaks into two fragments by itself
   (b) a light nucleus bombarded by thermal neutrons breaks up
   (c) a heavy nucleus bombarded by thermal neutrons breaks up
   (d) two light nuclei combine to give a heavier nucleus and possibly other products

4. The equation $4\,{}^{1}_{1}H \longrightarrow {}^{4}_{2}He^{2+} + 2e^{-} + 26\,MeV$ represents *(JEE 1983)*
   (a) β-decay
   (b) γ-decay
   (c) fusion
   (d) fission

5. (a) How much mass is lost per day by a nuclear reactor operated at a 10^9 watt power level?
   (b) If each fission releases 200 MeV, how many fissions occur per second to yield this power level?

6. Find energy released in the alpha decay,
   $$^{238}_{92}U \longrightarrow {}^{234}_{90}Th + {}^{4}_{2}He$$

   Given,
   $$M\left({}^{238}_{92}U\right) = 238.050784\ u$$
   $$M\left({}^{234}_{90}Th\right) = 234.043593\ u$$
   $$M\left({}^{4}_{2}He\right) = 4.002602\ u$$

7. Complete the nuclear reactions.
   (a) ${}^{6}_{3}Li + ? \longrightarrow {}^{7}_{4}Be + {}^{1}_{0}n$
   (b) ${}^{35}_{17}Cl + ? \longrightarrow {}^{32}_{16}S + {}^{4}_{2}He$
   (c) ${}^{9}_{4}Be + {}^{4}_{2}He \longrightarrow 3({}^{4}_{2}He) + ?$
   (d) ${}^{79}_{35}Br + {}^{2}_{1}H \longrightarrow ? + 2({}^{1}_{0}n)$

8. Consider the reaction ${}^{2}_{1}H + {}^{2}_{1}H = {}^{4}_{2}He + Q$. Mass of the deuterium atom $= 2.0141u$. Mass of helium atom $= 4.0024\ u$. This is a nuclear .... reaction in which the energy Q released is .... MeV. *(JEE 1996)*

9. The binding energies per nucleon for deuteron $({}_{1}H^{2})$ and helium $({}_{2}He^{4})$ are 1.1 MeV and 7.0 MeV respectively. The energy released when two deuterons fuse to form a helium nucleus $({}_{2}He^{4})$ is .... *(JEE 1988)*

Core Concepts

1. Classification of nuclei The nuclei have been divided in isotopes, isobars and isotones on the basis of number of protons (atomic number) or the total number of nucleons (mass number).

Isotopes The elements having the same number of protons but different number of neutrons are called isotopes. In other words, isotopes have same value of atomic number (Z) but different values of mass number (A). Almost every element has isotopes. Because of the same atomic number isotopes of an element have the same place in the periodic table. The isotopes of some elements are given below.

Element	Its isotopes	Number of protons	Number of neutrons
Hydrogen	$_1H^1$	1	0
	$_1H^2$	1	1
	$_1H^3$	1	2
Oxygen	$_8O^{16}$	8	8
	$_8O^{17}$	8	9
	$_8O^{18}$	8	10
Chlorine	$_{17}Cl^{35}$	17	18
	$_{17}Cl^{37}$	17	20
Uranium	$_{92}U^{235}$	92	143
	$_{92}U^{238}$	92	146

In nature, the isotopes of chlorine ($_{17}Cl^{35}$ and $_{17}Cl^{37}$) are found in the ratio 75.4% and 24.6%. When chlorine is prepared in laboratory, its atomic mass is found to be

$$M = (35 \times 0.754) + (37 \times 0.246) = 35.5$$

Note *Since, the isotopes have the same atomic number, they have the same chemical properties. Their physical properties are different as they have different mass numbers. Two isotopes, thus cannot be separated by chemical method, but they can be separated from the physical methods.*

Isobars The elements having the same mass number (A) but different atomic number (Z) are called isobars. They have different places in periodic table. Their chemical (as well as physical) properties are different.

$_1H^3$ and $_2He^3$, $_8O^{17}$ and $_9F^{17}$ are examples of isobars.

Isotones Elements having the equal number of neutrons ($A - Z$) are called isotones.

$_3Li^7$ and $_4Be^8$, $_1H^3$ and $_2He^4$ are examples of isotones.

2. Nuclear forces In nucleus the positively charged protons and the uncharged neutrons are held together in an extremely small space ($\approx 10^{-15}$ m) in spite of the strong electrostatic repulsion between the protons. Obviously, there are some strong attractive forces operating within the nucleus between the nucleons. The nuclear forces are non-electric and non gravitational forces. These forces are extremely short-range forces. They become operative only when the distance between two nucleons is a small multiple of 10^{-15} m. They do not exist when the distance is appreciably larger than 10^{-15} m and become repulsive when the distance is appreciably smaller than 10^{-15} m. Nuclear forces between protons and protons between neutrons and neutrons and between protons and neutrons are all essentially the same in magnitude. Thus, we can say that nuclear forces are charge independent.

Yukawa's meson theory of nuclear forces A Japanese scientist Yukawa in 1935 suggested that the nuclear forces are 'exchange forces. Which are produced by the exchange of new particles called π-mesons between nucleons. These particles were later on actually discovered in cosmic radiation. There are three types of π-mesons, π^+, π^- and π^0. There is a continuous exchange of π-mesons between protons and neutrons due to which they continue to be converted into one another. When a π^+-meson jumps from a proton to a neutron, the proton is converted into a neutron and the neutron is converted into a proton.

$$p - \pi^+ \longrightarrow n$$

and
$$n + \pi^+ \longrightarrow p$$

Conversely, when a π^--meson jumps from a neutron to a proton, then neutron is converted into a proton and the proton is converted into a neutron. Thus,

$$n - \pi^- \longrightarrow p$$

and
$$p + \pi^- \longrightarrow n$$

The exchange of π^+ and π^--mesons between protons and neutrons is responsible for the origin of nuclear forces between them. Similarly, nuclear forces between two protons and between two neutrons are generated by a continuous exchange of π^0-mesons between them. Thus, the basis of nuclear forces is the exchange of mesons and hence these are called 'exchange forces'.

3. **Size and shape of the nucleus** The Rutherford scattering experiment established that mass of an atom is concentrated within a small positively charged region at the centre which is called the nucleus of the atom. The nuclear radius is given by

$$R = R_0 \, A^{1/3}$$

Here, A is the mass number of the particular nucleus and $R_0 = 1.3$ fm (fermi) $= 1.3 \times 10^{-15}$ m. This means that the nucleus radius is of the order of 10^{-15} m.

Here, $R_0 = 1.3$ fm is the distance of closest approach to the nucleus and is also known as nuclear unit radius.

4. **Nuclear density** Let us consider the nucleus of an atom having the mass number A.

   Mass of nucleus $\approx A \times 1.67 \times 10^{-27}$ kg

   Volume of the nucleus $= \dfrac{4}{3} \pi R^3$

$$= \dfrac{4}{3} \pi \, (R_0 A^{1/3})^3 = \dfrac{4}{3} \pi R_0^3 A$$

   $\therefore$ Density of the nucleus, $\rho = \dfrac{\text{mass}}{\text{volume}}$

   or
$$\rho = \dfrac{A \times 1.67 \times 10^{-27}}{\dfrac{4}{3} \times \pi \times (1.3 \times 10^{-15})^3 \times A}$$

$$= 1.8 \times 10^{17} \text{ kg/m}^3$$

   Thus, density of a nucleus is independent of the mass number A and of the order of 10^{17} kg/m^3.

5. **Magic numbers** We know that the electrons in an atom are grouped in 'shells' and 'sub-shells'. Atoms with 2, 10, 18, 36, 54 and 86 electrons have all of their shells completely filled. Such atoms are unusually stable and chemically inert. A similar situation exists with nuclei also. Nuclei having 2, 8, 20, 28, 50, 82 and 126 nucleons of the same kind (either protons or neutrons) are more stable than nuclei of neighbouring mass numbers. These numbers are called as 'magic numbers'.

6. **Fundamental particles** The particles which are not constituted by any other particles are called fundamental particles. A brief discussion of important fundamental particles is as follows.

   (i) **Electron** It was discovered in 1897 by Thomson. Its charge is $-e$ and mass is 9.1×10^{-31} kg. Its symbol is e^- (or $_{-1}\beta^0$).

   (ii) **Proton** It was discovered in 1919 by Rutherford in artificial nuclear disintegration. It has a positive charge $+e$ and its mass is 1836 times $(1.673 \times 10^{-27}$ kg) the mass of electron. In free state, the proton is a stable particle. Its symbol is p^+. It is also written as $_1H^1$.

   (iii) **Neutron** It was discovered in 1932 by Chadwick. Electrically, it is a neutral particle. Its mass is 1839 times $(1.675 \times 10^{-27}$ kg) the mass of electron. In free state the neutron is unstable (mean life $\approx$ 17 minutes) but it constitutes a stable nucleus with the proton. Its symbol is n or $_0n^1$.

   (iv) **Positron** It was discovered by Anderson in 1932. It is the antiparticle of electron, i.e. its charge is $+e$ and its mass is equal to that of the mass of electron. Its symbol is e^+ (or $_{+1}\beta^0$).

   (v) **Antiproton** It is the antiparticle of proton. It was discovered in 1955. Its charge is $-e$ and its mass is equal to that of the mass of proton. Its symbol is p^-.

   (vi) **Antineutron** It was discovered in 1956. It has no charge and its mass is equal to the mass of neutron. The only difference between neutron and antineutron is that if they spin in the same direction, their magnetic momenta will be in opposite directions. The symbol for antineutron is $\bar{n}$.

   (vii) **Neutrino and antineutrino** The existence of these particles was predicted in 1930 by Pauli while explaining the emission of β-particles from radioactive nuclei, but these particles were actually observed experimentally in 1956. Their rest mass and charge are both zero but they have energy and momentum. These are mutually antiparticles of each other. They have the symbol ν and $\bar{\nu}$.

   (viii) **Pi-mesons** The existence of pi-mesons was predicted by Yukawa in 1935, but they were actually discovered in 1947 in cosmic rays. Nuclear forces are explained by the exchange of pi-mesons between the nucleons. pi-mesons are of three types, positive π-mesons (π^+), negative pi-mesons (π^-) and neutral π-mesons (π^0). Charge on $\pi^\pm$ is $\pm e$. Whereas mass of $\pi^\pm$ is 274 times the mass of electron. π^0 has mass nearly 264 times the electronic mass.

   (ix) **Mu-Mesons** These were discovered in 1936 by Anderson and Neddermeyer. These are found in abundance in the cosmic rays at the ground level. There are two types of mu-mesons. Positive mu-meson (μ^+) and negative mu-meson (μ^-). There is no neutral mu-meson. Both the mu-mesons have the same rest mass 207 times the rest mass of the electron.

   (x) **Photon** These are bundles of electromagnetic energy and travel with the speed of light. Energy and momentum of a photon of frequency ν are $h\nu$ and $\dfrac{h\nu}{c}$, respectively.

Antiparticles For every fundamental particle there exists an identical fundamental particle just opposite in some property. For example electron and positron are identical in all respects, except that charges on them are opposite.

The following table shows various particles and their antiparticles. Some particles are their own antiparticles. For example π^0 and γ.

Name of particle	Symbol	Antiparticle	Mass in comparison to mass of electron	Average life (in seconds) for the unstable particles
Electron	e^-	e^{+1}	1	stable
Proton	p^+	p^-	1836	stable
Neutron	n	$\bar{n}$	1839	1010
Neutrino	ν	$\bar{\nu}$	0	stable

Name of particle	Symbol	Antiparticle	Mass in comparison to mass of electron	Average life (in seconds) for the unstable particles
Pi-Mesons	π^+	π^-	274	2.6×10^{-8}
	π^0	π^0	264	0.9×10^{-16}
Mu-Mesons	μ^-	μ^+	207	2.2×10^{-6}
Photon	γ	γ	0	stable

7. If an unstable nucleus decays by two different processes and decay constants in two processes are λ_1 and λ_2, then effective value of λ is

$$\lambda = \lambda_1 + \lambda_2$$

Now, the above equation can also be written as

$$\frac{\ln 2}{T} = \frac{\ln 2}{T_1} + \frac{\ln 2}{T_2} \qquad (T = \text{half-life})$$

or

$$\frac{1}{T} = \frac{1}{T_1} + \frac{1}{T_2}$$

$\Rightarrow$

$$T = \frac{T_1 T_2}{T_1 + T_2}$$

Proof Suppose at some instant, the unstable nucleus has N number of nuclei, then

net rate of decay = decay in process 1 + decay in process 2

or

$$-\frac{dN}{dt} = \left(-\frac{dN}{dt}\right)_1 + \left(-\frac{dN}{dt}\right)_2$$

$\therefore$

$$\lambda N = \lambda_1 N + \lambda_2 N$$

or

$$\lambda = \lambda_1 + \lambda_2 \qquad \qquad \text{**Hence Proved.**}$$

Solved Examples

PATTERNED PROBLEMS

Type 1. *Based on radioactivity*

⊛ **Example 1** *At a given instant there are 25% undecayed radioactive nuclei in a sample. After 10 s the number of undecayed nuclei reduces to 12.5%. Calculate*
(a) mean life of the nuclei, (JEE 1996)
(b) the time in which the number of undecayed nuclei will further reduce to 6.25% of the reduced number.

Solution (a) In 10 s, number of nuclei has been reduced to half (25% to 12.5%). Therefore, its half-life is

$$t_{1/2} = 10 \text{ s}$$

Relation between half-life and mean life is

$$t_{\text{mean}} = \frac{t_{1/2}}{\ln 2} = \frac{10}{0.693} \text{ s}$$

$$t_{\text{mean}} = 14.43 \text{ s} \qquad\qquad \textbf{Ans.}$$

(b) From initial 100% to reduction till 6.25%, it takes four half-lives.

$$100\% \xrightarrow{t_{1/2}} 50\% \xrightarrow{t_{1/2}} 25\% \xrightarrow{t_{1/2}} 12.5\% \xrightarrow{t_{1/2}} 6.25\%$$

∴
$$t = 4\, t_{1/2} = 4\,(10)\text{s} = 40\text{s}$$

$$t = 40\text{s} \qquad\qquad \textbf{Ans.}$$

⊛ **Example 2** *A radioactive element decays by β-emission. A detector records n beta particles in 2 s and in next 2 s it records 0.75 n beta particles. Find mean life correct to nearest whole number. Given ln |2| = 0.6931, ln |3| = 1.0986.* (JEE 2003)

Solution Let n_0 be the number of radioactive nuclei at time $t = 0$. Number of nuclei decayed in time t are given by $n_0\,(1 - e^{-\lambda t})$, which is also equal to the number of beta particles emitted during the same interval of time. For the given condition,

$$n = n_0\,(1 - e^{-2\lambda}) \qquad\qquad \text{...(i)}$$

$$(n + 0.75n) = n_0\,(1 - e^{-4\lambda}) \qquad\qquad \text{...(ii)}$$

Dividing Eq. (ii) by Eq. (i), we get

$$1.75 = \frac{1 - e^{-4\lambda}}{1 - e^{-2\lambda}}$$

or
$$1.75 - 1.75\, e^{-2\lambda} = 1 - e^{-4\lambda}$$

∴
$$1.75\, e^{-2\lambda} - e^{-4\lambda} = \frac{3}{4} \qquad\qquad \text{...(iii)}$$

Let us take $e^{-2\lambda} = x$

Then, the above equation is

$$x^2 - 1.75\,x + 0.75 = 0$$

or

$$x = \frac{1.75 \pm \sqrt{(1.75)^2 - (4)\,(0.75)}}{2}$$

or

$$x = 1 \text{ and } \frac{3}{4}$$

∴ From Eq. (iii) either

$$e^{-2\lambda} = 1$$

or

$$e^{-2\lambda} = \frac{3}{4}$$

but $e^{-2\lambda} = 1$ is not acceptable because which means $\lambda = 0$.

Hence,

$$e^{-2\lambda} = \frac{3}{4}$$

or

$$-2\lambda \ln\,(e) = \ln\,(3) - \ln\,(4) = \ln\,(3) - 2\ln\,(2)$$

∴

$$\lambda = \ln\,(2) - \frac{1}{2}\ln\,(3)$$

Substituting the given values,

$$\lambda = 0.6931 - \frac{1}{2} \times (1.0986) = 0.14395 \text{ s}^{-1}$$

∴ Mean life, $t_{\text{mean}} = \dfrac{1}{\lambda} = 6.947$ s

∴ The correct answer is 7.   **Ans.**

◉ **Example 3** *A small quantity of solution containing* Na^{24} *radio nuclide* (*half-life* = 15 *h*) *of activity* 1.0 *microcurie is injected into the blood of a person. A sample of the blood of volume* 1 *cm*^{3} *taken after 5h shows an activity of* 296 *disintegrations per minute. Determine the total volume of the blood in the body of the person. Assume that the radioactive solution mixes uniformly in the blood of the person.*   (JEE 1994)

(1 *curie* = 3.7×10^{10} *disintegrations per second*)

Solution ∵ λ = Disintegration constant

$$\frac{0.693}{t_{1/2}} = \frac{0.693}{15} \text{ h}^{-1} = 0.0462 \text{ h}^{-1}$$

Let R_0 = initial activity = 1 microcurie = 3.7×10^4 disintegrations per second

r = Activity in 1 cm^3 of blood at $t = 5$ h

$= \dfrac{296}{60}$ disintegration per second

$= 4.93$ disintegration per second, and

R = Activity of whole blood at time $t = 5$ h

Total volume of blood should be

$$V = \frac{R}{r} = \frac{R_0 e^{-\lambda t}}{r}$$

Substituting the values, we have

$$V = \left(\frac{3.7 \times 10^4}{4.93}\right) e^{-(0.0462)(5)} \text{ cm}^3$$

$$V = 5.95 \times 10^3 \text{ cm}^3 \text{ or } V = 5.95 \text{ L} \qquad \textbf{Ans.}$$

◉ **Example 4** *A radioactive nucleus X decays to a nucleus Y with a decay constant* $\lambda_X = 0.1 \, s^{-1}$, *Y further decays to a stable nucleus Z with a decay constant* $\lambda_Y = 1/30 \, s^{-1}$. *Initially, there are only X nuclei and their number is* $N_0 = 10^{20}$. *Set up the rate equations for the populations of X, Y and Z. The population of Y nucleus as a function of time is given by* $N_Y(t) = \{N_0 \lambda_X / (\lambda_X - \lambda_Y)\} [\exp(-\lambda_Y t) - \exp(-\lambda_X t)]$. *Find the time at which* N_Y *is maximum and determine the populations X and Z at that instant.*

(JEE 2001)

Solution (a) Let at time $t = t$, number of nuclei of Y and Z are N_Y and N_Z. Then,
Rate equations of the populations of X, Y and Z are

$$\left(\frac{dN_X}{dt}\right) = -\lambda_X N_X \qquad \qquad \text{...(i)}$$

$$\left(\frac{dN_Y}{dt}\right) = \lambda_X N_X - \lambda_Y N_Y \qquad \qquad \text{...(ii)}$$

and
$$\left(\frac{dN_Z}{dt}\right) = \lambda_Y N_Y \qquad \qquad \text{...(iii)}$$

(b) Given, $N_Y(t) = \dfrac{N_0 \lambda_X}{\lambda_X - \lambda_Y} [e^{-\lambda_Y t} - e^{-\lambda_X t}]$

For N_Y to be maximum

$$\frac{dN_Y(t)}{dt} = 0$$

i.e
$$\lambda_X N_X = \lambda_Y N_Y \qquad \qquad \text{...(iv)} \qquad \text{[from Eq. (ii)]}$$

or
$$\lambda_X (N_0 e^{-\lambda_X t}) = \lambda_Y \frac{N_0 \lambda_X}{\lambda_X - \lambda_Y} [e^{-\lambda_Y t} - e^{-\lambda_X t}]$$

or
$$\frac{\lambda_X - \lambda_Y}{\lambda_Y} = \frac{e^{-\lambda_Y t}}{e^{-\lambda_X t}} - 1$$

$$\frac{\lambda_X}{\lambda_Y} = e^{(\lambda_X - \lambda_Y)t}$$

or
$$(\lambda_X - \lambda_Y) t \ln(e) = \ln\left(\frac{\lambda_X}{\lambda_Y}\right)$$

or
$$t = \frac{1}{\lambda_X - \lambda_Y} \ln\left(\frac{\lambda_X}{\lambda_Y}\right)$$

Substituting the values of λ_X and λ_Y, we have

$$t = \frac{1}{(0.1 - 1/30)} \ln\left(\frac{0.1}{1/30}\right) = 15 \ln(3)$$

or
$$t = 16.48 \text{ s} \qquad \textbf{Ans.}$$

(c) The population of X at this moment,

$$N_X = N_0\, e^{-\lambda_X t} = (10^{20})\, e^{-(0.1)(16.48)}$$
$$N_X = 1.92 \times 10^{19}$$
$$N_Y = \frac{N_X \lambda_X}{\lambda_Y} \qquad\qquad \text{[From Eq. (iv)]}$$
$$= (1.92 \times 10^{19})\, \frac{(0.1)}{(1/30)}$$
$$= 5.76 \times 10^{19}$$
$$N_Z = N_0 - N_X - N_Y$$
$$= 10^{20} - 1.92 \times 10^{19} - 5.76 \times 10^{19}$$

or $\qquad\qquad N_Z = 2.32 \times 10^{19}$

Type 2. *Based on nuclear physics*

● **Example 5** *In a nuclear reactor* ^{235}U *undergoes fission liberating* 200 *MeV of energy. The reactor has a* 10% *efficiency and produces* 1000 *MW power. If the reactor is to function for* 10 *yr, find the total mass of uranium required.* (JEE 2001)

Solution The reactor produces 1000 MW power or 10^9 J/s. The reactor is to function for 10 yr. Therefore, total energy which the reactor will supply in 10 yr is

$$E = (\text{power}) \, (\text{time})$$
$$= (10^9 \text{J/s}) \, (10 \times 365 \times 24 \times 3600 \, \text{s})$$
$$= 3.1536 \times 10^{17} \text{ J}$$

But since the efficiency of the reactor is only 10%, therefore actual energy needed is 10 times of it or 3.1536×10^{18} J. One uranium atom liberates 200 MeV of energy or $200 \times 1.6 \times 10^{-13}$ J or 3.2×10^{-11} J of energy. So, number of uranium atoms needed are

$$\frac{3.1536 \times 10^{18}}{3.2 \times 10^{-11}} = 0.9855 \times 10^{29}$$

or number of kg-moles of uranium needed are

$$n = \frac{0.9855 \times 10^{29}}{6.02 \times 10^{26}} = 163.7$$

Hence, total mass of uranium required is

$$m = (n)M = (163.7) \, (235) \text{ kg}$$

or $\qquad\qquad m \approx 38470 \text{ kg}$

or $\qquad\qquad m = 3.847 \times 10^4 \text{ kg}$

● **Example 6** *The element curium* $^{248}_{96}Cm$ *has a mean life of* 10^{13} *s. Its primary decay modes are spontaneous fission and α-decay, the former with a probability of* 8% *and the later with a probability of* 92%, *each fission releases* 200 *MeV of energy. The masses involved in decay are as follows* (JEE 1997) $^{248}_{96}Cm = 248.072220\ u,\ ^{244}_{94}Pu = 244.064100\ u\ and\ ^{4}_{2}He = 4.002603\ u.$ *Calculate the power output from a sample of* 10^{20} *Cm atoms. (* 1 *u* = 931 *MeV/c²)*

Solution The reaction involved in α-decay is

$$^{248}_{96}Cm \rightarrow\ ^{244}_{94}Pu +\ ^{4}_{2}He$$

Mass defect, $\quad\Delta m = $ mass of $^{248}_{96}Cm -$ mass of $^{244}_{94}Pu -$ mass of $^{4}_{2}He$

$$= (248.072220 - 244.064100 - 4.002603)\,u$$

$$= 0.005517\,u$$

Therefore, energy released in α-decay will be

$$E_\alpha = (0.005517 \times 931)\,MeV = 5.136\,MeV$$

Similarly, $E_{fission} = 200\,MeV$ (given)

Mean life is given as $t_{mean} = 10^{13}\,s = 1/\lambda$

∴ Disintegration constant $\lambda = 10^{-13}\,s^{-1}$

Rate of decay at the moment when number of nuclei are 10^{20}

$$= \lambda N = (10^{-13})\,(10^{20})$$

$$= 10^7 \text{ disintegration per second}$$

Of these, 8% are in fission and 92% are in α-decay.

Therefore, energy released per second

$$= (0.08 \times 10^7 \times 200 + 0.92 \times 10^7 \times 5.136)\,MeV$$

$$= 2.074 \times 10^8\,MeV$$

∴ Power output (in watt) $\quad=$ energy released per second (J/s)

$$= (2.074 \times 10^8)\,(1.6 \times 10^{-13})$$

$$= 3.32 \times 10^{-5}\,Js^{-1}$$

∴ Power output $= 3.32 \times 10^{-5}\,W$

⊙ ***Example 7*** *A nucleus X, initially at rest, undergoes alpha-decay according to the equation.* (JEE 1991)

$$^{A}_{92}X \rightarrow\ ^{228}_{Z}Y + \alpha$$

(a) *Find the values of A and Z in the above process.*

(b) *The alpha particle produced in the above process is found to move in a circular track of radius 0.11m in a uniform magnetic field of 3 T. Find the energy (in MeV) released during the process and the binding energy of the parent nucleus X.*

Given that m (Y) = 228.03 u, m $(^{1}_{0}n)$ = 1.009 u

$$m\,(^{4}_{2}He) = 4.003\ u,\ m(^{1}_{1}H) = 1.008\ u$$

Solution (a) $A - 4 = 228$

∴ $\qquad\qquad\qquad\qquad A = 232$

$$92 - 2 = Z$$

or $\qquad\qquad\qquad\qquad Z = 90$

(b) From the relation,

$$r = \frac{\sqrt{2Km}}{Bq} \quad\Rightarrow\quad K_\alpha = \frac{r^2 B^2 q^2}{2m}$$

$$= \frac{(0.11)^2 (3)^2\ (2 \times 1.6 \times 10^{-19})^2}{2 \times 4.003 \times 1.67 \times 10^{-27} \times 1.6 \times 10^{-13}}\,MeV$$

$$= 5.21\ MeV$$

From the conservation of momentum,

$$p_Y = p_\alpha \quad \text{or} \quad \sqrt{2K_Y m_Y} = \sqrt{2K_\alpha m_\alpha}$$

$$\therefore \qquad K_Y = \left(\frac{m_\alpha}{m_Y}\right) K_\alpha = \frac{4.003}{228.03} \times 5.21$$

$$= 0.09 \text{ MeV}$$

$\therefore$ Total energy released $= K_\alpha + K_Y = 5.3$ MeV

Total binding energy of daughter products

$$= [92 \times (\text{mass of proton}) + (232 - 92)(\text{mass of neutron}) - (m_Y) - (m_\alpha)] \times 931.48 \text{ MeV}$$
$$= [(92 \times 1.008) + (140)(1.009) - 228.03 - 4.003] \, 931.48 \text{ MeV}$$
$$= 1828.5 \text{ MeV}$$

$\therefore$ Binding energy of parent nucleus

$$= \text{binding energy of daughter products} - \text{energy released}$$
$$= (1828.5 - 5.3) \text{ MeV} = 1823.2 \text{ MeV}$$

⊙ **Example 8** *It is proposed to use the nuclear fusion reaction,*

$$^2_1 H + {}^2_1 H \rightarrow {}^4_2 He$$

in a nuclear reactor 200 MW rating. If the energy from the above reaction is used with a 25 per cent efficiency in the reactor, how many grams of deuterium fuel will be needed per day? (The masses of ${}^2_1 H$ and ${}^4_2 He$ are 2.0141 atomic mass units and 4.0026 atomic mass units respectively.)

(JEE 1990)

Solution Mass defect in the given nuclear reaction,

$$\Delta m = 2 \, (\text{mass of deuterium}) - (\text{mass of helium})$$
$$= 2 \, (2.0141) - (4.0026) = 0.0256$$

Therefore, energy released

$$\Delta E = (\Delta m)(931.48) \text{ MeV} = 23.85 \text{ MeV}$$
$$= 23.85 \times 1.6 \times 10^{-13} \text{ J} = 3.82 \times 10^{-12} \text{ J}$$

Efficiency is only 25%, therefore,

$$25\% \text{ of } \Delta E = \left(\frac{25}{100}\right)(3.82 \times 10^{-12}) \text{ J}$$

$$= 9.55 \times 10^{-13} \text{ J}$$

i.e. by the fusion of two deuterium nuclei, 9.55×10^{-13} J energy is available to the nuclear reactor.

Total energy required in one day to run the reactor with a given power of 200 MW,

$$E_{\text{Total}} = 200 \times 10^6 \times 24 \times 3600 = 1.728 \times 10^{13} \text{J}$$

$\therefore$ Total number of deuterium nuclei required for this purpose,

$$n = \frac{E_{\text{Total}}}{\Delta E / 2} = \frac{2 \times 1.728 \times 10^{13}}{9.55 \times 10^{-13}}$$

$$= 0.362 \times 10^{26}$$

$\therefore$ Mass of deuterium required $=$ (Number of g-moles of deuterium required) $\times$ 2 g

$$= \left(\frac{0.362 \times 10^{26}}{6.02 \times 10^{23}}\right) \times 2 = 120.26 \text{ g}$$

Miscellaneous Examples

Example 9 *Find the minimum kinetic energy of an α-particle to cause the reaction ^{14}N (α, p)^{17}O. The masses of ^{14}N, ^4He, ^1H and ^{17}O are respectively 14.00307 u, 4.00260 u, 1.00783 u and 16.99913 u.*

Solution Since, the masses are given in atomic mass units, it is easiest to proceed by finding the mass difference between reactants and products in the same units and then multiplying by 931.5 MeV/u. Thus, we have

$$Q = (14.00307 \text{ u} + 4.00260 \text{ u} - 1.00783 \text{ u} - 16.99913 \text{ u}) \left(931.5 \frac{\text{MeV}}{\text{u}}\right)$$

$$= -1.20 \text{ MeV}$$

Q-value is negative. It means reaction is endothermic.

So, the minimum kinetic energy of α-particle to initiate this reaction would be

$$K_{\min} = |Q| \left(\frac{m_\alpha}{m_N} + 1\right) = (1.20) \left(\frac{4.00260}{14.00307} + 1\right)$$

$$= 1.54 \text{ MeV} \qquad \qquad \textbf{Ans.}$$

Example 10 *Neon-23 decays in the following way,*

$$^{23}_{10}Ne \longrightarrow {}^{23}_{11}Na + {}^{0}_{-1}e + \bar{\nu}$$

Find the minimum and maximum kinetic energy that the beta particle ($_{-1}^{0}e$) can have. The atomic masses of ^{23}Ne and ^{23}Na are 22.9945 u and 22.9898 u, respectively.

Solution Here, atomic masses are given (not the nuclear masses), but still we can use them for calculating the mass defect because mass of electrons get cancelled both sides. Thus,

Mass defect $\Delta m = (22.9945 - 22.9898) = 0.0047 \text{ u}$

$\therefore \qquad\qquad Q = (0.0047 \text{ u}) (931.5 \text{ MeV/u})$

$$= 4.4 \text{ MeV}$$

Hence, the energy of beta particles can range from 0 to 4.4 MeV. $\qquad\qquad$ **Ans.**

Example 11 *The mean lives of an unstable nucleus in two different decay processes are 1620 yr and 405 yr, respectively. Find out the time during which three-fourth of a sample will decay.*

Solution Let at some instant of time t, number of nuclei are N. Then,

$$\left(\frac{-dN}{dt}\right)_{net} = \left(\frac{-dN}{dt}\right)_1 + \left(\frac{-dN}{dt}\right)_2$$

If the effective decay constant is λ, then

$$\lambda N = \lambda_1 N + \lambda_2 N$$

or $\qquad\qquad\qquad \lambda = \lambda_1 + \lambda_2 = \frac{1}{1620} + \frac{1}{405} = \frac{1}{324} \text{ year}^{-1}$

Now,
$$\frac{N_0}{4} = N_0 \, e^{-\lambda t}$$

∴
$$-\lambda t = \ln\left(\frac{1}{4}\right) = -1.386$$

or
$$\left(\frac{1}{324}\right) t = 1.386$$

∴
$$t = 449 \text{ yr} \qquad\qquad \textbf{Ans.}$$

● **Example 12** *In the chemical analysis of a rock the mass ratio of two radioactive isotopes is found to be* $100:1$. *The mean lives of the two isotopes are* 4×10^9 *years and* 2×10^9 *years, respectively. If it is assumed that at the time of formation the atoms of both the isotopes were in equal proportional, calculate the age of the rock. Ratio of the atomic weights of the two isotopes is* $1.02:1$.

Solution At the time of observation ($t = t$),

$$\frac{m_1}{m_2} = \frac{100}{1} \qquad\qquad \text{(given)}$$

Further it is given that
$$\frac{A_1}{A_2} = \frac{1.02}{1}$$

Number of atoms,
$$N = \frac{m}{A}$$

∴
$$\frac{N_1}{N_2} = \frac{m_1}{m_2} \times \frac{A_2}{A_1} = \frac{100}{1.02} \qquad\qquad \text{...(i)}$$

Let N_0 be the number of atoms of both the isotopes at the time of formation, then

$$\frac{N_1}{N_2} = \frac{N_0 \, e^{-\lambda_1 t}}{N_0 \, e^{-\lambda_2 t}} = e^{(\lambda_2 - \lambda_1) t} \qquad\qquad \text{...(ii)}$$

Eq. (i) and Eq. (ii), we have

$$e^{(\lambda_2 - \lambda_1) t} = \frac{100}{1.02}$$

or
$$(\lambda_2 - \lambda_1) t = \ln 100 - \ln 1.02$$

∴
$$t = \frac{\ln 100 - \ln 1.02}{\left(\dfrac{1}{2 \times 10^9} - \dfrac{1}{4 \times 10^9}\right)}$$

Substituting the values, we have
$$t = 1.834 \times 10^{10} \text{ yr} \qquad\qquad \textbf{Ans.}$$

● **Example 13** *A proton is bombarded on a stationary lithium nucleus. As a result of the collision, two α-particles are produced. If the direction of motion of the α-particles with the initial direction of motion makes an angle* $\cos^{-1}(1/4)$, *find the kinetic energy of the striking proton. Given, binding energies per nucleon of* Li^7 *and* He^4 *are 5.60 and 7.06 MeV, respectively.*
(Assume mass of proton $\approx$ *mass of neutron).*

Solution *Q*-value of the reaction is
$$Q = (2 \times 4 \times 7.06 - 7 \times 5.6) \text{ MeV} = 17.28 \text{ MeV}$$
Applying conservation of energy for collision,
$$K_p + Q = 2 K_\alpha \qquad \qquad \text{...(i)}$$
(Here, K_p and K_α are the kinetic energies of proton and α-particle respectively)

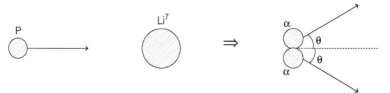

From conservation of linear momentum,
$$\sqrt{2 m_p K_p} = 2\sqrt{2 m_\alpha K_\alpha} \cos\theta \qquad \qquad \text{...(ii)}$$
$\therefore$
$$K_p = 16 K_\alpha \cos^2\theta = (16 K_\alpha)\left(\frac{1}{4}\right)^2 \qquad \qquad (\text{as } m_\alpha = 4 m_p)$$
$\therefore$
$$K_\alpha = K_p \qquad \qquad \text{...(iii)}$$
Solving Eqs. (i) and (iii) with $Q = 17.28$ MeV
We get
$$K_p = 17.28 \text{ MeV} \qquad \qquad \textbf{Ans.}$$

◉ **Example 14** *A ^{7}Li target is bombarded with a proton beam current of 10^{-4} A for 1 hour to produce ^{7}Be of activity 1.8×10^8 disintegrations per second. Assuming that one ^{7}Be radioactive nucleus is produced by bombarding 1000 protons, determine its half-life.*

Solution At time t, let say there are N atoms of ^{7}Be (radioactive). Then, net rate of formation of ^{7}Be nuclei at this instant is
$$\frac{dN}{dt} = \frac{10^{-4}}{1.6 \times 10^{-19} \times 1000} - \lambda N$$
or
$$\frac{dN}{dt} = 6.25 \times 10^{11} - \lambda N$$
or
$$\int_0^{N_0} \frac{dN}{6.25 \times 10^{11} - \lambda N} = \int_0^{3600} dt$$
where, N_0 are the number of nuclei at $t = 1$ h or 3600 s.
$\therefore$
$$-\frac{1}{\lambda} \ln\left(\frac{6.25 \times 10^{11} - \lambda N_0}{6.25 \times 10^{11}}\right) = 3600$$

λN_0 = activity of ^{7}Be at $t = 1$ h = 1.8×10^8 disintegrations/s
$\therefore$
$$-\frac{1}{\lambda} \ln\left(\frac{6.25 \times 10^{11} - 1.8 \times 10^8}{6.25 \times 10^{11}}\right) = 3600$$
$\therefore$
$$\lambda = 8.0 \times 10^{-8} \text{ sec}^{-1}$$
Therefore, half-life
$$t_{1/2} = \frac{0.693}{8.0 \times 10^{-8}} = 8.66 \times 10^6 \text{ s}$$

$$= 100.26 \text{ days} \qquad \qquad \textbf{Ans.}$$

⊚ **Example 15** A ^{118}Cd *radio nuclide goes through the transformation chain.*

$$^{118}Cd \xrightarrow[30\,min]{} {}^{118}\text{In} \xrightarrow[45\,min]{} {}^{118}Sn \;(stable)$$

The half-lives are written below the respective arrows. At time $t = 0$ *only Cd was present. Find the fraction of nuclei transformed into stable over 60 minutes.*

Solution At time $t = t$, $N_1 = N_0\, e^{-\lambda_1 t}$ and $N_2 = \dfrac{N_0 \lambda_1}{\lambda_2 - \lambda_1}(e^{-\lambda_1 t} - e^{-\lambda_2 t})$ (see Article 34.3)

∴
$$N_3 = N_0 - N_1 - N_2$$
$$= N_0\left[1 - e^{-\lambda_1 t} - \frac{\lambda_1}{\lambda_2 - \lambda_1}(e^{-\lambda_1 t} - e^{-\lambda_2 t})\right]$$

∴
$$\frac{N_3}{N_0} = 1 - e^{-\lambda_1 t} - \frac{\lambda_1}{\lambda_2 - \lambda_1}(e^{-\lambda_1 t} - e^{-\lambda_2 t})$$

$$\lambda_1 = \frac{0.693}{30} = 0.0231 \text{ min}^{-1}$$

$$\lambda_2 = \frac{0.693}{45} = 0.0154 \text{ min}^{-1}$$

and
$$t = 60 \text{ min}$$

∴
$$\frac{N_3}{N_0} = 1 - e^{-0.0231 \times 60} - \frac{0.0231}{0.0154 - 0.0231}(e^{-0.0231 \times 60} - e^{-0.0154 \times 60})$$

$$= 1 - 0.25 + 3\,(0.25 - 0.4)$$
$$= 0.31 \qquad\qquad\qquad\qquad\qquad \textbf{Ans.}$$

⊚ **Example 16** *Natural uranium is a mixture of three isotopes* $^{234}_{92}U$, $^{235}_{92}U$ *and* $^{238}_{92}U$ *with mass percentage* $0.01\%, 0.71\%$ *and* 99.28% *respectively. The half-life of three isotopes are* 2.5×10^5 *yr,* 7.1×10^8 *yr and* 4.5×10^9 *yr respectively. Determine the share of radioactivity of each isotope into the total activity of the natural uranium.*

Solution Let R_1, R_2 and R_3 be the activities of U^{234}, U^{235} and U^{238} respectively.

Total activity,
$$R = R_1 + R_2 + R_3$$

Share of U^{234},
$$\frac{R_1}{R} = \frac{\lambda_1 N_1}{\lambda_1 N_1 + \lambda_2 N_2 + \lambda_3 N_3}$$

Let m be the total mass of natural uranium.

Then,
$$m_1 = \frac{0.01}{100}\,m\,, \quad m_2 = \frac{0.71}{100}\,m \quad \text{and} \quad m_3 = \frac{99.28}{100}\,m$$

Now,
$$N_1 = \frac{m_1}{M_1}, \qquad N_2 = \frac{m_2}{M_2} \quad \text{and} \quad N_3 = \frac{m_3}{M_3}$$

where M_1, M_2 and M_3 are atomic weights.

∴
$$\frac{R_1}{R} = \frac{\left(\dfrac{m_1}{M_1}\right)\dfrac{1}{T_1}}{\dfrac{m_1}{M_1}\dfrac{1}{T_1} + \dfrac{m_2}{M_2}\cdot\dfrac{1}{T_2} + \dfrac{m_3}{M_3}\cdot\dfrac{1}{T_3}}$$

$$= \frac{\dfrac{(0.01/100)}{234} \times \dfrac{1}{2.5 \times 10^5 \text{ years}}}{\left(\dfrac{0.01/100}{234}\right)\left(\dfrac{1}{2.5 \times 10^5}\right) + \left(\dfrac{0.71/100}{235}\right)\left(\dfrac{1}{7.1 \times 10^8}\right) + \left(\dfrac{99.28/100}{238}\right)\left(\dfrac{1}{4.5 \times 10^9}\right)}$$

$$= 0.648 \approx 64.8 \%$$

Similarly, share of $\qquad\qquad U^{235} = 0.016\%$

and of $\qquad\qquad U^{238} = 35.184 \%$ **Ans.**

◉ **Example 17** *Uranium ores on the earth at the present time typically have a composition consisting of 99.3% of the isotope $_{92}U^{238}$ and 0.7% of the isotope $_{92}U^{235}$. The half-lives of these isotopes are 4.47×10^9 yr and 7.04×10^8 yr, respectively. If these isotopes were equally abundant when the earth was formed, estimate the age of the earth.*

Solution Let N_0 be number of atoms of each isotope at the time of formation of the earth ($t = 0$) and N_1 and N_2 the number of atoms at present ($t = t$). Then,

$$N_1 = N_0 e^{-\lambda_1 t} \qquad\qquad \text{...(i)}$$

and $\qquad\qquad N_2 = N_0 e^{-\lambda_2 t} \qquad\qquad \text{...(ii)}$

∴ $\qquad\qquad \dfrac{N_1}{N_2} = e^{(\lambda_2 - \lambda_1)t} \qquad\qquad \text{...(iii)}$

Further it is given that

$$\dfrac{N_1}{N_2} = \dfrac{99.3}{0.7} \qquad\qquad \text{...(iv)}$$

Equating Eqs. (iii) and (iv) and taking log on both sides, we have

$$(\lambda_2 - \lambda_1)\, t = \ln\left(\frac{99.3}{0.7}\right)$$

∴ $\qquad\qquad t = \left(\dfrac{1}{\lambda_2 - \lambda_1}\right) \ln\left(\dfrac{99.3}{0.7}\right)$

Substituting the values, we have

$$t = \frac{1}{\dfrac{0.693}{7.04 \times 10^8} - \dfrac{0.693}{4.47 \times 10^9}} \ln\left(\frac{99.3}{0.7}\right)$$

or $\qquad\qquad t = 5.97 \times 10^9$ yr **Ans.**

Exercises

LEVEL 1

Assertion and Reason

Directions : *Choose the correct option.*
(*a*) *If both* **Assertion** *and* **Reason** *are true and the* **Reason** *is correct explanation of the* **Assertion.**
(*b*) *If both* **Assertion** *and* **Reason** *are true but* **Reason** *is not the correct explanation of* **Assertion.**
(*c*) *If* **Assertion** *is true, but the* **Reason** *is false.*
(*d*) *If* **Assertion** *is false but the* **Reason** *is true.*
(*e*) *Both* **Assertion** *and* **Reason** *are false.*

1. **Assertion :** Rate of radioactivity cannot be increased or decreased by increasing or decreasing pressure or temperature.
   Reason : Rate depends on the number of nuclei present in the radioactive sample.

2. **Assertion :** Only those nuclei which are heavier than lead are radioactive.
   Reason : Nuclei of elements heavier than lead are unstable.

3. **Assertion :** γ-rays are produced by the transition of a nucleus from some higher energy state to some lower energy state.
   Reason : Electromagnetic waves are always produced by the transition process.

4. **Assertion :** If we compare the stability of two nuclei, then that nucleus is more stable whose total binding energy is more.
   Reason : More the mass defect during formation of a nucleus more will be the binding energy.

5. **Assertion :** In a nuclear process energy is released if total binding energy of daughter nuclei is more than the total binding energy of parent nuclei.
   Reason : If energy is released then total mass of daughter nuclei is less than the total mass of parent nuclei.

6. **Assertion :** 1 amu is equal to 931.48 MeV.
   Reason : 1 amu is equal to $\dfrac{1}{12}$th the mass of C^{12} atom.

7. **Assertion :** Between α, β and γ radiations, penetrating power of γ-rays is maximum.
   Reason : Ionising power of γ-rays is least.

Objective Questions

1. For uranium nucleus how does its mass vary with volume?
   (a) $m \propto V$
   (b) $m \propto 1/V$
   (c) $m \propto \sqrt{V}$
   (d) $m \propto V^2$

2. The half-life of a radioactive substance is 20 min. The approximate time interval $(t_1 - t_2)$ between the time t_1 when 2/3 of it has decayed and time t_2 when 1/3 of it had decayed is
   (a) 7 min   (b) 14 min   (c) 20 min   (d) 28 min

3. The binding energy per nucleon for deuteron $[{}^{2}_{1}\text{H}]$ and helium $[{}^{4}_{2}\text{He}]$ are 1.1 MeV and 7 MeV, respectively. The energy released when two deuterons fuse to form a helium nucleus is
(a) 32.4 MeV
(b) 23.6 MeV
(c) 16.2 MeV
(d) 11.8 MeV

4. In the nucleus of helium if F_1 is the nuclear force between two protons, F_2 is the force between two neutrons and F_3 is the force between a proton and a neutron. Then,
(a) $F_1 = F_2 = F_3$
(b) $F_1 > F_2 > F_3$
(c) $F_2 > F_3 > F_1$
(d) $F_2 = F_3 > F_1$

5. What are the respective number of α and β-particles emitted in the following radioactive decay?
$$\,^{200}_{90}X \rightarrow \,^{168}_{80}Y$$
(a) 6 and 8
(b) 6 and 6
(c) 8 and 8
(d) 8 and 6

6. If an atom of $^{235}_{92}\text{U}$, after absorbing a slow neutron, undergoes fission to form an atom of $^{138}_{54}\text{Xe}$ and an atom of $^{94}_{38}\text{Sr}$, the other particles produced are
(a) one proton and two neutrons
(b) three neutrons
(c) two neutrons
(d) one proton and one neutron

7. Nucleus A is converted into C through the following reactions,
$$A \rightarrow B + \alpha$$
$$B \rightarrow C + 2\beta$$
then,
(a) A and B are isotopes
(b) A and C are isobars
(c) A and B are isobars
(d) A and C are isotopes

8. The binding energy of α-particle is
$$(\text{if } m_p = 1.00785 \text{ u}, \ m_n = 1.00866 \text{ u and } m_\alpha = 4.00274 \text{ u})$$
(a) 56.42 MeV
(b) 2.821 MeV
(c) 28.21 MeV
(d) 32.4 MeV

9. $\dfrac{7}{8}$ th of the active nuclei present in a radioactive sample has decayed in 8 s. The half-life of the sample is
(a) 2 s
(b) 1 s
(c) 7 s
(d) $\dfrac{8}{3}$ s

10. The binding energies of the nuclei A and B are E_A and E_B, respectively. Three atoms of the element B fuse to give one atom of element A and an energy Q is released. Then, E_A, E_B and Q are related as
(a) $E_A - 3E_B = Q$
(b) $3E_B - E_A = Q$
(c) $E_A + 3E_B = Q$
(d) $E_B + 3E_A = Q$

11. The sun radiates energy in all directions. The average radiations received on the earth's surface from the sun is 1.4 kW/m^2. The average earth-sun distance is 1.5×10^{11} m . The mass lost by the sun per day is (1 day = 86400 s)
(a) 4.4×10^9 kg
(b) 7.6×10^{14} kg
(c) 3.8×10^{12} kg
(d) 3.8×10^{14} kg

12. A sample of radioactive substance loses half of its activity in 4 days. The time in which its activity is reduced to 5% is
(a) 12 days
(b) 8.3 days
(c) 17.3 days
(d) None of these

13. On bombardment of U^{235} by slow neutrons, 200 MeV energy is released. If the power output of atomic reactor is 1.6 MW, then the rate of fission will be
(a) 5×10^{16} per second
(b) 10×10^{16} per second
(c) 15×10^{16} per second
(d) 20×10^{16} per second

14. In a radioactive sample, the fraction of initial number of radioactive nuclei, which remains undecayed after n mean lives is
(a) $\dfrac{1}{e^n}$
(b) e^n
(c) $1 - \dfrac{1}{e^n}$
(d) $\left(\dfrac{1}{e-1}\right)^n$

15. A radioactive element is disintegrating having half-life 6.93 s. The fractional change in number of nuclei of the radioactive element during 10 s is
(a) 0.37
(b) 0.63
(c) 0.25
(d) 0.50

16. The activity of a radioactive sample goes down to about 6% in a time of 2 hour. The half-life of the sample in minute is about
(a) 30
(b) 15
(c) 60
(d) 120

17. What is the probability of a radioactive nucleus to survive one mean life?
(a) $\dfrac{1}{e}$
(b) $\dfrac{1}{e+1}$
(c) $1 - \dfrac{1}{e}$
(d) $\dfrac{1}{e} - 1$

18. In which sequence, the radioactive radiations are emitted in the following nuclear reactions?
$$_Z X^A \rightarrow {}_{Z+1}Y^A \rightarrow {}_{Z-1}K^{A-4} \rightarrow {}_{Z-1}K^{A-4}$$
(a) β, α and γ
(b) α, β and γ
(c) β, γ and α
(d) γ, α and β

19. A radioactive substance A disintegrates into a radioactive substance B. Let n_A and n_B denote the number of nuclei of A and B surviving against radioactive decay at any moment and λ_A and λ_B be the respective disintegration constants. The rate of change in number of nuclei of the substance B is given by
(a) $\dfrac{dn_B}{dt} = \lambda_A n_A - \lambda_B n_B$
(b) $\dfrac{dn_B}{dt} = -\lambda_A n_A + \lambda_B n_B$
(c) $\dfrac{dn_B}{dt} = -\lambda_A n_A - \lambda_B n_B$
(d) $\dfrac{dn_B}{dt} = \lambda_A n_A + \lambda_B n_B$

20. A gamma ray photon creates an electron-positron pair. If the rest mass energy of an electron is 0.5 MeV and the total kinetic energy of the electron-positron pair is 0.78 MeV, then the energy of the gamma ray photon must be
(a) 0.78 MeV
(b) 1.78 MeV
(c) 1.28 MeV
(d) 0.25 MeV

21. In the reaction $^2_1H + {}^3_1H \rightarrow {}^4_2He + {}^1n_0$, if the binding energies of ^2_1H, ^3_1H and ^4_2He are respectively a, b and c (in MeV), then the energy (in MeV) released in this reaction is
(a) $c + a - b$ (b) $c - a - b$
(c) $a + b + c$ (d) $a + b - c$

22. A radioactive sample has N_0 active atoms at $t = 0$. If the rate of disintegration at any time is R and the number of atoms is N, then the ratio R/N varies with time as

(a) 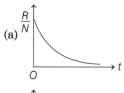   (b)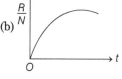

(c) 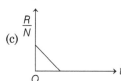   (d)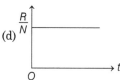

23. An atom of mass number 15 and atomic number 7 captures an α-particle and then emits a proton. The mass number and atomic number of the resulting product will respectively be
(a) 14 and 2   (b) 15 and 3
(c) 16 and 4   (d) 18 and 8

24. A radioactive nucleus is being produced at a constant rate α per second. Its decay constant is λ. If N_0 are the number of nuclei at time $t = 0$, then maximum number of nuclei possible are
(a) $\dfrac{\alpha}{\lambda}$ (b) $N_0 + \dfrac{\alpha}{\lambda}$

(c) N_0 (d) $\dfrac{\lambda}{\alpha} + N_0$

25. A nuclear reaction along with the masses of the particles taking part in it is as follows

$$\begin{array}{ccccccc} A & + & B & \rightarrow & C & + & D & + Q\text{ MeV} \\ 1.002 & & 1.004 & & 1.001 & & 1.003 \\ \text{amu} & & \text{amu} & & \text{amu} & & \text{amu} \end{array}$$

The energy Q liberated in the reaction is
(a) 1.234 MeV
(b) 0.931 MeV
(c) 0.465 MeV
(d) 1.863 MeV

Subjective Questions

Note You can take approximations in the answers.

1. The disintegration rate of a certain radioactive sample at any instant is 4750 disintegrations per minute. Five minutes later the rate becomes 2700 per minute. Calculate
(a) decay constant and
(b) half-life of the sample

2. A radioactive sample contains 1.00×10^{15} atoms and has an activity of 6.00×10^{11} Bq. What is its half-life?

3. Obtain the amount of ^{60}Co necessary to provide a radioactive source of 8.0 Ci strength. The half-life of ^{60}Co is 5.3 years?

4. The half-life of $^{238}_{92}$U against alpha decay is 4.5×10^9 year. How much disintegration per second occurs in 1 g of $^{238}_{92}$U ?

5. What is the probability that a radioactive atom having a mean life of 10 days decays during the fifth day?

6. In an ore containing uranium, the ratio of ^{238}U to ^{206}Pb nuclei is 3. Calculate the age of the ore, assuming that all the lead present in the ore is the final stable product of ^{238}U. Take the half-life of ^{238}U to be 4.5×10^9 years.

7. The half-lives of radioisotopes P^{32} and P^{33} are 14 days and 25 days respectively. These radioisotopes are mixed in the ratio of 4 : 1 of their atoms. If the initial activity of the mixed sample is 3.0 mCi, find the activity of the mixed isotopes after 60 years.

8. Complete the following reactions.
   (a) $^{226}_{88}$Ra $\rightarrow \alpha +$
   (b) $^{19}_{8}$O $\rightarrow ^{19}_{9}$F$+$
   (c) $^{25}_{13}$Al $\rightarrow ^{25}_{12}$Mg$+$

9. Obtain the binding energy of a nitrogen nucleus from the following data :
$$m_H = 1.00783 \text{ u}, \ m_N = 1.00867 \text{ u}, \ m\left(^{14}_{7}\text{N}\right) = 14.00307 \text{ u}$$
Give your answer in units of MeV. [Remember $1\,\text{u} = 931.5$ MeV/c^2]

10. 8 protons and 8 neutrons are separately at rest. How much energy will be released if we form $^{16}_{8}$O nucleus?

   Given :
$$\text{Mass of } ^{16}_{8} \text{ O atom} = 15.994915 \text{ u}$$
$$\text{Mass of neutron} = 1.008665 \text{ u}$$
$$\text{Mass of hydrogen atom} = 1.007825 \text{ u}$$

11. Assuming the splitting of U^{235} nucleus liberates 200 MeV energy, find
   (a) the energy liberated in the fission of 1 kg of U^{235} and
   (b) the mass of the coal with calorific value of 30 kJ/g which is equivalent to 1 kg of U^{235}.

12. $^{212}_{83}$Bi decays as per following equation.
$$^{212}_{83}\text{Bi} \rightarrow ^{208}_{81}\text{Tl} + ^{4}_{2}\text{He}$$
The kinetic energy of α-particle emitted is 6.802 MeV. Calculate the kinetic energy of Tl recoil atoms.

13. In a neutron induced fission of $_{92}$U^{235} nucleus, usable energy of 185 MeV is released. If $_{92}$U^{235} reactor is continuously operating it at a power level of 100 MW power, how long will it take for 1 kg of uranium to be consumed in this reactor?

LEVEL 2

Single Correct Option

1. The count rate observed from a radioactive source at t second was N_0 and at $4t$ second it was $\dfrac{N_0}{16}$. The count rate observed at $\left(\dfrac{11}{2}\right) t$ second will be

(a) $\dfrac{N_0}{128}$

(b) $\dfrac{N_0}{64}$

(c) $\dfrac{N_0}{32}$

(d) None of these

2. The half-lives of a radioactive sample are 30 years and 60 years for two decay processes. If the sample decays by both the processes simultaneously. The time after which, only one-fourth of the sample will remain is

(a) 10 years

(b) 20 years

(c) 40 years

(d) 60 years

3. Consider the nuclear fission reaction $W \rightarrow X + Y$. What is the Q-value (energy released) of the reaction?

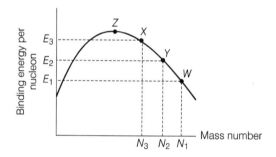

(a) $E_1 N_1 - (E_2 N_2 + E_3 N_3)$

(b) $(E_2 N_2 + E_3 N_3 - E_1 N_1)$

(c) $E_2 N_2 + E_1 N_1 - E_3 N_3$

(d) $E_1 N_1 + E_3 N_3 - E_2 N_2$

4. A radioactive element A of decay constant λ_A decays into another radioactive element B of decay constant λ_B. Initially, the number of active nuclei of A was N_0 and B was absent in the sample. The maximum number of active nuclei of B is found at $t = 2\,\dfrac{\ln 2}{\lambda_A}$. The maximum number of active nuclei of B is

(a) $\dfrac{N_0}{4}$

(b) $\dfrac{\lambda_A}{\lambda_B} N_0 e^{-\lambda_B t}$

(c) $\dfrac{\lambda_A}{\lambda_B} \dfrac{N_0}{4}$

(d) None of these

5. The energy released by the fission of a single uranium nucleus is 200 MeV. The number of fissions of uranium nucleus per second required to produce 16 MW of power is
(Assume efficiency of the reactor is 50%)

(a) 2×10^6

(b) 2.5×10^6

(c) 5×10^6

(d) None of these

6. A radioactive isotope is being produced at a constant rate A. The isotope has a half-life T. Initially, there are no nuclei, after a time $t >> T$, the number of nuclei becomes constant. The value of this constant is

(a) AT

(b) $\dfrac{A}{T} \ln 2$

(c) $AT \ln 2$

(d) $\dfrac{AT}{\ln 2}$

7. A bone containing 200 g carbon-14 has a β-decay rate of 375 decay/min. Calculate the time that has elapsed since the death of the living one. Given the rate of decay for the living organism is equal to 15 decay per min per gram of carbon and half-life of carbon-14 is 5730 years.

(a) 27190 years

(b) 1190 years

(c) 17190 years

(d) None of these

8. Two identical samples (same material and same amount) P and Q of a radioactive substance having mean life T are observed to have activities A_P and A_Q respectively at the time of observation. If P is older than Q, then the difference in their age is

(a) $T \ln \left(\dfrac{A_P}{A_Q} \right)$

(b) $T \ln \left(\dfrac{A_Q}{A_P} \right)$

(c) $T \left(\dfrac{A_P}{A_Q} \right)$

(d) $T \left(\dfrac{A_Q}{A_P} \right)$

9. A star initially has 10^{40} deuterons. It produces energy *via* the processes $^2_1\text{H} + {}^2_1\text{H} \rightarrow {}^3_1\text{H} + p$ and $^2_1\text{H} + {}^3_1\text{H} \rightarrow {}^4_2\text{He} + n$. Where the masses of the nuclei are $m\,(^2\text{H}) = 2.014$ amu, $m(p) = 1.007$ amu, $m(n) = 1.008$ amu and $m(^4\text{He}) = 4.001$ amu. If the average power radiated by the star is 10^{16} W, the deuteron supply of the star is exhausted in a time of the order of

(a) 10^6 s

(b) 10^8 s

(c) 10^{12} s

(d) 10^{16} s

10. Two radioactive samples of different elements (half-lives t_1 and t_2 respectively) have same number of nuclei at $t = 0$. The time after which their activities are same is

(a) $\dfrac{t_1 t_2}{0.693\,(t_2 - t_1)} \ln \dfrac{t_2}{t_1}$

(b) $\dfrac{t_1 t_2}{0.693} \ln \dfrac{t_2}{t_1}$

(c) $\dfrac{t_1 t_2}{0.693\,(t_1 + t_2)} \ln \dfrac{t_2}{t_1}$

(d) None of these

11. A nucleus X initially at rest, undergoes alpha decay according to the equation

$$^{232}_{Z}X \rightarrow {}^{A}_{90}Y + \alpha$$

What fraction of the total energy released in the decay will be the kinetic energy of the alpha particle?

(a) $\dfrac{90}{92}$

(b) $\dfrac{228}{232}$

(c) $\sqrt{\dfrac{228}{232}}$

(d) $\dfrac{1}{2}$

12. A stationary nucleus of mass 24 amu emits a gamma photon. The energy of the emitted photon is 7 MeV. The recoil energy of the nucleus is

(a) 2.2 keV

(b) 1.1 keV

(c) 3.1 keV

(d) 22 keV

13. A radioactive material of half-life T was kept in a nuclear reactor at two different instants. The quantity kept second time was twice of that kept first time. If now their present activities are A_1 and A_2 respectively, then their age difference equals

(a) $\dfrac{T}{\ln 2} \ln \dfrac{2A_1}{A_2}$

(b) $T \ln \dfrac{A_1}{A_2}$

(c) $\dfrac{T}{\ln 2} \ln \dfrac{A_2}{2A_1}$

(d) $T \ln \dfrac{A_2}{2A_1}$

14 What is the binding energy per nucleon of $_6C^{12}$ nucleus?

Given : Mass of C^{12} $(m_c) = 12.000$ u

Mass of proton $(m_p) = 1.0078$ u

Mass of neutron $(m_n) = 1.0087$ u

and $\qquad$ 1 amu $= 931.4 \dfrac{\text{MeV}}{c^2}$

(a) 5.26 MeV

(b) 6.2 MeV

(c) 4.65 MeV

(d) 7.68 MeV

15. Two radioactive substances A and B have decay constants 5λ and λ respectively. At $t = 0$ they have the same number of nuclei. The ratio of number of nuclei of A to those of B will be $\left(\dfrac{1}{e}\right)^2$ after a time interval

(a) $\dfrac{1}{4\lambda}$

(b) 4λ

(c) 2λ

(d) $\dfrac{1}{2\lambda}$

16. A radioactive nucleus of mass M emits a photon of frequency ν and the nucleus recoils. The recoil energy will be

(a) $h^2\nu^2/2Mc^2$

(b) zero

(c) $h\nu$

(d) $Mc^2 - h\nu$

17. A particular nucleus in a large population of identical radioactive nuclei did survive 5 half-lives of that isotope. Then, the probability that this surviving nucleus will survive the next half-life, is

(a) $\dfrac{1}{32}$

(b) $\dfrac{1}{5}$

(c) $\dfrac{1}{2}$

(d) $\dfrac{1}{10}$

18. The activity of a sample of radioactive material is A_1 at time t_1 and A_2 at time $t_2(t_2 > t_1)$. Its mean life is T.

(a) $A_1 t_1 = A_2 t_2$

(b) $\dfrac{A_1 - A_2}{t_2 - t_1} =$ constant

(c) $A_2 = A_1 e^{\left(\frac{t_1 - t_2}{T}\right)}$

(d) $A_2 = A_1 e^{\left(\frac{t_1}{t_2 T}\right)}$

19. The activity of a radioactive sample is measured as N_0 counts per minute at $t = 0$ and $\dfrac{N_0}{e}$ counts per minute at $t = 5$ min. The time (in minute) at which the activity reduces to half its value is

(a) $\log_e 2/5$

(b) $\dfrac{5}{\log_e 2}$

(c) $5 \log_{10} 2$

(d) $5 \log_e 2$

20. Two radioactive nuclei A and B have disintegration constants λ_A and λ_B and initially N_A and N_B number of nuclei of them are taken, then the time after which their undecayed nuclei are same is

(a) $\dfrac{\lambda_A \lambda_B}{(\lambda_A - \lambda_B)} \ln\left(\dfrac{N_B}{N_A}\right)$

(b) $\dfrac{1}{(\lambda_A + \lambda_B)} \ln\left(\dfrac{N_B}{N_A}\right)$

(c) $\dfrac{1}{(\lambda_B - \lambda_A)} \ln\left(\dfrac{N_B}{N_A}\right)$

(d) $\dfrac{1}{(\lambda_A - \lambda_B)} \ln\left(\dfrac{N_B}{N_A}\right)$

21. For a radioactive sample at given instant, number of active nuclei is N_0 and its decay constant is λ, then the **incorrect** relation is

(a) $N_0 \lambda$ = activity at given instant

(b) λ = decay probability per unit time of a nucleus

(c) after the next $\dfrac{1}{\lambda}$ time interval active nuclei in the sample will be $\dfrac{N_0}{e}$

(d) The half-life of the sample $= \dfrac{\ln 2}{\lambda}$

22. The half-life of radium is 1620 yr and its atomic weight is 226 kg/k-mol. The number of atoms that will decay from its 1 g sample per second will be (Avogadro number $N = 6.023 \times 10^{23}$ atom/mol)

(a) 3.61×10^{10}

(b) 3.6×10^{12}

(c) 3.11×10^{15}

(d) 31.1×10^{15}

More than One Correct Options

1. At $t = 0$, number of radioactive nuclei of a radioactive substance are x and its radioactivity is y. Half-life of radioactive substance is T. Then,

(a) $\dfrac{x}{y}$ is constant throughout

(b) $\dfrac{x}{y} > T$

(c) value of xy remains half after one half-life

(d) value of xy remains one fourth after one half-life

2. Choose the correct options.

(a) Isotopes have same number of atomic number

(b) Isobars have same atomic weight

(c) Isotones have same number of neutrons

(d) In neutral isotope atoms number of electrons are same

3. Choose the correct options.

(a) By gamma radiations atomic number is not changed

(b) By gamma radiations mass number is not changed

(c) By the emission of one α and two β particles isotopes are produced

(d) By the emission of one α and four β particles isobars are produced

4. Two radioactive substances have half-lives T and $2T$. Initially, they have equal number of nuclei. After time $t = 4T$, the ratio of their number of nuclei is x and the ratio of their activity is y. Then,

(a) $x = 1/8$ 　　(b) $x = 1/4$ 　　(c) $y = 1/2$ 　　(d) $y = 1/4$

5. Regarding the nuclear forces, choose the correct options.
   (a) They are short range forces
   (b) They are charge independent forces
   (c) They are not electromagnetic forces
   (d) They are exchange forces

6. Regarding a nucleus choose the correct options.
   (a) Density of a nucleus is directly proportional to mass number A
   (b) Density of all the nuclei is almost constant of the order of 10^{17} kg/m^3
   (c) Nucleus radius is of the order of 10^{-15} m
   (d) Nucleus radius $\propto A$

7. Assume that the nuclear binding energy per nucleon (B/A) *versus* mass number (A) is as shown in the figure. Consider a nucleus of $A = 110$. Fission of this nucleus results into 2 fragments.

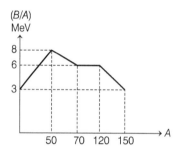

   Which of the following could possibly be the mass number of the resulting nuclei to release energy in fission?
   (a) 55 and 55   (b) 60 and 50
   (c) 100 and 10   (d) 90 and 20

Comprehension Based Questions

Passage : 1 (Q. No. 1 to 3)

The atomic masses of the hydrogen isotopes are
$$\text{Hydrogen } m(_1\text{H}^1) = 1.007825 \ amu$$
$$\text{Deuterium } m(_1\text{H}^2) = 2.014102 \ amu$$
$$\text{Tritium } m(_1\text{H}^3) = 3.016049 \ amu$$

1. The energy released in the reaction, $_1\text{H}^2 + _1\text{H}^2 \rightarrow _1\text{H}^3 + _1\text{H}^1$ is nearly
   (a) 1 MeV   (b) 2 MeV
   (c) 4 MeV   (d) 8 MeV

2. The number of fusion reactions required to generate 1 kWh is nearly
   (a) 10^8 (b) 10^{18}
   (c) 10^{28} (d) 10^{38}

3. The mass of deuterium, $_1\text{H}^2$ that would be needed to generate 1 kWh
   (a) 3.7 kg   (b) 3.7 g
   (c) 3.7×10^{-5} kg   (d) 3.7×10^{-8} kg

Passage : 2 (Q. No. 4 to 5)

A number of mass $M + \Delta m$ is at rest and decays into two daughter nuclei of equal mass $\dfrac{M}{2}$ each.

Speed of light is c.

4. The binding energy per nucleon for the parent nucleus is E_1 and that for the daughter nuclei is E_2. Then,

(a) $E_2 = 2E_1$ (b) $E_1 > E_2$

(c) $E_2 > E_1$ (d) $E_1 = 2E_2$

5. The speed of daughter nuclei is

(a) $c\dfrac{\Delta m}{M + \Delta m}$ (b) $c\sqrt{\dfrac{2\Delta m}{M}}$

(c) $c\sqrt{\dfrac{\Delta m}{M}}$ (d) $c\sqrt{\dfrac{\Delta m}{M + \Delta m}}$

Match the Columns

1. At $t = 0$, x nuclei of a radioactive substance emit y nuclei per second. Match the following two columns.

Column I	Column II
(a) Decay constant λ	(p) $(\ln 2)\,(x/y)$
(b) Half-life	(q) x/y
(c) Activity after time $t = \dfrac{1}{\lambda}$	(r) y/e
(d) Number of nuclei after time $t = \dfrac{1}{\lambda}$	(s) None of these

2. Corresponding to the graph shown in figure, match the following two columns.

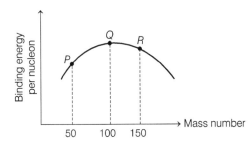

Column I	Column II
(a) $P + P = Q$	(p) energy is released
(b) $P + P + P = R$	(q) energy is absorbed
(c) $P + R = 2Q$	(r) No energy transfer will take place
(d) $P + Q = R$	(s) data insufficient

3. In the following chain,

$$A \rightarrow B \rightarrow C$$

A and B are radioactive, while C is stable. Initially, we have only A and B nuclei. There is no nucleus of C. As the time passes, match the two columns.

Column I	Column II
(a) Nuclei of $(A + B)$	(p) will increase continuously
(b) Nuclei of B	(q) will decrease continuously
(c) Nuclei of $(C + B)$	(r) will first increase then decrease
(d) Nuclei of $(A + C)$	(s) data insufficient

4. Match the following two columns.

Column I	Column II
(a) The energy of air molecules at room temperature	(p) 0.02 eV
(b) Binding energy of heavy nuclei per nucleon	(q) 2 eV
(c) X-ray photon energy	(r) 10 keV
(d) Photon energy of visible light	(s) 7 MeV

Subjective Questions

1. A F^{32} radio nuclide with half-life $T = 14.3$ hours is produced in a reactor at a constant rate $q = 2 \times 10^9$ nuclei per second. How soon after the beginning of production of that radio nuclide will its activity be equal to $R = 10^9$ disintegration per second?

2. Consider a radioactive disintegration according to the equation $A \rightarrow B \rightarrow C$. Decay constant of A and B is same and equal to λ. Number of nuclei of A, B and C are $N_0, 0, 0$ respectively at $t = 0$. Find

(a) number of nuclei of B as function of time t.

(b) time t at which the activity of B is maximum and the value of maximum activity of B.

3. Nuclei of a radioactive element A are being produced at a constant rate α. The element has a decay constant λ. At time $t = 0$, there are N_0 nuclei of the element.

(a) Calculate the number N of nuclei of A at time t.

(b) If $\alpha = 2N_0\lambda$, calculate the number of nuclei of A after one half-life of A, and also the limiting value of N as $t \rightarrow \infty$.

4. A solution contains a mixture of two isotopes A (half-life = 10 days) and B (half-life = 5 days). Total activity of the mixture is 10^{10} disintegration per second at time $t = 0$. The activity reduces to 20% in 20 days. Find (a) the initial activities of A and B, (b) the ratio of initial number of their nuclei.

5. A radio nuclide with disintegration constant λ is produced in a reactor at a constant rate α nuclei per second. During each decay energy E_0 is released.20% of this energy is utilized in increasing the temperature of water. Find the increase in temperature of m mass of water in time t. Specific heat of water is s. Assume that there is no loss of energy through water surface.

6. A stable nuclei C is formed from two radioactive nuclei A and B with decay constant of λ_1 and λ_2 respectively. Initially, the number of nuclei of A is N_0 and that of B is zero. Nuclei B are produced at a constant rate of P. Find the number of the nuclei of C after time t.

7. Polonium ($^{210}_{84}$Po) emits $^4_2$He particles and is converted into lead ($^{206}_{82}$Pb). This reaction is used for producing electric power in a space mission. Po^{210} has half-life of 138.6 days. Assuming an efficiency of 10% for the thermoelectric machine, how much ^{210}Po is required to produce 1.2×10^7 J of electric energy per day at the end of 693 days. Also find the initial activity of the material.

Given : Masses of nuclei

^{210}Po $= 209.98264$ amu, $\quad ^{206}$Pb $= 205.97440$ amu, $\quad ^4_2$He $= 4.00260$ amu,

1 amu $= 931$ MeV/c^2 and Avogadro's number $= 6 \times 10^{23}$/mol

8. A radio nuclide consists of two isotopes. One of the isotopes decays by α-emission and other by β-emission with half-lives $T_1 = 405$ s and $T_2 = 1620$ s, respectively. At $t = 0$, probabilities of getting α and β-particles from the radio nuclide are equal. Calculate their respective probabilities at $t = 1620$ s. If at $t = 0$, total number of nuclei in the radio nuclide are N_0. Calculate the time t when total number of nuclei remained undecayed becomes equal to $N_0/2$.

$\log_{10} 2 = 0.3010, \log_{10} 5.94 = 0.7742$ and $x^4 + 4x - 2.5 = 0, x = 0.594$

9. Find the amount of heat generated by 1 mg of Po^{210} preparation during the mean life period of these nuclei if the emitted alpha particles are known to possess kinetic energy 5.3 MeV and practically all daughter nuclei are formed directly in the ground state.

10. In an agricultural experiment, a solution containing 1 mole of a radioactive material ($T_{1/2} = 14.3$ days) was injected into the roots of a plant. The plant was allowed 70 h to settle down and then activity was measured in its fruit. If the activity measured was 1 μCi, what percentage of activity is transmitted from the root to the fruit in steady state?

Answers

Introductory Exercise 34.1

1. (b)	2. (a)	3. (a)	4. (c)	5. (c)
6. (b)	7. (a)	8. (b)	9. (d)	10. (a)
11. (b)	12. 3 days, 4.32 days		13. 9.36×10^9 nuclei	

14. (a) 1.55×10^{-5} /s, 12.4 h (b) 2.39×10^{13} atoms (c) 1.87 mCi   15. 1.16×10^3 s

16. $\dfrac{1}{4}$

Introductory Exercise 34.2

1. (c)	2. (b)	3. (d)	4. (c)

5. (a) 9.6×10^{-4} kg (b) 3.125×10^{19} 6. 4.27 MeV

7. (a) $^2_1 H$ (b) $^1_1 H$ (c) $^1_0 n$ (d) $^{79}_{36} Kr$ 8. Fusion, 24   9. 23.6 MeV

Exercises

LEVEL 1

Assertion and Reason

1. (b)	2. (d)	3. (c)	4. (d)	5. (a or b)	6. (d)	7. (b)

Objective Questions

1. (a)	2. (c)	3. (b)	4. (a)	5. (d)	6. (b)	7. (d)	8. (c)	9. (d)	10. (a)
11. (d)	12. (c)	13. (a)	14. (a)	15. (b)	16. (a)	17. (a)	18. (a)	19. (a)	20. (b)
21. (b)	22. (d)	23. (d)	24. (a)	25. (d)					

Subjective Questions

1. (a) 0.113 min^{-1} (b) 6.132 min
2. 19.25 min
3. 7.11×10^{-3} g
4. 1.23×10^4 dps
5. 0.39
6. 1.88×10^9 yr
7. 0.205 mCi
8. (a) $_{86}Rn^{222}$ (b) $\bar{e} + \bar{v}$ (c) $e^+ + v$
9. 104.72 MeV
10. 127.6 MeV
11. (a) 8.19×10^{13} J (b) 2.7×10^6 kg
12. 0.1308 MeV
13. 8.78 day

LEVEL 2

Single Correct Option

1. (b)	2. (c)	3. (b)	4. (c)	5. (d)	6. (d)	7. (c)	8. (b)	9. (c)	10. (a)
11. (b)	12. (b)	13. (c)	14. (d)	15. (d)	16. (a)	17. (c)	18. (c)	19. (d)	20. (c)
21. (b)	22. (a)								

More than One Correct Options

1. (a,b,d)   2. (a,b,c,d)   3. (a,b,c)   4. (b,c)   5. (a,b,c,d)   6. (b,c)   7. (a,b)

Comprehension Based Questions

1. (c)   2. (b)   3. (d)   4. (c)   5. (b)

Match the Columns

1. (a) → s   (b) → p   (c) → r   (d) → s
2. (a) → p   (b) → p   (c) → p   (d) → s
3. (a) → q   (b) → s   (c) → p   (d) → s
4. (a) → p   (b) → s   (c) → r   (d) → q

Subjective Questions

1. 14.3 h

2. (a) $N_B = \lambda N_0 (te^{-\lambda t})$ (b) $t = \dfrac{1}{\lambda}$, $R_{max} = \dfrac{\lambda N_0}{e}$

3. (a) $\dfrac{1}{\lambda}[\alpha - (\alpha - \lambda N_0)e^{-\lambda t}]$ (b) $\dfrac{3}{2}N_0, 2N_0$

4. (a) 0.73×10^{10} dps, 0.27×10^{10} dps (b) 5.4

5. $\dfrac{0.2\, E_0\left[\alpha t - \dfrac{\alpha}{\lambda}(1 - e^{-\lambda t})\right]}{ms}$

6. $N_c = N_0(1 - e^{-\lambda_1 t}) + P\left(t + \dfrac{e^{-\lambda_2 t} - 1}{\lambda_2}\right)$

7. 10 g, 4.57×10^{21} disintegrations/day

8. $\dfrac{1}{9}$, $\dfrac{8}{9}$, 1215 s

9. 1.55×10^6 J

10. 1.26×10^{-11} %

35

SEMICONDUCTOR

35.1 Introduction

Solids can be classified in three types as per their electrical conductivity. (i) conductors, (ii) insulators and (iii) semiconductors. In a conductor, large number of free electrons are present. They are always in *zig-zag* motion inside the conductor. In an insulator, all the electrons are tightly bound to the nucleus. If an electric field is applied inside a conductor, the free electrons experience force due to the field and acquire a drift speed. This results in an electric current. The conductivity of a conductor such as copper decreases as the temperature is increased. This is because as the temperature is increased, the random collisions of the free electrons with the particles in the conductor become more frequent. This results in a decrease in the drift speed and hence the conductivity decreases.

In insulators, almost zero current is obtained unless a very high electric field is applied. Semiconductors conduct electricity when an electric field is applied, but the conductivity is very small as compared to the usual metallic conductors. Silicon, germanium, carbon etc., are few examples of semiconductors.

Conductivity of silicon is about 10^{11} times smaller than that of copper and is about 10^{13} times larger than that of fused quartz. Conductivity of a semiconductor increases as the temperature is increased.

✅ *Extra Points to Remember*

- Before the discovery of transistors (in 1948) mostly vacuum tubes (also called valves) were used in all electrical circuits.

- The order of electrical conductivity (σ) and resistivity $\left(\rho = \dfrac{1}{\sigma} \right)$ of metals, semiconductors and insulators are given below in tabular form.

Table 35.1

S.No	Types of solid	ρ (Ω-m)	σ (Ω^{-1}-m^{-1})
1.	Metals	$10^{-2} - 10^{-8}$	$10^{2} - 10^{8}$
2.	Semiconductors	$10^{-5} - 10^{6}$	$10^{5} - 10^{-6}$
3.	Insulators	$10^{11} - 10^{19}$	$10^{-11} - 10^{-19}$

35.2 Energy Bands In Solids

To understand the energy bands in solids, let us consider the electronic configuration of sodium atom which has 11 electrons. The configuration is $(1s)^2$, $(2s)^2$, $(2p)^6$ and $(3s)^1$. The levels $1s$, $2s$ and $2p$ are completely filled. The level $3s$ is half filled and the levels above $3s$ are empty. Consider a group of N sodium atoms all in ground state separated from each other by large distances such as in sodium vapour. There are total $11N$ electrons. Each atom has two energy states in $1s$ energy level. So, there are $2N$ identical energy states lebelled $1s$ and all them are filled from $2N$ electrons. Similarly, energy level $2p$ has $6N$ identical energy states which are also completely filled. In $3s$ energy levels N of the $2N$ states are filled by the electrons and the remaining N states are empty.

These ideas are shown in the table given below.

Table 35.2

Energy level	Total available energy states	Total occupied states
1s	2N	2N
2s	2N	2N
2p	6N	6N
3s	2N	N
3p	6N	0

In the above discussion, we have assumed that N sodium atoms are widely spread and hence the electrons of one atom do not interact with others. As a result energy states of different states (e.g. 1s) are identical. When atoms are drawn closer to one another, electron of one atom starts interacting with the electrons of the neighbouring atoms of the same energy states. For example 1s electrons of one atom interact with 1s electrons of the other. Due to interaction of electrons, the energy states are not identical, but a sort of energy band is formed. These bands are shown in figure.

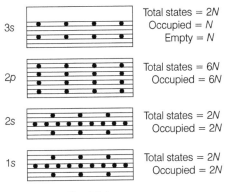

Fig. 35.1

The difference between the highest energy in a band and the lowest energy in the next higher band is called the **band gap** between the two energy bands.

Thus, we can conclude that energy levels of an electron in a solid consists of bands of allowed states. There are regions of energy, called gaps, where no states are possible. In each allowed band, the energy levels are very closely spaced. Electrons occupy states which minimize the total energy. Depending on the number of electrons and on the arrangement of the bands, a band may be fully occupied or partially occupied.

Now, electrical conductivity of conductors, insulators and semiconductors can be explained by these energy bands.

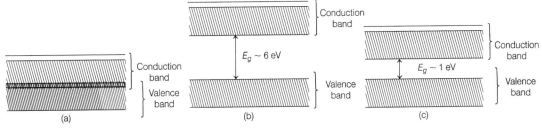

Fig 35.2   Energy band diagram for a (a) metal, (b) insulator and (c) semiconductor.
Note that one can have a metal either when the conduction band is partially filled or when the conduction and valence bands overlap in energy.

Conductors The energy band structure of a conductor is shown in figure (a). The last occupied band of energy level (called conduction band) is only partially filled. In conductors, this band overlaps with completely filled valence band.

Insulators The energy band structure of an insulator is shown in figure (b). The conduction band is separated from the valence band by a wide energy gap (e.g. 6 eV for diamond). But at any non-zero temperature, some electrons can be excited to the conduction band.

Semiconductors The energy band structure of a semiconductor is shown in figure (c). It is similar to that of an insulator but with a comparatively small energy gap. At absolute zero temperature, the conduction band of semiconductors is totally empty, and all the energy states in the valence band are filled. The absence of electrons in the conduction band at absolute zero does not allow current to flow under the influence of an electric field. Therefore, they are insulators at low temperatures. However at room temperatures some valence electrons acquire thermal energy greater than the energy gap E_g and move to the conduction band where they are free to move under the influence of even a small electric field. Thus, a semiconductor originally an insulator at low temperatures becomes slightly conducting at room temperature. Unlike conductors the resistance of semiconductors decreases with increasing temperature. We are generally concerned with only the highest valence band and the lowest conduction band. So, when we say valence band, it means the highest valence band. Similarly, when we say conduction band, it means the lowest conduction band.

⊗ **Example 35.1** *What is the energy band gap of : (i) silicon and (ii) germanium?*

Solution The energy band gap of silicon is 1.1 eV and of germanium is about 0.7 eV.

⊗ **Example 35.2** *In a good conductor, what is the energy gap between the conduction band and the valence band.*

Solution In a good conductor, conduction band overlaps with the valence band. Therefore, the energy gap between them is zero.

35.3 Intrinsic and Extrinsic Semiconductors

As discussed above, in semiconductors the conduction band and the valence band are separated by a relatively small energy gap. For silicon, this gap is 1.1 eV and for germanium it is 0.7 eV.

Silicon has an atomic number 14 and electronic configuration $1s^2, 1s^2, 2p^6, 3s^2, 3p^2$.

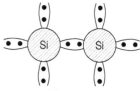

Fig. 35.3

The chemistry of silicon tells us that it has a valency 4. Each silicon atom makes covalent bonds with the four neighbouring silicon atoms. On the basis of bonds the atoms make with their neighbouring atoms, semiconductors are divided in two groups.

Intrinsic Semiconductors A pure (free from impurity) semiconductor which has a valency 4 is called an intrinsic semiconductor. Pure germanium, silicon or carbon in their natural state are intrinsic semiconductors. As discussed above, each atom makes four covalent bonds with their neighbouring atoms. At temperature close to zero, all valence electrons are tightly bound and so no free

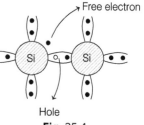

Free electron

Hole

Fig. 35.4

electrons are available to conduct electricity through the crystal. At room temperature, however a few of the covalent bonds are broken due to thermal agitation and thus some of the valence electrons become free. Thus, we can say that a valence electrons is shifted to conduction band leaving a **hole** (vacancy of electron) in valence band. In intrinsic semiconductors,

Number of holes = Number of free electrons   or $\boxed{n_h = n_e}$

Extrinsic Semiconductors The conductivity of an intrinsic semiconductor is very poor (unless the temperature is very high). At ordinary temperature, only one covalent bond breaks in 10^9 atoms of Ge. Conductivity of an intrinsic (pure) semiconductor is significantly increased, if some pentavalent or trivalent impurity is mixed with it. Such impure semiconductors are called extrinsic or doped semiconductors. Extrinsic semiconductors are again of two types (i) p-type and (ii) n-type.

(i) *p*-type semiconductors When a trivalent (e.g. boron, aluminium, gallium or indium) is added to a germanium or silicon crystal it replaces one of the germanium or silicon atom. Its three valence electrons form covalent bonds with neighbouring three Ge (or Si) atoms while the fourth valence electron of Ge (or Si) is not able to form the bond. Thus, there remains a hole (an empty space) on one side of the impurity atom.

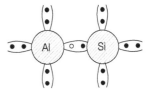

Fig. 35.5

The trivalent impurity atoms are called **acceptor atoms** because they create holes which accept electrons. Following points are worthnoting regarding p-type semiconductors.

(a) Holes are the majority charge carriers and electrons are minority charge carriers in case of p-type semiconductors or number of holes are much greater than the number of electrons.

$$\boxed{n_h \gg n_e}$$

(b) p-type semiconductor is electrically neutral.

(c) p-type semiconductor can be shown as

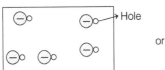   or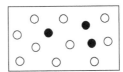

Fig. 35.6

(ii) *n*-type semiconductors When a pentavalent impurity atom (antimony, phosphorus or arsenic is added to a Ge (or Si) crystal it replaces a Ge (or Si) atom. Four of the five valence electrons of the impurity atom form covalent bonds with four neighbouring Ge (or Si) atoms and the fifth valence electron becomes free to move inside the crystal lattice. Thus, by doping pentavalent impurity number of free electrons increases.

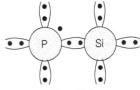

Fig. 35.7

The impurity (pentavalent) atoms are called **donor atoms** because they donate conduction electrons inside the crystal. Following points are worthnoting regarding n-type semiconductors,

(a) Electrons are the majority charge carriers and holes are minority or number of electrons are much greater than the number of holes

$$\boxed{n_e \gg n_h}$$

(b) *n*-type semiconductor is also electrically neutral.

(c) *n*-type semiconductor can be shown as

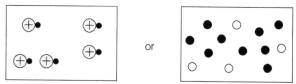

Fig. 35.8

Electrical Conduction through Semiconductors

When a battery is connected across a semiconductor (whether intrinsic or extrinsic) a potential difference is developed across its ends. Due to the potential difference an electric field is produced inside the semiconductor. A current (although very small) starts flowing through the semiconductor. This current may be due to the motion of (i) free electrons and (ii) holes. Electrons move in opposite direction of electric field while holes move in the same direction.

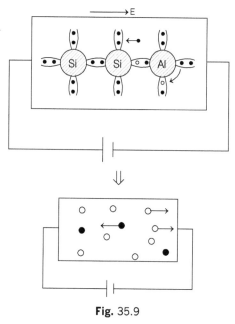

The motion of holes towards right (in the figure) take place because electrons from right hand side come to fill this hole, creating a new hole in their own position. Thus, we can say that holes are moving from left to right. Thus, current in a semiconductor can be written as,

$$i = i_e + i_h$$

But it should be noted that mobility of holes is less than the mobility of electrons.

Fig. 35.9

⊘ **Example 35.3** *C, Si and Ge have same lattice structure. Why is C insulator while Si and Ge intrinsic semiconductors?*

Solution *The energy gap between conduction band and valence band is least for Ge, followed by Si and highest for C. Hence, number of free electrons are negligible for C. This is why carbon is insulator.*

⊘ **Example 35.4** *In an n-type silicon, which of the following statements is true?*
(a) Electrons are majority carriers and trivalent atoms are the dopants.
(b) Electrons are minority carriers and pentavalent atoms are the dopants.
(c) Holes are minority carriers and pentavalent atoms are the dopants.
(d) Holes are majority carriers and trivalent atoms are the dopants.

Solution (c) Holes are minority charge carriers and pentavalent atoms are the dopants in an *n*-type silicon.

⊚ **Example 35.5** *Which of the statements given in above example is true for p-type semiconductors?*

Solution (d) Holes are majority carriers and trivalent atoms are the dopants in an *p*−type semiconductors.

INTRODUCTORY EXERCISE 35.1

1. Carbon, silicon and germanium have four valence electrons each. These are characterised by valence and conduction bands separated by energy band-gap respectively equal to $(E_g)_C$, $(E_g)_{Si}$ and $(E_g)_{Ge}$. Which of the following statements is true?
   (a) $(E_g)_{Si} < (E_g)_{Ge} < (E_g)_C$
   (b) $(E_g)_C < (E_g)_{Ge} > (E_g)_{Si}$
   (c) $(E_g)_C > (E_g)_{Si} > (E_g)_{Ge}$
   (d) $(E_g)_C = (E_g)_{Si} = (E_g)_{Ge}$

35.4 *p-n* **Junction Diode**

A *p*-type or *n*-type silicon crystal can be made by adding appropriate impurity as discussed above. These crystals are cut into thin slices called the wafer. Semiconductor devices are usually made of these wafers.

If on a wafer of *n*-type silicon, an aluminium film is placed and heated to a high temperature, aluminium diffuses into silicon.

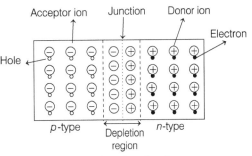

(a) Formation of *p-n* junction

In this way, a *p*-type semiconductor is formed on an *n*-type semiconductor. Such a formation of *p*-region on *n*-region is called the *p-n*-junction. Another way to make a *p-n* junction is by diffusion of phosphorus into a *p*-type semiconductor. Such *p-n* junctions are used in a host of semiconductor devices of practical applications. The simplest of the semiconductor devices is a *p-n* junction diode.

Biasing of a diode In a *p-n* junction diode, holes are majority carriers on *p*-side and electrons on *n*-side. Holes, thus diffuse to *n*-side and electrons to *p*-side.

This diffusion causes an excess positive charge in the *n* region and an excess negative charge in the *p* region near the junction. This double layer of charge creates an electric field which exerts a force on the electrons and holes, against their diffusion. In the equilibrium position, there is a barrier, for charge motion with the *n*-side at a higher potential than the *p*-side.

The junction region has a very low density of either *p* or *n*-type carriers, because of inter diffusion. It is called **depletion region.** There is a barrier V_B associated with it, as described above. This is called **potential barrier.**

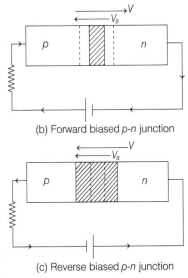

(b) Forward biased *p-n* junction

(c) Reverse biased *p-n* junction

Fig. 35.10

Now suppose a DC voltage source is connected across the *p-n* junction. The polarity of this voltage can lead to an electric field across the *p-n* junction that is opposite to the already present electric field. The potential drop across the junction decreases and the diffusion of electrons and holes is thereby increased, resulting in a current in the circuit. This is called **forward biasing.**

The depletion layer effectively becomes smaller. In the opposite case, called **reverse biasing** the barrier increases, the depletion region becomes larger, current of electrons and holes is greatly reduced.

Thus, the *p-n* junction allows a much larger current flow in forward biasing than in reverse biasing. This is crudely, the basis of the action of a *p-n* junction as a rectifier. The symbol of *p-n* junction diode is (p—⊙—n)

Diffusion Current and Drift Current

Because of concentration difference, holes try to diffuse from the *p*-side to the *n*-side at the *p-n* junction. This diffusion give rise to a current from *p*-side to *n*-side called **diffusion current.** Because of thermal collisions, electron-hole pair are created at every part of a diode.

However, if an electron-hole pair is created in the depletion region, the electron is pushed by the electric field towards the *n*-side and the hole towards the *p*-side. This gives rise to a current from *n*-side to *p*-side called the **drift current.**

Thus,
$$I_{df} \longrightarrow \text{from } p\text{-side to } n\text{-side}$$
$$I_{dr} \longrightarrow \text{from } n\text{-side to } p\text{-side}$$

When diode is unbiased $I_{df} = I_{dr}$ or $I_{net} = 0$.

When diode is forward biased $I_{df} > I_{dr}$ or I_{net} is from *p*-side to *n*-side.

When diode is reverse biased $I_{dr} > I_{df}$ or I_{net} is from *n*-side to *p*-side.

Characteristic Curve of a *p-n* Junction Diode

(a) Circuit for obtaining the characteristics of a forward biased diode and (b) Circuit for obtaining the characteristics of a reverse bias diode.

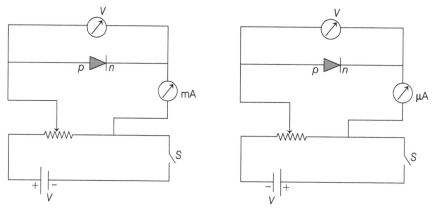

Fig. 35.11

When the diode is forward biased i.e. *p*-side is kept at higher potential, the current in the diode changes with the voltage applied across the diode. The current increases very slowly till the voltage across the diode crosses a certain value.

After this voltage, the diode current increases rapidly, even for very small increase in the diode voltage. This voltage is called the **threshold voltage or cut-off voltage.** The value of the cut-off voltage is about 0.2 V for a germanium diode and 0.7 V for a silicon diode.

When the diode is reverse biased, a very small current (about a few micro amperes) produces in the circuit which remains nearly constant till a characteristic voltage called the breakdown voltage, is reached. Then the reverse current suddenly increases to a large value. This phenomenon is called **avalanche breakdown.** The reverse voltage beyond which current suddenly increases is called the **breakdown voltage.**

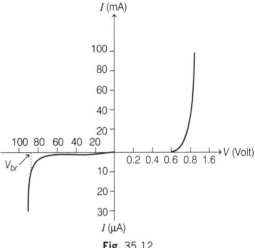

Fig. 35.12

⊛ **Example 35.6** *Can we take one slab of p-type semiconductor and physically join it to another n-type semiconductor to get p-n junction?*

Solution No. Any slab will have some roughness. Hence continuous contact at the atomic level will not be possible. For the charge carriers, the junction will behave as a discontinuity.

⊛ **Example 35.7** *Find current passing through 2 Ω and 4 Ω resistance in the circuit shown in figure.*

Solution In the given circuit diode D_1 is forward biased and D_2 reverse biased. Hence, D_1 will conduct but D_2 not. Therefore, current through 4 Ω resistance will be zero while through 2 Ω resistance will be, $\dfrac{10}{2} = 5$ A.

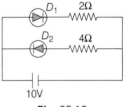

Fig. 35.13

INTRODUCTORY EXERCISE 35.2

1. In an unbiased *p-n* junction, holes diffuse from the *p*-region to *n*-region because
   (a) free electrons in the *n*-region attract them
   (b) they move across the junction by the potential difference
   (c) hole concentration in *p*-region is more as compared to *n*-region
   (d) All of the above

2. When a forward bias is applied to a *p - n* junction. It
   (a) raises the potential barrier
   (b) reduces the majority carrier current to zero
   (c) lowers the potential barrier
   (d) All of the above

35.5 **Junction Diode as a Rectifier**

A rectifier is a device which converts an alternating current (or voltage) into a direct (or unidirectional) current (or voltage). A *p-n* junction diode can work as an excellent rectifier. It offers a low resistance for the current to flow when it is forward biased, but a very high resistance when reverse biased. Thus, it allows current through it only in one direction and acts as a rectifier. The junction diode can be used either as an half-wave rectifier or as a full-wave rectifier.

(i) ***p-n* junction diode as half-wave rectifier** A simple rectifier circuit called the half-wave rectifier, using only one diode is shown in figure.

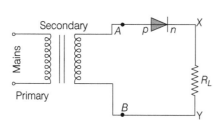

Fig. 35.14

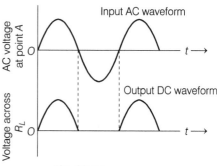

Fig. 35.15

When the voltage at *A* is positive, the diode is forward biased and it conducts and when the voltage at *A* is negative, the diode is reverse biased and does not conduct. Since, the diode conducts only in the positive half cycles, the voltage between *X* and *Y* or across R_L will be DC but in pulses. When this is given to a circuit called filter (normally a capacitor), it will smoothen the pulses and will produce a rather steady DC voltage.

(ii) ***p-n* junction diode as full-wave rectifier** Figure shows a circuit which is used in full-wave rectification. Two diodes are used for this purpose.

The secondary coil of the transformer is wound in two parts and the junction is called a Centre-Tap (CT). During one-half cycle D_1 is forward biased and D_2 is reverse biased. Therefore, D_1 conducts but D_2 does not, current flows from *X* to *Y* through load resistance R_L. During another half cycle D_2 is forward biased and D_1 reverse biased. Therefore, D_2 conducts and D_1 does not. In this half cycle also current through R_L flows from *X* to *Y*. Thus, current through R_L in both the half cycles is in one direction, i.e. from *X* to *Y*.

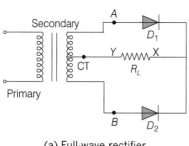

(a) Full-wave rectifier

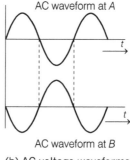

(b) AC voltage waveforms at points *A* and *B*

Fig. 35.16

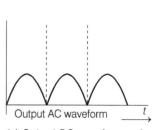

(c) Output DC waveforms of a full-wave rectifier.

Bridge rectifier Another full-wave rectifier called the bridge rectifier which uses four diodes is shown in figure.

For one-half cycle diodes D_1 and D_3 are forward biased and D_2 and D_4 are reverse biased. So, D_1 and D_3 conduct but D_2 and D_4 don't. Current through R_L flows from X to Y. In another half cycle D_2 and D_4 are forward biased and D_1 and D_3 are reverse biased. So, in this half cycle D_2 and D_4 conduct but D_1 and D_3 do not. Current again flows from X to Y through R_L. Thus, we see that current through R_L always flows in one direction from X to Y.

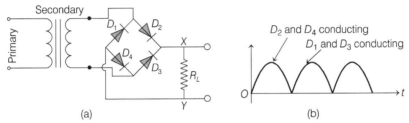

Fig. 35.17 (a) Bridge rectifier and (b) output waveforms for a bridge rectifier

Note *Even after rectification ripples are present in the output which can be removed upto great extent by a filter circuit. A filter circuit consists of a capacitor.*

⊘ **Example 35.8** *In half-wave rectification, what is the output frequency, if the input frequency is 50 Hz? What is the output frequency of a full-wave rectifier for the same input frequency?*

Solution A half-wave rectifier conducts once during a cycle. Therefore frequency of AC output is also the frequency of AC input i.e. 50 Hz. A full-wave rectifier rectifies both the half cycles of the AC output i.e. it conducts twice during a cycle.

So,   Frequency of AC output $= 2 \times$ frequency of AC input

$$= 2 \times 50 = 100 \, \text{Hz}$$ **Ans.**

⊘ **Example 35.9** *In the figure, the input is across the terminals A and C and the output is across B and D. Then the output is*

(a) zero

(b) same as the input

(c) full-wave rectified

(d) half-wave rectified

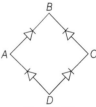

Fig. 35.18

Solution (c) During the half cycle when $V_M > V_N$, D_1 and D_3 are forward biased. Hence, the path of current is *MABPQDCNM*.

In the second half cycle, when $V_N > V_M$, D_2 and D_4 are forward biased while D_1 and D_3 are reverse biased. Hence, the path of current is *NCBPQDAMN*.

Therefore, in both half cycles current flows from P to Q from load resistance R_L. Or, it is a full-wave rectifier.

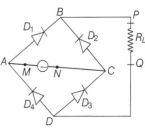

Fig. 35.19

35.6 Applications of *p-n* Junction Diodes

Zener Diode

A diode meant to operate under reverse bias in the breakdown region is called an **avalanche diode** or a **zener diode**. Such diode is used as a voltage regulator. The symbol of zener diode is shown in figure.

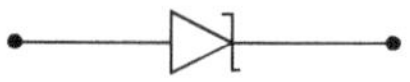

Fig. 35.20

Once the breakdown occurs, the potential difference across the diode does not increase even if, there is large change in the current. Figure shows a zener diode in reverse biasing.

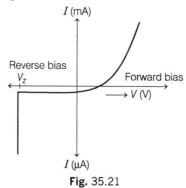

Fig. 35.21

An input voltage V_i is connected to the zener diode through a series resistance R such that the zener diode is reverse biased.

If the input voltage increases, the current through R and zener diode also increases. This increases the voltage drop across R without any change in the voltage across the zener diode. Similarly, if the input voltage decreases the current through R and zener diode also decreases. The voltage drop across R decreases without any change in the voltage across the zener diode.

Thus any increase/decrease in the input voltage results in increase/decrease of the voltage drop across R without any change in voltage across the zener diode (and hence across load resistance R_L). Thus, the zener diode acts as a voltage regulator.

We have to select the zener diode according to the required output voltage and accordingly the series resistance R.

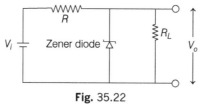

Fig. 35.22

Optoelectronic Devices

Semiconductor diodes in which carriers are generated by photons (photo excitation) are called optoelectronic devices. Examples of optoelectronic devices are, photodiodes, Light Emitting Diodes (LED) and photovoltaic devices, etc.

(a) Photodiodes Photodiodes are used as photodetector to detect optical signals. They are operated in reverse biased connections.

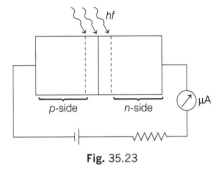

Fig. 35.23

When light of energy greater than the energy gap falls on the depletion region of the diode, electron-hole pairs are generated. Due to the electric field of junction, electrons and holes are separated before they recombine. Electrons reach n-side and holes reach p-side giving rise to an emf. When an external load is connected, current flows. The magnitude of the photocurrent depends on the intensity of incident light.

(b) Light Emitting Diode (LED) It is heavily doped p-n junction diode which under forward bias emits spontaneous radiation. LEDs that can emit red, yellow, orange, green and blue light are commercially available. These LEDs find extensive use in remote controls, burglar alarm systems, optical communications, etc.

Extensive research is being done for developing white LEDs which can replace incandescent lamps.

LED have the following advantages over conventional incandescent power lamps.

(i) Long life

(ii) Low operational voltage and less power

(iii) No warm up time is required. So fast on-off switching capability.

(c) Solar Cell It works on the same principle as the photodiode. It is basically a p-n junction which generates emf when solar radiation falls on the p-n junction. The difference between a photodiode and a solar cell is that no external bias is applied and the junction area is kept much larger for solar radiation to be incident because we require more power.

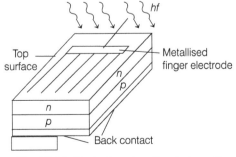

Fig. 35.24 Typical p-n junction Solar cell

The generation of emf by a solar cell (when light falls on it) is due to the following three processes.

(i) Generation Generation of electron-hole pairs due to light $(hf > E_g)$ falling on it.

(ii) Separation Separation of electrons and holes due to electric field of the depletion region.

(iii) Collection Electrons are swept to n- side and holes to p-side. Thus, p-side becomes positive and n-side becomes negative giving rise to photovoltage.

Solar cells are used to power electronic devices in satellites and space vehicles and also as power supply to some calculators.

⊘ **Example 35.10** *In a zener regulated power supply a zener diode with* $V_Z = 6.0\,V$ *is used for regulation. The load current is to be 4.0 mA and the unregulated input is 10.0 V. What should be the value of series resistor R?*

Solution Zener current I_Z should be sufficiently larger than load current I_L.

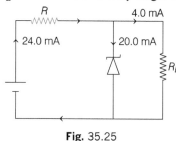

Fig. 35.25

Given, $\qquad\qquad\qquad\qquad\qquad I_L = 4.0\,\text{mA}$

So, let us take I_Z to be five times I_L or $I_Z = 20\,\text{mA}$

$$\text{Total current } I = I_Z + I_L = 24.0\,\text{mA}$$
$$\text{Input voltage } V_{\text{in}} = 10\,\text{V}$$
$$\text{Zener diode voltage } V_Z = 6\,\text{V}$$

∴ Voltage drop across resistance, $V_R = V_{\text{in}} - V_Z$

or $\qquad\qquad\qquad\qquad\qquad V_R = (10 - 6)\,\text{V} = 4\,\text{V}$

Now, $\qquad\qquad\qquad\qquad R = \dfrac{V_R}{I_R} = \dfrac{4}{24 \times 10^{-3}} = 167\,\Omega$

The nearest value of carbon resistor is $150\,\Omega$. So, a series resistor of $150\,\Omega$ is appropriate.

⊘ **Example 35.11** *The current in the forward bias is known to be more (in mA) than the current in the reverse bias (in μA). What is the reason then to operate the photodiodes in reverse bias ?*

Solution Let us take an example of p-type semiconductor.

Without illumination

number of holes $(n_h) \gg$ number of electrons (n_e) $\qquad\qquad\qquad\qquad$ ...(i)

This is because holes are the majority charge carriers in p-type semiconductor.

On illumination, let Δn_e and Δn_h are the excess electrons and holes generated.

$$\Delta n_e = \Delta n_h \qquad \qquad ...(ii)$$

From Eqs. (i) and (ii), we can see that

$$\frac{\Delta n_e}{n_e} >> \frac{\Delta n_h}{n_h}$$

From here, we can say that the fractional change due to illumination on the minority carrier dominated reverse bias current is more easily measurable than the fractional change in the forward bias current.

35.7 Junction Transistors

A junction transistor is formed by sandwiching a thin wafer of one type of semiconductor between two layers of another type. The *n-p-n* transistor has a *p*-type wafer between two *n*-type layers. Similarly, the *p-n-p* transistor has a *n*-type wafer between two *p*-type layers.

p-n-p Transistor

Figure shows a *p-n-p* transistor, in which a thin layer of *n*-type semiconductor is sandwiched between two *p*-type semiconductors. The middle layer (called the base) is very thin (of the order of 1 μm) as compared to the widths of the two layers at the sides. Base is very lightly doped. One of the side layer (called emitter) is heavily doped and the other side layer (called collector) is moderately doped. Figure (c) shows the symbol of *p-n-p* transistor.

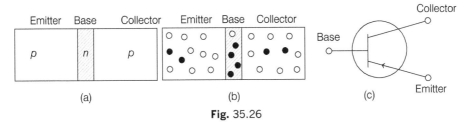

Fig. 35.26

n-p-n Transistor

In *n-p-n* transistor, *p*-type semiconductor is sandwiched between two *n*-type semiconductors. Symbol of *n-p-n* transistor is shown in figure (f).

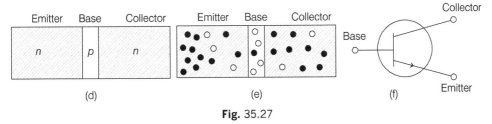

Fig. 35.27

More points about a transistor A transistor is basically a three-terminal device. Terminals come out from the emitter, base and the collector for external connections. In normal operation of a transistor, the emitter-base junction is always forward biased and collector-base junction is reverse biased.

The arrow on the emitter-base line shows the direction of current between emitter and base. In an *n-p-n* transistor for example, there are a large number of conduction electrons in the emitter and a large number of holes in the base. If the junction is forward biased the electrons will diffuse from emitter to the base and holes will diffuse from the base to the emitter. The direction of electric current at this junction is therefore from the base to the emitter. A transistor can be operated in three different modes.

(i) Common emitter (or grounded-emitter)

(ii) Common collector (or grounded-collector) and

(iii) Common base (or grounded-base)

In common emitter mode, emitter is kept at zero potential. Similarly in common collector mode collector is at zero potential and so on.

Working of a *p-n-p* Transistor

Let us consider the working of a *p-n-p* transistor in common base mode. In emitter (*p*-type) holes are in majority. Since, emitter-base is forward biased, holes move toward base. Few of them combine with electrons in the base and rest go to the collector. Since, base-collector is reverse biased, holes coming from base move toward the terminal of collector. They combine with equal number of electrons entering from collector terminal.

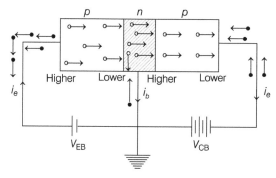

Fig. 35.28

Let us take an example with some numerical values.

Suppose 5 holes enter from emitter to base. This deficiency of 5 holes in emitter is compensated when 5 electrons emit from emitter and give rise to i_e. One out of five holes which reach the base combine with one electron entering from base (the equivalent current is i_b). Rest four holes enter the collector and move towards its terminal. On the other hand, 5 electrons which leave the emitter (as i_e) come to the base, emitter and collector junctions. One electron of it goes to base and rest four to collector. These four electrons give rise to i_c (the collector current) and combine with the four holes coming from the base, and thus circuit is complete. From the figure, we can see that,

$$i_e = i_c + i_b$$

Note that i_b is only about 2% of i_e, or roughly around 2% of holes coming from emitter to base combine with the electrons. Rest 98% move to collector.

Working of *n-p-n* Transistor

A common base circuit of an *n-p-n* transistor is shown in figure. Majority charge carriers in the emitter (*n*-type) are electrons. Since, emitter-base circuit is forward biased. The electrons rush from emitter to base. Few of them leave the base terminal (comprising i_b) and rest move to collector. These electrons finally leave the collector terminal (give rise to i_c). Electrons coming from base and from collector meet at junction O and they jointly move to emitter, which gives rise to i_e.

Thus, here also we can see that $\qquad i_e = i_b + i_c$

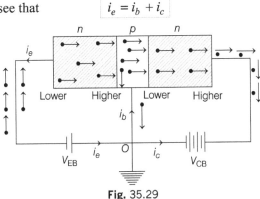

Fig. 35.29

Note *that although the working principle of p-n-p and n-p-n transistors are similar but the current carriers in p-n-p transistor are mainly holes whereas in n-p-n transistors the current carriers are mainly electrons. Mobility of electrons are however more than the mobility of holes, therefore n-p-n transistors are used in high frequency and computer circuits where the carriers are required to respond very quickly to signals.*

α **and** β**-parameters:** α and β-parameters of a transistor are defined as,

$$\alpha = i_c / i_e \quad \text{and} \quad \beta = i_c / i_b$$

As i_b is about 1 to 5% of i_e, α is about 0.95 to 0.99 and β is about 20 to 100. By simple mathematics we can prove that,

$$\beta = \frac{\alpha}{1-\alpha}$$

35.8 Transistor As An Amplifier

A transistor can be used for amplifying a weak signal.

When a transistor is to be operated as amplifier, three different basic circuit connections are possible. These are

(i) common base, (ii) common emitter and (iii) common collector circuits.

Whichever circuit configuration, the emitter-base junction is always forward biased, while the collector-base junction is always reverse biased.

(a) **Common base amplifier using a *p-n-p* transistor** In common base amplifier, the input signal is applied across the emitter and the base, while the amplified output signal is taken across the collector and the base. This circuit provides a very low input resistance, a very high output resistance and a current gain of just less than 1. Still it provides a good voltage and power amplification. There is no phase difference between input and output signals.

The common base amplifier circuit using a *p-n-p* transistor is shown in figure. The emitter base input circuit is forward biased by a low voltage battery V_{EB}. The collector base output circuit is reversed biased by means of a high voltage battery V_{CC}. Since, the input circuit is forward biased, resistance of input circuit is small. Similarly, output circuit is reverse biased, hence resistance of output circuit is high.

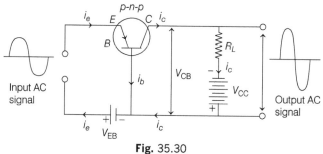

Fig. 35.30

The weak input AC voltage signal is superimposed on V_{EB} and the amplified output signal is obtained across collector-base circuit. In the figure we can see that,

$$V_{CB} = V_{CC} - i_c R_L$$

The input AC voltage signal changes net value of V_{EB}. Due to fluctuations in V_{EB}, the emitter current i_e also fluctuates which in turn fluctuates i_c. In accordance with the above equation there are fluctuations in V_{CB}, when the input signal is applied and an amplified output is obtained.

Current gain, Voltage gain and Power gain

(i) **Current gain** Also called AC current gain (α_{ac}), is defined as the ratio of the change in the collector current to the change in the emitter current at constant collector-base voltage.

Thus, $\qquad\qquad \alpha_{ac}$ or simply $\qquad \boxed{\alpha = \dfrac{\Delta i_c}{\Delta i_e}} \qquad\qquad (V_{CB} = \text{constant})$

As stated earlier also, α is slightly less than 1.

(ii) **Voltage gain** It is defined as the ratio of change in the output voltage to the change in the input voltage. It is denoted by A_V. Thus,

$$A_V = \frac{\Delta i_c \times R_{out}}{\Delta i_e \times R_{in}}$$

but $\dfrac{\Delta i_c}{\Delta i_e} = \alpha$, the current gain.

∴ $\qquad\qquad\qquad \boxed{A_V = \dfrac{a\, R_{out}}{R_{in}}}$

Since, $R_{out} \gg R_{in}$, A_V is quite high, although α is slightly less than 1.

(iii) **Power gain** It is defined as the change in the output power to the change in the input power.

Since $\qquad\qquad\qquad\qquad\qquad P = Vi$

Therefore, power gain = current gain × voltage gain

or $\qquad\qquad\qquad \boxed{\text{Power gain} = \alpha^2 \cdot \dfrac{R_{out}}{R_{in}}}$

✅ *Extra Points to Remember*

- The output voltage signal is in phase with the input voltage signal.
- The common base amplifier is used to amplify high (radio)-frequency signals and to match a very low source impedance (~20 Ω) to a high load impedance (~100 k Ω).

(b) **Common emitter amplifier using a *p-n-p* transistor** Figure shows a *p-n-p* transistor as an amplifier in common emitter mode. The emitter is common to both input and output circuits. The input (base-emitter) circuit is forward biased by a low voltage battery V_{BE}. The output (collector-emitter) circuit is reverse biased by means of a high voltage battery V_{CC}.

Since, the base-emitter circuit is forward biased, input resistance is low. Similarly, collector-emitter circuit is reverse biased, therefore output resistance is high. The weak input AC signal is superimposed on V_{BE} and the amplified output signal is obtained across the collector-emitter circuit.

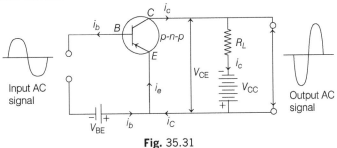

Fig. 35.31

In the figure we can see that, $$V_{CE} = V_{CC} - i_c R_L$$

When the input AC voltage signal is applied across the base-emitter circuit, it fluctuates V_{BE} and hence the emitter current i_e. This in turn changes the collector current i_c consequently V_{CE} varies in accordance with the above equation. This variation in V_{CE} appears as an amplified output.

Current Gain, Voltage Gain and Power Gain

(i) **Current gain** Also called ac current gain (β_{ac}), is defined as the ratio of the collector current to the base current at constant collector to emitter voltage.

$$\beta_{ac} \text{ or simply } \beta = \left(\frac{\Delta i_c}{\Delta i_b} \right) \qquad (V_{CE} = \text{constant})$$

(ii) **Voltage gain** It is defined as the ratio of the change in the output voltage to the change in the input voltage. It is denoted by A_V. Thus,

$$A_V = \frac{\Delta i_c \times R_{out}}{\Delta i_b \times R_{in}} \quad \text{or} \quad A_V = \beta \left(\frac{R_{out}}{R_{in}} \right)$$

(iii) **Power gain** It is defined as the ratio of change in output power to the change in the input power. Since,

$$P = Vi$$

Therefore, power gain = current gain × voltage gain   or $$\text{Power gain} = \beta^2 \left(\frac{R_{out}}{R_{in}} \right)$$

> ✅ *Extra Points to Remember*
> - The value of current gain β is from 15 to 50 which is much greater than α.
> - The voltage gain in common-emitter amplifier is larger compared to that in common base amplifier.
> - The power gain in common-emitter amplifier is extremely large compared to that in common base amplifier.
> - The output voltage signal is 180° out of phase with the input voltage signal in the common-emitter amplifier.

Transconductance *(g_m)* There is one more term called transconductance (g_m) in common-emitter mode. It is defined as the ratio of the change in the collector current to the change in the base to emitter voltage at constant collector to emitter voltage. Thus,

$$g_m = \left(\frac{\Delta i_c}{\Delta V_{BE}} \right) \qquad (V_{CE} = \text{constant})$$

The unit of g_m is Ω^{-1} or siemen (S). By simple calculation we can prove that,

$$g_m = \frac{\beta}{R_{in}}$$

Advantages of a transistor over a triode valve A transistor is similar to a triode valve in the sense that both have three elements. While the elements of a triode are, cathode, plate and grid. The three elements of a transistor are emitter, collector and base. Emitter of a transistor can be compared with the cathode of the triode, the collector with the plate and the base with the grid.

Transistor has following advantages over a triode valve

(i) A transistor is small and cheap as compared to a triode valve. They can bear mechanical shocks.

(ii) A transistor has much longer life as compared to a triode valve.

(iii) Loss of power in a transistor is less as it operates at a much lower voltage.

(iv) In a transistor no heating current is required. So, unlike a triode valve, a transistor starts functioning immediately as soon as the switch is opened. In case of valves, they come in operation after some time of opening the switch (till cathode gets heated).

Drawbacks of a transistor over a triode valve Transistor have following drawbacks as compared to valves.

(i) Since, the transistors are made of semiconductors they are temperature sensitive. We cannot work on transistors at high temperatures.

(ii) In transistors noise level is high. Keeping all the factors into consideration, transistors have replaced the valve from most of the modern electronic devices.

> ⊘ **Example 35.12** *The current gain of a transistor in a common base arrangement in 0.98. Find the change in collector current corresponding to a change of 5.0 mA in emitter current. What would be the change in base current?*
>
> *Solution* Given, $\alpha = 0.98$ and $\Delta i_e = 5.0 \text{ mA}$
>
> From the definition of, $\alpha = \dfrac{\Delta i_c}{\Delta i_e}$
>
> Change in collector current, $\Delta i_c = (\alpha)(\Delta i_e) = (0.98)(5.0) \text{ mA} = 4.9 \text{ mA}$
>
> Further, change in base current, $\Delta i_b = \Delta i_e - \Delta i_c = 0.1 \text{ mA}$ **Ans.**

⊛ **Example 35.13** *A transistor is connected in common emitter configuration. The collector supply is 8 V and the voltage drop across a resistor of* 800 Ω *in the collector circuit is 0.5 V. If the current gain factor* (α) *is 0.96, find the base current.*

Solution $\beta = \dfrac{\alpha}{1-\alpha} = \dfrac{0.96}{1-0.96} = 24$

The collector current is,

$$i_c = \frac{\text{voltage drop across collector resistor}}{\text{resistance}} = \frac{0.5}{800} \text{A} = 0.625 \times 10^{-3} \text{A}$$

From the definition of $\qquad\qquad\qquad \beta = \dfrac{i_c}{i_b}$

the base current $\qquad\qquad\qquad i_b = \dfrac{i_c}{\beta} = \dfrac{0.625 \times 10^{-3}}{24}$ A

$$= 26\,\mu\text{A} \qquad\qquad\qquad\qquad\qquad\qquad \textbf{Ans.}$$

⊛ **Example 35.14** *In a common emitter amplifier, the load resistance of the output circuit is 500 times the resistance of the input circuit. If* α = 0.98, *then find the voltage gain and power gain.*

Solution   Given α = 0.98 and $\dfrac{R_{\text{out}}}{R_{\text{in}}} = 500 \Rightarrow \beta = \dfrac{\alpha}{1-\alpha} = \dfrac{0.98}{1-0.98} = 49$

(i) Voltage gain $= (\beta)\dfrac{R_{\text{out}}}{R_{\text{in}}} = (49)(500) = 24500$

(ii) Power gain $= (\beta^2)\dfrac{R_{\text{out}}}{R_{\text{in}}} = (49)^2 (500) = 1200500$

INTRODUCTORY EXERCISE 35.3

1. For transistor action, which of the following statements are correct?
    (a) Base, emitter and collector regions should have similar size and doping concentrations
    (b) The base region must be very thin and lightly doped
    (c) The emitter junction is forward biased and collector junction is reverse biased
    (d) Both the emitter junction as well as the collector junction are forward biased

2. For a transistor amplifier, the voltage gain
    (a) remains constant for all frequencies
    (b) is high at high and low frequencies and constant in the middle frequency range
    (c) is low at high and low frequencies and constant at mid frequencies
    (d) None of the above

3. For a CE-transistor amplifier, the audio signal voltage across the collector resistance of 2 kΩ is 2 V. Suppose the current amplification factor of the transistor is 100. Find the input signal voltage and base current, if the base resistance is 1 kΩ.

35.9 **Digital Electronics and Logic Gates**

(i) **Binary system** There are a number of questions which have only two answers Yes or No. A statement can be either True or False. A switch can be either ON or OFF. These values may be represented by two symbols 0 and 1. In a number system, in which we have only two digits is called a binary system. (decimal system for example has ten digits).

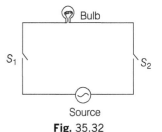

Bulb

S_1 S_2

Source

Fig. 35.32

In binary system usually we write 1 for positive response (e.g. when a switch is ON) and 0 for negative (when switch is OFF).

(ii) **Truth table** To understand the concept of truth table let us take an example. A bulb is connected to an AC source *via* two switches S_1 and S_2.

In binary system, we will write 0, if the switch (or bulb) is off and write 1 if it is on. Further let us write

A for state of switch S_1

B for state of switch S_2

and C for state of the bulb.

Now, let us make a table (called truth table) which is self explanatory.

Table 35.3

Switch S_1	Switch S_2	Bulb	A	B	C
Off	On	Off	0	1	0
On	Off	Off	1	0	0
Off	Off	Off	0	0	0
On	On	On	1	1	1

Exercise *Make a truth table corresponding to the circuit shown in figure.*

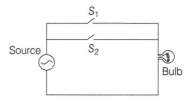

S_1

Source S_2

Bulb

Fig. 35.33

Table 35.4

Switch S_1	Switch S_2	Bulb	A	B	C
On	Off	On	1	0	1
Off	On	On	0	1	1
Off	Off	Off	0	0	0
On	On	On	1	1	1

(iii) **Logical function** A variable (e.g. state of a switch or state of a bulb) which can assume only two values (0 and 1) is called a logical variable. A function of logical variables is called a logical function. **AND, OR** and **NOT** represent three basic operations on logical variables.

'**AND' function** Suppose C is a function of A and B, then it will be said an 'AND' function when C has value 1 when both A and B have value 1. Truth table corresponding to Table 35.3 is an example of 'AND' function. The function is written as,

$$C = A \text{ and } B$$

AND function is also denoted as $C = A \cdot B$

'**OR' function** C, a function of A and B will be said an 'OR' function when C has value 1 when either of A or B has value 1. Truth table corresponding to Table 35.4 is an example of 'OR' function. The function is written as,

$$C = A \ \text{OR} \ B$$

OR function is also denoted as,

$$C = A + B$$

'**NOT' function** 'NOT' function is a function of a single variable.

A bulb is short circuited by a switch. If the switch is open, the current goes through the bulb and it is on. If the switch is closed the current goes through the switch and the bulb is off. The truth table corresponding to the above situation (or NOT function) is as under.

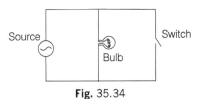

Fig. 35.34

Table 35.5

Switch	Bulb	A	B
Open	On	0	1
Closed	Off	1	0

'NOT' function is denoted as,

$$B = \text{NOT} \ A \ \text{ or } \ B = \overline{A}$$

⊙ **Example 35.15** *Write the truth table for the logical function* $D = (A \ OR \ B) \ AND \ B$.

Solution A OR B is a logical function, say it is equal to X, *i.e.,*

$$X = A \ \text{OR} \ B$$

Now, $D = X \ \text{AND} \ B$

The corresponding truth table is as under.

Table 35.6

A	B	$X = A \ OR \ B$	$D = (A \ OR \ B) \ AND \ B$
1	0	1	0
0	1	1	1
0	0	0	0
1	1	1	1

Note *that the given function can also be written as,*

$$D = (A + B) \cdot B$$

(iv) **Logic gates** Logic gates are important building blocks in digital electronics. These are circuits with one or more inputs and one output. The basic gates are OR, AND, NOT, NAND, NOR and XOR. As we know, in digital electronics only two voltage levels are present. Conventionally, these are 5V and 0V, referred to as 1 and 0 respectively or *vice-versa*. They are also referred as high and low.Figure given are the symbols of six basic gates.

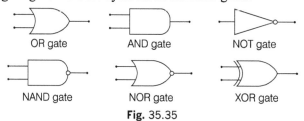

| OR gate | AND gate | NOT gate |

| NAND gate | NOR gate | XOR gate |

Fig. 35.35

OR gate The truth table of 'OR' gate is given below.

Table 35.7

A	B	X
0	0	0
0	1	1
1	0	1
1	1	1

The output X will be 1 (*i.e.,* 5V) when the A input is 1, OR when the B input is 1, OR when both are 1. This is written as,

$$X = A + B$$

$\rightarrow X = A + B$

Fig. 35.36

Figure shows construction of an OR gate using two diodes

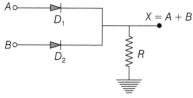

Fig. 35.37

When either of point A or point B (or both) has potential +5V, diodes D_1 or D_2 (or both) are forward biased and the potential at X is the same as the common potential at A and B which is 5V.

AND gate The truth table of 'AND' gate is given below.

Table 35.8

A	B	Y
0	0	0
0	1	0
1	0	0
1	1	1

The output X will be 1 (i.e. 5V) when both the inputs A and B is 1. This is written as,

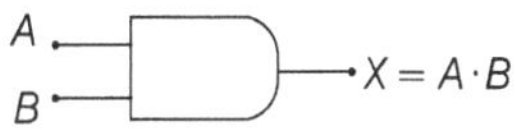

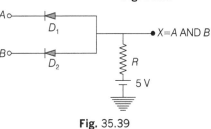

Fig. 35.38

$$X = A \cdot B$$

Figure shows construction for an AND gate using two diodes D_1 and D_2.

When potentials at A and B both are zero, then both the diodes are forward biased and offer no resistance. The potential at X in this position is equal to the potential at A or B i.e. 0. Thus $X = 0$, when both A and B are zero. Now suppose potential at A is zero but at B is 5V, then D_1 is forward biased. In this situation potential at X is also zero.

Fig. 35.39

Thus, $X = 0$ when $A = 0$. Similarly, we can see that $X = 0$ when $B = 0$. Lastly when potentials at both A and B are 5V, so that both the diodes are unbiased and there will be no current through R and the potential at X will be equal to 5V. Thus, $X = 1$ when A and B both are 1.

NOT gate This has one input and one output. The output is the inverse of the input. When the input A is 1, the output X will be 0 and *vice-versa*. The truth table for 'NOT' gate is given below.

Table 35.9

A	X
0	1
1	0

Fig. 35.40

Note *A NOT gate cannot be constructed with diodes. Transistor is used for realisation of a NOT gate, but at this stage students do not require it. A NOT gate is written as $X = \bar{A}$.*

NAND gate The function, $X = \text{NOT} \ (A \text{ and } B)$ of two logical variables A and B is called NAND function. It is written as $X = A$ NAND B. It is also written as,

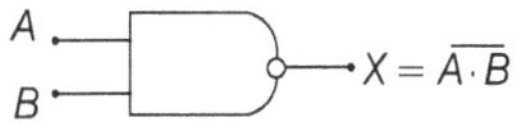

Fig. 35.41

$$X = \overline{A \cdot B}$$

or
$$X = \overline{AB}$$

The truth table of a 'NAND' gate is given below.

Table 35.10

A	B	A·B	$X = \overline{A \cdot B}$
0	0	0	1
0	1	0	1
1	0	0	1
1	1	1	0

NOR gate The function $X = \text{NOT} \ (A \text{ OR } B)$ is called a NOR function and is written as $X = A$ NOR B. It is also written as, $X = \overline{A + B}$. The truth table for a NOR gate is given below.

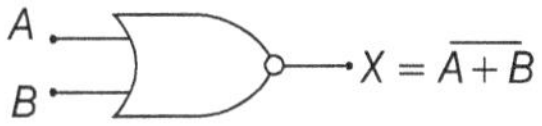

Fig. 35.42

Table 35.11

A	B	A + B	X = $\overline{A + B}$
0	0	0	1
0	1	1	0
1	0	1	0
1	1	1	0

XOR gate It is also called the exclusive OR function. It is a function of two logical variables A and B which evaluates to 1 if one of two variables is 0 and the other is 1. The function is zero, if both the variables are 0 or 1.

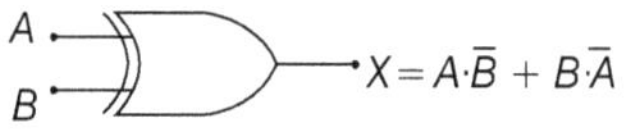

A —
B — $\rightarrow X = A \cdot \overline{B} + B \cdot \overline{A}$

Fig. 35.43

$$A \text{ XOR } B = A \cdot \overline{B} + \overline{A} \cdot B$$

The truth table for XOR is given below.

Table 35.12

A	B	$\overline{A}$	$\overline{B}$	$A \cdot \overline{B}$	$\overline{A} \cdot B$	$X = A \cdot \overline{B} + \overline{A} \cdot B$
0	0	1	1	0	0	0
0	1	1	0	0	1	1
1	0	0	1	1	0	1
1	1	0	0	0	0	0

● **Example 35.16** *Construct the truth table for the function X of A and B represented by figure shown here.*

A —
B — $\rightarrow X$

Fig. 35.44

Solution The output X in terms of the input A and B can be written as, $X = A \cdot (A + B)$
Let us make the truth table corresponding to this function.

Table 35.13

A	B	A + B	X = A·(A + B)
0	0	0	0
0	1	1	0
1	0	1	1
1	1	1	1

◎ **Example 35.17** *Make the output waveform (Y) of the OR gate for the following inputs A and B.*

Table 35.14

Time	A	B
For $t < t_1$	0	0
From t_1 to t_2	1	0
From t_2 to t_3	1	1
From t_3 to t_4	0	1
From t_4 to t_5	0	0
From t_5 to t_6	1	0
For $t > t_6$	0	1

Solution Output value Y corresponding to OR gate is given in the following table.

Table 35.15

Time	A	B	Y = A + B
For $t < t_1$	0	0	0
From t_1 to t_2	1	0	1
From t_2 to t_3	1	1	1
From t_3 to t_4	0	1	1
From t_4 to t_5	0	0	0
From t_5 to t_6	1	0	1
For $t > t_6$	0	1	1

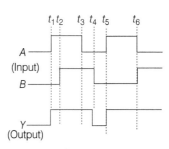

Fig. 35.45

Therefore, the waveform Y will be as shown in the figure.

◎ **Example 35.18** *Take A and B inputs similar to that in above example. Sketch the output waveform obtained from AND gate.*

Solution Output value, Y corresponding to AND gate is given in the following table.

Table 35.16

Time	A	B	Y = A · B
For $t < t_1$	0	0	0
From t_1 to t_2	1	0	0
From t_2 to t_3	1	1	1
From t_3 to t_4	0	1	0
From t_4 to t_5	0	0	0
From t_5 to t_6	1	0	0
For $t > t_6$	0	1	0

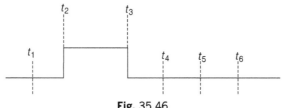

Fig. 35.46

Based on the above table, the output waveform Y for AND gate can be drawn as in figure 35.46.

INTRODUCTORY EXERCISE 35.4

1. Make the output waveform Y of the NAND gate for the following inputs A and B.

Table 35.17

Time	A	B
For $t < t_1$	1	1
From t_1 to t_2	0	0
From t_2 to t_3	0	1
From t_3 to t_4	1	0
From t_4 to t_5	1	1
From t_5 to t_6	0	0
For $t > t_6$	0	1

2. You are given two circuits. Identify the logic operation carried out by the two circuits.

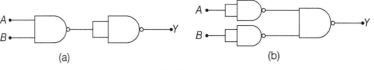

Fig. 35.47

Core Concepts

1. **Integrated Circuits** The short form of integrated circuit is IC. It is revolutionised the electronics technology. The entire electronic circuit (consisting of many passive components like R and C and active devices like diode and transistor) is fabricated on a small single block (called chip) of a semiconductor. Such circuits are more reliable and less shock proof compared to conventional circuits used before. The chip dimensions are as small as 1mm × 1mm or it could be even smaller than this.

   Depending on the nature of input signals, ICs are of two types.

   (i) Linear or analogue IC
   (ii) Digital IC

   Linear ICs process analogue signals which change over a range of values between a maximum and a minimum. The digital ICs process signals that have only two values. They contain circuits such as logic gates.

   IC is the heart of all computer systems. It is used in almost all electronic devices like, cell phones, televisions, cars etc.

   It was first invented in 1958 by **Jack Kilky** and he was awarded Nobel prize for this in the year 2000. Growth of semiconductor industry is very fast. From current trends it is expected that by 2020 computers will operate at 40 GHz and would be much smaller, more efficient and less expensive than present day computers.

2. **Feedback amplifier and transistor oscillator** In an amplifier, a sinusoidal input is given which gets amplified as an output. Hence, an external input is necessary to sustain AC signal in the output.

   In an oscillator, we get AC output without any external input signal. A portion of the output power is returned back (feedback) to the input (in phase) with the starting power. In other words, the output in an oscillator is self sustained.

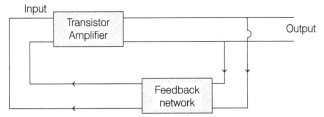

   Principle of a transistor amplifier with positive feedback working as an oscillator

3. In transistors, the base region is narrow and lightly doped, otherwise the electrons or holes coming from the input side (say emitter in CE-configuration) will not be able to reach the collector.

Solved Examples

⊛ **Example 1** *Sn, C, Si and Ge are all group XIV elements. Yet, Sn is a conductor, C is an insulator while Si and Ge are semiconductors. Why ?*

Solution It all depends on energy gap between valence band and conduction band. The energy gap for Sn is 0 eV, for C is 5.4 eV, for Si is 1.1 eV and for Ge is 0.7 eV.

⊛ **Example 2** *Three photodiodes D_1, D_2 and D_3 are made of semiconductors having band gaps of 2.5 eV, 2 eV and 3 eV, respectively. Which one will be able to detect light of wavelength 6000 $\overset{o}{A}$?*

Solution Energy of incident light

$$E \text{ (in eV)} = \frac{12375}{\lambda \text{ (in Å)}}$$

$$E = \frac{12375}{6000} \text{ eV}$$

or $\qquad\qquad\qquad E = 2.06 \text{ eV}$

For the incident radiation to be detected by the photodiode energy of incident radiation should be greater than the band gap. This is true only for D_2. Therefore only D_2 will detect this radiation.

⊛ **Example 3** *What is the range of energy gap (E_g) in insulators, semiconductors and conductors?*

Solution For insulators $E_g > 3$ eV, for semiconductors, $E_g = 0.2$ eV to 3eV while for conductors (or metals) $E_g = 0$.

⊛ **Example 4** *n-type extrinsic semiconductor is negatively charged, while p-type extrinsic semiconductor is positively charged. Is this statement true or false?*

Solution False. Intrinsic as well as extrinsic semiconductors are electrically neutral.

⊛ **Example 5** *What is resistance of an intrinsic semiconductor at 0K ?*

Solution At 0K number of holes (or number of free electrons) in an intrinsic semiconductor become zero. Therefore, resistance of an intrinsic semiconductor becomes infinite at 0 K.

⊛ **Example 6** *Consider an amplifier circuit using a transistor. The output power is several times greater than the input power. Where does the extra power come from?*

Solution The extra power required for amplified output is obtained from the DC source.

⊛ **Example 7** *A piece of copper and the other of germanium are cooled from the room temperature to 80 K. What will happen to their resistance?*

Solution Copper is conductor and germanium is semiconductor. With decrease in temperature resistance of a conductor decreases and that of semiconductor increases. Therefore resistance of copper will decrease and that of semiconductor will increase.

⊘ **Example 8** *A transistor has three impurity regions, emitter, base and collector. Arrange them in order of increasing doping levels.*

Solution The order of increasing doping levels is

$$\text{base} < \text{collector} < \text{emitter}.$$

⊘ **Example 9** *Name two gates which can be used repeatedly to produce all the basic or complicated gates.*

Solution NAND and NOR gates can be used repeatedly to produce all the basic or complicated gates. This is why these gates are called digital building blocks.

⊘ **Example 10** *A change of 8.0 mA in the emitter current brings a change of 7.9 mA in the collector current. How much change in the base current is required to have the same change 7.9 mA in the collector current ? Find the values of α and β.*

Solution We know that,

$$i_e = i_b + i_c$$

∴ $$\Delta i_e = \Delta i_b + \Delta i_c$$

or $$\Delta i_b = \Delta i_e - \Delta i_c$$

Substituting the given values of the question,

We have $\qquad \Delta i_b = (8.0 - 7.9)\ \text{mA} = 0.1\ \text{mA}$

Hence, a change of 0.1 mA in the base current is required to have a change of 7.9 mA in the collector current.

Further, $\qquad\qquad \alpha = \dfrac{i_c}{i_e} \text{ or } \dfrac{\Delta i_c}{\Delta i_e} = \dfrac{7.9}{8.0}$

$$= 0.99 \qquad\qquad \textbf{Ans.}$$

$$\beta = \dfrac{i_c}{i_b} \text{ or } \dfrac{\Delta i_c}{\Delta i_b} = \dfrac{7.9}{0.1}$$

$$= 79 \qquad\qquad \textbf{Ans.}$$

⊘ **Example 11** *A transistor is used in common-emitter mode in an amplifier circuit. When a signal of 20 mV is added to the base-emitter voltage, the base current changes by 20 μA and the collector current changes by 2 mA. The load resistance is 5 kΩ. Calculate (a) the factor β (b) the input resistance R_{in} (c) the transconductance and (d) the voltage gain.*

Solution (a) **Factor β**

$$\beta = \frac{\Delta i_c}{\Delta i_b}$$

Substituting the given values, we have

$$\beta = \frac{2 \times 10^{-3}}{20 \times 10^{-6}} = 100 \qquad\qquad \textbf{Ans.}$$

(b) Input Resistance R_{in}

$$R_{in} = \frac{\Delta V_{BE}}{\Delta i_b} = \frac{20 \times 10^{-3}}{20 \times 10^{-6}}$$

$$= 10^3 \ \Omega$$

$$= 1 \ k\Omega \qquad \text{Ans.}$$

(c) Transconductance g_m

$$g_m = \frac{\Delta i_c}{\Delta V_{BE}} = \frac{2 \times 10^{-3}}{20 \times 10^{-3}}$$

$$= 0.1 \ \text{mho} \qquad \text{Ans.}$$

(d) Voltage Gain A_V

$$A_V = \beta \left(\frac{R_{out}}{R_{in}} \right)$$

Substituting the values we have,

$$A_V = (100) \left(\frac{5 \times 10^3}{1 \times 10^3} \right)$$

$$= 500 \qquad \text{Ans.}$$

⊙ **Example 12** *An n-p-n transistor is connected in common-emitter configuration in which collector supply is 8V and the voltage drop across the load resistance of 800 Ω connected in the collector circuit is 0.8 V. If current amplification factor is 25, determine collector-emitter voltage and base current. If the internal resistance of the transistor is 200 Ω, calculate the voltage gain and the power gain.*
Solution The corresponding circuit is shown in figure.

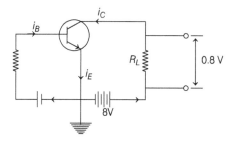

Voltage across $R_L = i_c \ R_L = 0.8$ V (given)

∴ $$i_c = \frac{0.8}{R_L} = \frac{0.8}{800} A = 1 \ \text{mA}$$

Further it is given that,

$$\beta = 25 = \frac{i_c}{i_b}$$

∴ $$i_b = \frac{i_c}{25} = 40 \ \mu A \qquad \text{Ans.}$$

Collector-Emitter Voltage (V_{CE})
Applying Kirchhoff's second law in emitter-collector circuit, we have

$$V_{CE} = (8 - 0.8) \ V = 7.2 \ V \qquad \text{Ans.}$$

Voltage gain (A_V)

Voltage gain,

$$A_V = \beta \left(\frac{R_{out}}{R_{in}} \right)$$

or

$$A_V = 25 \left(\frac{800}{200} \right) = 100$$ **Ans.**

Power gain

$$\text{Power gain} = \beta^2 \left(\frac{R_{out}}{R_{in}} \right) = (25)^2 \left(\frac{800}{200} \right) = 2500$$ **Ans.**

Note *Kirchhoff's laws can be applied in a transistor circuit in the similar manner as is done in normal circuits.*

◉ **Example 13** *An n-p-n transistor in a common-emitter mode is used as a simple voltage amplifier with a collector current of 4 mA. The positive terminal of a 8 V battery is connected to the collector through a load resistance R_L and to the base through a resistance R_B. The collector-emitter voltage $V_{CE} = 4\,V$, the base-emitter voltage $V_{BE} = 0.6\,V$ and the current amplification factor $\beta = 100$. Calculate the values of R_L and R_B.*

Solution Given, $i_c = 4$ mA

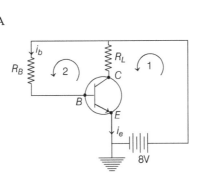

Applying Kirchhoff's second law in loop 1, we have

$$V_{CE} = 8 - i_c \, R_L$$

∴

$$R_L = \frac{8 - V_{CE}}{i_c} = \frac{8-4}{4 \times 10^{-3}}$$

$$= 1000 \; \Omega$$

$$= 1 \text{ k}\Omega$$ **Ans.**

Further,

$$\beta = \frac{i_c}{i_b}$$

∴

$$i_b = \frac{i_c}{\beta} = \frac{4 \times 10^{-3}}{100} \text{ A} = 40 \; \mu\text{A}$$

Now,

$$V_{BE} = 8 - i_b \, R_B$$

∴

$$R_B = \frac{8 - V_{BE}}{i_b}$$

$$= \frac{8 - 0.6}{40 \times 10^{-6}}$$

$$= 1.85 \times 10^5 \; \Omega$$ **Ans.**

⊚ **Example 14** *Let* $X = A \cdot \overline{BC}$. *Evaluate X for*

(a) $A = 1, B = 0, C = 1$,   (b) $A = B = C = 1$ *and*   (c) $A = B = C = 0$.

Solution (a) When, $A = 1, B = 0$ and $C = 1$

$$BC = 0$$
∴ $$\overline{BC} = 1$$
or $$A \cdot \overline{BC} = 1$$ **Ans.**

(b) When, $$A = B = C = 1$$
Then, $$BC = 1$$
or $$\overline{BC} = 0$$
∴ $$A \cdot \overline{BC} = 0$$ **Ans.**

(c) When, $$A = B = C = 0$$
Then, $$BC = 0$$
∴ $$\overline{BC} = 1$$
or $$A \cdot \overline{BC} = 0$$ **Ans.**

⊚ **Example 15** *Show that given circuit (a) acts as OR gate while the given circuit (b) acts as AND gate.*

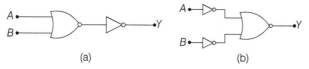

(a)   (b)

Solution (a) The first gate is NOR gate then NOT gate

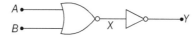

Thus, $X = \overline{A + B}$ and $Y = \overline{X}$

The truth table can be made as under.7

Table 35.18

A	B	A + B	$X = \overline{A+B}$	$Y = \overline{X}$
1	0	1	0	1
0	1	1	0	1
1	1	1	0	1
0	0	0	1	0

The last column of Y is similar to third column of $A + B$ which is the truth table corresponding to OR gate.

(b) First two gates are NOT gates and the last gate is NOR gate.

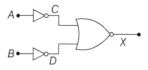

Thus, $$C = \overline{A} \text{ and } D = \overline{B}$$
$$X = \overline{C + D}$$

The truth table corresponding to this can be made as under.

Table 35.19

A	B	A·B	C = $\bar{A}$	D = $\bar{B}$	C + D	X = $\overline{C + D}$
1	0	0	0	1	1	0
0	1	0	1	0	1	0
1	1	1	0	0	0	1
0	0	0	1	1	1	0

The last column of X is similar to third column of $A \cdot B$, which is the truth table corresponding to AND gate.

⊙ **Example 16** *Write the truth table for the circuit given in figure consisting of NOR gates. Identify the logic operations (OR, AND, NOT) performed by the the circuits.*

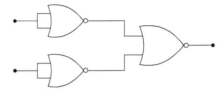

Solution The truth table corresponding to given circuit of logic gates is

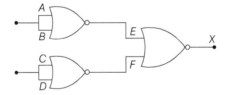

Table 35.20

A	B	A + B	E = $\overline{A + B}$	C	D	C + D	F = $\overline{C + D}$	E + F	X = $\overline{E + F}$
1	1	1	0	1	1	1	0	0	1
0	0	0	1	0	0	0	1	1	0

Corresponding to input columns of A, B, C and D we can see that output column of X is of AND gate,

$$X = A + B + C + D$$

Exercises

Single Correct Option

1. The conductivity of a semiconductor increases with increase in temperature because
  (a) number density of free current carriers increases
  (b) relaxation time increases
  (c) both number density of carriers and relaxation time decreases but effect of decrease in relaxation time is much less than increase in number density.
  (d) number density of current carriers increases, relaxation time decreases but effect of decrease in relaxation time is much less than increase in number density

2. In figure, assuming the diodes to be ideal,

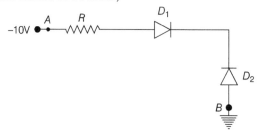

  (a) D_1 is forward biased and D_2 is reverse biased and hence current flows from A to B.
  (b) D_2 is forward biased and D_1 is reverse biased and hence no current flows from B to A and *vice-versa.*
  (c) D_1 and D_2 are both forward biased and hence current flows from A to B.
  (d) D_1 and D_2 are both reverse biased and hence no current flows from A to B and *vice-versa.*

3. Hole is
  (a) an anti-particle of electron
  (b) a vacancy created when an electron leaves a covalent bond
  (c) absence of free electrons
  (d) an artificially created particle

4. A 220 V AC supply is connected between points A and B. What will be the potential difference V across the capacitor?

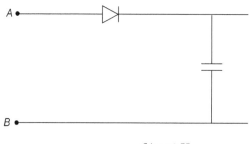

  (a) 220 V
  (c) 0V
  (b) 110 V
  (d) $220 \sqrt{2}$ V

More than One Correct Options

5. When an electric field is applied across a semiconductor,
   (a) electrons move from lower energy level to higher energy level in the conduction band.
   (b) electrons move from higher energy level to lower energy level in the conduction band.
   (c) holes in the valence band move from higher energy level to lower energy level.
   (d) holes in the valence band move from lower energy level to higher energy level.

6. Consider an *n-p-n* transistor with its base-emitter junction forward biased and collector base junction reverse biased. Which of the following statements are true?
   (a) Electrons crossover from emitter to collector.
   (b) Holes move from base to collector.
   (c) Electrons move from emitter to base.
   (d) Electrons from emitter move out of base without going to the collector.

7. In an *n-p-n* transistor circuit, the collector current is 10 mA. If 95 per cent of the electrons emitted reach the collector, which of the following statements are true?
   (a) The emitter current will be 8 mA.   (b) The emitter current will be 10.53 mA.
   (c) The base current will be 0.53 mA.   (d) The base current will be 2 mA.

8. In the depletion region of a diode,
   (a) there are no mobile charges
   (b) equal number of holes and electrons exist, making the region neutral
   (c) recombination of holes and electrons has taken place
   (d) immobile charged ions exist.

9. What happens during regulation action of a Zener diode?
   (a) The current and voltage across the Zener remains fixed.
   (b) The current through the series resistance (R) changes.
   (c) The Zener resistance is constant.
   (d) The resistance offered by the Zener changes.

10. The breakdown in a reverse biased *p-n* junction diode is more likely to occur due to
    (a) large velocity of the minority charge carriers if the doping concentration is small
    (b) large velocity of the minority charge carriers if the doping concentration is large
    (c) strong electric field in a depletion region if the doping concentration is small
    (d) strong electric field in the depletion region if the doping concentration is large.

Subjective Questions

11. Can the potential barrier across a *p-n* junction be measured by simply connecting a voltmeter across the junction?

12. Two car garages have a common gate which needs to open automatically when a car enters either of the garages or cars enter both. Devise a circuit that resembles this situation using diodes for this situation.

13. Two amplifiers are connected one after the other in series (cascaded). The first amplifier has a voltage gain of 10 and the second has a voltage gain of 20. If the input signal is 0.01 V, calculate the output AC signal.

14. A *p-n* photodiode is fabricated from a semiconductor with band-gap of 2.8 eV. Can it detect a wavelength of 6000 nm?

15. (i) Name the type of a diode whose characteristics are shown in figure.

(ii) What does the point P in figure represent?

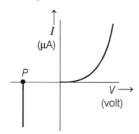

16. If the resistance R_1 is increased, how will the readings of the ammeter and voltmeter change?

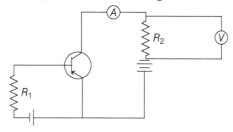

17. How would you set up a circuit to obtain NOT gate using a transistor?

18. Write the truth table for the circuit shown in figure. Name the gate that the circuit resembles.

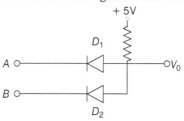

19. A Zener of power rating 1 W is to be used as a voltage regulator. If Zener has a breakdown of 5V and it has to regulate voltage which fluctuated between 3V and 7V, what should be the value of R for safe operation.

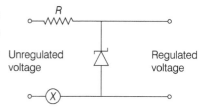

20. If each diode in figure has a forward bias resistance of $25\,\Omega$ and infinite resistance in reverse bias, what will be the values of the current I_1, I_2, I_3 and I_4?

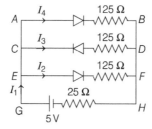

21. In the circuit shown in figure when the input voltage of the base resistance is 10 V. Find the values of I_b, I_c and β.

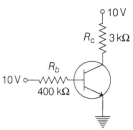

22. For the transistor circuit shown in figure, evaluate V_E, R_B and R_E. Given $I_C = 1$ mA, $V_{CE} = 3$ V, $V_{BE} = 0.5$ V, $V_{CC} = 12$ V and $\beta = 100$.

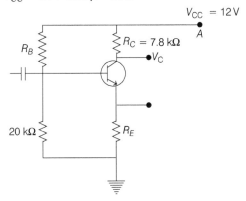

23. In the circuit shown in figure, find the value of R_C.

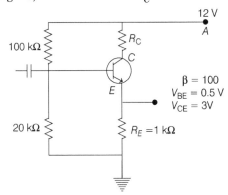

Answers

Introductory Exercise 35.1

   1. (c)

Introductory Exercise 35.2

   1. (c)   *2.* (c)

Introductory Exercise 35.3

   1. (b,c)   *2.* (c)   *3.* $V_i = 0.01$ V, $i_b = 10\,\mu$A

Introductory Exercise 35.4

1.

   2. (a) AND (b) OR

Exercises

1. (d)	*2.* (b)	*3.* (b)	*4.* (d)	*5.* (a,c)	*6.* (a,c)
7. (b,c)	*8.* (a,b,c)	*9.* (b,d)	*10.* (a,d)	*11.* No	*12.* OR gate
13. 2 V	*14.* No				

15. (i) Zener junction diode and solar cell (ii) Zener breakdown voltage

16. Both readings will decrease

18. AND gate

19. 10 Ω

20. $I_1 = 0.05$ A, $I_2 = 0.025$ A, $I_3 = 0$, $I_4 = 0.025$ A

21. $I_B = 25\,\mu$A, $I_C = 3.33$ mA, $\beta = 133$

22. $V_E = 1.2$ V, $R_B = 108$ kΩ, $R_E = 1.2$ kΩ

23. 0.56 kΩ

36

36.1 **Introduction**

Communication refers to the transfer of information or message from one point to another point. In modern communication systems, the information is first converted into electrical signals and then sent electronically. This has the advantage of speed, reliability and possibility of communicating over long distances. We are using these every day such as telephones, TV and radio transmission, satellite communication etc. Historically, long distance communication started with the advent of telegraphy in early nineteenth century. The milestone in trans-atlantic radio transmission in 1901 is credited to **Marconi.** However, the concept of radio transmission was first demonstrated by Indian physicist **JC Bose.** Satellite communication started in 1962 with the launching of **Telstar** satellite. The first geostationary satellite **Early Bird** was launched in 1965. Around 1970, optical fibre communication entered in USA, Europe and Japan. The basic units of any communication systems are shown in Fig. 36.1

The transmitter is located at one place. The receiver is located at some other place. Transmission channel connects the transmitter and the receiver. A channel may be in the form of wires or cables or it may be wireless. Transmitter converts message signals produced by the source of information into a form suitable for transmission through the channel.

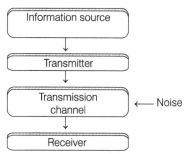

Fig. 36.1 Block diagram of communication system

In any communication system, a non-electrical signal (like voice signal) is first converted into an electrical signal by a device called **transducer.** Most of the speech or information signal cannot be directly transmitted to long distances. For this an intermediate step of **modulation** is necessary in which the information signal is loaded or superimposed on a high frequency wave which acts as a carrier wave.

> ⊘ *Extra Points to Remember*
>
> • There are basically two communication modes : point to point and broadcast.
>
> • **Point to point**   In this mode, communication takes place between a single receiver and transmitter. For example : telephonic call between two persons is a point to point communication.
>
> • **Broadcast**   In this mode, there are a large number of receivers corresponding to a single transmitter. Radio and television are examples of this type of communication.

36.2 **Different Terms Used in Communication System**

Following basic terminology is used in any communication system. Now let us discuss them in detail.

Electrical Transducer   As discussed earlier also a transducer converts a non-electrical signal (like a voice signal) into an electrical signal.

Signal   Any information in electrical form suitable for transmission is called a signal. Signals can be either analog or digital. Analog signals are continuous variations of voltage or current. Sine functions of time are fundamental analog signal. Digital signals are those which can take only discrete values. Binary system is extensively used in digital electronics. In binary system 0 corresponds to low level and 1 corresponds to high level of voltage or current.

Noise   Unwanted signals which are mixed with the main signals are referred as noise.

Transmitter   A transmitter makes the incoming message signal suitable for transmission through a channel.

Receiver   The signal sent by transmitter through channels is received by the receiver.

Attenuation   When the signal propagates from transmitter to receiver it loses some strength and it becomes weaker. This is known as attenuation.

Amplification   The signal received by receiver is weaker than the signal sent by transmitter (due to attenuation). The amplitude of this signal is increased by an amplifier. The energy needed for additional signal is obtained from a DC power source.

Range   This is the largest distance from the transmitter up to which signal can be received with sufficient strength.

Bandwidth   This is the width of the range of frequencies that an electronic signal uses on a given transmission medium. It is expressed in terms of the difference between the highest frequency signal component and the lowest frequency signal component.

Modulation   The low frequency message signals cannot be transmitted to long distances by their own. They are superimposed on a high frequency wave (also called a carrier wave). This process is called modulation.

Demodulation   This is reverse process of modulation. At the receiver end information is retrieved from the carrier wave. This process is known as demodulation.

Repeater   Repeaters are used to extend the range of a communication system. It is a combination of a receiver and a transmitter. Receiver (or a repeater) first receives the original signals, then amplifies it and retransmits it to other places (sometimes with a different carrier frequency).

36.3 Bandwidth of Signals

Message signals (such as voice, picture or computer data) have different range of frequencies. The type of communication system depends on the bandwidth (discussed in the above article). Some frequency range and their corresponding bandwidth are given below.

  (i) **For telephonic communication**   A bandwidth of 2800 Hz is required. As, the signals range from 300 Hz to 3100 Hz and their difference is 2800 Hz.

 (ii) **For music channels**   A bandwidth of approximately 20 kHz is required. Because, the audible range of frequencies extends from 20 Hz to 20 kHz and their difference is approximately 20 kHz.

(iii) **For TV signals**   A TV signal consists both audio and video. A bandwidth of approximately 6 MHz is required for its transmission.

36.4 Bandwidth of Transmission Medium

Like bandwidths of message signals different types of transmission media offer different bandwidths. Commonly used transmission media are optical fibres, free space and wire. The International Telecommunication Union (ITU) administers the present system of frequency allocations.

  (i) Coaxial cables offers a bandwidth of approximately 750 MHz.

 (ii) Optical fibres offers a frequency range of 1 THz to 1000 THz.

(iii) Communication through free space (using radio waves) offers a bandwidth varying from few hundreds of kHz to a few GHz. These frequencies are further subdivided for various services as given in following table.

Table 36.1

S.No.	Service	Frequency Bands
1.	AM radio broadcast	540 – 1600 kHz
2.	FM radio broadcast	88 – 108 MHz
3.	Television	54 – 890 MHz
4.	Cellular Phones	840 – 935 MHz
5.	Satellite communication	3.7 – 6.425 GHz

36.5 Propagation of Electromagnetic Waves or Communication Channels

Physical medium through which signals propagate between transmitting and receiving station is called the communication channel. There are basically two types of communications.

(i) Space communication

(ii) Line communication

As per syllabus, we are here discussing only space communication.

Space Communication

Consider two friends playing with a ball in a closed room. One friend throws the ball (transmitter) and the other receives the ball (receiver). There are three ways in which the ball can be sent to the receiver.

(a) By rolling it along the ground

(b) Throwing directly and

(c) Throwing towards roof and then reflected towards the receiver. Similarly, there are three ways of transmitting an information from one place to the other using physical space around the earth.

Line Communication

(a) Along the ground (ground waves).

(b) Directly in a straight line through intervening topographic space (space wave, or tropospheric wave or surface wave) and

(c) Upwards in sky followed by reflection from the ionosphere (sky wave).

These three modes are discussed below.

(i) **Ground Wave or Surface Wave Propagation** Information can be transmitted through this mode when the transmitting and receiving antenna are close to the surface of the earth.

The radio waves which progress along the surface of the earth are called ground waves or surface waves. These waves are vertically polarised in order to prevent short-circuiting of the electric component. The electrical field due to the wave induce charges in the earth's surface as shown in figure. As the wave travels, the induced charges in the earth also travel along it. This constitutes a current in the earth's surface. As the ground wave passes over the surface of the earth, it is weakened as a result of energy absorbed by the earth. Due to these losses, the ground waves are not suited for very long range communication. Further these losses are higher for high frequency. Hence, ground wave propagation can be sustained only at low frequencies (500 kHz to 1500 kHz).

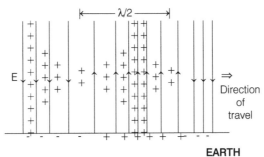

Fig. 36.2. Vertically polarised wave travelling over the surface of the earth. The solid lines represent the electric field (E) of the electromagnetic wave.

Space Wave Propagation or Tropospheric Wave Propagation Television signal (80 MHz to 200 MHz) waves neither follow the curvature of the earth nor get reflected by ionosphere. Surface wave or sky wave cannot be employed in television communication. Television signals can be reflected from geostationary satellite or tall receiver antennas.

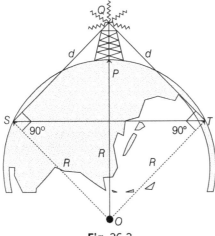

Fig. 36.3

Height of Transmitting Antenna The transmitted waves, travelling in a straight line, directly reach the receiver end and are then picked up by the receiving antenna as shown in figure. Due to finite curvature of the earth, such waves cannot be seen beyond the tangent points S and T.

Suppose h is the height of antenna PQ. Let R be the radius of earth.

Further, let $QT = QS = d$, $PQ = h$, $OQ = R + h$

From the right angled triangle OQT,

$$OQ^2 = OT^2 + QT^2$$

$$\therefore \qquad (R+h)^2 = R^2 + d^2$$

$$\therefore \qquad d^2 = h^2 + 2Rh$$

Since, $\qquad R >> h, \ h^2 + 2Rh \approx 2Rh$

$$\therefore \qquad \boxed{d \approx \sqrt{2Rh}}$$

This distance is of the order of 40 km. Area covered for TV transmission

$$\boxed{A = \pi d^2 = 2\pi Rh}$$

If height of receiving antenna is also given in the question, then the maximum line of sight distance d_M is given by

$$\boxed{d_M = \sqrt{2Rh_T} + \sqrt{2Rh_R}}$$

where, $\qquad h_T = $ height of transmitting antenna

and $\qquad h_R = $ height of receiving antenna

Further $\qquad \boxed{\text{population covered} = \text{population density} \times \text{area covered.}}$

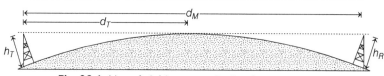

Fig. 36.4 Line of sight communication by space waves

● **Example 36.1** *A TV tower has a height of 60 m. What is the maximum distance and area up to which TV transmission can be received? (Take radius of earth as 6.4×10^6 m.)*

Solution (i) Distance $d = \sqrt{2Rh} = \sqrt{2 \times 6.4 \times 10^6 \times 60}$ m

$$= 27.7 \text{ km} \qquad \qquad \textbf{Ans.}$$

(ii) Area covered $= \pi d^2 = 2\pi Rh = (2 \times 3.14 \times 6.4 \times 10^6 \times 60)\,\text{m}^2$

$$= 2411 \text{ km}^2 \qquad \qquad \textbf{Ans.}$$

Sky Wave Propagation or Ionospheric Propagation If one wishes to send signals at far away stations, then either repeater transmitting stations are necessary or height of the antenna is to be increased. However much before the advent of satellites, radio broadcast covered long distances by the reflection of signals from the ionosphere. This mode of transmission is called ionospheric propagation or sky wave propagation.

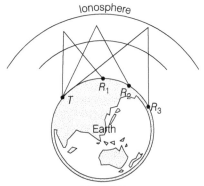

Fig. 36.5

$$T \rightarrow \text{Transmitter}, \quad R \rightarrow \text{Receiver}$$

The ionosphere extends from a height of 80 km to 300 km. The refractive index of ionosphere is less than its free space value. That is, it behaves as a rare medium. As, we go deep into the ionosphere, the refractive index keeps on decreasing. The bending of beam (away from the normal) will continue till it reaches critical angle after which it will be reflected back. The different points on earth receive signals reflected from different depths of the ionosphere. There is a critical frequency f_c (5 to 100 MHz) beyond which the waves cross the ionosphere and do not return back to earth.

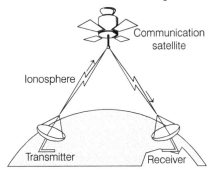

Fig. 36.6 Principle of satellite communication

Satellite Communication Long distance communication beyond 10 to 20 MHz was not possible before 1960 because all the three modes of communication discussed above failed (ground waves due to conduction losses, space wave due to limited line of sight and sky wave due to the penetration of the ionosphere by the high frequencies beyond f_c). Satellite communication made this possible.

The basic principle of satellite communication is shown in figure. A communication satellite is a spacecraft placed in an orbit around the earth. The frequencies used in satellite communication lie in UHF/microwave regions. These waves can cross the ionosphere and reach the satellite.

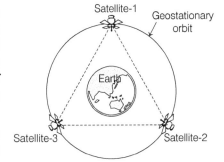

Fig. 36.7

For steady, reliable transmission and reception it is preferred that satellite should be geostationary. A geostationary satellite is one that appears to be stationary relative to the earth. It has a circular orbit lying in the equatorial plane of the earth at an approximate height of 36,000 km. Its time period is 24 hours.

If we use three geostationary satellites placed at the vertices of an equilateral triangle as shown in figure. The entire earth can be covered by the communication network.

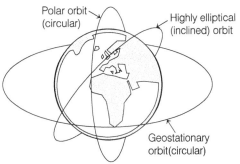

Fig. 36.8 A schematic diagram of various satellite orbits used in satellite communication

In addition to geostationary equatorial orbits, there are two more orbits which are being used for communication. These are

(a) **Polar circular orbit** This orbit passes over or very close to the poles. It is approximately at a height of 1000 km from earth.

(b) **Highly elliptical (inclined) orbits**

Remote Sensing

Remote sensing is an application of satellite communication. It is the art of obtaining information about an object or area acquired by a sensor that is not in direct contact with the target of investigation. Any photography is a kind of remote sensing. If we want to cover large areas for which information is required, we have to take photographs from larger distances. This is called aerial photography. Town and country planning can also be done by remote sensing.

A satellite equipped with appropriate sensors is used for remote sensing. Taking photograph of any object relies on the reflected wave from the object. We use visible light in normal photography. In principle, waves of any wavelength in the electromagnetic spectrum can be used for this purpose by using suitable sensors.

Some applications of remote sensing include meteorology (development of weather systems and weather forecasting), climatology (monitoring climate changes), and oceanography etc.

36.6 **Modulation**

In this section, we will discuss in detail about modulation. What is it ? What is the need of modulation or how the modulation is done etc.

No signal in general is a single frequency signal but it spreads over a range of frequencies called the signal bandwidth. Suppose we wish to transmit an electronic signal in the Audio Frequency (20 Hz-20 kHz) range over a long distance. Can we do it ? No it cannot because of the following problems.

   (i) **Size of antenna** For transmitting a signal we need an antenna. This antenna should have a size comparable to the wavelength of the signal. For an electromagnetic wave of frequency 20 kHz, the wavelength is 15 km. Obviously such a long antenna is not possible and hence direct transmission of such signal is not practical.

  (ii) **Effective power radiated by antenna** Power radiated by an antenna $\propto \dfrac{1}{(\lambda)^2}$.

      Therefore, power radiated by large wavelength would be small. For good transmission, we require high power and hence need of high frequency transmission is required.

 (iii) **Mixing up of signal from different transmitters** Another problem in transmitting baseband signals directly is of intermixing of different signals. Suppose many people are talking at the same time or many transmitters are transmitting baseband information signals simultaneously. All these signals will get mixed and there is no simple way to distinguish between them. A possible solution to all above problems is using communication at high frequencies and allotting a band of frequencies to each message signal for its transmission.

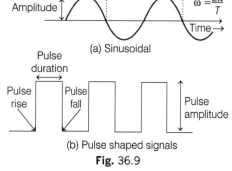

(a) Sinusoidal

(b) Pulse shaped signals

Fig. 36.9

Thus in the process of modulation the original low frequency information signal is attached with the high frequency carrier wave. The carrier wave may be continuous (sinusoidal) or in the form of pulses as shown in figure.

Modulation Types

Different types of modulation depend upon the specific characteristic of the carrier wave which is being varied in accordance with the message signal.

We know that a sinusoidal carrier wave can be expressed as

$$E = E_0 \sin (\omega t + \phi)$$

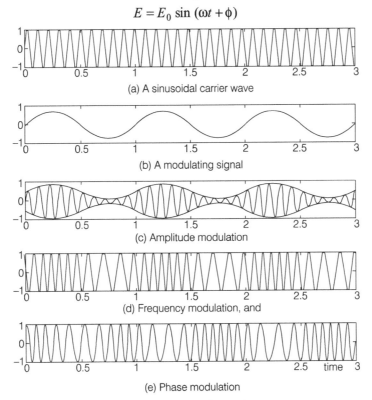

(a) A sinusoidal carrier wave

(b) A modulating signal

(c) Amplitude modulation

(d) Frequency modulation, and

(e) Phase modulation

Fig. 36.10 Modulation of a carrier wave

The three distinct characteristics are Amplitude (E_0), angular frequency (ω) and phase angle (ϕ). Either of these three characteristics can be varied in accordance with the signal. The three types of modulation are, amplitude modulation, frequency modulation and phase modulation.

Similarly, the characteristics of a pulse are, Pulse amplitude, pulse duration or pulse width and pulse position (time of rise or fall of the pulse amplitude).

Hence, different types of pulse modulation are, Pulse Amplitude Modulation (PAM), Pulse Duration Modulation (PDM) or Pulse Width Modulation (PWM) and Pulse Position Modulation (PPM).

In this chapter, we shall confine to amplitude modulation (of continuous wave or sinusoidal wave) only.

36.7 Amplitude Modulation

In this type of modulation, the amplitude of the carrier signal varies in accordance with the information signal. The information signal is superimposed on high frequency carrier wave. As a result, in the amplitude modulated carrier wave, amplitude no longer remains constant, but its envelope has similar sinusoidal variation as that of the low frequency or modulating signal. The carrier wave frequency ranges from 0.5 to 2.0 MHz. AM signals are noisy because electrical noise signals significantly affect this.

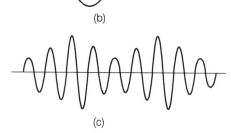

(a)

(b)

Let $C = A_c \sin \omega_c t$ represents a carrier wave

and $S = A_s \sin \omega_s t$ represents the signal wave

Then after making calculations we see that the modulated signal wave equation can be written as

$$m = A_c \sin \omega_c t + \frac{\mu A_c}{2} \cos (\omega_c - \omega_s) t$$

$$- \frac{\mu A_c}{2} \cos (\omega_c + \omega_s) t \qquad \ldots (i)$$

where, $\mu = \dfrac{A_s}{A_c}$ is called the **modulation index**. In

(c)

Fig. 36.11

practice, μ is kept ≤ 1 to avoid distortion.

In Eq. (i), $\omega_c - \omega_s$ and $\omega_c + \omega_s$ are respectively called the lower side and upper side frequencies.

The modulated signal therefore consists of the carrier wave of frequency ω_c plus two sinusoidal waves each with a frequency slightly different from ω_c, known as side bands.

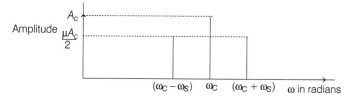

Fig. 36.12 A plot of amplitude *versus* ω for an amplitude modulated signal

> **Example 36.2** *A message signal of frequency* 10 *kHz and peak voltage of* 10 V *is used to modulate a carrier wave of frequency* 1 *MHz and peak voltage of* 20 V. *Determine*
> *(a) modulation index, (b) the side bands produced.*

Solution (a) **Modulation Index** $\mu = \dfrac{A_s}{A_c} = \dfrac{10}{20} = 0.5$ **Ans.**

(b) **Side Bands**   1 MHz = 1000 kHz

The side bands are, $(\omega_c - \omega_s)$ and $(\omega_c + \omega_s)$

or we can write $(f_c - f_s)$ and $(f_c + f_s)$

$\therefore$ $(f_c - f_s) = (1000 - 10) = 990$ kHz and

$(f_c + f_s) = (1000 + 10) = 1010$ kHz   **Ans.**

36.8 **Production of Amplitude Modulated Wave**

Amplitude modulation can be produced by a variety of methods. A simple method is shown in the block diagram of Fig.36.13.

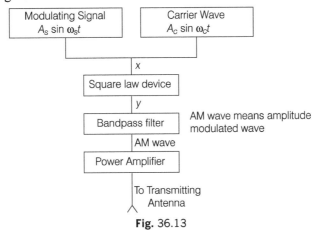

Fig. 36.13

In the y function shown in block diagram there is a DC term $\dfrac{C}{2}(A_c^2 + A_s^2)$ and sinusoids of frequencies $\omega_s, 2\omega_s, 2\omega_c, \omega_c - \omega_s$ and $\omega_c + \omega_s$. As shown in block diagram, this signal y is passed through a band pass filter which rejects DC and the sinusoids of frequencies $\omega_s, 2\omega_s$ and $2\omega_c$. After bandpass filter, the frequencies remaining are $\omega_c, \omega_c - \omega_s$ and $\omega_c + \omega_s$. The output (AM wave) of the band pass filter therefore is of the same form as Eq. (i) of previous article.

It is further to be noticed that this modulated signal cannot be transmitted as such. This signal is passed through a power amplifier and then the signal is fed to transmitter antenna.

36.9 **Detection of Amplitude Modulated Wave**

Signal received from the receiving antenna is first passed through an amplifier because the signal becomes weak in travelling from transmitting antenna to receiving antenna. For further processing, the signal is passed through intermediate frequency (IF) stage preceding the detection.

At this stage, the carrier frequency is usually changed to a lower frequency. The output signal from detector may not be strong enough. So, it is further passed through an amplifier for final use. The block diagram of all steps is shown in Fig. 36.14.

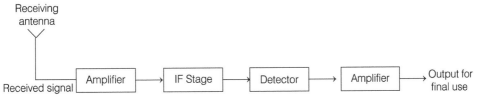

Fig. 36.14 Block diagram of a receiver

Inside the Detector

Detection is the process of recovering the signal from the carrier wave. In the previous two articles, we have seen that the modulated carrier wave contains the frequencies ω_c, $\omega_c + \omega_s$ and $\omega_c - \omega_s$. In order to obtain the original message signal $S\ (= A_s \sin \omega_s t)$ of angular frequency ω_s a simple method is shown in the form of a block diagram as shown below.

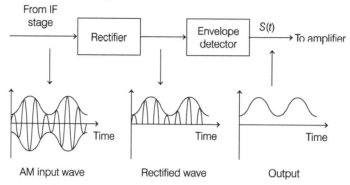

Fig. 36.15 Block diagram of a detector for AM signal

Note *that the quantity on y-axis can be current or voltage.*

> ✅ *Extra Points to Remember*
>
> • **The Internet** Everyone is well aware with internet. It has billions of users worldwide. It was started in 1960's and opened for public use in 1990's. Its applications include, E-mail, file transfer, website, E-commerce and chatting etc.
>
> • **Facsimile (FAX)** It first scans the image of contents of a document. Then those are converted into electronic signals. These electronic signals are sent to another FAX machine using telephone lines. At the destination, signals are reconverted into a replica of the original document.

Solved Examples

Example 1 *Name the device fitted in the satellite which receives signals from Earth station and transmits them in different directions after amplification.*

Solution Transponder.

Example 2 *An electromagnetic wave of frequency 28 MHz passes through the lower atmosphere of Earth and gets incident on the ionosphere. Shall the ionosphere reflects these waves?*

Solution Yes. The ionosphere reflects back electromagnetic waves of frequency less than 30 MHz.

Example 3 *Which waves constitute amplitude-modulated band?*

Solution Electromagnetic waves of frequency less than 30 MHz constitute amplitude-modulated band.

Example 4 *Give the frequency ranges of the following (i) High frequency band (HF) (ii) Very high frequency band (VHF) (iii) Ultra high frequency band (UHF) (iv) Super high frequency band (SHF).*

Solution (i) 3 MHz to 30 MHz (ii) 30 MHz to 300 MHz (iii) 300 MHz to 3000 MHz (iv) 3000 MHz to 30,000 MHz.

Example 5 *State the two functions performed by a modem.*

Solution (i) Modulation (ii) Demodulation.

Example 6 *Why is the transmission of signals using ground waves restricted up to a frequency of 1500 kHz?*

Solution This is because at frequencies higher than 1500 kHz, there is an increase in the absorption of signal by the ground.

Example 7 *How does the effective power radiated by an antenna vary with wavelength?*

Solution Power radiated by an antenna $\propto \left(\dfrac{1}{\lambda}\right)^2$.

Example 8 *Why is it necessary to use satellites for long distance TV transmission?*

Solution Television signals are not properly reflected by the ionosphere. So, reflection is affected by satellites.

Example 9 *Why long distance radio broadcasts use shortwave bands?*

Solution This is because ionosphere reflects waves in these bands.

Example 10 *What is a channel bandwidth?*

Solution Channel bandwidth is the range of frequencies that a system can transmit with efficient fidelity.

Example 11 *Give any one difference between FAX and e-mail systems of communication.*

Solution Electronic reproduction of a document at a distant place is known as FAX. In e-mail system, message can be created, processed and stored. Such facilities are not there in Fax system.

Example 12 *Why ground wave propagation is not suitable for high frequency?*

Solution At high frequency, the absorption of the signal by the ground is appreciable. So, ground wave propagation is not suitable for high frequency.

Example 13 *What is the purpose of modulating a signal in transmission?*

Solution A low frequency signal cannot be transmitted to long distances because of many practical difficulties. On the other hand, effective transmission is possible at high frequencies. So, modulation is always done in communication systems.

Example 14 *What is a transducer?*

Solution A device which converts energy in one form to another is called a transducer.

Example 15 *Why do we need a higher bandwidth for transmission of music compared to that for commercial telephone communication?*

Solution As compared to speech signals in telephone communication, the music signals are more complex and correspond to higher frequency range.

Example 16 *From which layer of the atmosphere, radio waves are reflected back?*

Solution The electromagnetic waves of radio frequencies are reflected by ionosphere.

Example 17 *Why sky waves are not used in the transmission of television signals?*

Solution The television signals have frequencies in 100-200 MHz range. As the ionosphere cannot reflect radio waves of frequency greater than 40 MHz back to the earth, the sky waves cannot be used in the transmission of TV signals.

Example 18 *Why are short waves used in long distance broadcasts?*

Solution The short waves (wavelength less than 200 m or frequencies greater than 1,00 kHz) are absorbed by the earth due to their high frequency but are effectively reflected by Flayer in ionosphere. After reflection from the ionosphere, the short waves reach the surface of earth back only at a large distance from the transmitter. For this reason, short waves are used in long distance transmission.

Example 19 *Define the term critical frequency in relation to sky wave propagation of electromagnetic waves.*

Solution The highest value of the frequency of radio waves, which on being radiated towards the ionosphere at some angle are reflected back to the earth is called critical frequency.

Example 20 *What mode of communication is employed for transmission of TV signals?*

Solution Space wave communication.

Exercises

Single Correct Option

1. Three waves A, B and C of frequencies 1600 kHz, 5 MHz and 60 MHz, respectively are to be transmitted from one place to another. Which of the following is the most appropriate mode of communication?
(a) A is transmitted *via* space wave while B and C transmitted *via* sky wave.
(b) A is transmitted *via* ground wave, B *via* sky wave and C *via* space wave.
(c) B and C are transmitted *via* ground wave while A is transmitted via sky wave.
(d) B is transmitted *via* ground wave while A and C are transmitted *via* space wave.

2. A 100 m long antenna is mounted on a 500 m tall building. The complex can become a transmission tower for waves with λ
(a) $\sim 400\,\text{m}$ (b) $\sim 25\,\text{m}$
(c) $\sim 150\,\text{m}$ (d) $\sim 2400\,\text{m}$

3. A speech signal of 3 kHz is used to modulate a carrier signal of frequency 1 MHz, using amplitude modulation. The frequencies of the side bands will be
(a) 1.003 MHz and 2.997 MHz   (b) 3001 kHz and 2997 kHz
(c) 1003 kHz and 1000 kHz   (d) 1 MHz and 0.997 MHz

4. A message signal of frequency ω_m is superposed on a carrier wave of frequency ω_c to get an amplitude modulated wave (AM). The frequency of the AM wave will be
(a) ω_m (b) ω_c
(c) $\dfrac{\omega_c + \omega_m}{2}$ (d) $\dfrac{\omega_c - \omega_m}{2}$

5. A basic communication system consists of
(A) transmitter   (B) information source   (C) user of information   (D) channel   (E) receiver
Choose the correct sequence in which these are arranged in a basic communication system.
(a) ABCDE   (b) BADEC
(c) BDACE   (d) BEADC

6. Which of the following frequencies will be suitable for beyond the horizon communication using sky waves?
(a) 10 kHz   (b) 10 MHz
(c) 1 GHz   (d) 1000 GHz

7. Frequencies in the UHF range normally propagate by means of
(a) ground waves   (b) sky waves
(c) surface waves   (d) space waves

8. Digital signals
(i) do not provide a continuous set of values
(ii) represent values as discrete steps
(iii) can utilize binary system and
(iv) can utilize decimal as well as binary systems

Which of the above statements are true?

(a) (i) and (ii) only

(b) (ii) and (iii) only

(c) (i), (ii) and (iii) but not (iv)

(d) All of (i), (ii), (iii) and (iv)

More than One Correct Options

9. A TV transmission tower has a height of 240 m. Signals broadcast from this tower will be received by LOS communication at a distance of (assume the radius of earth to be 6.4×10^6 m)

(a) 100 km

(b) 24 km

(c) 55 km

(d) 50 km

10. An audio signal of 15 kHz frequency cannot be transmitted over long distances without modulation because

(a) the size of the required antenna would be at least 5 km which is not convenient

(b) the audio signal cannot be transmitted through sky waves

(c) the size of the required antenna would be at least 20 km, which is not convenient

(d) effective power transmitted would be very low, if the size of the antenna is less than 5 km

11. Audio sine waves of 3 kHz frequency are used to amplitude modulate a carrier signal of 1.5 MHz. Which of the following statements are true?

(a) The sideband frequencies are 1506 kHz and 1494 kHz

(b) The bandwidth required for amplitude modulation is 6 kHz

(c) The bandwidth required for amplitude modulation is 3 MHz

(d) The sideband frequencies are 1503 kHz and 1497 kHz

12. In amplitude modulation, the modulation index μ, is kept less than or equal to 1 because

(a) $\mu > 1$ will result in interference between carrier frequency and message frequency, resulting into distortion.

(b) $\mu > 1$ will result in overlapping of both sidebands resulting into loss of information.

(c) $\mu > 1$ will result in change in phase between carrier signal and message signal.

(d) $\mu > 1$ indicates amplitude of message signal greater than amplitude of carrier signal resulting into distortion.

Subjective Questions

13. Compute the *LC* product of a tuned amplifier circuit required to generate a carrier wave of 1 MHz for amplitude modulation.

14. A carrier wave of peak voltage 12 V is used to transmit a message signal. What should be the peak voltage of the modulating signal in order to have a modulation index of 75%?

15. Which of the following would produce analog signals and which would produce digital signals?

(i) A vibrating tuning fork

(ii) Musical sound due to a vibrating sitar string

(iii) Light pulse

(iv) Output of NAND gate

16. Two waves *A* and *B* of frequencies 2 MHz and 3 MHz, respectively are beamed in the same direction for communication *via* sky wave. Which one of these is likely to travel longer distance in the ionosphere before suffering total internal reflection?

17. The maximum amplitude of an AM wave is found to be 15 V while its minimum amplitude is found to be 3V. What is the modulation index?

18. Why is an AM signal likely to be more noisy than a FM signal upon transmission through a channel?

19. Is it necessary for a transmitting antenna to be at the same height as that of the receiving antenna for line of sight communication? A TV transmitting antenna is 81 m tall. How much service area can it cover, if the receiving antenna is at the ground level?

20. A TV transmission tower antenna is at a height of 20 m. How much service area can it cover if the receiving antenna is (i) at ground level, (ii) at a height of 25 m? Calculate the percentage increase in area covered in case (ii) relative to case (i).

21. If the whole earth is to be connected by LOS communication using space waves (no restriction of antenna size or tower height), what is the minimum number of antennas required? Calculate the tower height of these antennas in terms of earth's radius?

22. The maximum frequency for reflection of sky waves from a certain layer of the ionosphere is found to be $f_{max} = 9(N_{max})^{1/2}$, where N_{max} is the maximum electron density at that layer of the ionosphere. On a certain day it is observed that signals of frequencies higher than 5 MHz are not received by reflection from the F_1 layer of the ionosphere while signals of frequencies higher than 8 MHz are not received by reflection from the F_2 layer of the ionosphere. Estimate the maximum electron densities of the F_1 and F_2 layers on that day.

23. A 50 MHz sky wave takes 4.04 ms to reach a receiver *via* re-transmission from a satellite 600 km above earth's surface. Assuming re-transmission time by satellite negligible, find the distance between source and receiver. If communication between the two was to be done by Line of Sight (LOS) method, what should be the size of transmitting antenna?

Answers

1. (b)	*2* (a)	*3.* (a)	*4.* (b)	*5.* (b)
6. (b)	*7.* (d)	*8.* (c)	*9.* (b,c,d)	*10.* (a,b,d)
11. (b,d)	*12* (b,d)	*13.* $2.53 \times 10^{-14} \, s^2$	*14.* 9 V	

15. (i) analog (ii) analog (iii) digital (iv) digital

16. 3 MHz　　　　　　　　　　*17.* 2/3

19. No, 3258 km^2　　　　　　　*20.* (i) 804 km^2 (ii) 3608 km^2 (iii) 349 %

21. Three, h = radius of earth　　　*22* $3.086 \times 10^{11} \, m^{-3}, 7.9 \times 10^{11} \, m^{-3}$

23. 170 km, 565 m

Hints & Solutions

29. Electromagnetic Waves

INTRODUCTORY EXERCISE 29.1

1.
$$i_d = \varepsilon_0 \frac{d\phi_E}{dt}$$

$$= \varepsilon_0 \frac{d}{dt}\left(E\frac{A}{2}\right)$$

$$= \frac{\varepsilon_0 A}{2}\frac{d}{dt}(E)$$

$$= \frac{\varepsilon_0 A}{2}\frac{d}{dt}\left(\frac{\sigma}{\varepsilon_0}\right)$$

$$= \frac{\varepsilon_0 A}{2}\frac{d}{dt}\left(\frac{q}{A\varepsilon_0}\right)$$

$$= \frac{1}{2}\frac{dq}{dt}$$

$$= \frac{i}{2} \qquad \left(\because \frac{dq}{dt}=i\right)$$

INTRODUCTORY EXERCISE 29.2

1. $c = \dfrac{1}{\sqrt{\varepsilon_0 \mu_0}}$ = speed of light in vacuum

$\therefore$ Unit of $\dfrac{1}{\sqrt{\varepsilon_0 \mu_0}}$ should be the unit of c or speed

or m/s.

Exercises

Single Correct Option

1. 11 eV energy radiation lies in UV range.

4. In case of perfectly non-reflecting surface,
$$\Delta p = \frac{E}{c}$$

where, $\quad E = 20 \times 30 \times 30 \times 60$

$$= 1.08 \times 10^6 \text{ J}$$

$$\therefore \qquad \Delta p = \frac{1.08 \times 10^6}{3 \times 10^8}$$

$$= 36 \times 10^{-4} \text{ kg-m/s}$$

More than One Correct Options

5. E, B and velocity of electromagnetic waves are mutually perpendicular.

2. There is a change in potential difference between the plates of capacitor.

Therefore, change in electric field between its plates. Now, change in electric field produces a magnetic field.

3. $\dfrac{E_0}{B_0} = c$

$\therefore \qquad B_0 = \dfrac{E_0}{c} = \dfrac{810}{3 \times 10^8}$

$$= 2.7 \times 10^{-6} \text{ T}$$

$$= 2.7 \, \mu\text{T}$$

4.
$$u_E = u_B = \frac{1}{2}\varepsilon_0 E^2$$

$$= \frac{1}{2}\varepsilon_0\left(\frac{E_0}{\sqrt{2}}\right)^2$$

$$= \frac{1}{4}\varepsilon_0 E_0^2$$

$$= \frac{1}{4}(8.86 \times 10^{-12})(50)^2$$

$$= 5.54 \times 10^{-9} \text{ J/m}^3$$

Total energy $= (u_E + u_B)$ (Given volume)
$$= 2 \times 5.54 \times 10^{-9} \times (10 \times 10^{-4})(0.50)$$

$$= 5.55 \times 10^{-12} \text{ J}$$

6. Every accelerated charged particle produces electromagnetic waves.

8. $\lambda = \dfrac{c}{f} = \dfrac{3 \times 10^8}{10^9} = 0.3$ m

This wavelength lies in radio waves region.

Subjective Questions

11. $\lambda = \dfrac{c}{f} = \dfrac{3 \times 10^8}{30 \times 10^6} = 10$ m

12. $\lambda = \dfrac{c}{f}$

$$\lambda_1 = \frac{3 \times 10^8}{7.5 \times 10^6} = 40 \text{ m}$$

$$\lambda_2 = \frac{3 \times 10^8}{12 \times 10^6} = 25 \text{ m}$$

13. $c = \dfrac{E_0}{B_0}$

$\quad E_0 = c B_0$

$\quad\quad = (3 \times 10^8)(510 \times 10^{-9})$

$\quad\quad = 153 \text{ V/m}$

14. (a) $C = \dfrac{\varepsilon_0 A}{d} = \dfrac{\varepsilon_0 (\pi R^2)}{d}$

$\quad\quad = \dfrac{(8.86 \times 10^{-12})(3.14)(0.12)^2}{5 \times 10^{-2}}$

$\quad\quad = 8 \times 10^{-12} \text{F} = 8 \text{ pF}$

$\quad V = \dfrac{q}{C}$

$\therefore \quad \dfrac{dV}{dt} = \dfrac{1}{C}\left(\dfrac{dq}{dt}\right) = \dfrac{i}{C}$

$\quad\quad = \dfrac{0.15}{8 \times 10^{-12}}$

$\quad\quad = 1.875 \times 10^{10} \text{ V/s}$

(b) $i_d = i_c = 0.15 \text{ A}$

15. (a) $c = \dfrac{E_0}{B_0}$

$\therefore \quad\quad B_0 = \dfrac{E_0}{c}$

$\quad\quad\quad \omega = 2\pi f$

$\quad\quad\quad c = v = \dfrac{\omega}{k}$

$\therefore \quad\quad\quad k = \dfrac{\omega}{c}$

$\quad\quad\quad \lambda = \dfrac{2\pi}{k}$

16. $X_C = \dfrac{1}{\omega C}$

With decrease in frequency, X_C will increase, so current will decrease.

Now,

$$i_d = i_c$$

i_c has decreased, so i_d will also decrease.

17. $\quad I_E = \dfrac{I}{2} = \dfrac{1}{2}\,\varepsilon_0 E^2 c$

$\quad\quad = \dfrac{1}{2}\,\varepsilon_0\left(\dfrac{E_0}{\sqrt{2}}\right)^2 c$

$\therefore \quad\quad E_0 = \sqrt{\dfrac{2I}{\varepsilon_0 c}}$

$\quad\quad = \sqrt{\dfrac{2 \times 2.5 \times 10^{14}}{8.86 \times 10^{-12} \times 3 \times 10^8}}$

$\quad\quad = 4.3 \times 10^8 \text{ N/C}$

Now, $\quad\quad c = \dfrac{E_0}{B_0}$

or $\quad\quad B_0 = \dfrac{E_0}{c}$

18. (a) $\quad\quad \lambda = \dfrac{c}{f}$

(b) $\quad\quad c = \dfrac{E_0}{B_0}$

or $\quad\quad B_0 = \dfrac{E_0}{c}$

(c) $u_E = \dfrac{1}{2}\,\varepsilon_0 E^2 = \dfrac{1}{2}\,\varepsilon_0\left(\dfrac{E_0}{\sqrt{2}}\right)^2 = \dfrac{1}{4}\,\varepsilon_0 E_0^2$

Similarly, $\quad u_B = \dfrac{B_0^2}{4\mu_0}$

After substituting the values we get,

$$u_E = u_B$$

19. $i_d = i_c = \dfrac{dq}{dt}$

$\quad\quad = -2\pi q_0 f \sin(2\pi f t)$

30. Reflection of Light

INTRODUCTORY EXERCISE 30.1

1.

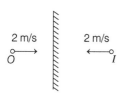

2 m/s → O   2 m/s ← I

$$|\mathbf{v}_{OI}| = 4 \text{ m/s}$$

2.

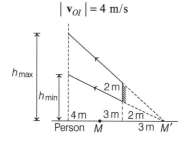

h_{max} h_{min} 2 m   4 m   3 m   2 m   Person M   3 m   M'

$$\frac{h_{min}}{10} = \frac{2}{3}$$

$$\therefore \quad h_{min} = \frac{20}{3} \text{ m}$$

$$\frac{h_{max}}{10} = \frac{4}{3}$$

$$\therefore \quad h_{max} = \frac{40}{3} \text{ m}$$

3.

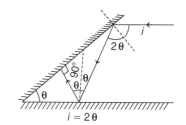

$$i = 2\theta$$

Exercises

LEVEL 1

Assertion and Reason

1.

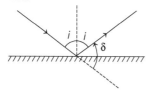

F

←— 20 cm —→ ←— 20 cm —→

Real object is in front of mirror, not at F. So, image is not at infinity.

2. Field of view of convex mirror is large.

3. $m = -2$, means image is real, inverted an 2-times magnified.

4.

$$\delta = 180° - 2i$$

For normal incidence, $i = 0°$

$$\therefore \qquad \delta = 180°$$

Objective Questions

1. Image is real and incident beam is convergent.

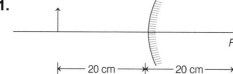

I   O

3. $\dfrac{1}{v} + \dfrac{1}{u} = \dfrac{1}{f}$ ...(i)

For virtual object u is positive and for concave mirror f is negative. Substituting these signs in Eq. (i), we can see that v is always negative or image is always real.

4. For real objects image formed by a convex mirror is always virtual, erect and diminished.

5. If object is placed at centre of curvature its image is also formed at centre of curvature.

6. The hour hand is lying between 3 and 4. So, on the mirror it will appear between 8 and 9.

The minute hand is lying at 25. So, on mirror it will appear at 35.

7.

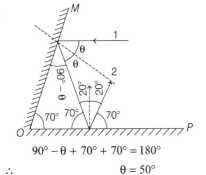

$$90° - \theta + 70° + 70° = 180°$$

∴ $$\theta = 50°$$

8.

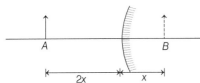

$$f = \frac{R}{2} = 30 \text{ cm}$$

$$\frac{1}{+x} + \frac{1}{-2x} = \frac{1}{+30}$$

∴ $$x = 15 \text{ cm}$$

Hence, $$AB = 3x = 45 \text{ cm}$$

9.

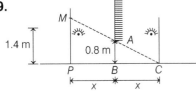

$$\frac{MP}{PC} = \frac{AB}{BC}$$

∴ $$\frac{MP}{2x} = \frac{0.8}{x}$$

or $$MP = 1.6 \text{ m} > 1.4 \text{ m}$$

Hence, the boy cannot see his feet.

10. Magnified image is formed only by concave mirror. But this image may be real or virtual.

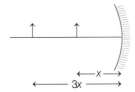

For real image,

$$2x = 80 \text{ cm}$$

∴ $$x = 40 \text{ cm}$$

$$\frac{1}{-120} + \frac{1}{-40} = \frac{1}{f}$$

Solving, we get $f = -30$ cm

Similarly, we can check for virtual image.

11. Let, $u = -x$

Then, $$v = +\frac{x}{n}$$

$$\frac{1}{(+x/n)} + \frac{1}{-x} = \frac{1}{+f}$$

Solving, we get $x = (n-1)f$

12. $$\frac{1}{v} + \frac{1}{-60} = \frac{1}{-24}$$

∴ $$v = -40 \text{ cm}$$

$$m = -\frac{v}{u} = -\frac{(40)}{(-60)} = \frac{-2}{3}$$

Image speed is m^2-times the object speed and opposite to the direction of object velocity.

13.

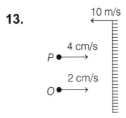

$$v_{PM} = 14 \text{ cm/s towards right}$$
$$v_{IM} = 14 \text{cm/s towards left}$$

So, actual speed of image $= 24$ cm/s towards left

∴ $$v_{IO} = 26 \text{ cm/s towards left.}$$

14. According to ray diagram as shown in figure

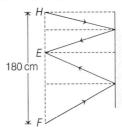

Length of mirror $= \dfrac{1}{2}(10 + 170)$

$$= 90 \text{ cm}$$

15. In case of concave mirror, $m = -2$

Also, $$m = \frac{f}{f-u} \implies -2 = \frac{-50}{-50-u}$$

∴ $$u = -75 \text{ cm}$$

16. Image of O from M_1 is at a distance of 8 cm to the left of M_1. This image is at a distance of 18 cm in front of M_2. So, its image is formed at a distance of 18 cm to the right of M_2.

First image of O from M_2 is at 2 cm behind M_2. So, it is at a distance of 12 cm from M_1. Hence, M_1 will make its image at a distance of 12 cm from M_1 towards left. This image is at a distance of 22 cm from M_2

17. Given, $AC = 60$ m

and $\angle BCB' = 90°$

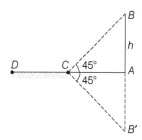

$\therefore \qquad \angle BCA = \dfrac{\angle BCB'}{2} = 45°$

$AB = AC = 60$ m

18. From the relation,

$$\dfrac{1}{v} + \dfrac{1}{u} = \dfrac{1}{f}$$

We have, $\dfrac{-dv}{v^2} - \dfrac{du}{u^2} = 0$

$\therefore \qquad dv = \dfrac{v^2}{u^2}(-du)$

$$= \left(\dfrac{20}{10}\right)^2 (0.1) = 0.4 \text{ cm}$$

19. For concave mirror,

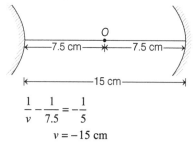

$$\dfrac{1}{v} - \dfrac{1}{7.5} = -\dfrac{1}{5}$$

$\therefore \qquad v = -15 \text{ cm}$

20. Image is magnified, so mirror is concave because convex mirror always makes diminished image. Further, image is erect and magnified. So, the object lies between P and F and its image is virtual.

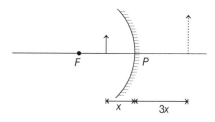

$4x = 80$ cm

$\Rightarrow \qquad x = 20$ cm

and $\qquad 3x = 60$ cm

Applying the mirror formula,

$$\dfrac{1}{f} = \dfrac{1}{v} + \dfrac{1}{u} = \dfrac{1}{+60} + \dfrac{1}{-20}$$

$\Rightarrow \qquad f = -30$ cm

21.

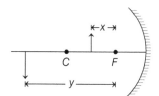

Applying the mirror formula,

$$\dfrac{1}{v} + \dfrac{1}{u} = \dfrac{1}{f}$$

or $\qquad \dfrac{1}{-(f+y)} + \dfrac{1}{-(f+x)} = \dfrac{1}{-f}$

$\Rightarrow \qquad \dfrac{f+x+f+y}{(f+x)(f+y)} = \dfrac{1}{f}$

$\Rightarrow \qquad 2f^2 + f(x+y) = f^2 + xy + f(x+y)$

$\Rightarrow \qquad f = \sqrt{xy}$

Subjective Questions

1. Reflected rays are neither converging nor diverging. Hence, mirror is a plane.

2. Image distance from plane mirror = object distance.

Lateral magnifications = 1

3.

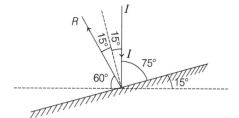

where, I = incident ray

R = reflected ray

Angle of incidence = 15°

Angle between reflected ray and horizontal = 60°

4.

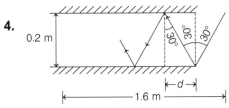

$$\therefore \quad \frac{d}{0.2} = \tan 30° = \frac{1}{\sqrt{3}}$$

$$d = \frac{0.2}{\sqrt{3}}$$

$$N = \frac{1.6}{d} = 8\sqrt{3}$$

$$= 13.85$$

Therefore, actual number of reflections required are 14.

5.

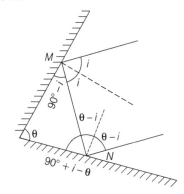

$$\delta_{\text{Total}} = \delta_M + \delta_N$$

$$= (180° - 2i) + [180° - 2\,(\theta - i)]$$

$$= 360° - 2\theta$$

6. Apply $\dfrac{1}{v} + \dfrac{1}{u} = \dfrac{1}{f}$

(a) $f = -10$ cm, $u = -25$ cm

Solving, we get $v = -16.7$ cm

Since, v is negative, image is in front of mirror. So, it is real. Similarly, we can solve for other parts.

7. (a) From O to F, image is real.

From F to P, image is virtual.

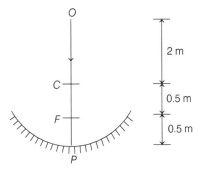

At O $\dfrac{1}{v} + \dfrac{1}{u} = \dfrac{1}{f}$

$$\therefore \quad \frac{1}{v} + \frac{1}{-3.0} = \frac{1}{-0.5}$$

$$v = -0.6 \text{ m}$$

(b) When object is at C and P, image coincides with object.

Using

$$s = \frac{1}{2}gt^2$$

or $$t = \sqrt{\frac{2s}{g}}$$

At C $t = \sqrt{\dfrac{2 \times 2}{9.8}} = 0.639$ s

At P $t = \sqrt{\dfrac{2 \times 3}{9.8}} = 0.782$ s

8. (a)

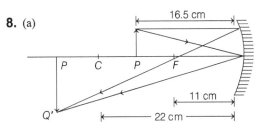

(b) Apply $\dfrac{1}{v} + \dfrac{1}{u} = \dfrac{1}{f}$ and $m = -\dfrac{v}{u}$

9. (a)

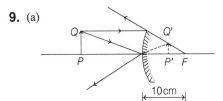

(b) Apply, $\dfrac{1}{v} + \dfrac{1}{u} = \dfrac{1}{f}$

and $\qquad m = -\dfrac{v}{u}$

10. O is placed at centre of curvature of concave mirror ($= 42$ cm). Therefore, image from this mirror I_1 will coincide with object O.

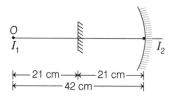

Now, plane mirror will make its image I_2 at the same distance from itself.

11.

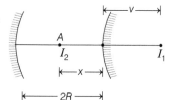

Using $\dfrac{1}{v} + \dfrac{1}{u} = \dfrac{1}{f}$

∴ $\qquad \dfrac{1}{-(y+f)} + \dfrac{1}{-(x+f)} = \dfrac{1}{-f}$

Solving this equation, we get

$$xy = f^2$$

12.

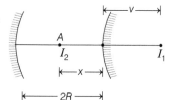

For convex mirror

$$\dfrac{1}{v} + \dfrac{1}{-x} = \dfrac{1}{+R/2}$$

∴ $\qquad \dfrac{1}{v} = \dfrac{2}{R} + \dfrac{1}{x}$ or $\qquad v = \dfrac{Rx}{R+2x}$

Now, applying mirror formula for concave mirror we have

$$\dfrac{1}{-(2R-x)} + \dfrac{1}{-(2R+v)} = \dfrac{1}{-R/2}$$

Solving this equation, we can find value of x.

13. (a) Image has to be taken on a screen. So, it should be real. Hence, mirror should be concave.

(b)

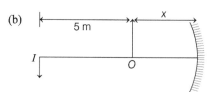

Image is 5 times magnified.

Hence, $\qquad |v| = 5|u|$

or $\qquad (5+x) = 5x$

Solving we get,

$\qquad x = 1.25$ cm

Now using,

$$\dfrac{1}{v} + \dfrac{1}{u} = \dfrac{1}{f} = \dfrac{2}{R}$$

We have,

$$\dfrac{1}{-6.25} - \dfrac{1}{1.25} = \dfrac{2}{R}$$

Solving we get,

$\qquad R = -2.08$ m

LEVEL 2

Single Correct Option

1.

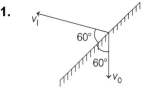

$$v_0 = v_I = \omega A = \left(\sqrt{\dfrac{k}{M}}\right) A$$

$$v_r = \sqrt{v_0^2 + v_I^2 - 2v_0 \cos 120°}$$

$$= \sqrt{3}\, A\, \sqrt{\dfrac{k}{M}}$$

2.

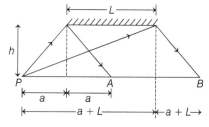

$$AB = PB - PA = 2(a+L) - 2a$$
$$= 2L = \text{constant}$$

3.

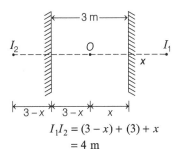

$$I_1 I_2 = (3 - x) + (3) + x$$
$$= 4 \text{ m}$$

Solving we get, $x = 1 \text{ m}$

4. Image of c will coincide with this.

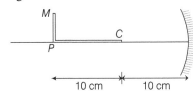

For P :

$$\frac{1}{v} + \frac{1}{-20} = \frac{1}{-5}$$

$\therefore$

$$v = -\frac{20}{3} \text{ cm}$$

$$m = -\frac{v}{u} = -\frac{(-20/3)}{(-20)} = -\frac{1}{3}$$

Length of image of PM :

$$I_1 = 10 \times \frac{1}{3} = \frac{10}{3} \text{ cm}$$

Length of image of PC :

$$I_2 = 10 - \frac{20}{3} = \frac{10}{3} \text{ cm}$$

$\therefore$

$$\frac{I_1}{I_2} = 1$$

5. $\dfrac{1}{v} + \dfrac{1}{-15} = \dfrac{1}{-10} \quad \Rightarrow \quad v = -30 \text{ cm}$

$$m = -\frac{v}{u} = -\frac{(-30)}{(-15)} = -2$$

$$|\Delta v| = m^2 |\Delta u| = (-2)^2 (2 \text{ mm})$$
$$= 8 \text{ mm}$$

6. Let i is the angle of incidence. Then, initial angle between incident ray and reflected ray will be $180° - 2i$. When mirror is rotated by $20°$, then reflected ray will rotate by $40°$.

$\therefore \qquad 180° - 2i \pm 40° = 45°$

Solving we get,

$$i = 47.5° \text{ or } 87.5°$$

The original angle was therefore

$$180° - 21° \text{ or } 85° \text{ or } 5°.$$

7.

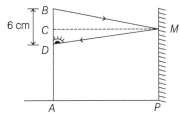

$$PM = AC = AD + DC$$
$$= AD + \frac{DB}{2} = 164 + \frac{6}{2} = 167 \text{ cm}$$

8. $a_{\text{LHS}} = a_1 = \dfrac{\text{Net pulling force}}{\text{Total mass}} = \dfrac{3 \, mg}{4 \, m} = \dfrac{3}{4} g$

$$a_{I_1} = 2a_1 = \frac{3}{2} g$$

$$a_{\text{RHS}} = a_2 = \frac{\text{Net pulling force}}{\text{Total mass}} = \frac{2 \, mg}{3 \, m}$$

$$= \frac{2}{3} g \quad \Rightarrow \quad a_{I_2} = 2a_2 = \frac{4}{3} g$$

The relative acceleration is therefore :

$$\frac{3}{2} g + \frac{4}{3} g = \frac{17}{6} g$$

9. $u_y = \sqrt{2} \sin 45° = 1 \text{ m/s}$

In vertical direction,

$$s_1 = \text{displacement of particle}$$
$$= (1)(0.5) - \frac{1}{2} g t^2 = 0.5 - \frac{1}{2} g t^2$$

$$s_2 = \text{displacement of mirror}$$
$$= -\frac{1}{2} g t^2$$

$\therefore$ Vertical distance of particle from mirror,

$$s = s_1 - s_2 = 0.5 \text{ m}$$

Hence, distance between particle and its image

$$= 25 = 1 \text{ m}$$

10. $\mathbf{v}_{OM} = \mathbf{v}_O - \mathbf{v}_M = (-\hat{\mathbf{i}} - 3 \hat{\mathbf{k}})$

$\therefore \qquad \mathbf{v}_{IM} = (-\hat{\mathbf{i}} + 3 \hat{\mathbf{k}}) = \mathbf{v}_I - \mathbf{v}_M$

or $\qquad \mathbf{v}_I = (-\hat{\mathbf{i}} + 3 \hat{\mathbf{k}}) + \mathbf{v}_M$

$$= (3 \hat{\mathbf{i}} + 4 \hat{\mathbf{j}} + 11 \hat{\mathbf{k}})$$

11.

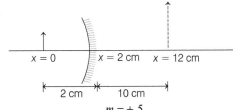

$$m = +5$$

$\therefore \quad v$ should be positive and 5 times $|u|$.

12. $90° - i\theta + 2r = 180°$

$$\therefore \quad r = \left(\frac{90° + i - \theta}{2}\right)$$

$$p = 180° - (90° - r) - 2i$$

$$= 180° - 90° + \left(\frac{90° + i - \theta}{2}\right) - 2i$$

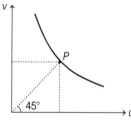

$$= \frac{180° - 4i + 90° + i - \theta}{2} = \left(\frac{270° - 3i - \theta}{2}\right)$$

$$m = p - \theta = 180° - (90° - i) - 2i$$

$$\therefore \quad \left(\frac{270° - 3i - \theta}{2}\right) - \theta = 90° - i$$

Substituting $\theta = 20°$, we get
$$i = 30°$$

13. Ray passing through c is only correct.

14. At P, $u = v$ which is possible only when $u = 2f$

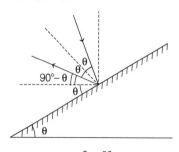

15. $\because v_{CM} = 8 \text{ m/s} \Rightarrow v_{IM} = 8 \text{ m/s}$

16. $90° - \theta + 2\theta = 90°$

$$\therefore \quad \theta = 0°$$

Angle of reflected ray with horizontal
$$= 90° - \theta = 90°$$

17.

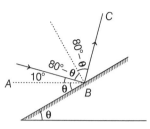

$$\angle ABC = 90°$$

$$\Rightarrow \quad 10° + (80° - \theta) + (80° - \theta) = 90°$$

$$\Rightarrow \quad \theta = 40°$$

18. Relative acceleration $= 0$

Relative velocity $= 2u \cos\theta$ in horizontal direction. Hence, motion of image of ball with respect to ball is a straight line and horizontal.

19.

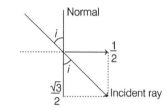

$$\tan i = \frac{1/2}{\sqrt{3}/2} = \frac{1}{\sqrt{3}} \quad \Rightarrow \quad i = 30°$$

More than One Correct Options

1. For real image,

Let $u = -x$, then $v = -2x$

$$\therefore \quad \frac{1}{-2x} + \frac{1}{-x} = \frac{1}{-20}$$

Solving, we get $x = 30$ cm.

For virtual image,

Let $u = -x$, then $v = +2x$

$$\therefore \quad \frac{1}{2x} + \frac{1}{-x} = \frac{1}{-20} \quad \text{or} \quad x = 10 \text{ cm}$$

2. Inverted and real image is formed by concave mirror.

Let $u = -x$, then $v = +x/2$

$$\therefore \quad \frac{1}{+x/2} + \frac{1}{-x} = \frac{1}{+f}$$

$$\therefore \quad x = 3f$$

Erect and virtual image is formed by convex mirror.

Let $u = -x$, then $v = +\dfrac{x}{2}$

$$\frac{1}{-x/2} + \frac{1}{-x} = \frac{1}{+f}$$

$$x = +f$$

3.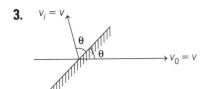

$$v_r = \sqrt{v^2 + v^2 - 2v \cdot v \cos 2\theta}$$
$$= 2\,v \sin \theta$$

4. Ray diagram is as shown in figure.

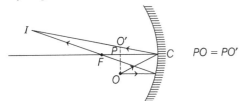

$$PO = PO'$$

5. $\dfrac{1}{v} + \dfrac{1}{-30} = \dfrac{1}{-20}$

Solving we get,
$$v = -60 \text{ cm}$$
$$m = \frac{v}{u} = -\frac{(-60)}{(-30)} = -2$$

Speed of image (in event -1) is m^2 times and m times in event-2.

6. In event -1

For concave mirror,
$$\frac{1}{v} + \frac{1}{-3f} = \frac{1}{-f} \quad \Rightarrow \quad v = -1.5f$$

For convex mirror,
$$\frac{1}{v} + \frac{1}{-3f} = \frac{1}{+f} \quad \Rightarrow \quad v = \frac{3}{4}f = 0.75f$$

For plane mirror,
$$v = +3f$$

In event-2

For concave mirror,
$$\frac{1}{v} + \frac{1}{-1.5f} = \frac{1}{-f}$$
$$\therefore \qquad v = -3f$$

For convex mirror,
$$\frac{1}{v} + \frac{1}{-1.5f} = \frac{1}{+f}$$
$$\therefore \qquad v = \frac{3f}{5} = 0.6f$$

For plane mirror,
$$v = +1.5f$$

Comprehension Based Questions

1.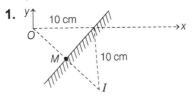

$$OM = MI$$

Coordinates of I are $(10 \text{ cm}, -10 \text{ cm})$.

2. Object is placed at centre at curvature of mirror. Hence, image is at the same point, real, inverted and of same size. Hence, coordinates are $(20 \text{ cm}, 0)$.

3. $\dfrac{1}{v} + \dfrac{1}{-20} = \dfrac{1}{+10}$

$$\therefore \qquad v = +\frac{20}{3} \text{ cm}$$
$$m = -\frac{v}{u} = -\frac{(+20/3)}{(-20)} = +\frac{1}{3}$$
$$\therefore \qquad I = 10\left(\frac{1}{3}\right) = \frac{10}{3} \text{ cm}$$
$$x = 10 - \frac{10}{3} = \frac{20}{3} \text{ cm}$$
and $\qquad y = 20 + \dfrac{20}{3} = \dfrac{80}{3} \text{ cm}$

4. Plane mirror forms image at equal distance on opposite sides.

Hence, $\qquad x = 0, y = 40 \text{ cm}$

Match the Columns

1. (a) $m = -2$ means image is real, inverted and 2-times magnified. So, mirror should be concave. Same logic can be given for other options also.

2. $\dfrac{1}{v} + \dfrac{1}{+u} = \dfrac{1}{f}$ (as u is positive for virtual objects)

$$\therefore \qquad \frac{1}{v} = \frac{1}{f} - \frac{1}{u}$$

For plane mirror, $f = \infty$. So, v is always negative. Hence, image is always real.

For concave mirror, f is negative. So, v is again negative. Therefore, image is always real.

For convex mirror, f is positive. So, v may be positive or negative.

Hence, image may be virtual or real.

3. (a) Image is inverted, real and diminished. Hence, mirror is concave.

Same logic can be applied for other options too.

4. (a) $\dfrac{1}{v} + \dfrac{1}{-20} = \dfrac{1}{-20}$

$\therefore$ $v = \infty$

$m = -\dfrac{v}{u} = \infty$

Same formulae can be applied for other options too.

5. (a) See the hint of Q.No-1 of more than one correct options section.

(b) Half size image is formed only in case of real image.

Let $u = -x$,

then $v = -\dfrac{x}{2}$

Now, $\dfrac{1}{-x/2} + \dfrac{1}{-x} = \dfrac{1}{-20}$

$\therefore$ $x = 60$ cm

In the similar manner, other options can be solved.

Subjective Questions

1.

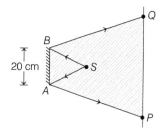

Insect can see the image of source S in the mirror, so far as it remains in field of view of image overlapping with the road.

Shaded portion is the field of view, which overlaps with the road upto length PQ.

By geometry we can see that, $PQ = 3AB = 60$ cm

$\therefore$ $t = \dfrac{\text{Distance}}{\text{Speed}} = \dfrac{60}{10} = 6$ s **Ans.**

2. Using mirror formula, $\left(\dfrac{1}{v} + \dfrac{1}{u} = \dfrac{1}{f}\right)$

$\dfrac{1}{v} - \dfrac{1}{50} = \dfrac{-1}{25}$

$\therefore$ $v = -50$ cm

$m = -\dfrac{v}{u} = -1$ **Ans.**

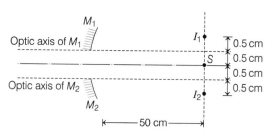

3. Using mirror formula $\dfrac{1}{v} + \dfrac{1}{u} = \dfrac{1}{f}$ for concave mirror first, we have

$\dfrac{1}{v} - \dfrac{1}{60} = \dfrac{1}{-40}$ $\quad\left(\because f = \dfrac{R}{2}\right)$

or $v = -120$ cm

First image I_1 at 120 cm from concave mirror will act as virtual object for plane mirror. Plane mirror will form real image of I_1 at S.

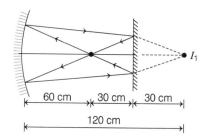

Ray diagram is shown in figure.

Distance between two mirrors is 90 cm. **Ans.**

4.

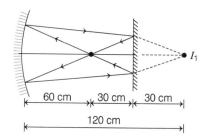

$\dfrac{FG}{BF} = \dfrac{IH}{BH} = \dfrac{HS}{BH}$

$\therefore$ $FG = (BF)\left(\dfrac{HS}{BH}\right)$

$= (5)\left(\dfrac{1.0}{0.5}\right) = 10$ m

$FC = 2 + 10 = 12$ m

The boy has dropped himself at point F. So, his velocity is 20 m/s in upward direction.

Let us first find the time to move from F to topmost point and then from topmost point to point C. From $s = ut + \dfrac{1}{2}at^2$, we have

$$-12 = (20t) + \frac{1}{2}(-10)\,t^2$$

Solving this equation we get, $t_1 = 4.53$ s.

Velocity of boy at point G,

$$v = \sqrt{(20)^2 - 2 \times 10 \times 10}$$

$$= 14.14 \text{ m/s} \qquad (\because\ v^2 = u^2 - 2gh)$$

Time taken to move the boy from G to topmost point and then from topmost point to G will be

$$t_2 = \frac{2v}{g} = 2.83 \text{ s}$$

$\therefore$ The required time is

$$t = t_1 - t_2 = 1.7 \text{ s} \qquad \textbf{Ans.}$$

5. Applying mirror formula for concave mirror first $\left(\dfrac{1}{v} + \dfrac{1}{u} = \dfrac{1}{f} \right)$ we have,

$$\frac{1}{v} - \frac{1}{110} = \frac{1}{-100}$$

$$v = -1100 \text{ cm}$$

$AI_1 = 100$ cm. Therefore, final image will be real and at distance 100 cm below point A at I_2.

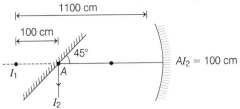

6. In 15 seconds, mirror will rotate 15° in clockwise direction.

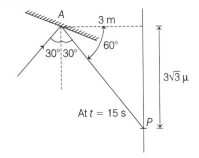

Hence, the reflected ray will rotate 30° in clockwise direction.

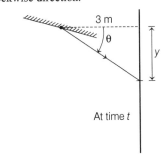

At time t

$$y = 3 \tan \theta$$

$\therefore$ $\qquad \dfrac{dy}{dt} = (3 \sec^2 \theta) . \dfrac{d\theta}{dt}$ ...(i)

Here, $\qquad \dfrac{dy}{dt} = v_P, \quad \dfrac{d\theta}{dt} = 2°$ per second

$$= \frac{2 \times \pi}{180} = \frac{\pi}{90} \text{ rad per second}$$

At $t = 15$ s and $\theta = 60°$

Substituting the values in Eq. (i), we have

$$v_P = \{3 \sec^2 60°\} \left\{ \frac{\pi}{90} \right\}$$

$$= 3 \times 4 \times \frac{\pi}{90}$$

$$= \frac{2\pi}{15} \text{ m/s} \qquad \textbf{Ans.}$$

7. (a) Differentiating the mirror formula, (with respect to time)

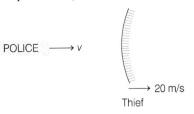

$$\frac{1}{v} + \frac{1}{u} = \frac{1}{f}$$

We get velocity of image,

$$v_I = (m)^2 v_O \qquad \text{...(i)}$$

Here, v_O = relative velocity of object with respect to mirror

v_I = relative velocity of image

m = linear magnification

Here, $v_O = (v - 20)$ m/s

$v_I = 1$ cm/s $= 0.01$ m/s

$$m = \frac{1}{10}$$

Substituting in Eq. (i) we have,

$$0.01 = \left(\frac{1}{10}\right)^2 (v - 20)$$

$$\therefore \qquad v = 21 \text{ m/s}$$

(b) $\dfrac{1}{v} + \dfrac{1}{u} = \dfrac{1}{f}$

Multiplying with u we get,

$$\frac{u}{v} + 1 = \frac{u}{f}$$

or $\qquad \dfrac{1}{m} = \dfrac{u}{f} - 1 = \dfrac{u - f}{f}$

$$\therefore \qquad m = \frac{f}{u - f}$$

Differentiating we have,

$$\left(\frac{dm}{dt}\right) = -\frac{f}{(u - f)^2} \cdot \frac{du}{dt} \qquad \ldots(\text{ii})$$

Using mirror formula to find u with magnification

$$m = \frac{1}{10} \text{ we get,}$$

$$\frac{1}{u/10} - \frac{1}{u} = \frac{1}{10}$$

or $\qquad u = 90 \text{ m}$ (with sign $u = -90$ m)

Substituting in Eq. (ii) we have,

$$\frac{dm}{dt} = -\frac{(10)}{(-90 - 10)^2}(-1)$$

$$= 10^{-3} \text{ per second} \qquad \textbf{Ans.}$$

Note $\quad u$ *is decreasing at a rate of* $v - 20$ *or* $(21 - 20)$
or 1 *m/s*

$$\therefore \qquad \frac{du}{dt} = -1 \text{ m/s}$$

8. (a) At $t = t$,

$$u = -(2f + x)$$
$$= -(2f + f \cos \omega t)$$

Using the mirror formula,

$$\frac{1}{v} + \frac{1}{u} = \frac{1}{f}$$

We have,

$$\frac{1}{v} - \frac{1}{2f + f \cos \omega t} = \frac{-1}{f}$$

$$\therefore \qquad v = -\left(\frac{2 + \cos \omega t}{1 + \cos \omega t}\right) f$$

i.e. distance of image from mirror at time t is

$$\left(\frac{2 + \cos \omega t}{1 + \cos \omega t}\right) f \qquad \textbf{Ans.}$$

(b) Ball coincides with its image at centre of curvature, i.e. at $x = 0$.

(c) At $t = T/2$

or $\qquad \omega t = \pi, x = -f$

i.e. $u = -f$ or ball is at focus. So, its image is at ∞.

$$m = \infty$$

9. Let the ray is incident at a point $P = (x_1, y_1)$ on the mirror. Then, slope at P,

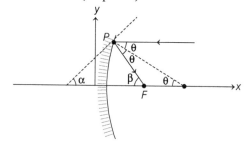

$$\tan \alpha = \left(\frac{dy}{dx}\right)_{(x_1, y_1)} = \frac{1}{4by_1} \qquad \ldots(\text{i})$$

$$\alpha = 90° - \theta \quad \text{and} \quad \beta = 2\theta$$

Now, the reflected ray is passing through $P(x_1 y_1)$ and has a slope $-\tan \beta$. Hence, the equation will be

$$\left(\frac{y - y_1}{x - x_1}\right) = -\tan \beta$$

$$= -\tan 2\theta = \frac{-2 \tan \theta}{1 - \tan^2 \theta}$$

$$\therefore \qquad y - y_1 = \frac{2 \cot \alpha}{1 + \cot^2 \alpha} (x_1 - x) \qquad \ldots(\text{ii})$$

Further, $\qquad x_1 = 4by_1^2 \qquad \ldots(\text{iii})$

At F, $\qquad x = 0 \qquad \ldots(\text{iv})$

From Eq. (i) to Eq. (iv),

we get $\qquad x = \dfrac{1}{8b}$

It shows that the coordinates of F are unique $\left(\dfrac{1}{8b}, 0\right)$.

Hence, the reflected ray passing through one focus and the focal length is $\dfrac{1}{8b}$. $\qquad$ **Hence proved.**

31. Refraction of Light

INTRODUCTORY EXERCISE 31.1

1. $_1\mu_2 \times {}_2\mu_3 \times {}_3\mu_1 = 1$

$\therefore \quad \dfrac{4}{3} \times \dfrac{3}{2} = \dfrac{1}{{}_3\mu_1} = {}_1\mu_3 \quad$ or $\quad _1\mu_3 = 2$

3. $\mu = \dfrac{c}{v} = \dfrac{c}{f\lambda} = \dfrac{3 \times 10^8}{6 \times 10^{14} \times 300 \times 10^{-9}} = 1.67$

INTRODUCTORY EXERCISE 31.2

1. $_1\mu_2 = \dfrac{\mu_2}{\mu_1} = \dfrac{\sin i_1}{\sin i_2} = \dfrac{\sin 60°}{\sin 30°} = \sqrt{3}$

2. $_1\mu_2 = 1.5 = \dfrac{\lambda_1}{\lambda_2}$

INTRODUCTORY EXERCISE 31.3

1. (a) $d_{app} = 10 + \dfrac{10}{1.5} = \dfrac{50}{3}$ cm

(b) $h_{app} = 10 + (1.5)(10) = 25$ cm

INTRODUCTORY EXERCISE 31.4

1. Total shift $= \left(1 - \dfrac{1}{\mu_1}\right)t_1 + \left(1 - \dfrac{1}{\mu_2}\right)t_2$

$= \left(1 - \dfrac{2}{3}\right)10 + \left(1 - \dfrac{1}{2}\right)10$

$= \dfrac{25}{3}$ cm

$\therefore$ Image distance $= 50 - \dfrac{25}{3} = \dfrac{125}{3}$ cm

INTRODUCTORY EXERCISE 31.5

1. All rays starting from centre pass undeviated as they fall normal to the surface.

2.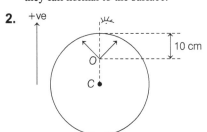

Using $\quad \dfrac{\mu_2}{v} - \dfrac{\mu_1}{u} = \dfrac{\mu_2 - \mu_1}{R}$, we get

$\dfrac{1}{v} - \dfrac{1.5}{-10} = \dfrac{1-1.5}{-15}$

Solving, we get $\quad v = -8.57$ cm

3.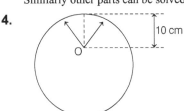

(a) Using $\quad \dfrac{\mu_2}{v} - \dfrac{\mu_1}{u} = \dfrac{\mu_2 - \mu_1}{R}$, we get

$\dfrac{1.5}{v} - \dfrac{1.0}{-20} = \dfrac{1.5 - 1.0}{+6}$

Solving, we get $\quad v = +45$ cm

Similarly other parts can be solved.

4.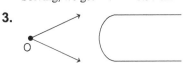

Using $\dfrac{\mu_2}{v} - \dfrac{\mu_1}{u} = \dfrac{\mu_2 - \mu_1}{R}$, we get

$\dfrac{1}{v} - \dfrac{4/3}{-10} = \dfrac{1 - 4/3}{-15}$

Solving, we get $\quad v = -9.0$ cm

5.

Using the equation

$\dfrac{\mu_2}{v} - \dfrac{\mu_1}{u} = \dfrac{\mu_2 - \mu_1}{R}$, we get

$\dfrac{1.44}{v} - \dfrac{1.0}{\infty} = \dfrac{1.44 - 1.0}{+1.25}$

$\therefore \qquad v = 4.0$ cm

INTRODUCTORY EXERCISE 31.6

1. $\dfrac{1}{v} - \dfrac{1}{u} = \dfrac{1}{f} = (\mu - 1)\left(\dfrac{1}{R_1} - \dfrac{1}{R_2}\right)$

$$\therefore \quad \frac{1}{-20} - \frac{1}{-60} = (1.65 - 1)\left(\frac{1}{-R} - \frac{1}{+R}\right)$$

Solving we get, $R = 39$ cm

2. $\dfrac{1}{-50} - \dfrac{1}{u} = \dfrac{1}{+30}$

Solving, we get $u = -18.75$ cm

$$m = \frac{v}{u} = \frac{(-50)}{(-18.75)} - 2.67$$

$$I = m(O) = 2.67 \times 2$$
$$= 5.33 \,\text{cm}$$

3.

$$\frac{1}{f_1} = (\mu - 1)\left(\frac{1}{+R_1} - \frac{1}{-R_2}\right) \qquad \ldots(\text{i})$$

$$\frac{1}{f_2} = (\mu - 1)\left(\frac{1}{+R_2} - \frac{1}{-R_1}\right) \qquad \ldots(\text{ii})$$

Solving these two equations, we can see that $f_1 = f_2$.

4.

When object is moved from O to F_1, its virtual, erect and magnified image should vary from O to $-\infty$.

5. (a) $\dfrac{1}{f} = \left(\dfrac{1.3}{1.8} - 1\right)\left(\dfrac{1}{-20} - \dfrac{1}{+20}\right)$

$$\therefore \qquad f = +36 \,\text{cm}$$

(b) Between O and F_1 image is virtual. Hence, for real image.

$$|\mu| < f \quad \text{or} \quad 36 \,\text{cm}$$

6.

7. $\because \quad \dfrac{1}{v} - \dfrac{1}{u} = \dfrac{1}{f}$

Differentiating this equation, we get

$$-v^{-2} \cdot dv + u^{-2} \cdot du = 0 \qquad (\text{as } f = \text{constant})$$

$$\therefore \qquad dv = \left(-\frac{v^2}{u^2}\right) \cdot du$$

8. It is just like a concave mirror.

$$|f| = 0.2 \,\text{m}$$
$$\therefore \qquad |R| = 0.4 \,\text{m}$$

Focal length of this equivalent mirror is

$$\frac{1}{F} = \frac{2\,(\mu_2/\mu_1)}{R_2} - \frac{2\,(\mu_2/\mu_1 - 1)}{R_1} \quad (\text{extra points})$$

$$= \frac{2\,(4/3)}{-0.4} - \frac{2\,(4/3 - 1)}{+0.4}$$

or $F = -0.12$ m or -12 cm

9. $|R| = 0.5$ m (from first case)

In the shown figure, object appears at distance

$$d = \mu_e(0.2) + 0.2$$

Now, for image to further coincide with the object,

$$d = |R|$$

Solving we get, $\mu_e = 1.5$

10. $O = \sqrt{I_1 I_2}$ \qquad (Displacement method)

$$= \sqrt{6 \times \frac{2}{3}} = 2 \,\text{cm}$$

11. Virtual, magnified and erect image is formed by convex lens.

Let $u = -x$

Then, $v = -3x$

Now, $\dfrac{1}{-3x} - \dfrac{1}{-x} = \dfrac{1}{+12}$

$$\therefore \qquad x = 8 \,\text{cm}$$

Distance between object and image

$$= 3x - x = 2x = 16 \,\text{cm}$$

12. Diminished erect image is formed by concave lens.

Let $u = -x$, then $v = -\dfrac{x}{2}$

Now, $|u| - |v| = 20$ cm

$$\therefore \qquad \frac{x}{2} = 20 \,\text{cm} \quad \text{or} \quad x = 40 \,\text{cm}$$

$$\therefore \qquad u = -40 \,\text{cm} \quad \text{and} \quad v = -20 \,\text{cm}$$

$$\frac{1}{f} = \frac{1}{-20} - \frac{1}{-40} \quad \text{or} \quad f = -40 \,\text{cm}$$

13. If an object is placed at focus of lens (= 10 cm), rays become parallel and fall normal on plane mirror. So, rays retrace their path.

INTRODUCTORY EXERCISE 31.7

1.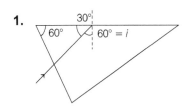

Critical angle $= i = 60° = \theta_C$

$$\sin \theta_C = \frac{\mu_R}{\mu_D} \quad \Rightarrow \quad \sin 60° = \frac{\mu}{\sqrt{3}}$$

Solving we get, $\mu = 1.5$

2. $\mu = \dfrac{c}{v} = \dfrac{3 \times 10^8}{2.3 \times 10^8} = 1.3$

$$\theta_C = \sin^{-1}\left(\frac{1}{\mu}\right) = \sin^{-1}\left(\frac{1}{1.3}\right) = \sin^{-1}(0.77)$$

3. (a) $\mu_1 \sin i_1 = \mu_2 \sin i_2 = \mu_2 \sin \theta_C$

$$(1.6)\sin\theta = (1.80)\left(\frac{1.30}{1.80}\right)$$

$$\therefore \qquad \theta = \sin^{-1}\left(\frac{13}{16}\right)$$

(b) If θ is decreased, then i_2 will decrease from the value θ_C. Hence, refraction will take place in medium-3.

INTRODUCTORY EXERCISE 31.8

1.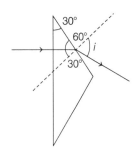

$$\mu = \frac{\sin i}{\sin 30°}$$

$$\therefore \qquad \sin i = \mu \sin 30°$$

$$= (1.6)\left(\frac{1}{2}\right) = 0.8$$

$$\therefore \qquad i = 53°$$

P ray deviates from its original path by an angle,

$$\delta = i - 30° = 23°$$

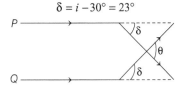

∴ Angle between two rays, $\theta = 2\delta$

$$= 46°$$

2.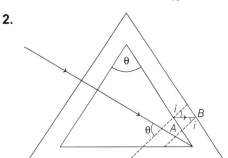

$$i = \theta_C$$

$$\therefore \qquad \sin i = \sin \theta_C = \frac{1}{\mu_g} = \frac{2}{3}$$

Applying Snell's law at point A,
We have

$$\mu_w \sin\theta = \mu_g \sin i$$

$$\therefore \qquad \frac{4}{3}\sin\theta = \frac{3}{2} \times \frac{2}{3}$$

$$\therefore \qquad \sin\theta = \frac{3}{4}$$

3. $\mu = \dfrac{\sin\left(\dfrac{A + \delta_m}{2}\right)}{\sin (A/2)}, \delta_m = 30°$

4. $i_1 = 0° \Rightarrow r_1 = 0°$ or $r_2 = A$

Now, $r_2 = \theta_C = A$

$$\therefore \qquad \sin A = \sin\theta_C = \frac{1}{\mu} = \frac{2}{3}$$

or $A = \sin^{-1}\left(\dfrac{2}{3}\right)$

5. $\delta = i_1 + i_2 - A$

$$30° = 60° + i_2 - 30°$$

$$\therefore \qquad i_2 = 0 \text{ or } r_2 = 0 \qquad \textbf{Hence proved.}$$

$$\Rightarrow \qquad r_1 = A = 30°$$

Now, $\mu = \dfrac{\sin i_1}{\sin r_1} = \dfrac{\sin 60°}{\sin 30°} = \sqrt{3}$

6. $\sqrt{2} = \dfrac{\sin i_1}{\sin (i_1/2)}$

$= \dfrac{2\sin (i_1/2)\cos (i_1/2)}{\sin (i_1/2)}$

Solving this, we get $i_1 = 90°$ and $r_1 = \dfrac{i_1}{2} = 45°$

At minimum deviation,

$$r_2 = r_1 = 45°$$

$\therefore$ $A = r_1 + r_2 = 90°$

7. From $\mu = \sin \left(\dfrac{A + \delta_m}{2}\right) / \sin (A/2)$

We can see that given deviation is the minimum deviation.

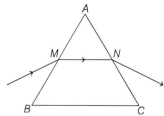

At minimum deviation, MN is parallel to BC is $\angle B = \angle C$.

8. ABC can be treated as a prism with angle of prism $A = 90°$. Condition of no emergence is

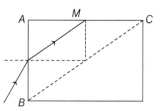

$$A \geq 2\theta_C$$

or $\sin \theta_C \leq \sin \left(\dfrac{A}{2}\right)$

or $\dfrac{1}{\mu} \leq \sin 45°$

or $\dfrac{1}{\mu} \leq \dfrac{1}{\sqrt{2}}$

$\therefore$ $\mu \geq \sqrt{2}$

9. $\theta_C = \sin^{-1}\left(\dfrac{1}{\mu}\right) = \sin^{-1}\left(\dfrac{1}{1.6}\right) = 38.7°$

$$r_2 = \theta_C = 38.7°$$

$\therefore$ $r_1 = A - r_2 = 45° - 38.7° = 6.3°$

Now applying, $\mu = \dfrac{\sin i_1}{\sin r_1}$

we can find i_1.

Exercises

LEVEL 1

Assertion and Reason

1. Shift due to a slab $= \left(1 - \dfrac{1}{\mu}\right) t$ is in the direction of ray of light. Hence, Ram appears nearer to Anoop by that much distance.

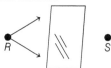

3. Image is formed at second focus (not the first focus).

4. $\dfrac{1}{F} = \dfrac{1}{f_1} + \dfrac{1}{f_2}$

$f_1 = $ Focal length of convex lens (+ ve)
$f_2 = $ Focal length of concave lens (– ve)

If $f_1 > |f_2|$, then F comes out to be negative. So, it becomes a diverging lens.

Negative power of a diverging lens is just for its diverging lens, nothing else.

5. If medium on both sides of the lens is same, then it doesn't matter, which side the object is kept.

6. $i = 45°$

For $\mu > \sqrt{2}$

or   1.414

$\Rightarrow$ $\theta_C < 45°$

$\therefore$ They get TIR on face AC.

7. $\dfrac{1}{f} = (\mu - 1)\left(\dfrac{1}{R} - \dfrac{1}{R}\right)$

$$f = \infty$$

$\therefore$ $P = \dfrac{1}{f} = 0$

8. When a diverging lens is immersed in a liquid, its diverging power will either decrease or it will become converging.

9. If λ is more, μ will be less as per Cauchy's formula $\left(\mu = A + \dfrac{B}{\lambda^2} \right)$. Therefore, focal length will be more.

10. Glass slab will shift the object towards mirror. If it comes between pole and focus image becomes virtual.

Objective Questions

2. Let image is n times in size.

Then, $\dfrac{1}{-12n} - \dfrac{1}{-12} = \dfrac{1}{f}$ ...(i)

$\dfrac{1}{+20n} - \dfrac{1}{-20} = \dfrac{1}{f}$ ...(ii)

Solving these two equations, we get
$$f = 16 \text{ cm}$$

3. $d_{app.} = \dfrac{d}{\mu}$

μ of red is least. So, $d_{app.}$ for red is maximum. So, they appear to be raised least.

4. $\theta_C = \sin^{-1}\left(\dfrac{1}{\mu} \right)$

μ for violet is maximum, so θ_C for violet is least.

5. $\dfrac{1}{f} = P = (\mu - 1)\left(\dfrac{1}{R_1} - \dfrac{1}{R_2} \right)$

$= (1.6 - 1)\left(\dfrac{1}{0.1} - \dfrac{1}{-0.1} \right)$

$= +12 \text{ D}$

6. $v = \dfrac{c}{\mu} = \dfrac{3 \times 10^8}{(4/3)} = 2.25 \times 10^8 \text{ m/s}$

7. After a certain angle all colours get total internally reflected.

8. Frequency does not change during refraction, but wavelength and speed decrease in a denser (here water) medium.

9. $\mu_1 \sin i_1 = \mu_3 \sin i_3$

$\therefore \quad \mu_1 \sin i = \mu_3 \sin r$ or $\dfrac{\sin i}{\sin r} = \dfrac{\mu_3}{\mu_1}$

10. $r_1 = i$ and $r_2 = 90° - r_1 = 90° - i$

Now, $\mu_R \sin i_R = \mu_D \sin i_D$

or $\dfrac{\mu_R}{\mu_D} = \sin \theta_C = \dfrac{\sin i_D}{\sin i_R} = \dfrac{\sin i}{\sin (90° - i)}$

or $\sin \theta_C = \dfrac{\sin i}{\cos i} = \tan i$

$\Rightarrow \quad \theta_C = \sin^{-1}(\tan i)$

11. At minimum deviation,
$$r_1 = r_2 = \dfrac{A}{2} = 30°$$

Now using, $\mu = \dfrac{\sin i_1}{\sin r_1}$ or $\sqrt{2} = \dfrac{\sin i_1}{\sin 30°}$

We get $i_1 = 45°$

12. $\dfrac{1}{0.2} = (1.5 - 1)\left(\dfrac{1}{R_1} - \dfrac{1}{R_2} \right)$ ...(i)

$\dfrac{1}{-0.5} = \left(\dfrac{1.5}{\mu} - 1 \right)\left(\dfrac{1}{R_1} - \dfrac{1}{R_2} \right)$ ...(ii)

Here, μ = refractive index of medium or liquid.
Dividing Eq. (i) by Eq. (ii), we get

$-5 = \dfrac{1}{(1.5/\mu) - 1}$

or $\mu = \dfrac{15}{8}$

13. From Snell's law,
$$\mu \sin i = \mu_4 \sin x$$

$\therefore \qquad \sin x = \dfrac{\mu}{\mu_4} \sin i$

14. Focal length of any one part will be $2f$.

$\therefore \qquad \dfrac{1}{F} = \dfrac{1}{2f} + \dfrac{1}{2f} + \dfrac{1}{2f} + \dfrac{1}{2f}$

or $\qquad F = \dfrac{f}{2}$

15. $t = n\lambda = \dfrac{n\lambda_0}{\mu}$ $\qquad \left(\text{as } \lambda = \dfrac{\lambda_0}{\mu} \right)$

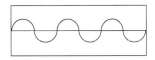

or $\qquad t \propto \dfrac{1}{\mu}$

$\therefore \qquad \dfrac{\mu_2}{\mu_1} = \dfrac{t_1}{t_2}$ or $\mu_2 = \dfrac{t_1}{t_2}\mu_1$

$= \left(\dfrac{5}{4} \right)\left(\dfrac{4}{3} \right) = \dfrac{5}{3}$

16. $\dfrac{1}{F} = \dfrac{1}{f_1} + \dfrac{1}{f_2} - \dfrac{d}{f_1 f_2}$

To behave like concave lens, F should be negative.

So, $\dfrac{d}{f_1 f_2} > \dfrac{1}{f_1} + \dfrac{1}{f_2}$

or $\dfrac{d}{f_1 f_2} > \dfrac{f_1 + f_2}{f_1 f_2}$

or $d > (f_1 + f_2)$ or $30\,\text{cm}$

17. Condition of no emergence from opposite face is

$$A > 2\theta_C$$

18. $r_2 = 0,\ r_1 = A$

$$\mu = \dfrac{\sin i_1}{\sin r_1} \approx \dfrac{i_1}{r_1} = \dfrac{i_1}{A} \quad \Rightarrow \quad i_1 = \mu A$$

19. $\mu = \dfrac{\sin\left(\dfrac{A + \delta_m}{2}\right)}{\sin (A/2)}$

Given, $\mu = \cot\left(\dfrac{A}{2}\right)$

Solving, we get $\sin = 180° - 2A$

20. Using the lens formula, we have

$$\dfrac{1}{v} - \dfrac{1}{-(f + x)} = \dfrac{1}{f}$$

$\therefore \qquad \dfrac{1}{v} = \dfrac{1}{f} - \dfrac{1}{(f + x)}$

$$= \dfrac{f + x - f}{f(f + x)} = \left(\dfrac{x}{f + x}\right)\left(\dfrac{1}{f}\right)$$

$$m = -\dfrac{v}{u}$$

$$= -\dfrac{\left(\dfrac{f + x}{x}\right)(f)}{-(f + x)}$$

$$= \dfrac{f}{x}$$

21. $\dfrac{1}{F} = \dfrac{1}{f_1} + \dfrac{1}{f_2} - \dfrac{d}{f_1 f_2}$

$$= \dfrac{f_1 + f_2}{f_1 f_2} - \dfrac{d}{f_1 f_2}$$

$$\dfrac{1}{F} = \dfrac{(f_1 + f_2) - d}{f_1 f_2}$$

$\therefore \qquad F = \dfrac{f_1 f_2}{(f_1 + f_2) - d}$ ...(i)

If d is doubled, focal length is doubled or denominator becomes half.

$\therefore \qquad (f_1 + f_2) - 2d = \dfrac{1}{2}[(f_1 + f_2) - d]$

or $\qquad (f_1 + f_2) = 3d$

Substituting in Eq. (i), we have

Originally,

$$F = \dfrac{f_1 f_2}{(f_1 + f_2) - d} = \dfrac{f_1 f_2}{3d - d} = \dfrac{f_1 f_2}{2d}$$

When d is made 4 times.

$$F' = \dfrac{f_1 f_2}{(f_1 + f_2) - 4d} = \dfrac{f_1 f_2}{3d - 4d} = -\dfrac{f_1 f_2}{d}$$

$$= -2F$$

22. $\dfrac{1}{24} = (1.5 - 1)\left(\dfrac{1}{R} - \dfrac{1}{2R}\right)$

$$R = 6\,\text{cm}$$

$\therefore \qquad 2R = 12\,\text{cm}$

23. **Lens formula:**

$$\dfrac{1}{v_1} - \dfrac{1}{-15} = \dfrac{1}{30}$$

$\Rightarrow \qquad v_1 = -30\,\text{cm}$

Mirror formula:

$$v_2 = -u_2 = -(-45) = 45\,\text{cm}$$

Lens formula:

$$\dfrac{1}{v_3} - \dfrac{1}{-60} = \dfrac{1}{30}$$

$\therefore \qquad v_3 = +60\,\text{cm}$

Hence, distance of final image from object

$$= 60 - 15 = 45\,\text{cm}$$

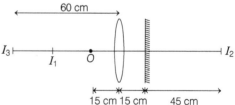

24. $n_1 \sin i_1 = n_3 \sin i_3$

$\therefore \quad (1)(\sin 45°) = \sqrt{2}\,\sin i_3$

$\Rightarrow \qquad \sin i_3 = \dfrac{1}{2}$ or $i_3 = 30°$

25. $\mu = \dfrac{\sin\left(\dfrac{A + \delta_m}{2}\right)}{\sin (A/2)}$

For small angled prism, $\sin \dfrac{A}{2} \approx \dfrac{A}{2}$

$\therefore \qquad \sin\left(\dfrac{A + \delta_m}{2}\right) = \dfrac{\mu A}{2}$

With increase in μ, $\sin\left(\dfrac{A+\delta_m}{2}\right)$ will increase.

Hence, δ_m will increase.

26. $n = \dfrac{\sin i}{\sin (i/2)} = \dfrac{2 \sin (i/2) \cos (i/2)}{\sin (i/2)}$

Solving we get, $i = 2 \cos^{-1} (n/2)$

27. If object is placed at focus of convex lens, rays become parallel and they are incident normally on plane mirror. So, ray of light will retrace its path.

28. $\mu = \dfrac{\sin i}{\sin r}$

$\Rightarrow \quad \sqrt{2} = \dfrac{\sin 45°}{\sin r} \quad$ or $\quad r = 30°$

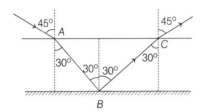

$\delta_{\text{Total}} = \delta_A - \delta_B + \delta_C$

$= (45° - 30°) - [180° - 2(30°)] + (45° - 30°)$

$= -90° \quad$ or $\quad |\delta_{\text{Total}}| = 90°$

29. $\mu = \dfrac{\sin\left(\dfrac{A+\delta_m}{2}\right)}{\sin\left(\dfrac{A}{2}\right)}$

30. $P_1 + P_2 = P$

$\therefore \qquad 5 + P_2 = 2 \qquad (P_1 = +5 \text{D})$

or $\qquad P_2 = -3$

$P \propto \dfrac{1}{f} \quad \Rightarrow \quad \dfrac{P_1}{P_2} = \dfrac{f_2}{f_1}$

or $\qquad \dfrac{5}{-3} = \dfrac{f_2}{f_1} \quad \Rightarrow \quad \dfrac{f_1}{f_2} = -\dfrac{3}{5}$

Now, $\dfrac{\omega_1}{f_1} + \dfrac{\omega_2}{f_2} = 0 \quad \Rightarrow \quad \dfrac{\omega_1}{\omega_2} = -\dfrac{f_1}{f_2} = \dfrac{3}{5}$

31. Image formed by convex lens I_1 should coincide at C_1, the centre of curvature C of convex mirror.

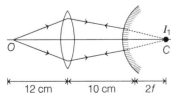

For convex lens,

$\dfrac{1}{+(10+2f)} - \dfrac{1}{-12} = \dfrac{1}{+10}$

Solving this equation we get, $f = 25$ cm

32. For convex lens,

$\dfrac{1}{v} - \dfrac{1}{-12} = \dfrac{1}{+20}$

$\Rightarrow \qquad v = -30$ cm

This image I_1 is therefore, $(30+10)$ cm or 40 cm towards left of plane mirror. Therefore, second image I_2 (by the plane mirror) will be formed 40 cm behind the mirror.

33. $\dfrac{1}{F} = \dfrac{1}{f_1} + \dfrac{1}{f_2} = \dfrac{1}{10} + \dfrac{1}{10}$

$\therefore \qquad F = 5$ cm

$\dfrac{1}{v} - \dfrac{1}{-7.5} = \dfrac{1}{+5}$

$\therefore \qquad v = +15$ cm

$m = \dfrac{v}{u} = \dfrac{+15}{-7.5} = -2$

$I = mO = (-2)(1 \text{ cm})$

$= -2$ cm

34. Applying, $\dfrac{\mu_2}{v} - \dfrac{\mu_1}{u} = \dfrac{\mu_2 - \mu_1}{R}$

$\therefore \qquad \dfrac{1}{v} - \dfrac{3/2}{+30} = \dfrac{1-3/2}{+20}$

or $\qquad \dfrac{1}{v} = \dfrac{1}{20} - \dfrac{3}{40}$

$\therefore \qquad v = 40$ cm

35. Between 1 and 3 there is no deviation.

Hence $\qquad \mu_1 = \mu_3$

Between 3 and 2

Ray to light binds towards normal. Hence, $\mu_2 > \mu_3$.

36. $A = \delta_m = 60° \quad \Rightarrow \quad \mu = \dfrac{\sin\left(\dfrac{A+\delta_m}{2}\right)}{\sin (A/2)}$

37. Critical angle,

$\sin C = \dfrac{1}{\mu}$

$\therefore \qquad C = \sin^{-1}\left(\dfrac{1}{\mu}\right)$

and μ decreases with increase in λ. Yellow, orange and red have larger wavelength than green, so μ will be less for these rays, so critical angle for these rays will be high, hence if green is just totally internally reflected then yellow, orange and red rays will emerge out.

38. $H = \mu h = \dfrac{4}{3} \times 18 = 24$ m

39. For air lens in glass,

$\dfrac{1}{f} = (_g\mu_a - 1)\left(\dfrac{1}{R_1} - \dfrac{1}{R_2}\right)$

$\phantom{\dfrac{1}{f}} = \left(\dfrac{2}{3} - 1\right)\left[\dfrac{1}{10} - \left(-\dfrac{1}{10}\right)\right]$

$\Rightarrow \qquad f = -15$ cm

So, nature of lens is diverging (concave).

40. $\mu_g \sin i = \mu_a \sin 90° = 1$

$\therefore \qquad \mu_g = \dfrac{1}{\sin i}$

41. Image is coinciding with P. Hence, P is placed at centre of curvature. Glass slab will produce shift the object at a distance of $\left(1 - \dfrac{1}{\mu}\right)t$ towards the mirror. So, we will have to shift the object by the same distance away from the mirror.

42. Apply $\dfrac{1}{f} = \dfrac{2(\mu_2/\mu_1)}{R_2} + \dfrac{2(\mu_2/\mu_1 - 1)}{R_1}$

43.

$\dfrac{1}{30} - \dfrac{1}{-u} = \dfrac{1}{f}$

or $\dfrac{1}{30} + \dfrac{1}{u} = \dfrac{1}{f}$ ...(i)

Similarly, $\dfrac{1}{120} + \dfrac{1}{u - 90} = \dfrac{1}{f}$ ...(ii)

Solving these two equations, we get

$f = 24$ cm

44.

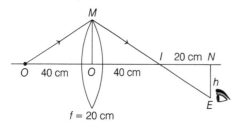

45. For TIR to take place,

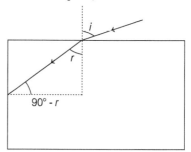

$\dfrac{h}{MO} = \dfrac{20}{40}$

$\Rightarrow \qquad h = \dfrac{MO}{2} = \dfrac{5}{2}$

$ = 2.5$ cm

$ 90° - r > \theta_C$

or $ r < 90° - \theta_C$

From the relation,

$n = \dfrac{\sin i}{\sin r}$

$\sin i = n \sin r$

Since, for TIR to take place $r < 90° - \theta_C$

$\therefore \qquad i < \sin^{-1}\{n \sin r\}$

or $\qquad i < \sin^{-1}\{n \cos \theta_C\}$

or $\qquad i < \sin^{-1}\left\{n\sqrt{1 - \dfrac{1}{n^2}}\right\}$

or $\qquad i < \sin^{-1}\left\{1.33\sqrt{1 - \dfrac{1}{(1.33)^2}}\right\}$

or $\qquad i < \sin^{-1}\{\sqrt{0.77}\}$

Note *For simplyfying the calculation, take* $1.33 = \dfrac{4}{3}$.

46. The reflected ray will rotate by an angle 2θ. For TIR to take place at water-air boundary,

$\sin 2\theta > \sin \theta_C$

or $\qquad \sin 2\theta > \dfrac{1}{\mu}$

$\therefore \qquad \theta > \dfrac{1}{2}\sin^{-1}\left(\dfrac{3}{4}\right)$

47. $\mu_A > \mu_B \quad \Rightarrow \quad C_1 < C_2$

$ \mu_B > \mu_C \quad \Rightarrow \quad C_2 < C_3$

$ \mu_C < \mu_A \quad \Rightarrow \quad C_3 > C_1$

The correct relation is therefore (d).

48. Applying $\dfrac{\mu_2}{v} - \dfrac{\mu_1}{u} = \dfrac{\mu_2 - \mu_1}{R}$, we have

$$\dfrac{3/2}{v} - \dfrac{1}{-15} = \dfrac{3/2 - 1}{+30}$$

$$\therefore \qquad \dfrac{3}{2v} = \dfrac{1}{60} - \dfrac{1}{15} = -\dfrac{1}{20}$$

$$\therefore \qquad v = -30 \text{ cm}$$

49. Critical angle between glass and water,

$$\sin\theta_C = \dfrac{\mu_w}{\mu_g} = \dfrac{4/3}{3/2} = \dfrac{8}{9}$$

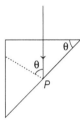

Now, total internal reflection will take place on face AC, if

$$\sin\theta > \sin\theta_c$$

or $$\sin\theta > \dfrac{8}{9}$$

50. In air, object lies between F and $2F$.

In liquid, focal length will become 4 times. So, object will now lie between optical centre and focus.

51. Condition of no emergence,

$$A > 2\theta_C$$

$$\therefore \qquad \theta_C < \dfrac{A}{2}$$

or $$45°$$

$$\therefore \qquad \sin\theta_C \text{ or } \dfrac{1}{\mu} < \sin 45° \text{ or } \dfrac{1}{\sqrt{2}}$$

For no emergence, $\mu > \sqrt{2}$

Subjective Questions

1. (a) $\mu = \dfrac{343}{1498} = 0.229$

(b) $\theta_C = \sin^{-1}(0.229) = 13.2°$

2. $t_1 = \dfrac{l}{v_1} = \dfrac{l}{c/\mu_1} = \dfrac{\mu_1 l}{e}$

$$\Rightarrow \qquad t_2 = \dfrac{\mu_2 l}{c}$$

$$\therefore \qquad t_2 - t_1 = (\mu_2 - \mu_1)\dfrac{l}{c}$$

$$= \dfrac{(1.63 - 1.47)(20)}{3 \times 10^8}$$

$$= 1.07 \times 10^{-8} \text{ s}$$

3. (a) $t_1 = \dfrac{l}{v_1} = \dfrac{l}{c/n_1} = \dfrac{n_1 l}{c} = $ minimum

$$= \dfrac{1.2 \times 10^{-6}}{3 \times 10^8}$$

$$= 4 \times 10^{-15} \text{ s}$$

(b) $\lambda = \dfrac{\lambda_0}{n}$

Number of wavelengths across any film,

$$N = \dfrac{l}{\lambda} = \dfrac{ln}{\lambda_0}$$

4. $\mu = \dfrac{\sin i}{\sin r}$

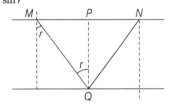

$$1.8 = \dfrac{\sin 60°}{\sin r}$$

Solving, we get $r = 28.8°$

$$MP = PQ \tan r$$

$$\therefore \qquad MN = 2(MP) = 2PQ \cdot \tan r$$

$$= 2 \times 6 \times \tan 28.8°$$

$$= 6.6 \text{ cm}$$

$$\mu = \dfrac{\sin 45°}{\sin r} = \dfrac{4}{3}$$

5. Dispersion power,

$$\omega = \dfrac{\mu_v - \mu_r}{\mu_y - 1}$$

6. For blue light,

$$\mu = \dfrac{\sin i_1}{\sin r_1}$$

or $$1.68 = \dfrac{\sin 65°}{\sin r_1}$$

Solving this equation, we get

$$r_1 = 32.6°$$

$$r_2 = A - r_1 = 27.4°$$

Again applying,

$$\mu = \dfrac{\sin i_2}{\sin r_2}$$

or $\qquad 1.68 = \dfrac{\sin i_2}{\sin 27.4°}$

Solving this equation, we get

$\qquad i_2 = 50.6°$

Now, $\quad \delta_B = i_1 + i_2 - A$

or $\qquad \delta_B = 65° + 50.6° - 60° = 55.6°$ ...(i)

For red light,

$\qquad 1.65 - \dfrac{\sin 65°}{\sin r_1}$

or $\qquad r_1 = 33.3°$

∴ $\qquad r_2 = A - r_1 = 26.7°$

Now, $\qquad 1.65 = \dfrac{\sin i_2}{\sin 26.7°}$

∴ $\qquad i_2 = 47.8°$

∴ $\qquad \delta_R = i_1 + i_2 - A$

or $\qquad \delta_R = 65° + 47.8° - 60° = 52.8°$ ...(ii)

From Eqs. (i) and (ii), we get

$\qquad \delta_B - \delta_R = 2.8°$

7. For plane surface, $h_{app} = \mu h = \dfrac{3}{2} \times 10 = 15\,\text{cm}$

This first image is at a distance, $(15 + 3)$ cm from the plane mirror. So, mirror will make its second image at a distance 18 cm below the mirror or 21 cm below the plane surface.

Now further applying,

$\qquad d_{app} = \dfrac{d}{\mu} = \dfrac{21}{1.5} = 14 \text{ cm}$

below the plane surface or 11 cm behind the mirror.

8.

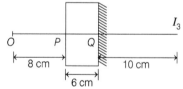

Applying h_{app} for first refraction,

$\qquad PI_1 = 8\mu \quad \text{(towards left)}$

$\qquad QI_1 = PQ + PI_1 = (6 + 8\mu)$

∴ $\qquad QI_2 = QI_1 = (6 + 8\mu)$, towards right.

$\qquad PI_2 = PQ + QI_2 = (12 + 8\mu)$

Applying $d_{app} = \dfrac{d}{\mu}$ for third and last refraction we have,

$\qquad PI_3 = \left(\dfrac{12 + 8\mu}{\mu} \right) = 16$

∴ $\qquad \mu = 1.5$

9.

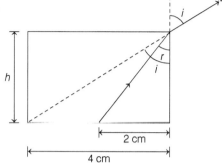

Applying, $\quad \mu = \dfrac{\sin i}{\sin r}$ we get

$\qquad \dfrac{4}{3} = \dfrac{4/\sqrt{16 + h^2}}{2/\sqrt{4 + h^2}}$

Solving this equation we get,

$\qquad h = 2.4\,\text{cm}$

10.

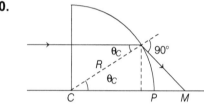

$\qquad \theta_C = \sin^{-1}\left(\dfrac{1}{n}\right) = \sin^{-1}\left(\dfrac{2}{3}\right) = 41.8°$

$\qquad CM = R \sec \theta_C = \dfrac{R}{\cos \theta_C}$

$\qquad \quad = \dfrac{5\,\text{cm}}{\cos 41.8°} = 6.7\,\text{cm}$

∴ $\quad PM = CM - CP = (6.7 - 5.0)$

$\qquad \qquad \qquad = 1.7\,\text{cm}$

Note *In critical case, angle in denser medium is θ_C and in rarer medium 90°.*

11.

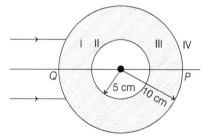

Apply $\qquad \dfrac{\mu_2}{v} - \dfrac{\mu_1}{u} = \dfrac{\mu_2 - \mu_1}{R}$ four times,

We have $\quad \dfrac{1.5}{v_1} - \dfrac{1.0}{\infty} = \dfrac{1.5 - 1.0}{+10}$

$\therefore \qquad\qquad v_1 = +30 \text{ cm}$

$\dfrac{1.0}{v_2} - \dfrac{1.5}{+25} = \dfrac{1.0 - 1.5}{-5.0}$

$\qquad\qquad v_2 = -6.25 \text{ cm}$

$\dfrac{1.5}{v_3} - \dfrac{1.0}{-3.75} = \dfrac{1.5 - 1.0}{-5.0}$

$\qquad\qquad v_3 = -4.1 \text{ cm}$

$\dfrac{1.0}{v_4} - \dfrac{1.5}{-9.1} = \dfrac{1.0 - 1.5}{-10}$

$\Rightarrow \qquad\qquad v_4 = -4.67 \text{ cm}$

$\therefore$ Final image is at 4.67 cm to the left of P.

12. Applying $\dfrac{\mu_2}{v} = \dfrac{\mu_1}{u} = \dfrac{\mu_2 - \mu_1}{R}$ we have,

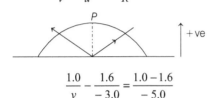

$\dfrac{1.0}{v} - \dfrac{1.6}{-3.0} = \dfrac{1.0 - 1.6}{-5.0}$

Solving we get, $\quad v = -2.42 \text{ cm}$

This is distance from P (downwards).

$\therefore$ Distance from observer $= 5 + 2.42$

$\qquad\qquad\qquad\qquad = 7.42 \text{ cm}$

13.

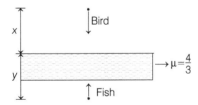

Given, $-\dfrac{dy}{dt} = 4 \text{ cm/s}$

Distance of bird as observed by fish

$Z = y + \mu x = y + \dfrac{4}{3} x$

$\therefore \quad \dfrac{-dZ}{dt} = \dfrac{-dy}{dt} + \dfrac{4}{3}\left(\dfrac{-dx}{dt}\right) \qquad \ldots\text{(i)}$

Given, $\quad \dfrac{-dZ}{dt} = 16 \text{ cm/s}$

Substituting in Eq. (i), we get

$\dfrac{-dx}{dt} = 9 \text{ cm/s}$

14. $f = \dfrac{d^2 - x^2}{4d}$ (displacement method)

$f = 16 \text{ cm}, x = 60 \text{ cm}$

Substituting the values, we get

$d = 100 \text{ cm}$

15. (a) $\dfrac{1}{f} = (\mu - 1)\left(\dfrac{1}{R_1} - \dfrac{1}{R_2}\right)$

$\therefore \qquad\qquad f \propto \left(\dfrac{1}{\mu - 1}\right)$

or $\quad \dfrac{f_1}{f_2} = \dfrac{\mu_2 - 1}{\mu_1 - 1} = \dfrac{1.7 - 1.0}{1.5 - 1.0} = 1.4$

(b) If refraction index of the liquid (or the medium) is greater than the refraction index of lens it changes its nature or converging lens behaves as diverging.

16.

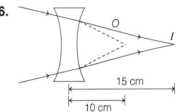

Using $\qquad \dfrac{1}{f} = \dfrac{1}{v} - \dfrac{1}{u},$

or $\qquad \dfrac{1}{f} = \dfrac{1}{+15} - \dfrac{1}{+10}$

Solving, we get $\quad f = -30 \text{ cm}$

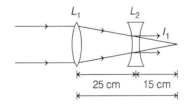

I_1 is formed at second focus of L_1 and first focus of L_2.

18. $\dfrac{\omega_1}{f_1} + \dfrac{\omega_2}{f_2} = 0$

$\therefore \qquad\qquad \left|\dfrac{\omega_1}{\omega_2}\right| = \left|\dfrac{f_1}{f_2}\right|$

Let 1-stands for flint glass and 2-stands for crown glass. Then,

$$\left|\frac{f_1}{f_2}\right| = \frac{3}{2} \text{ or } |f_1| = 1.5 |f_2|$$

Focal length of flint glass is more. So, its power is less. Combined focal length (and hence combined power) is positive. So, convex lens (converging lens) should be made up of crown glass (having more positive power).

Now, $\dfrac{1}{F} = \dfrac{1}{f_1} + \dfrac{1}{f_2}$

$\therefore \qquad \dfrac{1}{150} = \dfrac{1}{-1.5\,f} + \dfrac{1}{f}$

Solving this equation, we get

$$f_2 = f = 50 \text{ cm} \text{ and}$$
$$f_1 = -1.5, \ f = -75 \text{ cm}$$

19. Object is placed at distance $2f$ from the lens. Hence, image is also formed at distance $2f$ on other side. For mirror,

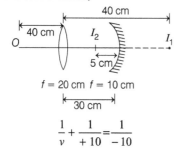

$f = 20 \text{ cm} \quad f = 10 \text{ cm}$

$\overleftarrow{} 30 \text{ cm} \overrightarrow{}$

$$\dfrac{1}{v} + \dfrac{1}{+10} = \dfrac{1}{-10}$$

Ray diagram is as shown below.

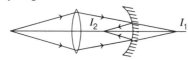

20. For second lens,

$$\dfrac{1}{v} - \dfrac{1}{-5} = \dfrac{1}{-20}$$

$\Rightarrow \qquad v = -4 \text{ cm}$

$f_1 = 10 \text{ cm} \qquad f_2 = -20 \text{ cm} \quad f_3 = 9 \text{ cm}$

For third lens,

$$\dfrac{1}{v} - \dfrac{1}{-(4+9)} = \dfrac{1}{+9}$$

$\therefore \qquad v = \infty$

21. See the result of sample example 31.30

$$R = \frac{h}{\sqrt{\mu^2 - 1}}$$

$$h = R\sqrt{\mu^2 - 1}$$

$$= (1 \text{ cm})\sqrt{(5/3)^2 - 1}$$

$$= \frac{4}{3} \text{ cm}$$

22. $\sin\theta_C = \dfrac{1}{\mu_1} = \dfrac{2}{3}$

Now, $\qquad \mu_1 \sin i_1 = \mu_2 \sin i_2$
or $\qquad \mu_1 \sin\theta_C = \mu_2 \sin\theta$

$\therefore \qquad \left(\dfrac{3}{2}\right)\left(\dfrac{2}{3}\right) = \left(\dfrac{4}{3}\right)\sin\theta$

or $\qquad \theta = \sin^{-1}\left(\dfrac{3}{4}\right)$

23. (a) $\dfrac{\omega_1}{f_1} + \dfrac{\omega_2}{f_2} = 0$

$\therefore \qquad \omega_2 = \left(-\dfrac{f_2}{f_1}\right)\omega_1$

$$= -\dfrac{(-30)}{(+20)}(0.18) = 0.27$$

(b) $\dfrac{1}{F} = \dfrac{1}{f_1} + \dfrac{1}{f_2} = \dfrac{1}{20} - \dfrac{1}{30}$

or $\qquad F = +60 \text{ cm}$

24. $\theta_C = \sin^{-1}\left(\dfrac{\mu_R}{\mu_D}\right) = \sin^{-1}\left(\dfrac{4/3}{3/2}\right) = \sin^{-1}(8/9)$

Water

Glass

$i = 0°$ $\qquad\qquad i = \theta_C$

$\therefore \qquad\qquad \delta_1 = 0°$
$\therefore \qquad\qquad \delta_2 = 90° - \theta_C$

$$\cos\delta_2 = \cos(90° - \theta_C) = \sin\theta_C = \frac{8}{9}$$

$\therefore \qquad\qquad \delta_2 = \cos^{-1}\left(\dfrac{8}{9}\right)$

25. (a) At minimum deviation,

$$r_1 = r_2 = \frac{A}{2} = 30°$$

Applying $\quad \mu = \dfrac{\sin i_1}{\sin r_1}$ or $\quad 1.5 = \dfrac{\sin i_1}{\sin 30°}$

We get $\qquad i_1 = 48.6°$

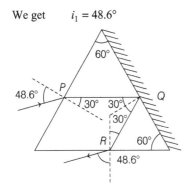

$$\delta_{\text{Total}} = \delta_P + \delta_Q + \delta_R$$
$$= (48.6° - 30°) + (180° - 2 \times 30°) + (48.6° - 30°)$$
$$= 157.2°$$

(b) $\dfrac{4}{3} \sin(48.6°) = 1.5 \sin r_1$

Solving we get, $r_1 = 41.8°$
$$r_2 = 60° - r_1 = 18.2°$$
$$r_3 = 60° - r_2 = 41.8°$$
$$\therefore \qquad i_3 = 48.6°$$

Hence,
$$\delta_{\text{Total}} = (48.6° - 41.8°) + (180° - 2 \times 18.2°)$$
$$+ (48.6° - 41.8°)$$
$$= 157.2°$$

LEVEL 2

Single Correct Option

1. $h_{\text{app}} = \mu h = \dfrac{4}{3} \times 2 = \dfrac{8}{3}$ m

Distance from mirror $= 1 + h_{\text{app}} = \dfrac{11}{3}$ m. So, mirror will make image at same distance ($= 11/3$ m from itself). Now in third refraction, depth of second image,
$$d = \dfrac{11}{3} + 1 = \dfrac{14}{3} \text{ m}$$
$$d_{\text{app}} = \dfrac{d}{\mu} = \dfrac{14}{3} \times \dfrac{3}{4} = \dfrac{7}{2} \text{ m}$$

The desired distance is therefore,
$$(d_{\text{app}} + h)$$
or $\qquad \left(\dfrac{7}{2} + 2 \right)$ m
or $\qquad \dfrac{11}{2}$ m

2. Applying, $\dfrac{\mu_2}{v} - \dfrac{\mu_1}{u} = \dfrac{\mu_2 - \mu_1}{R}$ we get,
$$\dfrac{1.5}{v} - \dfrac{1}{\infty} = \dfrac{1.5 - 1.0}{+ R}$$
$$\therefore \qquad v = + 3R$$

3.
$$\mu = \dfrac{\sin 60°}{\sin 30°} = \sqrt{3}$$

4. Refraction from first surface,
$$\dfrac{\mu_2}{v_1} - \dfrac{\mu_1}{\infty} = \dfrac{\mu_2 - \mu_2}{+ R}$$

Refraction from second surface,
$$\dfrac{\mu_3}{f} - \dfrac{\mu_2}{v_1} = \dfrac{\mu_3 - \mu_2}{- R} \qquad \text{(as } v_2 = f\text{)}$$

Adding these two equations, we get
$$\dfrac{\mu_3}{f} = \dfrac{\mu_2 - \mu_1}{R} - \dfrac{\mu_3 - \mu_2}{R}$$

Lens becomes diverging if f is negative or
$$\mu_3 - \mu_2 > \mu_2 - \mu_1$$
or $\qquad \mu_3 + \mu_1 > 2\mu_2$
Same result is obtained if parallel beam of light is incident from RHS.

5. In first case,
$$u = -16 \text{ cm, then } v = (+16n) \text{ cm}$$
$$\therefore \qquad \dfrac{1}{16n} - \dfrac{1}{-16} = \dfrac{1}{f} \qquad \text{...(i)}$$

In second case,
$$u = -6 \text{ cm, then } v = -(6n) \text{ cm}$$
$$\therefore \qquad \dfrac{1}{-6n} - \dfrac{1}{-6} = \dfrac{1}{f} \qquad \text{...(ii)}$$

Solving these two equations, we get
$$f = 11 \text{ cm}$$

6. $d_{\text{app}} = \dfrac{d}{(n_1/n_2)}$
$$\therefore \qquad d = \dfrac{n_2}{n_1} d_{\text{app}}$$
$$-\dfrac{d}{dt}(d) = \dfrac{n_2}{n_1}\left(-\dfrac{d}{dt} d_{\text{app}} \right) = \left(\dfrac{n_2}{n_1} \right) x$$
$$\dfrac{dv}{dt} = A\left[-\dfrac{d}{dt}(d) \right] = \dfrac{x \, \pi R^2 \, n_2}{n_1}$$

7. From geometry we can find that
$$r_2 = 53°$$
$$\theta_C = \sin^{-1}\left(\frac{1}{\mu}\right) = 37°$$

Since, $r_2 > \theta_C$, TIR will take place on the face AB
$$\delta = \delta_{AC} + \delta_{AB}$$
$$= 0 + 180° - 2r_2$$
$$= 180° - 2 \times 53° = 74°$$

8.

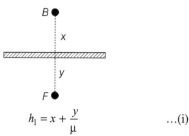

$$h_1 = x + \frac{y}{\mu} \qquad \ldots(i)$$
$$h_2 = y + \mu x \qquad \ldots(ii)$$

Eq. (i) can be written as
$$\frac{\mu x + y}{\mu} = h_1 \quad \text{or} \quad \frac{h_2}{\mu} = h_1 \quad \text{or} \quad \mu = \frac{h_2}{h_1}$$

9. $MC = QC - QM = (R - 0.3)$ cm
$$PC^2 = MC^2 + PM^2$$
$$R^2 = (R - 0.3)^2 + (3)^2$$

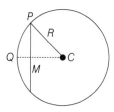

Solving this equation, we get
$$R = 15 \text{ cm}$$

10. See the hint of Q.No-5 of the same section. In that example,
$$f = \frac{16 + 6}{2} = 11 \text{ cm}$$

11. $\dfrac{1}{F_1} = \dfrac{1}{f_1} + \dfrac{1}{f_2}$
$$\frac{1}{F_2} = \frac{1}{f_1} + \frac{1}{f_2} - \frac{d}{f_1 f_2}$$
$$F_2 > F_1$$

So, image of distant object will be formed to the right of P.

12. $\mu = \dfrac{\sin\left(\dfrac{A + \delta_m}{2}\right)}{\sin(A/2)}$

μ and A for both rays are same. Hence, value of δ_m is also same for both rays.

13.
$$\theta_C = \sin^{-1}\left(\frac{1}{\mu}\right)$$
$$= \sin^{-1}\left(\sqrt{\frac{3}{7}}\right) = 40.9°$$
$$r_2 = \theta_C = 40.9°$$
$$r_1 = A - r_2 = 19.1°$$
$$\mu = \frac{\sin i_1}{\sin r_1}$$
$$\sqrt{\frac{7}{3}} = \frac{\sin i_1}{\sin r_1}$$

Solving this equation, we get $i_1 = 30°$

14. If object is placed at focus of plano-convex lens, then it will make rays parallel. Now, these rays fall normal on plane mirror. So, they retrace their path.

15. If object is placed at centre of the sphere, then all rays starting from C fall normal on spherical surface and pass understand.

16. $\sin \theta_C = \dfrac{\mu_R}{\mu_D} = \dfrac{6/5}{3/2} = \dfrac{4}{5}$
$$r_1 = 0°$$
$$\Rightarrow \qquad r_2 = <B = 90° - \theta$$
Now,
or $\qquad r_2 > \theta_c$
$$\sin r_2 > \sin \theta_C$$
$$\therefore \qquad \sin(90° - \theta) > \frac{4}{5}$$
or $\qquad \cos\theta > \dfrac{4}{5} \qquad \ldots(i)$
$$\cos 37° = \frac{4}{5}$$
From Eq. (i), we see that
$$\theta < 37°$$

17. From the first refraction, rays should become parallel. Or, image should formed at infinity.
Applying,
$$\frac{\mu_2}{u} - \frac{\mu_1}{u} = \frac{\mu_2 - \mu_1}{R}$$
$$\frac{3/2}{\infty} - \frac{1.0}{-x} = \frac{3/2 - 1.0}{+10}$$
Solving, we get
$$x = 20 \text{ cm}$$

18. (a) Two images are formed in case (i).
(b) One image is formed in case (ii).

(c) $\dfrac{1}{f_2} = (\mu - 1)\left(\dfrac{1}{-R} - \dfrac{1}{R}\right) = -\dfrac{2}{R}(\mu - 1)$ ...(i)

$\dfrac{1}{f_3} = \dfrac{1}{F_1} + \dfrac{1}{F_2}$

$\qquad = (\mu - 1)\left(\dfrac{1}{\infty} - \dfrac{1}{R}\right) + (\mu - 1)\left(\dfrac{1}{-R} - \dfrac{1}{\infty}\right)$ ...(ii)

From Eqs. (i) and (ii), we can see that $f_2 = f_3$.

19. $\dfrac{1}{f} = \dfrac{1}{OB} - \dfrac{1}{-OA} = \dfrac{1}{OB} + \dfrac{1}{OA}$

$\qquad f = \dfrac{(OA)\,(OB)}{AB + OB}$

$\therefore \qquad f = \dfrac{(OA)\,(OB)}{AB}$ ...(i)

Now, $\qquad AB^2 = AC^2 + BC^2$

or $\quad (OA + OB)^2 = AC^2 + BC^2$

or $\quad OA^2 + OB^2 + 2\,(OA)\,(OB) = AC^2 + BC^2$

$\therefore \quad (AC^2 - OC^2) + (BC^2 - OC^2)$

$\qquad\qquad\qquad + 2\,(OA)\,(OB) = AC^2 + BC^2$

Solving, we get

$\qquad\qquad (OA)\,(OB) = OC^2$

Substituting in Eq. (i), we get

$\qquad\qquad f = \dfrac{OC^2}{AB}$

20. Shift $= \left(1 - \dfrac{\mu_{\text{medium}}}{\mu_{\text{slab}}}\right) t$

$\qquad = \left[1 - \dfrac{4/3}{3/2}\right] \times 36 = 4$ cm

21. $\dfrac{h}{\mu} = \dfrac{21}{2}$ or $\dfrac{h}{(4/3)} = \dfrac{21}{2}$

Solving, we get $h = 14$ cm.

22. $m = -\dfrac{2\,\text{cm}}{1\,\text{cm}} = -2$

$\Rightarrow \qquad |v| = m\,|u|$

23. Using the equation,

$\dfrac{1}{F} = \dfrac{2\,(\mu_2/\mu_1)}{R_2} - 2\dfrac{(\mu_2/\mu_1 - 1)}{R_1}$

we get

$\dfrac{1}{-10} = \dfrac{2\,(1.5)}{\infty} - \dfrac{1\,(1.5 - 1)}{R_1}$

$\left(\text{as } F = \dfrac{R}{2}\right)$

Solving, we get $R_1 = 10$ cm.

24. For concave lens,

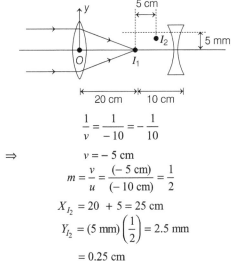

$\dfrac{1}{v} = \dfrac{1}{-10} = -\dfrac{1}{10}$

$\Rightarrow \qquad v = -5$ cm

$m = \dfrac{v}{u} = \dfrac{(-5\,\text{cm})}{(-10\,\text{cm})} = \dfrac{1}{2}$

$X_{I_2} = 20 + 5 = 25$ cm

$Y_{I_2} = (5\,\text{mm})\left(\dfrac{1}{2}\right) = 2.5$ mm

$\qquad\qquad = 0.25$ cm

25. $\angle i = 0°$ for all values of θ, as the rays fall normal to sphere at all points.

26. Cavity of placed at centre. Hence, image of cavity is also formed at centre, as all rays fall normal to surface at all points. (so pass undeviated).

Now, $\qquad m = \left(\dfrac{\mu_1}{\mu_2}\right)\left(\dfrac{v}{u}\right)$

$\qquad\qquad = \dfrac{(4/3)}{1}\left(\dfrac{1\,\text{m}}{1\,\text{m}}\right) = \dfrac{4}{3}$

27. $\dfrac{1}{f} = (1.5 - 1)\left(\dfrac{1}{20} - \dfrac{1}{-20}\right)$

$\Rightarrow \qquad f = +20$ cm

$$\frac{1}{v_1} - \frac{1}{-30} = \frac{1}{+20}$$

$$\therefore \qquad v_1 = +60 \text{ cm}$$

$$m_1 = \frac{v_1}{u_1} = \frac{+60}{-30} = -2$$

For second lens,

$$\frac{1}{v_2} - \frac{1}{-60} = \frac{1}{+20}$$

$$v_2 = +30 \text{ cm}$$

$$m_2 = \frac{v_2}{u_2} = \frac{(+30)}{(-60)} = -\frac{1}{2}$$

$$m = m_1 m_2 = 1$$

Final image is 30 cm to the right of second lens or 150 cm to the right of first lens.

$$m = 1$$

Hence, image height = object height

$$= 3 \text{ mm}$$

28. Apply $\dfrac{\mu_2}{v} - \dfrac{\mu_1}{v} = \dfrac{\mu_2 - \mu_1}{R}$

We get $\quad \dfrac{1}{v} - \dfrac{2}{-10} = \dfrac{1-2}{-10}$

Solving we get,

$$v = -10 \text{ cm}$$

29.

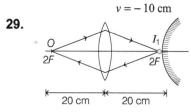

30. Shift $= \left(1 - \dfrac{1}{\mu}\right) t = \left(1 - \dfrac{2}{3}\right)(6) = 2 \text{ cm}$

For mirror, object distance = 50 − 2 = 48 cm.

So, mirror will make image at a distance 48 cm behind it. In return journey of ray of light, we will have to farther take 2 cm shift in the direction of ray of light.

So, image distance as observed by observer

$$= (50 + 48) - 2$$
$$= 96 \text{ cm}$$

31. Using $\dfrac{1}{v} - \dfrac{1}{u} = \dfrac{1}{f}$, we get

$$\frac{1}{+(f+40)} - \frac{1}{-(f+10)} = \frac{1}{+f}$$

Solving this equation, we get

$$f = +20 \text{ cm}$$

32. Applying Snell's law at point M, we get

$$n_1 = \frac{\sin\theta}{\sin(90° - \theta_C)} \quad \text{or} \quad \sin\theta = n_1 \cos\theta_C$$

$$= n_1\sqrt{1 - \sin^2\theta_C}$$

$$= n_1\sqrt{1 - \frac{n_2^2}{n_1^2}} = \sqrt{n_1^2 - n_2^2}$$

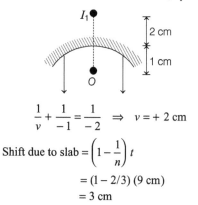

If angle of θ is less than this value, then angle of incidence at N will be greater than θ_C. Hence, TIR will take place at N.

33. Reflection from the concave mirror, I_1

$$\frac{1}{v} + \frac{1}{-1} = \frac{1}{-2} \quad \Rightarrow \quad v = +2 \text{ cm}$$

Shift due to slab $= \left(1 - \dfrac{1}{n}\right) t$

$$= (1 - 2/3)(9 \text{ cm})$$
$$= 3 \text{ cm}$$

Now, slab will make next image at a distance 3 cm from I_1 in the direction of ray of light, i.e. at O itself but it is virtual, as the ray of light has crossed the slab and we are making image behind the slab.

34.

$$\frac{\mu_2}{v} - \frac{\mu_1}{u} = \frac{\mu_2 - \mu_1}{-R}$$

$$\therefore \qquad \frac{\mu_2}{v} = \frac{\mu_1 - \mu_2}{R} + \frac{\mu_1}{u}$$

If $\mu_1 > \mu_2$ and u is positive (i.e. virtual object), then v is always positive or image is always real.

35.

$$\frac{1.5}{v} - \frac{1.0}{-u} = \frac{1.5 - 1.0}{+R}$$

or $$\frac{1.5}{v} = \frac{-1}{u} + \frac{1}{2R}$$

For image to real (for negative value of u) v should be positive.

Hence, $\dfrac{1}{u} < \dfrac{1}{2R}$ or $u > 2R$.

36.

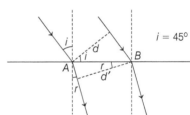

When object moves towards F to O virtual erect and magnified image moves from ∞ to O.

37. $\dfrac{1}{F} = \dfrac{1}{f_1} + \dfrac{1}{f_2} - \dfrac{d_2}{f_1/f_2}$

f_1 and f_2 both are negative. Hence, F is also negative. Object is real so combined lens (having negative focal length) will always make, its virtual image.

38. Using $\dfrac{\mu_2}{u} - \dfrac{\mu_1}{u} = \dfrac{\mu_2 - \mu_1}{R}$ we get

$$\frac{3/2}{\infty} - \frac{1.0}{-x} = \frac{3/2 - 1}{+60}$$

$\therefore$ $\qquad x = 120$ cm

Hence for $x = 120$ cm, rays of light become parallel to principal axis and fall normal to polished surface.

Hence, rays retrace their path.

39. $$\frac{1.6}{v_1} - \frac{1.0}{-2} = \frac{1.6 - 1.0}{+1.0}$$

$\Rightarrow$ $\qquad v_1 = 16$ m

$$\frac{2.0}{v_2} - \frac{1.0}{-2} = \frac{2.0 - 1.0}{+1.0}$$

$\therefore$ $\qquad v_2 = 4$ m

$\qquad I_2 I_2 = v_1 - v_2$

$\qquad\qquad = 12$ m

40. $\qquad \sqrt{3} = \dfrac{\sin 60^\circ}{\sin r}$

$\therefore$ $\qquad r = 30^\circ$

The asked angle,

$\qquad \theta = 180^\circ - i - r = 90^\circ$

41. $\dfrac{1}{-(f+1)} - \dfrac{1}{-(f-1)} = \dfrac{1}{f}$

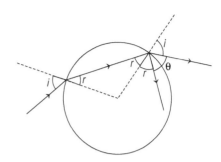

Solving, we get $f = (\sqrt{2} + 1)$ cm

42. $AB = \dfrac{d}{\cos i} = \dfrac{d'}{\cos r}$

$\therefore$ $\qquad d' = \dfrac{\cos r}{\cos i} d$ $\qquad$ ...(i)

Further, $\quad \sin r = \dfrac{\sin i}{\mu} = \dfrac{1}{\sqrt{2}\,\mu}$

Hence, $\quad \cos r = \sqrt{1 - \dfrac{1}{2\mu^2}} = \dfrac{\sqrt{2\mu^2 - 1}}{\sqrt{2}\,\mu}$

Substituting in Eq. (i), we have

$$d' = \frac{\sqrt{2\mu^2 - 1}}{\mu} \cdot d$$

43. $\qquad \dfrac{1}{3x} - \dfrac{1}{-x} = \dfrac{1}{+30}$

$\therefore$ $\qquad x = 40$ cm

and $\qquad 3x = 120$ cm

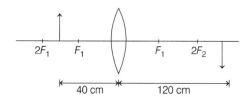

To decrease the magnification object should be moved towards $2F_1$.

Hence, image will move towards $2F_2$. Let displacement is y. Then,

$$2(40 + 5) = (120 - y)$$

$$\therefore \qquad y = 30 \, cm$$

44. In first case when sun is at infinity, i.e.

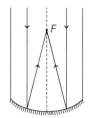 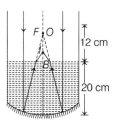

$$u = \infty$$

$$\frac{1}{f} = \frac{1}{-32} + \frac{1}{(-\infty)}$$

$$\therefore \qquad f = -32 \, cm$$

When water is filled in that tank upto a height of 20 cm, the image formed by the mirror will act as virtual object O for water surface.

$$\therefore \qquad BI = BO \times \frac{3}{4}$$

$$= 12 \times \frac{3}{4} = 9 \, cm$$

45. $\dfrac{1}{v} - \dfrac{1}{-u} = \dfrac{1}{+f}$

$$\therefore \qquad v = \frac{uf}{u - f}$$

or $\qquad \dfrac{v}{u} = m = \dfrac{f}{u - f}$

$$\therefore \qquad \frac{1}{m} = \left(\frac{1}{f}\right) u - 1$$

Comparing this with equation of straight line, $\dfrac{1}{f}$ is

the slope of line, which is $\dfrac{b}{c}$.

$$\therefore \qquad f = \frac{c}{b}$$

46.

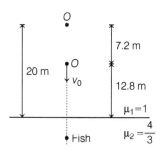

$$v_0 = \sqrt{2as} = \sqrt{2 \times 10 \times 7.2}$$

$$= 12 \, m/s = \text{Object speed}$$

Image distance,

$$v = \frac{\mu_2}{\mu_1} u = \frac{4/3}{1} u$$

$$\Rightarrow \qquad \frac{dv}{dt} = \frac{4}{3} \frac{du}{dt}$$

or $\qquad v_I = \frac{4}{3} v_0 = \frac{4}{3} \times 12$

$$= 16 \, m/s = \text{Image speed.}$$

47. $\mu = \dfrac{\sin \theta_1}{\sin \theta_3}$

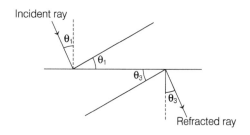

48. $\mu_1 \sin i_1 = \mu_2 \sin i_2$

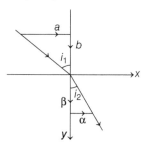

$$\therefore \qquad \frac{\mu_1 a}{\sqrt{a^2 + b^2}} = \frac{\mu_2 \alpha}{\sqrt{\alpha^2 + \beta^2}}$$

$$\sqrt{a^2 + b^2} = \sqrt{\alpha^2 + \beta^2} = 1$$

$$\therefore \qquad \mu_1 a = \mu_2 \alpha$$

49. Fish is observer and bird is object.

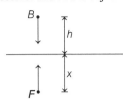

Apparent distance between F and B at some instant will be

$$y = (x + \mu h)$$

$$\left(-\frac{dy}{dt}\right) = \left(-\frac{dx}{dt}\right) + \mu\left(-\frac{dh}{dt}\right)$$

$$9 = 3 + \frac{4}{3}\left(-\frac{dh}{dt}\right)$$

∴ $$-\frac{dh}{dt} = 4.5 \text{ m/s}$$

50. When the ray passes into the rarer medium, the deviation is $\delta = \phi - \theta$. This can have a maximum value of $\left(\frac{\pi}{2}\right) - C$

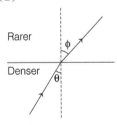

For $\theta = C$ and $\phi = \frac{\pi}{2}$

51. $f\,(\text{m}) = \dfrac{1}{P\,(\text{Dioptre})} = \dfrac{1}{0.66} = 1.515 \text{ m}$

or $f = 151.5$ cm

For short sightedness we need a concave lens so that images of all objects lie between O and F_2 or between O and f. Here, f is 151.5 cm. So, distant point of the eye is approximately 151.5 cm.

52. Let us say $PO = OQ = X$

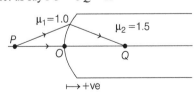

Applying $\dfrac{\mu_2}{v} - \dfrac{\mu_1}{u} = \dfrac{\mu_2 - \mu_1}{R}$

Substituting the values with sign

$$\frac{1.5}{+X} - \frac{1.0}{-X} = \frac{1.5 - 1.0}{+R}$$

(Distances are measured from O and are taken as positive in the direction of ray of light)

∴ $$\frac{2.5}{X} = \frac{0.5}{R}$$

∴ $$X = 5R$$

More than One Correct Options

1. For $n = 2m$, it is just like a slab.

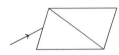

∴ Deviation = 0

For $n = 2m + 1$, it is just like an identical prism of larger size.

2. $\dfrac{\sin i_1}{\sin i_2} = \dfrac{v_1}{v_2}$

∴ $$\frac{\sin r}{\sin i} = \text{slope} = \frac{1}{\sqrt{3}} = \frac{v_y}{v_x}$$

∴ $$v_y = \frac{v_x}{\sqrt{3}}$$

Speed of light in medium-y is less. So, it is denser. TIR takes place when ray of travels from denser to rarer medium.

3. (a) If vacuum speed of light of all colours is same.

(b)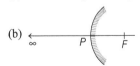

If object moves from ∞ to P, then its virtual, erect and diminished image move from F to P.

(c)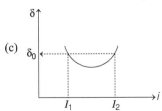

4. Displacement method of finding focal length of convex lens.

5. With increase in wavelength, refractive index gets decreased.

Comprehension Based Questions

1. Using the mirror formula,

$$\frac{1}{f} = \frac{1}{v} + \frac{1}{u} = \frac{1}{-40} - \frac{1}{10}$$

Solving we get,

$$f = -8 \text{ cm}$$

2. Focal length of lenses is

$$\frac{1}{F} = (1.8 - 1)\left(\frac{1}{\infty} - \frac{1}{-2R}\right)$$

$$+ (1.2 - 1)\left(\frac{1}{-2R} - \frac{1}{-R}\right)$$

$$F = 2R$$

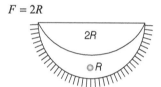

Now combined power of system,

$$P = 2P_L + P_m$$

or

$$-\frac{1}{f} = 2P_L + P_m$$

or

$$\frac{1}{8} = 2\left(\frac{1}{2R}\right) + \frac{2}{R}$$

or

$$R = 24 \text{ cm}$$

∴ Radius of curvature of common surface

$$= 2R = 48 \text{ cm}$$

3. Combined focal length of lens,

$$\frac{1}{f} = (1.2 - 1)\left(\frac{1}{+24} - \frac{1}{+48}\right)$$

$$+ (1.8 - 1)\left(\frac{1}{+48} - \frac{1}{\infty}\right)$$

$$= \frac{1}{48}$$

Now, combined power of system

$$P = 2P_L + P_M$$

∴

$$-\frac{1}{F} = 2\left(\frac{1}{f}\right) + \infty = 2\left(\frac{1}{48}\right)$$

∴

$$F = -24 \text{ cm}$$

Match the Columns

1. (c) and (d) $\dfrac{1}{v} - \dfrac{1}{u} = \dfrac{1}{f}$

∴

$$\frac{1}{v} = \frac{1}{u} + \frac{1}{f}$$

Between O and F_2 or between F_2 and $2F_2$, u is positive. So, v is also positive.

∴

$$m = \frac{u}{v} \quad \text{is positive}$$

Therefore, image is real (as v is positive) and erect (as m is also positive).

2. (a) $\dfrac{1}{v} - \dfrac{1}{u} = \dfrac{1}{-f}$

∴

$$\frac{1}{u} = \frac{1}{u} - \frac{1}{f}$$

Between O and F_1, u is positive and less than f. So, v is positive (therefore image is real). Further from

$$m = \frac{v}{u}$$

We can see that m is allow positive. So, it is erect also.

(b) $\dfrac{1}{v} - \dfrac{1}{u} = \dfrac{1}{-f}$ $\Rightarrow$ ∴ $\dfrac{1}{v} = \dfrac{1}{u} - \dfrac{1}{f}$

Between F_1 and $2F_1$, μ positive and greater than f. So, v negative (therefore image is virtual). Further from

$$m = \frac{v}{u}$$

We can see that m is negative so, image is inverted.

3. (a) and (b)

$$v = \frac{\mu_2}{\mu_1} u$$

$$\Rightarrow \qquad |v| < |u|$$

as

$$\mu_1 > \mu_2$$

i.e v and u are of same sign.

Or they are on same side of plane surface. From plane surface, if object is real, image is virtual and *vice-versa*.

(c) and (d)

$$v = \frac{\mu_1}{\mu_2} u$$

$$\Rightarrow \qquad |v| > |u|$$

Other explanations are same.

4. (a) $\dfrac{\mu}{v} - \dfrac{1}{-u} = \dfrac{\mu - 1}{-R}$

∴ $\dfrac{\mu}{v} = \dfrac{-1}{u} \dfrac{\mu - 1}{R}$

Therefore, v is always negative. Or image is always virtual.

(b) $\dfrac{\mu}{v} - \dfrac{1}{+u} = \dfrac{\mu - 1}{-R}$ or $\dfrac{\mu}{v} = \dfrac{1}{u} - \dfrac{\mu - 1}{R}$

So, v may be positive or negative. Hence, image may be real or virtual.

Same logic can be applied for two options. For them R is positive. In option (c), u is negative and in option (d) u is positive.

5. $\dfrac{1}{f_1}$ or $P_1 = (1.5 - 1)\left(\dfrac{1}{R_1} - \dfrac{1}{R_2}\right)$ ...(i)

$\dfrac{1}{f_2}$ or $P_2 = \left(\dfrac{1.5}{\mu_e} - 1\right)\left(\dfrac{1}{R_1} - \dfrac{1}{R_2}\right)$ ...(ii)

Dividing Eq. (ii) by Eq. (i), we get

$$P_2 = \left(\dfrac{3}{\mu_e} - 2\right) P_1 \qquad ...(iii)$$

(a) $\mu_e = 1.4$, then P_2 is positive and less than P_1.

Other options can be checked from Eq. (iii).

6. Concave lens can make only virtual, erect and diminished images of real objects.

Convex lens can make real, inverted and diminished size or real inverted and magnified or virtual, erect and magnified images of real objects.

Rest type of cases are possible with virtual, objects.

Subjective Questions

1. First draw a ray AA' until it intersects with the principal optical axis and find the centre of the lens C. Since, the virtual image is magnified, the lens is convex.

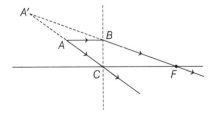

Draw a ray AB parallel to the principal optical axis. It is refracted by the lens so that it passes through its focus and its continuation passes through the virtual image. The ray $A'B$ intersects the principal optical axis at point F, the focus of the lens.

2. The paths of the rays are shown in figure. Since, the virtual image is diminished, the lens is concave.

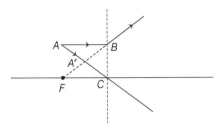

3. (a) $OA = 8.0$ cm

∴ $AI_1 = (n_g)(OA)$

$= \left(\dfrac{8}{5}\right)(8.0) = 12.8$ cm

For refraction at EG ($R = \infty$), using

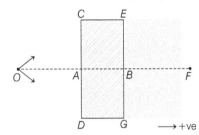

$\dfrac{n_2}{v} - \dfrac{n_1}{u} = \dfrac{n_2 - n_1}{R}$

∴ $\dfrac{4/3}{BI_2} - \dfrac{8/5}{-(12.8 + 3)} = 0$

∴ $BI_2 = -(15.8)(4/3)(5/8) = -13.2$ cm

∴ $FI_2 = 13.2 + 6.8 = 20.0$ cm **Ans.**

(b) **For face EF**

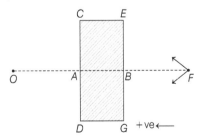

$\dfrac{8/5}{BI_1} - \dfrac{4/3}{-6.8} = 0$

∴ $BI_1 = -(6.8)(8/5)(3/4)$

$= -8.16$ cm

For face *CD*

$$\frac{1.0}{AI_2} - \frac{8/5}{-11.16} = 0$$

∴ $$AI_2 = -(11.16)(5/8)$$
$$= -6.975 \text{ cm}$$

∴ $$FI_2 = 8 + 6.975$$
$$= 14.975 \text{ cm} \qquad \textbf{Ans.}$$

4. The system behaves like a mirror of focal length given by

$$\frac{1}{F} = \frac{2(n_2/n_1)}{R_2} - \frac{2(n_2/n_1 - 1)}{R_1}$$

Substituting the values with proper sign.

$$\frac{1}{F} = \frac{2 \times 4/3}{-20} \qquad (\because R_1 = \infty)$$

or $$F = -7.5 \text{ cm} \qquad \textbf{Ans.}$$

i.e. system behaves as a concave mirror of focal length 7.5 cm.

5. $$\frac{1}{f} = (n-1)\left(\frac{1}{R_1} - \frac{1}{R_2}\right)$$

$$\frac{1}{10} = (1.5 - 1)\left(\frac{1}{R_1} - \frac{1}{-10}\right)$$

∴ $$R_1 = +10 \text{ cm}$$

Now using,

$$\frac{1}{v} + \frac{1}{u} = \frac{2(n_2/n_1)}{R_2} - \frac{2(n_2/n_1 - 1)}{R_1}$$

Substituting the values,

$$\frac{1}{v} + \frac{1}{-15} = \frac{2(1.5)}{-10} - \frac{2(1.5 - 1)}{+10}$$

∴ $$v = -3.0 \text{ cm} \qquad \textbf{Ans.}$$

6. Using lens formula, $$\frac{1}{v} - \frac{1}{u} = \frac{1}{f}$$

$$\frac{1}{v_1} - \frac{1}{-40} = \frac{1}{30}$$

∴ $$v_1 = 120 \text{ cm}$$

Shift due to the slab,

$$\Delta x = \left(1 - \frac{1}{\mu}\right)d = \left(1 - \frac{1}{1.8}\right)9 = 4 \text{ cm}$$

∴ $$u' = -(40 - \Delta x)$$
$$= -36 \text{ cm}$$

∴ $$\frac{1}{v_2} - \frac{1}{-36} = \frac{1}{30}$$

∴ $$v_2 = 180 \text{ cm}$$

Therefore, we will have to shift the screen a distance $x = v_2 - v_1 = 60$ cm away from lens. **Ans.**

7. $$\frac{1}{40} = (1.5 - 1)\left(\frac{1}{120} + \frac{1}{R_1}\right)$$

Solving we get, $R_2 = 24$ cm

Applying lens formula, for L_2

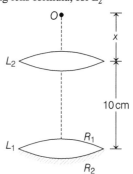

$$\frac{1}{v_1} + \frac{1}{x} = \frac{1}{20} \qquad \text{...(i)}$$

Using $\dfrac{\mu_2}{v} - \dfrac{\mu_1}{u} = \dfrac{\mu_2 - \mu_1}{R}$ for unsilvered side of L_1.

$$\frac{1.5}{-120} - \frac{1.0}{v_1 - 10} = \frac{1.5 - 1.0}{24} \qquad \text{...(ii)}$$

Solving Eqs. (i) and (ii), we get $x = 10$ cm **Ans.**

8. *Case* I $$\frac{1}{v} + \frac{1}{u} = \frac{1}{f}$$

∴ $$\frac{1}{v_1} - \frac{1}{30} = \frac{1}{-10}$$

∴ $$v_1 = -15 \text{ cm}$$

Case II Shift $= \left(1 - \dfrac{1}{\mu}\right)t = \left(1 - \dfrac{1}{1.5}\right)6 = 2$ cm

∴ $$\frac{1}{v_2} - \frac{1}{28} = \frac{1}{-10}$$

∴ $$v_2 = -15.55 \text{ cm}$$

∴ $$\Delta v = 0.55 \text{ cm} \qquad \textbf{Ans.}$$

9. Using $\dfrac{\mu_2}{v} - \dfrac{\mu_1}{u} = \dfrac{\mu_2 - \mu_1}{R}$, twice with $u = \infty$,

we have

$$\frac{1.5}{v_1} = \frac{1.5 - 1.4}{+20} \qquad \text{...(i)}$$

$$\frac{1.6}{v_2} - \frac{1.5}{v_1} = \frac{1.6 - 1.5}{-20} \qquad \text{...(ii)}$$

Solving Eqs. (i) and (ii), we get $f = v_2 = \infty$,
i.e. the system behaves like a glass plate.

10. First image will be formed by direct rays 1 and 2, etc.

$$PI_1 = \frac{PO}{\mu} = \frac{5}{1.5} = 3.33 \text{ cm} \qquad \textbf{Ans.}$$

Second image will be formed by reflected rays 3 and 4, etc.

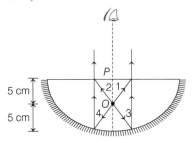

Object is placed at the focus of the mirror. Hence, I_2 is formed at infinity.

11. (a) Applying Snell's law at D,

$$\frac{4}{3}\sin i = \frac{3}{2}\sin 30°$$

$$\therefore \qquad i = 34.2° \qquad \textbf{Ans.}$$

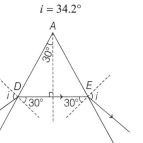

(b) $\delta = \delta_D + \delta_E = 2\delta_D$
$$= 2(i - 30°)$$
$$= 8.4° \qquad \textbf{Ans.}$$

12. $\sqrt{2} = \dfrac{\sin 45°}{\sin r}$

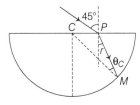

$$r = 30°$$

$$\theta_C = \sin^{-1}\left(\frac{1}{\mu}\right) = 45°$$

Applying sine law in $\triangle CPM$,

$$\frac{CP}{\sin \theta_C} = \frac{CM}{\sin (90° + r)}$$

$$\therefore \qquad \frac{CP}{(1/\sqrt{2})} = \frac{R}{\cos r} \qquad [R = \text{radius}]$$

$$\therefore \qquad CP = \sqrt{\frac{2}{3}}R$$

As we move away from C, angle PMC will increase. Therefore, $CP \not> \sqrt{\frac{2}{3}}R$. Same is the case on left side of C.

13. $\dfrac{1}{20} = (1.5 - 1)\left(\dfrac{1}{R} - \dfrac{1}{-R}\right)$

$$\therefore \quad R = 20 \text{ cm}$$

Applying $\dfrac{\mu_2}{v} - \dfrac{\mu_1}{u} = \dfrac{\mu_2 - \mu_1}{R}$ twice with the condition that rays must fall normally on the concave mirror.

$$\frac{1.5}{v_1} - \frac{1.2}{-40} = \frac{1.5 - 1.2}{+20} \qquad \text{...(i)}$$

$$\frac{2.0}{d - 80} - \frac{1.5}{v_1} = \frac{2.0 - 1.5}{-20} \qquad \text{...(ii)}$$

Solving Eqs. (i) and (ii), we get

$$d = 30 \text{ cm} \qquad \textbf{Ans.}$$

and $\qquad v_1 = -100 \text{ cm}$

The ray diagram is as shown in figure.

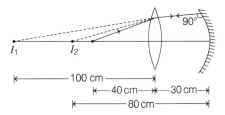

14. Using lens formula,

$$\frac{1}{36} - \frac{1}{-45} = \frac{1}{f}$$

$$\therefore \qquad f = 20 \text{ cm}$$

In the second case, let μ be the refractive index of the liquid, then

$$\frac{1}{48} - \frac{1}{-\left(5 + \dfrac{40}{\mu}\right)} = \frac{1}{20}$$

Solving this, we get
$$\mu = 1.37 \qquad \textbf{Ans.}$$

15. As the angles are small we can take,

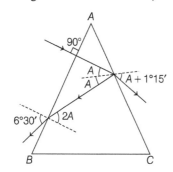

$$\sin\theta \approx \theta$$

Now,
$$\mu = \frac{A + 1°15'}{A}$$

$$= \frac{6°30'}{2A}$$

Solving this equation, we get

$$A = 2°$$

and
$$\mu = 1.62 \qquad \textbf{Ans.}$$

16. Using lens formula for L_2,

$$\frac{1}{v} - \frac{1}{-f/2} = \frac{1}{f}$$

or
$$v = -f$$

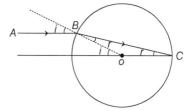

This f length will be along PP' from point O' (towards P).

∴
$$O'I_2' = f$$

On x-axis this distance will be $f \sec 60° = 2f$.
Since, $OO' = 2f$, therefore image will be formed at origin.

Note *A ray passing through O and then O′ goes undeviated.*

Therefore, I_1 and I_2 both should be on this line, which is also the x-axis. That's why for final image we have taken projection of $O'I_2'$ on x-axis.

17. For the lens, $u = -2.0$ m, $f = +1.5$ m

∴
$$\frac{1}{v} - \frac{1}{-2.0} = \frac{1}{1.5}$$

or
$$v = 6.0 \text{ m}$$

$$m = \frac{6.0}{-2.0} = -3.0$$

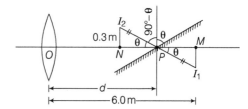

Therefore, y-coordinate of image formed by lens is $m(0.1) = -0.3$ m.

$$\frac{0.3}{NP} = \tan\theta = 0.3$$

∴
$$NP = MP = 1.0 \text{ m}$$

or
$$d = 6.0 - 1.0$$
$$= 5.0 \text{ m} \qquad \textbf{Ans.}$$

and x-coordinate of final image I_2 is
$$x = d - 1.0 = 4.0 \text{ m} \qquad \textbf{Ans.}$$

18. $BO = OC$

∴
$$\angle OBC = \angle BCO = r \qquad \text{(say)}$$

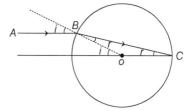

Let angle of incidence be i,
$$i = r + r = 2r \qquad \text{(external angle)}$$

∴
$$\mu = \frac{\sin i}{\sin r} = \frac{\sin 2r}{\sin r} \approx \frac{2r}{r} = 2 \qquad \textbf{Ans.}$$

19. $\delta_{\text{Total}} = \delta_{\text{Refraction}} + 2\delta_{\text{Reflection}} + \delta_{\text{Refraction}}$

or
$$\delta = (i - r) + 2(180° - 2r) + (i - r)$$
$$= 360° + 2i - 6r$$
$$= 360° + 2i - 6 \sin^{-1}\left(\frac{\sin i}{\mu}\right)$$

For deviation to be minimum, $\dfrac{d\delta}{di} = 0$

By putting first derivative of δ (w.r.t. i) equal to zero, we get the desired result.

20. (a) For refraction at first half lens $\left(\dfrac{1}{v} - \dfrac{1}{u} = \dfrac{1}{f} \right)$

$$\frac{1}{v} - \frac{1}{-20} = \frac{1}{15}$$

∴ $v = 60$ cm

Magnification, $m = \dfrac{v}{u} = \dfrac{60}{-20} = -3$

The image formed by first half lens is shown in figure (a).

$AB = 2$ mm, $A_1 B_1 = 6$ mm, $AO_1 = 20$ cm, $O_1 F = 15$ cm and $O_1 A_1 = 60$ cm.

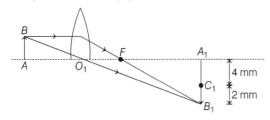

Point B_1 is 6 mm below the principal axis of the lenses. Plane mirror is 4 mm below it.

Hence, 4 mm length of $A_1 B_1$ (i.e. $A_1 C_1$) acts as real object for mirror. Mirror forms its virtual image $A_2 C_2$. 2 mm length of $A_1 B_1$ (i.e. $C_1 B_1$) acts as virtual object for mirror. Real image $C_2 B_2$ is formed of this part. Image formed by plane mirror is shown in figure (b).

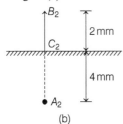

(b)

For the second half lens, $\dfrac{1}{v} - \dfrac{1}{-60} = \dfrac{1}{15}$

∴ $v = +20$

$m = \dfrac{v}{u} = \dfrac{20}{-60} = -\dfrac{1}{3}$

So, length of final image

$$A_3 B_3 = \frac{1}{3} A_2 B_2 = 2 \text{ mm}$$

Point B_2 is 2 mm below the optic axis of second half lens. Hence, its image B_3 is formed 2/3 mm above the principal axis. Similarly, point A_2 is 8 mm below the principal axis. Hence, its image is 8/3 mm above it. Therefore, image is at a distance of 20 cm

behind the second half lens and at a distance of 2/3 mm above the principal axis. The size of image is 2 mm and is inverted as compared to the given object. Image formed by second half lens is shown in figure (c).

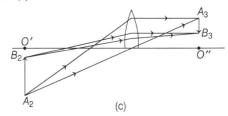

(c)

(b) Ray diagram for final image is shown in figure (d).

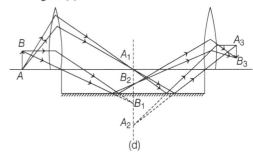

(d)

21. (i) $PO = OQ$

∴ $\angle OPQ = \angle OQP = r$ (say)

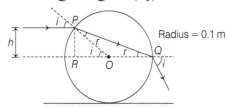

Also, $i = r + r = 2r$

In $\triangle POR$, $h = OP \sin i = 0.1 \sin i$

$= 0.1 \sin 2r$

or $h = 0.2 \sin r \cos r$ ...(i)

Also, $\sqrt{3} = \dfrac{\sin i}{\sin r} = \dfrac{2 \sin r \cos r}{\sin r}$

$= 2 \cos r$

∴ $r = 30°$

Substituting in Eq. (i), we get

$$h = 0.2 \times \frac{1}{2} \times \frac{\sqrt{3}}{2}$$

$= 0.086$ m

Hence, height from the mirror is

$0.1 + 0.086 = 0.186$ m

(ii) Use the principle of reversibility.

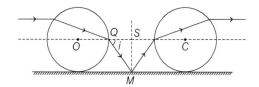

$$i = 2r = 60°$$

Now, $\dfrac{QS}{MS} = \cot i = \cot 60° = \dfrac{1}{\sqrt{3}}$

$\therefore \qquad QS = \dfrac{MS}{\sqrt{3}} = \dfrac{0.1}{\sqrt{3}}$

$\therefore$ The desired distance,

$$OC = 2 \times 0.1 + \dfrac{2 \times 0.1}{\sqrt{3}}$$

$$= 0.315 \qquad \textbf{Ans.}$$

22. $\dfrac{V_i}{V} = \dfrac{\rho_S}{\rho_L} = \dfrac{\rho}{2\rho} = \dfrac{1}{2}$

i.e. half the sphere is inside the liquid. For the image to coincide with the object light should fall normally on the sphere.

Using $\dfrac{\mu_2}{v} - \dfrac{\mu_1}{u} = \dfrac{\mu_2 - \mu_1}{R}$ twice, we have

$$\dfrac{3/2}{v_1} - \dfrac{1}{-8} = \dfrac{3/2 - 1}{+2}$$

$\therefore \qquad v_1 = 12 \text{ cm}$

Further, $\dfrac{4/3}{h-10} - \dfrac{3/2}{8} = \dfrac{4/3 - 3/2}{-2}$

Solving this equation, we get

$$h \approx 15 \text{ cm} \qquad \textbf{Ans.}$$

23. We have to see the image of O from the other side.

Applying, $\dfrac{\mu_2}{v} - \dfrac{\mu_1}{u} = \dfrac{\mu_2 - \mu_1}{R}$ twice, we have

$$\dfrac{\mu}{AI_1} - \dfrac{1}{-2R} = \dfrac{\mu - 1}{-R}$$

$\therefore \qquad AI_1 = \dfrac{2\mu R}{1 - 2\mu}$

Further, $\dfrac{1}{BI_2} - \dfrac{\mu}{(AI_1 - R)} = \dfrac{1 - \mu}{-R}$

Solving this equation, we get

$$BI_2 = -\dfrac{2R(4\mu - 1)}{3\mu - 1}$$

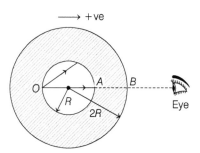

$\therefore$ Distance between the final image and object is

$$d = 3R - \dfrac{2R(4\mu - 1)}{3\mu - 1}$$

$$= \dfrac{(\mu - 1)R}{(3\mu - 1)} \qquad \textbf{Hence proved.}$$

24. $\delta_{\text{Total}} = \delta_P + \delta_Q$

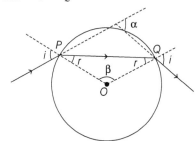

$\therefore \qquad \alpha = (i - r) + (i - r)$

or $\qquad i - r = \dfrac{\alpha}{2}$ ...(i)

Further, in $\triangle OPQ$,

$$r + r + \beta = 180°$$

$\therefore \qquad r = 90° - \dfrac{\beta}{2}$ ...(ii)

From Eq. (i),

$$i = r + \dfrac{\alpha}{2} = 90° + \left(\dfrac{\alpha - \beta}{2}\right)$$ ...(iii)

$$\mu = \dfrac{\sin i}{\sin r} = \dfrac{\sin\left[90° + \left(\dfrac{\alpha - \beta}{2}\right)\right]}{\sin\left(90° - \dfrac{\beta}{2}\right)}$$

$$= \dfrac{\cos\left(\dfrac{\beta - \alpha}{2}\right)}{\cos\left(\dfrac{\beta}{2}\right)}$$

or $\cos\left(\dfrac{\beta - \alpha}{2}\right) = \mu \cos \dfrac{\beta}{2}$ \qquad **Hence proved.**

25. $\theta = 90° - i$

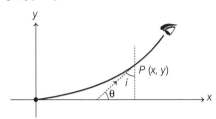

$$\tan \theta = \cot i$$

or $$\frac{dy}{dx} = \cot i \qquad \ldots(i)$$

$$\mu_0 \sin i_0 = \mu_P \sin i_P$$

(i) $\sin 90° = (\sqrt{1 + ay}) \sin i$

$\therefore \qquad \sin i = \dfrac{1}{\sqrt{1 + ay}}$

$\therefore \qquad \cot i = \sqrt{ay} = \dfrac{dy}{dx}$

$\therefore \qquad \displaystyle\int_0^y \frac{dy}{\sqrt{ay}} = \int_0^x dx \quad$ or $\quad x = 2\sqrt{\dfrac{y}{a}}$

Substituting $\qquad y = 2$ m,

and $\qquad\qquad a = 2.0 \times 10^{-6}$ m^{-1}

We get $\qquad\qquad x_{max} = 2000$ m $= 2$ km $\qquad$ **Ans.**

26. Applying, $\dfrac{\mu_2}{v} - \dfrac{\mu_1}{u} = \dfrac{\mu_2 - \mu_1}{R}$ twice, we have

$$\frac{\mu}{v_1} - \frac{1}{-2R} = \frac{\mu - 1}{R}$$

$\therefore \qquad\qquad v_1 = \dfrac{2\mu R}{2\mu - 3}$

Further, $\qquad \dfrac{1}{v_2} - \dfrac{\mu}{-(3R - v_1)} = \dfrac{1 - \mu}{R/2}$

$\therefore \qquad\qquad v_2 = \dfrac{R(9 - 4\mu)}{(10\mu - 9)(\mu - 2)} \qquad$ **Ans.**

Final image is real if, $v_2 > 0$.

As $10\mu - 9$ is always positive ($\mu > 1$). Therefore, for $v_2 > 0$, either $(9 - 4\mu)$ and $(\mu - 2)$ both should be greater than zero or both should be less than zero. For the first condition (when both > 0) $2 < \mu < 2.25$ and for the second condition (when both < 0), $\mu < 2$ and $\mu > 2.25$ which is not possible. Hence, μ should lie between 2 and 2.25.

32. Interference and Diffraction of Light

INTRODUCTORY EXERCISE 32.1

1. $\dfrac{I_1}{I_2} = \dfrac{9}{16}$, $\dfrac{I_{max}}{I_{min}} = \left(\dfrac{\sqrt{I_1/I_2}+1}{\sqrt{I_1/I_2}-1}\right)^2$

2. (a) $\dfrac{A_{max}}{A_{min}} = \dfrac{A_1 + A_2}{A_1 - A_2}$

(b) $\dfrac{I_{max}}{I_{min}} = \left(\dfrac{A_{max}}{A_{min}}\right)^2$

3. $\dfrac{\lambda}{4}$ path difference is equivalent to 90° phase difference

$\Rightarrow$ $\begin{aligned} A_{net} &= 5A_0 \\ I_{max} &= 25\,I_0 \end{aligned}$

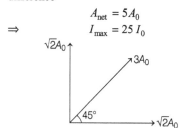

INTRODUCTORY EXERCISE 32.2

3. $I = I_{max} \cos^2 \dfrac{\phi}{2}$

$\dfrac{3}{4} I_{max} = I_{max} \cos^2 \dfrac{\phi}{2}$ or $\cos\dfrac{\phi}{2} = \dfrac{\sqrt{3}}{2}$

$\therefore$ $\dfrac{\phi}{2} = \dfrac{\pi}{6}$

$\therefore$ $\phi = \dfrac{\pi}{3} = \left(\dfrac{2\pi}{\lambda}\right)(\Delta x) = \dfrac{2\pi}{\lambda}\left(\dfrac{yd}{D}\right)$

$\therefore$ $y = \dfrac{\lambda D}{6d} = \dfrac{(600 \times 10^{-19})\,(1.2)}{(6)\,(0.25 \times 10^{-2})}$

$= 48 \times 10^{-6}\,\text{m} = 48\,\mu\text{m}$

4. $A_1 = 3A_2$

So, $I_1 = 9I_2$

Let $A_2 = A_0$ and $I_2 = I_0$

Then, $A_1 = 3A_0$ and $I_1 = 9I_0$

$A_{max} = (A_1 + A_2) = 4A_0$

and $I_{max} = 16I_0$

Now, $I = I_1 + I_2 + 2\sqrt{I_1 I_2}\,\cos\phi$

$= 9I_0 + I_0 + 2\sqrt{9I_0 \times I_0}\,\cos\phi$

$= 10I_0 + 6I_0\,\cos\phi$

$= 10 \times \dfrac{I_{max}}{16} + 6\left(\dfrac{I_{max}}{16}\right)\cos\phi$

$= \dfrac{5}{8}I_{max} + \dfrac{3}{8}I_{max}\,\cos\phi$

$= \dfrac{5}{8}I_{max} + \dfrac{3}{8}I_{max}\left(2\cos^2\dfrac{\phi}{2} - 1\right)$

$= \dfrac{1}{4}I_{max} + \dfrac{3}{4}I_{max}\cdot\cos^2\dfrac{\phi}{2}$

$= \dfrac{I_{max}}{4}\left(1 + 3\cos^2\dfrac{\phi}{2}\right)$

5. (a) $I = I_{max}\cos^2\dfrac{\phi}{2}$

$= I_0\cos^2 30°$ (as $\phi = 60°$)

$= \dfrac{3}{4}I_0$

(b) 60° phase difference is equivalent to $\dfrac{\lambda}{6}$ path difference.

6. $a_R = 2a\cos\dfrac{\phi}{2}$

(i) For $a_R = 2a$, $\phi = 0°$

(ii) For $a_R = \sqrt{2}a$, $\phi = 90°$ etc

Exercises

LEVEL 1

Assertion and Reason

1. The whole fringe pattern will shift upwards.

2. $I_{max} = (\sqrt{I_1} + \sqrt{I_2})^2$

and $I_{min} = (\sqrt{I_1} - \sqrt{I_2})^2$

When $I_1 = I_2 = I_0$, then

$I_{max} = 4I_0$ and $I_{min} = 0$

When slit of one width is slightly increased, then intensity due to that slit becomes greater than I_0. In that case, we can see that

$I_{max} > 4I_0$ and $I_{min} > 0$

4. At centre, path difference is maximum and this is equal to $S_1 S_2$. Then, path difference decreases as we move away on the screen. So, order of fringe also decreases. Hence, 11th order maxima occurs before 10th order maxima.

5. $d \sin \theta = 2\lambda$ (for second order maxima)

$$\sin \theta = 2\frac{\lambda}{d} = 2 \times \frac{1}{4} = \frac{1}{2}$$

$\therefore \qquad \theta = 30°$

For maxima, $d \sin \theta = n\lambda$

$\therefore \qquad n_{max} = \dfrac{d}{\lambda} = 4 \qquad$ (for $\theta = 90°$)

So, there are total 7 maxima corresponding to $n = 0, \pm 1, \pm 2$ and ± 3.

We cannot take $n = 4$, as it is for $\theta = 90°$, which is out of screen.

Objective Questions

3. Refractive index is slightly decreased.

4. $A = \sqrt{(8)^2 + (6)^2} = 10 \, \text{mm}$

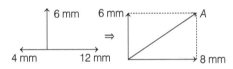

5. $\dfrac{I_{max}}{I_{min}} = \dfrac{(\sqrt{I_1/I_2} + 1)^2}{(\sqrt{I_1/I_2} - 1)^2} = \dfrac{49}{9}$

Solving, we get

$$\frac{I_1}{I_2} = \frac{25}{4}$$

6. $\dfrac{I_1}{I_2} = \beta^2$

So let, $I_2 = 1$ unit, then $I_1 = \beta$

$I_{max} = (\sqrt{I_1} + \sqrt{I_2})^2 = (1 + \beta)^2$

$I_{min} = (\sqrt{I_1} - \sqrt{I_2})^2 = (1 - \beta)^2$

$\qquad\qquad = I_{max} - I_{min} = 4\beta$

$I_{max} + I_{min} = 2(1 + \beta^2)$

$\therefore$ The asked ratio is $\dfrac{2\beta}{1 + \beta^2}$.

7. $d \sin \theta = \dfrac{\lambda}{2}$

$\therefore \qquad \theta = \sin^{-1}\left(\dfrac{\lambda}{2d}\right)$

$$= \sin^{-1}\left(\frac{5460 \times 10^{-10}}{2 \times 0.1 \times 10^{-3}}\right)$$

$$= 0.16°$$

8. 6th dark fringe distance in vacuum = 10th bright fringe distance in liquid.

$\therefore \qquad 5.5\,\omega = 10\,\omega'$

or $\qquad \dfrac{\omega}{\omega'} = \mu = \dfrac{10}{5.5} = 1.81$

9. $\quad \text{Shift} = \dfrac{(\mu - 1)tD}{d}$

$$= \frac{(1.5 - 1)(10 \times 10^{-6})(1.0)}{2.5 \times 10^{-3}}$$

$$= 2 \times 10^{-3} \, \text{m}$$

$$= 2 \, \text{mm}$$

10. $\omega = \dfrac{\lambda D}{d} \quad$ or $\quad \omega \propto \lambda$

ω will increase $\dfrac{6000}{4000}$

or $\quad$ 1.5 times.

Hence, number of fringes in same distance will decrease 1.5 times.

11. $\omega = \dfrac{\lambda D}{d}$

$\Rightarrow \qquad \Delta\omega = \dfrac{\lambda(\Delta D)}{d}$

$\therefore \qquad \lambda = \dfrac{(d)(\Delta\omega)}{\Delta D} = \dfrac{(10^{-3})(3 \times 10^{-5})}{5 \times 10^{-2}}$

$$= 0.6 \times 10^{-6} \, \text{m} = 6000 \, \text{Å}$$

12. Only fringe pattern will shift. Number of fringes on screen will remain unchanged.

13. $\qquad\qquad \lambda_{blue} < \lambda_{green}$

$\therefore \qquad\qquad \omega_{blue} < \omega_{green}$

14. At minima, $\sin\theta = m\dfrac{\lambda}{a}$

θ and a are same. Therefore,

$$(1)\lambda_1 = (3)\lambda_2$$

or $\qquad\qquad \lambda_1 = 3\lambda_2$

15. Wavelength in medium, $\lambda' = \dfrac{\lambda}{\mu}$

$$\Delta\phi = \left(\frac{2\pi}{\lambda'}\right)x = \frac{2\pi}{(\lambda/\mu)}$$

$$x = \frac{2\pi\mu x}{\lambda}$$

16. $I = 4I_0 \cos^2 \dfrac{\phi}{2}$

Given, $I = I_0$

$\therefore$ $\phi = \dfrac{2\pi}{3} = \dfrac{2\pi}{\lambda} \cdot \Delta x = \dfrac{2\pi}{\lambda} \left(\dfrac{yd}{D} \right)$

$\therefore$ $y = \dfrac{\lambda D}{3d}$

17. $\Delta I = (I_1 + I_2 + 2\sqrt{I_1 I_2} \cos \phi_1)$

$\qquad - (I_1 + I_2 + 2\sqrt{I_1 I_2} \cos \phi_2)$

$= 2\sqrt{I_1 I_2} (\cos \phi_1 \sim \cos \phi_2)$

18. θ (in radian) $= \dfrac{\lambda}{d}$

$\therefore$ $d = \dfrac{\lambda}{\theta}$

$= \dfrac{6 \times 10^{-7}}{\pi/180}$

$= 3.4 \times 10^{-5}$ m

19. $K = 4I_0, \ K' = 2I_0 = \dfrac{K}{2}$

20. $y = \dfrac{\omega}{4} = \dfrac{\lambda D}{4d} : \Delta x = \dfrac{yd}{D} = \dfrac{\lambda}{4} : \phi = \dfrac{2\pi}{\lambda} \cdot \Delta x = \dfrac{\pi}{2}$

$\dfrac{\phi}{2} = \dfrac{\pi}{4}$

Now, $I_2 = I_1 \cos^2 \dfrac{\phi}{2}$

or $\dfrac{I_1}{I_2} = \dfrac{1}{\cos^2 \phi/2} = 2$

Subjective Questions

1.

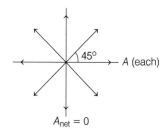

$A_{net} = 0$

2. (a) At centre path difference is zero. Therefore, construction interference will be obtained.

(b) $\dfrac{\lambda}{2} = 3$ m. At a distance, where path difference is $\dfrac{\lambda}{2}$ or 3 m destructive interference will be obtained.

$\begin{array}{ccc} \underset{A}{\circ} & \overset{1\,m}{\underset{P_1}{\circ}} & \overset{4\,m}{\underset{B}{\circ}} \end{array}$

$\begin{array}{ccc} \underset{A}{\circ} & \overset{4\,m}{\underset{P_2}{\circ}} & \overset{1\,m}{\underset{B}{\circ}} \end{array}$

At P_1 $\qquad BP_1 - AP_1 = 3\text{m} = \dfrac{\lambda}{2}$

At P_2 $\qquad AP_2 - BP_2 = 3\text{m} = \dfrac{\lambda}{2}$

3. $\because$ $\lambda = \dfrac{c}{f} = \dfrac{3 \times 10^8}{120 \times 10^6} = 2.5$ m

$\begin{array}{ccc} \underset{A}{\circ} & \overset{x}{\underset{P}{\circ}} & \overset{(9-x)}{\underset{B}{\circ}} \end{array}$

$\Delta x = (BP - AP) = (9 - 2x) = n\lambda$

$\therefore$ $x = \dfrac{9 - n\lambda}{2} = \dfrac{9 - 2.5n}{2}$

Now, substituting $n = 1, 2, \ldots$ etc.
We can find different values of x.

$x_1 = 3.25$ m for $n = 1$

$x_2 = 2.0$ m for $n = 2$

and $x_3 = 0.75$ m for $n = 3$

Similarly, we will get three points at same distance from other point B.

4. $\because$ $\omega = \dfrac{\lambda D}{d}$

$\therefore$ $\lambda = \dfrac{\omega d}{D} = \dfrac{(2.82 \times 10^{-3})(0.46 \times 10^{-3})}{2.2}$

$= 0.589 \times 10^{-6}$ m

≈ 590 nm

5. $\theta = \dfrac{\lambda}{d} = \dfrac{500 \times 10^{-9}}{2.0 \times 10^{-3}}$ radian

$\approx 0.014°$

6. Wavelength in water, $\lambda' = \dfrac{\lambda}{\mu}$

Fringe width, $\omega = \dfrac{\lambda' D}{d} = \dfrac{\lambda D}{\mu d}$

$= \dfrac{(700 \times 10^{-9})(0.48)}{(4/3)(0.25 \times 10^{-3})}$

$= 10^{-3}$ m

$= 1$ mm

7. Distance $= \dfrac{3\lambda_2 D}{d} - \dfrac{3\lambda_1 D}{d}$

$= \dfrac{3(\lambda_2 - \lambda_1)D}{d}$

$$= \frac{3 \times (600 - 480) \times 10^{-9} \times 1.0}{5.0 \times 10^{-3}}$$

$$= 7.2 \times 10^{-5} \text{ m}$$

$$= 0.072 \text{ mm}$$

8. $\Delta x = d \sin \theta = n\lambda$

$$n = \frac{d \sin \theta}{\lambda}$$

$$n_{max} = \frac{d}{\lambda} = \frac{4.0 \times 10^{-6}}{600 \times 10^{-9}}$$

$$= 6.66$$

Highest integer is 6.

9. $y = \omega_1 = \dfrac{\omega_2}{2}$

$$\therefore \qquad \frac{\lambda_1 D}{d} = \frac{\lambda_2 D}{2d}$$

$$\Rightarrow \qquad \lambda_2 = 2\lambda_1 = 1200 \text{ nm}$$

10. $d \sin \theta_1 = \dfrac{\lambda}{2}$

$$\sin \theta_1 = \frac{\lambda}{2d} = \frac{550 \times 10^{-9}}{2 \times 1.8 \times 10^{-6}}$$

$$\therefore \qquad \theta_1 = 8.78°$$

$$\frac{y_1}{D} = \tan \theta_1$$

$$\therefore \qquad y_1 = D \tan \theta_1$$

$$= 35 \tan 8.78°$$

$$= 5.41 \text{ cm}$$

$$d \sin \theta_2 = \frac{3\lambda}{2}$$

$$\therefore \qquad \sin \theta_2 = \frac{3\lambda}{2d} = \frac{3 \times 550 \times 10^{-9}}{2 \times 1.8 \times 10^{-6}}$$

$$\therefore \qquad \theta_2 = 27.27°$$

$$\therefore \qquad y_2 = D \tan \theta_2$$

$$= 35 \tan 27.27°$$

$$= 18 \text{ cm}$$

$$\Delta y = y_2 - y_1 = 12.6 \text{ cm}$$

11. $\lambda (\text{in Å}) = \sqrt{\dfrac{150}{E (\text{in eV})}}$

(de-Broglie wavelength of electron)

$$= \sqrt{\frac{150}{100}} = 1.22 \text{ Å}$$

$$\omega = \frac{\lambda D}{d} = \frac{(1.22 \text{ Å}) (3 \text{ m})}{(10 \text{ Å})}$$

$$= 0.366 \text{ m} = 36.6 \text{ cm}$$

12. (a) $\Delta x = \dfrac{yd}{D}$

and $\qquad \phi = \dfrac{2\pi}{\lambda} \cdot \Delta x$

$$= \frac{(2\pi) yd}{\lambda D}$$

$$= \frac{(2 \times 180) yd}{\lambda D} \text{ degree}$$

$$= \frac{360 \times 0.3 \times 10^{-3} \times 10 \times 10^{-3}}{546 \times 10^{-9} \times 1.0}$$

$$= 1978°$$

Now, $\quad I = I_0 \cos^2 \dfrac{\phi}{2}$

$$= 2.97 \times 10^{-4} I_0$$

$$\approx 3.0 \times 10^{-4} I_0$$

(b) $\omega = \dfrac{\lambda D}{d}$

$\therefore$ Number of fringes between central fringe and P

$$N = \frac{y}{\omega} = \frac{yd}{\lambda D}$$

$$= \frac{(10 \times 10^{-3}) (0.3 \times 10^{-3})}{(546 \times 10^{-9}) (1.0)}$$

$$= 5.49$$

So, bright fringes are five.

13. $\text{Shift} = \dfrac{(\mu - 1) tD}{d}$

$$S_1 = \frac{(1.6 - 1) (10 \times 10^{-6}) (1.5)}{1.5 \times 10^{-3}}$$

$$= 0.6 \times 10^{-2} \text{ m}$$

$$= 0.6 \text{ m}$$

$$S_2 = \frac{(1.2 - 1) (15 \times 10^{-6}) (1.5)}{1.5 \times 10^{-3}}$$

$$= 0.3 \times 10^{-2} \text{ m}$$

$$= 0.3 \text{ cm}$$

$$= \Delta S = S_1 - S_2$$

$$= 0.3 \text{ cm}$$

$$= 3 \text{ mm}$$

14. $\dfrac{\lambda (2D)}{d} = \dfrac{(\mu - 1) tD}{d}$ (fringe width = shift)

$$\therefore \qquad \lambda = \frac{(\mu - 1) t}{2}$$

$$= \frac{(1.6 - 1) (1.964 \times 10^{-6})}{2} \text{ m}$$

$$= 0.5892 \times 10^{-6} \text{ m} = 589 \text{ nm}$$

15. $\because$ $d = 2\,\text{cm}$

$$\omega = \frac{\lambda D}{d} = \frac{(500 \times 10^{-9})\,(100)}{2 \times 10^{-2}}$$

$$= 2.5 \times 10^{-3}\,\text{m} = 2.5\,\text{mm}$$

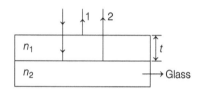

In this figure, P is in a dark fringe, as conditions of maxima and minima are interchanged.

Hence, next dark fringe will be obtained at a distance ω or 2.5 mm from P.

16. 1 and 2 both are reflected from denser medium.

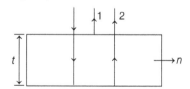

Hence,

$$2n_1 t = \frac{\lambda}{2} \quad \text{for first order minima}$$

or $\quad t_{\min} = \dfrac{\lambda}{4n_1} = \dfrac{650}{4 \times 1.42}$

$$= 114\,\text{nm}$$

17. (a) Ray-1 is reflected from a denser medium and ray-2 by a rarer medium.

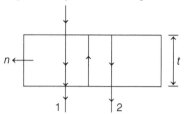

$\Delta x = 2nt = (2m - 1)\dfrac{\lambda}{2}$ for maximum intensity

$\therefore \quad \lambda = \dfrac{4\,nt}{(2m - 1)}$

$$= \frac{(4)(1.53)\,(485\,\text{nm})}{2m - 1}$$

$$= \left(\frac{2968}{2m - 1}\right)\text{nm}$$

For $\quad m = 1, \lambda = 2968\,\text{nm}$

For $\quad m = 2, \lambda = 989\,\text{nm}$

For $\quad m = 3, \lambda = 594\,\text{nm}$

For $\quad n = 4, \lambda = 424\,\text{nm}$

For $\quad n = 5, \lambda = 329\,\text{nm}$

Therefore, two wavelengths lying in the given range are 424 nm and 594 nm.

(b) Ray-1 and ray-2 are in same phase.

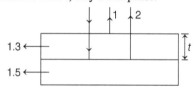

Hence,

$$\Delta x = 2nt = m\lambda \quad \text{(for maximum intensity)}$$

$\therefore \quad \lambda = \dfrac{2nt}{m} = \dfrac{(2)\,(1.53)\,(485\,\text{nm})}{m}$

$$= \left(\frac{1484}{m}\right)\text{nm}$$

Substituting $m = 1, 2, 3 \cdots$ etc,

$$\lambda_1 = 1484\,\text{nm}, \quad \lambda_2 = 742\,\text{nm},$$

$$\lambda_3 = 495\,\text{nm}, \quad \lambda_4 = 371\,\text{nm etc.}$$

Therefore, only wavelength lying in the given range is 495 nm.

18. Ray-1 and ray-2 both are reflected from denser medium. Hence, they are in phase.

$\therefore \quad 2\mu t = \dfrac{\lambda}{2}$ for minima

or $\quad t = \dfrac{\lambda}{4\mu} = \dfrac{600}{4 \times 1.3}$

$$= 1154\,\text{Å}$$

19. Ray-1 is reflected from denser medium and ray-2 from denser medium.

$\therefore \quad \Delta x = 2\mu t = \lambda = 800\,\text{nm}$ for destruction interference.

$\therefore \quad\quad\quad\quad \mu t = 400\,\text{nm}$

For constructive interference,

$$\Delta x = 2\,\mu t = (2n-1)\frac{\lambda}{2}$$

$$\therefore \qquad \lambda = \frac{4\mu t}{2n-1} = \frac{1600}{2n-1}$$

For $n = 1, \lambda = 1600\,\text{nm}$
For $n = 2, \lambda = 533\,\text{nm}$
For $n = 3, \lambda = 320\,\text{nm}$

The only wavelength lying in the given range is 533 nm.

20. $2\mu t = \lambda/2$

This is the condition for destructive interference.

$$\therefore \qquad t = \frac{\lambda}{4\mu} = \frac{3.0}{4 \times 1.5} = 0.5\,\text{cm}$$

21. Path difference produced by slab,

$$\Delta x = (\mu - 1)t = \frac{\lambda}{2}$$

$\dfrac{\lambda}{2}$ path difference is equivalent to 180° phase difference. Hence, maxima and minima interchange their positions.

LEVEL 2

Single Correct Option

1. $2\,I_0 = 4\,I_0\cos^2\left(\dfrac{\phi_1}{2}\right)$

$$\therefore \qquad \phi_1 = \frac{\pi}{2} = \left(\frac{2\pi}{\lambda}\right)(\Delta x_1) = \left(\frac{2\pi}{\lambda}\right)\left(\frac{y_1 d}{D}\right)$$

$$\therefore \qquad y_1 = \frac{\lambda D}{4d} = \frac{\beta}{4}$$

Further, $\qquad I_0 = 4 I_0 \cos^2\left(\dfrac{\phi_2}{2}\right)$

$$\therefore \qquad \phi_2 = \frac{2\pi}{3} = \left(\frac{2\pi}{\lambda}\right)(\Delta x_2)$$

$$= \left(\frac{2\pi}{\lambda}\right)\left(\frac{y_2 d}{D}\right)$$

$$\therefore \qquad y_2 = \frac{\lambda D}{3d} = \frac{\beta}{3}$$

$$\Delta y = y_2 - y_1 = \frac{\beta}{12}$$

2. At path difference λ, we get maximum intensity.

$$\therefore \quad I_{\max} = I$$

$$I_R = I_{\max} \cos^2\left(\frac{\phi}{2}\right)$$

$$\therefore \quad \frac{I}{4} = I\cos^2\left(\frac{\phi}{2}\right) \quad \text{or} \quad \cos\left(\frac{\phi}{2}\right) = \pm\frac{1}{2}$$

$$\therefore \qquad \frac{\phi}{2} = 60° \text{ or } 120°$$

$$\therefore \qquad \phi = 120° \text{ or } 240° \text{ or } \frac{2\pi}{3} \text{ and } \frac{4\pi}{3}$$

From the relation, $\Delta x = \left(\dfrac{\lambda}{2\pi}\right)\cdot\phi$

We see that,

$$\Delta x = \frac{\lambda}{3} \text{ and } \frac{2\lambda}{3}$$

3. Ray-1 is reflected from a denser medium ($\Delta\phi = \pi$) while ray-2 comes after reflecting from a rarer medium ($\Delta\phi = 0°$).

$$\therefore \quad \Delta x = 2\mu t = (2n-1)\frac{\lambda}{2} \text{ for maximum intensity.}$$

$$\text{or} \quad \lambda = \frac{4\mu t}{(2n-1)}$$

$$= \frac{4 \times 1.5 \times 500}{2n-1} = \left(\frac{3000}{2n-1}\right)\text{nm}$$

Substituting $n = 1, 2, 3 \cdots$ etc, we get $\lambda = 3000\,\text{nm}$, 1000 nm, 600 nm etc.

$$\therefore \quad \text{Answer is 600 nm.}$$

4. At points P, Q and R,

$$I = \frac{3}{4}\,I_{\max} = I_{\max}\cos^2\frac{\phi}{2}$$

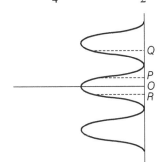

$$\therefore \qquad \frac{\phi}{2} = \frac{\pi}{6} \text{ and } \frac{5\pi}{6}$$

$$\therefore \qquad \phi = \frac{\pi}{3}$$

$$\text{and} \quad \frac{5\pi}{3} = \left(\frac{2\pi}{\lambda}\right)\Delta x = \left(\frac{2\pi}{\lambda}\right)\frac{yd}{D}$$

$\therefore \quad y_1 = OP = \dfrac{\lambda D}{6d} = \dfrac{6000 \times 10^{-10} \times 1 \times 10^3}{6 \times 10^{-3}}$ mm

$= 0.1$ mm

$y_2 = OQ = \dfrac{5\lambda D}{6d}$

$= 0.5$ mm

Now, the distance is either PR or 0.2 mm or PQ or 0.4 mm. Hence, the answer is 0.2 mm.

5. $\because \quad \theta = \dfrac{d}{D}$

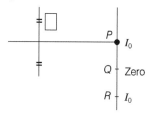

Third minima,

$y = \pm 2.5\,\omega = \pm 2.5 \left(\dfrac{\lambda D}{d}\right) = \pm \dfrac{2.5\lambda}{\theta}$

6. $\Delta x = \dfrac{yd}{D} = (\omega/4)\dfrac{d}{D} = \dfrac{\lambda}{4} \quad \left(\omega = \dfrac{\lambda D}{d}\right)$

$\phi = \left(\dfrac{2\pi}{\lambda}\right)\Delta x = \dfrac{\pi}{2}$ or $90°$

$I = I_{max} \cos^2 \dfrac{\theta}{2}$

$\therefore \quad \dfrac{I}{I_{max}} = \cos^2 45° = \dfrac{1}{2}$

or $\dfrac{I_{max}}{I} = 2$

7. Shift $= \dfrac{(\mu - 1)tD}{d}$

At $\mu = 1$, shift $= 0$

Therefore, intensity at centre is maximum or I_0.
As μ increases fringes shift upwards as shown in figure.

So, intensity at P first decreases to zero (as Q reaches at P), then it further increases to I_0 (as point R reaches to P).

8. $\dfrac{3}{4} I_{max} = I_{max} \cos^2 \dfrac{\phi}{2}$

$\therefore \quad \dfrac{\phi}{2} = \dfrac{\pi}{6}$ or

$\phi = \dfrac{\pi}{3} = \left(\dfrac{2\pi}{\lambda}\right)(\Delta x) = \left(\dfrac{2\pi}{\lambda}\right)(\mu - 1)\,t$

$\therefore \quad t = \dfrac{\lambda}{6\,(\mu - 1)} = \dfrac{6000 \times 10^{-10}}{6\,(1.5 - 1)}$

$= 0.2 \times 10^{-6}$ m $= 0.2\,\mu$m

9. $\Delta x_1 = (\mu_1 - 1), \Delta x_2 = (\mu_2 - 1)t$

$\therefore \quad \Delta x = (\mu_1 - \mu_2)\,t$

$= (1.52 - 1.40)\,(10400 \text{ nm})$

$= 1248$ nm

For maximum intensity,

$\Delta x = 1248 = n\lambda$

$\therefore \qquad \lambda = \dfrac{1248}{n} \qquad (n = 1, 2, 3\cdots)$

For $\qquad n = 2, \lambda = 624$ nm

and for $\qquad n = 3, \lambda = 416$ nm

10. $\Delta\phi = \left(\dfrac{2\pi}{\lambda/n_1}\right)L_1 - \left(\dfrac{2\pi}{\lambda/n_2}\right)L_2$

11. We will get four maximas corresponding to,

$\Delta X = \lambda, 2\lambda, 3\lambda$ and 4λ

Note At $x = 0$, $\quad \Delta x = 5\lambda$

and at $x = \infty$, $\quad \Delta x = 0$

12. Fringe width, $\beta = \dfrac{D\lambda}{d}$ i.e. $\beta \propto \lambda$

So, wavelength λ and hence fringe width β decreases 1.5 times when immersed in liquid. The distance between central maxima and 10th maxima is 3 cm in vacuum. When immersed in liquid it will reduce to 2 cm. Position of central maxima will not change while 10th maxima will be obtained at $y = 4$ cm.

13. For maximum intensity on the screen, path difference should be integer multiple of wavelength, i.e.

$d \sin \theta = n\lambda$

$\sin \theta = \dfrac{n\lambda}{d} = \dfrac{n(2000)}{7000} = \dfrac{n}{3.5}$

As, $(\sin \theta)_{max} = 1$

So, $\qquad n = 0, 1, 2, 3$

Thus, only seven maximas can be obtained on both sides of the screen.

14. Path difference between the waves reaching at P,
$$\Delta = \Delta_1 + \Delta_2$$
where, $\Delta_1 = $ initial path difference

$\Delta_2 = $ path difference between the waves after emerging from slits.

Now, $\Delta_1 = SS_1 - SS_2 = \sqrt{(D^2 + d^2)} - D$

and $\Delta_2 = S_1O - S_2O = \sqrt{(D^2 + d^2)} - D$

$\therefore \Delta = 2\{\sqrt{(D^2 + d^2)} - D\}$

$\qquad = 2\{(D^2 + d^2)^{1/2} - D\}$

$\qquad \approx 2\left\{\left(D + \dfrac{d^2}{2D}\right) - D\right\}$ from binomial expansion

$\qquad = \dfrac{d^2}{D}$

For obtaining minima at O, Δ must be equal to $(2n-1)\dfrac{\lambda}{2}$

i.e. $\dfrac{d^2}{D} = (2n-1)\dfrac{\lambda}{2}$

$\therefore \quad d^2 = \dfrac{(2n-1)\lambda D}{2}$

or $\quad d = \sqrt{\dfrac{(2n-1)\lambda D}{2}}$

For minimum distance, $n = 1$

So, $\quad d = \sqrt{\left(\dfrac{\lambda D}{2}\right)}$

15. P is actually 10th maxima with respect to point O.

$\therefore \quad S_1P - S_2P = 10\lambda$

or $\quad S_1B = 10\lambda = 10 \times 600 \times 10^{-9}$ m

$\qquad (S_2P \approx BP)$

$\qquad = 6 \times 10^{-6}$ m

16. Suppose P be the point on x-axis, where constructive interference is obtained.

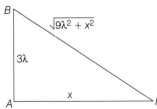

$\qquad BP - AP = 2\lambda$ or λ

$\therefore \quad \sqrt{9\lambda^2 + x^2} - x = 2\lambda$

$\therefore \qquad 9\lambda^2 + x^2 = x^2 + 4\lambda^2 + 4x\lambda$

$$x = \dfrac{5\lambda}{4}$$

Further, $\sqrt{9\lambda^2 + x^2} - x = \lambda$

$\therefore \qquad 9\lambda^2 + x^2 = x^2 + \lambda^2 + 2x\lambda$

$\therefore \qquad x = 4\lambda$

17. $I = I_{max}\cos^2\dfrac{\phi}{2}$ ...(i)

Given, $\quad I = \dfrac{I_{max}}{2}$ ...(ii)

$\therefore$ From Eqs. (i) and (ii), we have

$$\phi = \dfrac{\pi}{2}, \dfrac{3\pi}{2}, \dfrac{5\pi}{2}$$

Or path difference, $\Delta x = \left(\dfrac{\lambda}{2\pi}\right)\cdot\phi$

$\therefore \quad \Delta x = \dfrac{\lambda}{4}, \dfrac{3\lambda}{4}, \dfrac{5\lambda}{4} \cdots \left(\dfrac{2n+1}{4}\right)\lambda$

18. If two sources have a randomly varying phase difference ϕ, the resultant intensity will be $I_0 + I_0 = 2I_0$.

19. A fringe is a locus of points having constant path difference from the two coherent sources S_1 and S_2. It will be concentric circle.

20. $PR = d$

$\therefore \qquad PO = d\sec\theta$

and $\quad CO = PO\cos 2\theta = d\sec\theta\cos 2\theta$

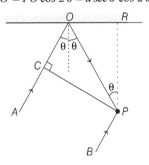

Path difference between the two rays is,

$\quad \Delta x = PO + OC = (d\sec\theta + d\sec\theta\cos 2\theta)$

Phase difference between the two rays is

$\Delta\phi = \pi$ (one is reflected, while another is direct)

Therefore, condition for constructive interference should be

$$\Delta x = \dfrac{\lambda}{2}, \dfrac{3\lambda}{2} \cdots$$

or $\qquad d\sec\theta\,(1+\cos 2\theta)=\dfrac{\lambda}{2}$

or $\qquad \left(\dfrac{d}{\cos\theta}\right)(2\cos^2\theta)=\dfrac{\lambda}{2}$

or $\qquad \cos\theta=\dfrac{\lambda}{4d}$

More than One Correct Options

1. (c) $\qquad I_{max}=(\sqrt{I_1}+\sqrt{I_2})^2$

$\qquad\qquad\quad I_{min}=(\sqrt{I_1}-\sqrt{I_2})^2$

When $\qquad I_1=I_2=I_0$

$\qquad\qquad\quad I_{max}=4I_0$

and $\qquad I_{min}=0$

When $\qquad I_2=\dfrac{I_0}{2}$,

then $\qquad I_{max}<4I_0$

and $\qquad I_{min}>0.$

2. $\Delta x_0=d\sin\theta=(10^{-3})\left(\dfrac{1}{2}\right)=5\times10^{-4}\,\text{m}=(10^3)\,\lambda$

Since, Δx_0 is integer multiple of λ, it will produce maximum intensity or $4I_0$ at O.

$$\omega=\dfrac{\lambda D}{d}=\dfrac{(5\times10^{-7})\,(2)}{(10^{-3})}$$

$$=10^{-3}\,\text{m}=1\,\text{mm}$$

At 4 mm, we will get 4th order maxima.

3. Fringe pattern shifts in the direction of slab. But,

$$\text{Shift}=\dfrac{(\mu-1)\,tD}{d}$$

So, actual shift will depend on the values of μ,t,D and d.

4. **For overlapping of maxima**

$$\dfrac{n_1\lambda_1 D}{d}=\dfrac{n_2\lambda_2 D}{d}$$

or $\qquad \dfrac{n_1}{n_2}=\dfrac{\lambda_2}{\lambda_1}=\dfrac{7}{5},\dfrac{14}{10}\cdots$

$\Rightarrow$ 14th order maxima of λ_1 will coincide with 10th order maxima of λ_2.

For overlapping of minima

$$\dfrac{(2n_1-1)\,\lambda_1 D}{2d}=\dfrac{(2n_2-1)\,\lambda_2 D}{2d}$$

$\therefore\qquad \dfrac{2n_1-1}{2n_2-1}=\dfrac{\lambda_2}{\lambda_1}=\dfrac{7}{5}$

(c) Option with $n_1=11$ and $n_2=8$ gives this ratio.

Match the Columns

1. $I=4I_0\cos^2\left(\dfrac{\phi}{2}\right)$

2. $\phi=\dfrac{2\pi}{\lambda}\Delta x$ and then apply,

$\qquad I=4I_0\cos^2\left(\dfrac{\phi}{2}\right)$

3.

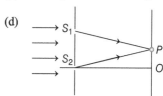

$\qquad\qquad Y\rightarrow$ maxima

$\qquad\qquad y\rightarrow$ minima

4. (a) Inclined rays and slab both will shift the fringe pattern upwards. So, zero order maxima will definitely lie about O.

(b) Inclined rays will shift the fringe pattern upwards, but slab will shift the fringe pattern downwards. Hence, zero order maxima may lie above O, below O or at O.

(c) Same explanations can be given for this option.

(d)

$\qquad\qquad \Delta X_p=0,$

$\qquad\qquad$ where $S_1P=S_2P$

5. $I=I_{max}=4I_0$

$\Rightarrow\qquad I_0=\dfrac{I}{4}$

(a) For $\qquad y=\dfrac{\lambda D}{2d},\ \Delta x=\dfrac{yd}{D}=\dfrac{\lambda}{2}$

$\therefore\qquad I_{S_3}=I_{S_4}=0$

$\qquad$ for $\Delta x=\lambda/2$

$\therefore\qquad I_0=0$

(b) For $y=\dfrac{\lambda D}{6d},\ \Delta x=\dfrac{yd}{D}=\dfrac{\lambda}{6}$

$\qquad \phi=\left(\dfrac{2\pi}{\lambda}\right)(\Delta x)=\dfrac{2\pi}{6}=60°$

Now, $I_{S_3} = I_{S_4} = I_{max} \cos^2 \dfrac{\theta}{2}$

$$= I \cos^2 30° = \dfrac{3}{4} I$$

$\therefore \qquad\qquad I_0 = 4 I_{S_3}$

or $\qquad\qquad I_{S_4} = 3I$

Same explanations can be given for (c) and (d) options.

Subjective Questions

1. $I_1 = 0.1 I_0$, $\ I_2 = 0.081 I_0$

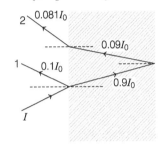

$\therefore \qquad \sqrt{\dfrac{I_1}{I_2}} = \dfrac{10}{9}$

$\therefore \qquad \dfrac{I_{max}}{I_{min}} = \left(\dfrac{\sqrt{I_1/I_2} + 1}{\sqrt{I_1/I_2} - 1} \right)^2$

$$= (19)^2$$

$$= 361 \qquad\qquad \textbf{Ans.}$$

2. $\because \qquad \mu = \dfrac{\sin i}{\sin r}$

$\therefore \qquad \dfrac{4}{3} = \dfrac{\sin 53°}{\sin r} = \dfrac{4/5}{\sin r}$

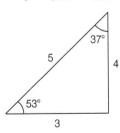

$\therefore \qquad \sin r = \dfrac{3}{5}$

$\therefore \qquad r = 37°$

Refer figure (a)

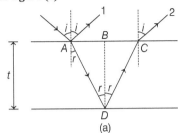

(a)

$\Delta x_1 =$ between 2 and 1 $= 2\,(AD)$

$$= 2 BD \sec r$$

$$= 2t \sec r$$

Their optical path $\Delta x_1 = 2\mu t \sec r$.

Refer figure (b)

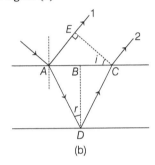

(b)

$\Delta x_2 = AC \sin i = (2t \tan r) \sin i$

$\therefore \ (\Delta x)_{net} = \Delta x_1 - \Delta x_2$

$$= 2\mu t \sec r - 2t (\tan r)(\sin i)$$

$$= 2 \times \dfrac{4}{3} \times t \times \dfrac{5}{4} - 2 \times t \times \dfrac{3}{4} \times \dfrac{4}{5}$$

$$= \dfrac{32}{15} t$$

Phase difference between 1 and 2 is π.

$\therefore$ For constructive interference,

$$\dfrac{32}{15} t = \dfrac{\lambda}{2}$$

or $\qquad t = \dfrac{15\lambda}{64} = \dfrac{15 \times 0.6}{64}$

$$= 0.14 \ \mu m \qquad\qquad \textbf{Ans.}$$

3. Applying lens formula, $\dfrac{1}{v} - \dfrac{1}{u} = \dfrac{1}{f}$

$$\dfrac{1}{v} + \dfrac{1}{15} = \dfrac{1}{10}$$

$\therefore \qquad\qquad v = 30 \text{ cm}$

$$m = \frac{v}{u} = \frac{30}{-15} = -2$$

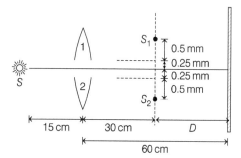

Distance between two slits,

$$d = 1.5 \text{ mm}, \ D = 30 \text{ cm}$$

Fringe width, $\omega = \dfrac{\lambda D}{d}$

$$= \frac{(5.0 \times 10^{-7})(0.3)}{(1.5 \times 10^{-3})}$$

$$= 10^{-4} \text{ m}$$

$$= 0.1 \text{ mm} \qquad \textbf{Ans.}$$

4. (a) $\because \qquad \Delta x = d \cos \theta$

$$\cos \theta = 1 - \frac{\theta^2}{2} \qquad \text{(When } \theta \text{ is small)}$$

$$\therefore \qquad \Delta x = d \left(1 - \frac{\theta^2}{2}\right)$$

$$= d \left(1 - \frac{y^2}{2D^2}\right)$$

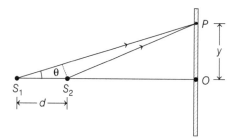

For *n*th maxima $\Delta x = n\lambda$

$\therefore \qquad\qquad y = $ radius of *n*th bright ring

$$= D \sqrt{2 \left(1 - \frac{n\lambda}{d}\right)} \qquad \textbf{Ans.}$$

(b) $d = 1000\lambda$

At O, $\qquad \Delta x = d = 1000\lambda$

i.e. at O, 1000 th order maxima is obtained.

Substituting $n = 998$ in, $y = D \sqrt{2\left(1 - \dfrac{n\lambda}{d}\right)}$

We get the radius of second closest ring

$$r = 6.32 \text{ cm} \qquad \textbf{Ans.}$$

(c) $n = 998$ \qquad\qquad\qquad\qquad **Ans.**

5. (a) The optical path difference between the two waves arriving at P is

$$\Delta x = \frac{y_1 d}{D_1} + \frac{y_2 d}{D_2}$$

$$= \frac{(1)(10)}{10^3} + \frac{(5)(10)}{2 \times 10^3}$$

$$= 3.5 \times 10^{-2} \text{ mm}$$

$$= 0.035 \text{ mm}$$

As, $\qquad \Delta x = 70\lambda$

$\therefore$ 70th order maxima is obtained at P.

(b) At O, $\Delta x = \dfrac{y_1 d}{D_1} = 10^{-2}$ mm

$$= 0.01 \text{ mm}$$

As $\qquad \Delta x = 20\lambda$

$\therefore$ 20th order maxima is obtained at O.

(c) $(\mu - 1) t = 0.01$ mm

$$\therefore \qquad t = \frac{0.01}{1.5 - 1} = 0.02 \text{ mm}$$

$$= 20 \text{ μm} \qquad \textbf{Ans.}$$

Since, the pattern has to be shifted upwards, therefore, the film must be placed in front of S_1.

6. (a) $\qquad d \sin \phi = \Delta x_1$

$$= (50 \times 10^{-4}) \sin 30°$$

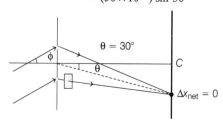

$$= 2.5 \times 10^{-3} \text{ cm}$$

$$\Delta x_2 = (\mu - 1) t$$

$$= \left(\frac{3}{2} - 1\right)(0.01)$$

$$= 5.0 \times 10^{-3} \text{ cm}$$

$$\Delta x_2 - \Delta x_1 = 2.5 \times 10^{-3} \text{ cm} = \Delta x_1 \qquad \text{(also)}$$

$\therefore$ Central maxima will be obtained at $\theta = 30°$ below C.

(b) **At** C $\Delta X_{net} = 2.5 \times 10^{-3}$ cm $= n\lambda$

$\therefore \quad n = \dfrac{2.5 \times 10^{-3}}{\lambda}$

$\quad = \dfrac{2.5 \times 10^{-3}}{500 \times 10^{-7}}$

$\quad = 50$ **Ans.**

(c) Number of fringes that will pass if we remove the slab

$= \dfrac{\text{Path difference due to slab}}{\lambda}$

$= \dfrac{5 \times 10^{-3}}{500 \times 10^{-7}}$

$= 100$ **Ans.**

7. (a) $(\Delta x)_{net} = 0$

$\therefore \quad \dfrac{y_1 d}{D_1} = \dfrac{y_2 d}{D_2}$

$\therefore \quad \dfrac{d/2}{1.5} = \dfrac{y}{2.0}$

or $\quad y = \dfrac{d}{1.5} = \dfrac{6}{1.5}$

$\quad = 4$ mm **Ans.**

(b) At O, net path difference,

$\Delta x = \dfrac{y_1 d}{D_1} = \dfrac{(d/2)\,(d)}{D_1}$

$\quad = \dfrac{(6 \times 10^{-3})^2}{2 \times 1.5} = 12 \times 10^{-6}$ m

$\quad = 120 \times 10^{-7}$ m

$\lambda = 6000$ Å

$\quad = 6 \times 10^{-7}$ m

As, $\Delta x = 20\lambda$, therefore at O bright fringe of order 20 will be obtained.

(c) $I = I_{max} \cos^2 \left(\dfrac{\phi}{2} \right)$

$\dfrac{3}{4} I_{max} = I_{max} \cos^2 \left(\dfrac{\phi}{2} \right)$

$\therefore \quad \dfrac{\phi}{2} = \dfrac{\pi}{6}$

$\phi = \dfrac{\pi}{3} = \left(\dfrac{2\pi}{\lambda} \right) (\mu - 1)\, t$

$\therefore \quad t = \dfrac{\lambda}{6\,(\mu - 1)} = \dfrac{6000}{6\,(1.5 - 1)}$

$\quad = 2000$ Å **Ans.**

8. (a) $\left(1 - \dfrac{1}{\mu} \right) t = \dfrac{3\lambda}{\mu}$

$\therefore \quad t = \dfrac{3\lambda}{(\mu - 1)} = \dfrac{3 \times 0.78}{1.3 - 1}$

$\quad = 7.8 \,\mu\text{m}$ **Ans.**

(b) **Upwards** $\dfrac{yd}{D} - \left(1 - \dfrac{1}{\mu} \right) t = \dfrac{4\lambda}{\mu}$

Solving, we get $y = 4.2$ mm **Ans.**

Downwards $t \left(1 - \dfrac{1}{\mu} \right) + \dfrac{yd}{D} = \dfrac{4\lambda}{\mu}$

Solving, we get $y = 0.6$ mm **Ans.**

33. Modern Physics - I

INTRODUCTORY EXERCISE 33.1

1. $E = \dfrac{hc}{\lambda}, P = \dfrac{h}{\lambda}$

2. Number of photons emitted per second,

$$N_1 = \frac{\text{Power of source}}{\text{Energy of one photon}} = \frac{P}{(hc/\lambda)} = \frac{P\lambda}{hc}$$

At a distance r, these photons are falling on an area $4\pi r^2$.

∴ Number of photons incident per unit area per unit time,

$$N_2 = \frac{N_1}{4\pi r^2} = \frac{P\lambda}{(4\pi r^2)\, hc}$$

3. $\lambda = \dfrac{h}{\sqrt{2qVm}} \quad \Rightarrow \quad \lambda \propto \dfrac{1}{\sqrt{qm}}$

$$\frac{\lambda_P}{\lambda_d} = \sqrt{\frac{(qm)_d}{(qm)_P}} = \sqrt{\frac{1 \times 2}{1 \times 1}} = \sqrt{2}$$

4. $\lambda = \dfrac{h}{\sqrt{2Km}} \quad \Rightarrow \quad \lambda \propto \dfrac{1}{\sqrt{m}}$

$$\frac{\lambda_d}{\lambda_\alpha} = \sqrt{\frac{m_\alpha}{m_d}} = \sqrt{\frac{4}{2}} = \sqrt{2}$$

5. Kinetic energy in magnetic field remains unchanged while in electric field it will increase. Further,

$$\lambda \propto \frac{1}{\sqrt{K}}$$

6. $\lambda = \dfrac{h}{mv}$

(a) $\lambda = \dfrac{6.63 \times 10^{-34}}{(46 \times 10^{-3})\,(30)}$

$= 4.8 \times 10^{-34}$ m

(b) $\lambda = \dfrac{6.63 \times 10^{-34}}{9.31 \times 10^{-31} \times 10^7}$

$= 7.12 \times 10^{-11}$ m

INTRODUCTORY EXERCISE 33.2

1. $Z = 3$ for doubly ionized atom $E \propto Z^2$

Ionization energy of hydrogen atom is 13.6 eV.

∴ Ionisation energy of this atom

$= (3)^2 (13.6)$

$= 122.4$ eV

2. $E_n = \dfrac{-13.6}{(n)^2} = -1.51 \quad \Rightarrow \quad n = 3$

Now, $\qquad L_n = n\left(\dfrac{h}{2\pi}\right)$

3. The expressions of kinetic energy, potential energy and total energy are

$$K_n = \frac{me^4}{8\varepsilon_0^2 n^2 h^2} \quad \Rightarrow \quad K_n \propto \frac{1}{n^2}$$

$$U_n = \frac{-me^4}{4\varepsilon_0^2 n^2 h^2} \quad \Rightarrow \quad U_n \propto -\frac{1}{n^2}$$

and $\quad E_n = \dfrac{-me^4}{8\varepsilon_0^2 n^2 h^2} \quad \Rightarrow \quad E_n \propto -\dfrac{1}{n^2}$

In the transition from some excited state to ground state, the value of n decreases, therefore kinetic energy increases, but potential and total energy decrease.

4.

First line of Balmer series — Second line of Balmer series

For hydrogen or hydrogen type atoms,

$$\frac{1}{\lambda} = RZ^2 \left(\frac{1}{n_f^2} - \frac{1}{n_i^2}\right)$$

In the transition from $n_i \longrightarrow n_f$,

∴ $\qquad \lambda \propto \dfrac{1}{Z^2 \left(\dfrac{1}{n_f^2} - \dfrac{1}{n_i^2}\right)}$

∴ $\qquad \dfrac{\lambda_2}{\lambda_1} = \dfrac{Z_1^2 \left(\dfrac{1}{n_f^2} - \dfrac{1}{n_i^2}\right)_1}{Z_2^2 \left(\dfrac{1}{n_f^2} - \dfrac{1}{n_i^2}\right)_2}$

$$\lambda_2 = \frac{\lambda_1 Z_1^2 \left(\dfrac{1}{n_f^2} - \dfrac{1}{n_i^2}\right)_1}{Z_2^2 \left(\dfrac{1}{n_f^2} - \dfrac{1}{n_i^2}\right)_2}$$

Substituting the values, we have

$$= \frac{(6561 \text{ Å}) (1)^2 \left(\dfrac{1}{2^2} - \dfrac{1}{3^2} \right)}{(2)^2 \left(\dfrac{1}{2^2} - \dfrac{1}{4^2} \right)} = 1215 \text{ Å}$$

∴ Correct option is (a).

5. The series in U-V region is Lyman series. Largest wavelength corresponds to minimum energy which occurs in transition from $n = 2$ to $n = 1$.

∴ $$122 = \frac{\dfrac{1}{R}}{\left(\dfrac{1}{1^2} - \dfrac{1}{2^2} \right)} \qquad \dots(i)$$

The smallest wavelength in the infrared region corresponds to maximum energy of Paschen series.

∴ $$\lambda = \frac{\dfrac{1}{R}}{\left(\dfrac{1}{3^2} - \dfrac{1}{\infty} \right)} \qquad \dots(ii)$$

Solving Eqs. (i) and (ii), we get
$$\lambda = 823.5 \text{ nm}$$

∴ Correct option is (b).

6. The first photon will excite the hydrogen atom (in ground state) to first excited state (as $E_2 - E_1 = 10.2 \text{ eV}$). Hence, during de-excitation a photon of 10.2 eV will be released. The second photon of energy 15 eV can ionise the atom. Hence, the balance energy, i.e. $(15 - 13.6) \text{ eV} = 1.4 \text{ eV}$ is retained by the electron. Therefore, by the second photon an electron of energy 1.4 eV will be released.

∴ Correct answer is (c).

7. In second excited state $n = 3$,

So, $$l_H = l_{Li} = 3 \left(\frac{h}{2\pi} \right)$$

while $E \propto Z^2$ and $Z_H = 1, Z_{Li} = 3$

So, $$|E_{Li}| = 9 |E_H|$$

or $$|E_H| < |E_{Li}|$$

8. Energy of infrared radiation is less than the energy of ultraviolet radiation. In options (a), (b) and (c), energy released will be more, while in option (d) only, energy released will be less.

9. For hydrogen and hydrogen like atoms,

$$E_n = -13.6 \frac{(Z^2)}{(n^2)} \text{ eV}$$

Therefore, ground state energy of doubly ionized lithium atom ($Z = 3$, $n = 1$) will be

$$E_1 = (-13.6) \frac{(3)^2}{(1)^2}$$
$$= -122.4 \text{ eV}$$

∴ Ionization energy of an electron in ground state of doubly ionized lithium atom will be 122.4 eV.

10. Shortest wavelength will correspond to maximum energy. As value of atomic number (Z) increases, the magnitude of energy in different energy states gets increased. Value of Z is maximum for doubly ionised lithium atom ($Z = 3$) among the given elements. Hence, wavelength corresponding to this will be least.

∴ Correct option is (d).

11. $5E - E = hf \Rightarrow E = \dfrac{hf}{4}$ ...(i)

Between 5E and 4E

$$5E - 4E = hf_1$$

∴ $$f_1 = \frac{E}{h} = \frac{f}{4} \qquad \text{[from Eq. (i)]}$$

Between 4E and E

$$4E - E = hf_2$$

∴ $$f_2 = \frac{3E}{h} = 3 \left(\frac{f}{4} \right) = \frac{3}{4} f$$

12. Longest wavelength means minimum energy.

$$(\Delta E)_{min} = E_3 - E_2$$
$$= -\frac{13.6}{9} + \frac{13.6}{4} = 1.9 \text{ eV}$$

$$\lambda \text{ (in Å)} = \frac{12375}{1.9} = 6513$$

or $$\lambda \approx 651 \text{ nm}$$

INTRODUCTORY EXERCISE 33.3

1. K_α transition takes place from $n_1 = 2$ to $n_2 = 1$

∴ $$\frac{1}{\lambda} = R (Z - b)^2 \left[\frac{1}{(1)^2} - \frac{1}{(2)^2} \right]$$

For K-series, $b = 1$

∴ $$\frac{1}{\lambda} \propto (Z - 1)^2$$

$$\Rightarrow \quad \frac{\lambda_{Cu}}{\lambda_{Mo}} = \frac{(Z_{Mo} - 1)^2}{(Z_{Cu} - 1)^2} = \frac{(42 - 1)^2}{(29 - 1)^2}$$

$$= \frac{41 \times 41}{28 \times 28} = \frac{1681}{784} = 2.144$$

2. Cut off wavelength depends on the applied voltage not on the atomic number of the target. Characteristic wavelengths depend on the atomic number of target.

3. $\dfrac{1}{\lambda} \propto (Z - 1)^2$

$\therefore \quad \dfrac{\lambda_1}{\lambda_2} = \left(\dfrac{Z_2 - 1}{Z_1 - 1}\right)^2 \quad$ or $\quad \dfrac{1}{4} = \left(\dfrac{Z_2 - 1}{11 - 1}\right)^2$

Solving this, we get $Z_2 = 6$

$\therefore$ Correct answer is (a).

4. Wavelength λ_k is independent of the accelerating voltage (V), while the minimum wavelength λ_c is inversely proportional to V. Therefore, as V is increased, λ_k remains unchanged whereas λ_c decreases or $\lambda_k - \lambda_c$ will increase.

5. The continuous X-ray spectrum is shown in figure.

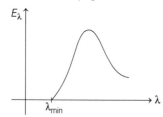

All wavelengths $> \lambda_{min}$ are found, where

$$\lambda_{min} = \dfrac{12375}{V \text{ (in volt)}} \text{ Å}$$

Here, V is the applied voltage.

6. $\Delta E = h\nu = Rhc \, (Z - b)^2 \left(\dfrac{1}{n_1^2} - \dfrac{1}{n_2^2}\right)$

For K-series, $b = 1$

$\therefore \quad \nu = Rc \, (Z - 1)^2 \left(\dfrac{1}{n_1^2} - \dfrac{1}{n_2^2}\right)$

Substituting the values,

$4.2 \times 10^{18} = (1.1 \times 10^7)(3 \times 10^8)(Z - 1)^2 \left(\dfrac{1}{1} - \dfrac{1}{4}\right)$

$\therefore \quad (Z - 1)^2 = 1697$

or $\qquad Z - 1 \approx 41$

or $\qquad Z = 42$

INTRODUCTORY EXERCISE 33.4

1. $K_{min} = 0$

and $\qquad K_{max} = E - W$

$= \dfrac{12375}{2000} - 3.0$

≈ 3.19 eV

2. $K_{max} = E - W = hf - hf_0$

$= h \, (f - f_0)$

$\therefore \qquad K_{max} \propto (f - f_0)$

3. $K_{max} = E - W$

$1.2 = E - W$ ...(i)

$4.2 = 1.5 \, E - W$ ...(ii)

Solving these equations, we get

$W = 4.8$ eV $= hf_0$

$\therefore \qquad f_0 = \dfrac{4.8 \times 1.6 \times 10^{-19}}{6.63 \times 10^{-34}}$

$= 1.16 \times 10^{15}$ Hz

4. Energy corresponding to 248 nm wavelength

$= \dfrac{1240}{248}$ eV $= 5$ eV

Energy corresponding to 310 nm wavelength

$= \dfrac{1240}{310}$ eV $= 4$ eV

$\dfrac{KE_1}{KE_2} = \dfrac{u_1^2}{u_2^2} = \dfrac{4}{1}$

$= \dfrac{5 \text{ eV} - W}{4 \text{ eV} - W}$

$\Rightarrow \qquad 16 - 4W = 5 - W$

$\Rightarrow \qquad 11 = 3W$

$\Rightarrow \qquad W = \dfrac{11}{3} = 3.67$ eV

$\simeq 3.7$ eV

5. Saturation current is proportional to intensity while stopping potential increases with increase in frequency.

Hence, $\qquad f_a = f_b$ while $I_a < I_b$

Therefore, the correct option is (a).

6. λ (in Å) $= \dfrac{12375}{W \text{ (eV)}}$

$= \dfrac{12375}{4.0}$ Å ≈ 3093 Å

or $\qquad \lambda \approx 309.3$ nm

or $\qquad \approx 310$ nm

Note λ(in Å) $= \dfrac{12375}{W \text{ (eV)}}$ *comes from* $W = \dfrac{hc}{\lambda}$

7. Stopping potential is the negative potential applied to stop the electrons having maximum kinetic energy. Therefore, stopping potential will be 4 V.

Exercises

LEVEL 1

Assertion and Reason

2. $E = \dfrac{hc}{\lambda}$ and $P = \dfrac{h}{\lambda}$

$\therefore \quad E$ and $P \propto \dfrac{1}{\lambda}$

Speed of all wavelengths (in vacuum) is c.

4. Energy of X-ray $> 13.6\,\text{eV}$

5. Already emitted electrons will repel the new electrons.

7. In case of wave it is possible.

8. Intensity = energy incident per unit area per unit time or $I = n(hf)$.

Here, n = number of photons incident per unit area per unit time.

f = frequency of incident photons. Hence, $I \propto nf$.

Hence, intensity can be increased either by increasing n or f. But saturation current only depends on n ($I_s \propto n$).

By increasing n and decreasing f, we can increase the saturation current even without increasing the intensity.

Objective Questions

2. $q\mathbf{E} + q\,(\mathbf{v} \times \mathbf{B}) = 0$

$\Rightarrow \qquad \mathbf{E} = -(\mathbf{v} \times \mathbf{B}) \quad \text{or} \quad \mathbf{B} \times \mathbf{v}$

$\mathbf{E}$, $\mathbf{B}$ and $\mathbf{v}$ are mutually perpendicular.

3. $K_{\max} = hf - W$

$K_{\max}$ *versus* f graph is a straight line of slope h (a universal constant)

4. $v \propto \dfrac{1}{n}$, $r \propto n^2$, $E \propto \dfrac{1}{n^2}$

5. $\qquad K_{\max} = 18 \times 10^3\,\text{eV}$

$\qquad\qquad = \dfrac{1}{2} m v_{\max}^2$

$\therefore \quad v_{\max} = \sqrt{\dfrac{2 \times 18 \times 10^3 \times 1.6 \times 10^{-19}}{9.1 \times 10^{-31}}}$

$\qquad\qquad = 8 \times 10^7\,\text{m/s}$

6. $(2\pi r_2) = 2\lambda_2$

$(2\pi r_3) = 3\lambda_3$

$\therefore \qquad\qquad \dfrac{\lambda_2}{\lambda_3} = \dfrac{3 r_2}{2 r_3} \qquad\qquad \ldots\text{(i)}$

Now, $\qquad\qquad r \propto n^2$

$\therefore \qquad\qquad \dfrac{r_2}{r_3} = \left(\dfrac{2}{3}\right)^2$

Substituting in Eq. (i), we get

$\qquad\qquad \dfrac{\lambda_2}{\lambda_3} = \dfrac{2}{3}$

7. $v_1^H = 2.19 \times 10^6\,\text{m/s} \approx \dfrac{c}{137}$

8. $E \propto \dfrac{Z^2}{n^2}$

$\therefore \qquad \dfrac{(-13.2) \times (Z)^2}{(2)^2} = -13.6$

$\therefore \qquad\qquad Z = 2$

9. $\lambda_{\min}\ (\text{in Å}) = \dfrac{12375}{V\ (\text{in volts})}$

For $\quad \lambda_{\min} = 1\text{Å}$

$\qquad\qquad V = 12375\,\text{V}$

$\qquad\qquad \approx 12.4\,\text{kV}$

10. $P = \dfrac{h}{\lambda}$

11. $\lambda = \dfrac{12375}{1.6} = 7734\,\text{Å}$

12. $U_1 = -27.2\,\text{eV}$

U_1 is assumed zero. Therefore, it is increased by $27.2\,\text{eV}$ at all points.

$E_\infty = 0$ under normal conditions.

Hence, in charged conditions it is $27.2\,\text{eV}$.

13. $E \propto \dfrac{1}{n^2}$

$\therefore \qquad E_5 = \dfrac{-13.6}{(5)^2} = -0.544\,\text{eV}$

15. $r_n \propto \dfrac{n^2}{Z} \quad \text{or} \quad r_n \propto \dfrac{1}{Z}$

16. $E_2 - E_1 = 40.8\,\text{eV}$

$\therefore \qquad \dfrac{E_1}{(2)^2} - E_1 = 40.8 \quad \text{eV}$

or $\qquad -\dfrac{3}{4} E_1 = 40.8 \quad \text{eV}$

or $\qquad\qquad E_1 = -54.4\,\text{eV}$

$\qquad\qquad |E_1| = 54.4\,\text{eV}$

17. $\because$ $\lambda = \dfrac{h}{\sqrt{2qVm}}$ $\Rightarrow$ $V = \dfrac{h^2}{2qm\lambda^2}$

18. $\lambda_{min} \propto \dfrac{1}{V} \propto V^{-1}$

% change in $\lambda_{min} = (-1)$ (% change in V) for small % changes

19. Frequency $\propto$ energy and energy $\propto Z^2$

20. $E \propto \dfrac{Z^2}{n^2}$

$\therefore$ $\dfrac{Z^2}{n^2} = 1$ or $n = Z = 3$

21. Longest wavelength of Lyman series means, minimum energy corresponding $n = 2$ to $n = 1$.

$\therefore$ $(E_2 - E_1)_H = (E_n - E_2)_{He^+}$

$\therefore$ $\dfrac{-13.6}{(2)^2} + \dfrac{13.6}{(1)^2} = \dfrac{-13.6(Z)^2}{n^2} + \dfrac{13.6(Z)^2}{(2)^2}$

Putting $Z = 2$, we get $n = 4$.

22. $E = \dfrac{12375}{3000} = 4.125\text{ eV}$

Since, $E < W$ no photoelectric effect will be observed.

23. $K_{max} = E - W = 2\text{ eV} = 3.2 \times 10^{-19}\text{ J}$

24. $m_e v_e = \dfrac{h}{\lambda}$

$\therefore$ $v_e = \dfrac{h}{\lambda m_e} = \dfrac{6.63 \times 10^{-34}}{(5200 \times 10^{-10}) \times 9.1 \times 10^{-31}}$

$\approx 1400\text{ m/s}$

25. In hydrogen atom, $E_2 - E_1 = 10.2\text{ eV}$

Since, $5\text{ eV} < 10.2\text{ eV}$

The electron cannot excite the hydrogen atom. The collision must be therefore elastic.

26. $\lambda = \dfrac{h}{\sqrt{2qVm}} \propto \dfrac{1}{\sqrt{qVm}}$

$\therefore$ $\dfrac{\lambda_\alpha}{\lambda_p} = \dfrac{\sqrt{q_p V_p m_p}}{\sqrt{q_\alpha V_\alpha m_\alpha}}$

$= \sqrt{\dfrac{1 \times 100 \times 1}{2 \times 800 \times 4}} = \dfrac{1}{8}$

$\therefore$ $\lambda_\alpha = \dfrac{\lambda_p}{8} = \dfrac{\lambda_0}{8}$

27. Energy, $E = eV = h\nu_{max} = \dfrac{hc}{\lambda_{min}}$

$\therefore$ $\lambda_{min} = \dfrac{hc}{eV}$

28. Since, atomic number is same,

$\lambda_1 = \lambda_2 = \lambda_3$ or $\lambda_2 = \sqrt{\lambda_1 \lambda_3}$

29. Here a depends on the transition states n_1 and n_2 and b depends upon the series.

30. $\Delta E = \dfrac{12375}{1085} = 11.4\text{ eV}$

Third Balmer line is corresponding to the transition,

$n = 5$ to $n = 2$.

$E_5 - E_2 = 11.4$

$\therefore$ $\dfrac{E_1}{(5)^2} - \dfrac{E_1}{(2)^2} = 11.4$

$E_1 = -54.28\text{ eV}$

$\therefore$ $|E_1| = 54.28\text{ eV}$

31. $eV_0 = \dfrac{hc}{\lambda_1} - W$ ...(i)

Similarly, $e(2V_0) = \dfrac{hc}{\lambda_2} - W$ ...(ii)

Subtracting Eq. (i) from Eq. (ii), we get

$eV_0 = \dfrac{hc(\lambda_1 - \lambda_2)}{\lambda_1 \lambda_2}$

$\therefore$ $V_0 = \dfrac{hc(\lambda_1 - \lambda_2)}{e\lambda_1 \lambda_2}$

$= \dfrac{(6.63 \times 10^{-34})(3 \times 10^8)(110)}{1.6 \times 10^{-19} \times 330 \times 220 \times 10^{-9}}$

$\approx 1.8\text{ volt}$

32. $\because$ $E = \dfrac{hc}{\lambda} - W$ ...(i)

$4E = \dfrac{hc}{\lambda/3} - W$ ...(ii)

Solving these equations, we get

$W = \dfrac{hc}{3\lambda}$

33. $\sqrt{f} \propto (Z - 1)$ for K-series

$\therefore$ $f \propto (Z - 1)^2$

$\dfrac{f_2}{f_1} = \dfrac{(Z_2 - 1)^2}{(Z_1 - 1)^2}$

$\therefore$ $f_2 = \left(\dfrac{Z_2 - 1}{Z_1 - 1}\right)^2 f_1$

$= \left(\dfrac{51 - 1}{31 - 1}\right)^2 f$

$= \dfrac{25}{9} f$

34. $\sqrt{f} \propto (Z - b) \sqrt{\left(\dfrac{1}{n_1^2} - \dfrac{1}{n_2^2}\right)^2}$

$\therefore \qquad$ Slope $\propto \sqrt{\dfrac{1}{n_1^2} - \dfrac{1}{n_2^2}}$

$\therefore \qquad \dfrac{\text{Slope}_1}{\text{Slope}_2} = \dfrac{\sqrt{1 - 1/9}}{\sqrt{1 - \dfrac{1}{4}}} = \sqrt{\dfrac{32}{27}}$

For K_β, $\qquad n_1 = 1, n_2 = 3$
For K_α, $\qquad n_1 = 1, n_2 = 2$

35. Energy of electrons $= 10000\,\text{eV}$

$\therefore \qquad \lambda_1 \text{ (in Å)} = \sqrt{\dfrac{150}{10000}} = 0.122$

$\qquad \lambda_2 \text{ (in Å)} = \dfrac{12375}{10000} \approx 1.2$

$\therefore \qquad \dfrac{\lambda_1}{\lambda_2} \approx 0.1$

36. $\qquad e(5V_0) = \dfrac{hc}{\lambda} - W \qquad$ ...(i)

$\qquad eV_0 = \dfrac{hc}{3\lambda} - W \qquad$ ...(ii)

Solving these equations, we get

$\qquad W = \dfrac{hc}{6\lambda}$

37. $eV_0 = 2h\nu_0 - h\nu_0$

$\therefore \qquad h\nu_0 = eV_0$

In second condition,

$\qquad eV = 3h\nu_0 - h\nu_0$
$\qquad\qquad = 2h\nu_0 = 2eV_0 \text{ or } V = 2V_0$

38. $\dfrac{1}{2}mv_1^2 = h\nu_1 - W$

$\qquad \dfrac{1}{2}mv_2^2 = h\nu_2 - W$

From these two equations, we can see that

$\qquad v_1^2 - v_2^2 = \dfrac{2h}{m}(\nu_1 - \nu_2)$

39.

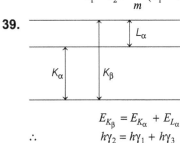

$\qquad E_{K_\beta} = E_{K_\alpha} + E_{L_\alpha}$
$\therefore \qquad h\gamma_2 = h\gamma_1 + h\gamma_3$
$\therefore \qquad \gamma_2 = \gamma_1 + \gamma_3$

40. $\lambda = \dfrac{h}{\sqrt{2Em}}$

where, $\qquad \lambda = \text{constant}$
$\therefore \qquad Em = \text{constant}$
or $\qquad E \propto \dfrac{1}{m}$

41. According to Bohr first postulate,

$\qquad mvr = \dfrac{nh}{2\pi}$

$\therefore \qquad 2\pi r = n\left(\dfrac{h}{mv}\right) = n\lambda$

For $n = 1$, $\lambda = 2\pi r$

42. $E \propto m$ and $r \propto \dfrac{1}{m}$

i.e. Energy will become two times and radius will become half.

43. Wave number is reciprocal of wavelength,

$\therefore \qquad \dfrac{1}{\lambda} = R\left[\dfrac{1}{n_1^2} - \dfrac{1}{n_2^2}\right]$

$\qquad = R\left[\dfrac{1}{2^2} - \dfrac{1}{4^2}\right] = R\left[\dfrac{1}{4} - \dfrac{1}{16}\right] = \dfrac{3R}{16}$

44. For $n = 3$ to $n = 2$ transition,

$\qquad \dfrac{1}{\lambda_1} = R\left[\dfrac{1}{2^2} - \dfrac{1}{3^2}\right] = \dfrac{5R}{36}$

For $n = 4$ to $n = 2$ transition,

$\qquad \dfrac{1}{\lambda_2} = R\left[\dfrac{1}{2^2} - \dfrac{1}{4^2}\right] = \dfrac{3R}{16}$

$\therefore \qquad \dfrac{\lambda_2}{\lambda_1} = \dfrac{20}{27}$

$\therefore \qquad \lambda_2 = \dfrac{20}{27}\lambda_1 = \dfrac{20}{27}\lambda_0$

45. $a = \omega^2 r$

$\qquad \omega = \dfrac{v}{r}, v \propto \dfrac{1}{n}$ and $r \propto n^2$

$\therefore \qquad \omega \propto \dfrac{1}{n^3}$ and $r \propto n^2$

$\qquad a \propto \dfrac{1}{n^4}$

$\qquad \dfrac{a_M}{a_L} = \left(\dfrac{2}{3}\right)^4 = \dfrac{16}{81}$

46. $\qquad K_1 = hf - W$

$\Rightarrow \qquad K_2 = 2hf - 2W$

$\therefore \qquad \dfrac{K_1}{K_2} = \dfrac{1}{2}$

47. As, $\lambda = \dfrac{h}{\sqrt{2qVm}}$

$\Rightarrow \qquad \lambda \propto \dfrac{1}{\sqrt{m}}$

$\qquad \dfrac{\lambda_1}{\lambda_2} = \sqrt{\dfrac{m_2}{m_1}}$

So, $\qquad \dfrac{\lambda_1}{\lambda_2} = \sqrt{\dfrac{M}{m}}$

$\Rightarrow \qquad \lambda_2 = \lambda_1 \sqrt{\left(\dfrac{m}{M}\right)}$

48. $P = \dfrac{E}{c}$

$\qquad F = \left(\dfrac{dP}{dt}\right) = \dfrac{dE/dt}{c}$

70% means 14 watt is absorbed ($\Delta P = P_i$) and 30% means 6 watt is reflected ($\Delta P = 2P_i$)

$\therefore \qquad F = \dfrac{14}{3 \times 10^8} + \dfrac{2(6)}{3 \times 10^8}$

$\qquad = 8.67 \times 10^{-8} \ \text{N}$

49. $\text{KE} = \dfrac{1}{4\pi\varepsilon_0} \dfrac{(2e)(92e)}{r_{\min}}$

$\therefore \qquad r_{\min} = \dfrac{(184 \ e^2)(1/4 \ \pi\varepsilon_0)}{\text{KE}}$

$\qquad = \dfrac{184 \times (1.6 \times 10^{-19})^2 (9 \times 10^9)}{5 \times 1.6 \times 10^{-13}}$

$\qquad = 5.3 \times 10^{-14} \ \text{m}$

$\qquad = 5.3 \times 10^{-12} \ \text{cm}$

50. $\dfrac{1}{\lambda} \propto Z^2 \quad \text{or} \quad \lambda \propto \dfrac{1}{Z^2}$

$\qquad \lambda_1 : \lambda_2 : \lambda_3 : \lambda_4 = \dfrac{1}{(1)^2} : \dfrac{1}{(1)^2} : \dfrac{1}{(2)^2} : \dfrac{1}{(3)^2}$

$\qquad = 36 : 36 : 9 : 4$

Subjective Questions

1.

$E_{L_\alpha} = E_{K_\beta} - E_{K_\alpha}$

$\therefore \qquad \dfrac{hc}{\lambda_{L_\alpha}} = \dfrac{hc}{\lambda_{K_\beta}} - \dfrac{hc}{\lambda_{K_\alpha}}$

or $\qquad \lambda_{L_\alpha} = \dfrac{\lambda_{K_\alpha} \lambda_{K_\beta}}{\lambda_{K_\alpha} - \lambda_{K_\beta}}$

$\qquad = \dfrac{0.71 \times 0.63}{0.71 - 0.63} = 5.59 \ \text{nm}$

2. $\lambda_{K_\alpha} = 0.71 \ \text{nm} = 7.1 \ \text{Å}$

$\qquad E_2 - E_1 = \dfrac{12375}{7.1} = 1743 \ \text{eV}$

$\therefore \qquad E_1 = E_2 - 1743$

$\qquad = -2870 - 1743$

$\qquad = -4613 \ \text{eV}$

$\qquad \lambda_{K_\beta} = 0.63 \ \text{nm}$

$\qquad = 6.3 \ \text{Å}$

$\qquad E_3 - E_1 = \dfrac{12375}{6.3}$

$\qquad = 1964 \ \text{eV}$

$\therefore \qquad E_3 = E_1 + 1964$

$\qquad = -4613 + 1964$

$\qquad = -2649 \ \text{eV}$

3. Number of photons incident per second

$\qquad = \dfrac{\text{Power}}{\text{Energy of one photon}}$

$\qquad = \dfrac{P}{(hc/\lambda)} = \dfrac{P\lambda}{hc}$

Number of electrons emitted per second

$\qquad = 0.1\% \ \text{of}$

$\qquad \dfrac{P\lambda}{hc} = \dfrac{P\lambda}{1000 \ hc}$

$\therefore$ Current = Charge (on photoelectrons per second)

$\qquad = \dfrac{P\lambda e}{1000 \ hc}$

$\qquad = \dfrac{(1.5 \times 10^{-3})(400 \times 10^{-9})(1.6 \times 10^{-19})}{(1000)(6.63 \times 10^{-34})(3 \times 10^8)}$

$\qquad = 0.48 \times 10^{-6} \ \text{A} = 0.48 \ \mu\text{A}$

4. (a) $p = \dfrac{E}{c} \quad \Rightarrow \quad E = pc$

(b) $\lambda = \dfrac{12375}{E \ (\text{in eV})} = \dfrac{12375}{1.54} = 8035 \ \text{Å}$

$\qquad \approx 804 \ \text{nm}$

So, this wavelength lies in ultraviolet region.

5. (a) $f = \dfrac{c}{\lambda}$

(b) $\because$ Number of photons emitted per second

$\qquad N_1 = \dfrac{\text{Power of source}}{\text{Energy of one photon}} = \dfrac{P}{hc/\lambda}$

$N_1 = \dfrac{P\lambda}{hc} = \dfrac{(75)\,(600 \times 10^{-9})}{(6.63 \times 10^{-34})\,(3 \times 10^{8})}$

$\approx 2.3 \times 10^{20}$ photons/s

6. (a) $E = hf \implies f = \dfrac{E}{h}$

(b) $\lambda = \dfrac{c}{f}$

7. (a) $K = \dfrac{p^2}{2m}$ or $K \propto p^2$

If momentum is doubled, kinetic energy becomes four times.

(b) $p = \dfrac{E}{c}$ or $E \propto p$ (for a photon)

If p is doubled, E will also become two times.

8. (a) Number of photons incident per second
= number of photons absorbed per second

$= \dfrac{\text{Power}}{\text{Energy of one photon}}$

$N = \dfrac{P}{hc/\lambda} = \dfrac{P\lambda}{hc}$

(b) Force = Rate of change of momentum =
(Number of photons absorbed per second) ×
(momentum of one photon)

$= \left(\dfrac{P\lambda}{hc}\right)\left(\dfrac{h}{\lambda}\right) = \dfrac{P}{c}$ $(\because P = \text{power})$

9. Force = Rate of change of momentum

$= 2\,[N\,]\left[\dfrac{h}{\lambda}\right]\cdot \cos 60^\circ$

N = number of photons striking per second

$\dfrac{h}{\lambda}$ = momentum of one photon.

10. (a) $\lambda = \dfrac{h}{p} \implies p = \dfrac{h}{\lambda}$

(b) λ (in Å) $= \sqrt{\dfrac{150}{\text{KE (in eV)}}}$

11. $v_{\text{rms}} = \sqrt{\dfrac{3RT}{M}} = v$ (say)

and $\lambda = \dfrac{h}{mv} = \dfrac{h}{m}\sqrt{\dfrac{M}{3RT}}$

Substituting the values, we get

$\lambda = \dfrac{6.63 \times 10^{-34}}{(2/6.02 \times 10^{23}) \times 10^{-3}}\sqrt{\dfrac{2 \times 10^{-3}}{3(8.31)\,(20 + 273)}}$

$= 1.04 \times 10^{-4}$ m $= 1.04$ Å

12. (a) $E_1 = -13.6$ eV

$\therefore$ KE $= |\,E_1\,| = 13.6$ eV

λ_1 (in Å) $= \sqrt{\dfrac{150}{\text{KE (in eV)}}}$ for an electron

$= \sqrt{\dfrac{150}{13.6}} = 3.32$Å

$2\pi r_1 = 2\pi(0.529\text{Å}) \approx 3.32$ Å

(b) $E_4 = \dfrac{E_1}{(4)^2} = \dfrac{-13.6}{(4)^2} = -0.85$ eV

$\lambda_4 = \sqrt{\dfrac{150}{0.85}}$ as KE $= |\,E_4\,| = 0.85$ eV

≈ 13.3 Å

$2\pi r_4 = 2\pi (n)^2 r_1$ (as $r \propto n^2$)

$= 53.15$ Å $\approx 4\lambda_4$

13. $E_n = E_1 = \dfrac{12375}{1023}$

or $\dfrac{-13.6}{(n)^2} + 13.6 = 12.1$

Solving this equation, we get $n = 3$

$\therefore$ Total possible emission lines $= \dfrac{n\,(n-1)}{2} = 3$

Longest wavelength means, minimum energy,
which is corresponding to $n = 3$ to $n = Z$

$\therefore$ $\lambda_{\max} = \dfrac{12375}{E_3 - E_2}$

Here, $E_3 - E_2 = -\dfrac{13.6}{(3)^2} + \dfrac{13.6}{(4)^2} = 1.9$ eV

$\therefore$ $\lambda_{\max} = \dfrac{12375}{1.9} = 6513$Å

14. In hydrogen atom,

$\Delta E_1 = E_3 - E_1 = 12.1$ eV

$E \propto Z^2$

$\therefore$ For $Z = 3$,

$\Delta E_2 = (3)^2\,\Delta E_1 = (3)^2\,(12.1)$

$= 108.9$Å

$\therefore$ $\lambda = \dfrac{12375}{108.9} \approx 113$ Å

15. $E_n - E_1 = \Delta E_1 + \Delta E_2$

$\therefore$ $\left[-\dfrac{13.6}{n^2} + 13.6\right](Z)^2 = \dfrac{12375}{1085} + \dfrac{12375}{304}$

Putting $Z = 2$ for He$^+$, we get $n = 5$

16. (a) Let these two levels are n_1 and n_2. Then,

$$-0.85 = -\frac{13.6\,(Z)^2}{n_1^2} \qquad \text{...(i)}$$

$$-0.544 = -\frac{13.6\,(Z)^2}{n_2^2} \qquad \text{...(ii)}$$

Total number of lines between n_2 and n_1 are given by

$$\frac{(n_2 - n_1)\,(n_2 - n_1 + 1)}{2} = 10 \qquad \text{...(iii)}$$

Solving these equations, we get

$$Z = 4,\, n_1 = 16 \quad \text{and} \quad n_2 = 20$$

(b) Smallest wavelength means maximum energy.

$$\Delta E_{\max} = E_{n_2} - E_{n_1}$$
$$= -0.544 + 0.85$$
$$= 0.306 \text{ eV}$$

$$\lambda_{\min} = \frac{12375}{0.306} = 40441 \text{Å}$$

17. (a) Ionization energy $= 15.6$ eV

∴ Ionization potential $= 15.6$ V

(b) $E_\infty - E_2 = 5.3$ eV

∴ $\lambda = \frac{12375}{5.3} = 2335$Å

(c) $E_3 - E_1 = 12.52$ eV

∴ Excitation potential is 12.52 V.

(d) $E_3 - E_1 = 12.52$ eV

∴ $\lambda = \frac{12375}{12.52}$ Å

$$= 988.41 \text{ Å}$$

∴ Wave number $= \frac{1}{\lambda} = \frac{1}{988.41 \times 10^{-10}}$ m^{-1}

$$= 1.01 \times 10^7 \text{ m}^{-1}$$

18. (a) Energy of photon $= \frac{12375}{8600}$ eV $= 1.44$ eV

∴ Internal energy after absorption

$$= -6.52 + 1.44 = -5.08 \text{ eV}$$

(b) Energy of emitted photon $= \frac{12375}{4200} = 2.946$ eV

Internal energy after emission $= -2.68 - 2.946$

$$= -5.626 \text{ eV}$$

19. $K_{\max}$ (in eV) $= E - W$

$$= \frac{12375}{2000} - 4.3$$

$$= 1.9 \text{ eV}$$

Therefore, stopping potential is 1.9 V.

20. $F = -\dfrac{dU}{dr} = -m^2\omega^2 r$

Now, $\dfrac{mv^2}{r} = |F| = m^2\omega^2 r$

or $v \propto r$

or $v = \alpha r$

Now, $m\,vr = n\dfrac{h}{2\pi}$

or $m\,(\alpha r)r = n\dfrac{h}{2\pi}$

∴ $r \propto \sqrt{n}$

21. $\Delta E_1 = 50\%$ of 50 keV $= 25$ keV

∴ $\lambda_1 = \dfrac{12375}{25 \times 10^3} = 0.495$ Å

$$= 49.5 \text{ pm}$$

$\Delta E_2 = 50\%$ of 25 keV

$$= 12.5 \text{ keV}$$

∴ $\lambda_2 = \dfrac{12375}{12.5 \times 10^3} = 0.99$Å

$$= 99 \text{ pm}$$

22. 26 pm $= 0.26$ Å

Now, $0.26 = \dfrac{12375}{V} - \dfrac{12375}{1.5\,V}$

23. Similar type of example is given in the theory.

24. Transition if from L-shell to K-shell.

$$\frac{1}{\lambda} = R\,(Z-1)^2 \left(\frac{1}{n_1^2} - \frac{1}{n_2^2}\right)$$

or $\dfrac{f}{c} = R\,(Z-1)^2 \left(\dfrac{1}{n_1^2} - \dfrac{1}{n_2^2}\right)$

or $\dfrac{4.2 \times 10^8}{3 \times 10^8} = 1.1 \times 10^7\,(Z-1)^2 \left(1 - \dfrac{1}{4}\right)$

Solving we get, $Z \approx 42$

25. (a) $P = Vi = (40 \times 10^3)\,(10 \times 10^{-3})$

$$= 400 \text{ W}$$

1% of 400 W is 4 W.

(b) Heat generated $= 400$ W $- 4$ W

$$= 396 \text{ W} = 396 \text{ J/s}$$

26. Stopping potential $= 10.4$ V

∴ $K_{\max} = 10.4$ eV

$E = W + K_{\max}$

$$= 1.7 + 10.4 = 12.1 \text{ eV}$$

$$\lambda = \frac{12375}{12.1} = 1022 \text{ Å}$$

12.1 eV is the energy gap between $n = 3$ and $n = 1$ in hydrogen atom.

27. $E = hf = \frac{(6.63 \times 10^{-34})(1.5 \times 10^{15})}{1.6 \times 10^{-19}}$ eV $= 6.21$ eV

$K_{max} = E - W = 6.21 - 3.7 = 2.51$ eV

28. $\lambda_0 = 5000$ Å

$$W = \frac{12375}{5000} = 2.475 \text{ eV}$$

Stopping potential is 3V. Therefore, $K_{max} = 3$ eV

$$E = W + K_{max} = 5.475 \text{ eV}$$

$$\lambda = \frac{12375}{5.475} = 2260 \text{ Å}$$

29. (a) $f_0 = f_A = 10 \times 10^{14}$ Hz $= 10^{15}$ Hz

(b) $W = |K_{max}|_c = 4$ eV

(c) $W = hf_0 \implies h = \frac{W}{f_0}$

30. $E_1 = \frac{12357}{3000} = 4.125$ eV

$$E_2 = \frac{12357}{6000} = 2.0625 \text{ eV}$$

Maximum speed ratio is 3 : 1. Therefore, maximum kinetic ratio is 9 : 1.

Now, $9 K_{max} = 4.125 - W$ ...(i)

$K_{max} = 2.0625 - W$ ...(ii)

Solving these two equations, we get

$W \approx 1.81$ eV and $K_{max} = 0.26$ eV

Putting $K_{max} = \frac{1}{2} m v_{max}^2$ we can find v_{max}. Here, m is the mass of electron.

31. $E = \frac{12375}{1800} = 6.875$ eV

K_{max} or $K = E - W$

$= 4.875$ eV

$$r = \frac{\sqrt{2Km}}{Bq}$$

$$= \frac{\sqrt{2 \times 4.875 \times 10^{-19} \times 9.1 \times 10^{-31}}}{5 \times 10^{-5} \times 1.6 \times 10^{-19}}$$

$= 0.148$ m

32. $f_{higher} = \frac{8 \times 10^{15}}{2\pi}$ s^{-1}

$$E = \frac{hf}{1.6 \times 10^{-19}} \text{ eV}$$

$$= \frac{(6.63 \times 10^{-34})(8 \times 10^{15})}{1.6 \times 10^{-19} \times 2\pi}$$

$= 5.27$ eV

$K_{max} = E - W$

$= 3.27$ eV

33. $f = \frac{\omega}{2\pi} = \frac{(1.57 \times 10^7)c}{2\pi}$

$$E = \frac{hf}{1.6 \times 10^{-19}} \text{ eV}$$

$$= \frac{(6.63 \times 10^{-34})(1.57 \times 10^7)(3 \times 10^8)}{1.6 \times 10^{-19} \times 2 \times \pi} \text{ eV}$$

$= 3.1$ eV

$K_{max} = E - W = 1.2$ eV

LEVEL 2

Single Correct Option

1. $\frac{mv^2}{r} = \frac{GMm}{r^2}$ ...(i)

$mvr = \frac{h}{2\pi}$ (for $n = 1$) ...(ii)

Solving these two equations, we can find v and r. Then,

$$E = \frac{1}{2} mv^2 - \frac{GMM}{r}$$

2. $\frac{M}{L} = \frac{q}{2m} =$ constant

$M \propto L$

and $L = \frac{nh}{2\pi}$

or $L \propto n$

$\therefore$ $M \propto n$

3. $i = qf = q\left(\frac{v}{2\pi r}\right)$

or $i \propto \frac{v}{r} \propto \frac{(1/n)}{(n)^2}$

or $i \propto \frac{1}{n^3}$

$$\frac{i_1}{i_2} = \left(\frac{n_2}{n_1}\right)^3 = (2)^3 = 8$$

4. $n_f = 6$

Total emission lines $= \frac{n_f(n_f - 1)}{2} = 15$

5. $A = \pi r^2$

$$A \propto r^2$$

or $\qquad A \propto n^4 \qquad$ (as $r \propto n^2$)

$\therefore \qquad \dfrac{A_n}{A_1} = (n)^4$

$$\ln\left(\dfrac{A_n}{A_1}\right) = 4 \ln(n)$$

Therefore, $\ln\left(\dfrac{A_n}{A_1}\right)$ *versus* $\ln n$ graph is a straight line of slope 4.

6. $B = \dfrac{\mu_0 i}{2\pi} \quad$ or $\quad B \propto \dfrac{i}{r}$

See the hint of Q.No. 4 of same section.

$$i \propto \dfrac{1}{n^3} \quad \text{and} \quad r \propto n^2$$

$\therefore \qquad B = \dfrac{1}{n^5}$

$\therefore \qquad \dfrac{B_1}{B_2} = \left(\dfrac{n_2}{n_1}\right)^5 = (2)^5 = 32$

7. $\dfrac{1}{\lambda} = R\left(1 - \dfrac{1}{4}\right) = \dfrac{3R}{4}$

$\therefore \qquad p = \dfrac{h}{\lambda}$

$$= \dfrac{3Rh}{4} = \text{momentum of photon}$$

From conservation of linear momentum,

Momentum of photon = Momentum of hydrogen atom

$\therefore \qquad \dfrac{3Rh}{4} = Mv$

$\Rightarrow \qquad v = \dfrac{3Rh}{4M}$

8. $T = \dfrac{2\pi r}{v} \quad$ or $\quad T \propto \dfrac{r}{v}$

or $\qquad T \propto \dfrac{(n^2/Z)}{(Z/n)}$

$\therefore \qquad T \propto \dfrac{n^3}{Z^2}$

$$\left(\dfrac{T_1}{T_2}\right) = \left(\dfrac{n_1}{n_2}\right)^3 = \left(\dfrac{Z_2}{Z_1}\right)^2$$

$$2 = \left(\dfrac{1}{2}\right)^3 \left(\dfrac{Z}{1}\right)^2$$

$\therefore \qquad Z = 4$

9.

$$\lambda_{2 \to 1} = \dfrac{12375}{10.2} \approx 1213 \, \text{Å}$$

10. For $K \geq 10.2$ eV electrons can excite the hydrogen atom (as $E_2 - E_1 = 10.2$ eV). So, collision may be inelastic.

11. $E_3 - E_1 = \dfrac{-13/6}{(3)^3} + 13.6 = 12.1$ eV

From momentum conservation,

Momentum of photon = Momentum of hydrogen atom

$\therefore \qquad \dfrac{E}{c} = mv$

or $\qquad v = \dfrac{E}{mc} = \dfrac{12.1 \times 1.6 \times 10^{-19}}{1.67 \times 10^{-27} \times 3 \times 10^8}$

$$= 3.86 \, \text{m/s}$$

12. $P = Vi = 150 \times 10^3 \times 10 \times 10^{-3} = 1500$ W

99% of $P = 1500 \times \dfrac{99}{100}$ J/s $= 1485$ J/s

$$= \dfrac{1485}{4.18} \, \text{cal/s}$$

$$\approx 355 \, \text{cal/s}$$

13. $E_4 - E_3 = 32.4$

$\therefore \qquad \dfrac{-13.6 \, (Z)^2}{(4)^2} + \dfrac{13.6 \, (Z)^2}{(3)^2} = 32.4$

Solving, we get

$$Z = 7$$

14. $E_n \propto \dfrac{1}{n^2} \quad$ and $\quad L_n \propto n$

15. $K = \dfrac{p^2}{2m}$

In collision, momentum p remains constant.

$\therefore \qquad K \propto \dfrac{1}{\text{mass}}$

After collision, mass has doubled. So, kinetic energy will remain $\dfrac{K}{2}$. Hence, loss is also $\dfrac{K}{2}$.

Now, $\dfrac{K}{2} = $ minimum excitation energy required.

$$\dfrac{K}{2} = 10.2 \, \text{eV} \quad \Rightarrow \quad K = 20.4 \, \text{eV}$$

16. $KE = |E| = 3.4$ eV

$$\lambda \text{ (in Å)} = \sqrt{\frac{150}{KE \text{ (in eV)}}}$$

$$= \sqrt{\frac{150}{3.4}}$$

$$= 6.6 \text{ Å}$$

17. $\Delta p = 2\left(\frac{h}{\lambda}\right) = \frac{2 \times 6.63 \times 10^{-34}}{5030 \times 10^{-10}}$

$$= 2.63 \times 10^{-27} \text{ kg-m/s}$$

18. $r_3 = (3)^2 \cdot r_1 = 9x$

Now, $3\lambda_3 = (2\pi r_3) = 18\pi x$

∴ $\lambda_3 = 6\pi x$

19. Minimum 10.2 eV energy is required to excite a hydrogen atom. In perfectly inelastic collision, maximum energy is lost.

∴ $\frac{1}{2}mv^2 = \frac{1}{2}(2m)\left(\frac{v}{2}\right)^2$

$$= 10.2 \times 1.6 \times 10^{-19}$$

$$\frac{1}{4}mv^2 = 1.632 \times 10^{-18}$$

∴ $v = \sqrt{\frac{1.632 \times 4 \times 10^{-18}}{1.67 \times 10^{-27}}}$

$$= 6.25 \times 10^4 \text{ m/s}$$

20. $\frac{1}{\lambda} = R\left(1 - \frac{1}{n^2}\right)$

∴ $\frac{R}{n^2} = R - \frac{1}{\lambda} = \frac{\lambda R - 1}{\lambda}$

∴ $n = \sqrt{\frac{\lambda R}{\lambda R - 1}}$

21. $\frac{M}{L} = \frac{q}{2m} = \frac{e}{2m}$

∴ $M = \left(\frac{e}{2m}\right)L$

$$= \left(\frac{e}{2m}\right)\left(\frac{nh}{2\pi}\right) = \left(\frac{neh}{4\pi m}\right)$$

22. $\lambda_\alpha - \lambda'_m = 3(\lambda_\alpha - \lambda_m)$

∴ $\frac{12375}{10.2 (Z-1)^2} - \frac{12375}{20 \times 10^3}$

$$= 3\left[\frac{12375}{10.2(Z-1)^2} - \frac{12375}{10 \times 10^3}\right]$$

Solving we get $Z = 29$

23. $\lambda_{ph} = \lambda_e$

∴ $\frac{h}{P_{ph}} = \frac{h}{P_e}$

∴ $P_{ph} = P_e$

∴ $\frac{E_{ph}}{c} = \frac{2E_e}{v}$

∴ $\frac{E_e}{E_{ph}} = \frac{v}{2c}$

24. Speed of electron in first orbit of hydrogen atom is given by

$$v = \frac{e^2}{2\varepsilon_0 h}$$

∴ $\frac{v}{c} = \frac{e^2}{2\varepsilon_0 hc}$

25. $E_1 = \frac{me^4}{8\varepsilon_0^2 h^2}$

$$f_n = \frac{v_n}{2\pi r_n} = \frac{(e^2/2\varepsilon_0 nh)}{(2\pi)\varepsilon_0 n^2 h^2/\pi me^2}$$

$$= \frac{me^4}{4\varepsilon_0^2 n^3 h^3} = \frac{8E_1 \varepsilon_0^2 h^2}{4\varepsilon_0^2 n^3 h^3}$$

$$= \frac{2E_1}{n^3 h}$$

26. $r = \frac{\sqrt{2Km}}{Bq} = \frac{\sqrt{2(E-W_0)m}}{eB}$

27. $mvr = \frac{h}{2\pi}$ (in first orbit)

∴ $v = \frac{h}{2\pi mr}$

$$a = \frac{v^2}{r} = \frac{h^2}{4\pi^2 m^2 r^3}$$

28. Decrease in kinetic energy = increase in potential energy

∴ $qV = \frac{1}{4\pi\varepsilon_0} \cdot \frac{Q \cdot q}{r}$

∴ $r = \frac{Q}{(4\pi\varepsilon_0)V}$

i.e. r is independent of q.

29. Number of photons emitted per second,

$$n_1 = \frac{\text{Power}}{\text{energy of one photon}}$$

$$= \frac{P}{hc/\lambda} = \frac{P\lambda}{hc}$$

Number of electrons emitted per second,

$$n_2 = \frac{n_1}{10^6} = \frac{P\lambda}{10^6 hc}$$

Current in μA,

$$i = (n_2 e) \times 10^6 = \frac{P\lambda e}{hc}$$

$$= \frac{5 \times 400 \times 10^{-9} \times 1.6 \times 10^{-19}}{6.6 \times 10^{-34} \times 3 \times 10^8}$$

$$= 1.6\,\mu A$$

30. de-Broglie wavelength, $\lambda \propto \dfrac{1}{\sqrt{T}}$

$$\frac{\lambda_1}{\lambda_2} = \sqrt{\frac{T_2}{T_1}}$$

$$\frac{\lambda_1}{\lambda_2} = \sqrt{\frac{273 + 927}{273 + 27}}$$

$$= \sqrt{\frac{1200}{300}} = 2$$

or $\qquad \lambda_2 = \dfrac{\lambda_1}{2}$

31. $\dfrac{mv^2}{a_0} = \dfrac{1}{4\pi\varepsilon_0}\dfrac{(e)(e)}{a_0^2} \quad\Rightarrow\quad v = \dfrac{e}{\sqrt{4\pi\varepsilon_0 ma_0}}$

32. $I = 0.2\,I_0 = I_0\,e^{-\alpha x}$

$$\Rightarrow \qquad \left(\frac{1}{5}\right) = e^{-\alpha x}$$

$$\Rightarrow \quad \ln 5 = \alpha x$$

or $\qquad x = \dfrac{\ln 5}{\alpha}$

33. As, $\qquad \lambda = \dfrac{h}{p}$

$$\Rightarrow \qquad \lambda - \Delta\lambda = \frac{h}{p + \Delta p}$$

$$\Rightarrow \qquad \frac{199\lambda}{200} = \frac{h}{p + \Delta p}$$

$$\Rightarrow \qquad p + \Delta p = \frac{200}{199}\,p$$

$$\Rightarrow \qquad p = 199\,\Delta p$$

More than One Correct Options

1. $R \propto n^2,\ v \propto \dfrac{1}{n}$ and $E \propto \dfrac{1}{n^2}$

2. $L \propto n,\ r \propto n^2$ and $T = \dfrac{2\pi r}{v}$

or $\quad T \propto \dfrac{r}{v} \propto \dfrac{n^2}{(1/n)}$ or $\quad T \propto n^3$

3. $\lambda = \dfrac{h}{p} = \dfrac{h}{mv} = \dfrac{h}{\sqrt{2Km}}$

$$\lambda \propto \frac{1}{m} \qquad \text{(if } v \text{ is same)}$$

$$\lambda \propto \frac{1}{\sqrt{m}} \qquad \text{(if } K \text{ is same)}$$

If change in potential energy is same, then change in kinetic energy is also same. But, this does not mean that kinetic energy is same.

4. $\dfrac{n_f\,(n_f - 1)}{2} = 6$

$$\Rightarrow \qquad n_f = 4$$

λ_1 and λ_4 are longer than λ_0.

λ_3, λ_5 and λ_6 belong to Lyman series.

5. $\sqrt{f} \propto (Z - b)$ ...(i)

If f *versus* Z is a straight line.

$$f = \frac{c}{\lambda}$$

Hence, $\dfrac{1}{\sqrt{\lambda}}$ *versus* Z is also a straight line.

Comprehension Based Questions

1. $E_1 = \dfrac{12375}{4950} = 2.5\,\text{eV}$

$\qquad K_1 = \text{maximum kinetic energy} = 0.6\,\text{eV}$

$\qquad W = E_1 - K_2 = 1.9\,\text{eV}$

2. $K_2 = 1.1\,\text{eV}$

$$E_2 = W + K_2 = 3.0 \ \text{eV}$$

$\therefore \qquad \lambda_2 = \dfrac{12375}{3.0} = 4125\,\text{Å}$

3. Magnetic field cannot change the kinetic energy of charged particle.

4. $K_{\max} = E - W = 2\,\text{eV}$

$$\lambda = \sqrt{\frac{150}{KE\ (\text{in eV})}},\ \text{for an electron}$$

$$= \sqrt{\frac{150}{2}} \approx 8.6\,\text{Å}$$

5. K_{max} is 2 eV. Hence, stopping potential is 2V. Photoemission stops when potential of sphere becomes 2V.

∴ $$2 = \frac{q}{4\pi\varepsilon_0 r}$$

∴ $$q = 8\pi\varepsilon_0 r$$

6. ∵ $q = ne = 8\pi\varepsilon_0 r$

∴ $$n = \frac{8\pi\varepsilon_0 r}{e}$$

$$= \frac{2 \times 8 \times 10^{-3}}{9 \times 10^9 \times 1.6 \times 10^{-19}}$$

$$= 1.11 \times 10^7$$

So, this much number of electrons are required to be ejected from the sphere.

Number of photons emitted per second,

$$N_1 = \frac{\text{Power of source}}{\text{Energy of one photon}}$$

$$= \frac{3.2 \times 10^{-3}}{5 \times 1.6 \times 10^{-19}}$$

$$= 4 \times 10^{15}$$

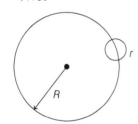

Number of photons incident on sphere per second,

$$N_2 = \left(\frac{N_1}{4\pi R^2}\right)(\pi r^2)$$

$$= \frac{N_1}{4R^2} r^2$$

$$= \frac{(4 \times 10^{15})(8 \times 10^{-3})^2}{4(0.8)^2} = 10^{11}$$

Number of photoelectrons emitted per second,

$$N_3 = \frac{N_2}{10^6} = 10^5$$

Now, $N_3 t = n$

∴ $$t = \frac{n}{N_3} = 111 \text{ s}$$

Match the Columns

2. For He^+, $Z = 2$

$$E \propto \frac{Z^2}{n^2}$$

—————— $E_2 = -3.4$ eV

—————— $E_1 = -13.6$ eV

H-atom

Ionisation energy from first, excited state of H-atom

$$= |E_2| = 3.4 \text{ eV} = E \qquad \text{(given)}$$

(a) $|E_1| = (13.6 \text{ eV})(2)^2$

$$= 16(3.4 \text{ eV}) = 16E$$

(b) $U_2 = 2E_2 = 2(-13.6)\dfrac{(2)^2}{(2)^2}$

$$= -8(3.4 \text{ eV}) = -8E$$

(c) $K_1 = |E_1| = 16E$

(d) $|E_2| = (13.6)\dfrac{(2)^2}{(2)^2}$

$$= 4(3.4 \text{ eV}) = 4E$$

3. $K_{max} = hf - W$

∴ K_{max} versus f graph is a straight line of slope h and intercept $-W$.

$$eV_0 = hf = W$$

∴ $$V_0 = \left(\frac{h}{e}\right)f - \frac{W}{e}$$

∴ V_0 versus f graph is again a straight line of slope $\dfrac{h}{e}$ and intercept $\dfrac{W}{e}$.

4. $T = \dfrac{2\pi r}{v}$

or $$T \propto \frac{r}{v} \propto \frac{n^2/Z}{Z/n}$$

∴ $$T \propto \frac{n^3}{Z^2}$$

$$L = \frac{nh}{2\pi} \quad \text{or} \quad L \propto n$$

$$v \propto \frac{Z}{n}$$

and $$r \propto \frac{n^2}{Z}$$

5. $\dfrac{1}{\lambda} \propto \left(\dfrac{1}{n_1^2} - \dfrac{1}{n_2^2} \right)$

or $\qquad \dfrac{\lambda_2}{\lambda_1} = \dfrac{(1/n_1^2 - 1/n_2^2)_i}{(1/n_1^2 - 1/n_2^2)_f}$

or $\qquad \lambda_2 = \dfrac{(1/4 - 1/16)\lambda}{(1/n_1^2 - 1/n_2^2)_f}$

$\qquad\qquad = \left(\dfrac{3}{16} \lambda \right) \left[\dfrac{1}{(1/n_1^2 - 1/n_2^2)_f} \right]$

(a) For first line of Balmer series,

$\qquad n_1 = 2, n_2 = 3 \quad \therefore \quad \lambda_2 = \left(\dfrac{27}{20} \right) \lambda$

(b) For third line of Balmer series,

$\qquad n_1 = 2, n_2 = 5 \quad \therefore \quad \lambda_2 = \left(\dfrac{25}{28} \right) \lambda$

(c) For first line of Lyman series,

$\qquad n_1 = 1, n_2 = 2 \quad \therefore \quad \lambda_2 = \dfrac{\lambda}{4}$

(d) For second line of Lyman series,

$\qquad n_1 = 2, n_2 = 3 \quad \therefore \quad \lambda_2 = \left(\dfrac{27}{128} \right) \lambda$

7. Stopping potential increases with increase in maximum kinetic energy of photoelectrons of frequency of incident light.

With increase in distance between cathode and anode, f remains unchanged.

$K_{max} = hf - W = eV_0$

If W is decreased, K_{max} and V_0 both will increase.

Subjective Questions

1. (a) Reduced mass of positronium and electron is $\dfrac{m}{2}$,

where, $m = $ mass of electron

$\qquad\qquad E \propto m$

$\therefore \qquad\qquad \lambda \propto \dfrac{1}{m}$

m has become half, so λ will become two times or 1312 nm or 1.31μm.

(b) $E \propto Z^2$

$\therefore \quad \lambda \propto \dfrac{1}{Z^2}$

For singly ionized helium atom $Z = 2$

$\therefore \qquad\qquad \lambda$ is $\dfrac{1}{4}$th

or $\qquad\qquad$ 164 nm

2. (a) $f = \dfrac{v}{2\pi r}$

$\qquad f_1 = \dfrac{(2.2 \times 10^6)}{(2\pi)(0.529 \times 10^{-10})}$

$\qquad\quad \approx 6.6 \times 10^{15}$ Hz

$\qquad v \propto \dfrac{1}{n}$ and $r \propto n^2$

$\qquad f \propto \dfrac{v}{r} \implies f \propto \dfrac{1}{n^3}$

$\therefore \qquad f_2 = \dfrac{f_1}{8}$

(b) $\Delta E = E_2 - E_1 = 10.2$ eV $= hf$

$\therefore \qquad f = \dfrac{10.2 \times 1.6 \times 10^{-19}}{6.6 \times 10^{-34}}$

$\qquad\quad \approx 2.46 \times 10^{15}$ Hz

(c) In option (a), we have found that

$\qquad f_2 = 0.823 \times 10^{15}$ Hz

$\qquad T_2 = \dfrac{1}{f_2}$

$\qquad N = \dfrac{t}{T_2} = tf_2 = (10^{-8})(0.823 \times 10^{15})$

$\qquad\quad = 8.23 \times 10^6$ revolutions

3. (a) $r \propto \dfrac{1}{m}$

$\therefore \qquad r = \dfrac{(r_1^H)}{m} = \dfrac{0.529 \times 10^{-10}}{207}$

$\qquad\quad = 2.55 \times 10^{-13}$ m

(b) $E \propto m$

$\therefore$ Ionization energy of given atom

$\qquad = (m)$ (ionization energy of hydrogen atom)

$\qquad = (207)(13.6$ eV$)$

$\qquad = 2815.2$ eV $= 2.81$ keV

4. (a) $E_n - E_1 = 12.5$

$\therefore \qquad -\dfrac{13.6}{n^2} + 13.6 = 12.5$

Solving we get, $n = 3.51$

Hence, electron jumps to $n = 3$. So, possible lines are between $n = 3$ to $n = 2$, $n = 3$ to $n = 1$ and between $n = 2$ to $n = 1$.

For $n = 3$ to $n = 2$,

$\qquad \Delta E = E_3 - E_2 = -\dfrac{13.6}{9} + \dfrac{13.6}{4}$

$\qquad\qquad = 1.9$ eV

$$\therefore \quad \lambda = \frac{12375}{1.9} \text{ Å} = 6513 \text{ Å}$$

$$\approx 651 \text{ nm}$$

Similarly, other wavelengths can also be obtained.

(b) $n = 3.51$ (in option-*a*)

A photon always transfers its energy completely. So, it cannot excite the ground state electrons to $n = 3$ (like and electrons excited it in part-a).

5. (a) $E = hf = (6.6 \times 10^{-34})(5.5 \times 10^{14})$

$$= 36.3 \times 10^{-20} \text{ J}$$

$$= 2.27 \text{ eV} \qquad \qquad \textbf{Ans.}$$

(b) Number of photons leaving the source per second,

$$n = \frac{P}{E} = \frac{0.1}{36.3 \times 10^{-20}}$$

$$= 2.75 \times 10^{17} \qquad \textbf{Ans.}$$

(c) Number of photons falling on cathode per second,

$$n_1 = \frac{0.15}{100} \times 2.75 \times 10^{17}$$

$$= 4.125 \times 10^{14}$$

Number of photoelectrons emitting per second,

$$n_2 = \frac{6 \times 10^{-6}}{1.6 \times 10^{-19}} = 3.75 \times 10^{13}$$

$$\therefore \quad \% = \frac{n_2}{n_1} \times 100$$

$$= \frac{3.75 \times 10^{13}}{4.125 \times 10^{14}} \times 100$$

$$= 9\% \qquad \qquad \textbf{Ans.}$$

6. $\dfrac{K_1}{K_2} = 5$

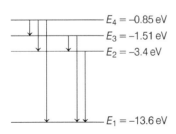

$$E_4 = -0.85 \text{ eV}$$
$$E_3 = -1.51 \text{ eV}$$
$$E_2 = -3.4 \text{ eV}$$

$$E_1 = -13.6 \text{ eV}$$

$$\therefore \quad \frac{\Delta E_1 - W}{\Delta E_2 - W} = 5 \qquad \qquad \text{...(i)}$$

Here, $\Delta E_1 = E_4 - E_1 = 12.75 \text{ eV}$
and $\Delta E_2 = E_3 - E_1 = 12.09 \text{ eV}$
Substituting in Eq. (i) and solving, we get

$$W = 11.925 \text{ eV} \qquad \qquad \textbf{Ans.}$$

7. **For shorter wavelength**

$$\Delta E = E_4 - E_3 = \frac{(-13.6)(3)^2}{(4)^2} - \left[\frac{(-13.6)(3)^2}{(3)^2} \right]$$

$$= 5.95 \text{ eV}$$

$$W = E - K_{\max} = (5.95 - 3.95) \text{ eV} = 2 \text{ eV}$$

For longer wavelength

$$\Delta E = E_5 - E_4 = \frac{(-13.6)(3)^2}{(5)^2} - \left[\frac{(-13.6)(3)^2}{(4)^2} \right]$$

$$= 2.754 \text{ eV}$$

$$\therefore \quad K_{\max} = E - W = 0.754 \text{ eV}$$

or stopping potential is 0.754 V. **Ans.**

8. Magnetic moment, $\mu = NiA = \left(\dfrac{e}{T} \right) (\pi r^2)$

$$\text{or} \qquad \mu = \left(\frac{e}{2\pi r/v} \right) (\pi r^2) = \frac{evr}{2} \qquad \text{...(i)}$$

We know that $\qquad mvr = \dfrac{nh}{2\pi} \qquad \qquad \text{...(ii)}$

Solving Eqs. (i) and (ii), we get

$$\mu = \frac{neh}{4\pi m} \qquad \qquad \textbf{Ans.}$$

Magnetic induction, $B = \dfrac{\mu_0 i}{2r} = \dfrac{\mu_0 e}{2rT}$

$$\text{or} \qquad B = \frac{\mu_0 ev}{(2r)(2\pi r)} = \frac{\mu_0 ev}{4\pi r^2} \qquad \text{...(iii)}$$

Substituting the values of v and r,

$$v = \frac{e^2}{2\varepsilon_0 nh} \quad \text{and} \quad r = \frac{\varepsilon_0 n^2 h^2}{\pi m e^2},$$

we get

$$B = \frac{\mu_0 \pi m^2 e^7}{8 \varepsilon_0 h^5 n^5} \qquad \qquad \textbf{Ans.}$$

9. Energy of electron in ground state of hydrogen atom is -13.6 eV. Earlier it had a kinetic energy of 2 eV. Therefore, energy of photon released during formation of hydrogen atom,

$$\Delta E = 2 - (-13.6) = 15.6 \text{ eV}$$

$$\therefore \quad \lambda = \frac{12375}{\Delta E} = \frac{12375}{15.6}$$

$$= 793.3 \text{ Å} \qquad \qquad \textbf{Ans.}$$

10. $U = -1.7$ eV

$$\therefore \quad E = \frac{U}{2} = -0.85 \text{ eV} = \frac{-13.6}{n^2}$$

$$\therefore \quad n = 4$$

Ejected photoelectron will have minimum de-Broglie wavelength corresponding to transition from $n = 4$ to $n = 1$.

$$\Delta E = E_4 - E_1 = -0.85 - (-13.6) = 12.75 \text{ eV}$$
$$K_{max} = \Delta E - W = 10.45 \text{ eV}$$

$$\therefore \quad \lambda = \sqrt{\frac{150}{10.45}} \text{ Å} \quad \text{(for an electron)}$$

$$= 3.8 \text{ Å} \qquad \text{Ans.}$$

11. (a) $\dfrac{n(n-1)}{2} = 3$

$$\therefore \quad n = 3$$

i.e. after excitation atom jumps to second excited state. Hence, $n_f = 3$. So, n_i can be 1 or 2. If $n_i = 1$, then energy emitted is either equal to or less than the energy absorbed. Hence, the emitted wavelength is either equal to or greater than the absorbed wavelength. Hence, $n_i \neq 1$.

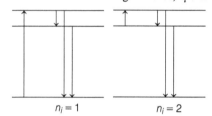

$$n_i = 1 \qquad\qquad n_i = 2$$

If $n_i = 2$, then $E_e \geq E_a$.
Hence, $\lambda_e \leq \lambda_b$

$$\therefore \qquad n_i = 2 \qquad \text{Ans.}$$

(b) $E_3 - E_2 = 68$ eV

$$\therefore \quad (13.6)(Z^2)\left(\frac{1}{4} - \frac{1}{9}\right) = 68$$

$$\therefore \qquad\qquad Z = 6 \qquad \text{Ans.}$$

(c) $\lambda_{min} = \dfrac{12375}{E_3 - E_1}$

$$= \frac{12375}{(13.6)(6)^2\left(1 - \dfrac{1}{9}\right)} = 28.43 \text{ Å} \qquad \text{Ans.}$$

(d) Ionization energy $= (13.6)(6)^2 = 489.6$ eV **Ans.**

$$\lambda = \frac{12375}{489.6} = 25.3 \text{ Å} \qquad \text{Ans.}$$

12. Pitch of helical path, $p = (v\cos\theta)\, T = \dfrac{vT}{2}$.

$$\text{(as } \theta = 60°\text{)}$$

$$T = \frac{2\pi m}{Bq} = \frac{2\pi}{B\alpha} \qquad \left(\alpha = \frac{q}{m}\right)$$

$$\therefore \qquad p = \frac{\pi v}{B\alpha}$$

or $$v = \frac{B\alpha p}{\pi} \qquad \qquad \text{...(i)}$$

$$\text{KE} = \frac{1}{2} mv^2 = E - W$$

$$\therefore \qquad W = E - \frac{1}{2} mv^2 \qquad \text{...(ii)}$$

Substituting value of v from Eq. (i) in Eq. (ii), we get

$$W = 4.9 - \frac{1}{2}$$

$$\times \frac{9.1 \times 10^{-31} \times (2.5 \times 10^{-3})^2 (1.76 \times 10^{11})^2}{\pi^2 \times 1.6 \times 10^{-19}}$$
$$\times (2.7 \times 10^{-3})^2$$

$$= (4.9 - 0.4) \text{ eV} = 4.5 \text{ eV} \qquad \text{Ans.}$$

13. (a) $\lambda = 1500\left(\dfrac{1}{1 - 1/p^2}\right)$

λ_{max} corresponds to least energetic photon with $p = 2$.

$$\therefore \quad \lambda_{max} = 1500\left(\frac{1}{1 - 1/4}\right) = 2000 \text{ Å} \qquad \text{Ans.}$$

λ_{min} corresponds to most energetic photon with $p = \infty$

$$\therefore \qquad \lambda_{min} = 1500 \text{ Å} \qquad \text{Ans.}$$

(b) $\lambda_{\infty - 1} = 1500$ Å

$$\text{———————} E_3 = -0.95 \text{ eV}$$
$$\text{———————} E_2 = -2.05 \text{ eV}$$

$$\text{———————} E_1 = -8.25 \text{ eV}$$

$$\therefore \quad E_\infty - E_1 = \frac{12375}{1500} \text{ eV}$$
$$= 8.25 \text{ eV}$$

$$\therefore \qquad E_1 = -8.25 \text{ eV} \qquad \text{(as } E_\infty = 0\text{)}$$
$$\lambda_{2-1} = 2000 \text{ Å}$$

$\therefore \qquad E_2 - E_1 = \dfrac{12375}{2000}$ eV

$= 6.2$ eV

$\therefore \qquad E_2 = -2.05$ eV

Similarly, $\lambda_{31} = 1500 \left(\dfrac{1}{1 - 1/9} \right)$

$= 1687.5$ Å

$\therefore \qquad E_3 - E_1 = \dfrac{12375}{1687.5}$ eV

$= 7.3$ eV

$\therefore \qquad E_3 = -0.95$ eV

(c) Ionization potential $= 8.25$ V   **Ans.**

14. (a) $K_1 = \dfrac{12375}{3000} - W$ ...(i)

$K_2 = \dfrac{12375}{1650} - W$ ...(ii)

$v_2 = 2v_1 \quad \therefore \quad K_2 = 4K_1$ ...(iii)

Solving these equations, we get

$W = 3$ eV

$\therefore$ Threshold wavelength,

$\lambda_0 = \dfrac{12375}{3} = 4125$ Å   **Ans.**

(b) Energy of photon in first case,

$= \dfrac{12375}{3000} = 4.125$ eV

or $\qquad E_1 = 6.6 \times 10^{-19}$ J

Rate of incident photons

$= \dfrac{P_1}{E_1} = \dfrac{0.388}{6.6 \times 10^{-19}}$

$= 5.88 \times 10^{17}$ per second

Number of electrons ejected

$= \dfrac{4.8 \times 10^{-3}}{1.6 \times 10^{-19}}$ per second

$= 3.0 \times 10^{16}$ per second

$\therefore$ Efficiency of photoelectrons generation

$= \dfrac{3.0 \times 10^{16}}{5.88 \times 10^{17}} \times 100$

$= 5.1\%$ **Ans.**

(c) $E_2 = \dfrac{12375}{1650} = 7.5$ eV

$= 12 \times 10^{-19}$ J

Therefore, number of photons incident per second

$n_2 = \dfrac{P_2}{E_2} = \dfrac{5.0 \times 10^{-3}}{12 \times 10^{-19}}$

$= 4.17 \times 10^{15}$ per second

Number of electrons emitted per second
($\eta = 5.1\%$)

$= \dfrac{5.1}{100} \times 4.17 \times 10^{15}$

$= 2.13 \times 10^{14}$ per second

$\therefore$ Saturation current in second case

$i = (2.13 \times 10^{14})\,(1.6 \times 10^{-19})$ A

$= 3.4 \times 10^{-5}$ A

$= 34$ μA   **Ans.**

15. Balmer Series

$\lambda_{32} = \dfrac{12375}{E_3 - E_2} = \dfrac{12375}{(13.6)\left(\dfrac{1}{4} - \dfrac{1}{9}\right)}$

$= 6551$ Å $= 655.1$ nm

$\lambda_{42} = \dfrac{12375}{E_4 - E_2} = \dfrac{12375}{(13.6)\left(\dfrac{1}{4} - \dfrac{1}{16}\right)}$

$= 4853$ Å

$= 485.3$ nm

$\lambda_{52} = \dfrac{12375}{E_5 - E_2} = \dfrac{12375}{(13.6)\left(\dfrac{1}{4} - \dfrac{1}{25}\right)}$

$= 4333$ Å

$= 433.3$ nm

First two lie in the given range. Of these λ_{42} corresponds to more energy.

$E = E_4 - E_2 = (13.6)\left(\dfrac{1}{4} - \dfrac{1}{16}\right)$

$= 2.55$ eV

$\therefore \qquad K_{max} = E - W = (2.55 - 2.0)$ eV

$= 0.55$ eV   **Ans.**

16. From the theory of standing wave, we can say that

$\dfrac{\lambda}{2} = (2.5 - 2.0) = 0.5$ Å   or $\lambda = 1$ Å

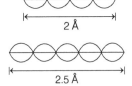

Therefore, least value of d required will correspond to a single loop.

$$\therefore \qquad d_{min} = \frac{\lambda}{2} = 0.5 \text{ Å} \qquad \textbf{Ans.}$$

Further for de-Broglie wavelength of an electron,

$$\lambda = \sqrt{\frac{150}{K \text{ (in eV)}}} \text{ Å}$$

$$\lambda = 1 \text{ Å}$$

$$\therefore \qquad K = 150 \text{ eV} \qquad \textbf{Ans.}$$

17. (a) Reduced mass

$$\mu = \frac{m_1 m_2}{m_1 + m_2} = \frac{(1837 m_e)(207 m_e)}{1837 m_e + 207 m_e}$$

$$= 186 m_e$$

$$= 186 \times 9.1 \times 10^{-31}$$

$$= 1.69 \times 10^{-28} \text{ kg} \qquad \textbf{Ans.}$$

(b) $E_n \propto m$

Here, reduced mass is 186 times mass of electron. Hence, ground state energy will also be 186 times that of hydrogen atom.

$$\therefore \qquad E_1 = 186(-13.6) \text{ eV}$$

$$= -2529.6 \text{ eV} \approx -2.53 \text{ keV} \qquad \textbf{Ans.}$$

(c) $E_2 = 186 (-3.4) \text{ eV} = -632.4 \text{ eV}$

$$\therefore \qquad \Delta E_{21} = 1897.2 \text{ eV}$$

$$\therefore \qquad \lambda_{21} = \frac{12375}{\Delta E_{21}} \text{ Å}$$

$$= \frac{12375}{1897.2} \text{ Å}$$

$$= 6.53 \text{ Å} \approx 0.653 \text{ nm} \qquad \textbf{Ans.}$$

18. Force of interaction between electron and proton is

$$F = -\frac{dU}{dr} = \frac{-k}{r}$$

Force is negative. It means there is an attraction between the particles and they are bound to each other. This force provides the necessary centripetal force for the electron.

$$\therefore \qquad \frac{mv^2}{r} = \frac{k}{r} \qquad \dots\text{(i)}$$

According to Bohr's assumption,

$$mvr = n\frac{h}{2\pi} \qquad \dots\text{(ii)}$$

Solving Eqs. (i) and (ii), we get

$$r = \frac{nh}{2\pi\sqrt{mk}} \quad \text{and} \quad v = \sqrt{\frac{k}{m}}$$

$$\therefore \qquad E = U + \frac{1}{2}mv^2 = k \ln r - \frac{k}{2} + \frac{k}{2} = k \ln r$$

Thus, $$r_n = \frac{nh}{2\pi\sqrt{mk}}$$

and $$E_n = k \ln \left\{ \frac{nh}{2\pi\sqrt{mk}} \right\} \qquad \textbf{Ans.}$$

19. (a) $$r = \frac{mv}{Be} \qquad \dots\text{(i)}$$

$$mvr = \frac{nh}{2\pi} \qquad \dots\text{(ii)}$$

Solving these two equations, we get

$$r = \sqrt{\frac{nh}{2\pi Be}}$$

and $$v = \sqrt{\frac{nhBe}{2\pi m^2}}$$

(b) $$K = \frac{1}{2}mv^2 = \frac{nhBe}{4\pi m} \qquad \textbf{Ans.}$$

(c) $$M = iA = \left(\frac{e}{T}\right)(\pi r^2)$$

$$= \frac{e}{\left(\frac{2\pi r}{v}\right)}(\pi r^2) = \frac{evr}{2}$$

$$= \frac{e}{2}\sqrt{\frac{nh}{2\pi Be}}\sqrt{\frac{nhBe}{2\pi m^2}}$$

$$= \frac{nhe}{4\pi m}$$

$$U = -MB \cos 180°$$

$$= \frac{nheB}{4\pi m}$$

Note Angle between **M** and **B** will be 180°. Think why?

(d) $$E = U + K = \frac{nheB}{2\pi m}$$

(e) $$|\phi| = B\pi r^2 = \frac{nh}{2e}$$

20. (a) and (b) When hydrogen atom is excited, then

$$eV = E_0 \left(\frac{1}{1} - \frac{1}{n^2} \right) \qquad \dots\text{(i)}$$

When ion is excited,

$$eV = E_0 Z^2 \left[\frac{1}{2^2} - \frac{1}{n_1^2} \right] \qquad \dots\text{(ii)}$$

Wavelength of emitted light,

$$\frac{hc}{\lambda_1} = E_0 \left(\frac{1}{1} - \frac{1}{n^2} \right) \qquad \dots\text{(iii)}$$

$$\frac{hc}{\lambda_2} = E_0 Z^2 \left(\frac{1}{1} - \frac{1}{n_1^2} \right) \qquad \ldots \text{(iv)}$$

Further it is given that

$$\frac{\lambda_1}{\lambda_2} = \frac{5}{1} \qquad \ldots \text{(v)}$$

Solving the above equations, we get

$$Z = 2,$$
$$n = 2,$$
$$n_1 = 4$$

and $\qquad V = 10.2 \text{ V}$ **Ans.**

(c) Energy of emitted photon by the hydrogen atom

$$= E_2 - E_1$$
$$= 10.2 \text{ eV} \qquad \textbf{Ans.}$$

and by the ion $= E_4 - E_1$

$$= (13.6)(2)^2 \left(1 - \frac{1}{16} \right)$$

$$= 51 \text{ eV} \qquad \textbf{Ans.}$$

21. $0.6 = \dfrac{12375}{4950} - W \qquad \ldots \text{(i)}$

$$1.1 = \frac{12375}{\lambda} - W \qquad \ldots \text{(ii)}$$

Solving above two equations, we get

$$W = 1.9 \text{ eV}$$

and $\qquad \lambda = 4125 \text{ Å} \qquad$ **Ans.**

22. $E = \dfrac{12375}{4000} = 3.1 \text{ eV}$

Number of photoelectrons emitted per second,

$$n = \left(\frac{1}{10^6} \right) \left(\frac{5}{3.1 \times 1.6 \times 10^{-19}} \right)$$

$$= 1.0 \times 10^{13} \quad \text{per second}$$

$\therefore \qquad i = ne$

$$= 1.0 \times 10^{13} \times 1.6 \times 10^{-19}$$

$$= 1.6 \times 10^{-6} \text{ A}$$

$$= 1.6 \, \mu\text{A} \qquad \textbf{Ans.}$$

23. (a) $E = \dfrac{12375}{4000} = 3.1 \text{ eV}$

Energy of electron after first collision

$E_1 = 90\%$ of $E = 2.79 \text{ eV}$ (as 10% is lost)

Energy of electron after second collision

$E_2 = 90\%$ of $E_1 = 2.51 \text{ eV}$

KE of this electron after emitting from the metal surface

$$= (2.51 - 2.2) \text{ eV} = 0.31 \text{ eV} \qquad \textbf{Ans.}$$

(b) Energy after third collision,

$$E_3 = 90\% \quad \text{of} \quad E_2 = 2.26 \text{ eV}$$

Similarly, $E_4 = 90\%$ of $E_3 = 2.03 \text{ eV}$

So, after four collisions it becomes unable for the electrons to come out of the metal.

34. Modern Physics-II

INTRODUCTORY EXERCISE 34.1

2. Penetrating power is maximum for γ-rays, then of β-particles and then α-particles because basically it depends on the velocity. However, ionization power is in reverse order.

3. Both the beta rays and the cathode rays are made up of electrons. So, only option (a) is correct.

(b) Gamma rays are electromagnetic waves.

(c) Alpha particles are doubly ionized helium atoms and

(d) Protons and neutrons have approximately the same mass.

Therefore, (b), (c) and (d) are wrong options.

4. During β-decay, a neutron is transformed into a proton and an electron. This is why atomic number (Z = number of protons) increases by one and mass number (A = number of protons + neutrons) remains unchanged during β-decay.

5. Following nuclear reaction takes place

$$_0n^1 \longrightarrow {}_1H^1 + {}_{-1}e^0 + \bar{v}$$

$\bar{v}$ is antineutrino.

6. From $R = R_0 \left(\dfrac{1}{2}\right)^n$

we have, $1 = 64 \left(\dfrac{1}{2}\right)^n$

or $\qquad n = 6 =$ number of half-lives

$\therefore \qquad t = n \times t_{1/2} = 6 \times 2 = 12\,h$

7. Activity of $S_1 = \dfrac{1}{2}$ (activity of S_2)

or $\qquad \lambda_1 N_1 = \dfrac{1}{2}(\lambda_2 N_2)$

or $\qquad \dfrac{\lambda_1}{\lambda_2} = \dfrac{N_2}{2N_1}$

or $\qquad \dfrac{T_1}{T_2} = \dfrac{2N_1}{N_2} \qquad \left(T = \text{half-life} = \dfrac{\ln 2}{\lambda}\right)$

Given, $\qquad N_1 = 2N_2$

$\therefore \qquad \dfrac{T_1}{T_2} = 4$

$\therefore$ Correct option is (a).

8. After two half-lives $\dfrac{1}{4}$ th fraction of nuclei will remain un-decayed. Or, $\dfrac{3}{4}$ th fraction will decay.

Hence, the probability that a nucleus decays in two half-lives is $\dfrac{3}{4}$.

9. Activity reduces from 6000 dps to 3000 dps in 140 days. It implies that half-life of the radioactive sample is 140 days. In 280 days (or two half-lives) activity will remain $\dfrac{1}{4}$ th of the initial activity.

Hence, the initial activity of the sample is

4×6000 dps $= 24000$ dps

Therefore, the correct option is (d).

10. $R = R_0 \left(\dfrac{1}{2}\right)^n \qquad \qquad \ldots(i)$

Here, $R =$ activity of radioactive substance after n half-lives $= \dfrac{R_0}{16}$ (given)

Substituting in Eq. (i), we get $n = 4$

$\therefore \qquad t = (n)\, t_{1/2} = (4)(100\,\mu s) = 400\,\mu s$

11. Using $\qquad N = N_0 e^{-\lambda t}$

where, $\qquad \lambda = \dfrac{\ln 2}{t_{1/2}} = \dfrac{\ln 2}{3.8}$

$\therefore \qquad \dfrac{N_0}{20} = N_0 e^{-\frac{\ln 2}{3.8}t}$

Solving this equation with the help of given data we find

$$t = 16.5 \text{ days}$$

$\therefore$ Correct option is (b).

12. $1000 = \left(\dfrac{1}{2}\right)^n 8000$

$\therefore \quad n = 3 =$ number of half-lives

These half-lives are equivalent to 9 days. Hence, one half-life is 3 days.

$t_{av} = 1.44\, t_{1/2} = 1.44 \times 3 = 4.32 \text{ days}$

13. $R_0 = \lambda N_0 \implies N_0 = \dfrac{R_0}{\lambda}$

where, $\qquad \lambda = \dfrac{\ln 2}{t_{1/2}}$

$$N = N_0 e^{-\lambda t}$$

Find $\qquad N_1 = N_0 e^{-\lambda t_1}$

and $\qquad N_2 = N_0 e^{-\lambda t_2}$

$\therefore$ Number of nuclei decayed in given

$$\text{time} = N_1 - N_2$$

14. (a) $R = R_0 e^{-\lambda t}$

$$R_0 = 10 \text{ mCi}$$
$$R = 8 \text{ mCi}$$
$$t = 4.0 \text{ h}$$

Find λ.

(b) $R_0 = \lambda N_0$. Find $N_0 = \dfrac{R_0}{\lambda}$

(c) Find $R = R_0 e^{-\lambda t}$

15. $R_0 = \lambda N_0$

$$6.0 \times 10^{11} = \lambda \ (10^{15})$$

$\therefore$ $\qquad \lambda = 6.0 \times 10^{-4} \text{ s}$

$$t_{1/2} = \frac{\ln 2}{\lambda} = \frac{0.693}{6.0 \times 10^{-4}}$$
$$= 1.16 \times 10^3 \text{ s}$$

16. In 200 minute time,

n_1 = number of half-lives of X
$$= \frac{200}{50} = 4$$

n_2 = number of half-lives of Y
$$= \frac{200}{100} = 2$$

$$\frac{N_X}{N_Y} = \frac{N_0 (1/2)^4}{N_0 (1/2)^2} = \frac{1}{4}$$

INTRODUCTORY EXERCISE 34.2

1. $4 \, ({}_2\text{He}^4) = {}_8\text{O}^{16}$

Mass defect, $\Delta m = \{4 \ (4.0026) - 15.9994\}$
$$= 0.011 \text{ amu}$$

$\therefore$ Energy released per oxygen nuclei
$$= (0.011) \ (931.48) \text{ MeV}$$
$$= 10.24 \text{ MeV}$$

$\therefore$ Correct answer is (c).

2. Heavy water is used as moderators in nuclear reactors to slow down the neutrons.

4. During fusion process two or more lighter nuclei combine to form a heavy nucleus.
Hence, the correct option is (c).

5. (a) $m(c)^2 = P \times t$

$\therefore$ $\quad m = \dfrac{P \times t}{c^2}$
$$= \frac{(10^9) \ (24) \ (3600)}{(3 \times 10^8)^2}$$
$$= 9.6 \times 10^{-4} \text{ kg}$$

(b) Number of fissions required per second
$$= \frac{\text{Energy required per second}}{\text{Energy released in one fission}}$$
$$= \frac{10^9}{200 \times 10^6 \times 1.6 \times 10^{-19}}$$
$$= 3.125 \times 10^{19}$$

6. Mass defect $\Sigma m_i - \Sigma m_f = \Delta m$
$$= (238.050784) - (234.043593 + 4.002602)$$
$$= 4.589 \times 10^{-3} \text{ u}$$

Energy released $= \Delta m \times 931.48 \text{ MeV}$
$$= 4.27 \text{ MeV}$$

8. $Q = (\Delta m$ in atomic mass unit$) \times 931.4 \text{ MeV}$
$$= (2 \times \text{mass of } {}_1\text{H}^2 - \text{mass of } {}_2\text{He}^4) \times 931.4 \text{ MeV}$$
$$= (2 \times 2.0141 - 4.0024) \times 931.4 \text{ MeV}$$
$Q \approx 24 \text{ MeV}$

9. $2 \, {}_1\text{H}^2 \longrightarrow {}_2\text{He}^4$

Binding energy of two deuterons,
$$E_1 = 2 [2 \times 1.1] = 4.4 \text{ MeV}$$

Binding energy of helium nucleus,
$$E_2 = 4 \ (7.0) = 28.0 \text{ MeV}$$

$\therefore$ Energy released $\Delta E = E_2 - E_1$
$$= (28 - 4.4) \text{ MeV} = 23.6 \text{ MeV}$$

Exercises

LEVEL 1

Assertion and Reason

1. Huge amount of energy is involved in any nuclear process, which cannot be increased or decreased by pressure or temperature.

2. Some lighter nuclei are also radioactive.

3. In moving from lower energy state to higher energy state electromagnetic waves are absorbed.

4. Total binding energy per nucleon is more important for stability.

6. $(1 \text{ amu}) (c^2) = 931.48 \text{ MeV}$

7. α-particles are heaviest. Hence, its ionizing power is maximum.

Objective Questions

1. Nuclear density is constant hence,

$$\text{mass} \propto \text{volume}$$

or $m \propto V$

2. $\frac{2}{3} N_0 = N_0 \, e^{-\lambda t_2}$

∴ $\lambda t_2 = \ln \left(\frac{3}{2} \right)$

$\left(\frac{\ln 2}{20} \right) t_2 = \ln (1.5) = 0.4$

or $t_2 = 11.7$ min

Similarly, $\frac{1}{3} N_0 = N_0 e^{-\lambda t_1}$

∴ $\lambda t_1 = \ln 3$

∴ $\frac{\ln 2}{20} t_1 = \ln 3 = 1.1$

$\Rightarrow t_1 = 31.7$ min

∴ $t_1 - t_2 \approx 20$ min

3. $2 \, (_1 H^2) \longrightarrow \, _2 He^4$

∴ $Q = 4 \,(7) - 4 \,(1.1) = 23.6$ MeV

5. Let $n - \alpha$ particles and $m - \beta$ particles are emitted. Then,

$$90 - 2n + m = 80 \qquad \ldots(i)$$
$$200 - 4n = 168 \qquad \ldots(ii)$$

Solving Eqs. (i) and (ii), we get

$$n = 8 \quad \text{and} \quad m = 6$$

7. By emitting one α-particle, atomic number decreases by 2. By emitting two β-particles, atomic number increases by 2. Hence,

$$Z_A = Z_C$$

or A and C are isotopes.

8. Binding energy $= (\Delta m) \times 931.5$ MeV

$$= [2 \times 1.00785 + 2 \times 1.00866 - 4.00274] \times 931.5$$
$$= 28.2 \text{ MeV}$$

9. Number of nuclei left $= \frac{1}{8}$ th

Now, $\frac{1}{8} = \left(\frac{1}{2} \right)^n$

∴ $n =$ number of half-lives

$= 3$

3 half-lives $= 8$ s

∴ 1 half-life $= \frac{8}{3}$ s

10. 3 atoms of $B \longrightarrow$ one atom of A

∴ $Q = E_A - 3E_B$

11. Intensity, $I = 1.4 \times 10^3 \, \frac{\text{watt}}{\text{m}^2}$

Area, $A = 4\pi R^2 = 4\pi (1.5 \times 10^{11})^2$

$$= 2.83 \times 10^{23} \text{ m}^2$$

∴ Power radiated $= IA$

$$= 3.96 \times 10^{26} \text{ watt}$$

Total energy radiated in 1 day,

$$E = (3.96 \times 10^{26} \times 86400) \text{ J}$$
$$= 3.42 \times 10^{31} \text{ J}$$

∴ Mass lost per day,

$$m = \frac{E}{c^2} = \frac{3.42 \times 10^{31}}{(3 \times 10^8)^2}$$
$$= 3.8 \times 10^{14} \text{ kg}$$

12. $\lambda = \frac{\ln 2}{t_{1/2}} = \frac{\ln 2}{4} \text{ day}^{-1}$

Now, apply

$$R = R_0 e^{-\lambda t}$$
$$\Rightarrow 5 = 100 e^{-\lambda t}$$

Substituting value of λ, we can find t.

13. Let N nuclei decay per second. Then,

$$N \,(200 \times 1.6 \times 10^{-13}) = 1.6 \times 10^6$$

Solving we get $N = 5 \times 10^{16}$ per sec

14. $\frac{N}{N_0} = e^{-\lambda t} = e^{-\lambda \left(\frac{n}{\lambda} \right)} = \frac{1}{e^n}.$

15. $\lambda = \frac{\ln 2}{t_{1/2}} = \frac{0.693}{6.93} = \frac{1}{10} \text{ sec}^{-1}$

$$N = N_0 e^{-\lambda t}$$

∴ $\frac{N}{N_0} = e^{-\lambda t} = e^{-\left(\frac{1}{10} \right) (10)}$

$$= e^{-1} \approx 0.63$$

16. Activity of atoms is 6.25% after four half-lives.

∴ Four half-lives ≈ 2 h $= 120$ min

∴ One half-life is 30 min.

17. Probability of survival,

$$P = \frac{\text{Number of nuclei left}}{\text{Initial number of nuclei}}$$
$$= \frac{N_0 e^{-\lambda t}}{N_0}$$

At $\qquad t = $ one mean life $= \dfrac{1}{\lambda}$

$$P = e^{-1} = \dfrac{1}{e}$$

18. From the emission of one β-particle, atomic number increases by 1and the mass number remains unchanged. So, the new values are $Z + 1$ and A.

From the emission of one α-particle, atomic number decreases by 2 and the mass number by 4. Therefore, the values are $Z - 1$ and $A - 4$.

Finally from the emission of one γ-ray, values of A and Z remain unchanged. Hence, the final values are $Z - 1$ and $A - 4$.

19.

$$+\dfrac{dn_B}{dt} = R_1 - R_2 = \lambda_a N_a - \lambda_b N_b$$

20. $E = (0.5 + 0.5 + 0.78)\, \text{MeV}$

$\qquad = 1.78\, \text{MeV}$

21. During fusion, BE of daughter nucleus is always greater than the total energy of the parent nuclei so energy released

$$= c - (a + b)$$
$$= c - a - b$$

22. $\qquad\qquad R = \lambda N$

$\therefore \qquad\qquad \dfrac{R}{N} = \lambda = \text{constant}$

So, graph between $\dfrac{R}{N}$ and t will be a straight line parallel to the time axis.

23. $_7 X^{15} + \alpha\text{-particle} \longrightarrow {}_9 Y^{19} - {}_1 H^1 \longrightarrow {}_8 Z^{18}$

24. Numbers are maximum, when rate of production = rate of disintegration

$\therefore \qquad\qquad \alpha = \lambda N$

$\Rightarrow \qquad\qquad N = \dfrac{\alpha}{\lambda}$

25. $Q = (1.002 + 1.004 - 1.001 - 1.003)(931.5)\, \text{MeV}$

$\qquad = 1.863\, \text{MeV}$

Subjective Questions

1. (a) $R = R_0 e^{-\lambda t}$

$\qquad R = 2700$ per minute, $R_0 = 4750$ per minute

$\qquad t = 5$ min

Find λ.

(b) $t_{1/2} = \dfrac{\ln 2}{\lambda}$

2. $R = \lambda N$

$\qquad 6 \times 10^{11} = 1.0 \times 10^{15} \lambda$

$\therefore \qquad \lambda = 6 \times 10^{-4}\, \text{s}$

$\qquad t_{1/2} = \dfrac{\ln 2}{\lambda} = \dfrac{0.693}{6 \times 10^{-4}}\, \text{s}$

$\qquad\qquad = 1155\, \text{s}$

$\qquad\qquad = 19.25\, \text{min}$

3. $\because \quad R = \lambda N$

$\therefore \quad N = \dfrac{R}{\lambda} = \dfrac{R}{(\ln 2)/t_{1/2}}$

$\qquad\qquad = \dfrac{R t_{1/2}}{\ln 2}$

$\qquad\qquad = \dfrac{(8 \times 3.7 \times 10^{10})\,(5.3)\,(365)\,(24)\,(3600)}{0.693}$

$\qquad\qquad = 7.14 \times 10^{19}$

$\qquad m = \dfrac{7.14 \times 10^9}{6.02 \times 10^{23}} \times 60\, \text{g}$

$\qquad\qquad = 7.11 \times 10^{-3}\, \text{g}$

4. $R = \lambda N = \left(\dfrac{\ln 2}{t_{1/2}}\right) N$

$\qquad = \dfrac{0.693}{4.5 \times 10^9 \times 365 \times 24 \times 3600} \left(\dfrac{1}{238}\right)(6.02 \times 10^{23})$

$\qquad = 1.23 \times 10^4\, \text{dps}$

5. $\dfrac{1}{\lambda} = 10\, \text{days}$

$\therefore \qquad\qquad \lambda = 0.1\, \text{day}^{-1}$

Probability of decay

$\qquad = \dfrac{\text{Number of atoms decayed}}{\text{Initial number of atoms}}$

$\qquad = \dfrac{N_0(1 - e^{-\lambda t})}{N_0} = 1 - e^{-\lambda t}$

$\qquad = 1 - e^{-0.1 \times 5}$

$\qquad = 0.39$

6. $\dfrac{U^{238}}{Pb^{206}} = \dfrac{3}{1}$

$\qquad N_0 = 3 + 1 = 4$

$\qquad N = 3$

$$N = N_0 e^{-\lambda t} \qquad \text{...(i)}$$

$$\lambda = \frac{\ln 2}{t_{1/2}} \qquad \text{...(ii)}$$

From Eqs. (i) and (ii), we get

$$t = 1.88 \times 10^9 \text{ yr}$$

7. $\lambda_1 = \dfrac{\ln 2}{T_1}$ \qquad $(T = \text{half-life})$

$$\lambda_2 = \frac{\ln 2}{T_2}$$

$$R_{01} + R_{02} = 8 \text{ mCi} \qquad \text{(given)}$$

$$\therefore \quad \lambda_1(4N_0) + \lambda_2(N_0) = 8 \text{ mCi}$$

From here we can find number

after $t = 60$ yr

$$R = R_1 + R_2$$

$$= (4\lambda_1 N_0)e^{-\lambda_1 t} + (\lambda_2 N_0)e^{-\lambda_2 t}$$

9. Binding energy $= \Delta m \times 931.5 \text{ MeV}$

$$= (7 \times 1.00783 + 7 \times 1.00867 - 14.00307)\, 931.5$$

$$= 104.72 \text{ MeV}$$

10. Energy released $=$ binding energy

$$= \Delta m \times 931.5 \text{ MeV}$$

$$= (8 \times 1.007825 + 8 \times 1.008665 - 15.994915)$$

$$\times 931.5$$

$$= 127.62 \text{ MeV}$$

11. (a) Number of nuclei in 1 kg of U^{235},

$$N = \left(\frac{1}{235}\right)(6.02 \times 10^{26})$$

$\therefore$ Total energy released

$$= (N \times 200) \text{ MeV}$$

$$= \left(\frac{1}{235}\right)(6.02 \times 10^{26})(200)(1.6 \times 10^{-13})$$

$$= 8.19 \times 10^{13} \text{ J}$$

(b) $\qquad m = \dfrac{8.19 \times 10^{13}}{30 \times 10^3} \text{ g}$

$$= 2.73 \times 10^9 \text{ g}$$

$$= 2.73 \times 10^6 \text{ kg}$$

12. From momentum of conservation,

$$p_1 = p_2$$

$$\therefore \quad \sqrt{2K_1 m_1} = \sqrt{2K_2 m_2}$$

$$\therefore \quad K_2 = \frac{K_1 m_1}{m_2}$$

$$= \frac{(6.802)(4)}{208}$$

$$= 0.1308 \text{ MeV}$$

13. Number of nuclei in 1 kg of uranium,

$$N = \left(\frac{1}{235}\right)(6.02 \times 10^{26})$$

Now, $\left(\dfrac{1}{235}\right)(6.02 \times 10^{26})(185 \times 1.6 \times 10^{-13})$

$$= (100 \times 10^6)t$$

$$\therefore \qquad t = 7.58 \times 10^5 \text{ s}$$

$$= \frac{7.58 \times 10^5}{60 \times 60 \times 24} \text{ day}$$

$$= 8.78 \text{ days}$$

LEVEL 2

Single Correct Option

1. $\dfrac{N_0}{16} = N_0 \left(\dfrac{1}{2}\right)^n \quad \Rightarrow \quad n = 4$

So, $3t$ times is equivalent to four half-lives. Hence, one half-life is equal to $\dfrac{3t}{4}$.

The given time $\dfrac{11}{2}t - t = \dfrac{9}{2}t$ is equivalent to 6 half-lives.

$$\therefore \qquad N = N_0 \left(\frac{1}{2}\right)^6 = \frac{N_0}{64}$$

2. $\lambda = \lambda_1 + \lambda_2$

$$\therefore \qquad \frac{\ln 2}{T} = \frac{\ln 2}{T_1} + \frac{\ln 2}{T_1} \qquad (T = \text{Half-life})$$

or $\qquad T = \dfrac{T_1 T_2}{T_1 + T_2} = 20 \text{ y}$

$\dfrac{1}{4}$th sample remains after 2 half-lives or 40 y.

3. Q-value $=$ Final binding energy

Initial binding energy

$$= E_2 N_2 + E_3 N_3 - E_1 N_1$$

4. N_B are maximum when

$$\lambda_B N_B = \lambda_A N_A$$

$$\therefore \qquad N_B = \frac{\lambda_A}{\lambda_B} \cdot N_A$$

The given time is equivalent to two half-lives of A. Hence,

$$N_A = \frac{N_0}{4}$$

$$\therefore \qquad N_B = \frac{\lambda_A}{\lambda_B}\left(\frac{N_0}{4}\right)$$

5. It means we are getting only 100 MeV of energy by the fission of one uranium nucleus.

Number of nuclei per second

$$= \frac{\text{Energy required per second}}{\text{Energy obtained by one fission}}$$

$$= \frac{16 \times 10^6}{100 \times 1.6 \times 10^{-13}} = 10^{18}$$

6. When the rate production = rate of disintegration, number of nuclei or maximum.

$$\therefore \qquad \lambda N = A$$

or $$\qquad \frac{\ln 2}{T} N = A$$

or $$\qquad N = \frac{AT}{\ln 2} = \text{maximum}$$

7. $R_0 = 15 \times 200 = 3000$ decay/min from 200 g carbon.

Using $$\qquad R = R_0 \left(\frac{1}{2}\right)^n$$

$$\therefore \qquad 375 = 3000 \left(\frac{1}{2}\right)^n$$

$$\therefore \quad n = \text{number of half-lives} = 3$$

$$\therefore \quad t = 5730 \times 3 = 17190 \text{ y}$$

8. $A_P = A_0 e^{-\lambda t_1}$

$$A_Q = A_0 e^{-\lambda t_2}$$

$$\lambda t_1 = \ln (A_0 / A_P)$$

$$\therefore \qquad t_1 = \frac{1}{\lambda} \ln (A_0 / A_P)$$

$$= T \ln (A_0 / A_P)$$

Similarly, $$\qquad t_2 = T \ln (A_0 / A_Q)$$

$$\therefore \qquad t_1 - t_2 = T \ln \left(\frac{A_Q}{A_P}\right)$$

9. Combining two given equations,
we have, $3_1 H^2 = 2 He^4 + p + n$

$$\Delta m = 3 \times 2.014 - 4.001 - 1.007 - 1.008$$

$$= 0.026 \text{ u}$$

Energy released by 3 deuterons

$$= 0.026 \times 931.5 \times 1.6 \times 10^{-13} \text{J}$$

$$= 3.9 \times 10^{-12} \text{J}$$

Now, $(10^{16} \times t) = \left(\frac{10^{40}}{3}\right)(3.9 \times 10^{-12})$

Solving we get,

$$t \approx 1.3 \times 10^{12} \text{ s}$$

10. $R_1 = R_2$

$$R_{01} e^{-\lambda_1 t} = R_{02} e^{-\lambda t}$$

$$\therefore \qquad \lambda_1 N_0 e^{-\lambda_1 t} = \lambda_2 N_0 e^{-\lambda_2 t} \qquad \ldots\text{(i)}$$

$$\lambda_1 = \frac{\ln 2}{t_1} = \frac{0.693}{t_1}$$

$$\lambda_2 = \frac{0.693}{t_2}$$

Substituting these values in Eq. (i), we can get the t.

11. $A = 232 - 4 = 228$

From conservation of momentum,

$$p_\alpha = p_\gamma = \sqrt{2 K_\alpha m_\alpha} = \sqrt{2 K_\gamma m_\gamma}$$

or $$\qquad \frac{K_\alpha}{K_\gamma} = \frac{m_\gamma}{m_\alpha} = \frac{228}{4}$$

$$\therefore \qquad K_\alpha = \left(\frac{228}{228 + 4}\right) K_{\text{Total}}$$

$$= \left(\frac{228}{232}\right) K_{\text{Total}}$$

12. From momentum of conservation,
momentum of photon = momentum of nucleus

$$\therefore \qquad \frac{E}{c} = \sqrt{2Km}$$

$$\therefore \qquad K = \frac{E^2}{2mc^2}$$

$$= \frac{(7 \times 1.6 \times 10^{-13})^2}{2 \times 24 \times 1.67 \times 10^{-27} \times (3 \times 10^8)^2} \text{ keV}$$

$$\times 1.6 \times 10^{-16}$$

$$= 1.1 \text{ keV}$$

13. Activity $A \propto$ Number of atoms

$$A_1 = A_0 e^{-\lambda t_1}$$

$$\therefore \qquad t_1 = \frac{1}{\lambda} \ln \left(\frac{A_0}{A_1}\right)$$

$$= \frac{T}{\ln 2} \ln \frac{A_0}{A_1}$$

$$A_2 = 2 A_0 e^{-\lambda t_2}$$

$$t_2 = \frac{T}{\ln 2} \ln \left(\frac{2 A_0}{A_2}\right)$$

$$t_1 - t_2 = \frac{T}{\ln 2} \left(\frac{A_0}{A_1} \times \frac{A_2}{2 A_0}\right)$$

$$= \frac{T}{\ln 2} \ln \left(\frac{A_2}{2 A_1}\right)$$

14. Binding energy per nucleon

$$= \left(\frac{6 \times 1.0078 + 6 \times 1.0087 - 12}{12} \right) \times 931.4$$

$$= 7.68 \text{ MeV}$$

15. $\frac{N_A}{N_B} = \frac{N_0 e^{-5\lambda t}}{N_0 e^{-\lambda t}} = \left(\frac{1}{e} \right)^2$

$\therefore \qquad\qquad e^{-4\lambda t} = e^{-2}$

or $\qquad\qquad 4\lambda t = 2$

or $\qquad\qquad t = \frac{1}{2\lambda}$

16. Momentum of a photon,

$$p = \frac{h\nu}{c}$$

Hence, recoil energy

$$E = \frac{p^2}{2M}$$

$\therefore \qquad\qquad E = \frac{\left(\frac{h\nu}{c} \right)^2}{2M}$

or $\qquad\qquad E = \frac{h^2 \nu^2}{2Mc^2}$

17. In next half-life further 50% nuclei will remain undecayed. So, probability of survival upto next half time is $\frac{1}{2}$.

18. $A_1 = A_0 e^{-\lambda t_1} = A_0 \, e^{\frac{t_1}{T}}$

$$A_2 = A_0 e^{\frac{t_2}{T}}$$

$\therefore \qquad\qquad \frac{A_2}{A_1} = e^{\left(\frac{t_1 - t_2}{T} \right)}$

$$A_2 = A_1 e^{\left(\frac{t_1 - t_2}{T} \right)}$$

19. $\qquad \frac{N}{N_0} = \left(\frac{1}{2} \right)^n = \left(\frac{1}{2} \right)^{t/T}$

Given, $\qquad\qquad N = \frac{N_0}{e}$

$\Rightarrow \qquad\qquad \frac{N_0}{eN_0} = \left(\frac{1}{2} \right)^{5/T}$

or $\qquad\qquad \frac{1}{e} = \left(\frac{1}{2} \right)^{5/T}$

Taking log on both sides, we get

$$\log 1 - \log e = \frac{5}{T} \log \frac{1}{2}$$

$$-1 = \frac{5}{T} (- \log 2)$$

$\Rightarrow \qquad\qquad T = 5 \log_e 2$

Now, let t' be the time after which activity reduces to half

$$\left(\frac{1}{2} \right) = \left(\frac{1}{2} \right)^{t'/5 \log_e 2}$$

$\Rightarrow \qquad\qquad t' = 5 \log_e 2$

20. $\qquad N_A e^{-\lambda_A t} = N_B e^{-\lambda_B t}$

$\therefore \qquad e^{(\lambda_B - \lambda_A)t} = \frac{N_B}{N_A}$

$\therefore \qquad t = \frac{1}{\lambda_B - \lambda_A} \ln \left(\frac{N_B}{N_A} \right)$

21. (a) Activity $-\frac{dN}{dt} = \lambda N_0$

(b) Decay probability $= \frac{N_0 (1 - e^{-\lambda t})}{N_0} = 1 - e^{-\lambda t}$

This probability in unit time will be $1 - e^{-\lambda}$.

(c) $\qquad N = N_0 e^{-\lambda t}$

At $t = \frac{1}{\lambda}$, $\quad N = \frac{N_0}{e}$

(d) $t_{\frac{1}{2}} = \frac{\ln 2}{\lambda}$

22. $\because \left(-\frac{dN}{dt} \right) = \lambda N$ ...(i)

$$\lambda = \frac{0.693}{T_{1/2}}$$

$$= \frac{0.693}{1620 \times 365 \times 24 \times 60 \times 60}$$ ...(ii)

and $\quad N = \frac{6.023 \times 10^{23}}{226}$ ...(iii)

$\therefore \left(-\frac{dN}{dt} \right) = \frac{0.693 \times 6.023 \times 10^{23}}{1620 \times 365 \times 24 \times 60 \times 60 \times 226}$

$$= 3.61 \times 10^{10}$$

More than One Correct Options

1. $y = \lambda x = \dfrac{\ln 2}{T} \cdot x$

$$\dfrac{x}{y} = \dfrac{1}{\lambda} = \text{constant}$$

$$\dfrac{x}{y} = \dfrac{T}{\ln 2}$$

or $\qquad \dfrac{x}{y} > T \qquad$ (as $\ln 2 = 0.693$)

Further, $\qquad xy = x(\lambda x) = \lambda x^2$

After one half-life, x remains half. Hence, x^2 remains $\dfrac{1}{4}$ th.

3. By the emission of an α-particle, atomic number decreases by 2 and by the emission of two particles atomic number increases by 2. Hence, net atomic number remains unchanged.

4. At $t = 4T$

Number of half-lives of first $n_1 = 4$ and number of half-lives of second $n_2 = 2$

$$\dfrac{N_1}{N_2} = x = \dfrac{N_0 (1/2)^4}{N_0 (1/2)^2} = \dfrac{1}{4}$$

$$y = \dfrac{R_1}{R_2} = \dfrac{\lambda_1 N_0 (1/2)^4}{\lambda_2 N_0 (1/2)^2}$$

$$= \dfrac{\lambda_1}{4\lambda_2} = \dfrac{T_2}{4T_1}$$

$$= \dfrac{2T}{4T} = \dfrac{1}{2}$$

6. $R = R_0 A^{1/3} \qquad$ or $\qquad R \propto A^{1/3}$

7. To release energy in a nuclear process, binding energy per nucleon should increase.

Comprehension Based Questions

1. Energy released $= (\Delta m) (931.48)$ MeV

$$= [2 \times 2.01102 - 3.0160 - 1.007825] \times 931.5$$

$$= 4.03 \text{ MeV} \approx 4 \text{ MeV}$$

2. Let N number of fusion reactions are required, then

$$N \times 4 \times 1.6 \times 10^{-13} = 10^3 \times 3600$$

$$N = 5.625 \times 10^{18}$$

3. In one fusion reaction two ${}^2_1 \text{H}$ nuclei are used. Hence, total number of ${}^2_1 \text{H}$ nuclei are $2N$.

or 1.125×10^{19} Mass in kg

$$= \left(\dfrac{1.125 \times 10^{19}}{6.02 \times 10^{26}} \right) (2) \text{ kg}$$

$$= 3.7 \times 10^{-8} \text{ kg}$$

4. After decay, the daughter nuclei will be more stable, hence binding energy per nucleon will be more than that of their parent nucleus.

5. By conservation of momentum,

$$0 = \dfrac{M}{2} v_1 - \dfrac{M}{2} v_2$$

$$v_1 = v_2 \qquad \qquad \text{...(i)}$$

$$\Rightarrow \quad \Delta mc^2 = \dfrac{1}{2} \cdot \dfrac{M}{2} \cdot v_1^2 + \dfrac{1}{2} \cdot \dfrac{M}{2} \cdot v_2^2 \quad \text{...(ii)}$$

$$\Rightarrow \quad \Delta mc^2 = \dfrac{M}{2} v_1^2$$

$$\Rightarrow \quad \dfrac{2\Delta mc^2}{M} = v_1^2$$

$$\Rightarrow \quad v_1 = c \sqrt{\dfrac{2\Delta m}{M}}$$

Match the Columns

1. $\left(-\dfrac{dN}{dt} \right) = \lambda N$

$$\therefore \qquad \qquad y = \lambda x$$

or $\qquad \qquad \lambda = \dfrac{y}{x}$

$$t_{1/2} = \dfrac{\ln 2}{\lambda} = (\ln 2)(x/y)$$

$$R = R_0 e^{-\lambda t}$$

$$= y e^{-\lambda (1/\lambda)} = y/e$$

$$R = \dfrac{y}{e} = \lambda N$$

$$\therefore \qquad N = \dfrac{y}{e\lambda} = \dfrac{y}{e(y/x)} = \dfrac{x}{e}$$

2. Energy is released when daughter nuclei lie towards peak of this graph, so that binding energy per nucleon or total binding energy in the nuclear process increases.

3. A will continuously decrease, but C will increase. $(A + B)$ will continuously decrease as C is formed only from A and B.

$$(C + B) = \text{Total} - A$$

A is continuously decreasing. Hence, $(C + B)$ will continuously increase.

4. (a) E is of the order of kT, where k = Boltzmann constant and $T \approx 300$ K

(c) λ to X-rays is of the order of $1\text{Å} - 100$ Å

$$E = \left[\frac{12375}{\lambda \ (\text{in Å})}\right] \text{in eV}$$

$$= \left[\frac{12.375}{\lambda}\right] \text{in keV}$$

where, λ is in Å.

(d) λ is of the order of 4000 Å $- 7000$ Å

Now, $E \ (\text{in eV}) = \dfrac{12375}{\lambda \ (\text{in Å})}$

Subjective Questions

1. $N = \dfrac{R}{\lambda} = \dfrac{10^9}{\dfrac{0.693}{14.3 \times 3600}} = 7.43 \times 10^{13}$

Now, $\dfrac{dN}{dt} = q - \lambda N$ or $\displaystyle\int_0^N \dfrac{dN}{q - \lambda N} = \int_0^t dt$

$\therefore \qquad N = \dfrac{q}{\lambda}\,(1 - e^{-\lambda t})$

Substituting the values,

$$7.43 \times 10^{13} = \frac{2 \times 10^9}{\dfrac{0.693}{14.3 \times 3600}}\,[1 - e^{-(0.693/14.3 \times 3600)t}]$$

Solving this equation we get,

$$t = 14.3 \text{ h} \qquad \textbf{Ans.}$$

2. (a)

	A	B	C
At $t = 0$	N_0	0	0
At t	N_1	N_2	N_3

Here, $\qquad N_1 = N_0 e^{-\lambda t}$ ...(i)

$$\frac{dN_2}{dt} = \lambda\,(N_1 - N_2)$$

or $\qquad \dfrac{dN_2}{dt} = \lambda N_0 e^{-\lambda t} - \lambda N_2$

or $\quad dN_2 + \lambda N_2 dt = \lambda N_0 e^{-\lambda t}$

$\therefore \quad e^{\lambda t} dN_2 + \lambda N_2 e^{\lambda t} dt = \lambda N_0 dt$

or $\qquad d(N_2 e^{\lambda t}) = \lambda N_0 dt$

$\therefore \qquad N_2 e^{\lambda t} = \lambda N_0 t + C$

At $t = 0$, $N_2 = 0$,

$\therefore \qquad\qquad C = 0$

$\therefore \qquad\qquad N_2 = \lambda N_0 (te^{-\lambda t})$

(b) Activity of B is

$$R_2 = \lambda N_2 = \lambda^2 N_0 (te^{-\lambda t})$$

For maximum activity, $\dfrac{dR_2}{dt} = 0$

$\therefore \qquad\qquad t = \dfrac{1}{\lambda}$ **Ans.**

$\therefore \qquad\qquad R_{\max} = \dfrac{\lambda N_0}{e}$ **Ans.**

3. (a) Let at time t, number of radioactive nuclei are N.

Net rate of formation of nuclei of A

$$\frac{dN}{dt} = \alpha - \lambda N$$

or $\qquad \dfrac{dN}{\alpha - \lambda N} = dt$

or $\qquad \displaystyle\int_{N_0}^{N} \dfrac{dN}{\alpha - N} = \int_0^t dt$

Solving this equation, we get

$$N = \frac{1}{\lambda}[\alpha - (\alpha - \lambda N_0)e^{-\lambda t}] \qquad \text{...(i)}$$

(b) (i) Substituting $\alpha = 2\lambda N_0$ and $t = t_{1/2} = \dfrac{\ln 2}{\lambda}$

in Eq. (i), we get $N = \dfrac{3}{2} N_0$

(ii) Substituting $\alpha = 2\lambda N_0$ and $t \to \infty$ in Eq. (i), we get

$$N = \frac{\alpha}{\lambda} = 2N_0$$

or $\qquad N = 2N_0$

4. (a) Let R_{A_0} and R_{B_0} be the initial activities of A and B. Then,

$$R_{A_0} + R_{B_0} = 10^{10} \text{ dps} \qquad \text{...(i)}$$

Activity of A after time $t = 20$ days (two half-lives of A) is

$$R_A = \left(\frac{1}{2}\right)^2 R_{A_0} = 0.25\, R_{A_0}$$

Similarly, activity of B after $t = 20$ days (four half-lives of B) is

$$R_B = \left(\frac{1}{2}\right)^4 R_{B_0} = 0.0625\, R_{B_0}$$

Now, it is given that $R_A + R_B = 20\%$ of 10^{10}

or $0.25 R_{A_0} + 0.0625 R_{B_0} = 0.2 \times 10^{10}$ dps ...(ii)

Solving Eqs. (i) and (ii), we get

$$R_{A_0} = 0.73 \times 10^{10} \text{ dps}$$

and $\quad R_{B_0} = 0.27 \times 10^{10} \text{ dps}$

(b) $\dfrac{R_{A_0}}{R_{B_0}} = \dfrac{\lambda_A N_{A_0}}{\lambda_B N_{B_0}} = \dfrac{(t_{1/2})_B}{(t_{1/2})_A} \cdot \dfrac{N_{A_0}}{N_{B_0}}$

$\therefore \quad \dfrac{N_{A_0}}{N_{B_0}} = \left(\dfrac{R_{A_0}}{R_{B_0}}\right) \dfrac{(t_{1/2})_A}{(t_{1/2})_B} = \left(\dfrac{0.73}{0.27}\right)\left(\dfrac{10}{5}\right)$

$= 5.4$

5. Let N be the number of radio nuclei at any time t. Then, net rate of formation of nuclei at time t is

$$\dfrac{dN}{dt} = \alpha - \lambda N$$

or $\displaystyle\int_0^N \dfrac{dN}{\alpha - \lambda N} = \int_0^t dt$

or $N = \dfrac{\alpha}{\lambda}(1 - e^{-\lambda t})$

Rate of formation $= \alpha$ Rate of decay $= \lambda N$

Number of nuclei formed in time $t = \alpha t$
and number of nuclei left after time

$$t = \dfrac{\alpha}{\lambda}(1 - e^{-\lambda t})$$

Therefore, number of nuclei disintegrated in time

$$t = \alpha t - \dfrac{\alpha}{\lambda}(1 - e^{-\lambda t})$$

$\therefore$ Energy released till time,

$$t = E_0\left[\alpha t - \dfrac{\alpha}{\lambda}(1 - e^{-\lambda t})\right]$$

But only 20% of it is used in raising the temperature of water.

So, $0.2\,E_0\left[\alpha t - \dfrac{\alpha}{\lambda}(1 - e^{-\lambda t})\right] = Q$

where, $Q = ms\Delta\theta$

$\therefore \quad \Delta\theta = $ increase in temperature of water $= \dfrac{Q}{ms}$

$\therefore \quad \Delta\theta = \dfrac{0.2\,E_0\left[at - \dfrac{a}{\lambda}(1 - e^{-\lambda t})\right]}{ms}$

6. We have for B $\dfrac{dN_B}{dt} = P - \lambda_2 N_B$

$\Rightarrow \quad \displaystyle\int_0^{N_B} \dfrac{dN_B}{P - \lambda_2 N_B} = \int_0^t dt$

$\Rightarrow \quad \ln\left(\dfrac{P - \lambda_2 N_B}{P}\right) = -\lambda_2 t$

$\Rightarrow \quad N_B = \dfrac{P(1 - e^{-\lambda_2 t})}{\lambda_2}$

The number of nuclei of A after time t is

$$N_A = N_0 e^{-\lambda_1 t}$$

Thus, $\dfrac{dN_c}{dt} = \lambda_1 N_A + \lambda_2 N_B$

$\Rightarrow \quad \dfrac{dN_c}{dt} = \lambda_1 N_0 e^{-\lambda_1 t} + P(1 - e^{-\lambda_2 t})$

$\Rightarrow \quad N_c = N_0(1 - e^{-\lambda_1 t}) + P\left(t + \dfrac{e^{-\lambda_2 t} - 1}{\lambda_2}\right)$

7. $^{210}_{84}\text{Po} \longrightarrow {}^{206}_{82}\text{Pb} + {}^{4}_{2}\text{He}$

$$\Delta m = 0.00564 \text{ amu}$$

Energy liberated per reaction $= (\Delta m)931 \text{ MeV}$
$= 8.4 \times 10^{-13} \text{ J}$

Electrical energy produced $= 8.4 \times 10^{-14} \text{ J}$

Let m g of ^{210}Po is required to produce the desired energy.

$$N = \dfrac{m}{210} \times 6 \times 10^{23}$$

$$\lambda = \dfrac{0.693}{t_{1/2}} = 0.005 \text{ per day}$$

$$\left(-\dfrac{dN}{dt}\right) = \lambda N = \dfrac{(0.005)(6 \times 10^{23}\,m)}{210} \text{ per day}$$

$\therefore$ Electrical energy produced per day

$$= \dfrac{(0.005)(6 \times 10^{23}\,m)}{210} \times 8.4 \times 10^{-14} \text{ J}$$

This is equal to $1.2 \times 10^7 \text{ J}$ (given)

$\therefore \qquad\qquad m = 10 \text{ g}$ **Ans.**

Activity at the end of 693 days is

$$R = \dfrac{0.005 \times 6 \times 10^{23} \times 10}{210}$$

$$= \dfrac{10^{21}}{7} \text{ per day}$$

$$= R_0\left(\dfrac{1}{2}\right)^n$$

Here, $n = $ number of half-lives $= \dfrac{693}{138.6} = 5$

$\therefore \qquad R_0 = R(2)^5 = 32 \times \dfrac{10^{21}}{7}$

$$= 4.57 \times 10^{21} \text{ per day}$$

Ans.

8. (i) At $t = 0$, probabilities of getting α and β particles are same. This implies that initial activity of both is equal. Say it is R_0.
Activity after $t = 1620$ s,

$$R_1 = R_0 \left(\frac{1}{2}\right)^{1620/405} = \frac{R_0}{16}$$

and $\quad R_2 = R_0 \left(\frac{1}{2}\right)^{1620/1620} = \frac{R_0}{2}$

Total activity, $R = R_1 + R_2 = \frac{9}{16} R_0$

Probability of getting α-particles,

$$= \frac{R_1}{R} = \frac{1}{9}$$

and probability of getting β-particles

$$= \frac{R_2}{R} = \frac{8}{9} \qquad \qquad \textbf{Ans.}$$

(ii) $R_{01} = R_{02}$

$\therefore \qquad \qquad \dfrac{N_{01}}{T_1} = \dfrac{N_{02}}{T_2}$

$\therefore \qquad \qquad \dfrac{N_{01}}{N_{02}} = \dfrac{1}{4}$

Let N_0 be the total number of nuclei at $t = 0$.

Then, $\qquad \qquad N_{01} = \dfrac{N_0}{5}$

and $\qquad \qquad N_{02} = \dfrac{4N_0}{5}$

Given that $\quad N_1 + N_2 = \dfrac{N_0}{2}$

or $\quad \dfrac{N_0}{5} \left(\dfrac{1}{2}\right)^{t/405} + \dfrac{4N_0}{5} \left(\dfrac{1}{2}\right)^{t/1620} = \dfrac{N_0}{2}$

Let $\qquad \left(\dfrac{1}{2}\right)^{t/1620} = x$

Then, above equation becomes

$$x^4 + 4x - 2.5 = 0$$

$\therefore \qquad \qquad x = 0.594$

or $\qquad \left(\dfrac{1}{2}\right)^{t/1620} = 0.594$

Solving, it we get

$$t = 1215 \text{ s.} \qquad \qquad \textbf{Ans.}$$

9. $N = \dfrac{10^{-3}}{210} \times 6.02 \times 10^{23}$

$\qquad = 2.87 \times 10^{18}$

During one mean life period 63.8% nuclei are decayed. Hence, energy released

$$E = 0.638 \times 2.87 \times 10^{18} \times 5.3 \times 1.6 \times 10^{-13} \text{ J}$$

$\qquad = 1.55 \times 10^6 \text{ J} \qquad \qquad \textbf{Ans.}$

10. $R_0 = \lambda N = \dfrac{0.693}{14.3 \times 3600 \times 24} \times 6.02 \times 10^{23}$ per sec

$\qquad = 3.37 \times 10^{17}$ per sec

After 70 hours activity,

$$R = R_0 e^{-\lambda t} = (3.37 \times 10^{17}) e^{-(0.693/14.3 \times 24)(70)}$$

$\qquad = 2.92 \times 10^{17}$ per sec

In fruits activity was observed $1 \mu\text{Ci}$ or 3.7×10^4 per sec. Therefore, percentage of activity transmitted from root to the fruit.

$$= \dfrac{3.7 \times 10^4}{2.92 \times 10^{17}} \times 100$$

$\qquad = 1.26 \times 10^{-11} \% \qquad \qquad \textbf{Ans.}$

35. Semiconductors

INTRODUCTORY EXERCISE 35.1

1. E_g Carbon $= 5.4$ eV

E_g Silicon $= 1.1$ eV

E_g Germanium $= 0.7$ eV

$\therefore$ $(E_g)_C > (E_g)_{Si} > (E_g)_{Ge}$

INTRODUCTORY EXERCISE 35.2

1. Hole diffusion from p to n side can be viewed as "electron diffusion" from n to p side.

Diffusion occurs due to difference in concentrations in different regions.

An electron (or hole) diffuses where its concentration is less.

2. Due to forward biasing depletion layer thickness decreases, potential barrier is reduced and diffusion of electrons from n to p side occurs.

INTRODUCTORY EXERCISE 35.3

1. In a transistor, base must be very thin and lightly doped so that all of the charge carriers are not combined in base and majority of them passes the reverse bias layer to collector side.

2. Voltage gain is maximum and constant for mid frequency range but is less for both low and high frequencies.

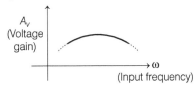

(b) We construct truth table to see the logical operation.

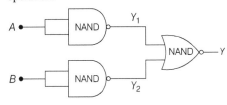

A	B	Y_1	Y_2	Y
0	0	1	1	0
1	0	0	1	1

A	B	Y_1	Y_2	Y
0	1	1	0	1
1	1	0	0	1

Clearly output resembles an 'OR' gate.

3. For given amplifier,

$$V_0 = 2\text{ V}, R_0 = 2\text{ k}\Omega$$
$$\beta_{ac} = 100, R_i = 1\text{ k}\Omega$$

We have, output voltage, $V_0 = I_C R_0$

$\Rightarrow$ I_C = collector current

$$= \frac{V_0}{R_0} = \frac{2}{2 \times 10^3} = 10^{-3}\text{ A}$$

$$= 1\text{ mA}$$

Also, current amplication $\beta = \dfrac{i_C}{i_B}$

$\Rightarrow$
$$i_B = \frac{i_C}{\beta} = \frac{10^{-3}}{100}\text{ A}$$

$$= 10^{-5}\text{ A} = 10 \times 10^{-6}\text{ A}$$

$$= 10\,\mu\text{A}.$$

and voltage amplification

$$A_V = \frac{\beta R_0}{R_i} = \frac{V_0}{V_i}$$

$\Rightarrow$
$$V_i = \frac{V_0 R_i}{\beta R_0} = \frac{2 \times 1 \times 10^3}{100 \times 2 \times 10^3}$$

$$= 10^{-2}\text{ volts} = 10\text{ mV}$$

INTRODUCTORY EXERCISE 35.4

1. Input waveforms are as shown

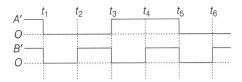

These are fed to an NAND gate,

Output waveform is as shown

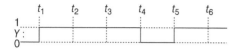

2. Truth table for the circuit given is

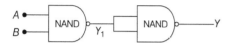

A	B	Y_1	Y
0	0	1	0
1	0	1	0
0	1	1	0
1	1	0	1

As the output resembles output of a AND gate so, given circuit behaves like an 'AND' gate.

Exercises

1. With increase in temperature, number of electrons reaching conduction band increases but, mean relation time decreases. Effect of decrease in relation time is much less than that of increase in number density of charge carriers.

2. For diode D_1,
$$V_p - V_n = -10 - 0 = -10\,\text{V}$$
So, D_1 is in reverse bias.
For diode D_2,
$$V_p - V_n = 0 - (-10) = 10\,\text{V}$$
So, D_2 is in forward bias.

3. Hole is a vacancy created by an electron moving from valance band to conduction band.

4. Capacitor is charged to maximum potential difference
$$\therefore \qquad V = V_{\text{max}} = V_{\text{rms}} \times \sqrt{2}$$
$$= 220\sqrt{2}\ \text{volts}$$

5. Electrons take the energy and move up to neat higher energy level both in conduction and valance band. So, a hole move downwards due to movement of electron.

6. In an n-p-n transistor,

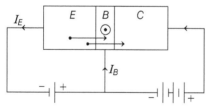

Electrons move from emitter to base and electrons which are not combined with holes in base region, crosses to collector side.

7. In an n-p-n transistor,
$$I_E = I_B + I_C$$

As $I_C = \dfrac{95}{100} I_E \quad \Rightarrow \quad I_E = \dfrac{100}{95} \times I_C$
$$= \dfrac{100}{95} \times 10\ \text{mA} = 10.53\ \text{mA}$$
So, $I_B = 0.53$ mA

8. Depletion zone is formed due to diffusion of e^- from n to p side. Due to diffusion positive immobile ions exists on n side and negative ions on p-side.

Recombination of e^- and holes takes place on p-side. This results in (n-side more positive than p-side) formation of a junction field and potential barrier across the depletion zone.

9. When applied voltage approaches zener potential diode breakdown to conduct excess current. This causes a change of current in series resistance.

10. Reverse breakdown may be "Avlanche break down" (breakdown due to high velocity collision of minority carrier) or it may be a zener breakdown (breakdown of bonds due to strong field).

11. No, it cannot be measured by using a voltmeter. Barrier potential is less than 0.2 V for germanium diode and is less than 0.7 V for silicon. Also there are no free charge carriers which provide 'current' for working of voltmeter.

12. An "OR" gate may be made to operate motor relays for garage gates.

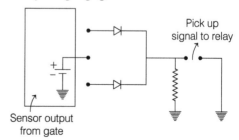

13. Such combination is called "Cascade" combination.

$$A_V = A_{V_1} \times A_{V_2}$$
$$\text{(net)}$$

$$= 10 \times 20 = 200$$

∴ V_0 = output voltage

$$= A_V \times V_i$$
$$\text{(net)}$$

$$= 200 \times 0.01$$

$$= 2\,\text{V}$$

14. We use, $E_g = \dfrac{hc}{\lambda} \Rightarrow E_g = \dfrac{1240\ \text{eV} \cdot \text{nm}}{600\ \text{nm}}$

$$\approx 2\ \text{eV}$$

So, photon energy is less than that required (2.8 eV). So, detector is not able to detect this wavelength.

15. (i) Diode is a rectifier diode.

(ii) Point P represents zener breakdown potential.

16. Given is a p-n-p CE configuration, when R_1 is increased, base current decreases as a result current also decreases.

Hence, both ammeter and voltmeter readings decreases.

17. A NOT gate can be formed by proper biasing of a transistor as shown.

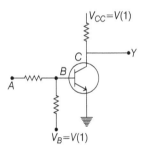

If input (A) is low (0), then the transistor is in cut off stage and output (Y) is same as $V_{CC} = V(1)$. If input (A) is high, then transistor current is in saturation and the net voltage at output (Y) is $V(0)$ or is in state 0.

18. Given is an AND gate, its truth table is

A	B	Y
0	0	0
1	0	0
0	1	0
1	1	1

19. Supply voltage may be 7 V and zener breakdown at 5 V.

So, voltage drop across resistance $R = 7 - 5 = 2\,\text{V}$.

Now power rating of zener = 1W.

So, current through zener must not exceed

$$I = \frac{P}{V} = \frac{1}{5}\text{A}$$

Hence, series resistance

$$R = \frac{V}{i} = \frac{2}{\frac{1}{5}} = 10\ \Omega.$$

20. Current flows only in branches AB and EF as diode of CD branch is in reverse bias. (∴ $I_3 = 0$)

So, given circuit is equivalent to

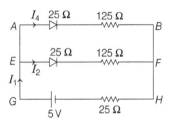

Current through cell is

$$i_1 = \frac{V}{R_{\text{Total}}} = \frac{5}{100} = 0.05\ \text{A}$$

Also by symmetry,

$$I_2 = I_4 = \frac{0.05}{2} = 0.025\ \text{A}$$

21. Given circuit is equivalent to

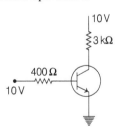

In base emitter loop,

$$V_B = I_B R_B$$

$$\Rightarrow \qquad I_B = \frac{V_B}{R_B} = \frac{10}{400 \times 10^3}$$

$$= 25 \times 10^{-6}\ \text{A}$$

$$= 25\ \mu\text{A}$$

In emitter-collector loop,

$$V_C = I_C R_C$$

$$\Rightarrow \qquad I_C = \frac{10}{3 \times 10^3}$$

$$= 3.33 \text{ mA}$$

and $\qquad \beta_{DC} = \dfrac{I_C}{I_B} = \dfrac{3.33 \text{ mA}}{25 \,\mu\text{A}}$

$$= 133$$

22. Consider the figure given here to solve this problem

$$I_C = I_E \qquad \text{[As base current is very small]}$$
$$R_C = 7.8 \text{ k}\Omega$$

From the figure, $I_C(R_C + R_E) + V_{CE} = 12$

$$(R_E + R_C) \times 1 \times 10^{-3} + 3 = 12$$
$$R_E + R_C = 9 \times 10^3 = 9 \text{ k}\Omega$$
$$R_E = 9 - 7.8 = 1.2 \text{ k}\Omega$$
$$V_E = I_E \times R_E$$
$$= 1 \times 10^{-3} \times 1.2 \times 10^3 = 1.2 \text{ V}$$

Voltage, $V_B = V_E + V_{BE} = 1.2 + 0.5 = 1.7$ V

Current, $I = \dfrac{V_B}{20 \times 10^3} = \dfrac{1.7}{20 \times 10^3}$

$$= 0.085 \text{ mA}$$

Resistance, $R_B = \dfrac{12 - 1.7}{\dfrac{I_C}{\beta} + 0.085} = \dfrac{10.3}{0.01 + 0.085}$

[Given, $\beta = 100$]

$$= 108 \text{ k}\Omega$$

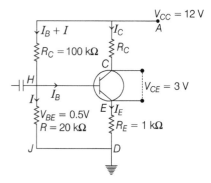

23. Consider the figure to solve this question,

$$I_E = I_C + I_B \text{ and } I_C = \beta I_B \qquad \text{...(i)}$$
$$I_C R_C + V_{CE} + I_E R_E = V_{CC} \qquad \text{...(ii)}$$
$$R I_B + V_{BE} + I_E R_E = V_{CC} \qquad \text{...(iii)}$$
$$I_E = I_C = \beta I_B$$

From Eq. (iii),

$$(R + \beta R_E) I_B = V_{CC} - V_{BE}$$
$$\Rightarrow \qquad I_B = \frac{V_{CC} - V_{BE}}{R + \beta R_E}$$
$$= \frac{12 - 0.5}{80 + 1.2 \times 100}$$
$$= \frac{11.5}{200} \text{ mA}$$

From Eq. (ii),

$$(R_C + R_E) = \frac{V_{CE} - V_{BE}}{I_C}$$
$$= \frac{V_{CC} - V_{CE}}{\beta I_B} \qquad (\because I_C = \beta I_B)$$
$$(R_C + R_E) = \frac{2}{11.5}(12 - 3) \text{ k}\Omega$$
$$= 1.56 \text{ k}\Omega$$
$$R_C + R_E = 1.56$$
$$R_C = 1.56 - 1 = 0.56 \text{ k}\Omega$$

36. Communication System

Exercises

Single Correct Option

1. Range of frequencies is as follows :
Ground wave : 300 Hz to 300 kHz
(it may go upto 3 MHz)
Sky wave : 300 kHz to 3 MHz
Space wave : 3 MHz to 300 GHz.

2. Length of antenna $\geq \dfrac{\lambda}{4} \Rightarrow l \geq \dfrac{\lambda}{4}$

$\Rightarrow \lambda \leq 4 \times l$ or $\lambda \leq 400$ m

3. Sideband frequencies are :
Lower sideband
$(LSB) = \omega_c - \omega_m$
$= 1 \times 10^6$ Hz $- 3 \times 10^3$ Hz
$= (1000 - 3) \times 10^3$ Hz
$= 2997$ kHz and $= 2.997$ MHz

Upper sideband
$(USB) = \omega_c + \omega_m$
$= 1 \times 10^6$ Hz $+ 3 \times 10^3$ Hz
$= 1003$ kHz $= 1.003$ MHz

4. Frequency of amplitude modulated wave is same as that of carrier wave.

5. Basic communication system is

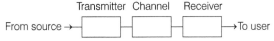

Transmitter Channel   Receiver
From source → [   ] [   ] [   ] →To user

6. Beyond horizon, a signal can reach *via* ionospheric reflection or sky wave mode. Frequency range suitable is 3 MHz to 30 MHz.

7. UHF band is in range of 150 to 900 MHz.
So, suitable mode of communication is "space wave mode".

8. Digital signals employs a discrete values of amplitudes which are coded using binary system.

9. In LOS communication maximum distance upto which a signals can be received from tower is
$d = \sqrt{2Rh} = \sqrt{2 \times 6.4 \times 10^6 \times 240}$
$\approx 55 \times 10^3$ m $= 55$ km

10. Wavelength of signal is
$\lambda = \dfrac{c}{F} = \dfrac{3 \times 10^8}{15 \times 10^3} = 20 \times 10^3$ m

So, size of antenna required
$= \dfrac{\lambda}{4}$ (at least)
$= 5 \times 10^3$ m $= 5$ km
Also, effective power radiated by antenna is very less.

11. $LSB = \omega_c = \omega_m$
$= 1.5 \times 10^6 - 3 \times 10^3 = 1497$ kHz
and $USB = \omega_c + \omega_m = 1503$ kHz
Bandwidth required
$= USB - LSB = 2\omega_m$
$= 2 \times 3$ kHz $= 6$ kHz

12. Due to over modulation $\mu > 1$, sidebands overlaps and fading (loss of information) may occur. Also when $\mu \approx 1$, distortion in carrier waveform occurs.

13. Frequency of signal obtained $= \dfrac{1}{2\pi\sqrt{LC}} = 1$ MHz
$\Rightarrow \quad LC = \dfrac{1}{(2\pi \times 10^6)^2}$
$\Rightarrow \quad LC = 0.25 \times 10^{-13}$ s^2
$\Rightarrow \quad LC = 2.5 \times 10^{-14}$ s^2

14. $\mu = $ modulation index
$= \dfrac{A_m}{A_c} \Rightarrow A_m = \mu \times A_c = 0.75 \times 12$
$= 9$ volts

15. Vibrating tuning fork and string produces all possible values of displacement hence, these signals are analog.
A light pulse and output of NAND gate gives only discrete values of output. So, signals are digital these.

16. Penetrating power of signal α frequency of signal.
So, 3 MHz signal travels longer distance in ionosphere.

17. Modulation index μ,
$= \dfrac{A_{max} - A_{min}}{A_{max} + A_{min}}$
($A = $ amplitude of modulated wave)
$\therefore \qquad \mu = \dfrac{15 - 3}{15 + 3} = \dfrac{12}{18} = \dfrac{2}{3}$

18. Man made noises and atmospheric interferences affect only amplitude of a signal.

So, an AM signal is more noisy than a FM signal.

19. In LOS communication, it is not necessary that transmitting antenna and receiving antenna are at same height. Only requirement is that there must not be any obstacle in between.

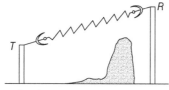

Given, $h = 81$ m

∴ Distance upto which transmission can be made
$$= d = \sqrt{2Rh}$$

and, area covered in broadcast
$$= \pi d^2 = 2\pi Rh$$
$$= 2 \times \pi \times 6.4 \times 10^6 \times 81 \; (m^2)$$
$$= 3258 \; km^2$$

20. (i) When receiver is at ground level, then service area covered
$$= \pi d^2 = \pi(\sqrt{2Rh})^2 = 2\pi Rh$$
$$= 2 \times \pi \times 6.4 \times 10^6 \times 20$$
$$\approx 804 \; km^2$$

(ii) When receiver is at height of 25 m, area covered
$$= \pi d_1^2 + \pi d_2^2$$
$$= \pi(\sqrt{2Rh_T})^2 + \pi(\sqrt{2Rh_R})^2$$
$$= 2\pi R(h_T + h_R)$$
$$= 2 \times \pi \times 6.4 \times 10^6 \times 45 \,(m^2)$$
$$\approx 3608 \; km^2$$

(iii) Percentage increase in area covered
$$= \frac{A_2 - A_1}{A_1} \times 100$$
$$= \frac{3608 - 804}{804} \times 100$$
$$\approx 349 \, \%$$

21.

22. From $f_{max} = 9(N_{max})^{\frac{1}{2}}$

$$\Rightarrow \quad N_{max} = \frac{f_{max}^2}{81}$$

$$\Rightarrow N_{max}\big|_{F_1} = \frac{(5 \times 10^6)^2}{81} = 0.3086 \times 10^{12} \; m^{-3}$$
$$= 3.086 \times 10^{11} \; m^{-3}$$

and $\quad N_{max}\big|_{F_2} = \frac{(8 \times 10^6)^2}{81}$
$$= 7.9 \times 10^{11} \; m^{-3}$$

23. Let the receiver is at point A and source is at B.

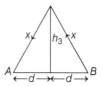

Velocity of waves $= 3 \times 10^8 \, m/s$

Time to reach a receiver $= 4.04$ ms $= 4.04 \times 10^{-3} s$

Let the height of satellite is
$$h_s = 600 \; km$$
Radius of earth $= 6400$ km
Size of transmitting antenna $= h_T$

We know that
$$\frac{\text{Distance travelled by wave}}{\text{Time}} = \text{Velocity of waves}$$

$$\frac{2x}{4.04 \times 10^{-3}} = 3 \times 10^8$$

or $\quad x = \dfrac{3 \times 10^8 \times 4.04 \times 10^{-3}}{2}$
$$= 6.06 \times 10^5 = 606 km$$

Using Pythagoras theorem,
$$d^2 = x^2 - h_s^2 = (606)^2 - (600)^2 = 7236$$

or $\qquad d = 85.06$ km

So, the distance between source and receiver $= 2d$
$$= 2 \times 85.06 = 170 \; km$$

The maximum distance covered on ground from the transmitter by emitted EM waves

$$d = \sqrt{2Rh_T} \quad \text{or} \quad \frac{d^2}{2R} = h_T$$

or size of antenna $h_T = \dfrac{7236}{2 \times 6400} = 0.565$ km

$$= 565 \, m$$

Ingram Content Group UK Ltd.
Milton Keynes UK
UKHW051142260423
420810UK00010B/451